Spicer and Pegler's
Book-keeping and Accounts

To Helen

Spicer and Pegler's Book-keeping and Accounts

Twenty-third Edition

Paul Gee, BA(Econ), FCA
Director of Training, Solomon Hare, Bristol

Butterworths
London, Dublin and Edinburgh
1996

United Kingdom	Butterworths, a Division of Reed Elsevier (UK) Ltd, Halsbury House, 35 Chancery Lane, LONDON WC2A 1EL, and 4 Hill Street, EDINBURGH EH2 3JZ
Australia	Butterworths Pty Ltd, SYDNEY, MELBOURNE, BRISBANE, ADELAIDE, PERTH, CANBERRA and HOBART
Canada	Butterworths Canada Ltd, TORONTO and VANCOUVER
Ireland	Butterworth (Ireland) Ltd, DUBLIN
Malaysia	Malayan Law Journal Sdn Bhd, KUALA LUMPUR
New Zealand	Butterworths of New Zealand Ltd, WELLINGTON and AUCKLAND
Singapore	Reed Elsevier (Singapore) Pte Ltd, SINGAPORE
South Africa	Butterworths Publishers (Pty) Ltd, DURBAN
USA	Michie Butterworth, CHARLOTTESVILLE, Virginia

A CIP Catalogue record for this book is available from the British Library.

ISBN 0 406 99088 3

Typeset by Phoenix Photosetting, Chatham, Kent
Printed and bound in Great Britain by Mackays of Chatham PLC, Chatham, Kent

ACKNOWLEDGMENTS

Extracts from exposure drafts, accounting standards and statements of recommended practice are reproduced by kind permission of the Accounting Standards Board and the International Accounting Standards Committee.

Extracts from the annual reports and accounts of the following companies are reproduced:

Albert Fisher Group plc
Argos plc
Argyll Group plc
Arjo Wiggins Appleton plc
BBA Group plc
Benson Group plc
Booker plc
Boots Company plc
Cadbury Schweppes plc
Chrysalis Group plc
Courts plc
Cowie Group plc
Dalgety plc
De La Rue plc
Fairway Group plc
First Choice Holdings plc
Galliford plc
Gestetner plc
Granada Group plc
Grand Metropolitan plc

Haynes Publishing plc
J Bibby & Sons plc
Lex Service plc
Lonrho plc
Lookers plc
Managanese Bronze
   Holdings plc
Norcros plc
Perry Group plc
Peter Black Holdings plc
Rank Organisation plc
Reckitt & Colman plc
Signet Group plc
Silentnight Holdings plc
Stakis plc
Tesco plc
Thorn EMI plc
Wessex Water plc
Williams Holdings plc
Wolseley plc

PREFACE

Spicer and Pegler's *Book-keeping and Accounts* first appeared 90 years ago. The text has enjoyed a reputation as a leader in financial accounting and reporting.

The lastest edition includes new chapters dealing with FRS 5, Reporting the substance of transactions, and listed company issues. Existing chapters have been extensively revised to reflect new Standards on capital instruments, fair values, acquisitions and mergers and related party disclosures. Accounting principles include the exposure draft of the ASB's Statement of Principles.

As with previous editions, the book includes a large selection of extracts from recently-published accounts of plcs. Many chapters have been restructured to enable easier access to desired topics.

It is hoped that the book will be useful and practical to a broad range of users, including students, practitioners and accountants in industry and commerce.

Once again I would like to thank Debbie Thom for her help in preparing the manuscript. Not least, I would like to thank my family for their patience and support.

Paul Gee
Bristol
May 1996

CONTENTS

ABBREVIATIONS

ACT	Advance corporation tax
ARD	Accounting reference date
ARP	Accounting reference period
ASB	Accounting Standards Board
ASC	Accounting Standards Committee
AVCO	Average cost
B/S	Balance sheet
CA	Companies Act
CBS	Consolidated balance sheet
CC	Current cost
CCA	Current cost accounting
CCAB	Consultative Committee of Accountancy Bodies
CCR	Current cost reserve
COSA	Cost of sales adjustment
CPL	Consolidated profit and loss account
CPP	Current (constant) purchasing power
CRC	Current replacement cost
CRR	Capital redemption reserve
DA	Depreciation adjustment
DTI	Department of Trade and Industry
ED	Exposure draft (of former ASC)
EC	European Community
EPS	Earnings per share
EV	Economic value
FCM	Financial capital maintenance
FDEPS	Fully diluted earnings per share
FIFO	First-in-first-out
FRC	Financial reporting council
FRED	Financial reporting exposure draft
FRRP	Financial Reporting Review Panel
FRS	Financial reporting standard
FY	Financial year
GA	Gearing adjustment
GAAP	Generally accepted accounting principles
HC	Historical cost
HCA	Historical cost accounting
IAS	International accounting standard
IASC	International Accounting Standards Committee
IPM	Investment period method
IRR	Investment revaluation reserve
IT	Income tax

LIBOR	London inter-bank offered rate
LIFO	Last-in-first-out
MCT	Mainstream corporation tax
MHC	Modified historical cost
MI	Minority interest
MWCA	Monetary working capital adjustment
NBV	Net book value
NCI	Net cash investment
NCRC	Net current replacement cost
NI	National insurance
NPSR	New profit-sharing ratio
NRV	Net realisable value
NV	Nominal value
OCM	Operating capital maintenance
OPSR	Old profit-sharing ratio
PAYE	Pay-as-you-earn
PCP	Permissible capital payment
PER	Price/earnings ratio
P/L	Profit and loss account
R + D	Research and development
RCA	Replacement cost accounting
ROCE	Return on capital employed
RPI	Retail price index
SFS	Summary financial statements
SORP	Statement of recommended practice
SSAP	Statement of standard accounting practice (issued by former ASC)
TR	Technical Release
UITF	Urgent Issues Task Force
VAT	Value added tax
WDA	Writing-down allowance
WDV	Written down value

A Partnership Accounts

1 PARTNERSHIP ACCOUNTS – 1

Key Issues

* The nature of partnership agreements
* Partners' accounts and the allocation of profits
* Goodwill – measurement and accounting adjustments
* Changes in partnership arrangements – admission of new partners
* Changes in partnership arrangements – departure, retirement or death of existing partners

---

1.1 INTRODUCTION

Partnership is defined by the Partnership Act 1890 as 'the relation which subsists between persons carrying on a business in common with a view of profit'. The participation in profits is not, however, of itself alone conclusive evidence of the existence of a partnership, since the relationship rests upon mutual intention.

Detailed considerations of partnership law are outside the scope of this book so no further reference will be made to the question of whether or not a partnership actually exists. It is, however, important to discuss the significance of the partnership agreement.

As the essence of partnership is mutual agreement, it is desirable for the partners to come to some understanding before entering into partnership as to the conditions upon which the business is to be carried on, and as to their respective rights and powers.

The Partnership Act 1890 lays down certain rules to be observed in the absence of agreement. The circumstances must determine whether these rules are applicable in the particular case, and since many matters should be decided which are not included in these rules, it is desirable that a formal agreement be entered into with a view to preventing disputes in the future. The advantages of a written agreement need no emphasis, and it is preferable that it should be under seal, since the character of a deed precludes contradiction by any party of the terms which have been agreed.

Even though a formal agreement is made, this does not preclude subsequent variation where changing circumstances demand it; such variation can always be effected with the consent of all the partners, which may be evidenced by an amending agreement, or inferred from a course of dealing.

(a) Clauses relating to accounting matters

The general provisions affecting questions of accounts that should be contained in all partnership agreements, apart from any special circumstances, are as follows:

(1) As to capital; whether each partner should contribute a fixed amount or otherwise.
(2) As to the division of profits and losses between the partners, including capital profits and losses.

(3) Whether the capitals are to be fixed, drawings and profits being adjusted on current accounts, or whether they are to be adjusted on the capital accounts.

(4) Whether interest on capital or on drawings, or both, is to be allowed or charged before arriving at the profits divisible in the agreed proportions, and if so, at what rate.

(5) Whether current accounts (if any) are to bear interest, and if so, at what rate.

(6) Whether partners' drawings are to be limited in amount.

(7) Whether partners are to be allowed remuneration for their services before arriving at divisible profits, and if so, the amounts thereof.

(8) That proper accounts shall be prepared at least once a year so that these shall be audited.

(9) That such accounts when duly signed shall be binding on the partners, but shall be capable of being reopened within a specified period on an error being discovered.

(10) The method by which the value of goodwill shall be determined in the event of the retirement or death of any of the partners.

(11) The method of determining the amount due to a deceased partner and the manner in which the liability to his personal representatives is to be settled eg by a lump sum payment within a specified period, by instalments of certain proportions etc, and the rate of interest to be allowed on outstanding balances.

(12) In the event of there being any partnership insurance policies, the method of treating the premiums thereon and the division of the policy money.

(b) Rights and duties of partners in the absence of a partnership agreement

The Partnership Act 1890 stipulates that the following rules apply in the absence of an agreement to the contrary (note that the rules are *not* mandatory).

The interests of partners in the partnership property, and their rights and duties in relation to the partnership shall be determined, subject to any agreement, express or implied, between the partners by the following rules:

(1) All the partners are entitled to share equally in the capital and profits of the business, and must contribute equally towards the losses, whether of capital or otherwise, sustained by the firm.

(2) The firm must indemnify every partner in respect of payments made and personal liabilities incurred by him:

   (a) in the ordinary and proper conduct of the business of the firm; or
   (b) in or about anything necessarily done for the preservation of the business or property of the firm.

(3) A partner is not entitled, before the ascertainment of profits, to interest on the capital subscribed by him.

(4) Every partner may take part in the management of the partnership business.

(5) No partner shall be entitled to remuneration for acting in the partnership business.

(6) No person may be introduced as a partner without the consent of all existing partners.

(7) Any difference arising as to ordinary matters connected with the partnership business may be decided by a majority of the partners, but no

change may be made in the nature of the partnership business without the consent of all existing partners.

(8) The partnership books are to be kept at the place of business of the partnership (or the principal place, if there is more than one), and every partner may, when he thinks fit, have access to and inspect and copy any of them.

1.2 PARTNERS' ACCOUNTS (CAPITAL, CURRENT, LOAN)

(a) Capital and current accounts

Where, as is usual, the partnership agreement provides for a fixed amount of capital to be contributed by each partner, it is preferable for the amounts thereof to be credited to the respective partners' capital accounts, and for partners' drawings, salaries, interest on capital and shares of profit to be dealt with in current accounts (see illustration below – Duck, Drake, Cygnet).

This enables a clear distinction to be made in the accounts between fixed capital (no part of which should be withdrawn, except by agreement) and undrawn profits. If partners' drawings, salaries, interest and shares of profit are passed through the capital accounts, the balances on these accounts will be constantly fluctuating, and there may be a danger of a partner's capital being depleted by drawings in excess of his share of profits etc, without particular attention being drawn to the fact.

(b) Partners' loan accounts

Where a partner makes an advance to the firm as distinct from capital, the amount thereof should be credited to a separate loan account and not to the partner's capital account. This is important, since under the Partnership Act 1890, advances by partners are repayable on dissolution in priority to capital.

Moreover, even in the absence of agreement on the point, a partner is entitled, under the Partnership Act 1890, to interest at 5% per annum on advances made to the firm, whereas he is not entitled to interest on capital.

Interest on a partner's advance or loan at the agreed rate (or, in the absence of agreement, at 5% per annum) should be credited to his current account, and debited to profit and loss account as an expense of the business in arriving at net profit. Interest on a partner's loan is as much a charge against the profits of a business as a loan from a third party. By contrast, interest on capital is an appropriation of profit, being in the nature of a preferential allocation of divisible profits.

1.3 ALLOCATION OF PARTNERSHIP PROFITS

The formula for allocation of partnership profits between the partners will usually be set out in the partnership agreement. The formula may take account of some or all of the following adjustments:

(a) Interest on capital.
(b) Interest on drawings.
(c) Partners' salaries.
(d) Profit-sharing ratios.

(a) Interest on capital

By making a notional charge against profits for interest at a fair commercial rate on the capital employed in a business, it can be seen whether the balance of profit remaining is sufficient to justify the continuance of the firm with unlimited liability, since the interest charged may be regarded as approximately the income the partners would have derived from the investment of their capital in securities involving little or no risk. Apart from this, however, where there are two or more partners with unequal capitals, the effect of charging interest on capital is to adjust the rights of the partners as between themselves as regards capital, giving each a reasonable return on his capital before dividing the balance of profit in the agreed proportions.

Where the capital is fixed, and the profits are shared in the same proportions as capital, the charging of interest makes no difference to the ultimate amount credited to each partner. Even in such cases, however, it may be desirable to charge interest for the first reason mentioned above.

Interest on capital should be calculated for the period during which the business has had the use of the capital, allowance being made for any additions or withdrawals during the period.

It may happen that the profits of the business in a particular year are less than the interest on capital credited to the partners. In such circumstances, unless the partnership agreement provides an alternative method, the interest should be charged in full, the resulting 'loss' being borne by the partners in the proportions in which they share profits. In this manner, the real result of the trading for the period is disclosed.

As already indicated, partners are not entitled to interest on capital unless the payment thereof is expressly authorised by the partnership agreement.

Illustration 1

A, B and C, sharing profits and losses equally, have capitals of £10,000, £5,000 and £2,000 respectively, on which they are entitled to interest at 5% per annum. The profits for the year, before charging interest on capital, amounted to £5,500. Show how the profits will be divided between the partners.

Statement of allocation of net profit (or appropriation account)

	Total	A	B	C
	£	£	£	£
Interest on capital	850	500	250	100
Balance of profits (shared equally)	4,650	1,550	1,550	1,550
Net profit, allocated between partners	5,500	2,050	1,800	1,650

(b) Interest on drawings

Frequently, partners make drawings in varying amounts and at irregular intervals, and in such cases, if interest is charged the rights of the partners are adjusted. In many cases, however, drawings are made by mutual agreement and no interest is charged at all.

Where interest is charged, it is usually calculated at a fixed rate per cent per annum from the date of each drawing to the date the accounts are closed and taken account of in the statement of allocation of net profit in a similar way to interest on capital.

(c) Partners' salaries

As already stated, in the absence of agreement no partner is entitled before arriving at the amount of divisible profits to remuneration for his services to the firm. In the following cases however, it may be desirable for the partnership agreement to provide for the payment of salaries to the partners:

(1) Where some of the partners take a greater or more effective part in the conduct and management of the business than others.

(2) Where there are junior partners, whom it is desired to remunerate by way of a fixed salary plus, perhaps, a small percentage of the profits.
(3) Where the partnership business is wholly managed by the partners, and it is desired to ascertain the true profit, after such a charge for managerial services had been made as would have been incurred had the business not been managed by the proprietors.

Where the agreement provides for the payment of salaries to partners, it should be appreciated that such payments, although designated salaries are, like interest on capital, merely in the nature of preferential shares of the divisible profit. The amounts of such salaries should therefore be taken into account in the statement of allocation of net profit.

Illustration 2

Duck, Drake and Cygnet carry on a retail business in partnership. The partnership agreement provides that:

(1) The partners are to be credited at the end of each year with salaries of £1,000 to Duck and £500 each to Drake and Cygnet, and with interest at the rate of 5% per annum on the balances at the credit of their respective capital accounts at the commencement of the year.
(2) No interest is to be charged on drawings.
(3) After charging partnership salaries and interest on capital, profits and losses are to be divided in the proportion: Duck, 50%; Drake, 30% and Cygnet, 20%; with the proviso, however, that Cygnet's share in any year (exclusive of salary and interest) shall not be less than £1,000, any deficiency to be borne in profit-sharing ratio by the other two partners.
  The trial balance of the firm at December 31 19X8 was as follows:

	Dr £	Cr £
Partners' capital accounts:		
Duck – Balance January 1 19X8		8,000
Drake – Balance January 1 19X8		5,000
Cygnet – Balance January 1 19X8		3,000
Partners' current accounts:		
Duck – Balance January 1 19X8		1,600
Drake – Balance January 1 19X8		1,200
Cygnet – Balance January 1 19X8		800
Sales		46,500
Trade creditors		3,700
Shop fittings at cost	3,600	
Shop fittings – provision for depreciation, January 1 19X8		1,400
Freehold premises – cost	6,000	
Leasehold premises – purchased during year	4,500	
Leasehold premises – additions and alterations	2,500	
Purchases	28,000	
Stock on hand, January 1 19X8	4,200	
Salaries and wages	6,400	
Office and trade expenses	4,520	
Rent, rates and insurance	1,050	
Professional charges	350	
Debtors	2,060	
Provision for doubtful debts, January 1 19X8		50
Balance at bank	4,370	
Drawings, other than monthly payments:		
Duck	1,700	
Drake	1,100	
Cygnet	900	
	71,250	71,250

You are given the following additional information:

(1) Stock on December 31 19X8 was valued at £3,600.
(2) A debt of £60 is to be written off, and the provision against the remaining debtors should be 5%.
(3) Salaries and wages include the following monthly drawings by the partners: Duck £50, Drake £30, Cygnet £25.
(4) Partners had during the year been supplied with goods from stock and it was agreed that these should be charged to them as follows: Duck £60 and Drake £40.
(5) On December 31, rates paid in advance and office and trade expenses owing were £250 and £240 respectively.
(6) Depreciation of shop fittings is to be provided at 5% per annum on cost.
(7) Professional charges include £250 fees paid in respect of the acquisition of the leasehold premises, which fees are to be capitalised.
(8) The cost of and the additions and alterations to the leasehold premises were to be written off over 25 years, commencing on January 1 in the year in which the premises were acquired.

You are required to prepare:

(a) the trading and profit and loss account for the year ended December 31 19X8;
(b) the balance sheet as at that date; and
(c) partners' current accounts in columnar form for the year ended December 31 19X8.

Solution

(a)   DUCK, DRAKE AND CYGNET TRADING AND PROFIT AND LOSS ACCOUNT
for the year ending 31 December 19X8

	£	£	£
Sales			46,500
Opening stock		4,200	
Purchases	28,000		
Goods supplied to partners	100		
		27,900	
		32,100	
Less closing stock		3,600	
			28,500
Gross profit			18,000
Salaries and wages		5,140	
Office and trade expenses		4,760	
Rent, rates and insurance		800	
Professional charges		100	
Bad debts		110	
Amortisation of leasehold premises		290	
Depreciation of shop fittings		180	
			11,380
Net profit			6,620

Statement of allocation of net profit

	Total £	Duck £	Drake £	Cygnet £
Interest on capital	800	400	250	150
Partners' salaries	2,000	1,000	500	500
Balance of profits (shared 50:30:20)	3,820	1,910	1,146	764
Provisional allocation of net profit	6,620	3,310	1,896	1,414
Adjustment to bring Cygnet's share of 'balance' of profit up to £1,000 (ie adjustment of 1,000 – 764) borne by Duck and Drake in ratio 5:3	–	(147)	(89)	236
Final allocation of net profit	6,620	3,163	1,807	1,650

(b) Balance sheet as at 31 December 19X8

	Cost £	Accumulated depreciation £	Net book value £
Fixed assets			
Freehold premises	6,000	–	6,000
Leasehold premises	7,250	290	6,960
Shop fittings	3,600	1,580	2,020
	16,850	1,870	14,980
Current assets			
Stock		3,600	
Debtors	2,000		
Less provision for doubtful debts	100		
		1,900	
Prepayments		250	
Cash at bank		4,370	
		10,120	
Less current liabilities			
Trade creditors	3,700		
Accrued expenses	240		
		3,940	
Net current assets			6,180
			21,160

Partners' accounts	Capital accounts £	Current accounts £	Total £
Duck	8,000	2,403	10,403
Drake	5,000	1,507	6,507
Cygnet	3,000	1,250	4,250
	16,000	5,160	21,160

(c) Partners' current accounts

	Duck £	Drake £	Cygnet £		Duck £	Drake £	Cygnet £
Drawings:							
Cash	2,300	1,460	1,200	Bal b/f	1,600	1,200	800
Goods	60	40	–	Share of net			
Bal c/f	2,403	1,507	1,250	profit	3,163	1,807	1,650
	4,763	3,007	2,450		4,763	3,007	2,450

1.4 GOODWILL

(a) Definition of goodwill

The following are some judicial definitions of goodwill:

(1) 'The goodwill of a business is the advantage, whatever it may be, which a person gets by continuing to carry on, and being entitled to represent to the outside world that he is carrying on a business, which has been carried on for some time previously.' (Warrington J, in *Hill v Fearis* [1950] 1 Ch 466.)

(2) '[Goodwill] is a thing very easy to describe, very difficult to define. It is the benefit and advantage of the good name, reputation and connection of a business. It is the attractive force which brings in custom. It is the one thing which distinguishes an old established business from a new business at its first start . . . Goodwill is composed of a variety of elements. It differs in its

composition in different trades and in different businesses in the same trade. One element may preponderate here, and another there.' (Lord Macnaughten in *IRC v Muller* [1901] AC 217.)

From the accountant's viewpoint, goodwill, in the sense of attracting custom, has little significance unless it has a saleable value. To the accountant, therefore, goodwill may be said to be that element arising from the reputation, connection or other advantages possessed by a business which enables it to earn greater profits than the return normally to be expected on the capital represented by the net tangible assets employed in the business. In considering the return normally to be expected, regard must be had to the nature of the business, the risks involved, fair management remuneration and any other relevant circumstances.

The goodwill possessed by a firm may be due, inter alia, to the following:

(a) The location of the business premises.
(b) The nature of the firm's products or the reputation of its service.
(c) The possession of favourable contracts, complete or partial monopoly etc.
(d) The personal reputation of the partners.
(e) The possession of efficient and contented employees.
(f) The possession of trade marks, patents or a well-known business name.
(g) The continuance of advertising campaigns.
(h) The maintenance of the quality of the firm's product, and development of the business with changing conditions.
(i) Freedom from legislative restrictions.

Goodwill is defined in SSAP 22 as 'the difference between the value of a business as a whole and the aggregate of the fair value of its separable net assets'. (See section 13.2.)

(b) Goodwill in partnership accounts

Although a firm may possess goodwill, it is not customary to raise an account for it in the books except to the extent that cash or other assets of the firm have been used to pay for it. It follows, therefore, that when goodwill exists and is unrecorded in the books, the capitals of the partners of the firm are understated to the extent of the value of their respective shares of the goodwill.

Even though a goodwill account may at some time have been raised in the books, the goodwill account would not be adjusted to give effect to every variation in its value, and in most cases, therefore, the partners' capitals are at all times understated or overstated in the books to some extent by their shares of the unrecorded appreciation or depreciation in the value of goodwill.

As the amount by which goodwill is undervalued (or overvalued) in the books is a profit (or a loss) to be shared by the partners in their agreed profit-sharing ratio, any alteration in the proportions in which profits and losses are shared, without first making an adjustment in the book value of goodwill, will result in an advantage to one or more partners and a disadvantage to others.

(c) Situations requiring adjustments in respect of goodwill

In each of the following cases, a change in the profit-sharing ratio takes place and therefore, unless a goodwill account already stands in the books at its correct value, some adjustment must be made:

(1) Upon the introduction of a new partner.
(2) Upon the retirement or death of a partner.
(3) Upon an agreed change in profit-sharing ratio between the partners.

These are dealt with later in the chapter under the respective headings.

(d) Methods of valuing goodwill

Various methods are advocated for the valuation of goodwill. In many cases the method adopted is a purely arbitrary one and is often governed by the custom of the particular trade in which the business is engaged. The more usual bases of valuation are as follows:

(1) *The average profits of a given number of past years multiplied by an agreed number*

Thus, 'three years' purchase of net profits' is commonly spoken of as the basis upon which goodwill is valued. This method is purely arbitrary and will frequently produce a figure for goodwill out of all proportion to its true value.

Illustration 3

The average net profit made by A, B and Co for the past five years has been £2,000 per annum before charging interest on capital and partners' salaries. The average capital employed in the business has been £10,000.

On the basis of three years' purchase of net profits, £6,000 would be payable for the goodwill of the firm. It is apparent, however, that no goodwill actually exists; in fact, there is a negative goodwill since no one would be prepared to pay £16,000 for a business which produces only £2,000 per annum before making any provision for fair remuneration to the proprietors in respect of their services to the business.

Allowing as little as £1,500 per annum for the services of the proprietors, only £500 per annum remains for interest on capital invested and, therefore, at, say 10% per annum, such a business would be worth as an investment only £5,000, irrespective of the fact that £10,000 was invested in it.

(2) *The average gross income of the business for a number of past years multiplied by an agreed number*

This method is frequently adopted by professional firms, but is subject to the same disadvantages as those described above. In many cases the gross income of certain years will have been inflated by business of a non-recurring nature, and therefore the purchaser will be paying for goodwill calculated on income which he himself will not enjoy. Furthermore, it is quite conceivable that the expenses incurred in earning the gross income may be so great that there is actually a loss, in which case a sum will be payable for the 'goodwill' of a business from which a loss is to be expected.

(3) *The capital value of an annuity for an agreed number of years of an amount equal to the average super profits of the business*

Super profits are the profits in excess of the amount necessary to pay a fair return upon the capital invested in the business, having regard to the nature of the business and the risks involved and a reasonable remuneration for the services of the partners who work therein.

Illustration 4

The average net profits expected in the future by A, B and Co are £10,000 per annum. The average capital employed in the business is £50,000.

The rate of interest expected from capital invested in this class of business, having regard to the risk involved, is 10%.

Fair remuneration to the partners of the firm in respect of their services to the business is estimated to be £2,500 per annum.

Valuation of goodwill

	£	£
Average annual profits		10,000
Less interest on capital employed at 10%	5,000	
partners' remuneration (say)	2,500	
		7,500
Annual super profit		2,500

It is now necessary to ascertain the present value of an annuity of £2,500 per annum for a suitable number of years. Alternatively, 'x years' purchase' of £2,500 may be taken as the value of goodwill, according to the number of years that could be regarded as necessary to build up such a goodwill, discounted by reference to the fact that any goodwill purchased is a wasting asset, since the influence of the vendor diminishes as that of the purchaser increases.

(4) *Excess of value of a business over value of tangible net assets*

The value of the business as a going concern is estimated by reference to the expected earnings and the yield required. From the figure arrived at the value of the net tangible assets is deducted, the difference being taken to represent the value of goodwill.

Illustration 5

	£
Estimated future annual profit	10,000
Less partners' remuneration	2,500
Available for interest on capital employed	7,500

Assuming a yield of 10% per annum is expected, the capital value of the business is £75,000. If the value of the net tangible assets of the business is £50,000, the goodwill is worth a maximum of £25,000. This figure may have to be discounted as the earning of super profits entails greater risks than the earning of the smaller amount required to provide a fair return on money invested in tangible assets.

1.5   CHANGES IN PARTNERSHIP ARRANGEMENTS: NEW PARTNERS

This can raise two particular problems:

(a) Adjustment for goodwill.
(b) Apportionment of profit.

(a) Adjustment for goodwill

It was stated above that if the value of goodwill is unrecorded in the books, the capital accounts of the partners are understated by the value thereof.

Illustration 6

Assume that the following is the balance sheet of the firm of A and B, who share profits in the proportion of two-thirds and one-third respectively.

	£	£	£
Fixed assets			
Land and buildings			5,250
Plant and machinery			3,075
			8,325

	£	£	£
Current assets			
Stock		4,500	
Debtors	3,000		
Less provision for doubtful debts	150		
		2,850	
Cash at bank		300	
		7,650	
Less creditors		3,975	
			3,675
			12,000
Capital accounts			
A			8,500
B			3,500
			12,000

The goodwill of the firm is valued at £6,000 and, therefore, the true capitals of A and B are £4,000 and £2,000 respectively more than the amounts standing to the credit of their capital accounts. As these increments arise from the fact that goodwill is not recorded in the books, it is apparent that some adjustment must be made in the event of the introduction of a new partner, in order that he shall not take a share of goodwill without payment.

There are two main methods of dealing with the goodwill.

Method 1 – raise an account for goodwill

An account is raised in the old firm's books for the full value of goodwill, the old partners' capital accounts being credited therewith in the proportions in which they share profits or losses. The new partner may or may not bring in capital according to the agreement. In any event, whatever he brings in will be credited to his capital account. The effect of this method is to increase the old partners' capital accounts to the extent of the value of goodwill previously unrecorded.

In the example above, assume that A and B agree to admit C into partnership, giving him a one-fifth share of profits; C to bring in capital to the extent of one-quarter of the combined capitals of A and B after adjustment for goodwill. A's and B's proportions of profit in the new firm are to be in the same ratio between themselves as before.

Assuming C brings in the required amount of cash, the following journal entries are relevant:

JOURNAL

	Dr £	Cr £
(1) Goodwill account	6,000	
Capital account of A		4,000
Capital account of B		2,000
Creation of goodwill as agreed on admittance of C into partnership		
(2) Cash	4,500	
Capital account of C		4,500

Capital in by C ($\frac{1}{4}$ of 12,500 + 5,500)

The balance sheet after the above transaction is:

	£
Fixed assets	
Goodwill	6,000
Land and buildings	5,250
Plant and machinery	3,075
	14,325

	£	£
Current assets		
Stock	4,500	
Debtors (net)	2,850	
Cash at bank	4,800	
	12,150	
Less creditors	3,975	
		8,175
		22,500
Capital accounts		
A		12,500
B		5,500
C		4,500
		22,500

Method 2 – no account retained for goodwill

No goodwill account is raised in the books, but the proportion of the agreed value of goodwill attributable to the incoming partner's share of profit is paid for by him in cash. The additional cash brought in by the new partner for the acquisition of a share of goodwill is credited to the capital accounts of the old partners in the proportions in which they shared profits before the introduction of the new partner, if the old partners continue to share profits as between themselves in the same proportions as they did before. The cash brought in by the new partner as his capital will be credited to his capital account in the normal manner.

Illustration 7

Assuming the same facts as for the previous example, but that no goodwill account is to be opened in the books on C's admission, the latter introducing £3,300 as his capital and £1,200 for his share of goodwill.

Show by journal entries the adjustments to be made on C's introduction, and the balance sheet of the new firm.

JOURNAL

	Dr £	Cr £
Cash	1,200	
Capital accounts:		
A ($\frac{2}{3}$)		800
B ($\frac{1}{3}$)		400

Payment by C for a one-fifth share in the goodwill.

Cash	3,300	
C Capital account		3,300

Capital introduced by C

Balance sheet after completion of transactions:

Fixed assets	
Land and buildings	5,250
Plant and machinery	3,075
	8,325

	£	£
Current assets		
Stock	4,500	
Debtors	2,850	
Cash at bank	4,800	
	12,150	
Less creditors	3,975	
		8,175
		16,500
Capital accounts		
A		9,300
B		3,900
C		3,300
		16,500

Workings

The simplest approach is to:

(1) Credit A and B with their goodwill shares in the old profit-sharing ratios (OPSR).
(2) Debit A, B and C with their goodwill shares in the new profit-sharing ratio (NPSR).

CAPITAL ACCOUNTS

	A £	B £	C £		A £	B £	C £
Goodwill account	3,200	1,600	1,200	Balances b/f	8,500	3,500	
				Goodwill a/c	4,000	2,000	
Balances c/f	9,300	3,900	3,300	Cash introduced:			
				For goodwill			1,200
				For capital			3,300
	12,500	5,500	4,500		12,500	5,500	4,500

GOODWILL ACCOUNT

	£		£
Capital accounts		Capital accounts:	
A ($\frac{2}{3} \times$ £6,000)	4,000	A ($\frac{8}{15} \times$ £6,000)	3,200
B ($\frac{1}{3} \times$ £6,000)	2,000	B ($\frac{4}{15} \times$ £6,000)	1,600
		C ($\frac{3}{15} \times$ £6,000)	1,200
	6,000		6,000

(b) Apportionment of profit

In order to apportion the profits or losses between the partners upon a change of personnel, or where the existing partners vary as between themselves the profit-sharing ratio, unless the change takes place at the financial year end of the business, it will be necessary for stock to be taken and work-in-progress valued, or alternatively for the profits for the year to be apportioned. If the profits are to be apportioned, they will be apportioned either on a time basis, or in proportion to the turnover of the periods prior to and after the change, or by a combination of these methods.

Illustration 8

Green and Blue were partners in a retail business sharing profits and losses: Green, two-thirds and Blue, one-third. Interest on fixed capitals was allowed at the rate of 6%

per annum, but no interest was charged or allowed on current accounts. Accounts were made up to 31 March in each year.

The following was the partnership trial balance as on 31 March 19X9:

	£		£	£
Leasehold premises		Fixed capital accounts:		
purchased 1 April 19X8	6,000	Green	3,000	
Purchases	16,400	Blue	2,000	
Motor vehicles at cost	3,400			5,000
Balance at bank	9,280	Current accounts:		
Salaries, including		Green	1,600	
partners' drawings	5,200	Blue	1,200	
Stock 31 March 19X8	4,800			2,800
Shop fittings at cost	1,200	Cash introduced – Black		5,000
Debtors	900	Sales (£14,000 to 30		
Professional charges	420	September 19X8)		35,000
Shop wages	2,200	Provisions for depreciation		
Rent, rates, lighting		on 1 April 19X8:		
and heating	1,240	Motor vehicles	1,200	
General expenses		Shop fittings	400	
(£1,410 for six months				1,600
to 30 September 19X8)	2,640	Creditors		4,280
	53,680			53,680

You are given the following additional information:

(1) On 30 September 19X8, Black was admitted as a partner and from that date, profits and losses were shared: Green, two-fifths, Blue, two-fifths and Black, one-fifth. For the purpose of these changes, the value of the goodwill of the firm was agreed at £12,000. No account for goodwill was to be maintained in the books, adjusting entries for transactions between the parties being made in their current accounts. On 1 October 19X8, Black had introduced £5,000 into the firm of which it was agreed £1,500 should comprise his fixed capital and the balance should be credited to his current account.

Any apportionment of gross profit was to be made on the basis of sales; expenses, unless otherwise indicated, were to be apportioned on a time basis.
(2) On 31 March 19X9, the stock was valued at £5,100.
(3) Provision was to be made for depreciation on the motor vehicles and shop fittings at 20% and 5% per annum respectively, calculated on cost.
(4) Salaries included the following partners' drawings: Green £600, Blue £480 and Black £250.
(5) At 31 March 19X9, rates paid in advance amounted to £260 and a provision of £60 for electricity consumed was required.
(6) A difference on the books of £120 had been written off at 31 March 19X9 to general expenses, which was later found to be due to the following errors:

   (i) sales returns of £80 had been debited to sales but had not been posted to the account of the customer concerned;
   (ii) the purchase journal had been undercast by £200.

(7) Professional charges included £210 paid in respect of the acquisition of the leasehold premises. These fees are to be capitalised as part of the cost of the lease, the total cost of which was to be written off in 25 equal annual instalments. Other premises, owned by Blue, were leased by him to the partnership at £600 per annum, but no rent had been paid or credited to him for the year to 31 March 19X9.
(8) Doubtful debts (for which full provision was required) as of 30 September 19X8 amounted to £120 and as of 31 March 19X9 to £160.

You are required to prepare:

(a) the trading and profit and loss account for the year ended 31 March 19X9;
(b) the balance sheet as on that date; and
(c) partners' current accounts, in columnar form.

Solution

(a)   MESSRS GREEN, BLUE AND BLACK TRADING, PROFIT AND
LOSS ACCOUNT

for the year ended 31 March 19X9

		£	£
Sales			
1.4.X8 to 30.9.X8			14,000
1.10.X8 to 31.3.X9			21,000
			35,000
Stock 1.4.X8		4,800	
Purchases (16,400 + 200)		16,600	
		21,400	
Less stock 31.3.X9		5,100	
			16,300
Gross profit			18,700

	£	*Period* *1.4.X8 to* *30.9.X8* £	*Period* *1.10.X8 to* *31.3.X9* £
Gross profit (allocated ratio 14:21)		7,480	11,220
Salaries (5,200 − 1,330)		1,935	1,935
Rent, rates, lighting and heating			
(1,240 + 600 + 60 − 260)		820	820
Shop wages		1,100	1,100
Professional charges (420 − 210)		105	105
General expenses (2,640 − 120)		1,410	1,110
Depreciation:			
Motor vehicles	680		
Shop fittings	60		
	740		
		370	370
Amortisation of lease $\frac{1}{25}$ of (6,000 + 210)		124	124
Provision for doubtful debts		120	40
Net profit c/d		1,496	5,616

Statement of allocation of net profit

	Total £	*Green* £	*Blue* £	*Black* £
Interest on capital				
6 m to 30.9.19X8	150	90	60	
6 m to 31.3.19X9	195	90	60	45
Balance of profits				
6 m to 30.9.19X8				
(1,496 − 150) in ratio 2:1:0	1,346	897	449	−
(5,616 − 195) in ratio 2:2:1	5,421	2,168	2,168	1,085
Totals	7,112	3,245	2,737	1,130

(b) Balance sheet as at 31 March 19X9

	Cost £	Depreciation £	Net book value £
Fixed assets			
Leasehold premises	6,210	248	5,962
Motor vehicles	3,400	1,880	1,520
Shop fittings	1,200	460	740
	10,810	2,588	8,222
Current assets			
Stock			5,100
Debtors (900 – 80)		820	
Less provision for doubtful debts		160	
			660
Prepayments			260
Cash at bank			9,280
			15,300
Less creditors (4,280 + 60)			4,340
Net current assets			10,960
			19,182

	Capital accounts £	Current accounts £	Total £
Partners' accounts			
Green	3,000	7,445	10,445
Blue	2,000	3,257	5,257
Black	1,500	1,980	3,480
	6,500	12,682	19,182

(c) Partners' current accounts

	Green £	Blue £	Black £		Green £	Blue £	Black £
Goodwill written down				Bal b/f	1,600	1,200	–
(NPSR)	4,800	4,800	2,400	Share of profit	3,245	2,737	1,130
Drawings	600	480	250	Goodwill written up			
Bal c/f	7,445	3,257	1,980	(OPSR)	8,000	4,000	–
				Rent	–	600	–
				Cash introduced	–	–	3,500
	12,845	8,537	4,630		12,845	8,537	4,630

OPSR = old profit-sharing ratio (2:1)
NPSR = new profit-sharing ratio (2:2:1)

1.6   CHANGES IN PARTNERSHIP ARRANGEMENTS: OUTGOING PARTNERS

(a) Introduction

In the absence of any agreement or uniform usage to the contrary a partner, on retirement, or the representative of a deceased partner, is entitled to have the partnership assets, including goodwill, revalued on a proper basis as at the date of the retirement or death, and any appreciation or depreciation so revealed is taken into account in computing the sum due to him or them. The total amount so ascertained to be due is normally a debt due by the firm to the retired partner or the representatives of the deceased partner.

An agreement may, however, be made between the partners whereby, in the event of the death or retirement of a partner, the remaining partners shall assume, personally, the liability for the amount due. In such circumstances, the debt is no longer due by the firm but by the partners individually in the ratio agreed upon.

(b) Repayment of amount owing by instalments

Upon the retirement or death of a partner, the value of his capital and share of the goodwill etc is ascertained, either in accordance with the provisions of the partnership agreement or by accounts taken at the date of the dissolution, and the amount so ascertained is paid out to him or his representatives forthwith, or credited to a loan account, and repaid by instalments, with interest running on the outstanding balance. It is important, where payment is not made at once, that the amount due should be credited to a loan account, and not retained in the books as capital, especially in the case of a retired partner, when retention of the amount due to him as capital might imply that he was still a partner.

Illustration 9

M, a partner in a firm, died on 31 March 19X8 and his share of capital and goodwill is ascertained to be £7,600. It was arranged that this should be paid out by annual instalments of £2,000 to include principal and interest on the outstanding balance at 5% per annum. The first payment is made one month after death, and succeeding payments are made on the anniversary of the date of death. Show the account in the firm's books relating thereto until completion. Ignore income tax, and make calculations to nearest £.

THE EXECUTORS OF M (DECEASED) ACCOUNT

			£				£
19X8				*19X8*			
30 April	Cash		2,000	31 March	Capital account		7,600
	Balance c/f		5,632	30 April	Interest, 1 month		32
			7,632				7,632
19X9				*19X8*			
31 March	Cash		2,000	1 May	Balance b/f		5,632
	Balance c/f		3,890	*19X9*			
				31 March	Interest, 11 mths		258
			5,890				5,890
19X10				*19X9*			
31 March	Cash		2,000	1 April	Balance b/f		3,890
	Balance b/f		2,085	*19X10*			
				31 March	Interest, 1 year		195
			4,085				4,085
19X11				*19X10*			
31 March	Cash		2,000	1 April	Balance b/f		2,085
	Balance c/f		189	*19X11*			
				31 March	Interest, 1 year		104
			2,189				2,189
19X12				*19X11*			
31 March	Cash		198	1 April	Balance b/f		189
				19X12			
				31 March	Interest, 1 year		9
			198				198

(c) Amount owing remains on as a loan to the firm

Where this course is adopted, the retired partner's capital must be transferred to a loan account. Usually, the rate of interest payable on this loan and the conditions of repayment are laid down in the partnership agreement or by a contract entered into at the date of retirement, but in the absence of agreement it is provided by s 42 of the Partnership Act 1890 that the retired partner is entitled to interest at 5% per annum, or such share of the profits as the court may determine to be attributable to the use of his share of the partnership assets. If a retired partner enforces his right to a share of profit in these circumstances, the court would deduct a reasonable sum for the services of the remaining partners for carrying on the business, before arriving at the profit to be divided.

Where an option is given to the continuing partners to purchase the share of the retired partner, and the option is exercised, the retired partner is not entitled to any further share of the profits. His capital is therefore transferred to the capital accounts of the continuing partners, who must pay him according to the terms of the agreement.

When it is agreed that the loan shall carry a rate of interest varying with the profits of the firm, or entitle the retired partner to a share of such profits, such an agreement will not of itself cause the retired partner to continue to be liable as a partner of the firm, provided that the contract is in writing and signed by or on behalf of all the parties thereto. If, however, the firm should become bankrupt, the retired partner will be a deferred creditor in respect of any loan made in such circumstances.

(d) Adjustments to asset values

When a partner retires, it does not follow that the balance of his capital account represents his true interest in the partnership, apart from the question of goodwill (to which reference has already been made), since some assets may have appreciated in value without any adjustment having been made in the books, whilst others may have been insufficiently depreciated, over-depreciated, or entirely written off. It will be necessary, therefore to correct these values, in order that the outgoing partner shall receive his true share. A revaluation account should be opened, to which all differences in values should be debited or credited, as the case may be, the resultant balance being divided among the partners according to the ratio in which they share profits and losses.

Illustration 10

Brown, Jones and Robinson, sharing profits and losses equally, had been trading for many years and Robinson decided to retire as at 31 December 19X8 on which date the balance sheet of the firm was as under:

	£	£
Fixed assets		
Freehold premises		8,000
Plant and machinery		4,000
Patents		6,000
		18,000
Current assets		
Stock	5,000	
Debtors	6,000	
Cash at bank	3,000	
	14,000	
Less creditors	8,000	
		6,000
		24,000

	£	£
Capital accounts		
Brown		10,000
Jones		8,000
Robinson		6,000
		24,000

The value of the goodwill was agreed at £8,000.

The freehold premises had increased in value as a result of general economic conditions, the value being agreed at £11,000. Plant and patents were respectively revalued at £3,600 and £5,300 and it was also agreed to provide 5% in respect of debtors, it having been the practice in the past only to write off bad debts actually incurred.

Show the adjusted balance sheet of the firm, and the amount to which Robinson would be entitled under the following alternative assumptions:

(1) The ongoing partners wish to retain the assets in the balance sheet at their revised valuations.
(2) The assets are to be reflected in the balance sheet at their previous valuations.

(1) Balance sheet reflecting revised valuations

	£	£	£
Fixed assets			
Freehold premises			11,000
Plant and machinery			3,600
Patents			5,300
Goodwill			8,000
			27,900
Current assets			
Stock		5,000	
Debtors	6,000		
Less provision	300		
		5,700	
Cash at bank		3,000	
		13,700	
Less creditors		8,000	
			5,700
			33,600
Capital accounts			
Brown			13,200
Jones			11,200
			24,400
Loan account			
Robinson			9,200
			33,600

Workings

REVALUATION ACCOUNT

	£	£		£
Plant		400	Goodwill	8,000
Patents		700	Freehold premises	3,000
Provision for bad debts		300		
Balance transferred to capital accounts				
Brown	3,200			
Jones	3,200			
Robinson	3,200			
	9,600			
	11,000			11,000

(2) Balance sheet retaining previous valuations

Although the above adjustments have been made in order to ascertain the amount due to Robinson, the remaining partners may not desire to disturb the existing book values, in which case the difference on revaluation (£9,600) would be written back to the capital accounts of Brown and Jones, in the proportions in which they will share profits and losses in future, the position then being:

	£	£
Fixed assets		
Freehold premises		8,000
Plant and machinery		4,000
Patents		6,000
		18,000
Current assets		
Stock	5,000	
Debtors	6,000	
Cash	3,000	
	14,000	
Less creditors	8,000	
		6,000
		24,000
Capital accounts		
Brown (13,200 – 4,800)		8,400
Jones (11,200 – 4,800)		6,400
		14,800
Loan account		
Robinson		9,200
		24,000

Note: alternative (2) has been shown for illustration purposes. While the partners may wish to exclude goodwill from the partnership balance sheet, any assets which have suffered a diminution in value (such as debtors, in this example) should be stated at a prudent amount (eg debtors, £5,700).

2 PARTNERSHIP ACCOUNTS – 2

> **Key Issues**
> * Situations involving dissolution of partnerships
> * Closing the partnership books on dissolution
> * Dissolution – the rule in *Garner v Murray*
> * Dissolution – piecemeal realisation
> * Amalgamation of separate businesses
> * Conversion of a partnership into a limited company

2.1 DISSOLUTION OF PARTNERSHIPS – GENERAL CONSIDERATIONS

(a) Basic principles

Upon the dissolution of a partnership, s 44 of the Partnership Act 1890 provides that the assets of the firm, including the sums (if any) contributed by the partners to make up losses or deficiencies of capital, must be applied in the following manner and order:

(1) In paying the debts and liabilities of the firm to persons who are not partners therein.
(2) In paying to each partner rateably what is due from the firm to him for advances as distinguished from capital.
(3) In paying to each partner the amount due to him in respect of his capital and current account balances.

In the absence of agreement to the contrary, the Partnership Act 1890 provides that the following shall be grounds for the dissolution of a partnership:

(1) The expiration of the term for which the partnership was entered into, if a fixed term was agreed upon.
(2) The termination of the adventure or undertaking, when a single adventure or undertaking was the purpose of the partnership.
(3) When one partner gives notice to the others of his intention to dissolve the firm.
(4) The death of a partner.
(5) The bankruptcy of a partner.
(6) The happening of an event which causes the partnership to become illegal.
(7) When a partner allows his share of the partnership to be charged for his separate debt.

(b) Formula for closing partnership books on dissolution

Apart from special circumstances, the following outline of the steps necessary to close the books of a partnership when the assets are sold en bloc, may be found useful:

(1) Open a realisation account, and debit thereto the book value of the assets, crediting the various asset accounts. The realisation account will also be debited with any expenses of realisation, and cash credited.

(2) Debit cash and credit realisation account with the amount realised on the sale of the assets.

Note: Should any of the assets be taken over at a valuation by any of the partners, debit such partners' capital accounts, and credit realisation account with the agreed price.

(3) Pay off the liabilities, crediting cash and debiting sundry creditors. Any discount allowed by creditors on discharging liabilities should be debited to the creditors' accounts and credited to realisation account.

(4) The balance of the realisation account will be the amount of the profit or loss on realisation, which will be divided between the partners in the proportion in which they share profits and losses and transferred to their capital accounts.

(5) Pay off any partners' advances as distinct from capital, first setting off any *debit* balance on the capital account of a partner against his loan account.

(6) The balance on the cash book will now be exactly equal to the balances on the capital accounts, provided they are in credit; credit cash and debit the partners' capital accounts with the amounts paid to them to close their accounts.

Should the capital account of any partner be in debit after being debited with his share of the loss, or credited with his share of the profit on realisation, the cash will be insufficient by the amount of such debit balance to pay the other partners the amounts due to them. If the partner whose account is in debit pays to the firm the amount of his indebtedness, the other partners' capital accounts can then be closed by the payment of cash. If, however, he is unable to do so, the deficiency must, according to the decision in *Garner v Murray*, be borne by the solvent partners, in proportion to their capitals, and not in the proportion in which they share profits and losses. The application of this rule is illustrated in section 2.2 below.

The following illustrations show the closing of the books on the dissolution of partnerships in varying circumstances:

(1) *Where, on dissolution, there is a profit on the realisation of the assets*

Illustration 1

X and Y are in partnership sharing profits – five-eighths and three-eighths. They agree to dissolve partnership, and their abridged balance sheet at the date of dissolution, 30 June 19X2, is as follows:

X AND Y BALANCE SHEET

June 30 19X2

	£	£		£
Capital accounts:			Premises	1,200
X	1,500		Stock	1,400
Y	1,300	2,800	Debtors	1,100
			Cash	600
Creditors		1,500		
		£4,300		£4,300

The dissolution is completed by December 31 19X2, the assets, other than cash, being sold en bloc and realising £4,500. Close the books of the firm.

REALISATION ACCOUNT

19X2		£	£	19X2		£
June 30	Sundry assets		3,700	Dec 31	Cash	4,500
Dec 31	Profit transferred					
	to capital accounts:					
	X ($\frac{5}{8}$)	500				
	Y ($\frac{3}{8}$)	300				
			800			
			£4,500			£4,500

SUNDRY CREDITORS

19X2		£	19X2		£
Dec 31	Cash	1,500	June 30	Balance b/f	1,500

X CAPITAL ACCOUNT

19X2		£	19X2		£
Dec 31	Cash	2,000	June 30	Balance b/f	1,500
			Dec 31	Realisation account:	
				profit	500
		£2,000			£2,000

Y CAPITAL ACCOUNT

		£			£
Dec 31	Cash	1,600	June 30	Balance b/f	1,300
			Dec 31	Realisation account:	
				profit	300
		1,600			1,600

CASH

		£			£	£
June 30	Balance b/f	600	Dec 31	Creditors		1,500
Dec 31	Realisation account	4,500		Capital accounts:		
				X	2,000	
				Y	1,600	
						3,600
		£5,100				£5,100

(2) *Where, on dissolution, the liabilities are paid in full, but there is a loss on the realisation of the assets*

Illustration 2

D, E and F, sharing profits and losses, one-half, one-third, and one-sixth respectively, dissolve partnership. At the date of dissolution their creditors amount to £2,300, and in the course of winding up a contingent liability of £200, not brought into the accounts, matured and had to be met. The capitals stood at £6,000, £4,000 and £1,500, respectively. D had lent to the firm as distinct from capital £2,000. The assets realised £10,000. Close the books of the firm.

REALISATION ACCOUNT

	£		£	£
Sundry assets	15,800	Cash		10,000
Contingent liability matured	200	Loss transferred to capital accounts:		
		D ($\frac{1}{2}$)	3,000	
		E ($\frac{1}{3}$)	2,000	
		F ($\frac{1}{6}$)	1,000	
				6,000
	£16,000			£16,000

SUNDRY CREDITORS

	£		£
Cash	2,500	Balance b/f	2,300
		Realisation account:	
		Contingent liability matured	200
	£2,500		£2,500

D LOAN ACCOUNT

	£		£
Cash	2,000	Balance b/f	2,000

D CAPITAL ACCOUNT

	£		£
Realisation account: loss	3,000	Balance b/f	6,000
Cash	3,000		
	£6,000		£6,000

E CAPITAL ACCOUNT

	£		£
Realisation account: loss	2,000	Balance b/f	4,000
Cash	2,000		
	£4,000		£4,000

F CAPITAL ACCOUNT

	£		£
Realisation account: loss	1,000	Balance b/f	1,500
Cash	500		
	£1,500		£1,500

CASH

	£		£
Realisation account	10,000	Creditors	2,500
		D loan account	2,000
		D capital account	3,000
		E capital account	2,000
		F capital account	500
	£10,000		£10,000

Note: the book value of the assets is equal to the sum of the capitals plus the creditors, viz £6,000 + £4,000 + £1,500 + £2,300 + £2,000 = £15,800.

(3) *Where, on dissolution, there is a loss on the realisation of the assets, placing one partner's capital account in debit, which amount he pays into the firm's account in cash*

Illustration 3

J and P are in partnership, with capitals of £700 and £100. The creditors are £2,300. The assets realise £1,900. Partners share profits and losses equally. Close the books of the firm, P having brought in the amount due by him.

REALISATION ACCOUNT

	£		£
Sundry assets	3,100	Cash	1,900
		Loss to capital accounts	
		J ($\frac{1}{2}$)	600
		P ($\frac{1}{2}$)	600
	£3,100		£3,100

J CAPITAL ACCOUNT

	£		£
Realisation account: loss	600	Balance b/f	700
Cash	100		
	£700		£700

P CAPITAL ACCOUNT

	£		£
Realisation account: loss	600	Balance b/f	100
		Cash	500
	£600		£600

CREDITORS

	£		£
Cash	2,300	Balance b/f	2,300

CASH

	£		£
Realisation account	1,900	Creditors	2,300
P capital account	500	J capital account	100
	£2,400		£2,400

Where, on dissolution, the assets are not sold en bloc, but are realised separately, or certain assets are taken over by partners on account of the sums due to them, it may be preferable, instead of transferring all the assets to a realisation account and crediting that account with the total proceeds, to credit each separate asset account with the amount at which it is sold or taken over, transferring the resultant profit or loss to a realisation profit and loss account, the ultimate balance of which will represent the net profit or loss on the dissolution.

Illustration 4

G and T, having carried on business as drapers and household furnishers at the same premises for a number of years, sharing profits and losses equally, decide to dissolve partnership.

At the date of dissolution, their abridged balance sheet was as follows:

	£	£		£	£
Capital accounts:			Goodwill		1,000
G	7,000		Freehold premises		8,000
T	8,000		Fixtures:		
		15,000	Drapery department	750	
Creditors		3,200	Furnishing department	400	
					1,150
			Debtors		1,050
			Stock:		
			Drapery department	1,600	
			Furnishing department	1,400	
					3,000
			Cash at bank		4,000
		£18,200			£18,200

The agreed terms were:

G was to take over the premises at £7,000, the drapery stock at £1,700, and drapery fixtures at £500.

T, having rented another shop nearby, was to take over the furniture stock at £1,500 and the fixtures of that department at £300.

Goodwill was to be written off.

Any loss on debtors was to be shared as to G, three-fifths, and T, two-fifths.

The creditors were to be paid by G.

The debtors realised £950, the proceeds being retained by G.

Prepare accounts, showing the final settlement between the partners.

REALISATION PROFIT AND LOSS ACCOUNT

	£	£		£	£
Goodwill written off		1,000	Profit on transfer of stock		200
Bad debts		100	Loss on debtors shared by agreement:		
Loss on transfer of:			G ($\frac{3}{5}$)	60	
Freehold premises	1,000		T ($\frac{2}{5}$)	40	
Fixtures	350	1,350			100
			Loss on realisation of other assets:		
			G, capital account	1,075	
			T, capital account	1,075	
					2,150
		£2,450			£2,450

CASH ACCOUNT

	£		£
Balance b/f	4,000	T, capital account	5,085
G, capital account	1,085		
	£5,085		£5,085

DEBTORS

	£		£
Balance b/f	1,050	G, proceeds of realisation	950
		Realisation profit and loss account	100
	£1,050		£1,050

FREEHOLD PREMISES

	£		£
Balance b/f	8,000	G, capital account	7,000
		Realisation profit and loss account	1,000
	£8,000		£8,000

FIXTURES

	£		£
Balance b/f			
Drapery	750	G, capital account	500
Furnishings	400	T, capital account	300
		Realisation profit and loss account	350
	£1,150		£1,150

STOCK

	£		£
Balance b/f		G, capital account	1,700
Drapery	1,600	T, capital account	1,500
Furnishings	1,400		
Realisation profit and loss			
account	200		
	£3,200		£3,200

CAPITAL ACCOUNTS

	G £	T £		G £	T £
Freehold premises	7,000	–	Balances b/f	7,000	8,000
Stock	1,700	1,500	Creditors taken over	3,200	–
Fixtures	500	300	Cash	1,085	–
Debtors	950	–			
Bad debts	60	40			
Loss on realisation	1,075	1,075			
Cash	–	5,085			
	£11,285	£8,000		£11,285	£8,000

2.2   DISSOLUTION OF PARTNERSHIPS – THE RULE IN GARNER V MURRAY [1904] 1 CH 57

(a) Background

This is the situation where, on dissolution, a partner's capital account is in debit and he is unable to discharge his indebtedness. (Contrast with the situation in section 2.1(b) above.)

Prior to the decision in *Garner v Murray* it was generally supposed that any loss occasioned by one of the partners of a firm being unable to make good a debit balance on his account should be borne by the remaining partners in the proportions in which they shared profits and losses.

In this case, however, it was held that a deficiency of assets occasioned through the default of one of the partners must be distinguished from an ordinary trading loss, and should be regarded as a debt due to the remaining partners individually and not to the firm.

The decision of the case gave rise to considerable controversy. The circumstances were as follows: Garner, Murray and Wilkins were in partnership under a parole agreement by the terms of which capital was to be contributed by them in unequal shares, but profits and losses were to be divided equally. On the dissolution of the partnership, after payment of the creditors and of advances made by two of the partners, there was a deficiency of assets of £635, in addition to which Wilkins' capital account was overdrawn by £263, which he was unable to pay. There was thus a total deficiency of £898, and the plaintiff claimed that this should be borne by the solvent partners, Garner and Murray, in their agreed profit-sharing ratio, viz equally. Mr Justice Joyce held, however, that each of the three partners was liable to make good his share of the £635 deficiency of assets, after which the available assets should be applied in repaying to each partner what was due to him on account of capital. Since, however, one of the 'assets' was the debit balance on Wilkins' account, which was valueless, the remaining assets were to be applied in paying to Garner and Murray rateably what was due to them in respect of capital, with the result that Wilkins' deficiency was borne by them in proportion to their capitals.

The effect of the decision is shown in the following illustration.

(b) Illustration 5

A, B and C, with unequal capitals, share profits and losses equally. They decide to dissolve partnership, and the following balance sheet shows the position of affairs after the assets have been realised and the liabilities discharged.

ABRIDGED BALANCE SHEET

	£		£
Capitals:		Cash	500
A	600	Capital C overdrawn	200
B	400	Deficiency of assets	300
	£1,000		£1,000

C is insolvent and is unable to contribute anything towards either his overdraft on capital or his share of the loss on realisation.

The loss on realisation of £300 should first be debited in profit-sharing ratio to the partners' accounts, thus reducing A's capital to £500 and B's to £300, and increasing C's deficit to £300.

If the ruling in *Garner v Murray* were followed strictly, A and B would introduce cash of £100 each to make good their shares of the deficiency and thus restore their capitals to £600 and £400 respectively. The balances then remaining in the books would be as shown by the reconstructed balance sheet given below.

BALANCE SHEET

	£		£
Capitals:		Cash	700
A	600	C's capital overdrawn	300
B	400		
	£1,000		£1,000

The only true asset, viz cash of £700, would now be divided between the solvent partners, A and B, in proportion to their capitals, viz:

		£
A ($\frac{6}{10}$ of £700)	=	420
B ($\frac{4}{10}$ of £700)	=	280
		£700

The only balances then remaining in the books would be the debit balance on C's capital account, £300, and the credit balances on the capital accounts of A and B, £180 and £120 respectively. As C is insolvent, the debit balance on his account will be written off against A and B, in the ratio of their respective capitals, viz £180 to A and £120 to B, thus closing their accounts.

As has been shown the net effect of the above treatment is to cause A and B to bear C's deficiency in proportion to their respective capitals. The introduction of cash by A and B to meet their share of the loss on realisation is unnecessary, as the balances on their capital account are sufficient to meet this loss. C's deficiency should be written off against the capital accounts of A and B in *capital* ratio, viz 6:4, after which the cash in hand will be exactly sufficient to repay to A and B the balances due to them on capital account, as shown hereunder.

CAPITAL ACCOUNTS

	A £	B £	C £		A £	B £	C £
Balance b/f			200	Balances b/f	600	400	
Realisation account–				A and B – C's			
loss	100	100	100	deficiency trans-			
C	180	120		ferred:			
Cash	320	180		A ($\frac{6}{10}$)			180
				B ($\frac{4}{10}$)			120
	£600	£400	£300		£600	£400	£300

2.3   DISSOLUTION OF PARTNERSHIPS – PIECEMEAL REALISATION AND INTERIM DISTRIBUTIONS

When assets are realised piecemeal, the partners may desire, as soon as all liabilities have been discharged, to withdraw immediately such cash as is available for division between them rather than wait until all the assets have been sold. In such circumstances, subject to any contrary agreement between the partners, the interim payments to the partners should be of such amounts that even though the remaining assets prove to be worthless no partner will receive more than the amount to which he is ultimately found to be entitled after being debited with his proper share of the total loss sustained on realisation of all the assets. To enable this to be done the proceeds of realisation of assets must first be applied in repaying to partners any sums necessary to reduce their capitals to amounts which will bear the same proportion to the total capital as those in which profits and losses are shared. Further realisations will then be shared in that ratio.

Illustration 6

A, B, C and D are in partnership, sharing profits in the ratio 3:2:1:4. It is decided to dissolve the firm on 1 January 19XX, on which date the balance sheet was as below:

	£	£
Fixed assets		
Land and buildings		8,500
Plant and machinery		7,921
Goodwill		3,000
Investments		2,000
		21,421
Current assets		
Stock	6,348	
Debtors	3,841	
Cash at bank	313	
	10,502	
Less creditors	6,923	
		3,579
		25,000

	£	£
Capital accounts		
A		7,000
B		4,000
C		3,000
D		4,000
		18,000
Leasehold redemption fund		2,000
General reserve		5,000
		25,000

The assets are realised piecemeal as under:

			£
January	10	Stock (part)	3,500
	14	Debtors (part)	2,932
	28	Investments	2,420
February	3	Goodwill	2,000
	21	Land and buildings	7,000
	21	Debtors (part)	500
	21	Stock (balance)	2,750
March	15	Plant and machinery	8,500
	15	Debtors (balance)	351

Subject to providing £500 to meet the probable expenses of realisation, the partners decide that after the creditors have been paid, all cash received shall be divided between them immediately.

The expenses of realisation, which are paid on March 15, amount to £400.

Prepare a statement showing how the distributions should be made, and show the realisation profit and loss account, cash account and partners' capital accounts. Calculations are to be made to the nearest £.

After transferring the general reserve to the partners' capital accounts in profit-sharing ratio the capitals of the partners will be:

	A £	B £	C £	D £	Total £
Balances, January 1	7,000	4,000	3,000	4,000	18,000
General reserve	1,500	1,000	500	2,000	5,000
	£8,500	£5,000	£3,500	£6,000	£23,000
The profit-sharing ratio is	3	2	1	4	10
The capital per unit of profit is	£2,833	£2,500	£3,500	£1,500	

D has the smallest capital in relation to his share of profit, viz £1,500 capital per unit of profit. If the capitals of the other partners were held on the same basis. A's capital would be £4,500, B's £3,000 and C's £1,500. A, B and C, therefore, have surplus capital over that of D of £4,000, £2,000 and £2,000 respectively, which surplus must be repaid to them before any payments are made to D.

	A £	B £	C £	D £	Total £
Balances as above	8,500	5,000	3,500	6,000	23,000
Capitals in profit-sharing ratio	4,500	3,000	1,500	6,000	15,000
Surplus capitals	£4,000	£2,000	£2,000	–	£8,000
The profit-sharing ratio between A, B and C is	3	2	1		
The surplus capital per unit of profit is	£1,333	£1,000	£2,000		

As between A, B and C, B has the smallest surplus capital in relation to his share of profit. If B's surplus capital of £2,000 were in the same proportion to the total surplus capital as his share of profit, the total surplus capital would be £6,000, of which A's share would be £3,000, B's £2,000 and C's £1,000. A and C therefore have surplus capital over B of £1,000 each, which must be repaid to them before any payment is made to B.

	A	B	C	D	Total
	£	£	£	£	£
Surplus capital as above	4,000	2,000	2,000	–	8,000
Surplus capitals in profit-sharing ratio (A,3; B,2; C,1)	3,000	2,000	1,000	–	6,000
Further surplus capital	£1,000	–	£1,000	–	£2,000

As between A and C, the profit-sharing ratio is 3:1 so that the further surplus per unit of profit is A, £333 and C, £1,000. If A's surplus of £1,000 represented three-quarters of the total surplus, C's share would be £333. C, therefore has a further surplus over A of £667 as shown hereunder.

	A	B	C	D	Total
	£	£	£	£	£
Surplus capital as above	1,000	–	1,000	–	2,000
Surplus capital in profit-sharing ratio (A,3; C,1)	1,000	–	333	–	1,333
Ultimate surplus capital	–	–	£667	–	£667

The amounts becoming available for distribution should accordingly be paid to the partners in the order of priority shown in the following statement.

	A	B	C	D	Total
	£	£	£	£	£
The first £667			667		667
The next £1,333 (A,3; C,1)	1,000		333		1,333
	1,000		1,000		2,000
The next £6,000 (A,3; B,2; C,1)	3,000	2,000	1,000		6,000
	£4,000	£2,000	£2,000	–	£8,000

After repayment of the above £8,000, the balances remaining on the capital accounts will be A £4,500, B £3,000, C £1,500 and D £6,000, these amounts being in the same proportion as that in which profits and losses are shared. By dividing all further realisations in this ratio, therefore, each partner will receive his proper share of the profit or bear his proper share of the loss.

STATEMENT OF ACTUAL DISTRIBUTIONS

19XX		Cash available £	A £	B £	C £	D £	Total £
	Balance b/f	313					
Jan 10	Realisation	3,500					
14	Realisation	2,932					
28	Realisation	2,420					
		9,165					
	Less creditors	6,923					
		2,242					
Jan 28	*Less* provided for expenses	500					
		1,742					
	Less to C	667	–	–	667	–	667
	Divisible between A and C in proportion of A,3; C,1	£1,075	806	–	269	–	1,075
			£806	–	£936	–	£1,742
19XX							
Feb 3	Realisations	2,000					
	Less balance of £1,333 to A and C in proportion of A,3; C,1	258	194	–	64	–	258
	Divisible between A, B and C in proportion of A,3; B,2; C1	£1,742	871	581	290	–	1,742
			£1,065	£581	£354	–	£2,000
19XX							
Feb 21	Realisations	10,250					
	Less balance of £6,000 to A, B and C in proportion of A,3; B,2; C,1	4,258	2,129	1,419	710	–	4,258
	Divisible between A, B, C and D in profit-sharing ratio of A,3; B,2; C,1; D,4	£5,992	1,798	1,198	599	2,397	5,992
			3,927	2,617	1,309	2,397	10,250
19XX							
Mar 15	Realisations	6,911					
	Add overprovision for expenses	100					
	Divisible between A, B, C and D in profit-sharing ratio A,3; B,2; C,1; D,4	£7,011	£2,103	£1,403	£701	£2,804	£7,011

The accounts will be closed as follows:

CASH ACCOUNT

			£				£
Jan	1	Balance b/f	313	Jan	2	Creditors	6,923
	15	Stock account	3,500			Capital accounts:	
	14	Debtors	2,932			A	806
	28	Investments	2,420			C	936
Feb	3	Goodwill	2,000	Feb	3	Capital accounts:	
	21	Land and buildings	7,000			A	1,065
		Debtors	500			B	581
		Stock	2,750			C	354
Mar	15	Plant and machinery	6,560		21	Capital accounts:	
		Debtors	351			A	3,927
						B	2,617
						C	1,309
						D	2,397
				Mar	15	Realisation profit and loss account:	
						expenses	400
						Capital accounts:	
						A	2,103
						B	1,403
						C	701
						D	2,804
			£28,326				£28,326

REALISATION PROFIT AND LOSS ACCOUNT

			£					£
Feb	3	Goodwill	1,000	Jan	28	Investments		420
	21	Land and buildings	1,500	Feb	21	Leasehold redemption		
		Stock	98			fund		2,000
		Plant and machinery	1,361	Mar	15	Loss transferred to		
		Debtors	58			capital accounts:		
		Cash – expenses of				A $(\frac{3}{10})$	£599	
		realisation	400			B $(\frac{2}{10})$	399	
						C $(\frac{1}{10})$	200	
						D $(\frac{4}{10})$	799	
								1,997
			£4,417					£4,417

CAPITAL ACCOUNTS

		A	B	C	D		A	B	C	D
		£	£	£	£	Jan 1	£	£	£	£
Jan 28	Cash	806	–	936	–	Balances b/f	7,000	4,000	3,000	4,000
Feb 3	Cash	1,065	581	354	–	General				
21	Cash	3,927	2,617	1,309	2,397	reserve	1,500	1,000	500	2,000
Mar 15	Loss on									
	realisation	599	399	200	799					
	Cash	2,103	1,403	701	2,804					
		8,500	5,000	3,500	6,000		8,500	5,000	3,500	6,000

Another, and more cautious, method is to treat the assets remaining unrealised after each realisation as completely valueless, and to charge each partner with his share of the notional loss in the agreed profit-sharing ratio. If a partner's capital is thereby thrown into debit, the amount thereof is charged to the other partners in proportion to their capitals, in accordance with the rule in *Garner v Murray*. The aggregate of the balances of the partners' capital accounts, after deducting the amounts of any previous distributions, will then equal the sum available for distribution. This process will be repeated on each realisation, with the result that after the final distribution, each partner will have borne his proper share of the ultimate loss and in no circumstances will any partner be required to repay anything.

Illustration 7

A, B, and C share profits in the proportion of one-half, one-third and one-sixth. Their balance sheet is as follows:

	£		£
A Capital account	3,000	Assets, *less* liabilities	8,000
B Capital account	3,000		
C Capital account	2,000		
	£8,000		£8,000

The partnership is dissolved, and the assets are realised as follows:

	£
First realisation	1,000
Second realisation	1,500
Third and final realisation	2,500
	£5,000

	£	A £	B £	C £	Total Distributions £
Capitals		3,000	3,000	2,000	
First realisation	1,000				
Balance of assets treated as loss	7,000	($\frac{1}{2}$) 3,500	($\frac{1}{3}$) 2,333	($\frac{1}{6}$) 1,167	
	£8,000	*Dr* £500	667	833	
A's debit balance divided between B and C in *capital* ratio (*Garner v Murray*)			($\frac{3}{5}$) 300	($\frac{2}{5}$) 200	
Distribution of first realisation			£367	£633	1,000
Capitals		3,000	3,000	2,000	
Second realisation	1,500				
Balance of assets treated as loss	5,500	($\frac{1}{2}$) 2,750	($\frac{1}{3}$) 1,833	($\frac{2}{6}$) 917	
	£7,000	250	1,167	1,083	
Less first distribution		–	367	633	
Distribution of second realisation		£250	£800	£450	1,500
Capitals		3,000	3,000	2,000	
Final realisation	2,500				
Balance of assets, being ultimate loss	3,000	($\frac{1}{2}$) 1,500	($\frac{1}{3}$) 1,000	($\frac{1}{6}$) 500	
	£5,500	1,500	2,000	1,500	

				Total
	A	B	C	Distributions
	£	£	£	£	£
Less first and second distributions		250	1,167	1,083
Distribution of final realisation	£1,250	£833	£417	2,500

The ultimate loss of £3,000 has thus been borne by the partners in the correct proportions.

The accounts will be closed as follows:

REALISATION ACCOUNT

	£			£
Net assets	8,000	Cash:		
		1st realisation		1,000
		2nd		1,500
		3rd		2,500
		Loss transferred to capital accounts:		
		A ($\frac{1}{2}$)	£1,500	
		B ($\frac{1}{3}$)	1,000	
		C ($\frac{1}{6}$)	500	
				3,000
	£8,000			£8,000

CASH ACCOUNT

	£		£
1st realisation	1,000	Capital accounts:	
		B	367
		C	633
2nd realisation	1,500	Capital accounts:	
		A	250
		B	800
		C	450
3rd realisation	2,500	Capital accounts:	
		A	1,250
		B	833
		C	417

CAPITAL ACCOUNTS

	A	B	C		A	B	C
	£	£	£		£	£	£
Cash 1st realisation		367	633	b/f	3,000	3,000	2,000
2nd realisation	250	800	450				
3rd realisation	1,250	833	417				
Realisation account: loss	1,500	1,000	500				
	3,000	3,000	2,000		3,000	3,000	2,000

The partners may, of course, agree between themselves on some other basis of distribution. One or other of the above methods should be used in the absence of agreement.

2.4 AMALGAMATION OF FIRMS

Where members of two or more partnerships decide to amalgamate, the transaction resolves itself into the dissolution of the existing partnerships and the formation of a new one. For the purposes of the amalgamation, it is probable that the goodwill and other assets of the original firms will be revalued, and the capitals of the respective partners adjusted by reference to the profit or loss arising on such revaluation, before arriving at the amount of capital introduced by each partner into the new firm. Where the capital of the new firm is a fixed amount, to be provided by the partners in specified proportions or sums, it may be necessary, after giving effect to the agreed revaluations of assets, for cash to be withdrawn or paid in by one or more of the partners in order to adjust the capitals to the agreed amounts.

Illustration 8

In similar type businesses, R and Y are in partnership as R, Y and Co, and V and B as V, B & Co. It was mutually agreed that as on January 1 19X9, the partnerships be amalgamated into one firm, Tints Co. The profit-sharing ratios in the various firms were and are to be as follows:

	R	Y	V	B
Old firms	4	3	3	2
New firm	6	5	4	3

As on December 31 19X8, the balance sheets of the firms were as follows:

	R, Y & Co £	V, B & Co £		R, Y & Co £	V, B & Co £
Capital accounts:			Property	7,400	10,000
R	15,300	–	Fixtures	1,800	1,400
Y	11,000	–	Vehicles	3,000	1,800
V	–	11,300	Stock	8,300	6,600
B	–	7,400	Investment	800	–
Creditors	5,200	6,000	Debtors	6,800	5,800
Bank overdraft	–	900	Bank balance	3,400	–
	£31,500	£25,600		£31,500	£25,600

The agreement to amalgamate contains the following provisions:

(1) Provision for doubtful debts at the rate of 5% be made in respect of debtors, and a provision for discount receivable at the rate of $2\frac{1}{2}$% be made in respect of creditors.

(2) Tints Co to take over the old partnership assets at the following values:

	R, Y & Co £	V, B & Co £
Stock	8,450	6,390
Vehicles	2,800	1,300
Fixtures	1,600	–
Property	10,000	–
Goodwill	6,300	4,500

(3) The property and fixtures of V, B & Co are not to be taken over by Tints Co. (These assets were sold for £13,500 cash on January 1 19X9.)

(4) Y to take over his firm's investment at a value of £760.

(5) The capital of Tints Co to be £54,000 and to be contributed by the partners in profit-sharing ratios, any adjustments to be made in cash.

Close the books of R, Y & Co and of V, B & Co and prepare the opening balance sheet of Tints Co.

R, Y & CO AND V, B & CO REALISATION ACCOUNTS

Debit side

		R, Y & Co £	V, B & Co £
Assets (at book values)			
Property		7,400	10,000
Fixtures		1,800	1,400
Vehicles		3,000	1,800
Stock		8,300	6,600
Investment		800	
Debtors		6,800	5,800
		28,100	25,600
Profit on realisation		8,400	5,750
Partners' capital accounts:			
Profit on realisation:			
R ($\frac{4}{7}$)	4,800		
Y ($\frac{3}{7}$)	3,600		
V ($\frac{3}{5}$)	3,450		
B ($\frac{2}{5}$)	2,300		
		£36,500	£31,350

Credit side

	R, Y & Co £	£	V, B & Co £	£
Creditors		5,200		6,000
Partners' capital account:				
Y – investment		760		
Tints Co:				
Assets taken over (at agreed values)				
Stock	£8,450		6,390	
Vehicles	2,800		1,300	
Fixtures	1,600		–	
Property	10,000		4,500	
Goodwill	6,300		5,510	
Debtors	6,460			
	35,610		17,700	
Less creditors	5,070	30,540	5,850	11,850
Cash – sale of property and fixtures				13,500
		£36,500		£31,350

PARTNERS' CAPITAL ACCOUNTS

	R £	Y £	V £	B £		R £	Y £	V £	B £
Realisation account:					Balances b/f	15,300	11,000	11,300	7,400
Investment taken over	2,100				Realisation account	4,800	3,600	3,450	2,300
Cash		760	2,750	700	Cash		1,160		
Transferred to Tints Co	18,000	15,000	12,000	9,000					
	£20,100	£15,760	£14,750	£9,700		£20,100	£15,760	£14,750	£9,700

CASH ACCOUNTS

	R, Y & Co £	V, B & Co £		R, Y & Co £	V, B & Co £
Balance brought forward	3,400		Balances brought forward		
Realisation account – sale of property and fixtures		13,500	Tints Co	2,460	900
Y	1,160		R		9,150
			V	2,100	2,750
			B		700
	£4,560	£13,500		£4,560	£13,500

TINTS CO

	R, Y & Co £	V, B & Co £	Capital accounts:	R, Y & Co £	V, B & Co £
Realisation account	30,540	11,850			
Cash	2,460	9,150	R $\frac{6}{18}$ of 54,000	18,000	
			Y $\frac{5}{18}$ of 54,000	15,000	
			V $\frac{4}{18}$ of 54,000		12,000
			B $\frac{3}{18}$ of 54,000		9,000
	£33,000	£21,000		£33,000	£21,000

TINTS CO BALANCE SHEET
as at 1 January 19X9

	£	£	£
Fixed assets (at cost)			
Goodwill			10,800
Property			10,000
Fixtures			1,600
Vehicles			4,100
			26,500
Current assets			
Stock		14,840	
Debtors	12,600		
Less provision for doubtful debts	630		
		11,970	
Cash at bank		11,610	
		38,420	
Less current liabilities			
Creditors	11,200		
Less provision for discounts receivable	280		
		10,920	
Net current assets			27,500
			54,000
Capital accounts			
R			18,000
Y			15,000
V			12,000
B			9,000
			54,000

2.5   CONVERSION OF A PARTNERSHIP INTO A LIMITED COMPANY

(a) Introduction

Frequently a private business is 'converted' into a newly-formed limited company. The partners give up their partnership stakes in exchange for shares in the company. This conversion is usually seen as a necessary stage of development of the growth of the business. A later stage may see the conversion of the private company into a public limited company (plc).

(b) Accounting entries – partnership books

Such a transaction will necessitate the books of the firm being closed, and new books being opened for the company. The following will be the procedure for closing the firm's books:

(1) Open a realisation account, and transfer to the debit thereof the book value of the assets taken over by the purchasing company, crediting the various asset accounts.

(2) Transfer to the credit of the realisation account the liabilities assumed by the company, debiting the respective liability accounts.

(3) Debit the purchasing company's account, and credit realisation account with the agreed purchase price of the net assets taken over by the company.

Note

The term 'net assets' means the assets less the liabilities.

(4) The balance on the realisation account, after debiting expenses (if any), will represent the profit or loss on realisation of the net assets, and will be transferred to the partners' capital accounts in the proportions in which they share profits and losses.

(5) Debit the accounts of the assets (eg cash, shares, debentures etc) received as purchase consideration, and credit the purchasing company's account.

(6) Pay off any liabilities not taken over by the new company, crediting cash and debiting the liability accounts.

(7) Distribute between the partners the shares, debentures etc received from the company in the proportions agreed between them, debiting their capital accounts and crediting the accounts of the shares, debentures etc.

(8) Any balances remaining on capital accounts must now be cleared by the withdrawal or payment in of cash.

Illustration 9

The firm of J, S and R decide to form a limited company, J, S & R Ltd, and transfer the business thereto. Their balance sheet is as follows:

J, S & R

Abridged balance sheet as at 30 June

	£	£		£	£
Capital accounts:			Freehold property		30,000
J	25,000		Plant		10,900
S	15,000		Fixtures, fittings		
R	10,000		and furniture		1,500
		50,000	Stock-in-trade		19,500
			Debtors	68,830	
Creditors		63,300	*Less* provision	2,000	
Loan on mortgage		20,000			66,830
			Cash at bank	4,500	
			Cash in hand	70	
					4,570
		£133,300			£133,300

They share profits — J, four-ninths, S, three-ninths, R, two-ninths. The purchase consideration was £85,000 (the company taking over all the assets and liabilities except the loan on mortgage) and was payable as to £25,000 in cash, £20,000 in 5% mortgage debentures, and £40,000 in ordinary shares. Expenses amounting to £600 were payable by the firm.

Assuming the transactions to have been carried through, and the loan on mortgage repaid, close the books of the firm, the debentures and shares being divided between the partners in the following proportions: J one-half, S one-quarter, R one-quarter.

REALISATION ACCOUNT

	£	£		£	£
Sundry assets		135,300	Provision for bad debts		2,000
Expenses		600	Creditors		63,300
Capital accounts, being profit:			J, S & R Ltd purchase		
			consideration		85,000
J ($\frac{4}{9}$)	6,400				
S ($\frac{3}{9}$)	4,800				
R ($\frac{2}{9}$)	3,200				
		14,400			
		£150,300			£150,300

LOAN ON MORTGAGE

	£		£
Cash	20,000	Balance b/f	20,000

J, S & R LTD

	£		£
Realisation account, purchase		Cash	25,000
consideration	85,000	Debentures in J, S & R Ltd	20,000
		Ordinary shares in J, S & R Ltd	40,000
	£85,000		£85,000

DEBENTURES IN J, S & R LTD

	£		£
J, S & R Ltd	20,000	J Capital account	10,000
		S	5,000
		R	5,000
	£20,000		£20,000

ORDINARY SHARES IN J, S & R LTD

	£		£
J, S & R Ltd	40,000	J Capital account, ($\frac{1}{2}$)	20,000
		S Capital account, ($\frac{1}{4}$)	10,000
		R Capital account, ($\frac{1}{4}$)	10,000
	£40,000		£40,000

J CAPITAL ACCOUNT

	£		£
Debentures in J, S & R Ltd	10,000	Balance b/f	25,000
Ordinary shares in J, S & R Ltd	20,000	Realisation account, profit	6,400
Cash	1,400		
	£31,400		£31,400

S CAPITAL ACCOUNT

	£		£
Debentures in J, S & R Ltd	5,000	Balance b/f	15,000
Ordinary shares in J, S & R Ltd	10,000	Realisation account, profit	4,800
Cash	4,800		
	£19,800		£19,800

R CAPITAL ACCOUNT

	£		£
Debentures in J, S & R Ltd	5,000	Balance b/f	10,000
Ordinary shares in J, S & R Ltd	10,000	Realisation account, profit	3,200
		Cash	1,800
	£15,000		£15,000

CASH ACCOUNT

	£		£	£
J, S & R Ltd	25,000	Loan on mortgage		20,000
Capital account: R	1,800	Expenses		600
		Capital accounts:		
		J	1,400	
		S	4,800	6,200
	£26,800			£26,800

Normally, where a partnership is converted into a limited company, the partners of the firm will agree as to the manner in which the shares, debentures etc of the company, received as purchase consideration, are to be divided between them. Where, however, the partners cannot agree upon such proportions, an independent valuation of the shares, debentures etc should be obtained and the profit or loss disclosed thereby divided between the partners in their profit-sharing ratio. The shares, debentures etc at their agreed valuation will then be divided between the partners in proportion to the adjusted balances on their capital accounts. If it is desired by the partners to share the profits of the company in the proportions in which the profits of the partnership were formerly divided, the shares, debentures etc should be allocated to the partners in their profit-sharing ratio, a cash adjustment being made between the partners in respect of any balances remaining due to or by them individually.

The accounting entries in the books of the company are discussed below.

(c) Accounting entries – books of the company

In the purchasing company's books, the assets acquired must be debited at acquisition values, which are often different from the book values shown in the vendor business's books; when a business is sold, assets are frequently revalued. Sometimes the purchasing company assumes trade liabilities as part of the purchase consideration; sometimes the company discharges the trade liabilities and collects the book debts as agent for the sellers; interest may be allowed or charged until final settlement between the purchasing company and the sellers is effected. Book debts are usually acquired at book values less an agreed provision for bad or doubtful debts; any excess received over the book values less the provision for doubtful debts is a capital profit in the purchasing company's books.

In addition to the purchase price of the tangible assets, a further sum is usually payable for goodwill. A company making a public issue for the purpose of acquiring a business must state in the prospectus the amount of the purchase consideration attributable to goodwill.

Goodwill is the excess of the total purchase consideration over the value of the other assets acquired, less the amount of any liabilities assumed by the company.

Summary of entries

The entries in the company's books necessary to record the purchase of the business are as follows:

Debit	Credit	Notes
Assets	Vendor's account	Assets acquired at acquisition values
Vendor's account	Liabilities	Liabilities acquired at acquisition values
Vendor's account	Share capital Share premium Debentures Cash	Purchase consideration
Goodwill	Vendor's account	Excess of purchase consideration over net assets required
Vendor's account	Capital reserve	Excess of net assets acquired over purchase consideration.

Note: any debtors taken over should be debited at book values and any provision for doubtful or bad debts should be credited to a provision for bad debts account.

Some accountants prefer to pass the purchase of a business through a purchase of business account, which replaces the vendor's account, being credited with the assets acquired and debited with the liabilities taken over and with the purchase consideration.

Illustration 10

A company takes over the following assets and liabilities of a private business:

	£
Leasehold property	7,000
Plant and machinery	3,000
Stock-in-trade	4,600
Sundry debtors	3,000
Cash	1,500
	19,100
Less trade creditors	2,100
	£17,000

The purchase consideration is £20,000 payable to the vendor as follows: £10,000 in ordinary shares of £1 each fully paid, £5,000 in 5% preference shares of £1 each fully paid, all issued at par, and the balance in cash. Show the opening journal entries in the books of the company.

JOURNAL

	Dr £	Cr £
Leasehold property	7,000	
Plant and machinery	3,000	
Stock-in-trade	4,600	
Sundry debtors	3,000	
Cash	1,500	
Goodwill	3,000	
Sundry creditors		2,100
Vendor (or purchase of business account)		20,000
Sundry assets and liabilities taken over as per contract dated	£22,100	£22,100

	£	£
Vendor (or purchase of business account)	20,000	
Ordinary share capital – 10,000 shares of £1 each fully paid		10,000
Preference share capital – 5,000 shares of £1 each fully paid		5,000
Cash		5,000
Discharge of purchase consideration as per contract dated	£20,000	£20,000

Note: the amount debited to goodwill account is the excess of the amount of the purchase consideration, £20,000, over the total amount of the assets acquired, less the amount of the liabilities assumed, £17,000.

Where the purchase consideration is less than the value at which the net assets stood in the books of the vendor, but the values of the assets taken over are correctly stated (as ascertained by revaluation), the surplus should be treated in the company's books as a capital reserve. The surplus is not available for distribution to shareholders and cannot be credited to a revenue reserve account.

The absence of a goodwill account indicates that no payment has been made for goodwill; it does not indicate that it is nonexistent.

(d) Preserving the previous rights of the partners in the new company

Where a partnership business is transferred to a limited company some difficulty may be experienced in capitalising the company so as to ensure that the rights of the partners are preserved. If the capitals of the partners are in the same ratio as that in which profits are shared, the problem is simplified, as the allotment to the partners of ordinary shares in that ratio will preserve the relationship as nearly as possible. Often, where the capitals are not held in profit-sharing ratio, the problem is complicated, particularly when taxation is considered.

The following illustration shows the effect on the books of a firm of the conversion of a private firm into a limited company, and also the entries in the books of the company:

Illustration 11

The X Company Ltd was formed to purchase the business of A and B, who share profits, two-thirds and one-third respectively, and whose balance sheet was as follows:

BALANCE SHEET A and B

	£	£		£	£
Creditors		2,700	Goodwill		1,000
Bills payable		900	Freehold property		5,000
Loan account		400	Plant and machinery		2,500
Capitals			Stock		3,000
A	8,000		Debtors	3,100	
B	5,000		*Less* provision for bad		
	———		debts	200	
		13,000		———	2,900
			Bills receivable		800
			Investments		600
			Cash		1,200
		£17,000			£17,000

The company takes over the assets at book value, with the exception of the freehold property, which is taken over at £6,000. The investments are retained by the firm, and sold by them for £450. They also discharge the loan of £400, but the company takes over the remaining liabilities.

The purchase consideration for the net assets taken over is fixed at £18,950, payable as follows: £9,500 5% debentures and 7,600 fully paid ordinary shares of £1 each, both at par, and the balance in cash. A and B agree to divide the assets forming the purchase consideration in proportion to the balance standing to the credit of their respective capital accounts, after the adjustments caused by the sale of the business and investments have been completed.

Show the ledger accounts closing the firm's books, and the journal entries opening the company's books.

FIRM'S BOOKS REALISATION ACCOUNT

	£		£
Freehold property	5,000	Creditors	2,700
Plant and machinery	2,500	Bills payable	900
Goodwill	1,000		
		Provision for bad debts	200
Stock	3,000	X Co Ltd	18,950
Debtors	3,100		
Bills receivable	800		
Cash	1,200		
Loss on investments	150		
Balance, being profit on			
realisation c/d	6,000		
	£22,750		£22,750

	£		£
Capital accounts:		Balance b/d	6,000
A ($\frac{2}{3}$)	4,000		
B ($\frac{1}{3}$)	2,000		
	£6,000		£6,000

X COMPANY LTD

	£		£
Realisation account	18,950	Debentures	9,500
		Ordinary shares	7,600
		Cash	1,850
	£18,950		£18,950

DEBENTURES IN X CO LTD

	£		£
X Co Ltd	9,500	A capital account $\frac{12}{19} \times$ £9,500	6,000
		B capital account $\frac{7}{19} \times$ £9,500	3,500
	£9,500		£9,500

ORDINARY SHARES IN X CO LTD

	£		£
X Co Ltd	7,600	A capital account $\frac{12}{19} \times$ £7,600	4,800
		B capital accounts $\frac{7}{19} \times$ £7,600	2,800
	£7,600		£7,600

CAPITAL ACCOUNTS

	A	B		A	B
	£	£		£	£
Balances c/d	12,000	7,000	Balances b/f	8,000	5,000
			Profit on realisation	4,000	2,000
	£12,000	£7,000		£12,000	£7,000
Debentures in X Co Ltd	6,000	3,500	Balances b/d	12,000	7,000
Shares in X Co Ltd	4,800	2,800			
Cash	1,200	700			
	£12,000	£7,000		£12,000	£7,000

CASH BOOK

	£		£
X Co Ltd	1,850	Loan account	400
Investments	450	Balance c/d	1,900
	£2,300		£2,300
	£		£
Balance b/d	1,900	A capital account $\frac{12}{19} \times$ £1,900	1,200
		B capital account $\frac{7}{19} \times$ £1,900	700
	£1,900		£1,900

INVESTMENTS

	£		£
Balance b/f	600	Cash	450
		Realisation account – loss	150
	£600		£600

LOAN

	£		£
Cash	400	Balance b/f	400

X COMPANY LTD'S BOOKS: JOURNAL

	Dr £	Cr £
Freehold property	6,000	
Plant and machinery	2,500	
Stock	3,000	
Debtors	3,100	
Bills receivable	800	
Cash	1,200	
Goodwill	6,150	
Creditors		2,700
Bills payable		900
Provision for bad debts		200
Vendors (or purchase of business account)		18,950
Assets and liabilities taken over as per contract dated	£22,750	£22,750

Note: the amount debited to goodwill account is the difference between the total of the assets, less the liabilities taken over, and the purchase consideration payable to the vendors.

	£	£
Vendors (or purchase of business account)	18,950	
Ordinary share capital		7,600
Debentures		9,500
Cash		1,850
7,600 ordinary shares of £1 each, and £9,500 5% debentures issued fully paid, and cash paid in settlement of purchase consideration as per contract dated	£18,950	£18,950

(e) Company collects debtors and settles creditors as agent for vendor

Sometimes a company on acquiring a business does not take over the book debts and liabilities of the vendor, but collects as agent the book debts and pays the liabilities out of the proceeds, accounting to the vendor for the balance; the company should provide special columns in its cash book, into which receipts from debtors and payments to creditors made on behalf of the vendor are entered, and from which they are posted to the personal accounts of the vendor's debtors and creditors. These postings, however, form no part of the double entry from the point of view of the company, since the accounts to which the amounts are posted are not in the company's ledgers. The double entry in the company's books for these transactions is completed by posting periodically the *totals* of the receipts and payments made on behalf of the vendor to the credit and debit respectively of the vendor's account. If the company wishes to continue to use the old debtors and creditors accounts, a line should be ruled across each account some distance below the last entry prior to the transfer, and the company's own transactions should be entered below this line, in order that the debts owing to and by the company may not be confused with those owing to and by the vendor.

If the company carries on the old debtors and old creditors accounts without a break, it has acquired debtors which it has debited to total debtors account. These must be credited to debtors suspense account since from the company's standpoint they are valueless. Similarly creditors are credited to total creditors account and debited to creditors suspense account. In the illustration below, by continuing to operate upon the vendor's debtors and creditors accounts, the ledger contains assets, £5,400, and liabilities, £3,700, which do not belong to the company, debtors suspense account is credited with £5,400, and creditors suspense account debited with £3,700. At the end of the accounting period, all transactions relating to these debtors and creditors are transferred in total from the sales ledger to the debtors suspense account and from the bought ledger to the creditors suspense account. Payments made to the vendor for debts collected or receipts from the vendor for liabilities met are passed through the current account with the vendor in the normal way.

Any balances remaining on the suspense accounts when the company prepares its balance sheet represent the amounts of the debtors and creditors of the vendor still appearing in the company's books, and must be deducted from the totals of the debtors and creditors respectively to arrive at the figures to be shown in the company's balance sheet.

Illustration 12

On January 1 YZ Ltd acquired the business of X, taking over all the assets with the exception of the book debts, which it undertook to collect on behalf of X, and out of the proceeds pay the liabilities owing at the date of the transfer. At that date the book debts amounted to £5,400 and the liabilities to £3,700

The company continued to operate on the old debtors and creditors accounts without a break, and at the following December 31 the total of the book debts amounted to £6,200, of which £400 represented debts owing to X, whilst the total creditors were £5,300, the whole of X's liabilities having been discharged. During the year, the company had written off £700 debts as bad, of which £300 was for X's debtors. Discounts allowed by the company during the year amounted to £680, of which £185 was allowed to X's debtors. Discounts allowed to the company amounted to £1,400 of which £104 was for pre-transfer liabilities.

Show the relevant ledger accounts in the company's books.

TOTAL DEBTORS ACCOUNT

	£
Dec 31 Balance	6,200

TOTAL CREDITORS ACCOUNT

	£
Dec 31 Balance	5,300

X's DEBTORS SUSPENSE ACCOUNT

	£		£
Dec 31 Bad debts account	300	Jan 1 Total debtors account –	
Discounts allowed account	185	debts not taken over from X	5,400
X's account – cash collected	4,515		
Balance c/d	400		
	£5,400		£5,400
		Jan 1 Balance b/d	400

X's CREDITORS SUSPENSE ACCOUNT

	£		£
Jan 1 Total creditors account –		Dec 31 Discounts received account	104
liabilities not taken over from X	3,700	X's account – cash paid	3,596
	£3,700		£3,700

X's ACCOUNT

	£			£
Dec 31 X's creditors suspense account – cash paid to creditors	3,596	Dec 31 X's debtors suspense account – cash received from debtors		4,515
Balance c/d	919			
	£4,515			£4,515
		Jan 1 Balance b/d		919

BAD DEBTS ACCOUNT

	£		£
Dec 31 Sundry debtors – debts written off	700	Dec 31 X's debtors suspense account – amounts applicable to X's debtors	300
		Profit and loss account	400
	£700		£700

DISCOUNTS ALLOWED ACCOUNT

	£		£
Dec 31 Sundry debtors – discounts allowed	680	Dec 31 X's debtors suspense account – discounts allowed to X's debtors	185
		Profit and loss account	495
	£680		£680

DISCOUNTS RECEIVED ACCOUNT

	£		£
Dec 31 X's creditors suspense account – discount received in respect of X's liabilities	104	Dec 31 Sundry creditors account – discounts received	1,400
Profit and loss account	1,296		
	£1,400		£1,400

Note: as a result of the above entries, there will appear in the company's balance sheet a liability to X of £919, whilst the sundry debtors will be £5,800, viz £6,200, less the credit balance of £400 carried down in the debtors suspense account. The bad debts and discounts transferred to the company's profit and loss account are reduced by the amounts transferred to the suspense accounts, and thus borne by the vendor.

B The financial reporting framework

3   COMPANY ACCOUNTS – BASIC CONSIDERATIONS

> **Key Issues**
> * Differences between partnerships and limited companies
> * Types of companies
> * Principal financial statements
> * Shares – main types
> * Reserves and provisions
> * Loan and debenture stock

3.1   DISTINCTIONS BETWEEN PARTNERSHIPS AND LIMITED COMPANIES

Company law today is embodied in the Companies Act 1985 as amended by the Companies Act 1989. In the future, further pieces of legislation can be expected as a result of membership of the European Community.

The majority of companies in the UK are limited liability companies, where the liability of each shareholder is limited to the amount unpaid on shares allotted. By contrast, the majority of partnerships in the UK are unlimited. The principal distinctions between unlimited partnerships and limited companies are set out in the table below:

Unlimited partnerships	Limited companies
1 No separate legal entity apart from its members.	Separate legal entity which is not affected by changes in its membership. A company may contract, sue and be sued in its own name and capacity.
2 Liability of each member for debts of the firm is unlimited.	If the company is limited by shares, each shareholder is limited to the amount he has agreed to pay to the company for shares allotted. If his shares are fully paid, he has no further liability.
3 Number of partners limited to 20 except for firms of solicitors, accountants, stockbrokers and certain other specified exceptions.	A private limited company may have only one member (referred to as a single member private limited company).
4 Every partner can normally take part in the management of the business; he can legally bind the firm by his action with the outside world within the scope of his real or apparent authority.	Rights of management are delegated to directors who alone can act on behalf of and bind the company.

5 Copies of accounts need not be filed with the Registrar of Companies.	Copies of accounts must be filed with the Registrar of Companies. Exemptions on amount of information to be filed are available to small and medium-sized companies (see chapter 10).
6 Although a written partnership agreement is desirable, it is not mandatory.	A company is required to have a memorandum and articles of association which define powers and duties of directors.
7 A partnership is subject to the Partnership Act 1890, which can be varied by mutual agreement.	A company is subject to the Companies Act 1985, the provisions of which cannot be varied.
8 The capital is contributed by the partners by agreement. The amount need not be fixed.	The authorised capital is fixed by the memorandum of association. It can be increased by passing an ordinary resolution. It can only be reduced by special resolution and sanction of the court.
9 A share in a partnership cannot be transferred except by the consent of all partners.	In public companies, shares are freely transferable. In private companies share transfers are subject to any restrictions imposed by the articles of association.
10 A partnership is not obliged to keep statutory books of account and an audit is not compulsory.	A company is required to keep specified accounting records and is subject to compulsory audit.
11 Profits are subject to income tax.	Profits are subject to corporation tax.

3.2   TYPES OF COMPANIES

The principal categories of companies are summarised in the diagram below:

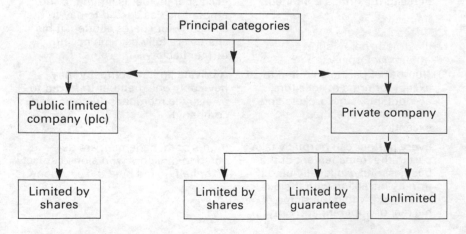

Notes

(a) A public limited company (plc) must be registered as such and have an authorised share capital in excess of £50,000. The title of the company must include the words public limited company or the abbreviation plc.

(b) A private company is any company which is not a plc, ie it is a residual category. A private company is not permitted to offer securities to the public.

(c) All companies are liable without limit for their debts. A company limited by shares is the most important category of company. In such a company, a shareholder is liable to pay to the company the amount (if any) which is due on the shares and which has not already been paid.

(d) Except for rare cases, a company limited by guarantee must be a private company. Furthermore, unless registered before 22 December 1980, a guarantee company cannot have share capital. In the usual situation, a shareholder is liable, when the company is wound up to contribute to the company's assets if needed for the purpose of discharging debts. The amount involved is limited to that specified in the memorandum of association.

(e) For an unlimited company, the liability of a shareholder arises only when the company goes into liquidation. In such an event, there is no limit on any individual shareholder to provide money towards the payment of debts.

3.3   FINANCIAL STATEMENTS OF COMPANIES

Special features of company financial statements include:

(a) Profit and loss account

The profit and loss account will be charged with directors' remuneration and auditors' remuneration. If the company has borrowings in the form of loan or debenture stock (see section 3.7 below), the profit and loss account will be charged with interest. Company profits are assessable to corporation tax and the profit and loss account thus includes a charge for tax on profits. Finally, the profit and loss account will show appropriations of profit, for example, dividends paid and proposed.

(b) Balance sheet

The balance sheet will include liabilities for tax and proposed dividends. It may also include long-term liabilities in the form of loan or debenture stock (see section 3.7 below). Finally, the 'capital' section of the balance sheet will include share capital and reserves.

Company financial statements to be presented to shareholders are subject to detailed disclosure requirements. These are dealt with in detail in chapter 4. The illustration below shows the preparation of accounts in a form suitable for presentation internally (e g to the directors). It is intended as a gentle introduction to chapter 4!

Illustration 1

The following trial balance for Hughes Ltd relates to the year ended 31 December 19X9:

	£'000	£'000
Sales		1,850
Purchases	940	
Wages and salaries	196	
Directors' remuneration	84	
Rent, rates and insurance	35	
Heat, light and water	42	
Auditors' remuneration	9	
Telephone, stationery and advertising	31	
Debenture interest	16	
Interest on bank overdraft	7	
Sundry expenses	24	
Dividend paid	30	
Freehold land and buildings		
−cost	1,094	
−accumulated depreciation		41
Plant and machinery		
−cost	193	
−accumulated depreciation		23
Stock at 1.1.X9	175	
Debtors and prepayments	273	
Cash in hand	18	
Creditors and accrued expenses		137
Bank overdraft		86
8% debenture stock 19X36		200
Called up share capital		
(50p ordinary shares)		100
Profit and loss account at 1.1.X9		730
	3,167	3,167

Additional information

(1) Depreciation for the year is to be provided as follows:

Plant and machinery	£16,000
Buildings	£11,000

(2) £123,000 is to be provided for the year in respect of corporation tax.
(3) Closing stock has been valued at £154,000 for accounts purposes.
(4) The directors propose a dividend of 25 pence per share.

Required
A profit and loss account for the year ended 31 December 19X9 and a balance sheet as at that date. Ignore the specific disclosure requirements of the Companies Act 1985.

Solution

PROFIT AND LOSS ACCOUNT OF HUGHES LTD

for the year ended 31 December 19X9

	£'000	£'000
Sales		1,850
Opening stock	175	
Purchases	940	
	1,115	
Less closing stock	154	
Cost of sales		961
Gross profit		889
Depreciation (16 + 11)	27	
Wages and salaries	196	
Directors' remuneration	84	
Rent, rates and insurance	35	
Heat, light and water	42	

	£'000	£'000
Telephone, stationery and advertising	31	
Auditors' remuneration	9	
Debenture interest	16	
Interest on bank overdraft	7	
Sundry expenses	24	
		471
Profit before tax		418
Taxation – corporation tax		123
Profit after tax		295
Dividends on ordinary shares		
Paid	30	
Proposed (25p × 200,000)	50	
		80
Retained profit		215
Balance brought forward		730
Balance carried forward		945

Balance sheet of Hughes Ltd as at 31 December 19X9

	£'000 Cost	£'000 Accumulated depreciation	£'000 Net Book value
Tangible fixed assets			
Freehold land and buildings	1,094	52	1,042
Plant and machinery	193	39	154
	1,287	91	1,196
Current assets			
Stock		154	
Debtors and prepayments		273	
Cash in hand		18	
		445	
Current liabilities			
Creditors and accrued expenses		137	
Taxation		123	
Dividend		50	
Overdraft		86	
		396	
Net current assets			49
			1,245
Creditors due in more than one year			
– 8% debenture stock 19X36			(200)
			1,045
Capital and reserves			
Ordinary share capital			100
Profit and loss account			945
			1,045

Workings

Accumulated depreciation:

Buildings	41 + 11 = 52
Plant and machinery	23 + 16 = 39

3.4   SHARE CAPITAL OF A COMPANY

The most common class of share capital is ordinary shares which carry votes. In principle a company may have more than one class of shares, including:

(a) Voting ordinary shares which carry the right to vote on all matters and to participate in surplus profits (on a distribution) or surplus assets (on a liquidation).
(b) Non-voting ordinary shares (occasionally referred to as 'A' ordinary shares) which have similar rights as for (a) above except that the ability to vote is restricted.
(c) Preference shares, which are entitled to a fixed amount of dividend in priority over ordinary shares, provided that there are profits available for distribution.
    Two further points are relevant:

    (1) preference shares are deemed to be cumulative unless they are designated as non-cumulative. Cumulative means that should a company be unable to pay a preference dividend in a particular year (because of lack of available profits), the entitlement is carried forward as a memorandum note outside the double entry system. Should available profits arise in a subsequent year, such arrears of preference dividends must be paid in priority to ordinary dividends; and
    (2) participating preference shares are a special type of share. They may have a prior entitlement to a fixed amount of dividend, and then a further entitlement, once ordinary shareholders have received a particular amount.

(d) Deferred or founders' shares – such shares carry votes but shareholders are not entitled to dividends until holders of ordinary shares have received a specified dividend. Such shares are fairly rare.

Note: FRS 4 classification of shares between equity and non-equity is dealt with in chapter 15.

3.5   ISSUE OF SHARES

(a) Journal entries relating to the issue of shares

Whenever an allotment of shares is made, an entry should be made in the journal, debiting an application and allotment account with the amount payable on application and allotment in respect of the shares so allotted, and (assuming the shares are issued at par) crediting share capital account. If more than one class of capital is being issued, separate accounts must be opened in the ledger for each class.

Similar entries must be made debiting the vendor or other persons, and crediting share capital account, in respect of all shares issued for a consideration other than cash.

When calls are made, an entry must be made debiting call account and crediting share capital account with the total amount due in respect of the call.

(b) Shares issued at a premium

A company may issue shares at a premium, i e for an amount in excess of their nominal value. Such an issue might be made by a successful company which has paid high dividends on its existing capital and where shares, as a result, already stand at a premium on the market. When shares are issued at a premium, whether for cash or otherwise, the premium must be credited to an account called 'the share premium account' unless the merger reserve provisions of the Companies Act 1985, s 131 apply (see section 25.4). The amount credited to share premium account can only be applied as follows:

(1) subject to the confirmation of the court, in a scheme for reduction of capital, as if it were paid-up share capital of the company;

(2) in paying up unissued shares of the company to be issued to the members as fully paid bonus shares;

(3) in writing off:

    (a) preliminary expenses; or

    (b) the expenses of, or commission paid or discount allowed on, any issue of shares or debentures of the company; and

(4) in providing for the premium payable on the redemption of debentures of the company. (The special application of the share premium account for the purchase or redemption of shares is dealt with in section 15.5.)

(c) Redeemable preference shares

The subject of redeemable preference shares in particular, and purchase and redemption of shares in general is dealt with in chapter 15.

3.6 RESERVES AND PROVISIONS

(a) Reserves

The term reserves may include the following:

(1) Reserves created by means of appropriation from profit and loss account. The reserves referred to below are voluntary reserves, ie the amounts transferred are at the discretion of the directors. These reserves may include the following:

    (i) general reserve;

    (ii) fixed asset replacement reserve;

    (iii) stock replacement reserve;

    (iv) debenture reserve.

There is no legal restriction on the use of any of these reserves to pay a dividend to the shareholders. However, the fact that a particular company has any of these reserves implies that the directors wish funds to be kept within the business for a future purpose (eg redemption of debentures) rather than be distributed as dividends.

(2) Share premium account (see section 3.5(b) above).

(3) Revaluation reserve (see section 12.7).

(4) Capital redemption reserve (see section 15.5).

(5) Merger reserve (see section 25.4).

(6) Reserves provided for by the articles of association.

(b) Provisions

This term is defined by the Companies Act 1985 and includes:

(1) Provision for depreciation or diminution in value of assets – this includes provision for depreciation, stock and doubtful debts. Such provisions are deducted from the asset heading to which they relate.

(2) Provisions for liabilities or charges – amounts retained as reasonably necessary for the purpose of providing for any liability or loss which is either:

(i) likely to be incurred, or
(ii) certain to be incurred but uncertain as to amount or date on which it will arise.

This includes provisions for redundancy and reorganisation, repairs and maintenance, warranty expenditure and deferred taxation.

Reserves and provisions are referred to in more detail in chapters 15 and 16.

3.7   ISSUE OF DEBENTURES

(a) Definition of a debenture

A debenture is a written acknowledgment of a debt by a company, usually under seal and generally containing provision for payment of interest and repayment of capital; a simple or naked debenture carries no charge on assets; a secured debenture carries either a fixed charge on a specific asset or a floating charge on all or some of the assets. All forms of loan stock are debentures.

(b) Fixed charge and floating charge

A fixed charge is a mortgage on specific assets, under which the company loses the right to deal with the assets charged, except with the consent of the mortgagee.

A floating charge is not a mortgage at all, since the charge is such that so long as the company continues to carry on its business and observe the terms of the charge, the directors are entitled to deal in any way they please in the ordinary course of business with the assets of the company, and may even make specific charges on property which, subject to the terms of the floating charge given, will have priority to the floating charge. The floating charge is a charge on a class of assets, present and future, which in the ordinary course of business is changing from time to time, and attaches to the property included therein in priority to the general liabilities of the company. The floating charge hovers over or 'floats' with the assets, until some event happens (e g default in repaying principal or interest) which crystallises or fixes the charge.

(c) More than one issue of debentures

A company may make more than one issue of debentures; issues subsequent to the first may rank pari passu (i e on an equal footing) with the original issue, or may confer a charge, subject to and following the first, according to whether the original debentures contained clauses allowing or forbidding subsequent pari passu issues. Where the debentures carry different priorities, they are usually designated first debentures, second debentures etc – a higher rate of interest usually being payable on those of lower rank to compensate for the lower degree of security.

(d) Limits on borrowing powers

A company can issue debentures within the limits of its borrowing powers, as set out in its memorandum and/or articles of association. A trading company's borrowing powers are implied unless there are provisions to the contrary in the memorandum or articles.

(e) Interest

Interest at the agreed rate is payable on the debentures whether the company makes profits or not, since the charge given covers both principal and interest. Income tax is deductible from the interest payable.

(f) Liquidation

In a liquidation, the debenture holders are entitled to the proceeds of their securities, if any, otherwise they rank equally with the unsecured creditors; if the proceeds of a security are insufficient to repay the debentures, the debenture holders rank as unsecured creditors for the balance still due to them.

(g) Accounting entries

The entries in the books of a company for an issue of debentures are similar to those on an issue of shares, instalment accounts being debited with the various instalments as they become due, and debentures account credited. If debentures are issued to the vendor as part of the consideration for a business acquired by the company, the vendor's account is debited and the debentures account credited. The appropriate entry must also be made in the register of charges kept by the company.

(h) Debentures issued at a premium

When debentures are issued at a premium, debenture account is credited with the nominal amount and debenture premium account with the premium. Debenture premium account can be shown in the balance sheet as a (revenue) reserve. The Companies Act does not specify the uses of the debenture premium account.

(i) Debentures issued at a discount

Debentures may be issued at a discount (rather than at par or nominal value) but must be redeemed either at par or at a premium. A holder will therefore make a capital profit on redemption. The interest payment will be adjusted to take account of this.

Accounting treatment is specified by FRS 4, Capital Instruments (see chapter 16).

(j) Redemption of debentures

Debentures may be irredeemable (i e the company may be under no obligation to repay the debentures at any specified date); but this is unusual, except in companies formed under special Act of Parliament.

Debentures may be redeemed either at the end of a given period or by annual drawings. The trust deed, or if there is no trust deed, then the debentures themselves, will contain provision for redemption.

Accounting treatment of redemption is specified by FRS 4, Capital Instruments (see chapter 16).

4 UK REGULATORY FRAMEWORK – DISCLOSURE, PREPARATION AND FILING REQUIREMENTS

Key Issues

* Importance of Companies Act 1985
  (as amended by the Companies Act 1989)
* Statutory formats for profit and loss account and balance sheet
* Principal disclosure requirements (including directors' report)
* Stock Exchange disclosure requirements

4.1 INTRODUCTION

The previous chapter dealt with the preparation of financial statements for internal use. We must now consider the preparation of financial statements for presentation to the shareholders in accordance with the requirements of the Companies Act 1985 (as amended by the Companies Act 1989).

This chapter also refers briefly to London Stock Exchange disclosure requirements for listed companies.

Chapter 5 deals with the overall regulatory framework which operates in the United Kingdom. Specific considerations relating to smaller companies are dealt with in chapter 10.

4.2 IMPACT OF EC DIRECTIVES

EC (European Community) Directives do not become mandatory until implemented by the individual member states of the EC. For example, the Fourth Directive on Company Accounts was adopted by the Council of Ministers in July 1978. This Directive dealt with the preparation, content and publication of accounts of individual companies. This Directive was eventually implemented by the Companies Act 1985.

The Seventh Directive on Group Accounts specifies the preparation, content and publication of group accounts. The Directive was adopted by the Council of Ministers in June 1983 and is reflected in the Companies Act 1985 as amended by the Companies Act 1989.

Other directives are outside the scope of this book.

4.3 THE PROFIT AND LOSS ACCOUNT AND BALANCE SHEET FORMATS

The formats are set out below. The following comments are relevant:

(a) The numbers and letters against items are for reference purposes in interpreting the requirements of the Act. They need not (and should not) be used in published company accounts.

(b) As vertical form accounts are almost universal in the UK, other possible layouts are not referred to.

(c) In the balance sheet and profit and loss account, any item identified by an arabic number may be shown on the face of the statement or relegated to the notes. All other items must be shown on the face of the balance sheet or profit and loss account.

(d) For the profit and loss account, two formats are possible. Both are used in practice. Of the two, format 1 (analysis by purpose) is more popular than format 2. Both formats are illustrated in an example later in the chapter.

(e) The balance sheet and profit and loss account should include items (provided they apply to the particular company) under the headings and in the sequence indicated in the formats. However, items indicated by arabic numbers may be shown in greater detail. Furthermore, the Act requires the directors to adapt arabic number items where the special circumstances of the business require such adaptation.

(f) A change in format (from one year to another) is only permitted if there are special reasons for a change eg a single company is taken over by a group which uses a different format for its profit and loss account. In such circumstances, disclosure is required of particulars and reasons for the change.

(g) Comparative figures are required for all items with the exception of the following:

(1) movement on fixed assets;
(2) details of substantial investments (shareholdings in excess of 10%);
(3) movement on provisions;
(4) movement on reserves;
(5) disclosure of transactions involving directors and others.

Companies Act 1985 formats

(1) *Profit and loss account* (analysis by purpose)

FORMAT 1	£	£
1 Turnover		X
2 Cost of sales		(X)
3 Gross profit or loss		X
4 Distribution costs		(X)
5 Administrative expenses		(X)
6 Other operating income		X
		X
7 Income from shares in group undertakings	X	
8 Income from participating interests	X	
9 Income from other fixed asset investments	X	
10 Other interest receivable and similar income	X	X
11 Amount written off investments		(X)
12 Interest payable and similar charges		(X)
– Profit or loss on ordinary activities before taxation		X
13 Tax on profit or loss on ordinary activities		(X)
14 Profit or loss on ordinary activities after taxation		X
15 Extraordinary income	X	
16 Extraordinary charges	(X)	
17 Extraordinary profit or loss	X	
18 Tax on extraordinary profit or loss	(X)	X
19 Other taxes not shown under the above items		(X)

20	Profit or loss for the financial year		X
	– Dividends	X	
	– Transfer to (from) reserves	X	(X)
			X
Profit and loss account brought forward			X
Profit and loss account carried forward			£XX

(2) *Profit and loss account* (analysis by type)

FORMAT 2

		£	£
1	Turnover		X
2	Change in stocks of finished goods and in work-in-progress		(X)
3	Own work capitalised		X
4	Other operating income		X
5	(a) Raw materials and consumables	X	
	(b) Other external charges	X	(X)
6	Staff costs:		
	(a) wages and salaries	X	
	(b) social security costs	X	
	(c) other pension costs	X	(X)
7	(a) Depreciation and other amounts written off tangible and intangible fixed assets	X	
	(b) Exceptional amounts written off current assets	X	(X)
8	Other operating charges		(X)
9	Income from shares in group undertakings	X	
10	Income from participating interests	X	
11	Income from other fixed asset investments	X	
12	Other interest receivable and similar income	X	X
13	Amount written off investments		(X)
14	Interest payable and similar charges		(X)
	– Profit or loss on ordinary activities before taxation		X
15	Tax on profit or loss on ordinary activities		(X)
16	Profit or loss on ordinary activities after taxation		X
17	Extraordinary income	X	
18	Extraordinary charges	(X)	
19	Extraordinary profit or loss	X	
20	Tax on extraordinary profit or loss	(X)	X
21	Other taxes not shown under the above items		(X)
22	Profit or loss for the financial year		X
	– Dividends	X	
	– Transfer to (from) reserves	X	
			(X)
			X
Profit and loss account brought forward			X
Profit and loss account carried forward			£XX

Note: Extraordinary items are unlikely to arise in practice following implementation of FRS 3 (see chapter 8).

(3) *Balance sheet* (vertical form)

			£	£	£
A	Called up share capital not paid				X
B	Fixed assets				
	I	Intangible assets			
		1 Development costs	X		
		2 Concessions, patents, licences, trade marks and similar rights and assets	X		
		3 Goodwill	X		
		4 Payments on account	X		
				X	
	II	Tangible assets			
		1 Land and buildings	X		
		2 Plant and machinery	X		
		3 Fixtures, fittings, tools and equipment	X		
		4 Payments on account and assets in course of construction	X		
				X	
	III	Investments			
		1 Shares in group undertakings	X		
		2 Loans to group undertakings	X		
		3 Participating interests	X		
		4 Loans to undertakings in which the company has a participating interest	X		
		5 Other investments other than loans	X		
		6 Other loans	X		
		7 Own shares	X		
				X	
	(Total of B)				X
C	Current assets				
	I	Stocks			
		1 Raw materials and consumables	X		
		2 Work-in-progress	X		
		3 Finished goods and goods for resale	X		
		4 Payments on account	X		
			X		
	II	Debtors			
		1 Trade debtors	X		
		2 Amounts owed by group undertakings	X		
		3 Amounts owed by undertakings in which the company has a participating interest	X		
		4 Other debtors	X		
		5 Called up share capital not paid	X		
		6 Prepayments and accrued income	X		
			X		
	III	Investments			
		1 Shares in group undertakings	X		
		2 Own shares	X		
		3 Other investments	X		
			X		
	IV	Cash at bank and in hand	X		
	(Total of C)			X	

		£	£	£
D	Prepayments and accrued income		X	
	(Total of C and D)		X	

E	Creditors: amounts falling due within one year		
	1 Debenture loans	X	
	2 Bank loans and overdrafts	X	
	3 Payments received on account	X	
	4 Trade creditors	X	
	5 Bills of exchange payable	X	
	6 Amounts owed to group undertakings	X	
	7 Amounts owed to undertakings in which the company has a participating interest	X	
	8 Other creditors including taxation and social security	X	
	9 Accruals and deferred income	X	
	(Total of E)		X

F	Net current assets (liabilities) (C + D − E)			X
G	Total assets less current liabilities (A + B + F)			X

H	Creditors: amounts falling due after more than one year		
	1 Debenture loans	X	
	2 Bank loans and overdrafts	X	
	3 Payments received on account	X	
	4 Trade creditors	X	
	5 Bills of exchange payable	X	
	6 Amounts owed to group undertakings	X	
	7 Amounts owed to undertakings in which the company has a participating interest	X	
	8 Other creditors including taxation and social security	X	
	9 Accruals and deferred income	X	(X)

I	Provisions for liabilities and charges		
	1 Pensions and similar obligations	X	
	2 Taxation, including deferred taxation	X	
	3 Other provisions	X	(X)

J	Accruals and deferred income		(X)
			£XX

K	Capital and reserves		
	I Called-up share capital		X
	II Share premium account		X
	III Revaluation reserve		X
	IV Other reserves		
	1 Capital redemption reserve	X	
	2 Reserve for own shares	X	
	3 Reserves provided for by the articles of association	X	
	4 Other reserves	X	X
	V Profit and loss account		X
			£XX

4.4 SUMMARY OF THE PRINCIPAL DISCLOSURE REQUIREMENTS FOR SINGLE COMPANIES

(a) Purpose of the checklist

The aim of the following checklist is to provide a guide to disclosure requirements for the more common reporting areas. All principal Companies Act requirements for single companies are referred to. At this stage of the book, however, only the more basic SSAP and Financial Reporting Standard requirements are listed. More advanced disclosure areas are dealt with in later chapters as follows:

(1) *Long-term contracts (chapter 14)*

(2) *Goodwill (chapter 13)*

(3) *Pension costs (chapter 20)*

(4) *Group accounts (chapters 21–28)*

(5) *Earnings per share (chapter 30)*

(6) *Cash flow statements (chapter 31)*

(7) *Segmental reporting (chapter 32)*

(b) Accounting policies

(1) *General*

— Disclosure of significant accounting policies – this would cover all areas, for example, stock valuation, depreciation of fixed assets, government grants, goodwill, development costs, deferred taxation and so on.
— Disclosure of use of true and fair override (5.7).

(2) *Depreciation*

For each major class of depreciable asset:

(i)   methods used;
(ii) useful lives or depreciation rates.

(3) *Development expenditure*

Statement and explanation of accounting policy

(4) *Goodwill*

(i)   explanation of accounting policy;
(ii) where goodwill is capitalised and amortised, write off period for each major acquisition.

(5) *Stocks and long-term contacts*

(i)   statement of accounting policies;
(ii) particular reference to method of ascertaining turnover and attributable profit (see chapter 14).

(6) *Deferred taxation*

Description of method of calculation.

(7) *Foreign currency translation*

(i)   method used to translate financial statements of foreign enterprises;
(ii) treatment of exchange differences (see chapter 28);
(iii) method used to translate transactions or assets denominated in foreign currencies.

(8) *Leasing – lessees*

Policies for accounting for operating leases and finance leases.

(9) *Leasing – lessors*

Policies for operating leases, finance leases and finance lease income (see chapter 18).

(c) Profit and loss items requiring disclosure

(1) *Turnover*

(i)   Analysis of turnover over:

(a) substantially different business activities;
(b) substantially different geographical markets.

(ii) Analysis of profit before tax between substantially different business activities.

(see also additional SSAP 25 disclosures, chapter 32).

(2) *Depreciation*

(i)   Total depreciation provided (including amortisation of intangibles).
(ii) Additional provisions for depreciation:

(a) temporary diminution in value of fixed asset investment;
(b) permanent diminution in value of any fixed asset;
(c) write back of provision considered no longer necessary;
Any of the above items in P/L must be shown by note.

(iii) Where assets revalued during current year, disclose the effect, if material, on the depreciation charge.

(3) *Expense items*

(i)   Charges for hire of plant and machinery.
(ii) Auditor's remuneration. (Companies other than small and medium-sized are required to disclose also the fee paid to auditors for non-audit work (eg corporate tax services.)
(iii) Interest payable:

(a) bank loans, overdrafts and other loans:

(1) repayable (other than by instalments) and due within five years of B/S date;
(2) repayable by instalments all of which are repayable within five years of B/S date;

(b) loans of any other kind.

(iv) Total amount of research and development expenditure charged in P/L analysed between current year's expenditure and amounts amortised from deferred expenditure.
(v) Amortisation charge for goodwill (if amortisation policy adopted, see chapter 13).

(4) *Particulars of staff*

(i)   Staff includes directors.
(ii) Average number of persons employed during year (determined on a weekly basis) and analysed within categories according to organisation of company's activities.
(iii) Staff costs disclosing:

    (a) wages;
    (b) social security costs;
    (c) other pension costs.

    SSAP 24, Accounting for pension costs, specifies further disclosure requirements (see chapter 20).

(5) *Directors' emoluments*

(i)   Aggregate of:

    (a) directors' emoluments;
    (b) directors' or past directors' pensions;
    (c) compensation to directors or past directors for loss of office.
    Items (a), (b) and (c) are to include benefits in kind.

(ii) Each item above to distinguish between:

    (a) amounts receivable in respect of services as director;
    (b) other emoluments (eg management remuneration).

(iii) Emoluments of chairman.
(iv) Emoluments of highest paid director (if in excess of chairman).
(v)   Numbers of directors whose emoluments fall in bands:

            0–£ 5,000
       £ 5,001–£10,000
       £10,001–£15,000 etc

Note: For purposes of (iii), (iv) and (v), emoluments should exclude employer's part of pension contributions.

(vi) Number of directors who have waived rights to emoluments and aggregate amount waived in year.

Notes
(1) If aggregate emoluments (as per (i) above) do not exceed £60,000, items (iii)–(vi) above need not be disclosed provided company is not part of a group.
(2) Items (iii), (iv) and (v) do not apply to directors whose duties were wholly or mainly outside UK during the year.
(3) The Companies Act 1989 extended the disclosure of directors' remuneration. The rules are complex and include disclosure of:

    (i)   amounts paid to obtain the services of a director ('golden hellos').
    (ii) consideration paid to third parties for the services of a person as a director.
    (iii) amounts paid to persons connected with, or bodies controlled by, a director.

(6) *Income items*

(i)   Income from listed investments.
(ii) If a substantial part of company's revenue, rents from lands.

(7) *Exceptional and extraordinary items*

(i)   Effect of transactions that are exceptional by virtue of size or incidence, though they fall within the ordinary activities of the company.
(ii) Particulars of extraordinary income or charges (disclose tax separately).
(iii) Prior year adjustments.
      Note impact of FRS 3 – see (10) below and chapter 8.

(8) *Taxation*

(i)   Basis of calculation of UK tax.
(ii) Particulars of special circumstances affecting tax liability; indication of extent to which tax charge is reduced by accelerated capital allowances.
(iii) State amounts for:

   (a) charge for UK corporation tax;
   (b) if greater than (a), charge for tax had double tax relief not been obtained;
   (c) charge for UK income tax;
   (d) amount of overseas tax;
   (e) tax attributable to franked investment income;
   (f) deferred taxation;
   (g) irrecoverable ACT;
   (h) relief for overseas taxation.

(iv) Amounts for (a)–(d) above to be stated separately in respect of tax on ordinary activities and tax on extraordinary items.

(9) *Other matters*

Amounts provided for the redemption of:

(i)   share capital.
(ii) loans.

(10) *Impact of FRS 3 – reporting financial performance*

(i)   disclosure of exceptional items;
(ii) note of historical cost profit (where difference is material);
(iii) statement of total recognised gains and losses;
(iv) reconciliation of movements in shareholders' funds.

   The impact of FRS 3 on accounts of smaller companies is likely to be slight.

(See chapter 8.)

(d) Balance sheet disclosures

(1) *Fixed assets – general points*

Unless indicated otherwise, the points below relate also to fixed asset investments and intangibles.

(i)   Cost or valuation: for each fixed asset category disclose:

   (a) aggregate at beginning of year;
   (b) revisions to valuation;
   (c) acquisitions;
   (d) disposals;
   (e) transfers between asset categories;
   (f) aggregate at end of year.

(ii) Cumulative depreciation: for each fixed asset category disclose:

(a) cumulative amount at beginning of year;
(b) amounts provided during the year;
(c) adjustments in respect of disposals;
(d) amount of any other adjustments during year;
(e) cumulative amount at end of year.

(iii) For fixed assets (other than listed investments) included on a valuation basis, state:

(a) the years and values involved (effectively analysis of aggregate cost or valuation at B/S date);
(b) for assets valued during financial year:

(1) names of valuers or particulars of their qualification;
(2) bases of valuation.

(iv) Land and buildings – analysis of NBV between:

(a) freehold;
(b) long leasehold; and
(c) short leasehold.

(v) For fixed assets included at a valuation state, either:

(a) aggregate cost and aggregate depreciation as would have been determined under historical cost rules; or
(b) difference between (a) and amounts actually included in B/S under modified historical cost.

(vi) If no record of original purchase price or production cost of asset:

(a) use value ascribed in earliest available record of its value after acquisition or production; or
(b) disclose particulars of such cases.

(vii) For investment properties, see below.

(2) *Investments*

(i) Disclosure rules (ii)–(iv) below apply whether fixed or current asset.
(ii) Disclose amount relating to listed investments (distinguishing between listed on recognised stock exchange and other listed investments).
(iii) The aggregate market value of the listed investments.
(iv) The market value of the listed investments and the stock exchange value in situation where market value is the higher of the two.
(v) Fixed asset investments included at a value determined on a basis that the directors consider appropriate: disclose particulars of the method of valuation and reasons for adopting it.
(vi) Nominal value of own shares held.

(3) *Significant shareholdings* (in excess of 10%)

(i) Situations:

(a) nominal value (NV) held exceeds NV of equity share capital of investee;
(b) NV held exceeds 10% of allotted share capital of investee;
(c) book value of investment exceeds 10% of assets of investor company.

(ii) Disclosure:

(a) name of the company;
(b) country in which incorporated if outside Great Britain;

    (c) its country of registration (England or Scotland) if different from the investing company;

    (d) identity and proportion of nominal value of each class of share held.

(iii) Comparatives not required.

(4) *Significant shareholdings* (in excess of 20%)

(i) Situations: NV of shares held exceeds 20% in NV of allotted share capital of investee.

(ii) Disclosure (additional to 10% plus requirements above):

    (a) aggregate amount of capital and reserves of investee as at B/S ending with or prior to that of investor;

    (b) profit or loss of investee.

(iii) Disclosure not required if investment accounted for by equity method of valuation.

(iv) Comparatives not required.

(5) *Intangible fixed assets*

(i) Development costs

    (a) separate disclosure under intangible fixed assets;

    (b) movements on deferred development expenditure;

    (c) amounts carried forward at beginning of year.

(ii) Goodwill

    (a) amount of goodwill for each material acquisition during the year.

    (b) if amortisation policy adopted (see chapter 13):

        (1) separate disclosure under intangible fixed assets;

        (2) movement on goodwill account (showing cost, accumulated amortisation and NBV at beginning and end of year);

        (3) period selected for amortising goodwill (for each major acquisition).

(Further aspects are discussed in chapter 13, and group accounts implications in chapter 25.)

(6) *Stocks and long-term contracts*

(i) Sub-classification of balance sheet figure into appropriate categories (see chapter 14).

(ii) If materially different, disclosure of difference between:

    (a) purchase price or production cost of stock in company's balance sheet using one of the specified methods such as FIFO, average cost etc; and

    (b) replacement cost at balance sheet date (or, if considered more appropriate by directors, the most recent actual purchase price or production cost).

(iii) Payments on account of orders to be shown in positions E3 or H3 of the Companies Act 1985 format to the extent that they are not shown as deductions from stock.

Note: Specific disclosure requirements relating to long-term contracts are dealt with in chapter 14.

(7) *Debtors*

For each item included under debtors: show separately amounts falling due after more than one year.

Note: possible disclosure implications of UITF 4 (see chapter 9).

(8) *Creditors*

(i) For each item shown under creditors, disclose:

   (a) aggregate amount of debts repayable (other than by instalments) more than five years after B/S date;
   (b) aggregate amount of debts repayable by instalments any of which fall due more than five years after the B/S date;
   (c) for each item in (b), the aggregate amount of instalments falling due after the five years.

(ii) For each debt required to be disclosed under (i)(c) above, disclose:

   (a) terms of payment or repayment and rate of interest payable; or
   (b) if above statement would be of excessive length, a general indication of the terms of payment or repayment and rates of interest payable.

(iii) For each item under creditors, supply:

   (a) aggregate amount of any debts in respect of which security has been given;
   (b) indication of nature of securities given.

(iv) Issues of debentures during the year – disclose:

   (a) reason for making issue;
   (b) classes of debentures Issued;
   (c) for each class, amount issued and consideration received by company.

(v) Particulars of redeemed debentures which company has power to reissue.

(vi) Where any of company's debentures are held by a nominee of or trustee for the company: state nominal amount of debentures and amount at which stated in the accounting records.

(vii) Convertible debenture loans:

   (a) amount of any convertible loans is required to be shown separately;
   (b) see share capital section (right to require allotment of shares to any person).

(9) *Capital instruments (FRS 4)*

(i) Debt:

   (a) analysis of debt between
      – in one year or less, or on demand
      – between one and two years
      – between two and five years
      – in five years or more;
   (b) convertible debt
      – separate disclosure on balance sheet
      – redemption dates and amounts
      – conversion dates and number of shares into which debt may be converted
      – whether conversion is at option of issuer or holder;
   (c) legal nature of any instrument if different from normal debt;
   (d) details where maturity of debt is assessed by reference to financing facilities.

(ii) Shareholders' funds:

   (a) total amount of shareholders' funds and split between equity and non-equity;
   (b) brief summary of rights of each class of shares;
   (c) aggregate dividends split between equity and non-equity elements.

(10) *Taxation*

(i)   Other creditors including taxation and social security (balance sheet items E8 and H8): show separate amount for taxation and social security.
(ii)   State amount of any provisions for taxation other than deferred taxation.
(iii) Disclose date of payment of corporation tax unless included as a current liability.
(iv)   Include ACT on proposed dividends as a current tax liability.
(v)   Deferred tax account balances to be shown separately in B/S:

(a) indicate nature and amount of major elements;
(b) description of method of calculation adopted.

(vi)   For each principal category of deferred taxation show:

(a) potential amount of deferred tax;
(b) amount provided within the account.

(vii) Recoverable ACT relating to proposed dividends:

(a) deduct from deferred tax account if available; failing which
(b) show ACT recoverable as a deferred asset.

(viii) Value of asset shown by way of note and differing from book value: disclose, if material, tax implications of realisation at valuation figure.

(ix)   Deferred tax relating to movements on reserve: show separately; disclose treatment.

(11) *Dividends*

(i)   State aggregate amount recommended for distribution as dividend.
(ii)   If arrears of fixed cumulative dividends, memorandum note of:

(a) amount of arrears;
(b) period for which dividends (or each class of dividends) are in arrear.

(See also (9)).

(12) *Provisions*

(i)   Where amounts transferred to any provision for liabilities and charges, disclose:

(a) amount of provision at beginning of year;
(b) amount transferred to the provision during the year;
(c) source and application of amounts so transferred;
(d) amount of provision at end of year.

(ii)   Where amounts are transferred from any provision for liabilities and charges except for purpose for which provision was established, disclose similar information as for (i) above.
(iii) Other provisions (B/S item I3): where amount of a provision is material, give particulars of each provision included under this heading.
(iv)   Comparatives not required.

(13) *Guarantees and other financial commitments*

(i)   Particulars of any charge on the assets of the company to secure the liabilities of any other person, including, where practicable, the amount secured.
(ii)   Any other contingent liability not provided for:

(a) amount or estimated amount of that liability (as at date on which financial statements are approved by board of directors);
(b) its legal nature;

   (c) whether any valuable security has been provided by the company in connection with the liability and if so, what;
   (d) the uncertainties which are expected to affect the ultimate outcome;
   (e) explain taxation implications of a contingency, where necessary for a proper understanding.

(iii) Capital commitments:

   (a) contracts for capital expenditure not provided for;
   (b) capital expenditure authorised by directors but not yet contracted for.

(iv) Pension commitment particulars:

   (a) pension commitments included under any provision shown in the B/S;
   (b) pension commitments for which no provision made;
   (c) where applicable, separate particulars of pension commitments relating wholly or partly to pensions payable to past directors.

Note: SSAP 24 disclosure requirements are dealt with in chapter 20.

(v) Particulars of any other financial commitments which:

   (a) have not been provided for; and
   (b) are relevant to assessing the company's state of affairs.

(14) *Share capital*

(i) Authorised share capital.
(ii) Allotted share capital:

   (a) where more than one class of shares allotted, number and aggregate nominal value of each class;
   (b) amount of allotted share capital;
   (c) amount of called-up share capital which has been paid up.

(iii) Allotted redeemable shares:

   (a) earliest and latest dates on which company has power to redeem;
   (b) whether redemption is mandatory or at option of company;
   (c) premium, if any, payable on redemption.

(iv) Shares allotted during the financial year:

   (a) reasons for making the allotment;
   (b) classes of shares allotted;
   (c) for each class of share;

     (1) number allotted,
     (2) aggregate nominal value,
     (3) consideration received by company.

(v) Options to subscribe for shares and any other rights to require allotment of shares to any person (including convertible loan stock):

   (a) number, description and amount of shares in relation to which right is exercisable;
   (b) period during which it is exercisable;
   (c) price to be paid for the shares allotted.

   (See also (9)).

(15) *Reserves*

(i) Where any amount is transferred to or from any reserves, disclose:

   (a) amount of reserves at beginning of year;
   (b) any amounts transferred to or from the reserves during the year.

(16) *Loans for acquisition of own shares*

Loans under the Companies Act 1985, s 153(4)(b) or (c) or s 155: where included under any B/S item, disclose aggregate amount of loans for each such item.

(17) *Government grants*

(i)   Effects of grants on the results for the period and/or the financial position.
(ii) Nature and effects of assistance other than grants (where applicable and if they materially affect the results).
(iii) Capital-based grants should be dealt with by the deferred credit method and not deducted from cost of asset. (Suitable position for deferred credit would be item J in the format, i e deferred income.)

(18) *Investment properties*

(i)   Valuation:

(a) name of valuer or particulars of qualifications;
(b) bases of valuation used;
(c) if appropriate, fact that valuer is employee or officer of the company.

(ii) Investment revaluation reserve:

(a) disclose prominently in financial statements;
(b) disclose movements during year.

(iii) Carrying value of investment properties: disclose prominently in financial statements.

(19) *Leasing and hire purchase*

The specific disclosure requirements are dealt with in chapter 18.

(20) *Post-balance sheet events*

For non-adjusting and window-dressing transactions, disclose:

(i)   nature of event;
(ii) estimate of financial effect;
(iii) tax implications.

(21) *Reporting the substance of transactions (FRS 5)*

(i)   Disclosure of a transaction should be sufficient to enable a user of financial statements to understand its commercial effect.
(ii) Where a transaction has resulted in assets or liabilities whose nature differs from that of items usually included under the relevant balance sheet heading, disclose the differences.
(iii) Refer to FRS 5 Application Notes for disclosures relating to:

(a) consignment stocks;
(b) factored debts;
(c) sale and repurchase agreements.

(22) *Related party disclosures (FRS 8)*

(i)   Disclosure of control:

(a) disclosure of controlling party and related party relationship;
(b) disclosure of ultimate controlling party (if different).

(ii) Disclosure of transactions and balances:

(a) names of transacting related parties;
(b) description of relationship;

   (c) description of transactions;
   (d) amounts involved;
   (e) any other element necessary for an understanding of the accounts;
   (f) amounts due to/from related parties at balance sheet date;
   (g) provisions against doubtful debts due from related parties;
   (h) amounts written off balances with related parties.

(23) *Disclosure of changes in accounting policies*

(i)   Disclose effect of change in accounting policy on:

   (a) results for current year (UITF 14);
   (b) results for preceding year (FRS 3).

(e) Cash flow statements

Disclosure requirements are dealt with in chapter 31.

(f) Directors' report – summary of matters to be disclosed

  (1) Principal activities of the company and any significant changes.
  (2) A fair review of the development of the business of the company during the financial year and of its position at the end of it.
  (3) Names of persons who were directors at any time during the year.
  (4) Significant changes in the fixed assets of the company during the year.
  (5) The difference, as precisely as is practicable, between the market value and the book value of land and buildings, where such difference is substantial.
  (6) Directors' interest in shares or debentures of this company or any other group company both at the beginning of the financial year (or date of appointment as director, if later) and at the end of the year.
  (7) Particulars of any important events which have occurred since the balance sheet date.
  (8) An indication of likely future developments in the business of the company.
  (9) An indication of the activities (if any) of the company in the field of research and development.
(10) Amount recommended to be paid by way of dividend.
(11) Amount to be carried to reserve.

(12) Charitable and political donations:

   (i) if combined amount exceeds £200, the split between charitable and political;
   (ii) details of any individual amount for political purposes where amount exceeds £200; name of recipient and amount given.

(13) Disabled persons – statement describing policies for:

   (i)   employment;
   (ii)   training;
   (iii) career development;
   (iv) promotion.

   (Not applicable to companies which employ fewer than 250 persons within the United Kingdom.)
(14) Particulars of acquisitions of company's own shares.
(15) If applicable, the fact that a company has purchased or maintained any insurance to indemnify any officer or auditor against liability incurred by him in relation to the company.

4.5   ILLUSTRATION   1 – VENEERING MANUFACTURERS LTD

(a) Basic data

The year end of Veneering Manufacturers Ltd is 30 June. The trial balance at 30 June 19X9 was as follows:

	£	£
100,000 8% (now 5.6% plus tax credit) cumulative preference shares of £1 each fully paid, redeemable at the company's option on January 1 19X30 at a premium of 25p per share (authorised £100,000)		100,000
400,000 ordinary shares of £1 each (authorised £500,000)		400,000
Freehold land and buildings, July 1 19X8 cost	414,900	
Additions during the year	20,000	
Plant and equipment (cost, £240,000) – see note	120,000	
Office furniture (cost, £30,000)	22,000	
Stock of raw materials, July 1 19X8	93,200	
Stock of finished goods, July 1 19X8	12,700	
Work-in-progress, July 1 19X8	9,200	
Debtors	107,600	
4% debenture (repayable at par, January 1 19X22) (secured by a floating charge)		150,000
Debenture interest, half-year to December 19X8 (gross), paid on January 1 19X9	3,000	
Dividends and interest:		
From unquoted investments received May 1 19X9 (cash received)		700
From quoted investments received June 20 19X9 (gross)		3,000
Share premium account		136,400
Unquoted investments at cost	32,000	
Quoted investments at cost (British government securities) (market value £71,000)	60,200	
Profit and loss account – balance July 1 19X8		30,900
Cash at bank and in hand	154,080	
Creditors		78,580
Sales		791,000
Purchases	319,600	
Carriage inwards	16,000	
Bank interest	2,900	
Wages and national insurance (factory)	137,900	
Plant hire (internal telephone system)	1,300	
Rates	5,000	
Repairs to premises	600	
Administrative salaries (including directors', £30,000)	61,300	
Salesmen's salaries (including directors', £40,000)	100,000	
Postage and telephone	1,800	
Printing and stationery	400	
Legal and professional charges	800	
Advertising	500	
Directors' fees	600	
Bank charges	100	
Salesmen's commissions	5,200	
Power and lighting (factory)	6,700	
Insurances – factory	7,200	
Insurances – office	400	
Repairs to plant	8,500	
Preference share dividend for half-year, due and paid on January 1 19X9	2,800	
Income tax account	900	
Corporation tax over-provided in previous year		1,400
ACT account	1,200	
Deposit interest received		38,600
	1,730,580	1,730,580

Illustration 1 – Veneering Manufacturers Ltd   81

The following adjustments are required:

(1) Accruals: £

    Power and lighting 2,400
    Salesmen's commissions 1,600
    Auditors' remuneration, including expenses (see also (19)) 1,000

(2) Doubtful debts provision 2,500
(3) Depreciation:

    Plant and equipment   10% straight-line on cost
    Office furniture   10% on reducing balance

(4) Corporation tax on profits for the year estimated at £67,000.
(5) Half-year's preference dividend (payable 1.7.19X9) is to be provided for.
(6) A final ordinary dividend of 5% (payable 31.7.19X9) is to be provided for.
(7) Closing stocks:

    Raw materials 76,400
    Work-in-progress 12,800
    Finished goods 40,100

(8) Prepayments:

    Factory insurances 1,100
    Rates 1,200

The following additional information is provided:

(9) The income tax position is:

INCOME TAX ACCOUNT

19X9		£	19X9		£
April 14	Bank	900	Jan 1	Debenture interest (tax deducted)	900
June 20	Quoted investment income account (tax deducted from un-franked investment income)	900	June 30	Corporation tax account	900
		1,800			1,800

(10) Corporation tax paid during the year amounted to £28,840, compared with £30,240 provided at the previous balance sheet date (i e £1,400 over-provided).
(11) At June 30 19X9, the company had placed contracts for heavy machinery for £80,000 and the Board has authorised, but not yet placed, a contract for a new storeroom for £30,000.
(12) During the year, the company acquired new plant for £10,000 and sold obsolete plant at written-down value (cost, £5,000; accumulated depreciation, £4,000). There were no acquisitions or disposals of office furniture.
(13) The unlisted investments relate to a 3% shareholding in a private company.
(14) There is no substantial difference between the purchase price or production costs of closing stocks, and their replacement cost or most recent prices at the balance sheet date.
(15) The historical cost of land and buildings at 1 July 19X8 was £200,000.
(16) The company acquired the business of G Huyton & Co on 18 August 19X9 for consideration in cash amounting to £139,500.

(17) *Staff details*
These details include relevant information relating to directors.

    (i) Administrative salaries include £4,017 in respect of social security costs and £3,675 in respect of other pension costs. Respective figures for salesmen's salaries are £7,095 and £6,042; for factory wages and national insurance, £10,538 and £8,473.
    (ii) Details of numbers of staff employed are:

Office and management	6
Selling and marketing	12
Manufacturing	21
	39

(18) *Directors' emoluments*

Details of directors' emoluments, exclusive of pension contributions are:

Williams (Chairman)	£5,500
Pace	£2,750
Slow	£15,930
Ruslow	£19,760
Harris	£12,750

(19) No fees were paid to the auditors other than those relating to audit work.

(b) Required

(1) A detailed manufacturing, trading and profit and loss account for the year ended 30 June 19X9, in a form suitable for presentation to the directors.
(2) A profit and loss account in a form suitable for presentation to the shareholders using both formats permitted by the revised Sch 4 of the Companies Act 1985.
(3) A balance sheet as at 30 June 19X9, in a form suitable for presentation to the shareholders.
(4) Notes for the profit and loss account and the balance sheet, including accounting policies.

Notes

(1) Ignore comparative figures and the requirements of SSAP 3 (earnings per share).
(2) Income tax should be taken at 30%, corporation tax at 50% and ACT at $\frac{3}{7}$. Deferred tax should be ignored.
(3) Ignore the requirement for a directors' report and a cash flow statement.

(c) Veneering Manufacturers Ltd

MANUFACTURING, TRADING AND PROFIT AND LOSS ACCOUNT

for the year ended 30 June 19X9 for presentation to the directors

	£	£
Materials:		
Stock at 1.7.19X8		93,200
Purchases		319,600
Carriage inwards		16,000
		428,800
Less stock at 30.6.19X9		76,400
		352,400
Wages and national insurance		137,900
Prime cost		490,300
Factory overheads:		
Power and lighting	9,100	
Insurance	6,100	
Repairs to plant	8,500	
Depreciation of plant	24,000	
		47,700
Factory cost of production		538,000
Work-in-progress, 30.6.19X9	12,800	
Work-in-progress, 30.6.19X8	9,200	
		(3,600)
Factory cost of finished goods produced		534,400

Illustration 1 – Veneering Manufacturers Ltd 83

	£	£
Sales:		791,000
Stock of finished goods at 1.7.X8	12,700	
Factory cost of finished goods produced	534,400	
	547,100	
Less stock of finished goods at 30.6.X9	40,100	
Cost of sales		507,000
Gross profit		284,000
Deposit interest received		38,600
Income from investments – quoted		3,000
– unquoted		1,000
		326,600
Administrative expenses:		
Rates	3,800	
Plant hire (internal telephones)	1,300	
Repairs to premises	600	
Insurances	400	
Depreciation of office furniture	2,200	
Directors' emoluments	30,600	
Salaries	31,300	
Auditors' remuneration	1,000	
Postage and telephone	1,800	
Printing and stationery	400	
Legal and professional charges	800	
	74,200	
Selling and distribution expenses:		
Salesmen's salaries	100,000	
Commissions	6,800	
Advertising	500	
	107,300	
Finance expenses:		
Debenture interest	6,000	
Bank interest	2,900	
Bank charges	100	
Provision for doubtful debts	2,500	
	11,500	
		193,000
Profit before tax		133,600
Taxation:		
Corporation tax		
Provided for the year	67,000	
Overprovided in previous year	(1,400)	
	65,600	
Tax credit on dividends received	300	
		65,900
Profit after tax		67,700
Dividends:		
Preference shares		
Paid	2,800	
Proposed	2,800	
Ordinary shares		
Proposed	20,000	
		25,600
Retained profit		42,100
Balance at 1.7.X8		30,900
Balance at 30.6.X9		73,000

(d) Veneering Manufacturers Ltd

PROFIT AND LOSS ACCOUNT
for the year ended 30 June 19X9
for presentation to the shareholders (format 1)

	£	£
Turnover		791,000
Cost of sales		507,000
Gross profit		284,000
Distribution costs	107,300	
Administrative expenses	76,800	184,100
		99,900
Income from fixed asset investments	1,000	
Other interest receivable	41,600	
		42,600
Interest payable		(8,900)
Profit on ordinary activities before taxation		133,600
Tax on profit on ordinary activities		65,900
Profit on ordinary activities after taxation		67,700
Dividends		25,600
Retained profit		42,100
Profit and loss account brought forward		30,900
Profit and loss account carried forward		73,000

Workings

(1) *Cost of sales and distribution costs*
Per detailed manufacturing account.

(2) *Administrative expenses*

	£
Per manufacturing account	74,200
Bank charges	100
Doubtful debts	2,500
	76,800

(e) Veneering Manufacturers Ltd

PROFIT AND LOSS ACCOUNT
for the year ended 30 June 19X9
for presentation to the shareholders (format 2)

	£
Turnover	791,000
Operating costs (see note)	691,100
Trading profit	99,900
Income from fixed asset investments	1,000
Other interest receivable	41,600
	42,600
Interest payable	(8,900)
Profit on ordinary activities before taxation	133,600
Tax on profit on ordinary activities	65,900
Profit on ordinary activities after taxation	67,700
Dividends	25,600
Retained profit	42,100
Profit and loss account brought forward	30,900
Profit and loss account carried forward	73,000

Illustration 1 – Veneering Manufacturers Ltd 85

NOTES – OPERATING COSTS

	£
Change in stocks of finished goods and work in progress	(31,000)
Raw materials and consumables	336,400
Other external charges	16,000
Staff costs	306,600
Depreciation	26,200
Other operating charges	34,600
Hire of plant and machinery	1,300
Auditors' remuneration	1,000
	691,100

Workings

(1) *Change in stocks*

	£
Finished goods	27,400
Work in progress	3,600
	31,000

(2) *Raw materials and consumables*

Opening stock	93,200
Purchases	319,600
Closing stock	(76,400)
	336,400

(3) *Other external charges*

Carriage	16,000

(4) *Staff costs*

Factory wages and NI	137,900
Directors' emoluments (admin)	30,600
Salaries (admin)	31,300
Salesmen's salaries and commission	106,800
	306,600

(5) *Depreciation*

Plant	24,000
Office furniture	2,200
	26,200

(6) *Other operating charges*

Power and lighting	9,100
Insurance	6,100
Repairs to plant	8,500
Rates	3,800
Repairs to premises	600
Insurances	400
Postage and telephone	1,800
Printing and stationery	400
Legal and professional	800
Advertising	500
Bank charges	100
Doubtful debts	2,500
	34,600

(f) Veneering Manufacturers Ltd

BALANCE SHEET

as at 30 June 19X9

	£	£	£
Fixed assets			
Tangible assets			550,700
Investments			32,000
			582,700
Current assets			
Stocks		129,300	
Debtors		116,870	
Investments		60,200	
Cash at bank and in hand		154,080	
		460,450	
Creditors: amounts falling due within one year			
Trade creditors	78,580		
Taxation and social security	74,370		
Proposed dividends	22,800		
Accruals and deferred income	8,000		
		183,750	
Net current assets			276,700
Total assets less current liabilities			859,400
Creditors: amounts falling due after more than one year			
Debenture loan			(150,000)
			709,400
Capital and reserves			£
Called-up share capital			500,000
Share premium account			136,400
Profit and loss account			73,000
			709,400

The financial statements were approved by the Board of Directors on 15 November 19X9.

Signed on behalf of the Board of Directors.

....

J Pace, director

(g) Notes to the accounts (part of the financial statements)

(1) *Accounting policies*
The accounts are prepared under the historical cost convention, modified to include the revaluation of freehold land and buildings.

(a) Depreciation is provided on all tangible assets, other than freehold land and buildings, at rates calculated to write off the cost of valuation, less estimated residual value, of each asset evenly over its expected useful life as follows:

Plant and machinery – 10% pa on a straight-line basis
Office furniture   – 10% pa on a reducing balance basis

Illustration 1 – Veneering Manufacturers Ltd 87

(b) Stock and work in progress — Stocks are stated at the lower of cost and net realisable value as follows:

Cost includes all costs incurred in bringing each product to its present location and condition and is determined as follows:

Raw materials – purchase costs on a first-in-first-out basis.

Work-in-progress and finished goods – cost of direct materials and labour, plus attributable overheads based on the normal level of activity.

Net realisable value is based on estimated selling price, less further costs expected to be incurred to completion and disposal.

(c) Turnover represents the invoiced amount of goods sold and services provided, stated net of credits and allowances and value added tax.

(d) The company operates a defined contribution scheme. The assets of the scheme are held separately from those of the company in an independently administered fund. The pension cost charge represents contributions payable by the company to the fund.

(2) *Profit on ordinary activities before tax*
This is stated after charging or crediting:

	£
Staff costs (see notes 3 and 4 below)	306,600
Auditors' remuneration	1,000
Depreciation	26,200
Hire of plant and machinery	1,300
Interest payable:	
Bank loans and overdrafts, wholly repayable within five years	2,900
Other loans	6,000
Interest receivable on deposit accounts	38,600
Income from investments:	
Listed	3,000
Unlisted	1,000

(3) *Staff costs*
Staff costs (including directors) were as follows:

	£
Wages and salaries	266,760
Social security costs	21,650
Other pension costs	18,190
	306,600

The average weekly number of employees, including directors, during the year was made up as follows:

	No
Office and management	6
Selling and marketing	12
Manufacturing	21
	39

(4) *Directors' remuneration*

	£
Fees	600
Other emoluments (including pension contributions)	70,000
	70,600

The emoluments of the chairman, excluding pension contributions, were £5,500 and of the highest paid director, excluding pension contributions, £19,760.

Other directors' emoluments, excluding pension contributions, fell within the following ranges:

	No
£ Nil–£ 5,000	1
£ 5,001–£10,000	–
£10,001–£15,000	1
£15,001–£20,000	1

£

(5) Tax on profit on ordinary activities
Based on the profit for the year:

Corporation tax at 50%	67,000
Tax credits attributable to dividends received	300
Corporation tax overprovided in previous years	(1,400)
	65,900

(6) Tangible fixed assets

	Total £	Freehold land and buildings £	Plant and machinery £	Fixtures, fittings and equipment £
Cost or valuation				
At 1 July 19X8	679,900	414,900	235,000	30,000
Additions	30,000	20,000	10,000	–
Disposals	(5,000)	–	(5,000)	–
At 30 June 19X9	704,900	434,900	240,000	30,000
Depreciation				
At 1 July 19X8	132,000	–	124,000	8,000
Provided during the year	26,200	–	24,000	2,200
Eliminated on disposals	(4,000)	–	(4,000)	–
At 30 June 19X9	154,200	–	144,000	10,200
Net book amounts at:				
30 June 19X9	550,700	434,900	96,000	19,800
30 June 19X8	547,900	414,900	111,000	22,000

For the freehold land and buildings included at valuation, comparable historical cost figures are:

At 1 July 19X8	£200,000
At 30 June 19X9	£220,000

(7) Investments

	£
Cost at 1 July 19X8 and at 30 June 19X9	
Listed investments (market value £71,000)	60,200
Unlisted investments	32,000
	92,200

(8) Stocks

Raw materials	76,400
Work-in-progress	12,800
Finished goods	40,100
	129,300

(9) Debtors

Trade debtors	105,100
Other debtors	9,470
Prepayments	2,300
	116,870

Other debtors includes a deferred asset – ACT recoverable.

(10) Debenture loan
The debenture loan bears interest at 4% and is repayable in 19X22.
   The loan is secured by a floating charge on the assets of the company.

Illustration 1 – Veneering Manufacturers Ltd 89

(11) *Called-up share capital*

	Authorised £	Allotted, issued and fully paid £
Ordinary shares of £1 each	500,000	400,000
8% (now 5.6% plus tax credit) Cumulative preference shares at £1 each	100,000	100,000
	600,000	500,000

The preference shares are redeemable at the company's option on 1 January 19X30 at a premium of 25p per share.

(12) *Post-balance sheet event*
On 18 August 19X9, the company acquired the business of G Huyton & Co for cash consideration of £139,500.

(13) *Capital commitments*

	£
Contracted	80,000
Authorised but not contracted	30,000

(14) *Contingent liabilities*

Guarantee of the bank overdraft of a supplier	£95,000

(15) *Pension commitments*
There is insufficient information for the purposes of a meaningful note.

Workings

(1) *Staff costs*

	Total £	Wages and salaries £	Social security costs £	Other pension costs £
Administrative salaries	61,300	53,608	4,017	3,675
Salesmen's salaries	100,000	86,863	7,095	6,042
Salesmen's commissions	6,800	6,800	–	–
Factory wages and national insurance	137,900	118,889	10,538	8,473
Directors' fees	600	600	–	–
	306,600	266,760	21,650	18,190

(2) *Directors' remuneration*

	Fees £	Other emoluments £
Administrative salaries	400	45,000
Salesmen's salaries	200	25,000
	600	70,000

(3) *Debtors*

	£	£
Trade debtors		107,600
Less provision for doubtful debts		2,500
		105,100
Other debtors – ACT recoverable		9,470
Prepayments:		
Factory insurances	1,100	
Rates	1,200	
		2,300
		116,870

(4)   MAINSTREAM CORPORATION TAX ACCOUNT (MCT)

	£		£
P/L (overprovided last year)	1,400	Bal b/d	30,240
Cash paid	28,840	P/L (this year charge)	67,000
IT a/c	900		
ACT a/c	1,200		
Bal c/d (67,000 – 900 – 1,200)	64,900		
	97,240		97,240

(5)   ADVANCE CORPORATION TAX ACCOUNT (ACT)

	£		£
Per trial balance ($\frac{3}{7}$ × 2,800 pref div)	1,200	MCT a/c	1,200
Bal c/d	9,470	Bal c/d	9,470
(see working below)			
	10,670		10,670

EXPLANATION OF CALCULATIONS
(i) *ACT asset and liability*

Proposed dividends	22,800
Dividends received	700
	22,100
ACT $\frac{3}{7}$ × 22,100	9,470

(ii) *ACT set-off*

Corporation tax on 19X9 profits		67,000
ACT paid (relating to dividends paid in 19X9)	1,200	
Income tax	900	
		2,100
Mainstream corporation tax liability		64,900

(This is explained in some detail in chapter 17.)
(iii) *Tax and social security payable within one year*

ACT	9,470
MCT	64,900
	74,370

4.6 ILLUSTRATION 2 – EXTRACT FROM ANNUAL REPORT AND ACCOUNTS OF THORN EMI PLC FOR THE YEAR ENDED 31 MARCH 1995

Directors' report for the year ended 31 March 1995

The Chairman's Statement together with the Financial Review and the review of business activities in this Annual Report contain details of the principal operations of the Group during the year and likely future developments.

Dividends

An interim dividend of 9.75p per share (1994: 9.0p) was paid in March 1995. The Board is recommending a final dividend of 26.75p per share (1994: 25.0p), payable on 6 October 1995 to ordinary shareholders on the register as at 15 August 1995, making a total of 36.5p (1994: 34.0p) for the full year. It is proposed that the retained loss of £49.4m be transferred to the profit and loss reserve.

Illustration 2 – Extract from annual report and accounts of THORN EMI plc 91

Scrip dividend

The scrip dividend scheme, which enables ordinary shareholders to elect to receive new ordinary shares in lieu of a cash dividend, continued to be of interest to certain shareholders. During the year under review, 466,537 new ordinary shares were issued under the scheme, which resulted in a cash saving to the company in respect of dividends forgone of approximately £4.7m. In addition, there was a cash flow saving in respect of advance corporation tax.

Details of the scrip dividend in respect of the final dividend for the year ended 31 March 1995 will be despatched to shareholders in August.

Research and development

The management of each of the Group's businesses is responsible for research and development in its particular area. These programmes are supported by the activities of the Central Research Laboratories. During the year, Group expenditure on research and development totalled £68.4m, of which customers funded £66.7m.

Fixed assets

The changes in fixed assets during the year are summarised in the Notes to the accounts.

The directors are of the opinion that the present value of the land and buildings of the company and its subsidiaries is in excess of net book value.

Share capital

Details of shares issued during the year are set out in Note 23.

As at 17 May 1995 the company had been notified of the following substantial interests of 3 per cent or more in its ordinary share capital:

The Capital Group Companies Inc.   18,636,042 (4.4%)
Prudential Corporation group of companies   14,793,841 (3.5%)

The company is not a close company within the meaning of the provisions of the Income and Corporation Taxes Act 1988.

Employment policies

THORN EMI, through the individual businesses and reinforced in the company's terms and conditions of employment, is committed to providing employment opportunities, including recruitment, access to training and promotion, without discrimination on the grounds of gender, nationality, ethnic or racial origin, non-job related disability or marital status.

The company views training and development of its employees as a priority.

THORN EMI positively encourages employee involvement and two-way communication throughout the Group, with each business unit responsible for setting up the necessary processes. Examples of this include joint management and employee committees on Health and Safety and other employment matters, in-house publications, attitude surveys and formal briefing groups. The UK Pension Fund, the largest in the Group, has wide employee representation on the Trustee Board and reports regularly to the membership, as do the smaller funds in other countries, as appropriate.

Share option schemes

Information on share options granted to employees is given in Note 23.

The 1984 executive share option scheme expired on 14 September 1994 and it is proposed to seek shareholder approval for a new executive share option scheme at the 1995 Annual General Meeting.

Charitable and political contributions

As indicated in the Corporate Activities section, charitable, sponsorship and fund-raising activities carried out during the year within the Group contributed in excess of £9.5m to charitable organisations and communities around the world. These included UK charitable donations amounting to £0.7m. No political contributions were made.

Directors and auditors

The present directors of the company are named on page 28 [not included in this extract]. All served as directors throughout the year.

Mr J D F Barnes retired as a director at the conclusion of the Annual General Meeting on 15 July 1994.

Mr S P Duffy, Mr J G Fifield and Sir Peter Walters now retire by rotation pursuant to Article 109 at the Annual General Meeting and, being eligible, each offers himself for re-election.

Mr Duffy has a service contract with the company which is terminable in normal circumstances at the option of the company on 24 months' prior notice in writing and by Mr Duffy on 12 months' prior notice in writing. Mr Fifield has a service contract with a subsidiary company which is terminable in normal circumstances by either party on 36 months' prior notice in writing. Sir Peter Walters does not have a service agreement with the company.

No director had a material interest in any contract of significance, other than a service contract, subsisting at the end of or during the year, involving any Group company. Details of directors' interests in the shares of the company are set out in Note 32.

Ernst & Young have expressed their willingness to continue in office as auditors and a resolution proposing their reappointment and authorising the directors to determine their remuneration will be put to the Annual General Meeting.

Directors' and officers' liability insurance

The company has maintained insurance to cover directors' and officers' liability as permitted by section 310(3) of the Companies Act 1985.

Corporate governance, going concern and internal financial control

The company has complied throughout the year with the provisions of the Code of Best Practice issued by the Committee on the Financial Aspects of Corporate Governance ('the Cadbury Committee') that were in effect during the year. Guidance for directors on reporting on internal control was issued in December 1994 but compliance with its provisions is not required until the company's next financial year.

The directors acknowledge their responsibility for the Group's system of internal financial control and, in advance of full compliance with paragraph 4.5 of the Code of Best Practice, a summary of the key elements is set out below.

The directors believe that the Group has adequate resources to continue in operational existence for the foreseeable future. For this reason, they continue to adopt the going concern basis in preparing the accounts.

Ernst & Young have reviewed the above statements, in so far as they relate to the paragraphs in the Code of Best Practice that the London Stock Exchange has specified for their review, and their report is set out on page 34 [not included in this extract].

The internal control system is subject to regular review by the Internal Audit Department. The independence of the internal audit function is safeguarded. All heads of internal audit have direct access to the Group finance director and the Audit Committee, and all internal audit reports are reviewed independently of the businesses concerned. The Audit Committee considers developments in THORN EMI's business environment and has reviewed the system of internal financial control based on reporting by management and both the Group's external and internal auditors. Any system of internal control can, however, only provide reasonable, and not absolute, assurance against material accounting errors or losses.

The directors hold regular meetings and a number of matters are specifically reserved for their approval. The Group has an established organisational structure with clearly defined lines of responsibility and reporting, all of which is supported by Group manuals which dictate policies and procedures applicable in common to all business units.

The Group has prepared both medium-term strategic plans, which focus on key business risks, and annual budgets. Formal procedures are in force which require Board and the operating businesses' approval of the medium-term strategic plans and the annual budget. The Group's performance is monitored against budget and all significant variances are investigated. There are also specific guidelines for capital and investment expenditure appraisal.

The strength of an internal control system is dependent on the quality and integrity of management and staff. The Group is committed to developing personnel of high quality and key executives and managers are required to sign an annual certificate of compliance with the Group manuals.

Annual General Meeting

The Annual General Meeting will be held at 11.30 am on Friday, 21 July 1995 at the London Marriott Hotel, Grosvenor Square, London W1.

As well as dealing with the routine business of the Annual General Meeting, resolutions will be put to the Meeting to authorise the directors to allot relevant securities and to disapply statutory pre-emption rights; to authorise the purchase of own shares; to authorise the directors to offer scrip dividends; and to approve the 1995 executive share option scheme and to authorise the directors to adopt and amend 'overseas schemes'.

A full explanation of the resolutions is set out in the separate letter from the Chairman contained in the document accompanying this Annual Report [not included in this extract] and the resolutions are set out in the Notice of Annual General Meeting in that document.

By Order of the Board
Robin Charlton
Secretary
23 May 1995

4.7   STOCK EXCHANGE DISCLOSURE REQUIREMENTS

The London Stock Exchange requires the annual report and accounts of a listed company to provide disclosures on the following areas:

(a)   explanation for significant differences from forecasts;
(b)   interest capitalised;
(c)   waiver of directors' emoluments;
(d)   waiver of dividends;
(e)   country of operation of each subsidiary undertaking;
(f)   details of associated undertakings;
(g)   details of non-executive directors;
(h)   compliance with corporate governance disclosures;
(i)   directors' interests in shares;
(j)   major interests in shares;
(k)   purchase by a company of its own shares;
(l)   interests in contracts;

(m) going concern statement;
(n) directors' remuneration details (Greenbury – see chapter 11).

4.8   PREPARATION OF ACCOUNTS AND FILING REQUIREMENTS

(a) Form and content

Company profit and loss accounts and balance sheets must comply with the Companies Act 1985 format requirements (see section 4.3). These must be accompanied by notes which comply with the disclosure requirements of the Companies Act 1985 as well as the relevant SSAPs and Financial Reporting Standards.

In addition to the accounts a directors' report is required (see section 4.6).

Large public limited companies which are quoted on the Stock Exchange frequently provide more than the minimum required (see chapter 11).

(b) Approval and signing

SSAP 17 (Accounting for post balance sheet events) requires the date on which the directors approve the financial statements to be disclosed in the financial statements.

The Companies Act 1985 requires the balance sheet to be approved and signed on behalf of the board by a director.

The directors' report must be approved by the board of directors and signed on behalf of the board either by a director or by the company secretary.

(c) Audit

Every company (except for dormant companies and small companies eligible for audit exemption must be audited by a registered auditor. The audit report must accompany the financial statements. Note that the audit requirement applies to unlimited companies and to companies limited by guarantee (see (f) below).

(d) Filing

The directors are required to file with the Registrar of Companies a copy of the annual accounts, directors' report and auditors' report. This requirement does not apply to unlimited companies (see (f) below).

Special concessions are available to small and medium-sized companies. The directors of these companies may file abbreviated accounts (previously referred to as modified accounts). The rules for abbreviated accounts are dealt with in chapter 10 (see section 10.4).

There is a time limit for filing of accounts. Private companies must file within ten months of the end of their reference period, public companies within seven months.

(e) Summary financial statements

The general rule is that all shareholders and debenture holders must be sent a copy of the full accounts.

However, in certain situations shareholders of Stock Exchange listed companies may choose to receive summary financial statements instead of full accounts (see section 11.8).

(f) Special types of companies

(i) *Unlimited companies*
Unlimited companies are required to prepare accounts, have them audited and deliver them to the shareholders. However, unlimited companies are exempt from the requirement to file accounts with the Registrar of Companies.

(ii) *Companies limited by guarantee*
The same requirements apply as for companies limited by share capital.

(iii) *Dormant companies*
The rules are very detailed. A key factor for a company to be classified as dormant is that during the period there must be no transactions required to be entered in the company's accounting records (except the special situation of the taking up of shares by subscribers to the memorandum).

In certain circumstances a dormant company may pass a special resolution exempting it from the obligation to appoint auditors.

4.9 SOME IMPORTANT LEGAL REQUIREMENTS

(a) Accounting reference dates and periods

(1) *Terminology*

(i) Accounting reference period (ARP) – the period by reference to which the financial statements have to be prepared and presented to members.

(ii) Accounting reference date (ARD) – the date on which the ARP ends.

(iii) Financial year (FY) – the period covered by the statutory profit and loss account, whether or not this is a year.

(2) *Accounting reference dates*
The Companies Act 1989 introduced some changes to the rules. Ignoring transitional provisions companies must notify the Registrar of Companies of their ARD within nine months of incorporation.
Failure to notify will mean an ARD of the last day of the month in which the anniversary of its incorporation falls. For example, a company incorporated on 8 October 1995 which failed to notify would have an ARD of 31 October. The first annual accounts would cover the period 8.10.95 to 31.10.96.

(3) *Accounting reference periods*
The first ARP begins on the date of incorporation and ends on the ARD, and is a period of more than six months and less than 18 months. Succeeding ARPs will be for 12 months unless appropriate notice is given of a change of ARD.

(4) *Financial years*
The FY of a company will usually be the same as its ARP. However, to cover special situations, the FY may begin or end on dates which are not more than seven days before or after the ARD.

(b) Accounting records

The Companies Act 1985 required accounting records to:

(1) be sufficient to show and explain the company's transactions;

(2) disclose with reasonable accuracy the company's financial position at any time; and
(3) enable the directors to ensure that any accounts which they are required to prepare comply with Companies Act 1985.

The records must contain:

(1) entries from day to day of all sums of money received and expended and the matters in respect of which the receipts and expenditure take place;
(2) a record of the company's assets and liabilities;
(3) for a trading or merchanting company dealing in goods:

   (i)   statements of stock held at the end of each financial year;
   (ii) all statements of stocktakings from which those statements of stock have been prepared; and
   (iii) statements of all goods sold and purchased in sufficient detail to identify the goods and the buyers and sellers ((iii) does not apply to goods sold by way of ordinary retail trade).

5   UK REGULATORY FRAMEWORK – REPORTING REGULATIONS

Key Issues

* Changes to the standard-setting process
* Mandatory requirements
* Current SSAPs, FRSs, and Consensuses (Abstracts)
* Contents of annual reports
* Terminology – financial statements or accounts?
* Overriding true and fair view
* Legal view on the role of Accounting Standards
* Revision of defective accounts
* Financial Reporting Review Panel
* Statements of Recommended Practice

5.1   BACKGROUND – IMPLEMENTATION OF THE DEARING COMMITTEE REPORT

(a) The recommendations of the Dearing Committee

The Consultative Committee of Accountancy Bodies (CCAB) appointed a Review Committee to be chaired by Sir Ronald Dearing to review and make recommendations on the standard-setting process. The Committee's report was published in November 1988.

The Committee recommended a three-tier structure:

(1) A Financial Reporting Council – this would make policy.
(2) An Accounting Standards Board – this would set and issue standards under its own authority.
(3) A Review Panel – this would monitor and enforce compliance.

Other recommendations included:

(1) A legal requirement for directors to confirm compliance with applicable accounting standards. This should extend to drawing attention to material departures from standards.
(2) New statutory powers to require revision of accounts which did not give a true and fair view.
(3) A task force to deal with emerging issues and to publish authoritative (but non-statutory) guidance.
(4) The need for a conceptual framework.

(b) Implementation

All of the above recommendations have either been implemented or are in the process of being acted upon:

(1) The Accounting Standards Board (ASB) and the Financial Reporting Council (FRC) came into existence in August 1990, replacing the former Accounting Standards Committee.

(2) In early 1991, the Financial Reporting Review Panel (FRRP) and the Urgent Issues Task Force (UITF) came into being.
(3) The accounts of all companies, other than small and medium-sized, must state whether they have been prepared in accordance with applicable accounting standards. Details of any material departures must be given, together with reasons.
(4) A mechanism for both compulsory and voluntary revision of defective accounts has been incorporated into the Companies Act 1985 (CA 1985).
(5) ASB has developed a conceptual framework – this was published at the end of 1995 in exposure draft form as the Statement of Principles (see chapter 5).

5.2   THE CURRENT REGULATORY STRUCTURE

(a) Key relationships

The relationship between the principal bodies may be illustrated as follows:

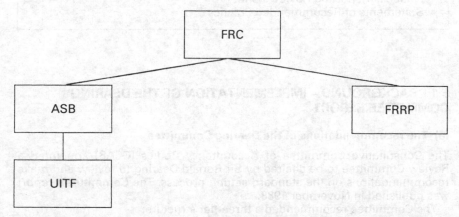

(1) The FRC is essentially a policy-making body which oversees the ASB and FRRP.
(2) The ASB develops and issues Financial Reporting Standards (FRSs). FRSs are gradually replacing the former Statements of Standard Accounting Practice (SSAPs).
(3) The UITF is a sub-committee of the ASB and issues short statements dealing with specific issues. These statements are referred to as 'Consensuses' or 'Abstracts' and are outlined in chapter 9.
(4) The FRRP examines the accounts of mainly larger and listed companies to consider whether those accounts comply with the Companies Act 1985. The FRRP's conclusions are published in the form of 'findings' (see section 5.10).

5.3   MANDATORY REQUIREMENTS

(a) Overview

All companies must comply with:

(1) The Companies Act 1985.
(2) Statements of Standard Accounting Practice (SSAPs) issued by the former Accounting Standards Committee (ASC). These are gradually being

replaced by FRSs from the ASB – eg SSAP 14 on Group Accounts was superseded by FRS 2, Accounting for subsidiary undertakings.
(3) Financial Reporting Standards (FRSs) issued by the Accounting Standards Board (ASB).
(4) Consensuses (Abstracts) issued by the Urgent Issues Task Force (UITF).
(5) When issued in definitive form, the Statement of Principles.

In addition, listed companies must also comply with the requirements of the London Stock Exchange.

(b) Companies Act 1985

Accounting principles and disclosure requirements are set out in the Companies Act 1985, as amended by the Companies Act 1989. From time to time the legal rules are extended as a result of the issue of Statutory Instruments (SIs).
  For example, SIs have been issued covering:

(1) Revision of defective accounts.
(2) Summary financial statements.
(3) Disclosure of fees paid to auditors for work other than audit work.
(4) Small company reporting and audit exemption.

(c) Statements of Standard Accounting Practice

The following SSAPs currently remain in force until replaced by Financial Reporting Standards:

SSAP 1 Accounting for the results of associated companies (revised 1982 and amended by the ASB's December 1990 statement).
SSAP 2 Disclosure of accounting policies.
SSAP 3 Earnings per share (revised August 1974).
SSAP 4 The accounting treatment of government grants (revised 1990).
SSAP 5 Accounting for value added tax.
SSAP 8 The treatment of taxation under the imputation system in accounts of companies (revised December 1977).
SSAP 9 Stocks and long-term contracts (revised September 1988).
SSAP 12 Accounting for depreciation (revised January 1987).
SSAP 13 Accounting for research and development (revised January 1989).
SSAP 15 Accounting for deferred taxation (revised May 1985).
SSAP 17 Accounting for post-balance sheet events.
SSAP 18 Accounting for contingencies.
SSAP 19 Accounting for investment properties.
SSAP 20 Foreign currency translation.
SSAP 21 Accounting for lease and hire purchase contracts.
SSAP 22 Accounting for goodwill (revised July 1989).
SSAP 24 Accounting for pension costs.
SSAP 25 Segmental reporting.

Notes:
(i) SSAP 15 has been amended to deal with the problem of deferred tax on post-retirement benefits.
(ii) SSAP 23 has been superseded by FRS 6 and FRS 7 for accounts periods commencing on or after 23 December 1994.

(d) Financial Reporting Standards

The ASB has issued the following mandatory statements:

(1) Interim Statement: Consolidated accounts. Note: parts of this statement have now been superseded by FRS 2.
(2) FRS 1 Cash flow statements.
(3) FRS 2 Accounting for subsidiary undertakings.

(4) FRS 3 Reporting financial performance.
(5) FRS 4 Capital instruments.
(6) FRS 5 Reporting the substance of transactions.
(7) FRS 6 Acquisitions and mergers.
(8) FRS 7 Fair values in acquisition accounting.
(9) FRS 8 Related party disclosures.

(e) UITF Consensuses (Abstracts)

The UITF has issued the following Consensuses or Abstracts:

3   Goodwill on disposal of a business.
4   Presentation of long-term debtors in current assets.
5   Transfers from current assets to fixed assets.
6   Accounting for post-retirement benefits other than pensions.
7   Guidance on the disclosure of the use of the true and fair override.
9   Accounting for operations in hyper inflationary economies.
10 Directors' share options.
11 Issuer call options.
12 Lessee accounting for reverse pensions and similar incentives.
13 Accounting for ESOP (Employee share ownership plans) trusts.
14 Disclosure of changes in accounting policy.
15 Disclosure of substantial acquisitions.

Certain of the above Abstracts are referred to in chapter 9.

5.4   EXPOSURE DRAFTS

(a) Issued by the former ASC

The following EDs remain in existence, although their status is uncertain following the demise of the ASC:

ED 47   Accounting for goodwill.
ED 51   Accounting for fixed assets and revaluations.
ED 52   Accounting for intangible fixed assets.
ED 55   Accounting for investments.

(b) Issued by the ASB

ASB has issued a number of Financial Reporting Exposure Drafts (FREDs). All but one, FRED 10 on cash flow statements, have been converted into FRSs.
    The ASB has given a ruling on the early adoption of FREDs. Until the FRED has been converted into a mandatory FRS, the requirements of any existing SSAPs remain in force. Companies who wish to provide additional information concerning proposals included in FREDs may do so in one of two ways:

(i) the information may be incorporated into the accounts as long as it does not conflict with the requirements of an existing Standard, or
(ii) the information may be provided in supplementary (or memorandum) form.

Companies which disregard the ASB's ruling may find themselves the subject of scrutiny by the Financial Reporting Review Panel.

5.5   CONTENTS OF ANNUAL REPORTS

The content of a particular annual report will vary considerably according to the size of the company or group concerned. The following attempts to give a broad indication of the possible ranges of information. Clearly it is important to appreciate what CA 1985, SSAPs and FRSs require as a minimum:

(a) Small private companies

The information presented to shareholders must include the:

(1) directors' report;
(2) balance sheet;
(3) profit and loss account;
(4) notes to the accounts; and
(5) auditors' report.

A cash flow statement (see chapter 31) will also be included unless the company claims the exemption under FRS 1.

Further considerations relating to small companies, including shareholders accounts under SI 2452 and abbreviated accounts, are dealt with in chapter 10.

(b) Large public companies

PLCs listed on the London Stock Exchange are required to comply with legal requirements, FRSs, SSAPs, UITF Abstracts and Stock Exchange requirements.

Annual reports of public groups frequently contain significantly more than the minimum requirements referred to above. These reports may include the elements referred to below. Note that items marked 'M' are mandatory, whilst those marked 'O' are optional.

Elements	*Contents*
Financial Statements (accounts)	* Balance sheet (M) * Profit and loss account (M) * Cash flow statements (M) * Statement of total recognised gains and losses (M) * Note of historical cost profits and losses (M) * Reconciliation of movements in shareholders' funds (M) * Accounting policies (M) * Other notes (M)
Reports	* Directors' report (M) * Chairman's/chief executive report (O) * Board and management committees ** (O) * Directors responsibilities ** (M) * Auditors' report (M)
Analytical information	* Division review (O) * Additional segmental information (M) * 5/10 year summaries (O)
Other information	* Shareholders profile (O)

** Examples of disclosure statements recommended by Cadbury Committee Report on Corporate Governance and the Greenbury Committee Report on Directors' Remuneration (see chapter 11).

5.6   FINANCIAL STATEMENTS

(a) Terminology

The term 'financial statements' is usually taken to include the balance sheet, profit and loss account and cash flow statement together with notes to the accounts. The term will include the additional statements and notes required by FRS 3, Reporting financial performance (see chapter 8).

Most large quoted companies refer throughout the directors' report, auditors' report and the various parts of the accounts to 'financial statements'. However, it is perfectly acceptable to refer to 'accounts' instead of 'financial statements'. For example, the audit reports of some quoted companies start off by saying '. . . we have audited the accounts and notes on p X to Y . . .'

(b) Accounting conventions

(1) Pure historical cost

Financial statements of UK companies are usually prepared on the basis of historical cost. This is taken to mean the monetary amount sacrificed or laid out at the date of acquisition. This basis is used both for asset measurement (eg fixed assets at historical cost less depreciation) and profit measurement (eg depreciation charge and cost of sales).

(2) Modified historical cost

However, it is common in the United Kingdom for companies to incorporate fixed asset valuations into their balance sheets. This means that under SSAP 12 (see chapter 12) the depreciation charge will be based on the revalued amount. On a sale of the asset, the profit or loss on sale will be determined by comparing:

(i)   proceeds of sale; and
(ii) net book value at the date of sale, based on revalued amount.

The implications of both these matters are important from the viewpoint of FRS 3, Reporting financial performance (see chapter 8).

(3) Current cost accounting

A very small number of companies present current cost accounting information (see chapter 33). These companies are mostly water, gas and electricity companies.

5.7   OVERRIDING TRUE AND FAIR VIEW

(a) The need to disclose additional information

The Companies Act 1985 provides that where compliance with the detailed requirements of its accounting provisions would not provide sufficient information to give a true and fair view, the additional information shall be given either:

(1)   in the accounts; or
(2)   in the notes.

(b) The true and fair override

This is an extremely important concept whose operation in practice has come under the scrutiny of the Urgent Issues Task Force (see section 9.5).

The concept applies to both the accounts of individual companies (CA 1985, s 226(5)) and the accounts of groups (CA 1985 s 227(6)) and in outline is as follows:

> If, because of the special circumstances of a company, compliance with any detailed requirement would prevent the financial statements from giving a true and fair view, the directors are required to depart from the detailed requirements.
> Disclose:
>
> (1) particulars of the departure;
> (2) reasons for the departure;
> (3) effect of the departure.

(c) Examples of the practical application of the true and fair override

An example of a frequently-used application is non-depreciation of investment properties by following SSAP 19 (see section 12.9) and departing from the normal statutory requirement to depreciate fixed assets.

5.8 LEGAL OPINION ON THE ROLE OF ACCOUNTING STANDARDS AND THE TRUE AND FAIR REQUIREMENTS

(a) The true and fair requirements

CA 1985 requires a company's (or group's) accounts to give a true and fair view of:

(i) the state of affairs at the end of the financial year and
(ii) the profit or loss for that financial year.

(b) The April 1993 legal opinion

This latest opinion was concerned with the impact of CA 1989 changes on the relationship between accounting standards and the true and fair requirement.

(c) The role of the Courts

Whether particular accounts satisfy the true and fair requirement is a question of law to be decided by the Courts. However, the opinion reiterates the point that the Court cannot make a decision without obtaining evidence regarding the practices and views of accountants.

(d) The status of accounting standards

Since August 1990, the responsibility for setting standards has rested with the Accounting Standards Board.

Paragraph 16 of the ASB's Foreword to Accounting Standards states: 'Accounting Standards are authoritative statements of how particular types of transactions and other events should be reflected in financial statements and accordingly compliance with accounting standards will normally be necessary for financial statements to give a true and fair view.'

The opinion considers that accounts which meet the true and fair requirements will in general follow rather than depart from standards and that departure is sufficiently abnormal to require to be justified. It is therefore likely that the Courts will hold that compliance with accounting standards is necessary to meet the true and fair requirement.

(e) Urgent Issues Task Force (UITF) Abstracts

The opinion considers that compliance with UITF Abstracts is also necessary to meet the true and fair requirement.

(f) True and fair – a dynamic concept

The opinion considers that 'true and fair' is a dynamic concept and that what is required to show a true and fair view is subject to 'continuous rebirth'.

5.9   REVISION OF DEFECTIVE ACCOUNTS

The Companies Act 1985 contains the following provisions relating to revision of defective accounts:

(1) a procedure for voluntary revision by the directors of annual accounts or directors' reports;
(2) a procedure for the Secretary of State (or a person authorised by him) to go to court to obtain an order requiring the revision of defective accounts. Should the court find that the accounts did not comply with the Companies Act 1985, it may order that all or part of the costs and expenses of preparing revised accounts are borne by those directors who were party to the approval of the defective accounts.

The revision should reflect the position at the date of preparation and approval of the original annual accounts. The revision is not intended as an updating of the accounts and should not take account of assets, liabilities, income or expenditure arising after that date.

Revisions are to be restricted to corrections of matters where the original accounts or report did not comply with requirements of the Companies Act 1985 and any consequential alterations.

(a) Voluntary revision – the options

The directors have a number of options for revising accounts which have been discovered not to comply with the Act. Taking into account the nature of the defect and the time which has elapsed since the defective statutory accounts and/or directors' report were issued, the directors may decide to:

(1) revise the accounts and/or directors' report by replacement of the original with a corrected set of accounts and/or report; or
(2) issue a supplementary note indicating the corrections to be made to the original accounts and/or report;
(3) Make corrections by means of a prior year adjustment to comparative figures in the following year's accounts.

Note: (3) is not referred to in the regulations. However, draft auditing guidelines issued in May 1991 suggested that (3) may frequently be the most effective means of correcting material errors during the course of preparing or auditing the company's next annual accounts.

The Act sets out detailed procedures which must be followed by directors and auditors. These are not referred to in this book.

(b) Voluntary revision – further considerations

Published accounts of several listed companies have come under scrutiny by FRRP. As indicated in section 5.10, where directors have agreed with Panel findings, the comparative figures of the accounts of the following years have been restated.

5.10 FINANCIAL REPORTING REVIEW PANEL (FRRP)

(a) Background

The Panel came into operation in 1991 as a result of implementation of the Dearing Committee proposals. Recent press releases have clarified the activities of the Panel as follows (extracts only):

> The remit of the Panel is to examine the annual accounts of public and large private companies to see whether they comply with the requirements of the Companies Act 1985. Within this framework a main focus is on material departures from accounting standards where such a departure results in the accounts in question not giving a true and fair view as required by the Act.
>
> Where a company's accounts are defective the Panel will wherever possible endeavour to secure their revision by voluntary means, but if this approach fails will make an application to the court under Section 245B of the Companies Act 1985 for an order compelling the revision. To date no court applications have been made.
>
> The Panel does not itself monitor or actively initiate scrutinies of company accounts for possible defects, but acts on matters drawn to its attention, either directly or indirectly.

(b) Issues raised

Example of issues raised include:

(1) Explicit non-compliance with Accounting Standards/Companies Act 1985 accounting requirements:

    (i)   Depreciation of buildings (SSAP 12);
    (ii) Cash flow statements (FRS 1);
    (iii) Exceptional items (FRS 3);
    (iv) Analysis of shareholders' funds between equity and non-equity.

(2) Unacceptable accounting policies (where the law is unclear or where no definitive Standards or Consensuses were operative at the date the accounts were approved by the directors):

    (i)   Deferred revenue expenditure;
    (ii) Deficits on property revaluation;
    (iii) reverse lease premiums.

(3) Change of accounting year end where the presentation of accounts did not comply with the Companies Act 1985 as regards the number of months included in the current period.

(4) Failure to disclose remuneration of certain directors.

(c) Follow-up by FRRP

The Panel discusses matters with the parties concerned (directors, auditors etc). Assuming the Panel's view is that the accounts failed to comply with requirements, it may be prepared to accept assurances from the directors. These could include assurances that:

(i) accounts of subsequent years will adhere to requirements;
(ii) where appropriate, the following year's published accounts will include a restatement of comparative figures.

Where such assurances are not forthcoming, the Panel may be prepared to make an application under the compulsory revision of defective accounts rules (see section 5.9).

Illustration – a recent FRRP finding

As is noted in the company's 1995 Preliminary results announcement made today, the Financial Reporting Review Panel has had under consideration the accounts of the company for the year ended 31st March 1994 and has discussed them with the company's directors.

Under the company's accounting policy for instalment and hire purchase transactions the total amount due under long-term credit agreements was included in turnover and operating profit and transfers were made to a deferred profit reserve; and the matter at issue was the conformity of this policy with the provisions of paragraphs 12 and 13 of Schedule 4, Companies Act 1985 and with the provisions of Statement of Standard Accounting Practice (SSAP) 21.

The Panel welcomes the change in accounting policy made by the company in its 1995 accounts, under which transfers to a deferred profit reserve will no longer arise, and on this basis regards its enquiry into the company's accounts for the year ended 31 March 1994 as being concluded.

(See also chapter 18, section 18.14.)

5.11 STATEMENTS OF RECOMMENDED PRACTICE

(a) Background

Statements of Recommended Practice (SORPs) were developed after 1986 by the former ASC as a new form of pronouncement, additional to SSAPs.

SORPs attempted to deal with areas not considered appropriate for SSAPs and could cover areas not considered essential in arriving at a true and fair view as well as areas which could be regarded as 'industry-specific'.

Whilst SSAPs were intended to be mandatory, SORPs were generally regarded as non-mandatory or advisory in nature.

The process for developing SORPs has changed – old SORPs are being superseded by new-style SORPs such as that relating to charities issued in 1995.

(b) ASB policy on development of SORPs

The ASB issued a detailed statement in October 1990 (ASB *Bulletin*, issue 4). The relevant extracts are reproduced below:

The Board believes that well prepared Statements of Recommended Practice (SORPs) have a useful part to play in the development of good financial reporting. It believes however that it must not allow its limited time and resources to be diverted from its central task, the development of accounting standards with a broad scope. It follows that, whilst the Board is anxious to play a part in the SORP process, its involvement must necessarily be a limited one. It has therefore concluded that it should proceed as follows.

(a) Because they do not have the statutory implications of accounting standards the Board does not believe it necessary to adopt the existing SORPs.

(b) In the future the Board will not issue its own SORPs. In the event that ASB's own authority is required to standardise practice within a specialised industry, the Board's preference is to issue an industry

standard. Before doing so, however, the Board will ensure that the issue cannot be resolved within existing accounting standards.
(c) Where appropriate, for example, for matters of pressing concern which can only be resolved within the framework of existing standards of accounting, the Board will address those issues separately.
(d) SORPs will be developed by bodies recognised by the Board to provide guidance on the application of accounting standards to specific industries. The Board will be prepared to recognise such bodies if they fall within its acceptance criteria. Recognition will turn on the size of the industry or sector in question; the Board being satisfied as to the representative nature of the body proposing to produce the SORP; and the body agreeing to follow the ASB's code of practice for the SORP development process.
The code of practice will be designed to ensure that the subject matter and general scope of the SORP has the ASB's prior approval; that there is adequate due process, including widespread public consultation; and that exposure drafts are submitted for consideration before publication.
(e) The Board will wish to stress the limited scope of its own involvement in the production of SORPs. The 'franking' of SORPs, as conducted by the former ASC, will therefore not be continued. Instead, where it is satisfied as to the particulars set out above, the Board will require to be appended to the SORP a 'negative assurance statement'. In essence this statement will make it clear that the Board is not approving the SORP but is rather confirming that it contains no fundamental points of principle which the Board considers unacceptable in the context of current accounting practice, that the SORP is not in conflict with any existing or currently contemplated accounting standard, and that the SORP has been prepared in accordance with the Board's code of practice.

The negative assurance statement that the Board will attach to SORPs which satisfy the above rules may vary in its wording according to the circumstances of the case. As an illustration however, a typical negative assurance statement might read as follows.

'THE ASB

The ASB has approved the XYZ Association (the Association) for the purpose of issuing recognised Statements of Recommended Accounting Practice (SORPs). This arrangement requires the XYZ Association to follow the ASB's code of practice for the production and issuing of SORPs.

The code of practice provides the framework to be followed by the Association for the development of SORPs, but does not entail a detailed examination of the proposed SORP by the ASB. However, a review of limited scope is performed.

On the basis of its review, the ASB has concluded that the SORP has been developed in accordance with the ASB's code of practice and does not appear to contain any fundamental points of principle which are unacceptable in the context of current accounting practice or to conflict with any existing or currently contemplated accounting standard.'

The above is an outline of the Board's intended approach. The Board is discussing the procedures with appropriate representative bodies.

(c) Examples of topics

SORPs cover a wide range of areas, for example:

(i)   charities;
(ii)   pension schemes;
(iii) higher education institutions;
(iv)   investment trusts.

6 UK REGULATORY FRAMEWORK – ACCOUNTING PRINCIPLES

Key Issues

* The Dearing report
* Fundamental accounting concepts and other principles
* Accounting policies
* Variations in accounting practice
* Conceptual framework – ASB Statement of Principles

6.1 BACKGROUND

SSAP2, Disclosure of accounting policies, was published in 1971. The Standard set out fundamental accounting concepts (see section 6.2) but did not seek to provide a conceptual framework to financial reporting.

The Dearing Report (see section 5.1) referred to the need for a conceptual framework. The ASB subsequently announced that it was drafting a Statement of Principles and this was published in December 1995 in exposure draft form (see section 6.7).

The first part of this chapter reviews SSAP 2 and includes an illustration of how a large company discloses its accounting policies. The latter part of the chapter covers the ASB's plans for the development of a conceptual framework, described as the 'Statement of Principles for Financial Reporting' (SOP).

6.2 FUNDAMENTAL ACCOUNTING CONCEPTS

SSAP 2 (Disclosure of accounting policies) refers to four basic assumptions underlying the periodic financial statements of enterprises. The term used to describe these broad assumptions is fundamental accounting concepts.

The concepts are:

(a) Going concern concept

This assumes that the enterprise will continue in operational existence for the foreseeable future. This means that there is no intention or necessity either to liquidate the entity or to curtail significantly its activities.

(b) Accruals concept

Revenue is included in accounts when earned rather than when money is received. Costs are included when incurred rather than when paid. Revenues dealt with in the profit and loss account are then matched with associated costs in order to determine profit.

Should the accruals concept conflict with the prudence concept (see below), the prudence concept prevails.

(c) Consistency concept

This assumes consistency of treatment of similar items within a particular accounting period as well as from one period to the next.

(d) Prudence concept

Revenues and profits are not anticipated. They are recognised in the profit and loss account only when realised either in the form of cash or of other assets (e g debtors) whose cash realisation can be determined with reasonable certainty.

Provision should be made for all known liabilities whether the amount of these is known with certainty or is a best estimate in the light of the information available. (Reference should also be made to SSAP 18, Accounting for contingencies.) (See chapter 17).

If financial statements are not drawn up on the basis of the above assumptions, the facts should be disclosed.

6.3   FURTHER ASSUMPTIONS AND PRINCIPLES

A number of other assumptions are frequently referred to, although these are not mentioned as such in SSAP 2. These include:

(a) Entity assumption

This assumes that for accounting measurement purposes, the business is regarded as a separate entity quite apart from its owners or proprietors. A business is regarded as owning the resources (assets) which it uses and as owing the claims (liabilities) against those assets. The assets and liabilities of the business are kept completely separate from those relating to the owners.

(b) Money measurement assumptions

This assumes that all assets, liabilities and transactions can be quantified in monetary terms.

(c) Stable standard of measurement assumption

Following on from (b), historical cost accounting assumes that transactions occurring over a period of time can be measured in terms of a single stable measuring unit, £ sterling. The obvious weaknesses of this assumption led to calls for some form of system of accounting for price changes (see chapter 33).

(d) Objectivity principle

This principle requires accounting to be carried out on an objective and factual basis. However, subjective opinions and estimates play an important part in historical cost accounting. Examples of subjectivity include estimated lives of fixed assets and net realisable value of stock items (see also section 6.4 below).

(e) Dual aspect principle

Every change in one element of an entity (assets, liabilities, equity) is accompanied by another change of a similar amount, but in an opposite direction. This principle underlies the basis of double-entry book-keeping.

(f) Substance over form

Transactions should be accounted for and presented in accordance with their substance and financial reality and not merely with their legal form. This principle is further discussed below (see chapter 7).

6.4 THE IMPORTANCE OF SUBJECTIVITY

Traditionally, financial statements have been based on the historical cost convention. The implications as far as the balance sheet and profit and loss account are concerned are:

(a) In the balance sheet, stock is stated at historical cost (unless it exceeds net realisable value) and fixed assets at historical cost less depreciation (unless fixed asset revaluations are incorporated into the balance sheet).

(b) In the profit and loss account, cost of sales is based on historical cost even though sales are expressed in current terms. Depreciation charges are based on historical costs of fixed assets possibly acquired several years ago.

A frequently quoted defence of historical cost accounting is that it is essentially factual and objective. However, it should be remembered that subjectivity does play an important role. For example:

(1) Calculation of depreciation of fixed assets requires subjective estimates of useful life and residual value (chapter 12).

(2) Calculation of profits on long-term contracts requires estimation of future costs, contract outcome and so on (chapter 14).

(3) Deferred tax provisions depend for their calculation on estimates of future capital expenditure (chapter 19).

6.5 SSAP 2 – DISCLOSURE OF ACCOUNTING POLICIES

This is probably the most important statement of standard accounting practice in that it deals with fundamental assumptions underlying the preparation of financial statements. Various aspects of the standard are dealt with below.

(a) Terminology

Three important terms are referred to:

Fundamental accounting concepts	Broad basic assumptions underlying the periodic financial statements of business enterprises. SSAP 2 names and defines four concepts: (1) going concern; (2) accruals; (3) consistency; (4) prudence.
Accounting bases	Methods developed for applying fundamental accounting concepts to financial transactions and items eg stock valuation methods, first-in-first-out, average cost.
Accounting policies	Specific accounting bases used by a particular business and regarded as appropriate to the circumstances of the business and suitable for the fair presentation of its results and financial position.

(b) Problems in applying fundamental concepts

A particular problem is caused by the fact that the financial effects of certain business transactions are spread over a number of years.

Examples include:

(1) Expenditure on the acquisition of tangible fixed assets: in order to apply the accruals concept, it is necessary to arrive at an estimate of the asset's useful economic life to the present owner. An element of commercial judgement is thus necessary to decide how much to charge as depreciation expense in the current period, and how much to carry forward in the balance sheet as unamortised cost.
(2) Sales of goods subject to warranties or guarantees: what, if anything, should be provided at the balance sheet date for the estimated expenditure likely to be incurred by the company in remedying defective goods?
(3) Long-term contracts: if the contract extends over several years, future events may cause an apparently profitable contract to turn into a loss-making contract.

Other such areas include deferred development expenditure and deferred taxation. All the above situations require consideration of future events of uncertain financial effect. Thus an element of commercial judgement is inevitable.

(c) Problems with the consistency concept

A number of earlier accounting standards have come in for criticism because of their apparent conflict with the consistency approach.

For example, SSAP 22 states that purchased goodwill should normally be eliminated from the accounts immediately on acquisition against reserves. However, the standard offers an alternative treatment – namely to regard goodwill as an intangible fixed asset subject to annual amortisation through the profit and loss account. Not only does the standard offer this choice of policies to a company but also permits a company to treat goodwill relating to different acquisitions in different ways. This alternative option has now been removed by the Companies Act 1989 amendments to the Companies Act 1985. A company must now apply a consistent goodwill policy to all acquisitions.

Fortunately the Accounting Standards Board is tackling this issue.

For example, on the subject of acquisitions and mergers, the Accounting Standards Board has replaced SSAP 23 with FRS 6 (see chapter 25). SSAP 23 permitted certain mergers to be accounted for by either acquisition accounting or merger accounting. By contrast, FRS 6 requires business combinations to be classified as either acquisitions or mergers to determine the appropriate consolidation approach. In those rare cases of mergers (see chapter 26), merger accounting will be mandatory.

In other areas, it is only a matter of time before 'option' Standards such as SSAP 22 and SSAP 13 (both of which offer alternative treatments), are replaced by FRSs which require a rigorous and consistent approach.

(d) Purposes and limitations of accounting bases

The accounting bases available to particular companies should provide:

(1) consistent, fair and (as far as is possible) objective solutions to situations where fundamental concepts are difficult to apply;
(2) an orderly framework within which to report the results and financial position of a business;
(3) limits to particular areas which are subject to the exercise of judgement.

It should be appreciated that:

(1) accounting bases are not intended as a substitute for the exercise of commercial judgement;
(2) generalised rules for the exercise of judgement are difficult (if not impossible) to develop. However, it may be possible to develop pragmatic rules for use in specific circumstances.

(e) Disclosure of accounting policies

In some areas of accounting, there may be more than one acceptable basis, for example, depreciation on a straight-line basis or depreciation on a reducing balance basis. Clear disclosure of accounting policies is essential to fair presentation since the choice of policy could have a significant effect on a company's reported results and position.

Since the issue of SSAP 2 in November 1971, a large number of exposure drafts and standards have been issued. These have had a significant effect in reducing the range of acceptable accounting bases. However, SSAP 2 reminds readers that 'the complexity and diversity of business renders total rigid uniformity of bases impracticable'.

An illustration of disclosure taken from the accounts of Cadbury Schweppes plc is shown in section (g) below.

(f) Standard accounting practice

(1) Any departures from the four fundamental accounting concepts should be fully disclosed. Unless such a disclosure is made, it will be assumed that the four concepts have been followed.
(2) Accounting policies used to deal with material or critical items should be disclosed.

(g) Extract from published accounts

Illustration

Extract from annual report of Cadbury Schweppes plc for the year ended 31 December 1994.

Accounting policies

a *Accounting convention*
The accounts are prepared under the historical cost convention modified for the revaluation of certain land and buildings. The accounts are prepared in accordance with applicable accounting standards.

b *Financial year*
The annual accounts are made up to the Saturday nearest to 31 December. Periodically this results in a financial year of 53 weeks.

c *Basis of consolidation*
The accounts are presented in the form of Group accounts and no profit and loss account is presented for Cadbury Schweppes plc itself as the exemption in section 230 of the Companies Act 1985 applies. The Group accounts consolidate the accounts of the parent company and its subsidiary undertakings after eliminating internal transactions and recognising the minority interests in those subsidiary undertakings.

d *Acquisition or disposal of subsidiary undertakings*
Results of subsidiary undertakings acquired during the financial year are included in Group profit from the effective date of control and those of undertakings disposed of up to the effective date of disposal. For this purpose the separable net assets, both tangible and intangible, of newly acquired subsidiary undertakings are incorporated into the accounts on the basis of the fair value to the Group as at the effective date of control. Goodwill, being any excess of the consideration over that fair value, is written off against reserves on consolidation. Upon disposal of a previously acquired business the

attributable amount of goodwill previously written off to reserves is included in determining the profit or loss on disposal.

e Foreign currencies

Assets and liabilities in foreign currencies are translated into sterling at the rates ruling at the end of the financial year except when covered by an open foreign exchange contract in which case the rate of exchange specified in the contract is used. Differences on exchange arising from the translation of both the opening balance sheets of overseas subsidiary undertakings (date of control in case of acquisition during the year) and foreign currency borrowings used to finance or hedge long term foreign investments are taken directly to reserves. All other profits and losses on exchange are credited or charged to operating profit. The results of overseas undertakings are translated into sterling at average rates. The exchange differences arising as a result of re-stating retained profits to closing rates are dealt with as movements on reserves.

f Turnover

This represents the invoiced value of sales (net of trade discounts) and royalties excluding inter-company sales, value added tax and sales taxes.

g Research and development expenditure

Expenditure is written off in the financial year in which it is incurred.

h Earnings per ordinary share

Earnings per ordinary share is calculated by dividing the profit on ordinary activities after taxation, minority interests and preference dividends by the weighted average number of shares in issue during the year.

i Taxation

Credit is taken for advance corporation tax paid to the extent that it is recoverable against the liability to corporation tax in the foreseeable future. Deferred taxation recoverable is recognised on long term timing differences arising from provisions for pensions and other post-retirement benefits. Provision is made for deferred taxation, using the liability method, on other timing differences to the extent that these amounts are regarded as likely to become payable in the foreseeable future.

The principal categories of timing differences are:

- the excess of book value of fixed assets over their tax written down value;
- income and expenditure in the accounts of the current year dealt with in other years for taxation purposes; and
- revaluation surpluses in respect of projected property sales on the assumption that the properties are sold at the revalued amounts.

j Stocks

Stocks are valued at the lower of average cost and estimated net realisable value. Cost comprises direct material and labour costs together with the relevant factory overheads on the basis of normal activity levels. In the case of cocoa, cost also reflects the use of the futures market on the basis of forecast physical requirements.

k Tangible fixed assets

Depreciation is charged on the original cost or subsequent valuation of assets (excluding freehold land and assets in course of construction). The principal rates, using the straight line method, are as follows:

- freehold buildings and long leasehold properties   2.5%
- plant and machinery   10%
- vehicles   12.5–20%
- office equipment   20%

Short leasehold properties are depreciated over the life of the lease. In specific cases higher depreciation rates are used eg high speed machinery, machinery subject to technological changes, any machinery with a high obsolescence factor. The rates used overseas are not materially different from the rates used above, but they vary according to local conditions and requirements. Investment and development grants are shown as deferred income, and credited to the profit and loss account by instalments on a basis consistent with the depreciation policy. Returnable containers are included in fixed assets at cost. Depreciation is charged to reflect estimated loss or breakage rates in each market. Interest costs incurred in funding major capital construction programmes are capitalised during the construction period.

l *Fixed assets held under leases*
Where assets are financed by leasing agreements that give rights approximating to ownership ('finance leases') the assets are treated as if they had been purchased outright and the corresponding liability to the leasing company is included as an obligation under finance leases. Depreciation on leased assets is charged to profit and loss account on the same basis as shown above. Leasing payments are treated as consisting of capital and interest elements and the interest is charged to profit and loss account. All other leases are 'operating leases' and the relevant annual rentals are charged wholly to profit and loss account.

m *Revaluation of properties*
Freehold and leasehold properties are revalued every five years and the surplus on book value is credited to the revaluation reserve. In subsequent years transfers are made to retained profits in order to amortise the surplus over the remaining useful lives of the properties. On disposal the profit or loss is calculated by reference to the net book value and any unamortised revaluation surplus is transferred from revaluation reserves to retained profits.

n *Intangibles*
Intangibles represent significant owned brands acquired since 1985 valued at historical cost. No amortisation is charged as the annual results reflect significant expenditure in support of these brands and the values are reviewed annually with a view to write down if a permanent diminution arises.

o *Associated undertakings*
All companies where the Group has significant influence, normally both board representation and ownership of 20% of the voting rights on a long term basis, are treated as associated undertakings. The carrying value of associated undertakings reflects the Group share of the net assets of the companies concerned. The share of their profits is included in operating profit.

p *Pensions*
The costs of providing pensions and other post-retirement benefits are charged to the profit and loss account on a consistent basis over the service lives of employees. Such costs are calculated by reference to actuarial valuations and variations from such regular costs are spread over the remaining service lives of the current employees. To the extent to which such costs do not equate with cash contributions a provision or prepayment is recognised in the balance sheet.

6.6   VARIATIONS IN ACCOUNTING PRACTICE

(a) Introduction

The programme of the former Accounting Standards Committee sought to eliminate the scope for variations in accounting practices, both within company annual reports and between one company and another.

Scope for variations in accounting practice still exists, but the number of possibilities has been reduced following the activities of the Accounting Standards Board.

(b) Examples

Areas which have been referred to include:

(1) Impact of fixed asset revaluations

Depreciation charges may be based on either historical cost or revalued amount (see section 12.5(e)).

(2) Long term contracts

Whether a particular contract of less than 12 months' duration is accounted for as long-term may well be a matter of fine judgement. In addition, for long-term contracts which are expected to be profitable, there are several acceptable ways of allocating profit over the life of the contract (see section 14.3).

(3) Group account matters

  (i)   previously, business combinations which satisfied the SSAP 23 merger conditions could be consolidated either on a merger accounting basis or on an acquisition accounting basis. FRS 6 has brought to an end this scope for variation in accounting practice.
  (ii) Where foreign subsidiaries are translated using the closing rate/net investment method, profit and loss account items may be translated at either average rate or closing rate.
  (iii) previously, under acquisition accounting there was scope for determining the extent to which provisions for losses and reorganisation costs could be taken into account under the fair value exercise. FRS 7 has introduced rules to bring this practice effectively to an end (see chapter 25).

(4) Extraordinary and exceptional items

Prior to the introduction of FRS 3, there was considerable scope for deciding whether items such as reorganisation costs should be treated as exceptional or extraordinary. FRS 3 has effectively outlawed extraordinary items.

(5) Intangible fixed assets

  (i)   Goodwill – purchased goodwill may be eliminated against reserves as soon as it arises. Alternatively it may be carried forward as an intangible fixed asset amortised over its useful life (see section 13.2).
  (ii) Development costs which satisfy the rigorous criteria of SSAP 13 may be written off to profit and loss account as they arise. Alternatively they may be capitalised as an intangible fixed asset amortised over a period (see section 13.3).

(6) Deferred revenue expenditure

  (i)   Certain borrowing costs may be capitalised as part of the cost of a fixed asset or they may be charged to profit and loss as incurred (see section 12.3).

(ii) Pre-opening expenses relating to new hotels or stores may be carried forward in the balance sheet and expenses over a period. Alternatively they may be written off as incurred.

(7) Post balance sheet events

Certain post balance sheet events which would normally be classified as non-adjusting may be treated as adjusting in special circumstances.

(c) Conclusion

The on-going work of the Accounting Standards Board should, over time, significantly reduce the scope for variation. This should be achieved by the impact of a combination of Financial Reporting Standards and the Statement of Principles.

6.7 TOWARDS A CONCEPTUAL FRAMEWORK

(a) The missing link

Standard-setting in the 1970s and 1980s took place in the absence of a so-called 'conceptual framework of accounting'. It is only in recent years that this subject has moved to the top of the agenda, mainly as a result of the Dearing Committee recommendations of 1988 and subsequent follow-up by the Accounting Standards Board.

(b) The Accounting Standards Board's statement of aims

The 'aims' are referred to as follows:

'The aims of the Accounting Standards Board . . . are to establish and improve standards of financial accounting and reporting, for the benefit of users, preparers and auditors of financial information'.

The statement of aims goes on to say that the Board intends to achieve its aims by:

1 Developing principles to guide it in establishing standards and to provide a framework within which others can exercise judgement in resolving accounting issues.
2 Issuing new accounting standards, or amending existing ones.
3 Addressing urgent issues promptly.

(c) The Statement of Principles

The principles in **(b)** above are referred to as the 'Statement of Principles'. The version of the Statement issued in December 1995, and referred to in the remainder of this chapter, is in exposure draft form.

(d) Status

The Statement of Principles, when issued in final form, will not override the requirements of accounting standards or of the law.

(e) Purpose

The Statement does not attempt to describe current practice. What it does seek to do is provide a 'basis from which current practice may evolve in a consistent and coherent manner that will improve the usefulness of financial statements'.

(f) The seven chapters

The Statement of Principles consists of seven chapters:

1 The objective of financial statements
2 The qualitative characteristics of financial information
3 The elements of financial statements
4 Recognition in financial statements
5 Measurement in financial statements
6 Presentation of financial information
7 The reporting entity

(g) The remainder of this section

The exposure draft version of the full statement is 132 pages long. In the Statement, the Principles themselves are highlighted in bold type. The principles are reproduced below, preceded by a brief commentary.

(h) The objective of financial statements (Chapter 1)

This chapter sets out general objectives (see principle 1.1 below) and refers to the information needs of various user groups, apart from investors including:

(1) employees
(2) lenders
(3) suppliers and other creditors
(4) customers
(5) government and government agencies
(6) the public.

The chapter puts into context the role of the four primary statements:

(i)   the profit and loss account
(ii)   the statement of recognised gains and losses (see chapter 8)
(iii) the balance sheet
(iv)   the cash flow statement (see chapter 31).

The principles are as follows. Note the key phrase 'financial adaptability' in principle 1.13 below.

Chapter 1 – the objective of financial statements

Extracts from exposure draft.

OBJECTIVE
The objective of financial statements is to provide information about the financial position, performance and financial adaptability of an enterprise that is useful to a wide range of users for assessing the stewardship of management and for making economic decisions. (Paragraph 1.1)

USERS AND THEIR INFORMATION NEEDS
Investors, as the providers of risk capital to the enterprise (and their advisers), are interested in information that helps them to assess the performance of management. They are also concerned with the risk inherent in, and return provided by, their investments, and need information that helps them to assess the ability for the enterprise to pay dividends, and to determine whether they should buy, hold or sell their investments. (Paragraph 1.5)

While not all the information needs of all users can be met by financial statements, there are needs that are common to all users: in particular, they all have some interest in the financial position, performance and financial adaptability of the enterprise as a whole. Financial statements that meet the needs of providers of risk capital to the enterprise will also meet most of the needs of other users that financial statements can satisy. This does not imply that other users are to be ignored: the information prepared for investors is useful as a frame of reference for other users, against which they can evaluate more specific information they may obtain in their dealings with the enterprise. (Paragraph 1.6)

FINANCIAL POSITION, PERFORMANCE AND FINANCIAL ADAPTABILITY
The economic decisions that are taken by users of financial statements require an evaluation of the enterprise's ability to generate cash and the timing and certainty of its generation. Evaluation of the ability to generate cash is assisted by focusing on the enterprise's financial position, performance and cash flows and using these in predicting expected cash flows and assessing financial adaptability. (Paragraph 1.9)

The financial position of an enterprise encompasses the economic resources it controls, its financial structure, its liquidity and solvency, and its capacity to adapt to changes in the environment in which it operates. Information on financial position is provided in a balance sheet. (Paragraph 1.10)

The performance of an enterprise comprises the return obtained by the enterprise on the resources it controls, including the cost of its financing. Information on performance is provided in a profit and loss account and a statement of total recognised gains and losses. (Paragraph 1.11)

Information on cash flows is provided in a cash flow statement. It provides an additional perspective on the performance of an enterprise by indicating the amounts and principal sources of its cash inflows and outflows. (Paragraph 1.12)

Financial adaptability consists of the ability of an enterprise to take effective action to alter the amount and timing of its cash flows so that it can respond to unexpected events and opportunities. All the primary financial statements provide information that is useful in evaluating the financial adaptability of the enterprise. (Paragraph 1.13)

(i) The qualitative characteristics of financial information (Chapter 2)

This chapter includes a number of crucial concepts – some familiar, others relatively new:

(1) materiality is referred to as a 'threshold quality'
(2) principles 2.16 and 2.18 underpin FRS 5, Reporting the substance of transactions (see chapter 7):

2.16 states that '. . . information must represent faithfully the effect of the transactions'.
2.18 refers to '. . . accounted for and presented in accordance with their substance and commercial effect and not merely their legal form . . .'.

(3) Para 2.39 (not a bold-type principle) refers to true and fair view as '. . . a dynamic concept whose content evolves in response to such matters as advances in accounting and changes in business practice.
Para 2.39 further adds:

'Although this Statement of Principles does not deal directly with the concept of a "true and fair view" it may be expected, together with accounting standards and other statements of the Board, to contribute over time to the evolution of the interpretation of that concept'.

Chapter 2 – the qualitative characteristics of financial information

Extracts from exposure draft.

QUALITATIVE CHARACTERISTICS

Qualitative characteristics are the characteristics that make the information provided in financial statements useful to users for assessing the financial position, performance and financial adaptability of an enterprise. (Paragraph 2.1)

Some qualitative characteristics relate to the content of the information contained in financial statements: others relate to how that information is presented. (Paragraph 2.2)

The primary qualitative characteristics relating to content are relevance and reliability. (Paragraph 2.3)

The primary qualitative characteristics relating to presentation are comparability and understandability. (Paragraph 2.4)

THRESHOLD QUALITY: MATERIALITY

Materiality is a threshold quality. If any information is not material, it does not need to be considered further. (Paragraph 2.6)

Information is material if it could influence users' decisions taken on the basis of the financial statements. If that information is misstated or if certain information is omitted the materiality of the misstatement or omission depends on the size and nature of the item in question judged in the particular circumstances of the case. (Paragraph 2.7)

CHARACTERISTICS RELATING TO CONTENT

Relevance

To be useful, information must be relevant to the decision-making needs of users. Information has the quality of relevance when it has the ability to influence the decisions of users by helping them evaluate past, present or future events or confirming, or correcting, their past evaluations. (Paragraph 2.8)

Predictive value and confirmatory value
Relevant information has either predictive value or confirmatory value. (Paragraph 2.10)

Choice of attribute
The choice of the attribute to be reported in financial statements should be based on its relevance to the economic decisions of users. (Paragraph 2.12)

Reliability

To be useful, information must also be reliable. Information has the quality of reliability when it is free from material error and bias and can be depended upon by users to represent faithfully what it either purports to represent or could reasonably be expected to represent. (Paragraph 2.13)

Faithful representation
Information must represent faithfully the effect of the transactions and other events it either purports to represent or could reasonably be expected to represent. (Paragraph 2.16)

Substance
If information is to represent faithfully the transactions and other events that it purports to represent, it is necessary that they are accounted for and presented in accordance with their substance and commercial effect and not merely their legal form. (Paragraph 2.18)

Neutrality
The information contained in financial statements must be neutral, ie free from bias. (Paragraph 2.19)

Prudence
Uncertainties are recognised by the disclosure of their nature and extent and by the exercise of prudence in the preparation of the financial statements. Prudence is the inclusion of a degree of caution in the exercise of the judgements needed in making the estimates required under conditions of uncertainty, such that income or assets are not overstated and expenses or liabilities are not understated. (Paragraph 2.20)

Completeness
The information in financial statements must be complete within the bounds of materiality and cost. (Paragraph 2.21)

CHARACTERISTICS RELATING TO PRESENTATION

Comparability

Users must be able to compare the financial statements of an enterprise over time to identify trends in its financial position and performance. Users must also be able to compare the financial statements of different enterprises to evaluate their relative financial position, performance and financial adaptability. It is therefore necessary for similar events and states of affairs to be represented in a similar manner. (Paragraph 2.23)

Consistency
Comparability requires the measurement and display of the financial effect of like transactions and other events to be carried out in a consistent way within each accounting period and from one period to the next, and also in a consistent way by different entities. Although consistency is necessary to attain comparability, it is not in itself always sufficient. (Paragraph 2.27)

Disclosures
A prerequisite of comparability is disclosure of the accounting policies employed in the preparation of the financial statements, and also any changes in those policies and the effects of such changes. (Paragraph 2.28)
  Because users wish to compare the financial position, performance and changes in financial position of an enterprise over time, it is important that the financial statements show corresponding information for one or more preceding periods. (Paragraph 2.29)

Understandability

An essential quality of the information provided in financial statements is that it should be readily understandable by users. (Paragraph 2.30)

Aggregation and classification
An important factor in the understandibility of financial information is the manner in which the information is presented. An understandable presentation requires that items are aggregated and classified in an appropriate way. (Paragraph 2.32)

Users' abilities

Financial information is generally prepared on the assumption that users have a reasonable knowledge of business and economic activities and accounting and a willingness to study the information with reasonable diligence. Information about complex matters that should be included in the financial statements because of its relevance to the economic decision-making needs of users should not be excluded merely on the grounds that it may be too difficult for some users to understand. (Paragraph 2.33)

(j) The elements of financial statements (Chapter 3)

The definitions of assets and liabilities are crucial to FRS 5, Reporting the substance of transactions (see chapter 7).

The definitions of gains, losses and ownership interest are important to FRS 3, Reporting financial performance (see chapter 8).

Chapter 3 – the elements of financial statements

Extracts from exposure draft.

The elements of financial statements are:
- assets
- liabilities
- ownership interest
- gains
- losses
- contributions from owners
- distributions to owners. (Paragraph 3.1)

Any item that does not fall within one of the definitions of elements should not be included in financial statements. (Paragraph 3.2)

ASSETS AND LIABILITIES

Assets are rights or other access to future economic benefits controlled by an entity as a result of past transactions or events. (Paragraph 3.5)

Liabilities are obligations of an entity to transfer economic benefits as a result of past transactions or events. (Paragraph 3.21)

OWNERSHIP INTEREST

Ownership interest is the residual amount found by deducting all of the entity's liabilities from all of the entity's assets. (Paragraph 3.39)

GAINS AND LOSSES

Gains are increases in ownership interest, other than those relating to contributions from owners. (Paragraph 3.47)

Losses are decreases in ownership interest, other than those relating to distributions to owners. (Paragraph 3.47)

CONTRIBUTIONS FROM OWNERS AND DISTRIBUTIONS TO OWNERS

Contributions from owners are increases in ownership interest resulting from investments made by owners in their capacity as owners. (Paragraph 3.49)

Distributions to owners are decreases in ownership interest resulting from transfers made to owners in their capacity as owners. (Paragraph 3.49)

(k) Recognition in financial statements (Chapter 4)

The concepts of 'recognition' and 'derecognition' are frequently referred to in FRS 5 – for example, when considering appropriate treatment of items such as consignment stock or debt factoring.

The importance of this chapter is likely to become increasingly apparent as further Standards evolve, replacing earlier SSAPs.

Illustration

Extract from annual report and accounts of Grand Metropolitan plc for the year ended 30 September 1995.

Accounting policies (extract)

Basis of preparation
The financial statements are prepared under the historical cost convention, modified by the revaluation of certain land and buildings, and comply with applicable UK accounting standards. Assets and liabilities are recognised in the financial statements where, as a result of past transactions or events, the group has rights or other access to future economic benefits controlled by the group, or obligations to transfer economic benefits.

Chapter 4 – recognition in financial statements

Extracts from exposure draft.

RECOGNITION
Recognition involves depiction of the element both in words and by a monetary amount, and the inclusion of that amount in the statement totals. (Paragraph 4.1)

The stages of recognition
The recognition of assets and liabilities falls into three stages:

(a) initial recognition;
(b) subsequent remeasurement; and
(c) derecognition. (Paragraph 4.5)

Recognition criteria

Initial recognition
An element should be recognised if:

(a) there is suffcient evidence that the change in assets or liabilities inherent in the element has occurred (including, where appropriate, evidence that a future inflow or outflow of benefit will occur); and
(b) it can be measured at a monetary amount with sufficient reliability. (Paragraph 4.6)

Subsequent remeasurement
A change in the amount at which an asset or liability is recorded should be recognised if:

(a) there is sufficient evidence that the amount of an asset or liability has changed; and
(b) the new amount of the asset or liability can be measured with sufficient reliability. (Paragraph 4.7)

Derecognition
An asset or liability should cease to be recognised if there is no longer sufficient evidence that the entity has access to future economic benefits or an obligation to transfer economic benefits (including, where appropriate, evidence that a future inflow or outflow of benefit will occur). (Paragraph 4.8)

Recognition of gains and losses
At any stage in the recognition process, where a change in total assets is not offset by an equal change in total liabilities or a transaction with owners, a gain or a loss will arise. (Paragraph 4.9)

THE RECOGNITION PROCESS

Past events
Recognition is triggered where a past event gives rise to a measureable change in the assets or liabilities of the entity. (Paragraph 4.11)

The event that triggers recognition must have occurred before the balance sheet date. (Paragraph 4.12)

To the extent that a past event has resulted in access to future economic benefits (or obligations to transfer economic benefits), assets (or liabilities) are recognised; to the extent that it has resulted in previously recognised access to future economic benefits (or obligations to transfer economic benefits) being transferred or ceasing to exist, assets (or liabilities) are derecognised; and to the extent that it has resulted in a flow of economic benefits in the current period (other than one relating to a transaction with owners), a gain or loss is recognised. (Paragraph 4.13)

Transactions
Transactions are arrangements under which services or interests in property are acquired by one entity from another. Where a transaction takes place it is necessary to recognise the assets and liabilities acquired. If the transaction is negotiated at arm's length and the consideration is monetary, transactions provide strong evidence of the amount of assets acquired. (Paragraph 4.15)

Where initial recognition is triggered by a transaction, any asset acquired or liability assumed will be measured at the amount inherent in the transaction (ie the amount of assets or liabilities given or received as consideration). (Paragraph 4.17)

Events other than transactions
Initial recognition of assets and liabilities and subsequent remeasurement may also be triggered by events other than transactions. (Paragraph 4.22)

Some of the events that trigger subsequent remeasurement involve the revaluation of the flow of benefits associated with an asset or liability. (Paragraph 4.24)

Derecognition
Derecognition is appropriate where a transaction or other past event has eliminated a previously recognised asset or liability or where the expectation of a future benefit flow on which recognition was originally based is no longer sufficiently strong to support continued recognition. (Paragraph 4.25)

THE RECOGNITION OF GAINS AND LOSES

The recognition of gains
The recognition of gains involves consideration of whether there is sufficient evidence that an increase in net assets (ie in ownership interest) had occurred before the end of the reporting period. (Paragraph 4.29)

The recognition of losses
The recognition of losses involves consideration of whether there is suffi-cient evidence that a decrease in ownership interest had occurred before the end of the reporting period. Prudence has the effect that less evidence

of occurrence and reliability of measurement is required for the recognition of a loss than for a gain. (Paragraph 4.32)

Where expenditure cannot justifiably be assumed to be associated with the generation of specific gains in the future, it should be recognised as a loss in the period in which it is incurred. (Paragraph 4.36)

SUFFICIENT EVIDENCE

The recognition criteria state that a necessary condition for initial recognition or subsequent remeasurement is that sufficient evidence exists to indicate that a change in an element has occurred. (Paragraph 4.37)

Uncertainty is countered by evidence – the more evidence there is about an item and the better the quality of that evidence, the less uncertainty there will be over its existence, nature and measurement, and the more reliable the item will be. (Paragraph 4.38)

SUFFICIENT RELIABILITY

The recognition criteria state that a necessary condition for initial recognition or subsequent remeasurement is that an element or a change in element can be measured with sufficient reliability. (Paragraph 4.40)

The use of reasonable estimates is a normal part of the preparation of financial statements and provided a reasonably reliable estimate can be made of the item it should be recognised. (Paragraph 4.41)

Reliability of measurement is affected by three factors:

(a) the ability to measure the benefits inherent in the item in monetary terms;
(b) the variability of the size of these benefits (both the spread of possible levels of benefit and the chance of any particular level of benefit occurring); and
(c) the existence of a minimum amount. (Paragraph 4.43)

(I) Measurement in financial statements (Chapter 5)

Chapter 5 considers various measurement systems under three main headings:

(a) historical cost;
(b) current values;
(c) adjusting for the effects of general inflation.

The chapter concludes by stating:

'The Board therefore believes that practice should develop by evolving in the direction of greater use of current values to the extent that this is consistent with the constraints of reliability and cost'.

Current value systems are discussed below in chapter 33 of this book.

Chapter 5 – measurement in financial statements

Extracts from exposure draft.

Initial recognition most commonly occurs as a result of a transaction such as the purchase of an asset. Assets and liabilities are, therefore, normally recorded initially at the transaction cost. At that time, the historical cost recorded is equal to current replacement cost. (Paragraph 5.3)

Remeasurement involves changing the monetary amount at which an asset or liability is recorded when the recognition criteria for a change are met. (Paragraph 5.4)

In a historical cost system subsequent remeasurement can involve the writing down of an asset to its recoverable amount and the amendment of the monetary amount of liabilities to the amount ultimately expected to be paid. (Paragraph 5.6)

Recoverable amount is the value of an asset in its most profitable use, i e the higher of net reliable value and value in use. Value in use is defined as the net present value of future cash flows obtainable as a result of an asset's continued use, including those resulting from its ultimate disposal. (Paragraph 5.7)

In a current value system of accounting, assets and liabilities are remeasured regularly so that changes in value are recorded as they occur, rather than simply when they are realised. (Paragraph 5.20)

The most important advantage for current value is its relevance to users who wish to assess the current state or recent performance of the business. (Paragraph 5.25)

In the case of assets, the appropriate current value is selected according to the value to the business rule. The value to the business rule values the assets at replacement (rather than historical) cost if the recoverable amount is higher, i e if the asset is one that the entity would replace. If replacement is not justified the asset is valued at recoverable amount. (Paragraph 5.35)

In the case of liabilities, use of the value to the business rule is an unnecessary complication because the various values will converge to a single current value and thus market values may be used. (Paragraph 5.36)

A real terms capital maintenance system improves the relevance of information because it shows current operating margins as well as the extent to which holding gains and losses reflect the effect of general inflation, so that users of real terms financial statements are able to select the particular information they require. (Paragraph 5.37)

Practice should develop by evolving in the direction of greater use of current values to the extent that this is consistent with the constraints of reliability and cost. (Paragraph 5.38)

(m) Presentation in financial statements (Chapter 6)

Chapter 6 sets out the role of the component parts of the financial statements and refers to the following:
(1) Statements of financial performance:

profit and loss account
statement of recognised gains and losses.

(See chapter 8 of this book).

(2) Statement of financial position:

the balance sheet.

(3) Statement of cash flows:

the cash flow statement (see chapter 31 of this book).

(4) Supplementary information:

Chapter 6 considers a number of kinds of supplementary information including:

(i)   an operating and financial review;
(ii)   information prepared from a different perspective from that adopted in the financial statements;
(iii) statistical information;
(iv) highlights and summary indications.

As regards listed companies, the increasingly important role of the operating and financial review is dealt with in chapter 11 of this book, section 11.7).

Chapter 6 – presentation in financial statements

Extracts from exposure draft.

Financial information is presented in the form of a structured set of financial statements comprising primary statements and supporting notes and, in some cases, supplementary information. (Paragraph 6.3)

THE COMPONENTS OF FINANCIAL STATEMENTS
The primary financial statements are currently:

(a) the profit and loss account;
(b) the statement of total recognised gains and losses;
(c) the balance sheet; and
(d) the cash flow statement. (Paragraph 6.11)

The notes and the primary financial statements form an integrated whole. The role of the notes is to amplify and explain the primary financial statements: disclosure of information in the notes to the financial statements does not correct or justify a misrepresentation or omission in the primary financial statements. (Paragraph 6.13)

Supplementary information may include voluntary or evolutionary disclosures and information that, perhaps because it is too subjective, is not suitable for inclusion in the primary financial statements and the notes. (Paragraph 6.17)

STATEMENTS OF FINANCIAL PERFORMANCE
The gains and losses that are recognised in respect of a period are reported in one of the statements of financial performance, ie the profit and loss account and the statement of total recognised gain and losses. (Paragraph 6.18)

In assessing the overall financial performance of an entity during a period, all gains and losses need to be considered. The individual components of total recognised gains and losses are often more significant than the total in itself. (Paragraph 6.20)

The statements of financial performance report only the gains and losses that arise in the period. (Paragraph 6.25)

Gains and losses on those assets and liabilities that are held on a continuing basis primarily in order to enable the entity's operations to be carried out are reported in the statement of total recognised gains and losses, and not in the profit and loss account. (Paragraph 6.27)

All other gains and losses are reported in the profit and loss account. (Paragraph 6.28)

A particular item should be reported separately if its disclosure is likely to be significant for appraising the stewardship of management, or as a factor in assessing or reassessing future performance and cash flows. (Paragraph 6.30)

Past results should be restated by way of a prior year adjustment only following the correction of a fundamental error in the recognition of gains and losses or a change in an accounting policy that would have affected the past results. (Paragraph 6.33)

BALANCE SHEET
The balance sheet (together with related notes) provides information about an entity's assets and liabilities and its ownership interest and shows their relationships to each other at a point in time. The balance sheet delineates the entity's resource structure (major classes and amounts of assets) and its financial structure (major classes and amounts of liabilities and ownership interest). (Paragraph 6.34)

CASH FLOW STATEMENT
A cash flow statement (together with its related notes) reflects an entity's cash inflows and outflows during a period, distinguishing those that are the result of operations and those that result from other activities. It provides useful information about the ways in which an entity's activities generate and use cash. (Paragraph 6.44)

SUPPLEMENTARY INFORMATION
The operating and financial review provides a commentary on the financial statements that discusses the entity's performance and the factors underlying its results and financial position, in order to assist users to assess for themselves the future potential of the business. (Paragraph 6.51)

Summary indicators may be useful as general indicators of the amount of investment or overall past performance. But in a complex business enterprise, summary amounts cannot, on their own, adequately describe an enterprise's financial position, performance or financial adaptability. (Paragraph 6.55)

(n) The reporting entity (Chapter 7)

Chapter 7 deals with the various ways an entity may invest in other entities. The chapter considers control and the varying degrees of influence in different investment situations.

The following are covered:

(1) relationship between parent and subsidiary
(2) acquisitions and mergers
(3) goodwill
(4) associates and joint ventures
(5) equity method of accounting
(6) proportional consolidation.

(See chapters 21–26 of this book.)

Chapter 7 – the reporting entity

Extract from exposure draft.

The reporting entity is the entity that is the subject of a given set of financial statements. (Paragraph 7.1)

DIFFERENT KINDS OF INVESTMENTS

Influence and nature of interest
The classification of investments needs to reflect the way in which they are used to further the business of the investor and the consequent effect on the investor's financial position, performance and financial adaptability. The two key factors for this purpose are the degree of influence of the investor and the nature of the investor's interest in the results, assets and liabilities of its investee. (Paragraph 7.4)

Control
Control describes the highest degree of influence that an investor can have over its investee. (Paragraph 7.9)

Control is the power to direct. To have control, whether of assets or of other entities, an entity must have both of the following abilities:

(a) the ability to deploy the economic resources, or direct the entities; and
(b) the ability to ensure that any resulting benefits accrue to itself (with corresponding exposure to losses) and to restrict the access of others to those benefits. (Paragraph 7.10)

PARENT AND SUBSIDIARY

Accounting for control and ownership
Consolidated financial statements recognise the parent's control of its subsidiaries. Consolidation is a process that aggregates the total assets, liabilities and results of the parent and its subsidiaries (the group) so that the consolidated financial statements present financial information about the group as a single reporting entity. (Paragraph 7.21)

Although control provides the basis for determining which investments should be consolidated, consolidated financial statements should also reflect the extent of outside ownership interests because they are an important factor in considering the parent's access and exposure to the results of its subsidiaries. (Paragraph 7.22)

CHANGES IN THE REPORTING ENTITY

Mergers
In rare circumstances a new economic unit is formed by entities merging together to form a new group. A merger is a business combination where no party to the combination in substance obtains control over any other or is otherwise seen to be dominant. Merger accounting reflects the uniting of interests by pooling the assets and liabilities of the individual merging entities at existing recognised values as the basis for the consolidated financial statements of the new entity. (Paragraph 7.29)

Acquisitions and goodwill
The membership of a group also changes as the parent entity acquires or loses control over entities, usually by acquiring or disposing of ownership interests. In order to represent an acquisition in consolidated financial statements the assets and liabilities of the acquired entity are brought in at their fair value (which is their cost to the group). The balance of the purchase consideration that is not recognised as an identifiable asset or as a liability in the post-acquisition fair value exercise is recognised as 'goodwill'. (Paragraph 7.32)

By including goodwill amongst the assets shown in the consolidated accounts the financial statements reflect the whole of the investment in the acquired entity. Goodwill is not in itself an asset of the group, but is the proportion of the purchase price of the underlying investment shown in the parent company's balance sheet that is not reflected in the consolidated financial statements in terms of identifiable assets and liabilities. (Paragraph 7.34)

ASSOCIATES AND JOINT VENTURES
Between investments that are controlled and passive investments lie investments where the investor has a participating interest and exercises significant influence (associates) and where the investor exercises joint control with the other investors (joint ventures). These intermediate investments are used as media through which the investor conducts part of its activities but, unlike subsidiaries, they do not operate directly as extensions to the investor's business because the investor does not control them. The investments where the investor has these special relationships need special treatment in its consolidated financial statements to reflect the effect of having an associate or a joint venture on the investor's financial position, performance and financial adaptability. (Paragraph 7.35)

Associates

An associate is an investment where the investor has a long-term beneficial interest, participating in its investment's operating and financial policies and exercising significant influence over them. (Paragraph 7.36)

Equity accounting for associates in the investor's consolidated financial statements reflects the investor's accountability for its share of their assets, liabilities and results and its exposure to the risks and rewards of their activities. (Paragraph 7.39)

Joint ventures

A joint venture is an entity jointly controlled with other venturers under a contractual agreement with a view to benefit. In most cases the venturers share in common the risks and rewards of their joint venture as a separate business. The venturer's interest in its joint venture relates to its share of that business as a whole and not to its share of the individual assets and liabilities and cash flows of the joint venture. In these cases the venturer should include the joint venture in its consolidated financial statements using the equity method. (Paragraph 7.40)

In some joint ventures each venturer has its own separate interest in the risks and rewards that derive either from its particular share of the fixed assets of the venture, or by its having a distinct share of the output or service of the joint venture and, in many cases, of its financing. In these cases proportional consolidation is the appropriate accounting treatment because the venturer's interest (and its risks and rewards) relate directly to its share of the underlying assets and liabilities (and cash flows) of the joint venture rather than its share in the joint venture itself as an entity. (Paragraph 7.41)

7 REPORTING THE SUBSTANCE OF TRANSACTIONS

Key Issues

* Background to FRS 5
* The concept of 'reporting substance'
* Recognition of assets and liabilities
* De-recognition
* FRS 5 and other standards
* Disclosure requirements
* Linked presentation
* Offset
* Consignment stocks
* Debt factoring
* Sale and purchase

7.1 HISTORICAL BACKGROUND

(a) The off balance sheet finance debate

For over twenty years, off balance sheet finance has been a significant financial reporting issue.

The publication in 1984 of SSAP 21, Leases and hire purchase transactions, marked an important step forward. Prior to SSAP 21 companies were not obliged to bring finance leased assets and related obligations into their balance sheets (see chapter 18, section 18.2).

However, following the issue of SSAP 21, a number of loopholes still remained. Some companies succeeded in reporting transactions in accordance with their strict legal form in situations when this conflicted with commercial substance.

(b) Accounting Standards Committee

The former Accounting Standards Committee used a number of advisory documents: a technical release dealing with off balance sheet finance, and two exposure drafts dealing with special purpose transactions and reporting substance.

(c) Accounting Standards Board

The Accounting Standards Board put this subject high up its agenda and issued an exposure draft, followed in 1994 by a Standard – FRS 5, Reporting the substance of transactions.

(d) The Statement of Principles

These principles, referred to in chapter 6, set the scene for FRS 5:

Paragraphs 2.16 and 2.18 of the draft Statement of Principles state:

2.16: Information must represent faithfully the effect of the transactions and other events it either purports to represent or could reasonably be expected to represent.

2.18: If information is to represent faithfully the transactions and other events that it purports to represent or could reasonably be expected to represent, it is necessary that they are accounted for and presented in accordance with their substance and commercial effect and not merely their legal form.

(e) FRS 5 – a Standard based on general principles

FRS 5 sets out general principles which are capable of being applied to a variety of transactions. In this respect, FRS 5 is different from other Standards. Until recently, most FRS 5 applications could be identified fairly readily. However, more less obvious applications of FRS 5 are now beginning to emerge. This process is likely to continue as FRS 5 plays an increasingly central-stage role.

7.2   THE SUBSTANCE OF TRANSACTIONS

(a) Reporting substance

The basic message of FRS 5 is clear – paragraph 14 of the Standard requires the 'A reporting entity's financial statement should report the substance of the transactions into which it has entered'.

(b) Commercial effect and legal form

FRS 5 is aimed at 'more complex transactions whose substance may not be readily apparent'. The Standard states that 'the true commercial effect of such transactions may not be adequately expressed by their legal form and, where this is the case, it will not be sufficient to account for them merely by recording that form . . .' (Summary to FRS 5 para (b)).

A long-standing practical illustration of the 'commercial effect over legal form' principle is the accounting treatment of fixed assets under hire purchase and finance lease arrangements (see also 7.3(a)).

A further illustration is debt factoring. Some companies factor debts as an alternative source of finance to a bank loan or overdraft. The legal form of the transaction is that the debts are 'sold' or assigned over to the factoring company. However, in most debt factoring arrangements, the commercial effect is that the transaction is a financing one and not an asset disposal. Accordingly, FRS 5 would normally require monies received from the factoring company to be separately presented as a source of finance. However, in very restricted cases, linked presentation might be appropriate (see section 7.9).

7.3   FEATURES OF MORE COMPLEX TRANSACTIONS

Certain transactions of a more complex nature may include the following features:

(a) Separation of legal title from benefits and risks

As an example, the legal title to a finance lease remains with the lessor although the risks and benefits associated with the asset pass to the lessee. SSAP 21 requires the party having the benefits and risks relating to the underlying property to recognise an asset in its balance sheet even though it does not have legal title.

(b) Linking of transactions

A transaction may be linked with others in such a way that the overall commercial effect can only be understood by considering the series as a whole. FRS 5 gives an example of a sale of goods where there is a commitment to repurchase. The repurchase price is set at costs (including interest) incurred by the other party in holding the goods. The transaction should be accounted for as a financial transaction – the original asset remains on the balance sheet whilst the 'proceeds of sale' is accounted for as finance, ie as a balance sheet liability.

(c) Inclusion of options

The transaction may include options or conditions on terms that make it highly likely that the option will be exercised or the conditions fulfilled.

FRS 5 requires the commercial effect of the options or conditions to be assessed in order to determine what assets and liabilities exist.

7.4   APPLYING THE PRINCIPLES OF FRS 5

(a) General principle

FRS 5, para 14 requires the accounts of a reporting entity such as a company to report the substance of the transactions into which it has entered. Para 14 extends this general principle as follows:

(1) All aspects and implications of a transaction should be identified. Greater weight should be given to those more likely to have a commercial effect in practice.

For example, a legal agreement such as a consignment stock agreement may contain a large number of terms (see 7.11). It will be necessary to analyse these terms and decide which ones are important in practice. This analysis will form the basis of deciding the appropriate accounting treatment.
(2) A group or series of transactions that achieves or is designed to achieve an overall commercial effect should be viewed as a whole. For example, a sale of property where the seller is committed to repurchasing the property at a later date should be looked at in terms of its overall effect, not as two separate transactions (see 7.3(b)).

(b) Application notes

The FRS gives extensive criteria for identifying the substance of transactions as well as a lengthy appendix running to 67 pages with application notes on five specific areas:

(1) consignment stock
(2) sale and repurchase agreements
(3) factoring debts
(4) securitised assets
(5) loan transfer.

These application notes are referred to later in the chapter.

7.5   RECOGNITION OF ASSETS AND LIABILITIES

(a) Recognition

This term refers to the process of incorporating an item into a primary statement, such as the balance sheet, under an appropriate heading. For example, if a company enters into a hire purchase arrangement, recognition refers to bringing a fixed asset and related creditor on to the balance sheet.

(b) FRS 5 criteria

For an asset or liability to be recognised in the balance sheet, three criteria must be satisfied. These relate to:

(1) identification;
(2) existence;
(3) monetary measurement.

(FRS 5 paras 16 and 20).

(1) *Identification test*

Assets are defined as 'rights or other access to future economic benefits controlled by an entity as a result of past transactions or events' (FRS 5, para 2).

Liabilities are defined as 'an entity's obligations to transfer economic benefits as a result of past transactions or events' (FRS 5, para 4).

(2) *Existence test*

This requires sufficient evidence of the existence of the item (including, where appropriate, evidence that a future inflow or outflow of benefits will occur) (FRS 5, para 20(a)).

(3) *Monetary measurement test*

This requires that the item can be measured at a monetary amount with sufficient reliability (FRS 6, para 20(b)).

Assets such as stock (SSAP 9) and purchased goodwill (SSAP 22) would satisfy the three tests above. However, internally-generated goodwill would be unable to satisfy the monetary measurement condition, and so should not be recognised as an asset.

(c) Examples

Some illustrations of how FRS 5 might be applied include:

(1) A finance lease – if this satisfied the SSAP 21 'risks and rewards of ownership' test (which is re-enforced by the FRS 5 'substance' test), the related asset and obligation would be included on the balance sheet.
(2) An operating lease, for example a contract hire arrangement – this would satisfy the FRS 5 tests above. In principle therefore, FRS 5 would require a '50% asset' (i e where the finance element of rentals is equivalent to 50% of the overall cost of the asset) to come on the balance sheet together with the related obligation. However the more detailed requirements of SSAP 21 override in accordance with FRS 5, para 13. Operating leases – provided they satisfy the spirit as well as the letter of SSAP 21 – should not be recognised, i e they will continue to remain off balance sheet for the foreseeable future. (See also section 7.7).
(3) Consignment stocks of cars held by a dealer – in principle, this could go either way. Application Note A gives guidance as to whether the stock is an

asset of the dealer at delivery (i e 'recognition') or whether the stock is not an asset of the dealer at delivery (i e 'no recognition'). This is referred to in detail later in this chapter.

(4) A company constructs a specialised item of machinery for its eventual use as a fixed asset. Once complete and ready for use, the item should be capable of satisfying the above recognition test. Direct costs together with a proportion of manufacturing overheads would be part of the measured 'monetary amount'.

7.6 DE-RECOGNITION

(a) De-recognition

This refers to ceasing to recognise an item in the balance sheet.

(b) FRS 5 criteria

Where a transaction satisfies both of the conditions below, the asset should cease to be recognised in the balance sheet:

(1) The transaction transfers to a third party all significant rights or other access to benefits relating to that asset.
(2) The transaction transfers to a third party all significant exposure to the risks inherent in those benefits (FRS 5, para 22).

(c) Examples

(1) A straightforward sale of goods – the asset stock would be 'de-recognised' and removed from the balance sheet. The transaction has passed access to benefits and exposure to risks on to the purchaser.
(2) Sale of goods with a commitment to repurchase – the first transaction cannot be considered in isolation, it is part of a 'series of transactions . . . designed to achieve an overall commercial effect'. If the repurchase price is based on the original sale price plus interest, then from the viewpoint of both parties, the substance of the transaction is financing. The access to benefits and exposure to risks remain throughout with the original seller. Stock remains on the balance sheet, 'de-recognition' is inappropriate. The so-called 'income' received is dealt with as borrowings.
(3) A manufacturing company sells its fleet of 40 motor vehicles to a contract hire company. The vehicles are then leased back under a traditional contract hire arrangement. From the viewpoint of the seller the transaction satisfies the 'de-recognition' test, for example the significant exposure to risks relating to residual value has been passed on to the contract hire company.
(4) Sale and operating leaseback of a freehold building, where the original seller retains a repurchase option – it will be necessary to assess whether the option terms make it 'highly likely that the option will be exercised . . .' (FRS 5, para 47(c)). If this is the assessment, the sale will *not* result in a de-recognition and the property will remain on the balance sheet. This is further referred to later in this chapter. The accounting treatment of a profit or loss on sale is dealt with in SSAP 21.
(5) Sale and leaseback, where the lease is classified under SSAP 21 as a finance lease – clearly 'de-recognition' is not appropriate. The treatment of profit or loss on sale is dealt with in SSAP 21.
(6) A trading company enters into a debt factoring arrangement – in principle this may or may not result in 'de-recognition'. In practice, the substance of most factoring arrangements is likely to be that of financing rather than

disposal of assets, in which case 'de-recognition' is not applicable. Significant exposure to risks of slow payment of debtors remains with the trading company. Slow payment results in higher finance charges paid to the factor. A further risk is that the amount received depends on the realisation of the debtor balances. Debtors would remain on the balance sheet until cash is collected from the customer.

(7) Discounting of bills of exchange with recourse – when a company discounts bills receivable with a bank, it has not transferred the significant risks relating to possible non-payment by the original debtor. The company should, therefore, leave bills receivable on the balance sheet until the bill has matured and been collected by the bank. In other words, separate presentation should be adopted – similar to the treatment for most debt factoring arrangements.

Illustration 1

Extracts from annual report and accounts of J Bibby & Sons plc for the year ended 30 September 1995

Accounting policies (extract)

Accounting for the substance of transactions
Where bills or leases are discounted with recourse to the Group, then the transactions are brought onto the balance sheet within debtors and creditors.

Notes (extracts)

	Consolidated		Company	
	1995	*1994*	*1995*	*1994*
	£000's	*£000's*	*£000's*	*£000's*
Debtors				
Amounts falling due within one year:				
Trade debtors	118,683	113,839	–	–
Amounts due from subsidiaries	–	–	10,811	4,866
Other debtors	6,893	5,397	110	10
Prepayments and accrued income	5,079	5,504	91	987
Bills and leases discounted with recourse	20,354	21,241	–	–
	151,009	145,981	11,012	5,863
Amounts falling due after more than one year:				
Amounts due from subsidiaries	–	–	67,690	20,767
Other debtors	3,353	3,689	330	528
Bills and leases discounted with recourse	517	508	–	–
	3,870	4,197	68,020	21,295
	154,879	150,178	79,032	27,158
Creditors and provisions				
Amounts falling due within one year:				
Trade creditors	61,032	63,192	–	–
Amounts due to subsidiary companies	–	–	–	450
Social security and payroll taxes	5,182	6,190	–	–
Other creditors	20,389	17,349	486	408
Accruals and deferred income	26,096	27,351	1,112	4,616
Bills and leases discounted with recourse	20,354	21,241	–	–
Repurchase obligations	5,428	4,236	–	–
	138,481	139,559	1,598	5,474

7.7 RELATIONSHIP WITH OTHER STANDARDS

(a) General rule

FRS 5, para 13 sets out the overriding rule:

'Where the substance of a transaction or the treatment of any resulting asset or liability falls not only within the scope of this FRS but also directly within the scope of another FRS, a Statement of Standard Accounting Practice ("SSAP"), or a specific statutory requirement governing the recognition of assets or liabilities, the standard or statute that contains the more specific provision(s) should be applied.'

(b) Example – relationship with SSAP 21

As regards SSAP 21, the leasing standard, concern has been expressed on the likely impact of FRS 5 on issues such as operating/finance lease classification; and sale and leaseback arrangements, including those entered into some years ago.

Paragraph 45 of FRS 5 is the only part of the Standard which deals explicitly with leasing issues. This states:

'The relationship between SSAP 21 "Accounting for leases and hire purchase contracts" and FRS 5 is particularly close. In general, SSAP 21 contains the more specific provisions governing accounting for stand-alone leases that fall wholly within its parameters, although the general principles of the FRS will also be relevant in ensuring that leases are classified as finance or operating leases in accordance with their substance. However, for some lease arrangements, and particularly for those that are merely one element of a larger arrangement, the FRS will contain the more specific provisions. An example is a sale and leaseback arrangement where there is also an option for the seller/lessee to repurchase the asset; in this case the provisions of Application Note B are more specific than those of SSAP 21.'

This is further referred to in chapter 18.

(c) Example – relationship with SSAP 13

The accounting treatment of deferred development expenditure, satisfying the stringent SSAP 13 capitalisation criteria, is a further illustration of the play-off between the general principles of FRS 5 and the more specific provisions of another standard.

The general principles of FRS 5 would require such expenditure to be recognised in the balance sheet as an asset. However, para 13 of FRS 5 allows SSAP 13 to override and thus allows companies the option of capitalisation or immediate write-off.

7.8 DISCLOSURE REQUIREMENTS

(a) General requirements

FRS 5 has two key paragraphs dealing with disclosure requirements for more complex transactions. Paragraphs 30 and 31 of the FRS state:

'30 Disclosure of a transaction in the financial statements, whether or not it has resulted in assets or liabilities being recognised or ceasing to be recognised, should be sufficient to enable the user of the financial statements to understand its commercial effect.

31 Where a transaction has resulted in the recognition of assets or liabilities whose nature differs from that of items usually included under the relevant balance sheet heading, the differences should be explained.'

(b) Specific applications

FRS 5 application notes deal with detailed disclosures on areas such as consignment stocks, sale and repurchase arrangements and debt factoring.

7.9   LINKED PRESENTATION FOR CERTAIN NON-RECOURSE FINANCE ARRANGEMENTS

(a) Applicability

Linked presentation is a very specific aspect of FRS 5 and is likely to apply to only a relatively few companies.

Linked presentation applies to a transaction that is in substance a financing transaction but where the financing effectively 'ring-fences' the item. For example, where the transaction relates to debt factoring, the finance received will be repaid only out of the proceeds generated by the debtors. The company which has factored the debtors has a strictly limited exposure to loss – it is linked to a fixed monetary amount.

A linked presentation effectively shows the finance on the face of the balance sheet as a deduction from the gross amount of the item it finances.

Illustration 2

Extract from annual reports and accounts of Arjo Wiggins Appleton plc for the year ended 31 December 1994.

Balance sheets (extract)

	Group		Company	
	1994 *£m*	*1993* *£m*	*1994* *£m*	*1993* *£m*
Fixed assets				
Tangible assets	**1,097.9**	1,090.4	**1.0**	1.7
Investments:				
Security deposit	**62.5**	–	–	–
Other investments	**132.3**	116.5	**1,495.5**	1,520.2
	194.8	116.5	**1,495.5**	1,520.2
	1,292.7	1,206.9	**1,496.5**	1,521.9
Current assets				
Stocks	**475.7**	364.6	–	–
Debtors:				
Debts factored without recourse	–	29.7	–	–
Less: non-returnable proceeds	–	(27.0)	–	–
	–	2.7	–	–
Other debtors	**769.3**	641.6	**221.3**	238.9
	769.3	644.3	**221.3**	238.9
Investments	**8.8**	62.0	–	–
Cash at bank and in hand	**125.1**	180.5	**0.1**	–
	1,378.9	1,251.4	**221.4**	238.9

	Group 1994 £m	1993 £m	Company 1994 £m	1993 £m
Creditors: amounts falling due within one year				
Short-term borrowings	**235.7**	321.6	**2.6**	83.6
Other creditors	**721.1**	591.5	**44.3**	35.9
	956.8	913.1	**46.9**	119.5
Net current assets	**422.1**	338.3	**174.5**	119.4
Total assets less current liabilities	**1,714.8**	1,545.2	**1,671.0**	1,641.3

(b) Conditions

A linked presentation can only be used if certain stringent criteria can be satisfied including the following:

(1) the finance will be repaid only from proceeds generated by the specific item it finances (or by transfer of the item itself) and there is no possibility whatsoever of a claim on the entity being established other than against funds generated by that item (or the item itself); and
(2) there is no provision whatsoever whereby the entity may either keep the item on repayment of the finance or re-acquire it at any time.

Additional conditions are contained in FRS 5, para 27. These are extremely stringent and likely to be difficult to satisfy in practice.

7.10 OFFSET

The general principle is that assets and liabilities should not be offset.

Debit and credit balances should be aggregated into a simple net item where:

(a) they do not constitute separate assets and liabilities, and
(b) the following three conditions are satisfied:

   (i) The reporting entity and another party owe each other determinable monetary amounts, denominated either in the same currency, or in different but freely convertible currencies.
   (ii) The reporting entity has the ability to insist on a net settlement.
   (iii) The reporting entity's ability to insist on a net settlement is assured beyond doubt.

Illustration 3

Extract from annual report and accounts of Reckitt & Colman plc for the year ended 31 December 1994.

Accounting policies (extract)

Accounting convention
The accounts are prepared under the historical cost convention and in accordance with applicable UK Accounting Standards and the Companies Act 1985, except for the treatment of stock units. As explained in Note 31 the directors have invoked the true and fair view override and disclosed the stock units as part of shareholder's funds.

The group has adopted the provisions of Financial Reporting Standards FRS 6 (Acquisitions and Mergers) and FRS 7 (Fair Values in Acquisition Accounting). UITF 6 (Accounting for post-retirement benefits other than pensions) and FRS 5 (Reporting the Substance of Transactions) have been implemented and the accounts of the previous year have been restated accordingly.

140   *Reporting the substance of transactions*

Note 20: Aggregate bank loans and overdrafts

	1994 Group £m	1993 Group £m	1994 Parent £m	1993 Parent £m
Repayable in full within one year*	**122.99**	83.44	**86.40**	56.71
Repayable between one and five years	**142.47**	144.16	**103.63**	94.33
	265.46	227.60	**190.03**	151.04
Timing of repayments				
In one year or less, or on demand (Note 16)	**122.99**	84.70	**86.40**	56.71
Due after more than one year (Note 17):				
Between one and two years	**63.09**	37.88	**38.93**	37.66
Between two and five years	**79.38**	105.02	**64.70**	56.67
	142.47	142.90	**103.63**	94.33
	265.46	227.60	**190.03**	151.04

£142.47m (1993, £144.16m) of the amounts shown as payable between one and five years are repayable within twelve months of the balance sheet date, but as they are drawn under committed facilities they are classified in the table above on the basis of the expiry dates of the facilities.

Contingent liabilities in respect of bills of exchange discounted by subsidiary undertakings at 31 December 1994 were £1.75m (1993, £1.02m).

The 1993 figures for aggregate bank loans and overdrafts for the group and parent have been increased by £70.90m to comply with FRS 5.

*Bank loans and overdrafts repayable within 90 days amounted to £44.55m (1993, £42.52m) (Note 24).

7.11   CONSIGNMENT STOCKS

(a) The key issues involved

The trade most likely to be affected by this aspect of FRS 5 is motor dealerships. The manufacturer transfers motor vehicles to the dealer but retains legal title until, say, cash has been paid over. The key issue is to determine whether, at the point of physical transfer, the manufacturer has in substance passed on the risks and rewards of ownership to the dealer.

From the dealer's viewpoint, is the commercial substance of the transaction:

(1) a purchase of stock on extended credit terms; or
(2) are the vehicles simply being 'loaned' by the manufacturer to facilitate a sale?

It is essential to determine whether, at the point of physical transfer, the manufacturer has in substance passed on the risks and rewards of ownership to the dealership.

Risks of ownership would include obsolescence risks (models becoming out of date) and risks of slow movement (thus having to finance stocks prior to achieving a sale). Benefits of ownership would include fixing purchase price on delivery with opportunity to sell at a profit.

(b) FRS 5 guidance

FRS 5 Application note A includes the following table as guidance.

For example, if the features of the consignment stock arrangement are more in line with those in the right-hand column, this would indicate that the consignment stock should be included on the dealer's balance sheet.

Indications that the stock is not an asset of the dealer at delivery	Indications that the stock is an asset of the dealer at delivery
Manufacturer can require the dealer to return stock (or transfer stock to another dealer) without compensation, or Penalty paid by the dealer to prevent returns/transfers of stock at the manufacturer's request.	Manufacturer cannot require dealer to return or transfer stock, or Financial incentives given to persuade dealer to transfer stock at manufacturer's request.
Dealer has unfettered right to return stock to the manufacturer without penalty and actually exercises the right in practice.	Dealer has no right to return stock or is commercially compelled not to exercise its right of return.
Manufacturer bears obsolecence risk, e g: – obsolete stock is returned to the manufacturer without penalty; or – financial incentives given by manufacturer to prevent stock being returned to it (e g on a model change or if it becomes obsolete).	Dealer bears obsolescence risk, e g: – penalty charged if dealer returns stock to manufacturer; or – obsolete stock cannot be returned to the manufacturer and no compensation is paid by manufacturer for losses due to obsolecence.
Stock transfer price charged by manufacturer is based on manufacturer's list price at date of transfer of legal title.	Stock transfer price charged by maunfacturer is based on manufacturer's list price at date of delivery.
Manufacturer bears slow movement risk, e g: – transfer price set independently of time for which dealer holds stock, and there is no deposit.	Dealer bears slow movement risk, e g: – dealer is effectively charged interest as transfer price or other payments to manufacturer vary with time for which dealer holds stock; or – dealer makes a substantial interest-free deposit that varies with the levels of stock held.

(c) Disclosure requirements

(1) Where stock is regarded in substance as an asset of the dealer:
   (a) Recognise stock on balance sheet of dealer with corresponding liability to the manufacturer. Comparative figures are required.
   (b) Deduct any deposit paid from the liability, classifying difference as a trade creditor.
   (c) Notes to the accounts should explain:
      – nature of arrangement;
      – amount of consignment stock included in the balance sheet;
      – main terms under which stock held including terms of any deposit.
   (d) Where necessary comparative figures should be restated.

(2) Where stock is not regarded in substance as an asset of the dealer:
   (a) Do not include stock on dealer's balance sheet until transfer of title has crystallised.
   (b) Include any deposit under 'other debtors'.
   (c) Notes similar to those in (1) above including the value of consignment stock held at year end.
   (d) Note that comparative information should be given.

(d) Illustrations – extracts from annual reports and accounts

1 *Wolseley plc for the year ended 31 July 1994*

Note 14 – Stocks

The main categories of stocks are:	1994	1993
	£000	£000
Raw materials	14,393	12,422
Work in progress	6,561	6,023
Finished goods	9,601	9,729
Goods purchased for resale	479,924	363,358
	510,479	391,532

The current replacement cost of stocks does not materially differ from the historical cost stated above.

   Certain subsidiary undertakings have consignment stock arrangements, in the ordinary course of business, with suppliers. Inventory drawn from consignment stock is generally invoiced to the companies concerned at the price ruling at the date of drawdown. The value of such stock, at cost, which has been excluded from the balance sheet in accordance with the application notes included in FRS 5, amounted to £9.228m (1993 £5.640m).

2 *Lookers plc for the year ended 30 September 1994*

Accounting policies – Note 6
Stocks are valued at the lower of cost and net realisable value.
   Deposits paid for vehicles on consignment represent bulk deposits paid to manufacturers.

Note 10 – restatement of 1993 comparatives
During the current financial year FRS 5 (Reporting the Substance of Transactions) became effective. Interest bearing consignment vehicles and motability buy-back vehicles are now included as part of total stocks.
   The related liabilities are included in trade and other creditors respectively. Other creditors due after more than one year relate to motability buy-back vehicles due to return between one and three years.
   Previously these vehicles and the related liabilities were excluded from the balance sheet.
   The interest charged on consignment vehicles is now included in interest payable and not in cost of sales. This has no effect on the profit before taxation.
   As a result, the comparatives for 1993 have been restated. The effect of this can be seen in notes 3, 12, 14 and 15.

	1994	1993
	£000	£000
Goods for resale	30,372	29,135
Bulk deposit for vehicles on consignment	1,806	1,882
Interest bearing consignment vehicles	2,880	4,431
Motability buy-back vehicles	10,186	11,730
	45,244	47,178

In accordance with FRS 5, interest bearing consignment vehicles and motability buy-back vehicles for both years are now included in stocks.

3 *Lex Service plc for the year ended 31 December 1994*

Consignment stock
Balance sheet footnote

Note. In accordance with Financial Reporting Standard 5 'Reporting the Substance of Transactions' certain vehicle consignment stock has been brought on to the balance sheet and the comparatives have been restated (note 16).

Note 16

	Group		Lex Service plc	
	1994	1993	1994	1993
		(restated)		
	£m	£m	£m	£m
Vehicles	155.5	140.8	–	1.2
Vehicle parts	23.9	25.3	–	–
	179.4	166.1	–	1.2
Work in progress	1.3	0.9	–	–
Raw materials and consumables	1.3	1.3	–	–
	182.0	168.3	–	1.2

In accordance with Financial Reporting Standard 5 'Reporting the Substance of Transactions', vehicle consignment stock amounting to £16.5m million has been brought onto the balance sheet together with an associated creditor. The comparative figures have been adjusted to reflect additional stock of £5.1 million at 26 December 1993. This consignment stock has been acquired under agreements with finance companies at interest rates between 1% and 6% over finance house rates. Deposits paid in respect of this stock previously reported as debtors, have been reclassified as stock to the extent that the benefits and risks of holding the stock have been passed to the Group.

In addition, the Group held consignment stock with a cost of £66.1 million (1993 – £71.1 million), in respect of which the benefits and risks of holding the stock had not been passed to the Group. This stock was held under agreements providing interest free periods ranging from 5 to 180 days.

4 *Cowie Group plc for the year ended 31 December 1994*

Note 13 – Stocks

	The Group		The Company	
	1994	1993	1994	1993
	£000	£000	£000	£000
Raw materials and consumables	379	7	5	7
Work in progress	56	152	–	85
Finished goods and goods for resale	60,608	60,436	181	47,459
Deposits with motor manufacturers	8,447	6,406	–	4,088
	69,490	67,001	186	51,639

Where vehicles on consignment are deemed in substance to be assets of the Group they have been included in Stocks. The principal determining criterion is whether the assets bear interest. The Group has included £4,734,000 (1993: £5,810,000) of consignment stock in finished goods and a corresponding amount in trade creditors.

5 *Signet Group plc, year ended 28 January 1995*

Note 14 – Stocks
Subsidiary undertakings held £43,517,000 of consignment stock as at 28 January 1995 (1994: £41,003,000) which is not recorded on balance sheet. The principal terms of the consignment agreements, which can generally be terminated by either side, are such that the Group can return any or all of the stock to the relevant suppliers without financial or commercial penalties and the supplier can vary stock prices.

7.12   DEBT FACTORING AND INVOICE DISCOUNTING

(a) Background

Debt factoring is a widely used method of financing and can be referred to using a number of different terms (for example 'invoice discounting'). It is one of the topics dealt with in the application notes which are part of FRS 5.

(b) Key issue

The key issue is to determine whether a particular debt factoring arrangement is:

(1) a sale transaction – unlikely in most cases as it would be necessary to demonstrate that all significant benefits and risks had been transferred to the factor; or
(2) a borrowing or financing transaction where the company's debts are used as collateral.

(c) Evaluating the treatment of debt factoring and invoice discounting arrangements

FRS 5 suggests that two key questions should be asked (Application Note C, para C4):

(1) Does the seller have access to the benefits of the factored debts and exposure to the risks inherent to those benefits?
(2) Does the seller have a liability to repay amounts received from the factor?

In theory, the following are three possible responses:

(1) The seller has transferred all significant benefits and risks relating to the debts and has no obligation to repay the factor:
    – the appropriate accounting treatment is 'de-recognition'. This would remove the factored debts from the balance sheet and show no liability in respect of any proceeds received from the factor.
    This treatment is likely to be appropriate only in very rare cases.
(2) The seller has retained significant benefits and risks relating to the debts. However its downside exposure to loss is limited – there is no question of doubt on this:
    – the appropriate accounting treatment is 'linked presentation'. This would show the proceeds received from the factor as a deduction from the factored debts. The two elements and the net effect would be shown within a single asset caption.
    In view of the stringent criteria required by FRS 5, linked presentation is likely to be relatively uncommon. Its use is likely to be restricted to special situations involving a small minority of listed companies.
(3) In all other cases, i e where debtors are used to obtain finance:
    – 'separate presentation' is the appropriate accounting treatment. This shows the factored debt as an asset (as previously); and shows a corresponding liability within creditors (this relates to the proceeds received from the factor).
    Application Note C includes a table giving guidance as to appropriate treatment. In practice, for most factoring and invoice discounting arrangements, separate presentation is likely to be required.

In a typical with-recourse arrangement, the 'seller' retains both slow payment risk (incurring higher finance charges paid to the factor) and bad debt risk.

In a non-recourse arrangement, the factor may be taking the bad debt risk by providing bad debt protection. However, where the factor's charges are linked to bank base rates and take into account speed of payment by debtors, the 'seller' company has effectively retained a significant risk, i e risk of slow payment. Separate presentation will still be appropriate.

Confidential invoice discounting arrangements fall within the scope of FRS 5 and are subject to the same disclosure requirements in the shareholders' accounts.

(d) Accounting and disclosure requirements

De-recognition

(1) remove the factored debts from the balance sheet;
(2) no liability will be shown in respect of proceeds received from the factor;
(3) the profit and loss account will reflect the difference between the carrying amount of the debts and proceeds received on the sale of those debts to the factoring house.

Linked presentation

(1) deduct proceeds received from gross amount of factored debts (after providing for bad debts, credit protection charges and any accrued interest) – show this offset on the face of the balance sheet;
(2) notes to the accounts should disclose:
   (a) the main terms of the arrangement;
   (b) the gross amount of factored debts outstanding at the balance sheet date;
   (c) the factoring charges recognised in the period, analysed as appropriate;
   (d) statement by directors that the entity is not obliged to support any losses, nor does it intend to do so;
   (e) statement that the provider of finance has agreed that it will seek repayment of finance only to the extent that sufficient funds are generated by the specific item it has financed and that it will not seek recourse in any other form.

Separate presentation

(1) the gross amount of factored debts should be shown on the seller's balance sheet within assets;
(2) liabilities should include an amount in respect of proceeds received from the factor;
(3) the interest element of the factor's charges should be accrued and included in the profit and loss account;
(4) other factoring costs should be similarly accrued;
(5) the notes to the accounts should disclose the amount of factored debts outstanding at the balance sheet date.

Note also that CA 1985 Sch 4 para 48(4) requires disclosure of the aggregate amount of creditors in respect of which security has been given by the company, and the nature of the security.

Illustration 4

Extract from annual report and accounts of Benson Group plc for the year ended 31 May 1995.

Notes to the accounts

Creditors – amounts falling due within one year	Group 1995 £000	Group 1994 £000	Company 1995 £000	Company 1994 £000
Bank overdraft and acceptance credits	4,495	3,008	4,449	2,636
Invoice discounting	2,033	1,372	–	–
Hire purchase and leasing liabilities	520	540	35	22
Trade creditors	9,056	5,897	–	–
Amounts owed to subsidiary undertakings	–	–	1,393	1,137
Other creditors and accruals	1,672	927	408	312
Corporation tax	88	221	43	98
Other tax and social security	1,127	1,109	108	107
Proposed dividend	–	300	–	300
	18,991	13,374	6,436	4,612

The Group has provided its bankers with cross guarantees and debentures to provide fixed and floating charges on substantially all of the assets of the Group as security for the bank overdraft and acceptance credits.

Hire purchase and leasing liabilities are secured on the related assets.

Advances under invoice discounting are secured on the related trade debtors of £3,849,000 (1994: £2,644,000) and guaranteed by Benson Group plc.

Interest payable and similar charges	1995 £000	1994 £000
Bank overdraft and acceptance credits	370	209
Invoice discounting	242	171
Hire purchase and finance lease agreements	141	148
Other	12	2
	765	530

7.13   SALE AND REPURCHASE AGREEMENTS

(a) Background

Sale and repurchase agreements are arrangements under which assets are sold by one party to another on terms that provide for the seller to repurchase the asset in certain circumstances. This area can be complex, covering a diverse range of agreements. A key practical point is to be able to recognise sales agreements which include repurchase options or commitments. It will then be necessary to establish to what extent FRS 5 will be relevant.

(b) Features

The main features of sale and repurchase agreements will include:

(1) Sale price – this may be:
   (a) market value;
   (b) another agreed price.
(2) Nature of the repurchase provision – possibilities are:
   (a) unconditional commitment for both parties;
   (b) an option for the seller to repurchase (a call option);
   (c) an option for the buyer to resell to the seller (a put option);
   (d) a combination of put and call options.
(3) The repurchase price – this may:
   (a) be fixed at the outset;
   (b) vary with the period for which the asset is held by the buyer;
   (c) be the market price at the time of repurchase.
(4) Other provisions – for example the use of an asset by the seller whilst in the ownership of the buyer.

(c) Examples

Sale and repurchase agreements may cover a broad spectrum of possibilities including, for example:

(1) sale and leaseback of property with a commitment to repurchase at a future date;
(2) sale and leaseback of property with an option for the seller to repurchase at a future date;
(3) sale of new machinery with a commitment to repurchase in a few years' time in a substantially depreciated state.

(d) Applying the principles of FRS 5

(i) Sale and leaseback of property with a commitment to repurchase

In a straightforward case, the substance of a sale and repurchase agreement will be that of a secured loan. An example of this would be where the seller has an unconditional commitment to repurchase the original asset from the buyer at the original sale price plus interest. In this case the seller has retained all significant rights to benefits relating to the asset and all significant exposure to risk. The seller also has a liability to the buyer for the whole of the proceeds received. The 'sales' arrangement should be accounted for by showing the original asset on its balance sheet together with a liability for the amounts received from the buyer.

(ii) Sale and leaseback of property with a call option for the seller to repurchase

The key point to consider here is whether there is a genuine commercial possibility that the option will be exercised. In this situation the agreement gives the buyer no rights to require the seller to repurchase. An exception would be, for example, where the seller defaulted on the terms of the lease.

For this purpose it is important to assume that the seller will act in accordance with its best economic interest, taking account of factors such as option price and value of property. For example if there is no genuine commercial possibility that the option will fail to be exercised, the substance of the transaction is that of a secured loan with the benefits and risks of the asset remaining with the seller. The property and the related creditor should continue to appear on the seller's balance sheet.

Illustration 5

Extract from annual report and accounts of Stakis plc for the year ended 2 October 1994.

Directors' report (extract)

. . . The 1993 Accounts have been restated to comply with Financial Reporting Standard 5, by reaccounting for a hotel sale and leaseback in 1990. As a result Hotels operating profit increased by £0.9 million and interest charges by £2.0 million, and a property was brought onto the balance sheet at a valuation of £18.1 million together with a lease creditor of £20.7 million, the difference being adjusted on shareholders' funds.

Notes to the accounts (extracts)

Change in accounting treatment of prior year transaction

As a result of Financial Reporting Standard 5, the accounting for a hotel sale and leaseback in 1990 has been revised and the 1993 comparative figures adjusted accordingly by restoring the property to the balance sheet at valuation of £18.1m, incorporating a lease creditor of £20.7m and applying the difference to reduce the 1993 profit and the opening reserves in that year by £1.1m and £1.5m respectively. This change in accounting treatment has reduced the 1994 profit by £1.1m.

(iii) Sale of new asset and commitment to repurchase in a substantially depreciated state

The substance of the overall arrangement may be:

(1) sale of a new item of machinery; and
(2) a residual interest in the machinery – amounted for by including a stock item and associated creditor.

Illustration 6

Extract from annual report and accounts of J Bibby and Sons plc for the year ended 30 September 1995.

Accounting policies (extract)

Accounting for the substance of transactions
Where bills or leases are discounted with recourse to the Group, then the transactions are brought onto the balance sheet within debtors and creditors. Where Group companies enter into commitments to repurchase equipment at specified dates, then the residual interest in the equipment is included within stock and the repurchase obligation is included within creditors.

Note 8 – Stocks

	1995 £000's	1994 £000's
Industrial	40,157	38,824
Materials handling	31,900	25,260
Capital equipment	58,948	48,453
Agricultural	–	564
	131,005	113,101
Raw materials	17,553	20,183
Work in progress	8,336	8,470
Finished goods	85,184	67,985
Livestock	–	142
Residual interests in equipment	19,932	16,321
	131,005	113,101

In the opinion of the directors, the replacement cost of stocks is not materially different from the value of stock as listed above.

Note 10 – Creditors and provisions

	Consolidated 1995 £000's	Consolidated 1994 £000's	Company 1995 £000's	Company 1994 £000's
Amounts falling due within one year:				
Trade creditors	61,032	63,192	–	–
Amounts due to subsidiary companies	–	–	–	450
Social security and payroll taxes	5,182	6,190	–	–
Other creditors	20,389	17,349	486	408
Accruals and deferred income	26,096	27,351	1,112	4,616
Bills and leases discounted with recourse	20,354	21,241	–	–
Repurchase obligations	5,428	4,236	–	–
	138,481	139,559	1,598	5,474

Note 12 – Creditors and provisions

	Consolidated		Company	
	1995	1994	**1995**	1994
	£000's	£000's	**£000's**	£000's
Amounts falling due after more than one year:				
Fair value provisions	–	1,143	–	–
Amounts due to subsidiaries	–	–	**20,749**	–
Pension provisions	**24,287**	22,157	–	–
Other creditors	**1,812**	2,287	**600**	1,200
Bills and leases discounted with recourse	**517**	508	–	–
Repurchase obligations	**14,504**	12,085	–	–
	41,120	38,180	**21,349**	1,200

The fair value provisions relate to the acquisition of Finanzauto in 1992.

7.14 FURTHER COMPLICATIONS

(a) Quasi-subsidiaries

The area of quasi-subsidiaries is complex and likely to be relevant to only a small proportion of listed companies. The summary to FRS 5 refers to quasi-subsidiaries as follows:

'Sometimes assets and liabilties are placed in an entity (a "vehicle") that is in effect controlled by the reporting entity but does meet the legal definition of a subsidiary. Where the commercial effect for the reporting entity is no different from that which would result were the vehicle a subsidiary, the vehicle will be a "quasi-subsidiary".' (FRS 5 summary para 1.)

Illustration 7

Extract from annual report and accounts of Lonrho plc for the year ended 30 September 1994.

Accounting policies (extract)

The objective of FRS 5 is to ensure that the commercial effect of transactions and any resulting assets, liabilities, gains and losses, are reported in the financial statements of the company concerned.

The Lonrho Group has a 19 per cent interest in Masterdrive Limited which is a vehicle leasing company. The remaining 81 per cent interest in the company is owned by Lombard North Central PLC, which provided the finance for the vehicles. It is considered that Masterdrive Limited is a quasi-subsidiary under the terms of FRS 5 and, therefore, the assets and liabilities of the company are consolidated in the 1994 accounts and the comparative figures have been adjusted accordingly. The effect on the balance sheet is to increase net borrowings by £39m in 1994 (1993 – £30m) and to increase fixed assets by £40m (1993 – £30m). There is no effect on profit before taxation or earnings per share in either 1993 or 1994.

Note 14 – Quasi-subsidiary

The Lonrho Group has a 19 per cent interest in Masterdrive Limited, a vehicle leasing company which is considered to be a quasi-subsidiary under the terms of FRS 5. The assets and liabilities of the company are consolidated in the 1994 accounts and the comparative figures restated accordingly.

The summary financial statements of Masterdrive Limited are:

	1994 £m	1993 £m
Profit and loss account		
Turnover	19	16
Operating profit	3	2
Net interest payable	(3)	(2)
Profit before taxation	–	–
Taxation	1	–
Profit for the year	1	–

There are no recognised gains or losses for the year other than the profits shown above.

Balance sheet		
Tangible assets	40	30
Debtors	3	3
Creditors: amounts falling due within one year		
Loans	(14)	(12)
Other	(3)	(3)
Creditors: amounts falling due after more than one year		
Loans	(25)	(18)
Shareholders' funds	1	–

Cash flow statement		
Net cash inflow from operating activities	13	12
Returns on investments and servicing of finance	(2)	(3)
Purchase of assets	(26)	(18)
Sale of assets	6	6
Net cash outflow before financing	(9)	(3)
Net cash inflow from financing	(9)	(3)

(b) Application Notes D and E

(i) Application Note D – securitised assets

Application Note D describes securitisation as a means by which providers of finance fund a specific block of assets rather than the general business of a company. The assets that have been most commonly securitised in the UK are household mortgages. Other receivables such as credit card balances, hire purchase loans and trade debts are sometimes securitised, as are non-monetary assets such as property and stocks.

The Application Notes apply to all kinds of assets. In view of its specialised application, no further reference is made here.

(ii) Application Note E – loan transfers

Application Note E deals with the transfer of interest-bearing loans to an entity other than a special purpose vehicle. Again, no further reference is made here.

(c) UITF 13 – Accounting for ESOP trusts

'ESOP' stands for employee share ownership plan. An ESOP trust is a trust set up by a sponsoring company to enable its employees to obtain shares in the company. The overall scheme is usually part of an employee's remuneration package – the trust may enable employees to exercise share options at a future date or to receive shares by way of gift following a specified period of service with the company.

An ESOP trust is a separate legal entity and can thus purchase shares in the sponsoring company – something which the sponsoring company is itself prohibited from doing.

UITF 13 requires the sponsoring company of an ESOP trust to recognise certain assets and liabilities of the trust on its own balance sheet whenever it has de facto control of the shares held by the ESOP trust and bears their benefits or risks.

Illustration 8

Extract from annual report and accounts of Silentnight Holdings plc for the year ended 31 January 1995 (pre-UITF 13).

Accounting policies (extract)

Employee share ownership plan (ESOP)
The assets and liabilities of Silentnight Share Scheme Trustee Limited (the Company's ESOP trust) are recognised as the assets and liabilities of Silentnight Holdings plc.

Note 12 (extracts)

12. Investments held as fixed assets

		Group		Company	
		1995	1994	1995	1994
		£000's	£000's	£000's	£000's
Interest in associated undertaking	(i)	403	597	–	–
Investment in subsidiary undertakings	(ii)	–	–	21,857	19,637
Investment in own shares	(iii)	3,329	–	3,329	–
		3,732	597	25,186	19,637

(iii) Investment in own shares
At the extraordinary general meeting held on 21 June 1994 it was resolved that the Silentnight Holdings plc Executive Share Option Scheme be adopted. Further to this resolution, Silentnight Share Scheme Trustee Limited was established and during the year it acquired 1,460,000 ordinary shares in the company, at an average cost of £2.28 per share. Options on all these shares have been granted to 21 senior executives, 4 of whom are directors of the company, at a price of £2.33. Options granted to directors of the company are disclosed in the Directors' Report. Options are generally exercisable only if the percentage growth in earnings per share of the company over a three year period is at least 6% greater than the percentage increase in inflation over the same period.

Silentnight Share Scheme Trustee Limited has waived the right to dividends (other than 0.01 pence per share) on the shares which it owns.

Under FRS 5 (Reporting the Substance of Transactions) and as recommended in the draft UITF abstract 'Accounting for ESOP Trusts', the assets and liabilities of an ESOP (employee share ownership plan) trust are required to be recognised as the assets and liabilities of the sponsoring company. The administration costs of the ESOP trust are charged to the profit and loss account as they accrue.

7.15   COMPREHENSIVE ILLUSTRATION

Extract from annual report and accounts of Gestetner Holdings plc for the year ended 31 December 1994.

Financial review (extract)

Off balance sheet finance
The requirements of FRS 5, Reporting the Substance of Transactions, impact the Group in three areas:

- sale of finance lease receivables
- cash offsetting and back to back arrangements
- factoring of receivables.

Sale of finance lease receivables
Where the Group retains a significant element of the risk/reward attaching to finance lease receivables sold on through various finance houses, the asset is retained on balance sheet in its entirety. Most commonly, this would be where the Group retains some of the bad debt risk. In previous years, to the extent that provision had not been made for this recourse liability, this had been disclosed in the Report & Accounts as a contingent liability (1993: £2.8m).

The effect of this accounting treatment is to gross up the Group's balance sheet (receivables and secured creditors) by £69m at 31 December 1994 (1993: £95m).

Cash offsetting and back to back arrangements
In instances where cross company cash pooling arrangements are in place with certain banks, or where bank lending is secured by cash deposits, the accounting treatment in previous years has been to net down cash balances against borrowings. Under FRS 5, unless the Group subsidiary as well as the bank has a legal right to offset these balances, netting down is not permitted.

This grossed up the Group's balance sheet (cash and borrowings) by £69m at 31 December 1994 (1993: £128m).

Factoring of receivables
Where the Group retains any bad debt risk under such arrangements, the asset is retained on the balance sheet in its entirety.

This grossed up the Group's balance sheet (debtors and borrowings) by £7m at 31 December 1994 (1993: £18m).

Accounting policies (extract)

Refinancing of finance lease and other receivables
Finance lease and other receivables are periodically sold to third party finance companies. Where all significant risks and rewards of ownership of such receivables are transferred to a third party, the receivables are treated as sold and removed from the balance sheet. However, where some of the risks and rewards of ownership are retained, the receivables are reclassified as secured assets offset by a secured liability. The majority of such sales relate to finance lease receivables and the liability is separately identified on the face of the balance sheet as customer lease financing (secured). The liability in respect of sales of other receivables is included within other creditors.

This represents a change of accounting policy with respect to those sales where some of the risks and rewards of ownership are retained, following the introduction of Financial Reporting Standard 5, Reporting the Substance of Transactions. In previous years, such receivables were treated as sold and removed from the balance sheet with a note included within contingencies of any limited recourse liability not provided against. The 1993 balance sheet has been restated.

Cash offsetting
The Group has various arrangements with its bankers whereby loans taken from a bank are offset by cash deposits placed with the same bank in such a manner that the bank has the legal ability to insist on a net settlement in all situations of default. In those situations where the Group has an equal legal ability to insist on a net settlement, the loan is reduced by the amount of the cash deposit. In all other circumstances, the cash deposit and the loan are disclosed separately within the respective balance sheet headings, secured against each other.

This represents a change of accounting policy following the introduction of Financial Reporting Standard 5, Reporting the Substance of Transactions. In previous years, all the cash deposits where a bank had the legal ability to insist on a net settlement were offset against the respective loans. The 1993 balance sheet has been restated.

Note 37

Restatement of the 1993 balance sheet following the introduction of Financial Reporting Standard 5, Reporting the Substance of Transactions

	Published 1993 £m	Finance lease receivables £m	Other receivables £m	Cash offsetting £m	Restated 1993 £m
Tangible assets	80.2	1.5	–	–	81.7
Investments	4.7	–	–	–	4.7
Stocks	212.3	–	–	–	212.3
Debtors	348.6	93.9	18.2	–	460.7
Cash at bank and in hand	79.6	–	(9.8)	128.1	197.9
Convertible loan stock	(37.9)	–	–	–	(37.9)
Loans and overdrafts	(170.6)	6.1	(13.0)	(128.1)	(305.6)
Customer lease financing (secured)	–	(102.3)	–	–	(102.3)
Other creditors	(280.2)	(0.7)	4.6	–	(276.3)
Provisions for liabilities and charges	(41.1)	1.1	–	–	(40.0)
	195.6	(0.4)	–	–	195.2

8 REPORTING FINANCIAL PERFORMANCE

```
Key Issues
* Background to FRS 3
* Exceptional items
  - usual cases
  - special cases
* Profit or loss on disposal of fixed assets
* Continuing and discontinued operations
* Statement of total recognised gains and losses
* Note of historical cost profits and losses
* Reconciliation of movements in shareholders' funds
* Reserve movements
* Reserves note
* Prior period adjustments
* Comparative figures
```

8.1 BACKGROUND TO FRS 3

Prior to the issue in 1974 of SSAP 6 (Extraordinary items and prior year adjustments) some companies adopted the practice referred to as 'reserve accounting'. An example of this was where items of an extraordinary nature, such as costs relating to discontinued activities, were dealt with through reserves as opposed to the profit and loss account. A principal aim of SSAP 6 was to limit reserve accounting to specified situations. Unfortunately SSAP 6 came in for widespread criticism during the late 1980s, due to the manipulation by some companies of the use of extraordinary items. The Accounting Standards Board soon came to the view that there was little point in making further changes to SSAP 6. SSAP 6 was subsequently replaced by FRS 3, Reporting Financial Performance.

8.2 OVERVIEW OF FRS 3

The key areas of FRS 3 include:

(1) Presentation in the profit and loss account:

    (i) items such as turnover, cost of sales, gross profit, operating expenses and operating profit are to be analysed between:

        (a) continuing operations (disclosing separately the effect of acquisitions during the year),
        (b) discontinuing operations;

    (ii) exceptional items, (apart from three specific categories (see section 8.4(b)) to be taken into account in arriving at operating profit.

(2) Presentation and measurement of profit on disposal of fixed assets – this is particularly important for companies who incorporate fixed asset revaluations into the accounts (see section 8.4(c)).

(3) Treatment of extraordinary items – FRS 3 effectively makes extraordinary items almost extinct.
(4) Additional statements and notes:

  (i) statement of total recognised gains and losses;
  (ii) note of historical cost profits and losses;
  (iii) reconciliation of movement in shareholders' funds.

8.3 CONTINUING AND DISCONTINUED OPERATIONS

FRS 3 sets out detailed criteria to be followed in deciding whether particular business disposals and terminations are to be regarded as 'discontinued'. The Standard also specifies the extent to which provisions can be set up in the balance sheet relating to the year prior to discontinuance.

This area of the Standard is particularly complex and will apply mostly to large quoted groups which are regularly involved in acquisitions, disposals and business closures. As this part of FRS 3 is concerned particularly with consolidated accounts, it is dealt with in chapter 25.

8.4 EXCEPTIONAL AND EXTRAORDINARY ITEMS

(a) Exceptional items – usual treatment

These are defined by FRS 3 as follows:

(1) Exceptional items: These are material items which derive from events or transactions that fall within the ordinary activities of the reporting entity and which individually or, if of a similar type, in aggregate, need to be disclosed by virtue of their size or incidence if the financial statements are to give a true and fair view.
(2) Ordinary activities: These are any activities which are undertaken by a reporting entity as part of its business and such related activities in which the reporting entity engages in furtherance of, incidental to, or arising from, these activities. Ordinary activities include the effects on the reporting entity of any event in the various environments in which it operates, including the political, regulatory, economic and geographical environments, irrespective of the frequency or unusual nature of the events.

  Apart from the three categories referred to in (b) below, exceptional items should be included under the relevant statutory heading such as cost of sales or distribution costs.

  Exceptional items will thus usually be taken into account in arriving at operating profit. The company must decide whether exceptional items are to be disclosed on the face of the profit and loss account or referred to by way of note. An example would be an abnormal loss on a long-term contract included under cost of sales.

Illustration 1

	1994 £	1993 £
Note 4		
Operating profit is arrived at after charging		
Depreciation		
Staff costs		
Exceptional items – continuing operations:		
reorganisation and related costs	166,000	–

Illustration 2

2 *Operating (loss)/profit*
Continuing

	£
Turnover	1,173,010
Cost of sales	(861,450)
Exceptional cost of sales	(15,700)
Gross profit	295,860
Distribution costs	(241,750)
Administrative costs	(125,430)
Exceptional administrative costs	(59,700)
Operating (loss)/profit	(131,020)

4 *Exceptional items*

(a) Within cost of sales – continuing operations	
– Additional stock provision	15,700
(b) Within administrative costs – continuing operations	
– Write-off of computer asset	59,700

Illustration 3

	£'000
Turnover – continuing operations	2,318
Cost of sales	1,852
Gross profit	466
Net operating expenses	(264)
Exceptional bad debt charge	(35)
Operating profit – continuing operations	167

(b) Exceptional items – the three special categories

Any exceptional items which fall within one of the three categories below must be shown below the figure of operating profit but before interest payable and receivable. The three special categories are:

(1) Profits or losses on the sale or termination of an operation. This could apply to the profit or loss on the sale of a subsidiary.
(2) Costs of a fundamental reorganisation or restructuring which have a material effect on the nature and focus of the reporting entity's operations.

(These two aspects are dealt with in chapter 25.)

(3) Profits or losses on the disposal of fixed assets. This item does not include profits and losses which are little more than marginal adjustments to depreciation previously charged.

Illustration 4

	£'000
Non-operating items:	
Continuing operations:	
Loss on fixed asset disposal	310
Reorganisation expenses	86
Discontinued operations:	
Loss on withdrawal from businesses	185
	581

A further illustration is provided at the end of this chapter.

(c) Profit or loss on disposal of fixed assets

The profit or loss on disposal of a fixed asset should be recognised in the accounts of the period in which the disposal takes place. The profit or loss should be calculated by comparing:

(i) the net sales proceeds, and
(ii) the net carrying amount.

The net carrying amount will be based on either:

(i) historical cost, less any provision, less depreciation (historical cost accounting rules), or
(ii) valuation less depreciation (alternative accounting rules).

Illustration 5

A company acquired an asset in 19X2 at a cost of £120,000. The asset was revalued in 19X6 at £250,000 the surplus of £130,000 being transferred to revaluation reserve.

The asset was sold in 19X8 for proceeds of £400,000. Ignore depreciation.

Under FRS 3 the profit on sale included in the profit and loss account is £150,000 (£400,000 − £250,000). Any amount previously held in revaluation reserve (£130,000) now becomes realised and is accounted for by making a transfer within reserves of £130,000. The £130,000 has no effect on the reported profit for the year but does form part of the cumulative realised profit in the balance sheet and is thus available as distributable profit.

(d) Extraordinary items

FRS 3 defines extraordinary items as follows:

> Extraordinary items:
>
> Material items possessing a high degree of abnormality which arise from events or transactions that fall outside the ordinary activities of the reporting entity and which are not expected to recur. They do not include exceptional items nor do they include prior period items merely because they relate to a prior period.

Paragraph 48 of the explanation section to FRS 3 makes the following comment: '... in view of the extreme rarity of such items no examples are provided...' Even if a loss falls within the revised definition of extraordinary items it will come within the revised definition of earnings per share (see section 30.2).

8.5 STATEMENT OF TOTAL RECOGNISED GAINS AND LOSSES

FRS 3 requires a statement of total gains and losses to be included as a primary statement. The statement should be given the same prominence as the balance sheet, the profit and loss account and the cash flow statement.

In the illustration in (c) above, the surplus on revaluation during 19X6 amounted to £130,000. This would be included in the statement of total recognised gains and losses. Assuming the profit and loss account showed profit for the financial years of £253,427 and £313,562 respectively, the statement would appear as follows:

Illustration 6

Statement of total recognised gains and losses

	19X6 £	19X5 £
Profit for the financial year	253,427	313,562
Unrealised surplus on revaluation of property	130,000	–
Total gains and losses relating to the year	383,427	313,562

Many smaller companies do not incorporate fixed asset revaluations into their accounts. A statement of total recognised gains and losses will not be required provided the company includes a note at the bottom of the profit and loss account.

Illustration 7

The company has no recognised gains or losses other than the profit (loss) for the period.

A final point – gains recognised in previous periods (eg revaluation surpluses) and which are realised this year should not be included in the current year statement of total recognised gains and losses.

8.6   NOTE OF HISTORICAL COST PROFITS AND LOSSES

This note, required by FRS 3, provides a reconciliation between:

(1) Reported profit before tax (where, say, depreciation charges are based on revalued amounts); and
(2) Profits measured on the basis of unmodified (ie pure) historical cost.

The note is effectively an abbreviated restatement of the profit and loss account on the basis that no asset revaluation has been made. Its aim is to put companies that have revalued assets on a more comparable basis with those who have not.

A key consideration here is the impact of incorporating fixed asset revaluations into the accounts. This practice, sometimes referred to as modified historical cost, can have two important effects:

(1) On disposal of a revalued asset – considered above.
(2) On the depreciation charge – where revaluations are incorporated into the accounts, SSAP 12 requires the depreciation charge to be based upon the revalued amount (see section 12.7(d)).

The note required by FRS 3 should include two pieces of information:

(1) a reconciliation of the reported profit on ordinary activities before tax to the equivalent historical cost amount; and
(2) the retained profit for the financial year reported on a historical costs basis.

Illustration 8

Note of historical costs profits and losses

	19X8 £	19X7 £
Reported profit on ordinary activities before taxation	454,217	396,543
Realisation of property revaluation gains of previous years	130,000	–
Difference between a historical cost depreciation charge and the actual depreciation charge of the year calculated on the revalued amount	2,000	–
Historical cost profit on ordinary activities before taxation	586,217	396,543
Historical cost profit for the year retained after taxation, minority interests, extraordinary items and dividends	196,250	177,130

This note is not required if the difference between the two profit before tax figures is not material.

8.7 RECONCILIATION OF MOVEMENTS IN SHAREHOLDERS' FUNDS

A note is required reconciling the opening and closing totals of shareholders' funds. Using the figures in section 8.5 for 19X6 and 19X5, and assuming:

(1) dividends of £90,000 and £80,000;
(2) purchase of shares during 19X6 of £50,000;
(3) shareholders' funds at 1.1.X5 of £627,201;

the statement could appear as follows:

Illustration 9

Reconciliation of movements in shareholders' funds

	19X6 £	19X5 £
Profit for the financial year	253,427	313,562
Dividends	(90,000)	(80,000)
	163,427	233,562
Other recognised gains and losses	130,000	–
Purchase of shares during the year	(50,000)	
Net addition to shareholders' funds	243,427	233,562
Shareholders' funds at 1 January	860,763	627,201
Shareholders' funds at 31 December	1,104,190	860,763

In straightforward cases, e g where the only movement on shareholders' funds related to retained profit (loss), a separate statement may not be necessary.

8.8 RESERVE MOVEMENTS

FRS 3 states that '. . . Gains and losses may be excluded from the profit and loss account only if they are specifically permitted or required to be taken directly to reserves by this or other accounting standards, or, in the absence of a relevant accounting standard, by law'.
Examples that would fall within the above statement include:

(1) FRS 3:

(i)   surplus and deficits on fixed assets revaluations; or
(ii) realisation of property revaluation gains of previous years;
(iii) the difference between historical cost depreciation charge and the actual depreciation charge of the year calculated on the revalued amount.

(2) SSAP 20 – certain exchange differences required to be taken direct to reserves.
(3) SSAP 19 – changes in value of investment properties.
(4) SSAP 22 – immediate write-off of goodwill against reserves (required where the write-off option is selected).
(5) Amounts required by law to be charged direct to share premium account:

(i)   preliminary expenses;
(ii) commission on issue of shares or debentures and discount on issue of debentures;
(iii) premium on redemption of shares or debentures (if permitted by the Companies Act 1985);
(iv) purchase by company of own shares (other than out of proceeds or new issue of shares).

8.9   RESERVES NOTE

This is not an additional requirement of FRS 3 – it is the usual statutory note which shows the movement on each category of reserves.

Illustration 10

Reserves note

	Share premium account £	Revalu- ation reserve £	Profit & loss account £	Total £
At 1 July 19X3	150,000	296,000	532,000	978,000
Transfer from profit and loss account	–	–	297,550	297,550
Transfer of realised profits – disposal of assets	–	(80,000)	80,000	–
– depreciation	–	(2,000)	2,000	–
Surplus on property revaluations	–	115,000	–	115,000
At 30 June 19X4	150,000	329,000	911,550	1,390,550

Explanatory notes:
(1) The £80,000 relates to a revaluation surplus, first created several years ago, and realised in the current year on the sale of the asset. The £80,000 now forms part of the company's distributable profits.
(2) The £115,000 relates to a revaluation surplus created this year. The amount would also appear in this year's statement of total recognised gains and losses.
(3) The depreciation adjustment of £2,000 represents the difference between the depreciation charges based on revaluation and historical cost respectively.

8.10   PRIOR PERIOD ADJUSTMENTS

(a) Definition

Prior period adjustments are material adjustments applicable to prior periods arising from changes in accounting policies or from the correction of fundamental errors. They do not include normal recurring adjustments or corrections of accounting estimates made in prior periods.

(b) Accounting treatment

FRS 3 requires prior period adjustments to be accounted for by:

restating the comparative figures for the preceding period in the primary statements (i e balance sheet, profit and loss account, statement of total recognised gains and losses), and adjusting the opening balance of reserves for the cumulative effect.

The cumulative effect of the adjustments should also be noted at the foot of the statement of total recognised gains and losses of the current period.
The effect of prior period adjustments on the results for the preceding period should be disclosed where practicable.

Illustration 11

The example below relates to a change in the accounting treatment of expenditure on major software and developments projects. In previous years such expenditure was capitalised and amortised over ten years. The new policy is to write off such expenditure as it is incurred. This policy is to be first adopted in the accounts for the year ended 30 June 1995.

The calculations and relevant disclosures are set out below – please note that for simplicity, taxation has been ignored.

(i) Relevant information

The movement on intangible fixed assets under the old policy was as follows:

	£
1 July 1993 b/f	22,000
Expenditure	13,000
Charge to p/l	(8,600)
1 July 1994	26,400

Expenditure for the year ended 30 June 1995 amounted to £15,000. Had the old policy been continued in 1995, the charge to p/l would have amounted to £7,200 compared with a charge under the new policy of £15,000 i e an increase of £7,800.

Assume that the previously reported shareholders funds at 30 June 1994 were made up as follows:

	£
Ordinary share capital	50,000
Profit and loss reserves	120,400
	170,400

(ii) Prior year adjustment

Had the new policy been in operation last year, the intangible fixed assets shown at £26,400 at 30 June 1994 would not have been capitalised.

The prior year adjustment at 1 July 1994 to therefore £26,400.

The effect of adopting the new policy is to reduce shareholders funds at 1 July 1994 by £26,400 i e to £144,000.

(iii) Relevant disclosures

The relevant disclosures required, so far as information permits, are as follows:

Statement of recognised gains and losses

	1995 £	Restated 1994 £
Profit for the financial year	x	x
Total recognised gains and losses relating to the year	x	x
Prior year adjustment	(26,400)	
Total gains and losses recognised since last annual report	xx	

Reconciliation of movements in shareholders' funds

	1995 £	Restated 1994 £
Profit for the financial year	x	x
Dividends	(x)	(x)
Net addition to shareholders' funds	x	x
Opening shareholders' funds (originally £170,400 before deducting prior year adjustment of £26,400)	144,000	x
Closing shareholders' funds	xx	xx

Reserves note

	Profit and loss account £
At 1 July 1994	
– as previously reported	120,400
Prior year adjustment	26,400
– as restated	94,000
Retained profit for the year	x
At 30 June 1995	xx

Accounting policy note (extract)
Change of accounting policy

In prior years, the Group has capitalised expenditure on major software and development projects where it believed that a sustainable value had been created. However, in line with current prevailing accounting practice it is now felt that a more appropriate policy is to write off all such expenditure as incurred. Prior years' figures have been restated to bring them into line with this policy. The effect is to reduce shareholders' funds as at 30 June 1994 by £26,400 and to reduce operating and pre-tax profits for 1995 by £7,800 (1994, £4,400).

(See also chapter 9, section 9.7.)

8.11   COMPARATIVE FIGURES

The general requirement is for comparative figures to be given for all items in the primary statements and notes specifically required by FRS 3. This therefore extends to: the statement of total recognised gains and losses; the note of historical cost profits and loss; and the reconciliation of movements in shareholders' funds.

For the first year for which a company adopts FRS 3, comparative amounts for the previous year may need to be restated (in respect of profit and loss accounts items) or be provided (in the case of new statements or notes, such as the statement of total recognised gains and losses).

8.12   ILLUSTRATION – SMALL COMPANY

The accounts extracts below are based on a small company which has incorporated fixed asset revaluations into its account and which has followed FRS 3:

PROFIT AND LOSS ACCOUNT
for the year ended 31 December 19X6

	19X6 £	19X6 £	19X5 £	19X5 £
Turnover		896,743		763,257
Cost of sales		302,195		269,042
Gross profit		594,548		494,215
Distribution costs	73,050		67,100	
Administrative expenses	105,216		103,050	
		178,266		170,150
Operating profit		416,282		324,065
Profit on sale of property		65,000		–
Profit on ordinary activities before interest		481,282		324,065
Interest receivable		8,964		2,510
		490,246		326,575
Interest payable and similar charges		11,063		8,055
Profit on ordinary activities before tax		479,183		318,520
Tax on profit on ordinary activities		95,130		82,120
Profit for the financial year		384,053		236,400
Dividends		70,000		50,000
Retained profit for the financial year		314,053		186,400

STATEMENT OF TOTAL RECOGNISED GAINS AND LOSSES

	19X6 £	19X5 £
Profit for the financial year	384,053	236,400
Unrealised surplus on revaluation of properties	22,500	50,000
Total recognised gains and losses relating to the year	406,553	286,400

NOTE OF HISTORICAL COST PROFITS AND LOSSES

	19X6 £	19X5 £
Reported profit on ordinary activities before taxation	479,183	318,520
Realistion of property revaluation gains of previous year	41,000	–
Difference between historical cost depreciation charge and the actual depreciation charge of the year calculated on the revalued amount	3,500	3,200
Historical cost profit on ordinary activities before taxation	523,683	321,720

	19X6 £	19X5 £
Historical cost profit for the year retained after taxation and dividends	358,553	189,600

RECONCILIATION OF MOVEMENTS IN SHAREHOLDERS' FUNDS

	19X6 *£*	*19X5* *£*
Profit for the financial year	384,053	236,400
Dividends	70,000	50,000
	314,053	186,400
Other recognised gains and losses relating to the year	22,500	50,000
Net addition to shareholders' funds	336,553	236,400
Shareholders' funds at 1 January	1,641,032	1,404,632
Shareholders' funds at 31 December	1,977,585	1,641,032

RESERVES

	Share premium account *£*	*Revaluation reserve* *£*	*Profit and loss account* *£*	*Total* *£*
At 1 January 19X6	100,000	143,500	897,532	1,141,032
Transfer from profit and loss account of the year	–	–	314,053	314,053
Transfer of realised profits	–	(44,500)	44,500	–
Surplus on property revaluation	–	22,500	–	22,500
At 31 December 19X6	100,000	121,500	1,256,085	1,477,585

Working: Transfer of realised profits

$$(£3,500 + £41,000) = £44,500$$

Further illustrations including the effect of acquisitions, discontinued operations and exceptional items are included in chapter 25.

9 THE URGENT ISSUES TASK FORCE (UITF)

Key Issues

* Status of UITF Abstracts
* Abstracts issued to date
* UITF 4, long-term debtors
* UITF 5, transfers from current assets to fixed assets
* UITF 7, true and fair override
* UITF 12, reverse premiums
* UITF 14, disclosure of changes in accounting policy

9.1 INTRODUCTION

The UITF is a committee of the ASB. Its main role is to assist the ASB in areas where an accounting standard or a Companies Act provision exists but where unsatisfactory or conflicting interpretations have developed or seem likely to develop. The UITF has the task of providing interpretations of accounting standards and legal requirments in relation to newly emerging issues.

Consensus pronouncements (or Abstracts) should be regarded as part of the corpus of practices forming the basis for determining what constitutes a true and fair view.

Consensus pronouncements may be taken into account by the Financial Reporting Review Panel in deciding whether to call financial statements for review.

9.2 ABSTRACTS ISSUED TO DATE

The following had been issued as at 31 March 1996:

UITF 3   Goodwill on disposal of a business.
UITF 4   Presentation of long-term debtors in current assets.
UITF 5   Transfers from current assets to fixed assets.
UITF 6   Post-retirement benefits other than pensions.
UITF 7   Disclosure of the use of the true and fair override in company accounts.
UITF 9   Accounting for operations in hyper-inflationary economies.
UITF 10 Disclosure of directors' share options.
UITF 11 Accounting for issuer call options.
UITF 12 Lessee accounting for reverse premiums.
UITF 13 Accounting for ESOP trusts.
UITF 14 Disclosure of changes in accounting policy.
UITF 15 Disclosure of substantial acquisitions.

Certain of the above Abstracts are referred to in other chapters, for example:

UITF 3   Chapter 25, section 25.8
UITF 4   Chapter 14, section 14.4
UITF 13 Chapter 7, section 7.14
UITF 6   Chapter 20, section 20.22
UITF 10 Chapter 11, section 11.6
UITF 7   Chapter 5, section 5.7

Of the remaining Abstracts those of wider practical application are referred to below.

9.3   UITF 4 – PRESENTATION OF LONG-TERM DEBTORS

(a) Limitations of Companies Act 1985 disclosures

For debtors, the Companies Act 1985 requires separate disclosure of amounts falling due after more than one year. Unlike creditors, however, this split does not show up on the face of the balance sheet. In the balance sheet formats the sub-total of net current assets may thus include an element of non-current debtors.

(b) UITF 4

In most cases the Consensus accepts that it will be satisfactory to disclose the size of debtors due after more than one year by way of note.

The Consensus is particularly concerned with instances where the amount of the non-current debtor(s) is so material in relation to net current assets that its amount should be separately disclosed on the face of the balance sheet.

Examples of significant long-term debtors could include:

(1) a pension fund surplus;
(2) part of the trade debtors of lessors (i e finance receivable);
(3) deferred consideration receivable relating to fixed assets investment sales.

(c) Acceptable disclosure methods

(1) Analysis of debtors on the face of the balance sheet:

BALANCE SHEET EXTRACT

Current assets	£
Stocks	186,000
Debtors	
– due within one year	112,530
– due in more than one year	42,500
Bank balances and cash	7,600
	348,630

(2) Disclosure related to the net current assets/liabilities figure:

BALANCE SHEET EXTRACT

Current assets	£
Stock	186,000
Debtors	155,030
Bank balances and cash	7,600
	348,630
Creditors: amounts falling due within one year	195,780
Net current assets (including amounts falling due after more than one year of £42,500 (1992 – £X)	152,850

Further illustrations are included in section 14.4 of chapter 14.

9.4 UITF 5 – TRANSFERS FROM CURRENT ASSETS TO FIXED ASSETS

(a) Introduction

An asset, e g a trading property, may start off on acquisition as a current asset. Management may subsequently decide to retain the property as an investment property, held on a continuing basis as a fixed asset.

In these circumstances the UITF is concerned that the property might be transferred from current to fixed assets at book value, without regard to its value at the date of transfer. Management might then write-down the property by means of a debit to revaluation reserve, thus avoiding a charge to the profit and loss account.

(b) UITF 5

To avoid the above, UITF 5 lays down certain ground rules:

(1) the effective date of transfer is the date of management's change of intent – this date should not be backdated;
(2) the current asset accounting rules (i e lower of cost and net realisable value) should be applied up to this date;
(3) the asset should be transferred at the lower of cost and net realisable value – if NRV is below cost, the diminution in value should be charged to the profit and loss account;
(4) subject to (3), the fixed asset will be held at either:

   (i) cost (under the historical cost accounting rules in CA 1985), or
   (ii) valuation (under the alternative accounting rules in CA 1985).

9.5 UITF 7 – TRUE AND FAIR OVERRIDE

(a) Background

The purpose of UITF 7 is to give guidance on the interpretation of the statutory requirement to give particulars of any departure from the Companies Act accounting provisions made in order to give a true and fair view, together with the reasons for any such departure and its effect.

The UITF had regarded this as an area where disclosure by companies was often varied and inadequate.

(b) True and fair override

The UITF refers to the override as follows:

> The Companies Act 1985, as amended ('the Act') provides, both for individual company accounts and for group accounts, that if in special circumstances compliance with any of the provisions of the Act as to the matters to be included in a company's accounts (or notes thereto) is inconsistent with the requirement to give a true and fair view of the state of affairs and profit or loss, the directors shall depart from that provision to the extent necessary to give a true and fair view. Where this true and fair view override is used the Act requires that 'particulars of any such departure, the reasons for it and its effect shall be given in a note to the accounts.' The Act gives no further elaboration of this requirement.

The UITF interprets the above disclosure requirements as follows:

(1) 'Particulars of any such departure' – a statement of the treatment which the Act would normally require in the circumstances and a description of the treatment actually adopted;
(2) 'the reasons for it' – a statement as to why the treatment prescribed would not give a true and fair view;

(3) 'its effect' – a description of how the position shown in the accounts is different as a result of the departure, normally with quantification, except (i) where quantification is already evident in the accounts themselves (an example of which might be a presentation rather than a measurement matter, such as an adaption of the headings in the Act's format requirements not covered by paragraph 3(3) of schedule 4), or (ii) whenever the effect cannot reasonably be quantified, in which case the directors should explain the circumstances.

(c) Where should the disclosure be given?

The UITF requires the necessary disclosures to be given in one of two ways:

(1) in the note required by the Companies Act 1985 referring to compliance with accounting standards and particulars of any material departure; or
(2) a cross-reference to the note required by (1).

Illustration 1 – Extracts from annual reports and accounts

(a) The Boots Company plc for the year ended 31 March 1995

Extract from note 12

In accordance with SSAP 19, no depreciation is provided in respect of investment properties. This represents a departure from the Companies Act 1985 requirements to provide for the systematic annual depreciation of fixed assets. However, these properties are held for investment, rather than consumption, and the directors consider that the adoption of the above policy is necessary to give a true and fair view.

(b) Wessex Water plc for the year ended 31 March 1994

Extract from statement of accounting policies

Grants and contributions
Grants and contributions in respect of specific expenditure on non-infrastructure fixed assets are treated as deferred income and recognised in the profit and loss account over the expected useful economic lives of the related assets.

  Grants and contributions relating to infrastructure assets have been deducted from the cost of those assets. This is not in accordance with the Companies Act 1985 which requires assets to be stated at their purchase price or production cost. The departure from the requirements of the Act is, in the opinion of the directors, necessary to give a true and fair view. This is because infrastructure assets are not depreciated and the grants and contributions would not be recognised in the profit and loss account.

(c) Norcos plc for the year ended 31 March 1994

(i) Extract from balance sheet

		Group	
		1994	1993
	note	£'000	£'000
Fixed assets			
Tangible assets	11	113,209	111,587
Investments	12	16,689	14,291
Properties for disposal	13	25,660	44,983
		155,558	170,861
Long term debtors			
Pension fund prepayment	23	41,864	39,242
Current assets			
Stocks	14	58,810	51,577
Debtors	15	84,971	81,073
Cash at bank and in hand		8,004	1,786
		151,785	134,436

(ii) Extract from note 15 (Debtors)

The pension fund prepayments have been presented separately on the face of the company and Group balance sheets rather than included as part of current assets. In the opinion of the directors, this departure from the format of Schedule 4 of the Companies Act 1985 is required to give a true and fair view of the state of affairs of the company and Group at 31 March 1994, since to present the pension fund prepayment as part of current assets would not fairly reflect the true liquidity position of the company and Group. If the formats included in Schedule 4 of the Companies Act 1985 were adopted the pension fund prepayment would be included as part of current assets resulting in an increase in Group net current assets to £93,918,000 (1993 – £77,283,000) and the net current assets of Norcros plc to £71,567,000 (1993 – £71,985,000).

9.6   UITF 12 – LESSEE ACCOUNTING FOR REVERSE PREMIUMS AND SIMILAR INCENTIVES

(a) Aim

This abstract deals with the accounting treatment for incentives offered to a lessee to sign up an operating lease.

(b) Example

Examples of such incentives include:

(i)   an up-front cash payment to the lessee (a reverse premium);
(ii) a rent-free period;
(iii) a contribution to lessee costs such as fitting out or relocation.

(c) Accounting treatment

UITF 12 requires that, irrespective of the form the benefit takes, benefits received and receivable by a lessee as an incentive to sign the lease should be spread by the lessee on a straight-line basis over the shorter of:

(i)   the lease term; and
(ii) the period from the start of the lease up to the review date on which the
       rent is first expected to be adjusted to the prevailing market rate.
(See also section 18.6.)

Illustration 2

Lessor Ltd is negotiating a 20 year lease with Lessee Ltd. The rent is subject to review at the end of years 5, 10 and 15.
  An appropriate market rental for years 1 to 5 would normally be £200,000 per annum. However Lessor Ltd is prepared to accept a total rental for that period of £900,000. The 'discount' of £100,000 could be presented in various forms:

(a) a reverse premium of £100,000;
(b) a contribution to fitting out costs of £100,000;
(c) a rent-free period for the first six months.

Whatever form the incentive takes, the annual charge for years 1 to 5 should amount to £180,000. This assumes that the rent review mechanism adjusts the rental to the prevailing market rate.

Accounting policy note – reverse premiums

Reverse premiums are treated as deferred income and released to the profit and loss account over the period up to the first rent review of the lease concerned.

Illustration 3

Extract from annual report and accounts of The Boots Company plc for the year ended 31 March 1995.

a Change in accounting policy

The group has implemented the provisions of Urgent Issues Task Force Abstract No. 12 'Lessee accounting for reverse premiums and similar incentives' (UITF 12). This requires all benefits received by a lessee as an incentive to sign a lease, whatever form they may take, to be credited to the profit and loss account on a straight line basis over the lease term or, if shorter than the full lease term, over the period to the review date on which the rent is first adjusted to the prevailing market rate. Previously, cash incentives were either credited directly to the profit and loss account or to tangible fixed assets and released to the profit and loss account through a reduction in the depreciation charge, depending on the size and nature of the incentive received. The benefits of rent free periods were taken as they arose.

All benefits received since 1 April 1988 have been restated in accordance with UITF 12 and comparative figures have been restated accordingly. The impact on the results for the year to 31 March 1994 is shown below. The effect on the balance sheet at 31 March 1994 is to increase tangible fixed assets by £10.7m, debtors by £.4m and creditors by £11.1m with no net amount on reserves.

9.7   UITF 14 – DISCLOSURE OF CHANGES IN ACCOUNTING POLICY

FRS 3 requires disclosure of the effect on the results for the preceding period following a change in accounting policy. UITF 14 additionally requires disclosure of:

(a) indication of effect on current year's results; or
(b) where appropriate, a statement that the effect on the current year is
   (i)   immaterial, or
   (ii) similar to quantified effect on prior year; or
(c) where appropriate, a statement that is not practicable to give effect on current year, together with reasons.

The Abstract does not discuss the reasons for a change in accounting policy. This important aspect is covered in the UITF's Information Sheet No. 15, issued at the same time as the Abstract. This makes the key point that '. . . directors of companies contemplating a possible change of policy should ensure that the reasons for any change are compelling'.

10 SPECIAL CONSIDERATIONS FOR SMALLER COMPANIES

Key Issues

* Principal reporting requirements
* The importance of classification as 'small' or 'medium-sized'
* Statutory definitions
* Transitional provisions
* Implications of changing size
* Shorter-form of accounts for shareholders – the SI 2452 option
* Abbreviated accounts
* Concessions offered by particular accounting standards
* Legal considerations
* Small/medium-sized parent companies

10.1 REPORTING REQUIREMENTS – AN OVERVIEW

(a) Companies Act 1985 (CA 1985)

In principle, CA 1985 accounting requirements apply equally to small and large companies. However, several important concessions are available for smaller companies and groups, for example:

(1) Small companies may present shareholders with a shorter form of accounts in accordance with statutory instrument SI 2452 (see section 10.3).

(2) Small and medium-sized companies may file abbreviated accounts with the Registrar of Companies (see section 10.4).

(3) Small and medium-sized groups may claim exemption from the preparation of group accounts (see chapter 24).

(4) Most companies with a turnover of under £350,000 are entitled to exemption from statutory audit. This is outside the scope of this book and not referred to further.

(b) Accounting Standards and Consensuses

General requirements of Accounting Standards and UITF Consensuses or Abstracts apply equally to smaller companies. However, certain concessions and exemptions are available. These are referred to in section 10.5.

10.2 STATUTORY DEFINITIONS

(a) Importance of classification as 'small' or 'medium-sized'

(1) Small companies may present shareholders with shorter-form accounts in accordance with SI 2452 (see section 10.3).
(2) Small and medium-sized companies may file abbreviated accounts with the Registrar of Companies (see section 10.4).
(3) Small and medium-sized groups may claim exemption from the preparation of group accounts (see section 24.11).
(4) Small companies may claim exemption from the preparation of cash flow statements under FRS 1 (see section 31.1).
(5) Small and medium-sized companies are not required to disclose fees paid to their auditors for work other than audit work.
(6) Exemptions from segmental reporting disclosures under SSAP 25 are linked to a multiple of the medium-sized limits (see section 32.4).

(b) Small company

A company is regarded as 'small' for CA 1985 purposes provided it satisfies two sets of requirements:

(1) Two out of three of:

    (i) turnover £2.8m
    (if the company's financial year is other than 12 months, the above limit must be adjusted proportionately);
    (ii) total assets £1.4m
    (total assets means fixed assets plus current assets without deducting any liabilities);
    (iii) Number of employees 50.

(2) Legal status: whatever its size, a company cannot be regarded as small for these purposes if it falls within one of the following categories:
    (i) public company;
    (ii) banking, insurance or financial services company (the Act refers to an authorised person under the Financial Services Act 1986);
    (iii) a member of a group which includes a public company or a banking, insurance or financial services company.

Illustration 1

A Ltd is a small private company, part of the following group structure:

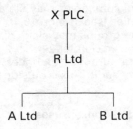

A Ltd is a member of an ineligible group (which includes X plc). A Ltd is not regarded as a 'small' company for CA 1985 purposes.

(c) Medium-sized company

The respective limits for size are:

(i)   turnover £11.2m (previously £8m);
(ii) total assets £5.6m (previously £3.9m);
(iii) number of employees 250.

The same considerations for legal status apply as for small companies.

(d) Implications of changing size

Similar rules apply for both small and medium-sized companies. For clarity of explanation the notes below refer to small companies. The illustrative examples below, however, show the effect of changing size on the filing status of small and medium-sized companies.

A newly-incorporated company will qualify as small in its first year provided it meets the relevant criteria in that year. It will still qualify as small in year 2 even if it does not meet the size criteria in year 2.

An established company may qualify as small for abbreviated company accounts exemptions in one of four ways:

(a) small company size requirements satisfied this year and last year; or
(b) although small company size requirements not satisfied this year, they were satisfied in the two previous years (the one year of grace rule); or
(c) small company size requirements satisfied this year but not last year (however treated small last year for filing purposes on the basis of paragraph (b)); or
(d) small company size requirements satisfied last year but not this year (however, last year qualified as small as under paragraph (c).

Illustration 2 – long established company

S refers to small company size.

	(a)	(b)	(c)	(d)
1991	S	S	S	S
1992	S	S	S	S
1993	Not S	S	S	Not S
1994	S	S	Not S	S
1995	S	Not S	S	Not S

The four columns refer to the four ways referred to above. In all cases, the company qualifies as small for 1995.

10.3 SHORTER FORM OF ACCOUNTS FOR SHAREHOLDERS (SI 2452)

(a) Background

Statutory Instrument, SI 2452, dealing with accounts of small and medium-sized companies offers an opportunity for small (but not medium-sized) companies and groups – directors may opt to circulate to shareholders a shorter form of directors' report and accounts. This exemption is quite distinct from the facility to file abbreviated accounts with the Registrar of Companies (see section 10.4).

(b) Minimum information required

For companies wishing to take maximum advantage of the concessions offered by SI 2452, the following is the minimum information which may be presented to shareholders:

(1) a shorter form of directors' report;
(2) a less detailed balance sheet;
(3) fewer notes to the accounts.

The concessions are dealt with below. Individual companies may take advantage of as many or as few of these concessions as they choose.

(c) Special considerations for directors and auditors

Where a company takes advantage of any or all of the exemptions above:

(1) The directors should make a statement immediately above the signature on the balance sheet, to the effect that in preparing the accounts, the directors have taken advantage of the special exemptions applicable to small companies on the grounds that the company is small.
(2) The directors should also make a similar statement, above the signature on the directors report, to the effect that in preparing the directors' report the directors have taken advantage of the special exemptions applicable to small companies on the grounds that the company is small.
(3) The audit report must state whether, in the opinion of the auditors, the annual accounts have been properly prepared in accordance with the provisions of the Companies Act 1985 applicable to small companies.

(d) Directors' report concessions

SI 2452 provides that certain discosures, otherwise required in full form directors' reports may be excluded in cases where a company has properly indicated that it has taken advantage of the exemptions.

The directors' report of a small company need not give any of the following information (references are to sections of CA 1985 or paragraphs of CA 1985, Sch 7):

(1) a fair review of the development of the business (s 234(a));
(2) recommended dividend and transfer to reserves (s 234(b));
(3) significant changes in fixed assets (para 1(1));
(4) for property assets, any substantial differences between market value and amount at which included in balance sheet (para 1(21));
(5) insurance effected for officers or auditors (para 5(a));
(6) miscellaneous disclosures:

    (i)   particulars of important post-balance sheet events (para 6(a)),
    (ii) indication of likely future developments in the business (para 6(b)),
    (iii) indication of research and development activities (para 6(c));

Two other areas of disclosure would not be applicable to small companies in any event:

(1) health, safety and welfare at work disclosures (para 10);
(2) employee involvement disclosures (para 11).

(e) The shorter form balance sheet

If a small company decides to take advantage of the exemptions, it may combine certain sub-headings which would otherwise be shown separately either on the face of the balance sheet or in the notes to the accounts.

The minimum sub-headings permitted by SI 2452 are as follows:

ILLUSTRATION – SHORTER FORM BALANCE SHEET

Format 1

A   Called up share capital not paid

B   Fixed assets
 I Intangible assets
  1 Goodwill
  2 Other intangible assets
 II Tangible assets
  1 Land and buildings
  2 Plant and machinery etc
 III Investments
  1 Shares in group undertakings and participating interests
  2 Loans to group undertakings and undertakings in which the company has a participating interest
  3 Other investments other than loans
  4 Others

C   Current assets
 I Stocks
  1 Stocks
  2 Payments on account
 II Debtors
  1 Trade debtors
  2 Amounts owed by group undertakings in which the company has a participating interest
  3 Others
 III Investments
  1 Shares in group undertakings
  2 Other investments
 IV Cash at bank and in hand

D   Prepayments and accrued income

E   Creditors: amounts falling due within one year
  1 Bank loans and overdrafts
  2 Trade creditors
  3 Amounts owed to group undertakings and undertakings in which the company has a participating interest
  4 Other creditors

F   Net current assets (liabilities)

G   Total assets less current liabilities

H   Creditors: amounts falling due after more than one year
  1 Bank loans and overdrafts
  2 Trade creditors
  3 Amounts owed to group undertakings and undertakings in which the company has a participating interest
  4 Other creditors

I   Provisions for liabilities and charges

J   Accruals and deferred income

K   Capital and reserves
 I Called-up share capital
 II Share premium account
 III Revaluation reserve
 IV Other reserves
 V Profit and loss account

(f) Combined sub-headings

Examples of sub-headings which may be combined include:

(1) 'Plant and machinery', 'fixtures, fittings, tools and equipment' and 'payments on accounts and assets in course of construction' may be combined under a single heading: 'Plant and machinery etc'.
(2) Regarding creditors: amounts falling due within one year: 'debenture loans', 'payments received on account', 'bills of exchange payable', 'other creditors including taxation and social security', 'accruals and deferred income' may be combined under a single heading: 'other creditors'.

(g) Notes to the accounts

A small company may take advantage of the special exemptions and omit the following information from the notes to the accounts. The paragraph references in brackets refer to Sch 4 of CA 1985:

(1) contingent right to allotment of shares (para 40);
(2) particulars of debentures issued during the year (para 41);
(3) the analysis of land and buildings between freehold/leasehold and long lease/short lease (para 44);
(4) separate disclosure of the provision for deferred tax from the provision for any other taxation (para 47);
(5) where the company has given a security in respect of creditors of the company, an indication of the nature of the securities given (para 48(4)(b)) (note that it will still be necessary to disclose the aggregate amount of the creditors for which security has been given);
(6) loans payable in more than five years – the terms of the repayment and the interest on the loan (para 48(2));
(7) aggregate of proposed dividends (para 51(3));
(8) separate statement of certain items of income and expenditure (para 53):

   (i)   analysis of interest charges (para 53(2)),
   (ii) income from listed investments (para 53(4)),
   (iii) rents from land (para 53(5)),
   (iv) charges for hire of plant and machinery (para 53(6)),
   (v) amounts set aside for redemption of shares and loans (para 53(3));

(9) detailed particulars of the tax charge (para 54);
(10) particulars of staff (para 56):

   (i)   number employed and analysis,
   (ii) staff costs and analysis;

(11) any material difference between the stock figure in the balance sheet and the comparable figure on a replacement cost basis (para 27(3));
(12) analysis of turnover between different classes of business and geographical markets supplied; analysis of profit before tax between different classes of business (para 55) (note that this segmented information may only be omitted if the notes disclose the percentage of turnover which has been supplied to geographical markets outside the United Kingdom – a negative statement is not required);
(13) the following directors' remuneration disclosures are *not* required:

   (i)   the breakdown of aggregate remuneration between:

      1 emoluments for services as director (i e directors fees) and
      2 remuneration relating to the management of the company (this total would include, for example, the salary of the sales director);

   (ii) emoluments of the Chairman;
   (iii) emoluments of the highest paid director (if greater than the Chairman);

(iv) banding of emoluments (0 – £5,000, £5,001 – £10,000 etc);
(v) details of emoluments waived;
(vi) details of pensions and directors and past directors.
Note that the following disclosure *will* still be required:

(i) aggregate amount of directors' emoluments;
(ii) aggregate amount of compensation paid to directors for loss of office;
(iii) aggregate amount of sums paid to third parties in respect of directors services.

(h) Practical illustration

The example below relates to the directors' report and accounts of Smallco Ltd. The company qualifies as a small company and has taken full advantage of the exemptions offered by SI 2452.

Illustration 3

The report and accounts below would be presented to the shareholders. It would be up to the company to decide whether to file these accounts with the Registrar or whether to file abbreviated accounts.

Directors report of Newco Ltd (extracts)

Miminum information would include:

Principal activity
The principal activity of the company in the year under review was the manufacture of office equipment.

Directors
The directors of the company in office during the year and their interests in the issued share capital were as follows:

	£1 Ordinary Shares	
	30.6.X9	1.7.X8
A Williams	20	20
B Williams	20	20
C Williams	60	60

Re-appointment of Auditors

Statement that in preparing the directors report the directors have taken advantage of the special exemptions applicable to small companies.

Signature of Directors or Secretary.

Balance sheet (ignoring comparative figures)

BALANCE SHEET

As at 30 June 19X9

	£	£	£
Fixed assets			
Tangible assets			550,700
Investments			32,000
			582,700
Current assets			
Stocks		129,300	
Debtors		116,870	
Investments		60,200	
Cash at bank and in hand		182,920	
		489,290	

Creditors: amounts falling due within one year

Trade creditors	78,580	
Other creditors	69,110	
		147,690

Net current assets	341,600
Total assets less current liabilities	924,300
Creditors: amounts falling due after more than one year	
Other creditors	214,900
	709,400
Capital and reserves	
Called up share capital	500,000
Share premium account	136,400
Profit and loss account	73,000
	709,400

In preparing these accounts, the directors have taken advantage of the special exemptions applicable to small companies on the grounds that the company is small.

The accounts were approved by the Board of Directors on . . .

Signed on behalf of the Board of Directors.

Profit and loss account (ignoring comparative figures)

PROFIT AND LOSS ACCOUNT

For the year ended 30 June 19X9

	£	£
Turnover		791,000
Cost of sales		507,000
Gross profit		284,000
Distribution costs	107,300	
Administrative expenses	76,800	184,100
		99,900
Income from fixed asset investments	1,000	
Other interest receivable	41,600	
		42,600
Interest payable		(8,900)
Profit on ordinary activities before taxation		133,600
Tax on profit on ordinary activities		65,900
Profit on ordinary activities after taxation		67,700
Dividends		25,600
Retained profit		42,100
Profit and loss account brought forward		30,900
Profit and loss account carried forward		73,000

Notes to the accounts – (ignoring comparative figures)

These would include:

(i) *Accounting Policies*
(a) Accounting Convention
    The accounts have been prepared under the historical cost convention.
(b) Cash Flow Statement
    The company has taken advantage of the exemption conferred by Financial Reporting Standard 1, from presenting a cash flow statement as it qualifies as a small company.

(c) Depreciation
Depreciation is provided on all tangible assets, other than freehold land at rates calculated to write off the cost of valuation, less estimated residual value of each asset evenly over its expected useful life as follows:
Plant and machinery – 10% pa on a straight-line basis
Office furniture – 10% pa on a reducing balance basis

(d) Stock and work-in-progress
Stocks are stated at the lower of cost and net realisable value as follows:
Costs includes all costs incurred in bringing each product to its present location and condition and is determined as follows:
Raw materials – purchase costs on a first-in first-out basis.
Work-in-progress and finished goods – cost of direct materials and labour, plus attributable overheads based on the normal level of activity.
Net realisable value is based on estimated selling price, less further costs expected to be incurred to completion and disposal.

(e) Turnover
Turnover represents the invoiced amount of goods sold and services provided, stated net of credits and allowances and value added tax.

(f) Pension Costs
The company operates a defined contribution scheme. The assets of the scheme are held separately from those of the company in an independently administered fund. The pension cost charge represents contributions payable by the company to the fund.

(ii) *Operating Profit*

The operating profit is stated after charging:

	£
Auditors remuneration	1,000
Depreciation	26,200
Directors' remuneration	70,600

(iii) *Tangible fixed assets*

	Land and buildings £	Plant and machinery etc £	Total £
Cost			
At 1 July 19X8	414,900	265,000	679,900
Additions	20,000	10,000	30,000
Disposals	–	(5,000)	(5,000)
At 30 June 19X9	434,900	270,000	704,900
Depreciation	£	£	£
At 1 July 19X8	10,000	122,000	132,000
Provided during the year	2,000	24,200	26,200
Estimated on disposals	–	(4,000)	(4,000)
At 30 June 19X9	12,000	142,200	154,200
Net book amounts at			
30 June 19X9	422,900	127,800	550,700
30 June 19X8	404,900	143,000	547,900

(iv) *Debtors falling due within one year*

	£
Trade debtors	105,100
Others	11,770
	116,870

(v) *Creditors: amounts falling due after more than one year*

Other creditors includes £150,000 repayable in 19X2 in respect of which a security has been given by the company.

(vi) *Capital commitments*

	£
Contracted	80,000
Authorised but not contracted	30,000

(vii) *Contingent liabilities*

	£
Guarantee of the bank overdraft of a supplier	95,000

Summary of exclusions

The following is a summary of the items that would have appeared in a full-form set of accounts for the above company. They all fall within the exemption headings set out in SI 2452:

(a) Directors' Report

    (i)   fair review of business
    (ii)   dividends
    (iii) transfers to reserve
    (iv) asset values

(b) Balance sheet

    (i)   Creditors due within one year
         Taxation and Social Security; proposed dividends; accruals and deferred income: combined as 'other creditors'
    (ii)   Creditors due after one year
         Debenture loans; tax and Social Security: combined as 'other creditors'.

(c) Profit and loss account
    No difference, as details appear in the notes to the accounts.

(d) Notes to the accounts

    (i)   Staff costs including pension costs and number of employees
    (ii)   Hire of plant and machinery
    (iii) Segment information (turnover and profits)
    (iv) Split of interest payable between bank loans and overdrafts; other loans
    (v)   Income from listed investments
    (vi) Emoluments of Chairman, highest paid director and bands of £5,000
    (vii Analysis of tax charge
    (viii) Plant and machinery; fixtures fittings and equipment: combined as 'plant and machinery etc'
    (ix) Breakdown of stock figure
    (x)   Other debtors; prepayments: combined as 'others'
    (xi) Debenture loan; interest rate, repayment terms; nature of security given (eg floating charge)

10.4   ABBREVIATED ACCOUNTS

(a) Filing concessions

Under the Companies Act 1985, smaller companies (as defined) may file less information with the Registrar of Companies than larger companies.

Smaller companies fall into two categories, each with a separate set of concessions. These categories are small and medium-sized respectively.

(b) Qualifying conditions

The Companies Act 1985 definitions of 'small' and 'medium-sized' were referred to in section 10.2 above.

(c) Parent companies

Special considerations relating to parent companies with subsidiaries are referred to in section 10.8 below.

(d) Small company abbreviated accounts

The minimum information which may be filed by a small company is as follows:

(1) A balance sheet in abbreviated form, containing only items designated in the formats by letters or roman numerals.
(2) Notes relating to the following matters:

    (i)   accounting policies;
    (ii)   share capital;
    (iii) particulars of allotments of shares and debentures;
    (iv) particulars of debts
           – payable in more than five years
           – debts which are secured;
    (v)   loans and transactions with directors and officers;
    (vi) information on subsidiaries;
    (vii) ultimate parent company;
    (viii) movement on fixed assets;
    (ix) basis of translation of foreign currency amounts into sterling; corresponding figures.

Note: A small company need not file a profit and loss account, a directors' report and information regarding directors' emoluments.

Illustration 4

Illustration of abbreviated accounts for a small company

Please note that the special auditors' report has not been reproduced below.

SMALL COMPANY LIMITED – ABBREVIATED BALANCE SHEET
as at 31 December 19X3

NOTES	19X3		19X2	
	£	£	£	£
Fixed assets				
Tangible assets		92,400		73,200
Investments		9,500		12,000
		101,900		85,200
Current assets				
Stocks	37,350		36,300	
Debtors	69,500		54,050	
Cash at bank and in hand	22,300		19,700	
	129,150		110,050	
Creditors – amounts falling due within one year	103,100		91,750	
Net current assets		26,050		18,300
Total assets less current liabilities		127,950		103,500
Creditors – amounts falling due after more than one year		(20,000)		(20,000)
Provisions for liabilities and charges		(2,600)		(1,700)
		105,350		81,800

Capital and reserves

Called-up share capital	30,000	30,000
Share premium account	10,000	10,000
Revaluation reserve	15,000	5,500
Profit and loss account	50,350	36,300
	105,350	81,800

Advantage is taken of the exemptions conferred by Part 3 of Schedule 8 of the Companies Act 1985 with respect to the delivery of individual accounts. In the opinion of the directors, the company is entitled to those exemptions on the grounds that it has met the qualifications for a small company specified in Sections 246 and 249.

> Signed on behalf of the Board of Directors
> A. Jones, Director
>
> ....
> (Signature)

Notes to the abbreviated accounts

(1) *Accounting policies*

(i)   Accounting Convention – the accounts are prepared under the historical cost convention, modified to include the revaluation of land and buildings.

(ii) Depreciation – this is provided on all tangible fixed assets other than freehold land, at rates calculated to write off the cost or valuation, less estimated residual value, of each asset evenly over its expected useful life, as follows:

Freehold buildings	– over 50 years
Plant and equipment	– over 10 years
Fixtures and fittings	– over 5 years
Motor vehicles	– over 4 years

(iii) Stocks and work-in-progress – these are valued on a 'first-in-first-out' basis, at the lower of cost and net realisable value. As regards work-in-progress and finished goods, cost includes attributable production overheads.

(iv) Deferred taxation – deferred taxation is provided on the liability method on the tax effects of all timing differences other than those which are not expected to reverse in the future.

(2) *Tangible fixed assets*

Cost or valuation

At 1 January 19X3	180,400
Additions	54,100
At 31 December 19X3	234,500

Accumulated depreciation

At 1 January 19X3	107,200
Provision	25,400
At 31 December 19X3	132,600

Net book value

At 31 December 19X3	101,900
At 31 December 19X2	73,200

(3) *Creditors*

(i)   Amounts falling due within one year – included in this amount is a bank overdraft of £30,000 (19X2 – £25,000) which is secured. (For accounting periods ending on or after 16 November 1992, abbreviated accounts of small companies need no longer disclose the nature of the security.)

(ii) Amounts falling due after more than one year – at 31 December 19X3, creditors include an amount of £15,000 repayable in eight years' time (31 December 19X2 – £15,000 repayable in nine years' time). This amount is secured. The balance of the total is repayable within five years and is unsecured.

(4) *Called-up share capital*

	19X3 £	19X2 £
Authorised		
30,000 shares of £1 each	30,000	30,000
Allotted and Fully Paid		
30,000 shares of £1 each	30,000	30,000

(e) Medium-sized company abbreviated accounts

The minimum requirements include:

(1) a full balance sheet (without modification);
(2) an abbreviated form of profit and loss account – effectively starting with the gross profit or loss:

    (i) in format 1, the items of turnover, cost of sales, gross profit and other operating income may be combined into a single figure described as gross profit,

    (ii) in format 2, the items turnover, change in stocks of finished goods and work-in-progress, own work capitalised, other operating income, raw materials and consumables and other operating charges may be combined into a single figure described as gross profit;

(3) full notes except for turnover and profit or loss before taxation by class of business and geographical markets;
(4) a directors' report;
(5) a special auditor's report (see (f) below).

A medium-sized company is required to include a cash flow statement (FRS 1).

(f) Special auditor's report

Any small or medium-sized company which files abbreviated accounts (i e accounts which fall short in any respect of those presented to shareholders) must include also a special auditor's report, as well as the appropriate statutory declaration by the directors.

(g) Directors' statement

A statement should appear above the director's signatures to the effect that advantage is taken of the exemptions on the grounds that the company is small or medium-sized.

(h) Problem areas

Examples of cases where qualifying conditions may have been incorrectly applied include:

(i) asset criteria incorrectly measured by reference to assets after deducting creditors due within one year;
(ii) financial services companies wrongly treated as small companies;
(iii) failure to apply rules regarding changing company size where company moves through size thresholds (e g turnover £2.8m);
(iv) failure to understand meaning of term ineligible group, eg a small private company may be ineligible because it is part of a group which somewhere includes a plc;
(v) treating a small unlisted plc as 'small' purely on the basis of size;
(vi) treating a parent company as small purely on the basis of size when in fact it heads up a medium-sized group (see section 10.8);

(vii) attempting to file abbreviated group accounts. Only individual companies can qualify for abbreviated accounts exemption;
(viii) failing to take account of the length of accounting period, ie periods of other than 12 months.

10.5   CONCESSIONS OFFERED BY PARTICULAR ACCOUNTING STANDARDS

The main concessions include:

(a) FRS 1 (Cash flow statements)

Small companies (ie companies entitled to file abbreviated accounts as small companies) may claim exemption from preparing a cash flow statement (see section 31.1).

(b) FRS 2 (Accounting for subsidiary undertakings)

Small and medium-sized groups may claim exemption from the preparation of group accounts (see section 24.11). FRS 2 merely repeats the exemption offered by the Companies Act 1985.

(c) FRS 3 (Reporting financial performance)

No exemptions are offered to smaller companies as such. However, the circumstances of many such companies are such that certain FRS 3 disclosures will not be required (see chapter 8).

(d) SSAP 13 (Research and development)

Certain of the disclosure requirements relating to total research and development expenditure need not be applied by an entity that:

(1) is not a plc or a special category company under s 257 (essentially banks and insurance companies); and
(2) satisfies the medium-sized company criteria multiplied by a factor of 10 (see section 13.3(i)).

(e) SSAP 25 (Segmental reporting)

Small and medium-sized companies are exempt from several of the discosure requirements of SSAP 25, segmental reporting (see section 32.7).

(f) SSAP 3 (Earnings per share)

SSAP 3 is mandatory for listed companies only.

10.6   EXEMPTIONS FROM STANDARDS – RECENT DEVELOPMENTS

The Consultative Committee of Accountancy Bodies (CCAB) has published two consultative documents on the application of accounting standards to small companies:

(a) Exemptions from standards on grounds of size or public interest – November 1994.
(b) Designed to fit – a Financial Reporting Standard for Smaller Entities – December 1995.

The earlier paper proposed that all small companies – small for abbreviated accounts purposes – should be exempt from compliance with all accounting standards except for SSAPs 4 (grants), 9 (stocks), 13 (research and development), 17 (post balance sheet events), 18 (contingencies) and UITF 7 (true and fair override).

The recent paper advocates a quite different approach – that the accountancy profession should have a more focused approach for smaller entities and should create a specific Financial Reporting Standard to meet the sector's needs.

The discussion paper includes a draft Financial Reporting Standard for Smaller Entities (FRSSE). This covers most topics which could be relevant to individual companies (not groups), for example:

(a) stocks
(b) depreciation
(c) taxation
(d) goodwill
(e) pensions
(f) leases
(g) related party disclosures
(h) foreign currency translation
(i) cash flow statements.

10.7 LEGAL CONSIDERATIONS

(a) Accounting concessions

The concessions for shorter-form accounts, abbreviated accounts and group accounts exemption were referred to above.

(b) Disclosure concessions

(1) The Companies Act 1989 introduced a new requirement for companies to state in their accounts whether the accounts have been prepared in accordance with applicable accounting standards. Companies which depart from accounting standards will be required to disclose:

   (i) particulars of any material departure from those standards;
   (ii) reasons for the departure.

   Small and medium-sized private companies, as defined by the 1985 Act, are exempt from the above disclosure requirements.
(2) Small and medium-sized companies are not required to disclose fees paid to their auditors for work other than audit work.

(c) Filing of accounts

All private companies (not just those which are small or medium-sized) have ten months to file accounts, compared with seven months for PLCs (see section 4.8(d)).

(d) Loans to directors

The rules for loans to directors are less stringent for private companies than for PLCs. These are not dealt with in this text.

(e) Distributable profit rules

The rules for private companies are less stringent than those for PLCs (see section 15.7).

(f) Share purchases

Private companies are permitted to purchase or redeem shares out of capital, subject to compliance with CA 1985 requirements (see section 15.5(h)).

10.8   PARENT COMPANIES

A parent company will only be treated as 'small' for abbreviated accounts purposes if the group it heads up is small. Parent company disclosures are referred to in section 24.11.

11 EXTERNAL REPORTING – LISTED COMPANY ISSUES

Key Issues

* Publication of non-statutory accounts
* Interim reports
* Corporate governance disclosures
* Greenbury – directors' remuneration
* Operating and financial review
* Summary financial statements

11.1 OVERVIEW

This chapter is concerned with external reporting by larger and listed companies. Some of the issues referred to below – including corporate governance, directors' remuneration and financial reviews – relate to annual reports and accounts. However, interim reports and summary financial statements are also referred to.

11.2 STOCK EXCHANGE DISCLOSURE REQUIREMENTS

The Stock Exchange's Yellow Book specifies disclosure requirements in annual reports – additional to those required by the Companies Act 1985. These were referred to in section 4.7 of chapter 4.

11.3 PUBLICATION OF NON-STATUTORY ACCOUNTS

(a) Introduction

This section is concerned with the situation where a company publishes, other than as part of its full statutory accounts, any balance sheet or profit and loss account relating to a financial year.

Non-statutory accounts were previously referred to as 'abridged accounts' (not to be confused with 'abbreviated accounts', chapter 10, section 10.4).

Non-statutory accounts may include the following:

(1) Preliminary announcements:
    preliminary announcements to the Stock Exchange, covering a financial year.
(2) Certain interim reports:
    interim reports for Stock Exchange purposes usually cover a six-month period (see section 11.4 below) and would not therefore normally count as non-statutory accounts. However, if such statements contain comparative figures for a full year they would count as non-statutory accounts and come within the scope of the Companies Act 1985.
(3) Reporting to employees:
    summary accounts relating to a financial year and contained in annual reports to employees.

(b) Publication

A body corporate is to be regarded as publishing any balance sheet or other account if it publishes, issues or circulates it or otherwise makes it available for public inspection in a manner calculated to invite members of the public generally, or any class of members of the public, to read it.

(c) Requirements where non-statutory accounts are published

The published non-statutory accounts must contain a statement which refers to the following matters:

(1) that the accounts are not full (statutory) accounts;
(2) whether full (statutory) individual or group accounts have been delivered to the Registrar of Companies;
(3) whether the company's auditors have made a report on the full (statutory) accounts for a period to which the non-statutory accounts relate;
(4) whether the report in (3) was unqualified.

The non-statutory accounts must not include the audit report on the statutory accounts.

11.4 STOCK EXCHANGE REQUIREMENTS – INTERIM REPORTS TO SHAREHOLDERS

(a) Introduction

Once a company's securities have been admitted to listing on The London Stock Exchange, that company is obliged to follow specified continuing obligations.
   One such continuing obligation is that a company must prepare a half-yearly report on its activities and profit or loss during the first six months of each financial year. This report should either be sent to shareholders or inserted in two national daily newspapers.

(b) Accounting and audit requirements

The figures in the half-yearly or interim reports are the sole responsibility of the directors.
   The accounting policies applied to the interim figures should be consistent with those for the annual accounts. Where a change in policy is proposed, the Quotations Department of The Stock Exchange should be consulted as regards periods to be covered by the interim report. The figures in the interim report are unaudited.
   However, directors should ensure that the accounting policies applied to interim accounts are consistent with those used for annual accounts.

(c) Minimum contents of an interim report

The Stock Exchange's Listing Rules require the following:

(1) *Figures in table form*

The following figures in table form for the interim period and for the corresponding previous period should be included:

(i)   net turnover;
(ii)   profit or loss before taxation and extraordinary items;

(iii)　tax on profits (showing separately UK tax; overseas tax; associated companies' tax);

(iv)　minority interests;

(v)　profit or loss attributable to shareholders before extraordinary items;

(vi)　extraordinary Items (net of taxation);

(vii)　profit or loss attributable to shareholders;

(viii)　rates and amounts of dividends paid and proposed;

(ix)　earnings per share (in pence).

(2) *Explanatory statement*

The report should include an explanatory statement relating to the group's activities and profit or loss during the relevant period. This must include any significant information enabling investors to make an informed assessment of the trend of the group's activities and profit or loss together with an indication of any special factor which has influenced those activities and the profit or loss during the period in question. The statement should enable a comparison to be made with the corresponding period of the preceding financial year.

As far as possible, the statement should refer to the group's prospects in the current financial year.

(3) *Audit status*

The report must state the fact that the accounting information given in the half-yearly report has not been audited and reference should be made to the Companies Act 1985.

Extract from 1996 Interim Report of Peter Black Holdings plc

Chairman's Statement
1 February 1996

In the first half of our financial year, underlying profit before taxation increased by 6.2% to £8.2 million (1994 – £7.7 million, excluding an exceptional profit on disposal), on sales of £69.3 million. Last year's sales of £69.5 million, on continuing activities, included a contribution of approximately £4.6 million from the Keighley based slipper and casual footwear manufacturing facility which was closed in May 1995. On a comparable basis sales increased 6.8%. Profit before taxation on continuing activities increased by 8.1%. Earnings per share, before exceptional items, rose 6.4% to 10.13p (1994 – 9.52p).

Our balance sheet remains strong despite an increase in capital expenditure to £5.5 million in the first half year. This included a £3.8 million payment for the new Healthcare manufacturing facility. At 2 December 1995 the Group had net cash resources of £3.5 million.

The further progress demonstrated by these results, combined with our confidence in the growth prospects for the business, underpin the Board's decision to declare an increase in the interim dividend from 1.26p to 1.37p.

Personal care
In line with our expectations, this Division has again achieved a substantial advance in profitability and sales.

Toiletries and Cosmetics benefited from improved operating efficiency and from our policy of concentrating on enhanced rather than basic product. Highlights were the sales of skin care products, fragrances and gifts. Our customer base in the UK has been broadened and the growing demand for our products from overseas is an exciting prospect for the future.

The new English Grains Healthcare factory at Swadlincote is now operational, resulting in the entire business being consolidated on one site. It is the most advanced facility of its kind in Europe. The transfer of production from the old plant to the new was a complicated operation and has had, as anticipated, a temporary adverse impact on capacity. This constraint is progressively disappearing and the expected improvements in production efficiency are materialising. Our brands, supported by effective advertising and promotion, have maintained their position of leadership in the market. The ranges of private label products we produce for the major multiple retailers continue to be improved and extended.

Footwear & accessories

It has been widely reported that clothing sales had a difficult Autumn season in the face of consumer restraint and an unusual weather pattern. Against this background, our Footwear business also had a disappointing six months. In addition, sales were affected by the closure, in the second half of last year, of the Keighley based slipper and casual footwear manufacturing facility. The downturn in sales was largely offset by the substantial advance in our Accessories business (handbags, textile toiletries, small leather goods, gifts and promotional items) whose results exceeded our expectations.

Our Import business is well positioned to progress as a result of the outstanding sources of supply in Italy, India and the Far East, which we have identified and developed over recent years. We continue to refine our management systems in order to respond most effectively to Marks & Spencer's clear commitment to expand its share of the footwear market. Intense competition, together with lower than planned sales of ladies boots, combined to make it a difficult six months for Newbold, our only UK production facility.

The substantial progress achieved by Accessories is based on innovative design and the ability to source product from centres of excellence overseas. Highlights were the small leather goods manufactured to our design and specification in India and the ranges of gifts covering sport and outdoor leisure, which sold extremely well in the Christmas selling season.

Distribution

This Distribution achieved a commendable increase in business.

The investment in recent years in management systems and facilities has provided us with the ability to develop unique logistical solutions for both companies within the Group and third party customers.

In order to optimise sales, retailers demand a high level of service which involves the flexibility to respond promptly to changing patterns of demand. The specialist niche which we have identified has now enabled us to include amongst our customers Savacentre and Safeway, for whom we handle certain non-food distribution. Peter Black Distribution's efficient management of the peak Christmas despatches played a vital part in the achievement of the Group's progressive results.

Board appointment

We were delighted that Peter Glynn-Jones joined the Board as a Non-Executive Director on 18 January 1996. As Managing Director of Strategic Development Worldwide for SmithKline Beecham Consumer Healthcare, his global experience will greatly assist the international expansion of our Personal Care business.

Prospects

Our management and financial resources are sharply focused on the manufacture and marketing of Healthcare, Beauty and Fashion products. In the years towards the Millennium there are significant growth opportunities for these areas of business. In addition, we consider this relatively broad base to be a strength in that it gives the Group extra resilence in times of economic uncertainty.

The development of new ranges in our Personal Care Division is ongoing and we are confident that progress can be maintained. Our new Healthcare factory will enable us to meet the growing demand for vitamins, dietary supplements and herbal remedies. In Footwear & Accessories, our policy of sourcing globally from centres of excellence enables us to meet, without inhibitions, the demands of the market. Our dedicated approach to Distribution continues to provide the companies within the Group with a competitive edge. The developments of third party customers is gathering momentum and the prospects for growth are encouraging.

We remain confident that the current progressive trend can be maintained.

Gordon L Black

Notes

1. Preparation of financial statements

The interim financial statements have been prepared on the basis of the accounting policies set out in the group's 1995 annual report and are unaudited.

The figures for the year ended 3 June 1995 are abridged from the group's statutory accounts for that year which received an unqualified auditors' report and have been filed with the Registrar of Companies.

In accordance with Financial Reporting Standard No. 3, the results of the Leisure business have been classified as discontinued.

2. Analysis of activities

	Six months ended 2 December 1995 £'000	Six months ended 3 December 1994 £'000	Year ended 3 June 1995 £'000
Turnover			
Personal care	28,172	26,724	49,119
Footwear & accessories	37,637	39,823	70,242
Distribution	3,489	2,959	5,267
	69,298	69,506	124,628
Profit before taxation			
Personal care	4,667	4,131	7,082
Footwear & accessories	2,839	2,964	4,664
Distribution	702	490	733
	8,208	7,591	12,479

Balance sheet

	as at 2 December 1995 £'000	as at 3 December 1994 £'000	as at 3 June 1995 £'000
Fixed assets			
Tangible assets	41,912	40,589	37,971
Current assets			
Investments	–	1,050	–
Stocks	18,919	17,495	17,555
Debtors	18,168	17,646	12,228
Cash at bank and in hand	11,793	13,255	17,140
	48,880	49,446	46,923
Current liabilities			
Creditors: *amounts falling due within one year*	(35,626)	(36,515)	(34,680)
Net current assets	13,254	12,931	12,243
Net assets	55,166	53,520	50,214
Capital and reserves			
Called up share capital	13,878	13,812	13,860
Share premium account	1,808	1,547	1,734
Revaluation reserve	4,419	6,219	4,419
Capital reserve	(10,330)	(10,330)	(10,330)
Profit and loss account	45,391	42,272	40,531
Equity shareholders' funds	55,166	53,520	50,214
Creditors include:			
Loan notes	8,250	8,250	8,250

Interim results

	Six months ended 2 December 1995 £'000	Six months ended 3 December 1994 £'000	Year ended 3 June 1995 £'000
Turnover			
Continuing operations	69,298	69,506	124,628
Discontinued operations	–	356	356
	69,298	69,862	124,984
Operating profit			
Continuing operations	8,364	7,675	12,501
Discontinued operations	–	136	136
	8,364	7,811	12,637
Profit and disposal of discontinued operation	–	627	627
Loss on closure of business	–	–	(3,847)
Profit before interest	8,364	8,438	9,417
Net interest payable	(156)	(84)	(22)
Profit before taxation	8,208	8,354	9,395
Taxation	(2,586)	(2,473)	(3,149)
Profit after taxation	5,622	5,881	6,246
Dividends	(762)	(696)	(2,802)
Profit retained	4,860	5,185	3,444
Earnings per share	10.13p	10.66p	11.31p
Profit on disposal of discontinued operation	–	(1.14p)	(1.13p)
Loss on closure of business	–	–	5.47p
Adjusted earnings per share	10.13p	9.52p	15.65p
Dividend per share	1.37p	1.26p	5.05p

Earnings per share is based on earnings of £5,622,000 (1994 – £5,881,000) available for distribution to the holders of 55,480,184 (1994 – 55,173,070) ordinary shares, being the average number of shares in issue during the period.

The interim dividend of 1.37p will be paid on 30 April 1996 to shareholders on the register at close of business on 19 March 1996.

11.5   CORPORATE GOVERNANCE DISCLOSURES

The Cadbury Committee report on the Financial Aspects of Corporate Governance was published in December 1992. A listed company is required to state whether or not it has complied throughout the accounting period with the Code of Best Practice.

Illustration 1

The extract below is taken from the annual report and accounts of the Granada Group plc for the year ended 30 September 1995.

In the opinion of the directors, the company fully complied throughout the 52 weeks ended 30 September 1995 with the Code of Best Practice in the Report of the Committee on the Financial Aspects of Corporate Governance ('the Cadbury Report').

The structure of the Board and its various standing committees is as follows:

The Board

The Board currently consists of seven executive and three non-executive directors and meets regularly throughout the year. A formal schedule of matters reserved for the decision of the Board covers key areas of the Group's affairs including overall Group strategy, acquisition and divestment policy, approval of budgets, major capital expenditure projects and general treasury and risk management policies. Procedures have been established to enable directors to obtain independent professional advice. The Board has delegated specific responsibilities to committees, as described below.

The Audit Committee

The Audit Committee comprises all the non-executive directors, is chaired by Michael Orr and normally meets four times a year. The Committee reviews the Company's interim and annual financial statements before submission to the Board for approval. The committee also reviews regular reports from management and the external auditors on accounting and internal control matters. Where appropriate, the committee monitors the progress of action taken in relation to such matters. The committee also recommends the appointment and reviews the fees of external auditors.

The Remuneration Committee

The Remuneration Committee also comprises all the non-executive directors and it is chaired by Ian Martin. On pages 51 and 54 [not reproduced in this book] of this report and accounts is the Report of the Remuneration Committee on the policies they apply and on directors' remuneration packages.

The Nomination Committee

The Nomination Committee is chaired by Alex Bernstein and comprises in addition all the non-executive directors and Gerry Robinson. This Committee meets as required and is authorised to propose to the Board new appointments of executive and non-executive directors.

The Administration and Finance Committee

The Administration and Finance Committee comprises the executive directors and meets as required to conduct the Company's business within the clearly defined limits delegated by the Board and subject to those matters reserved for the Board.

The Granada Pension Scheme

The corporate trustee of the Granada Pension scheme – the principal UK scheme – is Granada Trust Corporation Limited, which is chaired by Graham Parrott and whose directors include representatives nominated by the employee members of the Scheme. The management of the investments of the Scheme has been delegated to six independent investment managers and the trustees are advised by independent actuaries and auditors. Members of the Scheme receive annually a statement of their accrued benefits and a Trustees' Report. The Actuaries and Consultants, William M Mercer Limited, will advise the trustee if any actions are necessary to ensure full compliance with the provisions of the Pensions Act 1995 once the detailed regulations are published.

Going concern

After making appropriate enquiries, the directors consider that the Group has adequate resources to continue in operational existence for the foreseeable future. For this reason, they continue to adopt the going concern basis in preparing the financial statements.

Internal financial control

The directors have overall responsibility for the Group's system of internal financial control and have established a framework designed to provide reasonable but not absolute assurance against material mis-statement or loss. The key procedures supporting such a framework are detailed below.

Financial reporting – a rolling three year strategic review process is part of a comprehensive planning system together with an annual budget approved by the Board. The results of operating units are reported monthly, compared with their individual budgets and forecast figures are reviewed on a month by month basis.

Control environment – financial controls and procedures including information system controls are detailed in policies and procedures manuals for all major subsidiaries. As the overall quality of internal financial control across the Group is directly related to the controls in individual operating units, it is a requirement for the managers of operating units and divisions to confirm each year in writing the quality of internal financial control in their area.

Functional reporting – the risks facing the business are assessed on an ongoing basis. A number of key areas, such as treasury and corporate taxation matters are subject to regular review by the directors. Other important areas, such as, detailed insurance risk management and legal matters come under the direct control of the executive directors and are reviewed on a continuous basis. In addition at the end of each financial year, managers of operating units and divisions are also required to provide a schedule of identified risks and action taken to minimise exposure.

Investment appraisal – the Group has a clearly defined framework for controlling capital expenditure including appropriate authorisation levels beyond which such expenditure requires the approval of the Board. There is a prescribed format for capital expenditure applications which places a high emphasis on the commercial and strategic logic for the investment and due diligence requirements in the case of business acquisitions. As a matter of routine, projects are also subject to a post investment appraisal after an appropriate period.

The directors have reviewed the effectiveness of the system of internal financial control in operation during the period covered by this report.

Auditors' confirmation

The auditors, KPMG, have confirmed that in their opinion: with respect to the directors' statements on internal financial control and going concern the directors have provided the disclosures required by paragraphs 4.5 and 4.6 of the Code (as supplemented by the related guidance for directors) and such statements are not inconsistent with the information of which they are aware from their audit work on the financial statements; and that the directors' statement on page 22 [not reproduced] appropriately reflects the company's compliance with the other paragraphs of the Code specified by the Listing Rules for their review. They have carried out their review in accordance with the relevant Bulletin issued by the Auditing Practices Board, which does not require them to perform any additional work necessary to express a separate opinion on the effectiveness of either the company's system of internal financial control or corporate governance procedures, or on the ability of the Group to continue in operational existence.

11.6   THE GREENBURY COMMITTEE ON DIRECTORS' REMUNERATION

(a) Stock Exchange implementation

The Greenbury Committee reported in July 1995. The Stock Exchange subsequently made important changes in October 1995 to the part of the listing rules dealing with directors' remuneration. For accounts periods ending on or after 31 December 1995, a company's annual report and accounts should include a report to shareholders by the remuneration committee giving specified details on directors' remuneration. A summary of the main disclosures is set out below.

(b) Summary of main disclosures

In outline, the main disclosures required by the Stock Exchange are as follows:

(1) a statement of the company's policy on executive directors' remuneration;
(2) the amount of each element in the remuneration package giving details for each director by name. Possible sub-headings include:

   (i)   basic salary and fees;
   (ii) estimated money value of benefits in kind;

(iii) annual bonuses;
(iv) compensation for loss of office, payments for breach of contract etc.;
(v) totals for each director – this year and last year.

(3) generally the information should be in tabular form together with explanatory notes;
(4) share option details in accordance with UITF 10;
(5) details of any long-term incentive schemes;
(6) explanation and justification of any element of remuneration, apart from basic salary, which is pensionable;
(7) details of service contracts with a notice period exceeding one year;
(8) for directors proposed for election or re-election:

(i)   unexpired term of service contract; or
(ii) statement that the person does not have a service contract.

Illustration 2 (pre-Stock Exchange implementation of Greenbury)

Extract from annual report and accounts of Manganese Bronze Holdings plc for the year ended 31 July 1995.

Note 30 – Directors

(a) Remuneration
The remuneration committee of the board, comprising the Chairman, the non-executive directors and the Chief Executive, is responsible for determining the remuneration of the directors and the Group's senior executive management. The Chairman and other non-executive directors receive fees and expenses but no other benefits. The remuneration of the executive directors consists of basic salary, a performance related bonus, pension and other benefits. Bonuses are awarded based on targets related to profits and the attainment of budgets.

Analysis of directors' remuneration (excluding share options)

	Basic salary/fees 1995 £	Bonus 1995 £	Other benefits 1995 £	Pension contributions 1995 £	Total 1995 £	Total 1994 £
Executive						
Jamie Borwick	112,000	28,000	7,910	14,187	162,097	140,395
Bill Gillespie	85,000	21,250	5,168	11,689	123,107	49,979
Barry Widdowson	85,000	29,800	8,450	11,900	135,150	109,544
Michael Williams	85,000	8,500	4,470	10,767	108,737	95,877
Non-executive						
Hugh Lang *Chairman*	48,333	–	–	–	48,333	40,000
Somerset Gibbs	12,500	–	–	–	12,500	12,500
Christopher Ross	1,335	–	–	–	1,335	–
William Salomon	15,000	–	–	–	15,000	15,000
Brian Smith	–	–	–	–	–	10,625
Rod Turner	12,500	–	–	–	12,500	48,032
	456,668	87,550	25,998	48,543	618,759	521,952

None of the directors of the Company has any contract or agreement with the company or any of its subsidiaries apart from service contracts. The comparative figures have been restated to take account of annual bonuses paid during the year ended 31 July 1995 in respect of the year ended 31 July 1994.

Emoluments of the Directors (excluding pension contributions) including the Chairman were in the following ranges:

£		*1995*	*1994*
0 – 5,000		one	–
10,001 – 15,000		three	three
30,001 – 35,000		–	one
40,001 – 45,000		–	one
45,001 – 50,000		one	one
85,001 – 90,000		–	one
90,001 – 95,000		–	one
95,001 – 100,000		one	–
110,001 – 115,000		one	–
120,001 – 125,000		one	one
145,001 – 150,000		one	–

(b) Share options

	Number at 1 August 1994	Options granted/ (exercised)	Number at 31 July 1995	Exercise price (pence)	Date exercisable	Expiry date
Bill Gillespie	100,000	–	100,000	152.0	30 March 1997	30 March 2004
Barry Widdowson	49,000	–	49,000	103.0	7 January 1994	7 January 2001
	51,000	–	51,000	87.5	29 March 1996	29 March 2003
Michael Williams	50,000	–	50,000	103.0	7 January 1994	7 January 2001
	50,000	–	50,000	87.5	29 March 1996	29 March 2003

(c) Directors' interests

The interests of the directors in the ordinary share capital of the company, as shown by the register maintained for that purpose, are as follows:

	31 July 1995 Shares	31 July 1995 Options	31 July 1994 Shares	31 July 1994 Options
Beneficial Interests				
Hugh Lang	25,000	–	20,000	–
Jamie Borwick	266,195	–	266,195	–
Family companies of Mr Borwick	333,227	–	333,227	–
Bill Gillespie	4,544	100,000	–	100,000
Barry Widdowson	14,532	100,000	9,859	100,000
Michael Williams	15,000	100,000	9,859	100,000
Somerset Gibbs	4,000	–	4,000	–
Christopher Ross	–	–	–	–
Rod Turner	6,900	–	6,900	–
William Salomon	–	–	–	–
Non-beneficial Interests				
Jamie Borwick	1,153,316	–	1,153,316	–

11.7   OPERATING AND FINANCIAL REVIEW

(a) Overview

ASB has published a Statement recommending listed companies to provide supplementary information in the form of an Operating and Financial Review (OFR).

The aim is to provide an objective discussion which analyses and explains the main features underlying the results and financial position. The exercise is principally one of communication – getting across the underlying message of the accounts.

For many large companies, much of the relevant information is already being provided (for example in a chief executive's report).

(b) Scope

The Statement is not mandatory but ASB, the Hundred Group of Finance Directors and the Stock Exchange hope that it will be widely adopted.

The proposals are aimed at listed companies (particularly the larger ones) and other large corporations where there is a legitimate public interest in their accounts.

(c) Format

The Statement encourages directors to develop the presentation of the OFR in a way that will best complement the format of the annual report.

The OFR may be presented as a stand-alone document. Alternatively, the OFR may be incorporated within the structure of one or more other sections (for example, the Chief Executive's report).

The ASB's Statement sets out essential features of an OFR. This includes discussion of confidentiality and commercially sensitive information.

The OFR should cover two main areas – operating review and financial review. The Statement gives guidance on typical matters which could be covered under each area.

(d) Operating Review

The main aim of this section is to enable the user to understand the main influences on the overall results and how they interrelate. The review should explain the main factors which have varied in the past or which are expected to change in the future.

The principal sub-section of the operating review could include:

(i)   operating results for the period (new products, market share, changes in turnover, new activities etc.);
(ii) dynamics of the business – factors and influences which may have a major effect on future results (product liability, health and safety, patents etc.);
(iii) investment for the future (capital expenditure, marketing and advertising campaigns, research, technical support to customers etc.);
(iv) profit for the year, total recognised gains and losses, dividends, earnings per share.

(e) Financial Review

The main aim of this section is to explain the capital structure of the business, its treasury policy, its liquidity position and its financing requirements.

Principal sub-sections could include:

(i)   capital structure and treasury policy;
(ii) taxation;
(iii) funds from operating activities and other sources of cash;
(iv) current liquidity;
(v)   going concern;
(vi) balance sheet value (strengths and sources of the business not reflected in the balance sheet).

11.8   SUMMARY FINANCIAL STATEMENTS

(a) Introduction

Listed companies are permitted to send summary financial statements (SFSs) to those of their shareholders who do not wish to receive full statutory accounts.

The notes below give a guide to the general requirements but do not deal with such matters as how the company determines whether particular share-holders wish to receive SFSs instead of full statutory accounts.

(b) Matters to be referred to in summary financial statements

The main matters required to be referred to include:

(1) a 'health warning' – this is a paragraph which commences with: 'This summary financial statement does not contain sufficient information to allow for a full understanding of the results and state of affairs . . .';
(2) the SFS must be approved by the board of directors and be signed on behalf of the board by a director whose name is clearly stated;
(3) the SFS must contain a 'conspicuous statement' to the effect that members are entitled to demand a copy of the full statutory accounts free of charge;
(4) the SFS must include a special audit report.

Illustration 3

Extract from summary financial statement of Argos plc for the 52 weeks ended 31 December 1994.

(a) Summary group profit and loss account (for the 52 week period ended 31 December 1994)

	1994 £000	1993 £000
Turnover (excluding VAT)	1,257,404	1,109,692
Operating profit	91,911	76,206
Net interest receivable	8,315	7,253
Profit on ordinary activities before taxation	100,226	83,459
Taxation	(33,632)	(28,109)
Profit for the financial period	66,594	55,350
Dividends (paid and proposed)	(31,561)	(23,973)
Retained profit for the period	35,033	31,377
Earnings per share	22.3p	18.6p
Total dividends per share	10.5p	8.0p

The emoluments of the directors were £1.5 million (1993: £1.3 million).
    There are no recognised gains or losses in 1994 or 1993 other than the profit for those periods as shown above, and accordingly, a statement of total recognised gains and losses is not presented.
    The profit and loss account relates solely to continuing operations, as defined in FRS 3.

(b) Summary group balance sheet (at 31 December 1994)

	1994 *£000*	*1993* *£000*
Fixed assets	138,260	123,318
Current assets		
Stock (goods for resale)	182,369	166,442
Debtors	41,354	31,568
Cash and liquid funds	358,985	298,089
	582,708	496,099
Creditors – due within one year	418,438	357,262
Net current assets	164,270	138,837
Total assets less current liabilities	302,530	262,155
Provisions for liabilities and charges	7,742	8,375
Net assets	294,788	253,780
Equity capital and reserves	294,788	253,780

This summary financial statement was approved by the board on 27 March 1995 and signed on its behalf by M J Smith.

(c) Summary directors' report

This summary financial statement does not contain sufficient information to allow for a full understanding of the results of the Group and state of affairs of the company or the Group. For further information the full annual accounts, the auditors' report on those accounts and the directors' report should be consulted, as this statement is only a summary of the information given in full in those documents.

If you wish to receive, free of charge, a copy of the full directors' report and accounts, please write to the Company's registrar at the address to be found on page 16.

Summary directors' report – 52 weeks to 31 December 1994
The directors have pleasure in presenting this summary financial statement for the 52 week period ended 31 December 1994.

Principal activities and business review
The principal activity of the Group is the retailing of consumer durable goods through catalogue stores. The statement by the chairman on pages 2 and 3 and the operating review on pages 4 to 10 report on the progress made in the period under review and outline future developments.

Results and dividends
The consolidated accounts cover the 52 week period ended 31 December 1994. The Group profit for the financial period was £66.6 million. Of this, £7.9 million was used for the payment of the interim dividend at 2.65p per share, £23.7 million has been provided for the final dividend of 7.85p per share, and the balance of £35.0 million is retained profit.

The proposed final dividend is payable on 17 May 1995 to shareholders whose names are on the Register of Members at close of business on 13 April 1995.

Auditors' report
The auditors' report on the full accounts for the 52 week period ended 31 December 1994 is unqualified and does not contain a statement under either s 237(2) or s 237(3) of the Companies Act 1985.

Directors' details
In accordance with articles 89 and 95 of the Company's Articles of Association, Sir Richard Lloyd, Mr Birch, Mr O'Callaghan and Mr Stewart will retire at the forthcoming

annual general meeting and offer themselves for re-election. A list of directors who served throughout the period appears on page 11. In addition, Sir Richard Lloyd was appointed a director of the Company on 1 January 1995.

Annual general meeting
The notice convening the annual general meeting for 9 May 1995 is enclosed. The notes to the notice explain the special business of the meeting.

(d) Statement by the auditors to the members of Argos plc

We have audited the summary financial statement as set out on page 12 to 14 [not reproduced].

Respective responsibilities of directors and auditors
The summary financial statement is the responsibility of the directors. Our responsibility is to report to you our opinion as to whether the statement is consistent with the annual accounts and directors' report.

Basis of opinion
We conducted our audit in accordance with Auditing Standards issued by the Auditing Practices Board. The audit of a summary financial statement comprises an assessment of whether the statement contains all information necessary to ensure consistency with the annual accounts and directors' report and of whether the detailed information required by law has been properly extracted from those documents and included in the summary statement. Our report on the company's annual accounts includes information on the responsibilities of directors and auditors relating to the preparation and audit of accounts and on the basis of our opinion on the accounts.

Opinion
In our opinion the summary financial statement set out on pages 12 to 14 [not reproduced] is consistent with the annual accounts and the directors' report of Argos plc for the 52 week period ended 31 December 1994 and complies with the requirements of section 251 of the Companies Act 1985 and the regulations made thereunder.

Coopers & Lybrand, Chartered Accountants and Registered Auditors, London, 27 March 1995

C Balance sheet considerations

12 TANGIBLE FIXED ASSETS

Key Issues

* Definition of fixed asset
* Recognition test
* Determination of purchase price or production cost
* Enhancement costs (repair or improvement?)
* Capitalisation of borrowing costs
* Treatment of capital-based grants
* Depreciation
  – meaning
  – purpose
  – methods
  – changes in methods and asset lives
  – effect of revaluation
* Permanent diminution in value
* Disposal of fixed assets
  – carrying amount based on historical cost
  – carrying amount based on revaluation
* Investment properties
* Disclosures in financial statements

12.1 DEFINITION AND CLASSIFICATION

(a) Definition

A fixed asset may be defined as an asset that:

(1) is held by an enterprise for use in the production or supply of goods and services, for rental to others or for administrative purposes and may include items held for the maintenance or repair of such assets; and
(2) has been acquired or constructed with the intention of being used on a continuing basis; and
(3) is not intended for sale in the ordinary course of business.

(b) Main headings

Fixed assets may be classified under three main headings:

(1) tangible fixed assets – land and buildings, plant and machinery, fixtures and equipment;
(2) intangible fixed assets – goodwill, patents, licences, trademarks, development costs etc;
(3) investments.

(c) Scope of this chapter

The chapter is concerned with tangible fixed assets including investment properties. Chapter 18 deals with fixed assets leased under finance leases.

Intangible fixed assets are dealt with in chapter 13, while investments are dealt with in chapter 27.

12.2   DETERMINING COST

(a) Basic principles

Under the historical cost convention, the cost of a fixed asset may be defined either as:

(1) its purchase price; or
(2) its production cost.

Cost would also include any expenditure incurred in bringing the fixed asset to a working condition for its intended use at its intended location.

(b) Costs included

The following are examples of costs which may usually be taken into account in determining purchase price or production cost:

(1) purchased buildings

    (i)   purchase price (excluding land)
    (ii) repairs, alterations and improvements needed to bring into use for the buildings' intended purpose.

(2) constructed buildings

    (i)   cost of work sub-contracted
    (ii)   material, labour costs
    (iii) supervision costs
    (iv)   direct production overheads
    (v)   other incidental costs including professional fees
    (vi)   a proportion of indirect overheads to the extent that they relate to the period of production.

(3) plant and machinery purchased

    (i)   purchase price
    (ii)   freight and duty
    (iii) installation costs.

(4) self-constructed plant and machinery

    (i)   labour
    (ii)   materials
    (iii) appropriate production overheads.

(5) fixtures and fittings, e g show-cases, shelves, counters, shelving, display fixtures, safes, office equipment, furniture – purchase price or production cost.

(6) machine tools – capitalise but keep separate from the related machine as they are likely to have a shorter life.

(7) hand tools

    (i)   capitalise – record in a separate tool account, or
    (ii) write off in year of purchase.

(8) computer equipment

    (i)   hardware costs
    (ii) software costs

        (a) capitalise – but write off over relatively short period, or
        (b) write off as incurred.

(9) payments on account – note separate balance sheet heading (where material).

(10) assets in course of construction – note separate balance sheet heading (separate column in fixed asset schedule).

(c) Costs excluded

The following costs are usually excluded:

(1) administrative and general overheads;
(2) costs of relocating machinery within a factory or to another location;
(3) costs arising from inefficiencies (e g, idle capacity, industrial disputes).

(d) Enhancement costs

Expenditure relating to improvements to fixed assets should be capitalised. The key is to establish whether the expenditure will increase the expected future benefits from the existing fixed asset beyond its previously assessed standard of performance.

The following are examples of such future benefits:

(1) a significant lengthening of the asset's useful life over and above that which would follow from repairs and maintenance;
(2) an increase in the productive capacity of the asset;
(3) a substantial improvement in the quality of output;
(4) a substantial reduction in previously assessed operating costs;
(5) a substantial increase in the open market value of the fixed asset.

A common example of costs which would fall within the above requirements would be adaptation works to buildings.

12.3 CAPITALISATION OF INTEREST

(a) Conditions for capitalisation of borrowing costs

In certain circumstances, the interest cost of borrowed funds may be included in the production cost of an asset (eg a fixed asset or long-term contract work in progress).

The necessary conditions and disclosure requirements are set out in the Companies Act 1985.

These include:

(1) the interest cost must relate to capital borrowed to finance the production, ie it should normally relate to a specific source of finance. However, the main business of some companies may be several property development projects. In these circumstances it may be reasonable to apportion general interest charges between these projects;
(2) the interest cost must accrue in respect of the production period.

More detailed conditions are likely to be included in a future accounting standard. For example, a policy of capitalising or not capitalising such borrowing costs should be applied consistently for all qualifying fixed assets.

(b) Companies Act 1985 requires the following to be disclosed:

(1) the fact that such interest is capitalised;
(2) the amount of capitalised interest.

In addition, Stock Exchange listed companies must disclose:

(1) the amount of interest capitalised in the year;
(2) the treatment of any tax relief.

(c) Accounting policy note

Illustration 1

Interest costs incurred during the construction period on major fixed asset additions are capitalised and form part of the total asset cost. Depreciation is charged on the total cost including such interest.

12.4   GOVERNMENT GRANTS FOR CAPITAL EXPENDITURE

(a) Introduction

SSAP 4 (revised July 1990) deals with acounting for government grants. SSAP 4 is also dealt with in chapter 19, section 19.4. The note below deals with the situation of a grant which is made as a contribution towards expenditure on fixed assets.

(b) Standard accounting practice

SSAP 4 states that in principle two methods may be acceptable:

(1) to treat the amount of the grant as deferred income. The deferred income should be credited to profit and loss account over the expected useful economic life of the related asset on a basis consistent with the depreciation policy. This method is recommended as it accords with the requirements of the Companies Act 1985;
(2) to deduct the amount of the grant from the purchase price or production cost of the related asset, with a consequent reduction in the annual charge for depreciation. This method is not recommended as it is prohibited by the requirements of the Companies Act 1985. It was, however, referred to in chapter 9, section 9.5(b), with regard to the true and fair override.

(c) Acceptable treatment

Illustration 2

Manufacturers Ltd acquired an item of machinery on 1 January 19X3 at a cost of £100,000. The company received an investment grant of £20,000. The asset is to be depreciated over five years on a straight-line basis.
  Show the relevant ledger accounts and financial statements extracts for 19X3 and 19X4.

(1) Ledger accounts

Fixed assets – cost

	£'000		£'000
1.1.X3 Cash	100,000		

Fixed assets – accumulated depreciation

	£'000			£'000
		31.12.X3 P/L		20,000
31.12.X4 Bal c/d	40,000	31.12.X4 P/L		20,000
	40,000			40,000

Investment grants – deferred income

		£'000			£'000
31.12.X3	P/L	4,000	1.1.X3 Cash		20,000
	Bal c/d	16,000			
		20,000			20,000
31.12.X4	P/L	4,000	Bal b/d		16,000
	bal c/d	12,000			
		16,000			16,000

(2) Financial statements extracts

(i) *Accounting policy note*

Capital based investment grants are included in the accounts as deferred income and released to revenue over five years, being the estimated average useful life of the asset which attracted the grant.

(ii) *Balance sheet (extracts)*

	31 December	
	19X3	19X4
	£'000	£'000
Fixed assets		
– tangible assets	80	60
Deferred income		
– investment grants	16	12

(iii) *Profit and loss account notes*

	19X3	19X4
	£'000	£'000
Profit on ordinary activities is stated after charging		
Depreciation	20	20
Less: release from deferred income		
– investment grants	4	4
	16	16

	19X3 £'000	19X4 £'000
(iv) *Balance sheet notes*		
Tangible fixed assets		
Cost at 1 January	–	100
Additions	100	–
At 31 December	100	100
Depreciation		
At 1 January	–	20
Provided during year	20	20
At 31 December	20	40
Net book amount	80	60
Deferred income – investment grants		
Balance at 1 January	–	16
Grants received	20	
Released to profit and loss a/c	(4)	(4)
Balance at 31 December	16	12

Illustration 3

Extract from annual report and accounts of J Bibby & Sons plc for the year ended 30 September 1995.

Accounting policies (extract)

Fixed assets
Depreciation is calculated to write off fixed assets by equal annual instalments over their estimated useful lives. Freehold land is not depreciated.

The estimated lives of the assets are:

	Years		*Years*
Freehold buildings	10–50	Plant and machinery	3–20
Leasehold buildings	50*	Vehicles	3–10
* or the period of the lease, if less			

   Investment and regional development grants receivable in respect of expenditure on fixed assets are credited to the profit and loss account over the lives of the assets on which the grants were received. Investments in subsidiaries are reflected at the lower of cost and net asset value at acquisition in the accounts of the Company.

Balance sheet (extract)

	Notes	Consolidated 1995 £000's	1994 £000's	Company 1995 £000's	1994 £000's
Fixed assets					
Tangible assets	6	**157,611**	151,182	–	–
Investments	7	**950**	111	**157,986**	155,635
		158,561	151,293	**157,986**	155,635
Current assets					
Deferred taxation asset due after more than one year	19	**9,941**	12,218	–	–
Stocks	8	**131,005**	113,101	–	–
Debtors	9	**154,879**	150,178	**79,032**	27,158
Taxation		**–**	–	**1,531**	782
Cash		**28,055**	14,460	**8,544**	33,957
		323,880	289,957	**89,107**	61,897

Current liabilities
Amounts falling due within one year

Creditors and provisions	10	**138,481**	139,559	**1,598**	5,474
Taxation		**4,911**	2,472	–	–
Dividends		**6,252**	3,125	**6,252**	3,125
Short term borrowings	11	**29,204**	45,013	**1,752**	12,417
		178,848	190,169	**9,602**	21,016
Net current assets		**145,032**	99,788	**79,505**	40,881

Amounts falling due after more than one year

Creditors and provisions	12	**41,120**	38,180	**21,349**	1,200
Taxation		**1,274**	1,340	–	–
Loans	13	**88,886**	51,524	**46,126**	24,103
Investment grants	14	**1,033**	1,283	–	–
		132,313	92,327	**67,475**	25,303
Net assets		**171,280**	158,754	**170,016**	171,213

12.5 DEPRECIATION

(a) SSAP 12 – Accounting for depreciation

SSAP 12 was issued in revised form in January 1987. The standard applies to all fixed assets except for investment properties (see section 12.9), goodwill (see section 13.2), development costs (see section 13.3) and fixed asset investments. Note that the standard applies to all intangibles other than goodwill and development costs and so includes patents, licences, trademarks, publishing titles and so on.

(b) Definition of depreciation

Depreciation is defined in SSAP 12 as: the measure of the wearing out, consumption or other reduction in the useful economic life of a fixed asset, whether arising from use, effluxion of time or obsolescence through technology and market changes.

(c) Purpose of depreciation

The primary purpose of depreciation is to allocate a fair proportion of the cost of a fixed asset over the asset's expected useful life.

More specifically, SSAP 12 requires that provision for depreciation of fixed assets with finite useful lives should be made as follows: allocate cost (or revalued amount) less estimated residual value as fairly as possible over the number of years expected to benefit from the use of the asset.

A further aspect referred to by some accountants is replacement of fixed assets at the end of their useful lives. By making a depreciation charge, funds which might otherwise be distributed as dividend are retained within the business. Note, however, that the standard does not regard adequacy of funds for asset replacement as a main purpose of providing depreciation. The guidance notes to SSAP 16 (subsequently withdrawn) stated:

> ... As with historical cost, the provision of cash to replace individual assets in the future is a matter for financial management and remains outside the ambit of the accounting system.

The conclusion, therefore, is that depreciation is concerned primarily with cost allocation in accordance with the accruals concept.

(d) Calculating depreciation

The following three factors need to be taken into account:

(1) cost (or valuation when an asset has been revalued in the financial statements);
(2) the nature of the asset and the length of its expected useful life to the business having due regard to the incidence of obsolescence;
(3) estimated residual value.

(e) Cost or valuation of an asset

The carrying amount of a fixed asset may be based on either historical cost or valuation.

(1) Historical cost – where an asset is purchased from an outside supplier, historical cost is an objective figure. Where a company constructs fixed assets for continuing use in the business historical cost includes all those costs incurred in bringing the assets to their present location and conditions and thus includes a proportion of production overheads as well as direct material and labour costs. In some circumstances a proportion of borrowing costs may also be included (see section 12.3).
(2) Valuation – a company may revalue fixed assets at a subsequent date and substitute a revaluation figure in place of historical cost.

(f) Residual value

SSAP 12 defines this as the realisable value of the asset at the end of its useful economic life based on prices prevailing at the date of acquisition or revaluation, where this has taken place. Realisation costs should be deducted in arriving at the residual value.

(g) Useful life

Useful life may be:

(1) predetermined, as in leaseholds;
(2) directly governed by extraction or consumption (eg mineral deposits);
(3) dependent on the extent of use;
(4) reduced by economic or technological obsolescence (eg specialised machinery manufacturing products for which there is no longer demand).

Useful life refers to useful economic life as far as the present owner is concerned and not the asset's total economic useful life.

Determination of useful life inevitably involves the exercise of judgement by management and should be reviewed annually. Where management considers that an original estimate of useful life needs to be revised, the unamortised cost of the asset should be charged to profit and loss account over the revised remaining useful life.

(h) Depreciation methods

The method selected should be the one most appropriate to the type of asset and its use in the business. The principal methods are set out below:

(1) *Straight-line (fixed instalment) method*
    Under this method, cost (or valuation) less estimated residual value is allocated over the asset's estimated useful life on a straight-line basis.

Illustration 4

Plant and machinery was acquired on 1.1.19X6 at a cost of £70,000. Estimated useful life and residual value were four years and £5,000 respectively.

Annual depreciation charge

$$= \frac{£70,000 - £5,000}{4} = £16,250$$

(2) *Reducing balancing method*

The depreciation charge is calculated by applying a percentage rate to the accounts written down value of the asset.

In examination questions, the depreciation rate is given. However, the rate may be calculated by applying the following formula:

$R = C(1 - D)^L$
R = residual value
C = cost
D = depreciation rate
L = economic useful life

Applying the formula to the figures in the above illustration:

$£5,000 = £70,000 (1 - D)^4$
$(1 - D)^4 = 0.0714285$
$1 - D = 0.516973$
$D = 0.483027$

		£
Check	Cost at 1.1.19X6	70,000
	Depreciation charge 19X6	
	48.3027% × 70,000	33,812
	Acs WDV at 31.12.X6	36,188
	Depreciation charge 19X7	
	48.3027% × £36,188	17,480
	Acs WDV at 31.12.X7	18,708
	Depreciation charge 19X8	
	48.3027% × £18,708	9,036
	Acs WDV at 31.12.X8	9,672
	Depreciation charge 19X9	
	48.3027% × £9,672	4,672
	Acs WDV at 31.12.X10	5,000

Note: At the end of its useful life, the accounts written down value equals the estimated residual value.

Advantages claimed for the reducing balance method include the following:

(1) the method reflects the more rapid fall in value of particular assets (e g cars) in their earlier years;

(2) the higher charge for depreciation in the early years of an asset's life balances out with lower repair charges. Correspondingly, as an asset becomes old, the lower depreciation charges balance out with higher repair charges.

(3) *Output or usage method*

This method apportions the cost of a fixed asset in relation to the output or usage each year. The method may be useful where the output or usage varies significantly from one year to another.

Illustration 5

A machine which cost £20,000 on 1.1.19X5 has an estimated life of three years. Its total life in machine hours is 2,700 hours, expected to arise as follows:

19X5	1,500
19X6	800
19X7	400
	2,700

Depreciation charges under this method (ignoring residual value) would be:

	£
19X5 $\dfrac{1,500}{2,700} \times £20,000$	11,111
19X6 $\dfrac{800}{2,700} \times £20,000$	5,926
19X7 $\dfrac{400}{2,700} \times £20,000$	2,963
	20,000

(4) *Annuity or rising charges method*

The capital locked up in the asset is regarded as earning interest; a constant annual charge for depreciation is credited to the asset account, so calculated that during the life of the asset it will write off its cost (less any scrap value) plus the interest earned. The interest earned is debited to the asset account; it is calculated at a fixed rate per cent, but on the reducing balance. Actuarially, the cost of the asset is regarded as providing an annuity during its life, the value of the annuity being the annual charge to depreciation.

This is the most scientific system when investment is not desired outside the business, but may be criticised from the viewpoint that it introduces an uncertain element i e the rate of interest, which is bound to be arbitrarily arrived at, and also that it is not sufficiently conservative in the early years, so that if obsolescence supervenes, the true depreciation will not have been provided; but the latter objection can be met by shortening the estimated life on which the calculations are based. The annuity system is particularly applicable to long leases, where no additions are made to the asset during its life. It is not generally used for plant, since, when additions are made from time to time, these would at once necessitate further calculations.

Illustration 6

A lease costs £6,000 for a term of seven years. Depreciation by the annuity method at $6\frac{1}{2}\%$ per annum, calculations being taken to the nearest £, would be:

Workings

(i) *Notional depreciation charge*

The annual amount of depreciation under this system is calculated from actuarial tables compiled for the purpose employing the formula:

$$\frac{i}{1-(1+i)^{-n}} = \text{Periodic rest of annuity whose present value is 1}$$

where i is the annual rate of interest and n is the number of years of the term. Consequently, the annual depreciation is:

$$\text{£6,000} \times \frac{6.5/100}{1-(1+6.5/100)^{-7}}$$

$$= 6,000 \times \frac{6.5}{100\,(1-1/1.554)}$$

$$= 6,000 \times 0.1823 = \text{£1,094 to the nearest £.}$$

(ii) *Notional interest credit*

	B/F	Notional interest $6\frac{1}{2}\%$	Notional depreciation (working (i))	C/F
19X1	6,000	390	(1,094)	5,296
19X2	5,296	344	(1,094)	4,546
19X3	4,546	295	(1,094)	3,747
19X4	3,747	244	(1,094)	2,897
19X5	2,897	188	(1,094)	1,991
19X6	1,991	129	(1,094)	1,026
19X7	1,026	68	(1,094)	–

(iii) *Summary – depreciation charge in profit and loss account*

	Total £
19X1	704
19X2	750
19X3	799
19X4	850
19X5	906
19X6	965
19X7	1,026
	6,000

(5) *Choice of method*

ED 37 issued in March 1985 (and subsequently superseded by SSAP 12 revised) stated:

> ... management should select the method regarded as most appropriate to the type of asset and its use in the business, so as to allocate depreciation as fairly as possible to the periods expected to benefit from the use of the asset. Although the straight-line method is the simplest to apply it may not always be the most appropriate.

(i) Change in method

A change in method is only allowed if the new method will give a fairer presentation of results and financial position.

Where the depreciation method is changed, the unamortised cost (i e cost less depreciation to date) should be written off over the remaining number of years' useful life.

If the change in method has a material effect on the profit for the year, the effect of the change should be disclosed.

(j) Supplementary depreciation

If a company wishes to provide depreciation in excess of that based on the carrying amount of the asset, the excess should not be charged to profit and loss account. It may, however, be treated as an appropriation of profit and credited to a specified fixed asset replacement reserve.

(k) Depreciation of buildings

The requirement to depreciate applies just as much to buildings as to other categories of fixed assets. SSAP 12 points out that buildings have a limited economic life. For example, although the physical life of a building may be extended almost indefinitely, its economic life may be restricted by reference to technological and environmental changes. A building may become techno-logically obsolete and therefore may need to be replaced by a more modern building.

The fact that the market value of a building exceeds the net book value does not remove the need to record a depreciation charge in the profit and loss account. Only if estimated residual value (measured at current price levels) is expected to equal or exceed existing net book value is no depreciation charge required.

Two points are worth mentioning:

(1) Investment properties, as defined in SSAP 19, should not be depreciated (see section 12.9).
(2) Depreciation is not necessary if failure to depreciate would not have a material effect on the accounts. For example, if a brewery group had a comprehensive and systematic programme to carry out maintenance work on its licensed houses, it might be able to argue that such mainte-nance expenditure kept estimated residual value very close to existing net book value. Several companies have successfully advanced this argu-ment, particularly those in the licensed and hotel trades.

(l) The importance of subjective judgement

Several subjective estimates enter into the calculation of the depreciation charge. For example:

(1) original estimation of the useful life of a fixed asset;
(2) annual review of useful life;
(3) estimate of residual value;
(4) recognition of permanent diminution in value (see below);
(5) revaluation – where depreciation is based on revalued amount (see section 12.7).

12.6   PERMANENT DIMINUTION IN VALUE

(a) Introduction

There may be situations where the unamortised cost of a fixed asset is unlikely to be recovered in full. An example of such a situation could be where a fixed asset has become technologically obsolete.

(b) Definition

A possible definition of a *permanent diminution* in the value of a fixed asset is a diminution in the amount recoverable from its future use and subsequent disposal which is not expected to reverse in the foreseeable future.

(c) Situations

A permanent diminution in value is caused by an irreversible change in circumstances. The following are possible examples of such circumstances:

(1) significant technological developments;
(2) physical damage;
(3) structural changes in external economic conditions leading to reduced demand for the output produced by the fixed asset;
(4) a change in the law or the environment relating to the fixed asset.

(d) Illustration 7

The net book value at 31.12.19X6 of a group of fixed assets was arrived at as follows:

	£
Cost	280,000
Accumulated depreciation (Four years at 10%)	112,000
Net book value at 31.12.19X6	168,000

During 19X7, it has become apparent that the machines will only be used for a further two years, as the goods produced by the machines have suffered a permanent fall in demand.

At 31.12.19X7, an assessment was made of anticipated future net cash inflows expected to be generated. These were as follows:

19X8	30,000
19X9	15,000
	45,000

No further goods will be produced after this date, and the machinery is expected to be worthless on account of its specialised nature.

The effect on the financial statements will be as follows:

Year ended 31.12.X7
Profit and loss account: depreciation charge
(£168,000–£45,000)   £123,000
Balance sheet (net book value)   £45,000

Years ending 31.12.X8 and 19X9
Depreciation charge £22,500 per annum
(assuming straight-line depreciation is appropriate)

If subsequently the reasons for making the provision no longer apply, the provision should be written back to profit and loss account to the extent that it is no longer necessary.

12.7 REVALUATION OF FIXED ASSETS

(a) Background

UK accounting practice has always permitted companies to incorporate fixed asset revaluations into their balance sheets. This practice, sometimes referred to as 'modified historical cost', is permitted by the Companies Act 1985 under the alternative accounting rules.

(b) Revaluation policy

UK companies may therefore carry assets in the balance sheet at either:

(1) historical cost less accumulated depreciation; or
(2) revaluation less accumulated depreciation since the date of revaluation.

However, companies are unlikely to revalue *all* assets annually (except for investment properties, see section 12.9) and may not extend revaluation to all categories of fixed assets. Companies are therefore given considerable discretion as to how they may apply modified historical cost. Companies are required to disclose in the directors' report significant differences between market values and book values of property assets.

(c) The viewpoint of the former ASC

The explanatory note to SSAP 12 states:

> It has, however, become increasingly common for enterprises to revalue their fixed assets, in particular freehold and leasehold property, and to incorporate these revalued amounts in their financial statements. This gives useful and relevant information to users of accounts. This statement does not prescribe how frequently assets should be revalued but, where a policy of revaluing assets is adopted, the valuations should be kept up to date.

In May 1990, the ASC issued an exposure draft ED 51 – Accounting for fixed assets and revaluations. The ASB has also published a discussion paper on the subject.

(d) The requirements of SSAP 12

Where assets are revalued, and the revaluation is reflected in the balance sheet, SSAP 12 requires the depreciation charge to be based on the revalued amount.

In the year of change, disclosure by way of note is required of the breakdown of the new charge between that applicable to historical cost (or historical revaluation) and that applicable to the current change in valuation.

Illustration 8

A company acquired an asset on 1.1.19X2 at a cost of £100,000. The useful life of the asset was estimated as 10 years with a nil residual value at the end of that period. Depreciation is provided on a straight-line basis.

At 31.12.X4, the net book value of the asset is £70,000 (cost £100,000 less accumulated depreciation of £30,000). Suppose the asset is revalued at £84,000 and the remaining useful life still assumed to be seven years.

Revaluation surplus should be credited with £14,000 and the depreciation charge for 19X5 onwards should be £12,000 per annum (ie £84,000 ÷ 7).

Several important points may be made:

(1) The depreciation charge in the profit and loss account should be related to the carrying amount in the balance sheet. Once a revaluation is incorporated in the balance sheet, depreciation charges relating to periods after this date should be based on revalued amount. In particular, no part of the depreciation charge should be set directly against reserves. In the above illustration, profit and loss account should be debited with £12,000. It would not be acceptable to debit £10,000 to profit and loss account and the remaining £2,000 to revaluation reserve (the so-called split depreciation method).

(2) The effect of the revaluation has been to increase the annual depreciation charge by £2,000 (ie £12,000 less £10,000).

(3) Each year (from 19X5 onwards) the company should make a transfer within reserves of £2,000 ie taking £2,000 out of revaluation reserve and into profit and loss reserves as follows:

	Profit and loss account £	Revaluation reserve £
Balance 1.1.X5	X	14,000
Transfer within reserves	2,000	(2,000)
Retained profit 19X5	X	X
Balance 31.12.X5	X	X

Each year £2,000 of the revaluation reserve becomes realised and thus forms part of distributable profit (see section 15.7(i)). At the end of the

asset's useful life the part of the revaluation reserve relating to that asset should no longer exist.
(4) Depreciation charged prior to the revaluation should not be written back to profit and loss account except to the extent that it relates to a provision for permanent diminution in value which is subsequently found to be unnecessary, ie £14,000 must be credited to revaluation reserve (as indicated above) and not profit and loss account.

(e) Further illustration

(1) The details

A company owns a freehold building. The building is used by the company for its own operations and is therefore not to be treated as an investment property under SSAP 19.
At 1.1.X2, the relevant balances and the breakdown between land and buildings were:

	£	£
Land		150,000
Buildings:		
Cost	75,000	
Depreciation (8 years at 2%)	12,000	63,000
Net book value		213,000

The building was revalued on the last day of the year at £320,000. The valuer allocated the valuation as follows:

	£
Land	230,000
Buildings	90,000
	320,000

This revaluation was to be incorporated into the balance sheet at 31.12.X2. The remaining useful life of the building was left unchanged at 41 years.
Required: show the effect of the above information on the financial statements for the year.

(2) Workings

(i) Calculation of surplus on revaluation
Since the revaluation takes place on the last day of the year, the depreciation charge for the whole year is based on historical cost ie 2% × £75,000 = £1,500.

For 19X3 and subsequent years, the depreciation charge will be $\frac{£90,000}{41}$ ie £2,195.

The surplus on revaluation may be calculated as follows:

	£
Net book value at 31.12.X2	211,500
(213,000 − 1,500)	
Revaluation figure	320,000
So surplus on revaluation	108,500

Attributable:	
Land (230,000 − 150,000)	80,000
Buildings (90,000 − (63,000 − 1,500))	28,500
	108,500

(ii) Effect of revaluation on depreciation charge of subsequent years

Part of charge applicable to:	£
Historical cost	1,500
$\frac{1}{41} \times £28,500$	695
Total charge	2,195

(3) Effect on financial statements

(i) Fixed asset schedule (extract)
 Cost or revaluation

	£
Cost at 1.1.X2	225,000
Adjustment on revaluation	95,000
Revaluation at 31.12.X2	320,000

Depreciation	
At 1.1.X2	12,000
Provided during the year	1,500
Adjustment on revaluation (13,500)	(13,500)
At 31.12.X2	–

Net book value	
31.12.X2	320,000
31.12.X1	213,000

(ii) Profit and loss account (extract)
 Depreciation charge   1,500

(iii) Revaluation reserve account
 Movement on account   108,500

(iv) Comparable historical cost figures (Companies Act 1985 disclosure)

	£
Cost	225,000
Depreciation	13,500
	211,500

Additional comments

(1) The Companies Act 1985 requires information to be given regarding details of revaluations which took place during the year (eg name of valuer or qualification, basis of valuation).
(2) The part of the total revaluation reserve attributable to buildings (£28,500) may be amortised over the remaining life of the buildings (41 years) and dealt with each year as a transfer within reserves (as previously discussed).

(f) Revaluation deficits

This topic is not covered by any accounting standard, but is under consideration by the Accounting Standards Board.
  A previous exposure draft, ED 36, subsequently withdrawn, stated:

> ... deficits on the revaluation of fixed assets should be debited to the profit and loss account for the year to the extent that they exceed any surplus held in reserves and identified as relating to previous revaluations of the same assets.

The treatment of revaluation deficits is far from clear. One view is that it is necessary to consider the position for each individual asset and not to consider a class of assets (the portfolio approach). The position will need to be clarified in a future accounting standard.

(g) The desirability of modified historical cost (MHC)

An advantage claimed for MHC is that the inclusion in the balance sheet of up-to-date property values helps to overcome a major limitation of historical cost accounts during a period of rising prices.
  However, the practice of MHC creates several problems including:

(1) Lack of comparability between companies as regards revaluation policies. Some companies may extend MHC to several classes of fixed assets while others restrict revaluation to particular asset classes such as property assets. Some companies may state all their fixed assets at historical cost less depreciation. Frequency of revaluation is also likely to differ as between companies.

(2) Two companies may be identical in all respects and experience the same transactions and cash flows. Because one company adopts MHC and the other does not, they could report markedly differing profit figures because of different figures for depreciation charges and profit on sale of assets. Earnings per share could also look quite different. Would company analysts be able to allow for this and come to the correct conclusion that both companies had performed identically? There is evidence to show that this is a particular problem area. Difficulties caused by MHC are now becoming apparent.

As indicated above, a future standard will establish detailed ground rules concerning company policy, frequency of revaluations, those able to carry out valuations and so on.

12.8 DISPOSAL OF FIXED ASSETS

(a) Carrying amount based on historical cost

Profit or loss on disposal is calculated by comparing net disposal proceeds and the net carrying amount (ie historical cost of purchase or production less accumulated depreciation). Under FRS 3, the gain or loss on disposal, if material, would be treated as an exceptional item (see section 8.4).

(b) Carrying amount based on revaluation

FRS 3 requires profit or loss on sale to be determined by comparing proceeds of sale with net book value (derived from a previous revaluation) at the date of sale.

Illustration 9

A company acquired a building in 19X2 at a cost of £120,000. The building was revalued in 19X6 at £250,000. The revaluation was reflected in the accounts and £130,000 credited to revaluation reserve as an unrealised surplus. The building was subsequently sold in 19X8 for proceeds of £400,000. Ignore depreciation.

The profit on sale may be calculated as follows:

£400,000 − £250,000, ie £150,000. Assuming the profit on sale is to be regarded as an exceptional item, the profit and loss account would disclose an exceptional profit of £150,000. The amount of £130,000 hitherto included in revaluation reserve would then be transferred by means of a movement within reserves (ie no entry would be made in the actual profit and loss account) to profit and loss reserves.

12.9 INVESTMENT PROPERTIES (SSAP 19)

(a) Background

The general principle established by SSAP 12, and confirmed by the Companies Act 1985, is that fixed assets with a restricted useful life should be subject to a depreciation charge.

The majority of fixed assets are used by the company for its own use in its business operations. However, certain types of property assets, referred to as investment properties, are held for their investment potential. Such properties have not usually been depreciated and have been excluded from the requirements of SSAP 12.

The definition and accounting treatment of investment properties are covered by SSAP 19.

(b) Definition

An investment property:

(1) *is* an interest in land and/or buildings in respect of which construction work and development work has been completed *and* which is held for its investment potential. It must be shown that the disposal of such a property would not materially affect any manufacturing or trading operations of the enterprise; and
(2) does *not* include:

    (i) property owned and occupied by the company for its own purposes;
    (ii) property let to, and occupied by, another group company. (*Note:* this does not exclude property let to an associated company provided that rental income is determined on an arm's length basis.)

(c) Accounting treatment

The main features are as follows:

(1) A current value accounting system which reflects the fact that the main interest is in the current values of properties and changes therein.
(2) Investment properties should not be subject to periodic depreciation charges.

    There is an important exception to this. Investment properties held on leases with less than 20 years to run at the balance sheet date should be depreciated. This is to avoid a situation which might otherwise occur whereby a company purchased a short lease, charged the amortisation direct to reserves (investment revaluation reserve) but credited any rentals received on the letting to profit and loss account.

(3) Investment properties (including those held on leases with less than 20 years to run) should be included in the balance sheet at their open market value.
(4) Changes in valuation from one balance sheet date to the next should be credited or debited to investment revaluation reserve (IRR). If the total balance on IRR is insufficient to cover an overall deficit on all investment properties, the excess should be charged to profit and loss account.

(d) Disclosure

The following should be disclosed in the financial statements:

(1) names of valuers or particulars of their qualifications;
(2) basis of valuation;
(3) whether valuations have been made by employees or officers;
(4) prominent disclosure of investment properties, IRR and movements thereon;
(5) historical cost information relating to revalued assets.

(e) Companies Act 1985 implications

Under the Act, fixed assets with a limited useful economic life should be subject to periodic depreciation charges.

However, the Act also has a true and fair view requirement which overrides specific requirements. Should this apply (as it does with SSAP 19), a note to the accounts should give 'particulars of that departure, the reasons for it, and its effect' (see also UITF 7, section 9.5).

Illustration 10

Extract from annual report and accounts of The Boots Company plc for the year ended 31 March 1995.

Note 12 – Tangible fixed assets (extract)

	£m
Land and buildings include investment properties as follows	
Valuation	
At 1 April 1994	93.3
Additions	41.4
Reclassification	(1.0)
Revaluation surplus	6.6
At 31 March 1995	**140.3**

Investment properties were valued on the basis of open market value at 31 March 1995 by the group's own professionally qualified staff.

In accordance with SSAP 19, no depreciation is provided in respect of investment properties. This represents a departure from the Companies Act 1985 requirements to provide for the systematic annual depreciation of fixed assets. However, these properties are held for investment, rather than consumption, and the directors consider that the adoption of the above policy is necessary to give a true and fair view.

12.10   DISCLOSURE REQUIREMENTS – A SUMMARY

(a) SSAP 12 – Accounting for depreciation

(1) the depreciation methods used;
(2) the useful lives or the depreciation rates used;
(3) total depreciation allocated for the period;
(4) the gross amount of depreciable assets and the related accumulated depreciation.

Other disclosure requirements, where material:

(1) in the event of a change in depreciation method, the effect on profit in the year of change as well as reasons for the change;
(2) in the event of fixed asset revaluations, the effect of the revaluation on the depreciation charge for the year of revaluation.

(b) SSAP 19 – Accounting for investment properties

(1) names of valuers or particulars of their qualifications;
(2) basis of valuation;
(3) whether valuations have been made by employees or officers;
(4) prominent disclosure of investment properties, IRR and movements thereon;
(5) historical cost information relating to revalued assets.

(c) Companies Act 1985

(1) financial statements

   (i)   fixed assets movements (cost, accumulated depreciation etc) and analysis
   (ii) depreciation charge
   (iii) analysis of cost/valuation between years of valuation and values
   (iv) for a year in which a valuation takes place, names of valuers (or details of their qualifications) and bases of valuation
   (v)   for assets held at valuation, comparable historical cost figures.

(2) directors' report

   (i)   significant changes in fixed assets during the year
   (ii) substantial differences between market values and book values of land and buildings.

(3) Yellow Book (Stock Exchange requirements for listed companies)

   (i)   interest capitalised during year
   (ii) treatment of tax relief on capitalised interest.

Illustration 11

Extract from annual report and accounts of Argyll Group plc for the year ended 1 April 1995.

Statement of accounting policies (extract)

Tangible fixed assets
Tangible fixed assets are stated at cost less accumulated depreciation, Plant, equipment and vehicles which are leased but provide the group with substantially all the benefits and risks of ownership are capitalised at the original cost to the lessor.
   The costs of operating leases of land and buildings and other assets are charged to the profit and loss account as incurred. Surpluses on sale and operating leaseback of properties are recognised as income in the year of disposal.
   Interest costs relating to the financing of freehold and long leasehold developments are capitalised at the weighted average cost of the related borrowings up to the date of completion of the project.
   Freehold land is not depreciated unless, in the opinion of the directors, a permanent diminution in value has occurred.
   Depreciation is provided to write off the cost of other tangible fixed assets over their estimated economic lives on a straight-line basis as follows:

Freehold and long leasehold buildings – maximum of 40 years
Short leasehold buildings   – maximum of 40 years or term of lease if less
Plant and equipment   – 4 years to a maximum of 8 years
Motor cars and commercial vehicles   – 4 years to a maximum of 6 years
Computer hardware and software   – 4 years to a maximum of 6 years

   In the case of poor performing or proposed replacement stores, additional depreciation is provided over the remaining estimated life to write down to net realisable value.
   The group's policy is to maintain its properties to a high standard through a continual programme of refurbishment and maintenance.

Illustration 12

Extract from the annual report and accounts of T Cowie Group plc for the year ended 31 December 1994.

Note 11 – Tangible fixed assets

	Land & Buildings £000	Plant, Company Vehicles, Buses & Coaches £000	Fixtures & Fittings £000	Contract Hire Vehicles £000	Total £000
(a) The Group					
Cost or Valuation					
At 1 January 1994	49,857	36,856	5,782	443,147	535,642
Acquisitions	5,455	35,402	5	30,414	71,276
Additions	755	19,536	520	182,560	203,371
Disposals	(496)	(18,121)	(822)	(158,917)	(178,356)
At 31 December 1994	55,571	73,673	5,485	497,204	631,933
Comprising					
Cost	13,221	73,673	5,485	497,204	589,583
Valuation 1992	27,700	–	–	–	27,700
Valuation 1993	14,650	–	–	–	14,650
	55,571	73,673	5,485	497,204	631,933
Accumulated depreciation					
At 1 January 1994	632	14,602	3,761	150,467	169,462
Acquisitions	–	22,687	–	–	22,687
Amounts provided	432	6,911	607	100,577	108,527
Disposals	(98)	(5,203)	(756)	(89,078)	(95,135)
At 31 December 1994	966	38,997	3,612	161,966	205,541
Net book amounts					
At 31 December 1994	54,605	34,676	1,873	335,238	426,392
At 1 January 1994	49,225	22,254	2,021	292,680	366,180

The net book amount of assets held under finance leases, included in plant, company vehicles, buses and coaches and contract hire vehicles is £5,896,000 and £203,000 respectively.

The depreciation provided in the year in respect of those assets is £730,000 and £328,000 respectively.

	1994 £000	1993 £000
Net book amount of land and buildings comprises:		
Freehold	**50,572**	44,584
Long leasehold	**3,076**	3,119
Short leasehold	**957**	1,522
	54,605	49,225

On an historical cost basis land and buildings would have been included at cost of £60,917,000 and accumulated depreciation of £1,027,000.

13 INTANGIBLE FIXED ASSETS

Key Issues

* Regulatory framework
* Goodwill
  – background
  – accounting rules
  – effect of different treatments
  – disclosures
* Research and development
  – classification and examples
  – considerations for capitalisation
  – accounting rules
  – disclosures
* Accounting for intangibles
  – the search for a standard
* Published accounts illustrations

13.1 INTRODUCTION

(a) Statutory headings

Companies Act 1985 Sch 4 includes the following sub-headings for intangible fixed assets:

(1) development costs;
(2) concessions, patents, licences, trade marks and similar rights and assets;
(3) goodwill.

(b) Definition

ED 52-Accounting for intangible fixed assets, provides the following definition of an intangible fixed asset: a fixed asset that is non-monetary in nature and without physical substance.

(c) Regulatory framework

(1) Companies Act 1985

    (i)   format headings – these were referred to in (a) above.
    (ii) accounting rules – there are two important rules:

        (a) intangibles such as concessions, patents, licences, trade marks and similar rights and assets may only be included in the balance sheet in either of the following situations:

            (1) the assets were acquired for valuable consideration and are not effectively part of goodwill, or
            (2) the assets were created by the company itself. (Note that the Companies Act 1985 prevents non-purchased or internally generated goodwill from being included on the balance sheet).

(b) intangible assets (other than goodwill) may be included at their current cost. This alternative to historical cost is permitted by the alternative accounting rules of Schedule 4. It is not clear whether this statutory rule effectively permits companies to revalue intangible fixed assets (in a similar way to tangibles) within the historical cost framework. Opinion is divided and ED 52 attempts to limit the circumstances in which the alternative would be permitted.

(2) SSAPs

Accounting standards deal with research and development (SSAP 13), and goodwill (SSAP 22). There is also an exposure draft, ED 52, dealing with accounting for intangible fixed assets. These statements are referred to below.

(d) Illustrations

The following are examples of some intangible fixed asset headings which have appeared in the accounts of several listed PLCs:

(1) goodwill;
(2) development costs;
(3) brand names;
(4) patents, trade marks and other product rights;
(5) trade values of retail outlets;
(6) betting office licences;
(7) mailing list expansion;
(8) deferred launch costs;
(9) know-how agreement;
(10) programmes, film rights and stores;
(11) newspaper titles;
(12) publishing copyright;
(13) publishing rights and titles, databases, exhibition rights and other similar intangible assets.

13.2   ACCOUNTING FOR GOODWILL

(a) Background

For over 15 years, the Accounting Standards Committee sought to produce a widely acceptable standard on accounting for goodwill.

The most recently issued standard, SSAP 22, was extended in July 1989 to include additional disclosure requirements. At the same time ASC was reappraising the situation and in February 1990 issued an exposure draft, ED 48. The Accounting Standards Board has published a discussion paper and a working paper (see 13.2(r)).

(b) Factors contributing to goodwill

An established business may possess advantages such as the following:

(1) superior management team;
(2) effective advertising;
(3) market dominance;
(4) established list of customers;
(5) experienced work-force;
(6) good relations with suppliers;
(7) reputation of products;
(8) strategic location, and so on.

(c) Definitions

Goodwill is defined by SSAP 22 as the difference between the value of a business as a whole and the aggregate of the fair values of its separable net assets.

Fair value is the amount for which an asset or liability could be exchanged in an arm's length transaction. Separable net assets are essentially those assets which can be sold or disposed of separately from the rest of the business.

(d) Classification of goodwill

Possible types of goodwill may be illustrated diagrammatically as follows:

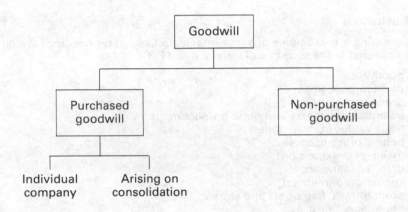

Non-purchased goodwill is sometimes referred to as inherent goodwill or internally generated goodwill.

(e) Special characteristics of goodwill

Several features distinguish goodwill from other assets, including:

(1) goodwill cannot be sold as a separate asset apart from the rest of the business;
(2) the value of goodwill may fluctuate from day to day;
(3) the value and existence of goodwill are subjective;
(4) the value of goodwill has no reliable relationship to costs which may have been incurred in its creation.

(f) Measurement problems

(1) *Purchased goodwill*

Purchased goodwill results from a definitive market transaction. Consequently, it is capable of objective and consistent appraisal. However, the value of goodwill reflects the valuation at the valuation date only. As mentioned above, the value of goodwill may subsequently fluctuate.

(2) *Non-purchased goodwill*

This presents considerable valuation problems. Such goodwill does not result from a definitive market transaction and cannot be appraised objectively and consistently. This is one important reason why non-purchased goodwill is not recognised in financial statements of companies.

(g) Measurement of purchased goodwill

Goodwill is defined as the difference between:

(1) the fair value of a business as a whole; and
(2) the aggregate of the fair values of its separable net assets. Thus it is important to consider fair values of property assets. In addition the fair value of intangibles other than goodwill (such as patents, licences and trade marks), should be taken account of even if they do not appear in the balance sheet of the purchased company.

(h) Main requirements of SSAP 22

The principal requirements are as follows:

(1) Non-purchased goodwill should not be recognised in financial statements.
(2) Purchased goodwill should not be carried in the balance sheet as a permanent item.
(3) Purchased goodwill should be treated in one of the following ways:

    (i) The preferred method is that goodwill should be eliminated on acquisition by immediate write-off against reserves, without any entry in the profit and loss account.
    (ii) A permitted alternative is to treat purchased goodwill as an intangible fixed asset and to amortise it through the profit and loss account over its useful economic life.

SSAP 22 permits different methods to be used for different acquisitions.

(i) Immediate write-off against reserves

The standard does not specify which particular reserve may be used. The following is a guide to what may be regarded as acceptable:

(1) profit and loss reserves;
(2) capital reserve arising on consolidation;
(3) merger reserve under CA 1985, s 131 (see section 25.4).

Goodwill should not be written off against revaluation reserve or share premium account.

Note that some companies have passed a special resolution and sought the permission of the court to have the share premium account cancelled and redesignated as a special reserve. Goodwill may then be written off against the special reserve.

(j) SSAP 22 and the amortisation method

(1) *Balance sheet*

(i) Goodwill should be classified as an intangible fixed asset.
(ii) Goodwill should not be revalued upwards.
(iii) Goodwill should be reduced for any permanent diminution in value.

(2) *Profit and loss account*

The annual amortisation charge should be taken into account in arriving at the profit on ordinary activities before tax.

(3) *Amortisation basis*

Under this method, goodwill should be amortised in a systematic basis over the useful life of the goodwill. No maximum period is specified.

The useful life should be estimated at the time of acquisition and should take account of:

(i)   expected changes in products, markets or technology;
(ii)   expected period of future service of certain employees;
(iii) expected future demand, competition or other economic factors which may affect current advantages.

Guidance is given in SSAP 22, App 1. Note that useful life may be subsequently shortened but should not be lengthened.

(k) Negative goodwill

Any excess of the aggregate of the fair values of the separable net assets acquired over the fair value of the consideration given should be credited direct to reserves.

SSAP 22 points out that the amounts allocated to the relevant separable net assets will need to be reviewed particularly carefully to ensure that fair values attributed to them are not overstated.

(I) Arguments for and against the two main approaches

	Method	Arguments for	Arguments against
(1)	Immediate write-off direct to reserves.	(1) Goodwill is not like any other asset – it cannot be realised separately and to show it in the balance sheet is of little value to users of accounts. (2) To exclude goodwill from the balance sheet is to treat purchased and non-purchased goodwill in a consistent way. (3) Permitted by Companies Act 1985. (4) This method is more widely used than any other by large companies.	(1) If a purchaser paid valuable consideration for the goodwill, it is difficult to dispute that it is an asset. (2) Inconsistent treatment in the P/L between purchased goodwill (no effect) and non-puchased goodwill (where expenditures are charges to P/L).
(2)	Intangible fixed asset – with amortisation.	(1) Goodwill is an asset on which capital has been expended in exchange for a number of years' future earnings – this cost should be allocated to the periods expected to benefit (accruals concept). (2) Approach of EC Fourth Directive and permitted by Companies Act 1985. (3) Recognised that purchased goodwill is eventually replaced by non-purchased goodwill.	(1) Possible double-charge to P/L – amortisation of purchased goodwill – expenditures incurred in building up non-purchased goodwill. (2) Economic useful life is difficult to determine – amortisation period is subjective.

(m) Other approaches to accounting for goodwill

These include:

(1) Intangible fixed asset with no amortisation – it is often argued that purchased goodwill does not fall in value as it is maintained by the on-going operations of the business. Against this it is argued that the value of purchased goodwill diminishes over time and is replaced by internally generated goodwill. Internally generated goodwill is never recognised in financial statements. This method is not permitted by SSAP 22 or Companies Act 1985.

(2) Permanent deduction from shareholders' funds (the dangling debit) – this method is prohibited by Companies Act 1985 as it involves offsetting assets against shareholders' funds. The goodwill is carried forward indefinitely in successive balance sheets.

(3) Negative goodwill write-off reserve – a reserve is created with an initial value of zero and goodwill is written off against it. This method is regarded by many accountants as artificial but it is not illegal.

Illustration 1

Profit of Appleton Ltd for 19X8 is £200. Balance brought forward is £600 so carried forward is £800. Revaluation reserve is £350 and share capital is £500.

Purchased goodwill arising during the year is £100. Useful life is regarded as 10 years.

The effect of the various methods on reported profits and balance sheets may be summarised as follows:

P/L	Amortisation through profit and loss account	Fixed asset without amortisation	Write-off against reserves	Dangling debit	Negative goodwill write-off reserve
	£	£	£	£	£
Reported profit	190	200	200	200	200
Balance b/f	600	600	600	600	600
Balance c/f	790	800	800	800	800

B/S EXTRACTS					
Intangible fixed assets					
Goodwill	90	100	–	–	–
Capital and reserves					
Share capital	500	500	500	500	500
Profit and loss	790	800	700	800	800
Goodwill write-off reserve	–	–	–	–	(100)
Revaluation reserve	350	350	350	350	350
	1,640	1,650	1,550	1,650	1,550
Goodwill	–	–	–	(100)	–
	1,640	1,650	1,550	1,550	1,550

The distinction between the dangling debit and the goodwill write-off reserve is a very fine one!

(n) Disclosure requirements

The principal disclosures required by SSAP 22 are:

(1) Accounting policy for goodwill.
(2) For each material acquisition during the year: the amount of goodwill recognised.

(3) For companies which amortise goodwill for some or all of their acquisitions:

    (i) goodwill should be included in the balance sheet under intangible fixed assets;

    (ii) movements during the year on cost and accumulated amortisation together with net book values;

    (iii) amortisation charge in the profit and loss account;

    (iv) for each major acquisition, the amortisation period.

(4) For each material acquisition:

    (i) fair value of consideration (see section 25.6);

    (ii) amount of goodwill and method of dealing with it;

    (iii) whether goodwill has been written off against merger reserve (see section 25.4) or carried forward in the balance sheet as an intangible fixed asset;

    (iv) a fair value table showing book values and fair value adjustments made on consolidation. Adjustments relating to revaluations, provisions for future trading losses and accounting policy alignments should be separately disclosed and explained. This is considered further in chapter 25 under acquisition accounting.

    (v) movements on provisions set up on acquisition (again, see section 25.6) disclosing amounts used, released unused or applied for another purpose and the extent to which provisions proved to be unnecessary.

In principle, disclosures (i) to (v) should be given for each material acquisition. However, where acquisitions are material in total but not individually, the disclosures may be given on a combined or aggregate basis.

(5) For each material disposal of a previously acquired business or business segment:

    (i) profit or loss on disposal;

    (ii) amount of purchased goodwill attributable to business/segment disposed of, how the goodwill has been treated in calculating profit or loss on disposal.

(o) Companies Act 1985 implications

(1) Goodwill may only be treated as an intangible fixed asset if the goodwill was acquired for valuable consideration.

(2) As regards goodwill in the accounts of an individual company, it may only be treated as an asset if it is systematically written off over a period not exceeding its useful economic life. In this event, disclosure is required of:

    (i) the write-off period;

    (ii) the reason for choosing that period.

This restriction does not apply to consolidation goodwill as this is covered by the EC Seventh Directive on group accounts.

(3) The dangling debit treatment is effectively outlawed, but the Companies Act 1985 does not appear to prohibit immediate write-off of goodwill against reserves (the goodwill would have to be written off as it arose so that no asset ever appeared in the balance sheet).

(4) Any asset figure would require to be written down in the event of permanent diminution in value.

(p) Effect on distributable profits

The concept of distributable profits can only be related to individual companies. The accounting treatment of goodwill arising on consolidation has no effect on the distributable profits of individual companies.

Purchased goodwill in the accounts of an individual company has a limited useful economic life. As regards the Companies Act 1985 the elimination of this goodwill must ultimately constitute a realised loss.

The appendix to SSAP 22 suggests that the calculation of distributable profits should reflect the concept of amortisation of goodwill over a number of years. Where a company adopts an amortisation policy the profit and loss account balance for the year automatically achieves this.

Where, however, goodwill is written off against reserves in the year of acquisition, the profit and loss account in the balance sheet will differ from that which would result from the use of the amortisation method. Despite this the distributable profits should be the same irrespective of the different accounting treatments of goodwill.

(q) Criticisms of SSAP 22

As indicated in section 13.2(a) accounting for goodwill proved to be a major problem area for ASC.

SSAP 22 indicates a clear preference for the immediate write-off against reserves method. Nevertheless the standard is open to criticism in permitting two radically different approaches to accounting for goodwill. Furthermore, while companies are required to follow the consistency concept set out in SSAP 2 they are permitted to use different accounting treatments for the goodwill arising on purchase at different times in the year.

(r) Recent proposals

ASB published a Working Paper on goodwill and intangible assets in Autumn 1995. At the end of September, ASB held public hearings to determine whether its proposals would command an acceptable degree of support.

The Working Paper's key proposals are as follows:

(1) The focus is on the treatment of purchased goodwill and purchased intangible assets. The ASB has no plans to consider the recognition in balance sheets of internally developed intangible assets.
(2) The approach to purchased intangible assets has been reconsidered. The approach now proposed would allow an acquirer, in allocating the original cost of acquisition, to recognise intangible assets separately from purchased goodwill provided their fair value can be measured reliably.
(3) The proposed approach aims to align the treatment of purchased goodwill and intangible assets as far as possible, especially when the two are very similar in nature, and to preclude the opportunities for 'accounting arbitrage' between the two categories.
(4) Goodwill and intangible assets having finite lives would be depreciated over such lives.
(5) Goodwill and intangible assets believed to have indefinitely long lives would not be depreciated.
(6) All recognised balances of goodwill and intangible assets would be reviewed for impairment at each year-end. The extent of this review would be minimal for goodwill and intangible assets having a life that does not exceed twenty years and fuller otherwise. For goodwill and intangible assets having a life of more than twenty years or an indefinite life the fuller review would involve an assessment of future cash flows.
(7) There would be a rebuttable presumption that goodwill has a finite life that does not exceed twenty years.

13.3 ACCOUNTING FOR RESEARCH AND DEVELOPMENT EXPENDITURE

(a) Background

The accounting treatment of research and development expenditure illustrates possible conflict between the accruals and prudence concept.

On the one hand, R + D expenditure in the current period may lead to higher revenues (or lower costs) in subsequent periods than would otherwise have been the case.

On the other hand, there are considerable uncertainties regarding the amount of benefits (let alone whether such benefits will actually materialise) and the timing of benefits.

A general principle has been established which effectively requires expenditure to be written off as it arises unless its relationship to revenue of a future period can be established with reasonable certainty.

(b) Definitions

(1) *Pure (or basic) research:*

Experimental or theoretical work undertaken primarily to acquire new scientific or technical knowledge for its own sake rather than directed towards any specific aim or application.

(2) *Applied research:*

Original or critical investigation undertaken in order to gain new scientific or technical knowledge and directed towards a specific practical aim or objective.

(3) *Development:*

Use of scientific or technical knowledge in order to produce new or substantially improved materials, devices, products or services, to install new processes or systems prior to the commencement of commercial production or commercial applications, or to improve substantially those already produced or installed.

(c) Examples of research and development activity

(1) General principle

Research and development activity is distinguished from non-research based activity by the presence or absence of an appreciable element of innovation. If the activity departs from routine and breaks new ground it should normally be included; if it follows an established pattern it should normally be excluded.

(2) The following are examples of activities that would normally be included in research and development:

  (i)   experimental, theoretical or other work aimed at the discovery of new knowledge, or the advancement of existing knowledge;
  (ii) searching for applications of that knowledge;
  (iii) formulation and design of possible applications for such work;
  (iv) testing in search for, or evaluation of, product, service or process alternatives;
  (v)   design, construction and testing of pre-production prototypes and models and development batches;
  (vi) design of products, services, processes or systems involving new technology or substantially improving those already produced or installed;
  (vii) construction and operation of pilot plants.

(3) The following are examples of activities that would normally be excluded from research and development:

  (i)   testing and analysis either of equipment or product for purposes of quality or quantity control;
  (ii) periodic alterations to existing products, services or processes even though these may represent some improvement;
  (iii) operational research not tied to a specific research and development activity;
  (iv) cost of corrective action in connection with breakdowns during commercial activity;
  (v)   legal and administrative work in connection with patent applications, records and litigation and the sale or licensing of patents;
  (vi) activity, including design and construction engineering, relating to the construction, relocation, rearrangement or start-up of facilities or equipment other than facilities or equipment whose sole use is for a particular research and development project;
  (vii) market research.

(d) Accounting treatment – pure and applied research expenditure

This expenditure should be written off as incurred since any possible future benefits are difficult to assess.

(e) Accounting treatment – development expenditure

Development expenditure *may* (*not* must) be capitalised as an intangible asset and amortised over a period of time if *all* of the following conditions can be satisfied:

(1) There is a clearly defined project.
(2) The related expenditure is separately identifiable.
(3) The outcome of such a project has been assessed with reasonable certainty as to:

  (i)   its technical feasibility; and
  (ii) its ultimate commercial viability considered in the light of factors such as likely market conditions (including competing products), public opinion, consumer and environmental legislation.

(4) If further development costs are to be incurred on the same project the aggregate of such costs together with related production, selling and administration costs is reasonably expected to be more than covered by related future revenues.
(5) Adequate resources exist, or are reasonably expected to be available, to enable the project to be completed and to provide any consequential increases in working capital.

The basic principle is that development expenditure may be deferred to the extent that its recovery can reasonably be regarded as assured. It is also important to carry out an annual balance sheet date review of unamortised expenditure to ensure that the conditions referred to above are still capable of being satisfied. Irrecoverable expenditure should be written off immediately. Each project should be considered individually. Finally, consistency of accounting treatment between development projects should be paramount.

(f) Capitalised development costs – basis of amortisation

Amortisation should start in the period in which commercial production of the product or process commences.

Development costs should be allocated over accounting periods by reference to:

(1) the sale or use of the product or process; *or*
(2) the period over which the product or process is expected to be sold or used.

(g) Further considerations

(1) The cost of fixed assets used for R + D purposes should be capitalised and depreciated.
(2) Expenditure in locating and exploiting mineral deposits does not come within the scope of SSAP 13.
(3) Where companies enter into a firm contract to carry out development work on behalf of third parties, or to develop and manufacture at an agreed price calculated to reimburse development expenditure, such expenditure should be included in work in progress.

(h) Disclosure requirements

The disclosure requirements of SSAP 13 are:

(1) the accounting policy should be stated and explained;
(2) movements on deferred development expenditure and the amount carried forward at the beginning and end of the period should be disclosed;
(3) deferred development expenditure should be separately disclosed under intangible fixed assets;
(4) the total research and development charge in the profit and loss account should be disclosed and analysed between:

    (i)   current year expenditure;
    (ii) amounts amortised from deferred expenditure (but see (i) below).

(i) Implications for smaller companies

Certain companies are exempt from the disclosures in (h)(4) above. These are companies which do not fall within any of the following categories:

(1) public limited companies (whether listed or not) or subsidiaries of PLCs;
(2) special category companies (banks, insurance companies) or subsidiaries of these;
(3) companies which exceed the medium-sized criteria multiplied by a factor of ten (ie two out of three of: turnover £112m, gross assets £56m, employees 2,500).

(j) Companies Act 1985 implications

(1) Development costs may be capitalised in special circumstances (presumably those specified in SSAP 13). Disclosure is required of:

    (i)   the period over which the costs are to be written off;
    (ii) the reasons for capitalising the development costs.

(2) Costs of research may not be capitalised under any circumstances.

13.4 ILLUSTRATIONS FROM PUBLISHED ACCOUNTS

Illustration 2

Extract from annual report and accounts of Wessex Water plc for the year ended 31 March 1994.

Accounting policies (extract)

Business development expenditure
Expenditure incurred by the Group attributable to business development projects is deferred in circumstances where, in the opinion of the directors, there exists a reasonable expectation that a project will lead to the recovery of attributable expenditure through future commercial success. Deferred business development expenditure is amortised over the period during which the related future income is expected to arise. Unamortised expenditure is reviewed on a regular basis and its recoverability reassessed. Where doubt exists as to the continued recoverability of such expenditure it is written off.

Illustration 3

Extract from annual report and accounts of Reckitt & Colman plc for the year ended 31 December 1994.

Intangible assets and goodwill

On the acquisition of businesses, the purchase consideration is allocated over the fair value of the underlying net tangible assets, significant intangible assets (wholly comprising trade marks) and goodwill. Goodwill is deducted from reserves. Trade marks are not amortised, as it is considered that their useful economic lives are not limited. Their carrying value is reviewed annually by the directors to determine whether there has been any permanent diminution in value and any reductions in value are taken to the profit and loss account.

The profit or loss arising on the disposal of businesses previously acquired is recognised in the accounts after taking into account any goodwill arising on acquisition which has not been previously written off in the profit and loss account.

Illustration 4

Extract from annual report and accounts of Chrysalis Group plc for the year ended 31 August 1994.

Accounting policies (extract)

Deferred development expenditure
Pre-contract development expenditure is written off in the period in which it is incurred except where it relates to a clearly defined contract, the outcome of which has been assessed with reasonable certainty as to its success and commercial viability. In such cases the expenditure is deferred to the extent that its recovery can be reasonably regarded as assured and the cost is written off against revenue over the period of the contract.

14 STOCKS AND DEBTORS

14.1 STOCKS AND LONG-TERM CONTRACTS – OVERVIEW

(a) Principal objectives of SSAP 9

SSAP 9 (Stocks and long-term contracts) was issued in 1975 and revised in 1988. The objectives of the original version of SSAP 9 were:

(1) to define practices of stock valuation;
(2) to narrow the differences and variations as between different companies;
(3) to ensure adequate disclosure in financial statements.

To a large extent, SSAP 9 has succeeded in achieving these aims. Aspects (2) and (3) are also covered by the Companies Act 1985.

(b) Stock categories

SSAP 9 stock categories may be illustrated diagrammatically as follows:

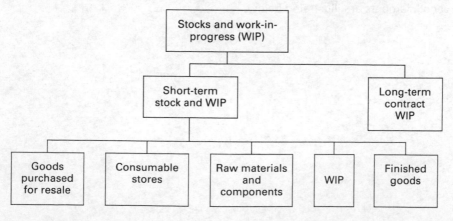

Section 14.2 of this chapter is concerned principally with short-term stocks while section 14.3 deals with long-term contract work-in-progress.

The Companies Act 1985 balance sheet formats refer to:

(1) raw materials and consumables;
(2) work-in-progress;
(3) finished goods and goods for resale;

but do not refer specifically to long-term WIP.

14.2   SHORT-TERM STOCKS AND WORK-IN-PROGRESS

(a) Basic concepts

The fundamental accounting concepts of SSAP 2 apply to stock valuation as follows:

(1) Going concern – the stock figure in the balance sheet implicitly assumes that the business will continue in operational existence in the foreseeable future, and that stock will be used or realised in an orderly manner in the operations of the business.
(2) Accruals – cost of sales (based as far as possible on actual costs incurred) are matched against sales revenues of the year in which the revenue arises, in order to determine business income.
(3) Prudence – stock should be stated in the balance sheet at net realisable value (NRV) in those specific cases where NRV is expected to be less than historical cost.
(4) Consistency – stock valuation bases should be consistently applied as between different stock categories and from one accounting period to the next.

The basis of stock valuation under both SSAP 9 and the Companies Act 1985 is that individual stock items (or groups of similar items) should be valued for accounts purposes at the lower of cost and net realisable value.

(b) Elements of cost

The overriding principle is that costs to be included in the stock valuation should relate to expenditure which has been incurred in the normal course of business bringing the product or service to its present location and condition.

These costs will include both purchase costs and conversion costs. Relevant cost elements are illustrated below:

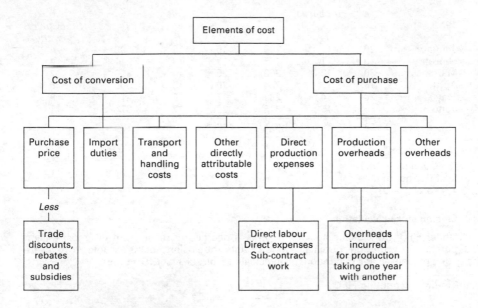

(c) Net realisable value (NRV)

NRV is defined as actual or estimated selling price, net of any trade discount and after deducting any further costs expected to be incurred in completing, marketing, selling or distributing the product. Problems in determining NRV are discussed below in (e).

(d) Cost flow assumptions

In a perfect world, when an item is sold the actual purchase or production costs of that item should be matched against sales in order to determine profit. This might be feasible for a garage selling cars but it is hardly practicable for a manufacturer of Widgets!

In the frequent situations where it is not practicable to relate actual expenditure incurred to specific stock items, an approximate method must be used. However, the standard requires management to ensure that whatever method is chosen provides the fairest practicable approximation to actual costs incurred in bringing the product to its present location and condition.

Possible approaches are discussed below and their acceptability or otherwise under SSAP 9 and the Companies Act 1985 referred to.

(1) *First-in-first-out (FIFO)*

Under FIFO, cost of stocks and work-in-progress is calculated on the basis that the quantities in closing stock represent the latest purchases or production.

Illustration 1

A trader's purchases and sales for the six months ended 30 June 19X8 were as follows:

| 19X8 | Purchases | | | Sales | | | Stock level |
	Q	P £	T £	Q	P £	T £	(quantity)
January	20	10	200	16	12	192	4
February	15	11	165	17	13	221	2
March	30	12	360	25	14	350	7
April	18	13	234	20	15	300	5
May	20	14	280	17	16	272	8
June	25	15	375	22	17	374	11
	128		1,614	117		1,709	

KEY
Q = Quantity (units)
P = Price per unit
T = Total (P × Q)

Closing stock calculation

Under FIFO, the closing stock of 11 units is deemed to result from the most recent purchases. As the June purchases were 25 units, the closing stock is assumed to relate to June purchases at £15 per unit, giving closing stock of 11 × £15 = £165.

Trading accounting FIFO

	£	£
Sales		1,709
Purchases	1,614	
Less closing stock	165	
Cost of sales		1,449
Gross profit		260

FIFO is a widely used stock valuation base and is acceptable under both SSAP 9 and the Companies Act 1985.

(2) *Last-in-first-out (LIFO)*

Under LIFO, cost of stocks and work-in-progress is calculated on the basis that the quantities in closing stock represent the earliest purchases or production.

Illustration 2

Using the same data as for the FIFO illustration, closing stock is calculated as follows:

COMPUTATION OF COST OF SALES AND CLOSING STOCK FIGURES UNDER THE LIFO ASSUMPTION

19X8	Cost of sales		£	Closing stock at month end (memorandum note)		
January	18 at £10		160	4 at £10	=	£40
February	17	15 at £11 = 165				
		2 at £10 = 20	185	2 at £10	=	£20
March	25 at £12		300	2 at £10 5 at £12		£80
April	20	18 at £13 = 234				
		2 at £12 = 24	258	2 at £10 3 at £12		£56
May	17 at £14		238	2 at £10 3 at £12 3 at £14		£98
June	22 at £15		330	2 at £10 3 at £12 3 at £14 3 at £15		£143

Total cost of sales £1,471

Trading account – LIFO

	£	£
Sales		1,709
Purchases	1,614	
Less closing stock	143	
Cost of sales		1,471
Gross profit		238

Note: Calculations
LIFO calculations are rather detailed compared with FIFO. The main problem from a computational viewpoint is that in certain months, physical stock levels fall (eg February and April). In these months, costs of sales draws in purchase prices of earlier months.

COMMENTS ON ACCEPTABILITY OF LIFO

SSAP 9 states that LIFO cost of sales does not bear a reasonable relationship to actual costs obtaining during the period. For this reason, SSAP 9 does not usually regard LIFO as an acceptable valuation basis. However, the Companies Act 1985 permits the use of LIFO, as long as the directors consider it to be appropriate to the circumstances of the company. In practice, this provision has little practical importance in view of the restrictive terms of SSAP 9.

(3) *Average cost (AVCO)*

Under AVCO, cost of stocks and work-in-progress is calculated by applying an average price to the number of units on hand.

The average price may be computed in various ways, each of which may result in differing figures for closing stock. Possible approaches include:

(i) a continuous calculation (eg every month, by means of computer program);
(ii) a periodic calculation (eg six-monthly or yearly);
(iii) a moving period calculation.

Illustration 3

Using the above figures and using an average for the six-month period:

Average purchase cost per unit $= \dfrac{£1,614}{128} = £12.60$

Closing stock $= 11 \times £12.60 = £139$

Trading account – average cost

	£	£
Sales		1,709
Purchases	1,614	
Less closing stock	139	
Cost of sales		1,475
Gross profit		234

(4) *Comments on the usefulness of the above three methods*

Both FIFO and AVCO are widely used in the UK and are regarded as acceptable by both SSAP 9 and the Companies Act 1985. Although LIFO is permitted in certain cases by the Companies Act 1985, it is not considered generally acceptable under SSAP 9.

During periods of rising prices, FIFO may give an exaggerated impression of profitability, in that sales revenues (measured in current price terms) are matched with cost of sales (measured in terms of price levels possibly several months previously). However, FIFO may give a balance sheet stock figure which reflects current prices.

LIFO, on the other hand may give a balance sheet stock figure which is misleading as it could relate to prices of earlier periods (eg in the earlier illustration, two units of stock are valued at £10 per unit). When it comes to profit measurement, in some situations, LIFO may give a measure of profit which is a fair reflection of the capability of a business to make a distribution without impairing its future earning capacity. LIFO may result in the matching together of sales and cost of sales both in terms of current price levels. However, a drawback of LIFO is that where stock levels fall (as in the earlier illustration), cost of sales will reflect some items measured at price levels of earlier periods.

AVCO is acceptable from a practical viewpoint although it suffers from theoretical drawbacks during inflationary periods as regards profit measurement.

(5) *Other methods of stock valuation*

These include:

(i) UNIT COST

Unit cost is the cost of purchasing or manufacturing identifiable units of stock. This method is acceptable because it goes directly to actual costs rather than some approximation thereof. This method is appropriate for stock items such as jewellery and motor vehicles.

(ii) BASE STOCK

Certain types of businesses eg sugar refiners, require a certain minimum physical quantity of stock for continuous operations. This stock must be identified in terms of a predetermined number of units of stock which are then valued for balance sheet purposes at a fixed unit value. Such stock may be classified under tangible fixed assets.

Any excess of physical quantities over this number is valued on the basis of some other method such as FIFO or AVCO. Should the number of stock units fall below the predetermined minimum, stocks are valued on the basis of fixed unit value.

The base stock method is permitted by the Companies Act 1985 provided that:

(a) the overall value is not material to assessing the company's state of affairs; and
(b) the quantity, value and composition are not subject to material variation.

SSAP 9 does not regard base stock as a generally acceptable basis, although base stock has been used by companies such as Tate and Lyle.

(iii) REPLACEMENT COST

Replacement cost is the cost at which an identical asset could be purchased or manufactured. Replacement cost is not acceptable under the historical cost convention, as it does not derive from actual costs incurred. However, some companies have drawn up their statutory accounts on a current cost basis. Fixed asset and stock figures are then derived from replacement costs.

(iv) STANDARD COST

SSAP 9, App 2 states that cost is calculated on the basis of periodically predetermined costs calculated from management's estimates of expected levels of costs and of operations and operational efficiency and the related expenditure.

Where standard costs are used they should be reviewed frequently to ensure they bear a reasonable relationship to actual costs obtained during the period, in which case the approach is acceptable under both SSAP 9 and the Companies Act 1985.

(v) SELLING PRICE LESS MARGIN

Some retail stores use selling price less an estimated profit margin as a means of valuing stocks. This is acceptable, provided it can be shown that the method gives a reasonable approximation to actual cost.

(e) Problem areas

Two particular problem areas regarding stock valuation are allocation of production overheads and determination of net realisable value.

(1) *Allocation of production overheads*

Stock and work-in-progress should be valued for accounts purposes at the lower of cost and net realisable value. Cost should include all expenditure incurred in the normal course of business in bringing the product or service to its present location and condition.

These costs will include production overheads such as factory rent and rates and depreciation of plant and machinery, even though such costs accrue on a time basis.

Production overheads are defined in SSAP 9 as overheads incurred in respect of materials, labour or services, based on the normal level of activity taking one year with another.

In determining the normal level of activity SSAP 9, App 1 suggests that the following factors should be taken into account:

(i) the volume of production which the facilities are intended to achieve;
(ii) the budgeted level of activity for the current and following year;
(iii) the level of activity actually achieved in the current and previous years.

The following points may be added:

(a) It can be argued that in the present climate, key factors must be actual activity levels in current and previous years.
(b) The cost of unused capacity should be written off in the current year if the reduction in activity or trade of a company is considered to be permanent.
(c) Abnormal conversion costs (eg exceptional spoilage, idle capacity and other losses) should be excluded from stock valuation and should be charged to the profit and loss account of the period in which they are incurred.

Problems may also arise in determining whether particular overheads relate to the production, selling or administration function. Any arbitrary apportionment should reasonably have regard to the materiality of the amounts involved.

(2) *Determination of net realisable value*

(i) SITUATIONS WHERE APPLICABLE

SSAP 9 refers to the following situations where net realisable value is likely to be below cost:

(a) increase in cost or fall in selling price;
(b) physical deterioration of stocks;
(c) marketing decisions to manufacture and sell at a loss;
(d) errors in production or purchasing.

In addition, SSAP 9 refers to the situation of stock held which is unlikely to be sold within the usual turnover period. The likely delay in realising the stock increases the possibility of situations (a) to (c) occurring. This should be borne in mind when considering net realisable value.

(ii) CONSIDERATIONS IN DETERMINING NRV

(a) *Formula approach*. It may be possible to determine NRV by using a formula and applying it to cost of items. The formula should be based on predetermined criteria which take account of age and movements of stock and estimated scrap values. The provision should then be reviewed in the light of any special circumstances which cannot be built into the formula.
(b) *Effect of finished goods valuation on raw materials*. If it is decided that finished goods stocks should be written down below cost, it is important that related raw material and sub-assembly stocks should be reviewed for possible write-down.
(c) *Post-balance sheet events*. Events between the balance sheet date and the date of approval of the financial statements by the directors should be taken into account in determining whether NRV is below cost.
   In certain cases, it may not be necessary to reduce cost of raw materials to a lower figure of realisable value. These would be cases where the finished product could be sold at a profit after allowing for inclusion of raw materials at cost price.

(f) Disclosure in financial statements

Disclosure requirements in the financial statements are specified in SSAP 9 and the Companies Act 1985. The disclosure requirements below relate to all stock categories with the exception of long-term contract work-in-progress.

(1) *Accounting policies*

The accounting policies used to determine cost and net realisable value should be disclosed.

(2) *Analysis of stocks total*

SSAP 9 requires that stocks and work-in-progress should be sub-classified in balance sheets or in notes to the financial statements in a manner which is appropriate to the business and so as to indicate the amounts held in each of the main categories. This is also effectively required by the Companies Act 1985 (see balance sheet formats).

(3) *Further disclosure*

In addition to the above disclosures, the Companies Act 1985 requires a note to the accounts disclosing the difference if material between:

(i)   the balance sheet value of stock;
(ii) the comparable figure determined either on replacement cost at the balance sheet date or on the most recent actual purchase price or production cost (but purchase price or production cost may only be used if they appear to the directors to constitute the more appropriate standard of comparison).

(4) *Consignment stocks*

These are dealt with in chapter 7.

14.3   LONG-TERM CONTRACTS

(a) Definition

The definition of long-term contract in SSAP 9 is as follows:

> . . . a contract entered into for the design, manufacture or construction of a single substantial asset or the provision of a service (or of a combination of assets or services which together constitute a single project) where the time taken substantially to complete the contract is such that the contract activity falls into different accounting periods. A contract that is required to be accounted for as long-term by this accounting standard will usually extend for a period exceeding one year. However, a duration exceeding one year is **not an essential feature** of a long-term contract. **Some** contracts with a shorter duration than one year **should** be accounted for as long-term contracts **if** they are sufficiently material to the activity of the period that **not to record turnover and attributable profit would lead to a distortion of the period's turnover and results** such that the financial statements would not give a true and fair view, provided that the policy is applied consistently within the reporting entity and from year to year. (Emphasis added.)

(b) Implications

The old SSAP 9 was inflexible – contracts of less than twelve months' duration were automatically treated as short-term and had to be accounted for by the completed contract method, turnover and profits only being picked up in the year of completion.

Under the revised version of SSAP 9, a true and fair view may require some contracts of say nine to ten months' duration to be treated as long-term contracts with turnover and profits being spread over the life of the contract. These could include contracts which possess the usual characteristics of long-term contracts, for example: detailed contract specification, some sub-contract work, staged payment terms and a fairly substantial time period.

A final point is that in these cases it is likely that the bulk of contract work will be completed by the time the financial statements are approved by the directors.

Illustration 4

Fitters Ltd commenced a shop-fitting contract on 1 May 19X8 and completed it on 31 March 19X9. The accounts for the year ended 31 December 19X8 were approved by the directors on 1 October 19X9.

The contract price was £220,000 and costs amounted to £88,000 giving a total contract profit of £132,000.

Amounts invoiced and received were as follows:

	Invoiced £	Received £
Y.E. 31.12.X8	130,000	80,000
Y.E. 31.12.X9	90,000	140,000
	220,000	220,000

Assuming costs and contract activity accrue evenly on a time basis, how might the contract be reflected in the financial statements for the two years?

In theory, there are two approaches:

(1) the completed contract method; and
(2) the percentage of completion method.

Under method 1, turnover and profits would be reported in 19X9, the year of completion. Under the previous version of SSAP 9, this method would have been mandatory as the duration of the contract was less than twelve months.

Under method 2, turnover and profits would be spread over the life of the contract. Thus profits of £96,000 ($\frac{8}{11} \times 132,000$) would be reported in 19X8 and £36,000 ($\frac{3}{11} \times 132,000$) in 19X9.

The effect of the two methods on the financial statements for the two years would be as follows:

(1) Completed contract method

	19X8 £	19X9 £
Profit and loss account		
Sales	–	220,000
Cost of sales	–	88,000
Gross profit	–	132,000
Balance sheet		
Creditors		
Costs ($\frac{8}{11} \times 88,000$)	64,000	–
Payments received on account	130,000	–
	66,000	–
Trade debtors		
(130,000 – 80,000)	50,000	–

(2) Percentage of completion method

	19X8 £	19X9 £
Profit and loss account		
Sales	160,000	60,000
Cost of sales	64,000	24,000
Gross profit	96,000	36,000
Balance sheet – debtors		
Amounts recoverable on contracts		
(see below) (160,000 – 130,000)	30,000	–
Trade debtors (130,000 – 80,000)	50,000	–
	80,000	–

Notes
(i)   amounts recoverable on contracts is treated in substance as a debtor.
(ii) under SSAP 9, the percentage of completion method may be claimed to give a truer and fairer view of profit and contract activity than the completed contract method and would be recommended in this case. The outcome of the contract would be apparent at the time the financial statements were approved by the directors.

(c) Fundamental accounting concepts

The four concepts specified in SSAP 2 are particularly relevant to the accounting treatment of long-term contracts.

Also of particular interest is the possible conflict between the accruals concept and the prudence concept.

(1) *Going concern concept*

In view of the time period for completion of many long-term contracts, adequacy of financial resources is particularly important.

(2) *Accruals concept*

Such a long-term contract may extend over several accounting periods: the accruals concept would require profits to be allocated over these periods.

The method described below (see (e)), which achieves this, is sometimes referred to as the percentage of completion method. The alternative view, that profit should not be included in profit and loss account until the contract is complete, is not considered appropriate for long-term contracts, as it could distort comparison of profits as between successive accounting periods. This latter approach is sometimes referred to as the completed contract method and in normal circumstances may only be used for short-term work-in-progress. (See section 14.2.)

(3) *Prudence concept*

In view of the considerable uncertainties surrounding the outcome of the contract, no profits should be recognised until such outcome can be assessed with reasonable certainty.

Clearly, the trade-off between the accruals concept and the prudence concept relies to a large extent on subjective judgement. Two companies may take significantly differing viewpoints!

(4) *Consistency concept*

In view of possible conflicts between accruals and prudence, it is essential that a company is consistent as between different contracts, and between successive accounting periods.

(d) Determining turnover

SSAP 9 states that for long-term contracts, turnover should be ascertained in a manner appropriate to the stage of completion of the contract, the business and the industry in which it operates.

SSAP 9, App 1, para 23 refers to two principal methods of ascertaining turnover:

(1) By reference to valuation of the work carried out to date (presumably balance sheet date). Under this method, sometimes referred to as the cost-based approach, all costs may be included in the profit and loss account as cost of sales with no costs left to be included in the balance sheet stock figure.

(2) By reference to valuation at specific points in the contract. Paragraph 23 refers to '. . . specific points during a contract at which individual elements of work done with separately ascertainable sales values and costs can be identified and appropriately recorded as turnover (eg because delivery or customer acceptance has taken place)'.

The paragraph concludes that the Standard does not provide a definition of turnover in view of the different methods of ascertaining it. However, it does require disclosure of the means by which turnover is ascertained (see illustration in (h) below).

The standard also indicates that the question of how much turnover to recognise is independent of whether and how much profit should be taken. For example, in the case of a loss-making contract, turnover should be based on activity during the year. Loss provisions will be reflected in cost of sales.

(e) Calculating profits – two possible methods

Where the outcome of the contract can be assessed with reasonable certainty before completion, the standard requires the prudently calculated attributable profit to be included in the profit and loss account.

SSAP 9 does not say how this should be calculated but there seem to be two broad approaches:

(1) comparison of value of work to a particular date (often the balance sheet date) with costs incurred to that date;
(2) taking a proportion of estimated total profit over the life of the contract. This proportion should be calculated using an indicator of completion eg costs to date/estimated total cost or some appropriate physical measure such as labour hours.

The terms of the contract may give a guide as to which method is more appropriate.

The calculation for method (2) may be carried out as follows:

(i) Calculate estimated profit over life of contract:

Total sales value of contract		X
Total costs (including overheads) to date	X	
Total estimated further costs required to complete contract	X	
Estimated further costs of guarantee and rectification work	X	X
∴ Total estimated profit on contract		X

Note: This procedure should be followed even if there is no intention of taking any profit to the credit of profit and loss account, since it may indicate the possibility of a contract turning in a loss. In this event, further investigation of figures is required.

(ii) Calculate attributable profit (ie cumulative profit earned to date).

Attributable profit (AP) = degree of completion % × total estimated profit.

Degree of completion (or indicator of performance) may be calculated in several ways including:

(a) costs incurred as proportion of total costs;
(b) surveys which measure work performed;
(c) completion of physical portion of contract work.

(iii) Profit reported this year.

This is calculated as attributable profit less profit taken up in previous years.

Note: The profit recognised this year will not necessarily represent the proportion of the total profit on the contract which corresponds with the amount of work carried out in the period. It is also likely to reflect the effect of changes in circumstances during the year which affect the total profit estimated to accrue on completion.

(f) Further factors to be considered

The following points are referred to in SSAP 9. Certain of them reflect once again possible conflict between accruals and prudence.

(1) The profit taken up in a particular period should reflect the proportion of work carried out at the accounting date (accruals).
(2) Attributable profit is that part of total profit estimated to arise over the life of the contract which fairly reflects the proportion of work completed to date (accruals).
(3) There can be no attributable profit until the outcome of the contract can be assessed with reasonable certainty. SSAP 9 suggests that a company should define the earliest point for each particular contract before any attributable profit is taken up (prudence).

   In the early stages of an apparently profitable contract it may not be possible to assess the outcome with reasonable certainty and the client thus decides to take no profit. However, progress after the end of the accounting period could be taken into account. An excessively prudent policy regarding taking of profit may not be acceptable as it may distort the truth and fairness of the accounts.
(4) If a company considers that the contract outcome can be assessed with reasonable certainty before the contract is completed, attributable profit should be taken up, but judgement should be exercised with prudence (accruals/prudence).
(5) In some contracts it will be necessary to take account of 'known equalities of profitability in the various stages of a contract'. For example, a contract may have four phases – A, B and D which are 'own work' only and C which is a significantly less profitable phase consisting mainly of sub-contract work. Profit allocation between different periods should reflect these profitability variations.
(6) SSAP 9 recognises that there are certain businesses which carry out contracts where the outcome cannot reasonably be assessed before completion. In these situations, profit should not be taken up prior to completion (prudence).
(7) Once it is expected that a contract will turn in a loss, full provision for the loss should be reflected in the current period financial statements (prudence).

Illustration 5

Contractors plc is engaged in a number of long-term contracts. The following summarised details refer to three particular long-term contracts which were in progress at 31 December 19X6.

	Contract A £'000	Contract B £'000	Contract C £'000
Total contract price	700	400	800
Cost incurred to 31.12.X6	400	30	500
Estimated total costs to complete (allowing for contingencies)	790	300	570
Progress payments invoiced	390	40	600
Amounts received relating to above progress payments invoiced	350	20	450

To what extent should profits and losses be recognised up to 31 December 19X6? Dealing with each contract in turn:

Contract A
This contract indicates a foreseeable loss of £90,000. SSAP 9 requires the full amount of the loss to be reflected in the 19X6 financial statements. Clearly it is important to ensure that estimated total costs of £790,000 have been determined on a prudent basis.
    Loss-making contracts are further considered in (I) below.

Contract B
This contract is expected to make a total profit of £100,000 (i e £400,000 less £300,000). However, since the contract is at a relatively early stage, it can be argued that the outcome of the contract cannot be assessed with reasonable certainty. On prudence grounds, therefore, the contract should be included in the balance sheet at cost of £30,000 less progress payments invoiced of £40,000. The £10,000 excess may be regarded as a creditor.

Contract C
This contract is expected to produce a total profit of £230,000. The contract is well advanced and it can be argued that its profitable outcome can be assessed with reasonable certainty. Once again, it is important to establish that estimated total costs of £570,000 have been arrived at on a prudent basis and allow for contingencies.
    With the limited information available, the best way of determining attributable profit may be to use cost to date divided by expected total costs as an indicator of progress.
    On this basis, attributable profit would be calculated as:

$$\frac{£500,000}{£570,000} \times £230,000 = £201,755$$

say, £201,000

Clearly, given more information, other indications of progress might be available. A useful approach might be to use more than one method, each method providing a cross-check on the other.
    The profit reported in current year profit and loss account would be attributable profit (£201,000 using the method above) less any profit recognised in previous years.

Illustration 6

Contract 187 has a fixed contract price of £200,000. Total contract costs are estimated at £160,000 and thus total profits at £40,000.
    At the end of 19X7, the contract is estimated to be 60% complete. The company's policy is to calculate attributable profit by applying degree of completion to estimated total profit. The effect on the 19X7 profit and loss account would be:

		£
Turnover	(60% × 200,000)	120,000
Cost of sales	(60% × 160,000)	96,000
Gross profit	(60% × 40,000)	24,000

Suppose that costs incurred to complete in 19X8 amounted to £74,000 (as opposed to 40% × 160,000 = 64,000 expected). The effect on the 19X8 profit and loss account would be:

		£
Turnover	(40% × 200,000)	80,000
Cost of sales	(actual costs)	74,000
Gross profit	(balancing figure)	6,000

Note: the profit recognised in 19X8 reflects the effect of changes in circumstances during 19X8 which affects the total profit on completion (see (n) on interpretation).

Illustration 7

Facts as in example 6 except that the contract is only 15% complete at the end of 19X7 and company policy is to recognise no profit on contracts which are less than 25% complete at the year-end. Total contract costs turn out to be £160,000 as estimated.

Note that where no profit is to be recognised in the year, turnover should be calculated as a proportion of total contract value using a zero estimate of profit.

Profit and loss extracts for the two years would be as follows:

	19X7 £	19X8 £	Total £
Turnover			
15% × 160,000 (based on cost)	24,000		
£200,000 − £24,000		176,000	200,000
Cost of sales			
15% × 160,000	24,000		
160,000 − 24,000		136,000	160,000
Gross profit	−	40,000	40,000

(Again, see **(m)** below on interpretation.)

(g) Variations and claims

The appendix to SSAP 9 makes the following suggestions:

Aspect	Suggested approach
Variations (additional work).	Make conservative estimate of effect on sales value.
Foreseen claims or penalties against contractor.	Ensure allowed for in further costs of guarantee and rectification.
Settlement of claims by contractor arising from circumstances not envisaged in the contract or arising as an indirect consequence of approved variations.	Only provide for in sales value if negotiations in advanced stage *and* written evidence of acceptability and amount.

(h) Disclosure requirements for long-term contracts

The main disclosure requirements of SSAP 9 are as follows. The examples in (l) below illustrate some of the requirements.

(1) A suitable description for long-term contracts would be 'at net cost less foreseeable losses and payments on account'.

Net cost is effectively total costs incurred less amounts transferred to the profit and loss account in respect of work carried out to date.

(2) The policy for ascertaining turnover and attributable profit should be stated.

Illustration of disclosure

STOCKS AND WORK-IN-PROGRESS

Stocks and work-in-progress are stated at the lower of cost and net realisable value. Cost includes direct materials and labour together with a proportion of production overheads.

Long-term contract work-in-progress is stated at costs incurred, net of amounts transferred to cost of sales in respect of work recorded as turnover. Profit on long-term contracts is taken as work is carried out provided that the final outcome can be assessed with reasonable certainty. Full provision is made for all known or expected losses as soon as they are foreseen.

TURNOVER

Turnover which is stated net of value added tax represents the value of services provided to third parties except in respect of long-term contract work-in-progress where turnover represents the sales value of work done in the year including amounts not invoiced.

---

(3) Specific disclosures for long-term contracts.

    (i) If cumulative turnover (ie total turnover recorded since commencement of contract) exceeds total payments on account, the excess represents an 'amount recoverable on contracts' and should be separately disclosed within debtors (see (i) below).

    (ii) If payments on account exceed cumulative turnover (considering a particular contract) the excess is classified as a deduction from any balance on that contract in stocks. Any residual balance in excess of cost is classified with creditors.

    (iii) Long-term contract balances should be separately disclosed within the balance sheet heading 'stock'. The following should be disclosed separately:

        (1) net cost less foreseeable losses;
        (2) applicable payments on account.

    (iv) The amount by which the provision or accrual for foreseeable losses exceeds the costs incurred (after transfers to cost of sales) should be included within either provisions for liabilities and charges or creditors as appropriate.

(i) Amounts recoverable on contracts

Appendix 3 of SSAP 9 points out that an 'amount recoverable on contracts' may not have the contractual status of a debtor in strict legal form. The accruals concept should not preclude debtors and creditors from being recorded where this is necessary to reflect the substance of a transaction (see chapter 7).

Counsel's opinion obtained by ASC confirms that 'amounts recoverable on contracts' should be classified under debtors and cannot be classified under stocks.

(j) Example of calculations and disclosures

The following data relates to Hayseed plc, a construction company. Details relating to contract 467 are as follows. All figures are £'000.

		Year		
	1	*2*	*3*	*4*
Degree of completion at end of year	25%	60%	85%	100%
Contract price (as updated)	800	850	900	980
Estimated cost (as updated)	500	560	650	730
Estimated total profits	300	290	250	250
Costs to date (actual)	135	350	570	730
Payments on account (invoiced)	160	490	790	980
Payments on account (received)	130	480	720	980

Attributable profit is calculated by applying a suitable measure or indicator of completion to the estimated total profit over the life of the contract. No profit is recognised by the company until a contract is at least 60% complete.

Required: Show how the above contract might be presented in the profit and loss account, balance sheet and notes of Hayseed for each of years 1 to 4 in accordance with SSAP 9 revised.

Suggested solution

(1) *Workings*

(i) Reported Profit

Year		£'000
1	no profit (assume contract not sufficiently advanced to assess outcome of contract with reasonable certainty)	
2	(60% × 290,000)	174
3	(85% × 250,000 = 213,000) − 174,000	39
4	(250,000 − 213,000)	37
	Total	250

(Other methods of calculating attributable profit could include consideration of value of work done up to the balance sheet date.)

(ii) Cost of sales calculations

Year		£'000
1	(25% × 500,000)	125
2	(60% × 560,000 = 336,000) − 125,000	211
3	(85% × 650,000 = 552,000) − 336,000	216
4	(730,000 − 552,000)	178
	Total	730

(iii) Stocks at year end (costs not traded)

Year		£'000
1	Cost incurred	135
	Transfer cost of sales	125
	Closing stock	10
2	Costs incurred	215
		225
	Transfer cost of sales	211
	Closing stock	14
3	Costs incurred	220
		234
	Transfer cost of sales	216
	Closing stock	18
4	Costs incurred	160
		178
	Transfer cost of sales	178
	Closing stock	−

Note: Alternative methods could include direct calculations of stock, transferring remaining costs to cost of sales

(iv) Turnover calculation

Year		£'000	£'000
1	No profit recognised, so base on cost of sales		125
2	Cumulative turnover 60% × 850,000 less recognised in year 1	510 125	385
3	Cumulative turnover 85% × 900,000 less recognised in years 1 and 2	765 510	255
4	Cumulative turnover (= contract price) less recognised in years 1, 2 and 3	980 765	215
	Total		980

(v) Balance sheet figures

(a) Debtors – payments on account

Year		£'000
1	(160,000 – 130,000)	30
2	(490,000 – 480,000)	10
3	(790,000 – 720,000)	70

(b) Other balances

	Year 1 £'000	2 £'000	3 £'000
Stock (cost not traded)	10	14	18
Debtors – amounts recoverable (510 – 490)		20	
Creditors – applicable payments on account			
(160 – 125)	(35)	–	
(790 – 765)			(25)
Net total	(25)	34	(7)

(vi) The above amounts would be presented each year as follows:

Year
1   £25,000 (excess of payments on account over stock) in creditors
2   £14,000 in stock; £20,000 in debtors under sub-heading 'amount recoverable on contracts'
3   £7,000 in creditors (as under 1 above)

(2) *Extracts from financial statements*

(i) Profit and loss account extracts

	Year 1 £'000	2 £'000	3 £'000	4 £'000	Total £'000
Turnover	125	385	255	215	980
Costs of sales	125	211	216	178	730
Gross profit	–	174	39	37	250

Comment: The actual contract profit of £250,000 is recognised as follows:

Year	£'000	%	Degree of completion
1	–	–	25
2	174	69.6	35
3	39	15.6	25
4	37	14.8	15
	250	100.0	100

Hayseed does not recognise profit in the early stages of a contract on the grounds that the contract outcome cannot be assessed with reasonable certainty. This results in the recognition of a disproportionate amount of profit in year 2. In addition in year 3 the company has revised its estimate of expected total profit downwards from £290,000 to £250,000. This has resulted in the recognition of a relatively low proportion of profit in year 3 to the benefit of year 2.

(ii) Balance sheet extracts

	Year		
	1	*2*	*3*
	£'000	*£'000*	*£'000*
Debtors – payments on account	30	10	70
– amounts recoverable on contracts	–	20	–
Stocks	–	14	–
Creditors	25	–	7

(k) Loss-making contracts

Where a contract is expected to result in a loss, the total expected loss (not just the part which is deemed to have occurred to date) should be recognised in the financial statements as soon as it is foreseen.

The disclosure implications are as follows:

(1) The first step is to deduct the accrual or provision for foreseeable loss from the work-in-progress figure for that particular contract, thus reducing it to net realisable value.

(2) Any loss in excess of the work-in-progress should be classified either:

(i) as an accrual within creditors; or
(ii) under provisions for liabilities and charges,

depending on circumstances.

(l) Contracts expected to result in losses

Where it is expected that the contract as a whole will result in a loss, the whole amount of the loss should be accounted for as soon as it is recognised.

Where unprofitable contracts are of such a magnitude that they can be expected to absorb a considerable part of the company's capacity for a considerable period, then the loss calculation should also reflect related overhead expenses expected to be incurred during the period to completion.

Illustration 8

A company commenced work at the beginning of the year on a long-term contract. At the end of year 1 the following information is available:

	£
Total contract price	650,000
Estimated costs to completion	850,000
Degree of completion	40%
Costs to date	350,000
Progress payments invoiced	290,000

Required: Extracts from financial statements for year 1.

(1) Profit and loss account for year 1

	£
Turnover (40% × 650,000)	260,000
Cost of sales (350,000 + (850,000 – 350,000) – 60% × 650,000)	460,000
Loss	200,000

Note: The foreseeable loss over the duration of the contract is £200,000 (£850,000 – £650,000). The full amount of this loss should be reflected in the profit and loss account in accordance with the accruals concept.

Illustration 9

Accounting policies

Stocks
The basis of valuation is as follows:

(i)   Raw materials, bought-in-goods, bottles, cases, pallets and consumable stores at the lower of cost and net realisable value on a first in, first out basis.
(ii) Work-in-progress and finished stocks at the lower of cost, which includes an appropriate element of production overhead costs, and net realisable value.

Costs include all expenditure incurred in bringing each product to its present condition and location. Net realisable value is based on estimated selling prices less further costs expected to be incurred in bringing the stocks to completion and disposal.

Note 12 – stocks

	19X2 £m	19X1 £m
Raw materials	39	32
Work-in-progress	60	53
Finished stocks	113	112
Consumable stores	37	40
	249	237

The replacement cost of stocks approximates to the value at which they are stated in the accounts.

Illustration 10

Accounting policies

Stocks
Stocks are valued at the lower of cost and net realisable value; due allowance is made for obsolete and slow moving items. Cost is based upon 'First in, First out' or 'Moving Average' and includes, where appropriate, a proportion of production overheads. Development land has been valued at its cost of acquisition and development.

Note 13 – stocks

	19X1		19X0	
	Group £'000	Parent Company £'000	Group £'000	Parent Company £'000
Materials	23,812	5,549	29,470	7,600
Consumable stores	11,743	7,743	12,490	8,794
Work-in-progress	10,796	3,769	11,952	4,647
Finished products	33,118	1,374	26,100	1,310
Development land	1,352	–	742	–
	80,821	18,435	80,754	22,351

The Group replacement cost of stocks is £82,982,000 (1990: £81,903,000)

Illustration 11

Note 14 – stocks

	The Group		The Company	
	19X1 £'000	19X0 £'000	19X1 £'000	19X0 £'000
Raw materials and consumables	24	114	24	34
Work-in-progress	83	89	32	47
Finished goods and goods for resale	33,385	28,125	22,671	19,097
Deposits with motor manufacturers	2,946	3,930	2,946	3,930
Property investment held for resale	7,407	6,544	–	–
	43,845	38,802	25,673	23,108

Illustration 12

Accounting policies

Turnover and recognition of profit and losses
Turnover represents the value of work invoiced to customers, excluding value added tax plus the value of the work done but not invoiced on long-term contracts. Profits on contracts are only recognised after the final account has been agreed with the client or in the case of long-term contracts an interim account has been agreed and the outcome of the contract can be assessed with reasonable certainty. Provision is made in full for anticipated future losses on uncompleted contracts.

Stocks and work-in-progress
Stocks and work-in-progress are stated at the lower of cost, including an appropriate proportion of attributable overheads, and net realisable value less amounts received and receivable. Long-term contracts are included at net cost after deducting foreseeable losses and payments on account.

Illustration 13

Accounting policies

Income recognition
Profit is recognised on houses when contracts are exchanged and building is substantially complete. Profit is recognised on commercial property developments or units of development when they are substantially complete and subject to binding and unconditional contracts of sale and where legal completion has occurred shortly thereafter. Where the sale price is conditional upon letting, profit is restricted by reference to the space unlet.
   Profit in respect of construction is recognised when the contract is complete.
   In the case of contracts that are regarded as long term, profit is recognised during execution provided a binding contract for sale exists and the outcome can be foreseen with reasonable certainty.

(m) Interpretation and analysis

Where a company is engaged in a significant amount of long-term contract activity, the relationship between aggregate figures for gross profit and turnover may be distorted by factors such as:

(a) contracts in early stages of completion where company policy is not to take any profit at that point;
(b) contracts whose outcome cannot be assessed with reasonable certainty before the conclusion of the contract;
(c) contracts where profitability varies significantly between different stages;
(d) loss-making contracts.

Illustration 14

Accounting policies (extracts)

4 *Turnover*
Turnover comprises the sum of:

(a) deliveries made and services rendered during the year at fixed prices or at estimated prices where fixed prices are not agreed;
(b) price adjustments arising from revision of estimated prices or settlement of prices which in previous years were estimated;
(c) the estimated selling value of work done on major long-term development and similar contracts.

In the case of long duration contracts calling for a series of items to be delivered throughout the period of the contract, turnover is taken on each delivery.

Intra-group transactions are not included except as shown in the activity analysis and geographical analysis of turnover.

5 *Profit*
Profit is taken when turnover is recognised and, in the case of long duration contracts calling for a series of items to be delivered throughout the period of the contract, profit is taken on each delivery, based on the estimated overall profitability. Changes in estimates of overall profitability are adjusted against current year profits to the extent that they relate to current and prior year deliveries. Losses are provided for in full as soon as they become likely. Thus, profits for the year are not necessarily related to turnover, particularly if adjustments are made on very large contracts which account for a substantial part of turnover.

9 *Stocks*
(a) Work-in-progress, manufactured parts, raw materials and bought out stocks are valued at the lower of cost and estimated realisable value.
(b) Costs of manufactured parts and work-in-progress against customers' contracts comprise prime cost plus full overheads (including administration, distribution and selling expenses). The costs of other manufactured parts and work-in-progress comprise prime cost plus production overheads.
(c) Progress payments received from customers are deducted from stock and work-in-progress to the extent of the value of the work carried out and any excess is shown as customers' advances.
(d) Certain initial costs, including design, development, specific tooling and learning, on risk-sharing contracts, where final sales quantities are still to be determined, are carried forward and amortised over prudent estimates of sales. To the extent that such costs are not covered by firm orders they are shown as deferred costs in work-in-progress.

14.4   DEBTORS

(a) Introduction

Companies Act 1985, Sch 4 formats for debtors include the following headings:

1. Trade debtors
2. Amounts owed by group companies
3. Amounts owed by related companies
4. Other debtors
5. Called up share capital not paid
6. Prepayments and accrued income

Separate disclosure is required of any parts of the above which are not considered to be recoverable within twelve months of the balance sheet date. See also UITF 4 (section 9.3).

Illustration 15

Extract from annual report and accounts of Williams Holdings plc for the year ended 31 December 1994.

Balance sheet (extract)

Consolidated Balance Sheet at 31 December 1994

	Notes	1994 £m	1993 £m
Fixed assets			
Tangible assets	12	**368.0**	340.3
Investments	13	**2.5**	3.5
		370.5	343.8
Current assets			
Stocks	14	**213.6**	185.7
Debtors:			
Falling due within one year	15	**266.6**	213.4
Falling due after more than one year	15	**185.4**	180.0
		452.0	393.4
Investments and other assets for sale	16	**5.6**	8.3
Cash		**191.8**	76.2
		863.0	663.6
Creditors: amounts falling due within one year			
Borrowings and finance leases	17	**(9.3)**	(12.6)
Other creditors	17	**(394.0)**	(322.7)
		(403.3)	(335.3)
Net current assets		**459.7**	328.3
Total assets less current liabilities		**830.2**	672.1
Creditors: amounts falling due after more than one year			
Borrowings and finance leases	18	**(244.5)**	(256.4)
Other creditors	18	**(1.0)**	(1.1)
		(245.5)	(257.5)
Provisions for liabilities and charges	20	**(100.2)**	(95.5)
Net assets		**484.5**	319.1

(b) Factored debts

Debt factoring is dealt with in chapter 7.

(c) Deferred revenue expenditure

Deferred revenue expenditure is not referred to in either Companies Act 1985 or any statement of standard accounting practice and is referred to in the accounts of only a small minority of companies.

Those companies which carry forward such costs in the balance sheet usually include them within debtors (see illustration below). Some companies have, however, classified this type of expenditure as an intangible fixed asset.

Illustration 16

Accounting policies

Interest, internal professional fees and pre-opening expenses:
Interest on capital employed on land awaiting development and on the construction and major redevelopment of hotels and restaurants and internal professional costs incurred until these enterprises start to trade are capitalised as part of the costs of construction. In addition, pre-opening and development expenses incurred up to the commencement of full trading are deferred and written off over five to ten years. Expenses incurred on major information technology projects are capitalised and written off over five years.

15 ACCOUNTING FOR SHAREHOLDERS FUNDS

> **Key Issues**
>
> * Share capital
> * Reserves
> * FRS 4 – Capital instruments
> * Redemption of shares
>   – FRS 4
>   – CA 1985
> * Realised profits
> * Distributable profits

15.1 SHARE CAPITAL

(a) Statutory disclosure requirements – CA 1985

The disclosure requirements of the Companies Act 1985 were referred to in chapter 4. In summary form these are:

(1) Authorised share capital.
(2) Allotted share capital:

    (i) where more than one class of shares allotted, number and aggregate nominal value of each class;
    (ii) amount of allotted share capital;
    (iii) amount of called-up share capital which has been paid up.

(3) Allotted redeemable shares:

    (i) earliest and latest dates on which company has power to redeem;
    (ii) whether redemption is mandatory or at option of company;
    (iii) premium, if any, payable on redemption.

(4) Shares allotted during the financial year:

    (i) reasons for making the allotment;
    (ii) classes of shares allotted;
    (iii) for each class of share:

        (a) number allotted,
        (b) aggregate nominal value,
        (c) consideration received by company.

(5) Options to subscribe for shares and any other rights to require allotment of shares to any person (including convertible loan stock):

    (i) number, description and amount of shares in relation to which right is exercisable;
    (ii) period during which it is exercisable;
    (iii) price to be paid for the shares allotted.

Illustration 1

Extract from annual report and accounts of Manganese Bronze Holdings plc for the year ended 31 July 1995.

Note 22 – share capital

	Number	£000
Authorised Share Capital		
Ordinary shares of 25p each	25,439,892	6,360
$8\frac{1}{4}$% (now 5.775% plus tax credit) cumulative preference shares of £1 each	890,027	890
Issued Share Capital		
Allotted fully paid ordinary shares of 25p each:		
Ordinary shares in issue at 1 August 1994	16,491,436	4,122
Ordinary shares issued	36,000	9
Ordinary shares in issue at 31 July 1995	**16,527,436**	**4,131**
$8\frac{1}{4}$% (now 5.775% plus tax credit) cumulative preference shares of £1 each	890,027	890
Total called up share capital		5,021

During the year 36,000 ordinary shares with a nominal value of £9,000 were issued for cash under the Executive Share Option Scheme, with a related share premium of £28,080. The preference shares have cumulative rights to dividends, no voting rights and priority to the ordinary shares for repayment of capital on winding up.

As at 31 July 1995 the options outstanding under the Executive Share Option Scheme were as follows:

Date of Grant	*Exercise price*	*Outstanding*
7 January 1991	103.0p	289,000
29 March 1993	87.5p	321,000
6 November 1993	113.0p	31,000
30 March 1994	152.0p	115,000
		756,000

The options are excercisable normally between three and ten years of the date of grant.

(b) Bonus shares, scrip or capitalisation issues

(1) Introduction

When a company has substantial undistributed profits on profit and loss account or other reserve account, the total capital employed in the business tends to be obscured. Such accumulations are usually represented by fixed assets or permanent working capital.

To bring the issued share capital into proper relationship with the capital employed in the business, the accumulations can be capitalised and applied in paying up the amounts due on shares to be issued to the members as bonus shares.

Cash is not involved in a bonus issue and a bonus issue of shares adds nothing to the net assets of the company; it divides the capital employed in the business into a larger number of shares. This can be explained by an illustration.

Illustration 2

A company's summarised balance sheet is as follows:

Share capital in £1 shares	£100,000	Sundry assets less creditors	£150,000
Reserves	50,000		

If the assets and goodwill are fully valued, each £1 share is worth £1.50. On the profits being capitalised, if the bonus shares are issued at par, the share capital becomes £150,000 in £1 shares. Each share is now worth £1, but each shareholder has 50 per cent more shares. The shareholders are no better off.

(2) *Implications*

On The Stock Exchange a bonus issue is often considered a bull point and it is common for a bonus issue to be followed by an increased dividend. A bonus issue attracts attention to the company's shares and often increases dealings in the shares which forces up the market value and enables shareholders who wish to do so to realise an immediate profit.

Seldom will the net assets as shown in the balance sheet reflect the true market value of the shares, which will depend primarily on the income they yield and growth prospects. The company may have paid a dividend of 12% and if a reasonable yield were 6% the shares would possibly be quoted round about £2 each, and the total value of the capital would be £200,000. The real value of the shares after the bonus issue would still be £200,000, or 133p each, if it is anticipated that the company will only distribute the same amount of profits as before and will reduce the rate of dividend proportionately, i e to 8%. The market, however, will usually gamble on the dividend not being reduced so much and may quote the shares at, say, £1.50 or £1.75 in the expectation of 9% or more being paid. A member who shares in this expectation might then sell part of his shares, while retaining the anticipation of the same income.

(3) *Accounting entries*

Consider a company having a reserve of £25,000 and a paid-up capital of £100,000 in £1 shares, which resolves to pay a bonus of 20% out of its reserve by the issue of one fully paid share for each five shares held.

The journal entries would be as follows:

	£	£
Reserve account	20,000	
Bonus account		20,000
Bonus of 20% payable out of the reserve account in fully paid shares as per resolution dated . . .		
Bonus account	20,000	
Share capital account		20,000
Issue of 20,000 shares of £1 each fully paid in satisfaction of bonus at the rate of one share for every five held		

15.2 RESERVES – A SUMMARY

(a) Companies Act 1985

The balance sheet formats include:

K Capital and reserves
  I   Called-up share capital   X
  II Share premium account   X
  III Revaluation reserve   X
  IV Other reserves
      1 Capital redemption reserve   X
      2 Reserve for own shares   X
      3 Reserves provided for by the articles of association   X
      4 Other reserves   X   X
  V Profit and loss account   X

                   £XX

Additionally, where any amount is transferred to or from any reserves, disclosure is required of:

(1) amount of reserves at beginning of year;
(2) any amounts transferred to or from the reserves during the year.

(b) References to reserves in this book

(1) overview (section 3.6)
(2) revaluation reserve (section 12.7)
(3) investment property revaluation (section 12.9)
(4) merger reserve (section 25.4)
(5) capital redemption reserve (section 15.5)
(6) permitted reserve movements (section 8.8)

Illustration 3

Extract from annual report and accounts of Cowie Group plc for the year ended 31 December 1994.

Note 21 – Reserves

	Capital Redemption Reserve Fund £000	Share Premium Account £000	Special Reserve £000	Revaluation Reserve £000	Profit and Loss Account £000	Total £000
(a) The Group						
At 1 January 1994	50	30,129	10,411	938	86,876	128,404
Goodwill eliminated on current year acquisitions	–	–	(10,411)	–	(2,732)	(13,143)
Goodwill eliminated on acquisition made in the previous year	–	–	–	–	(453)	(453)
Arising on issue of shares	–	9	–	–	–	9
Retained profit for the year	–	–	–	–	18,784	18,784
At 31 December 1994	50	30,138	–	938	102,475	133,601
(b) The Company						
At 1 January 1994	50	30,129	10,411	745	38,564	79,899
Goodwill eliminated on current year acquisitions	–	–	(10,411)	–	(1,803)	(12,214)
Goodwill eliminated on acquisition made in the previous year	–	–	–	–	(453)	(453)
Arising on issue of shares	–	9	–	–	–	9
Retained profit for the year	–	–	–	–	3,487	3,487
At 31 December 1994	50	30,138	–	745	39,795	70,728

15.3 FRS 4 – CAPITAL INSTRUMENTS

(a) Introduction

The stated aim of FRS 4 is 'to secure clear and appropriate distinctions in the balance sheet between the various kinds of financial instruments and to ensure that their respective costs are properly reflected in the profit and loss account'.

The term 'capital instruments' refers to all instruments that are issued as a means of raising finance including:

(1) shares
(2) debentures
(3) loans and debt instruments
(4) options and warrants that give the holder the right to subscribe for or obtain capital instruments.

The Standard applies to all financial statements intended to give a true and fair view (whether or not these relate to companies).

(b) Classification of shares under FRS 4

Shares must be classified either as equity or non-equity.

(1) *Non-equity*

These are defined as shares which possess *any* of the following three characteristics.

(1) Any of the rights of the shares to receive payments (whether in respect of dividends, in respect of redemption or otherwise) are for a limited amount that is not calculated by reference to the company's assets or profits or the dividends on any class of equity share.
(2) Any of their rights to participate in a surplus in a winding up are limited to a specific amount that is not calculated by reference to the company's assets or profits and such limitation had a commercial effect in practice at the time the shares were issued or, if later, at the time the limitation was introduced.
(3) The shares are redeemable either according to their terms, or because the holder, or any party other than the issuer, can require their redemption.

Thus, any shares that have a right to a dividend payment or to a redemption payment that is for a limited amount will be regarded as non-equity shares.

Participating preference shares are entitled to a fixed dividend plus a proportion of dividend paid on equity shares. This type of preference share is referred to in the Application Notes which states that such shares are non-equity in accordance with FRS 4. Paragraph 13 of FRS 4 defines the term 'participating dividend'.

(2) *Equity shares*

Equity shares are a residual category, i e shares other than non-equity shares.

(c) Balance sheet analysis of shareholders' funds

The disclosure requirements of FRS 4 are as follows:

(1) the total amount of shareholders funds should be shown on the face of the balance sheet;
(2) the total in (1) should be analysed between:

   (i)   amount attributable to equity interest; and
   (iii) amount attributable to non-equity interests.

The analysis may be given on the balance sheet or in the notes. If given by way of note the balance sheet caption should state that the total of shareholders funds includes non-equity interests.

A further analysis is required for (ii) above giving the total for each class of non-equity shares. Note, however, that FRS4 does not require any of the individual components of shareholders funds such as share premium or revaluation reserve to be analysed between equity and non-equity interests.

Illustration 4

Part of balance sheet

	Note	£'000	£'000
Net assets		11,446	10,240
Capital and reserves			
Called up share capital	16	1,774	1,774
Revaluation reserve	17	1,417	1,417
Other reserves	17	581	581
Profit and loss account	18	7,674	6,468
Shareholders' funds		11,446	10,240
Attributable to equity shareholders		11,360	10,154
Attributable to non-equity shareholders		86	86

These accounts were approved by the board of directors on . . . and were signed on its behalf by:

...

Director

(d) Profit and loss account disclosures

The following profit and loss account information should be given:

(1) aggregate dividends for each class or shares giving sub-totals for:

    (i) dividends on equity shares;
    (ii) participating dividends (ie for participating preference shares the participating element of the dividend as opposed to the fixed element;
    (iii) other dividends on non-equity shares.

(2) any other appropriation of profit in respect of non-equity shares. This could relate to the annual build-up of the premium payable on redemption in some years time.

Where the above information is given by way of note, the P/L caption should make it clear that the above such amounts are included.

Illustration 5

Part of the profit and loss account

	Note	£'000	£'000
Profit on ordinary activities before taxation		1,621	579
Tax on profit on ordinary activities	6	(5)	(123)
Profit for the financial year		1,616	456
Dividends paid and proposed (including non-equity)	8	(410)	(291)
Retained profit for the year		1,206	165

Note 8 – Dividends

	1994 £'000	1993 £'000
Non-equity shares		
Preference and pre-preference dividends paid	4	4
Equity shares		
Ordinary shares:		
Interim paid 10p (1993 – 5p)	169	84
Final proposed 14p (1993 – 12p)	237	203
	410	291

(e) Additional disclosures for non-equity shares

For each class of non-equity shares, the notes to the accounts should give a brief summary of:

(1) rights to dividends;
(2) dates at which shares are redeemable and amounts payable on redemption;
(3) priority and amounts receivable on a winding-up;
(4) voting rights.

For shares with unusual rights and characteristics, further information may need to be given. The main sources for the above information will be the company's Articles (as amended, if appropriate) and any special agreements.

Illustration 6

Note 16 – share capital (part of note)

5% pre-preference shares of £1 each
The rights of the pre-preference shareholders include entitlement to receive a cumulative dividend, preferential to all other classes of shares, at a rate of 5% per annum on the paid up capital. The shareholders are entitled on a winding-up or otherwise to a repayment of paid-up capital, in priority to all other classes of shares.
   At a general meeting, the voting rights of pre-preference shareholders are as follows: on a show of hands, one vote per member; on a poll, holders of pre-preference shares have nine votes per share compared with one vote for every ordinary share held by members.

5% preference shares of £1 each
The rights of the preference shareholders include entitlement to receive a cumulative dividend at the rate of 5% per annum on paid up capital. This dividend entitlement ranks after that of the pre-preference shareholders but is in priority to the other remaining classes of shares.
   Except in restricted circumstances, the shares do not carry an entitlement to vote at a general meeting.

'A' ordinary shares of £1 each
These have the same rights as ordinary shares apart from voting rights. Except in restricted circumstances, the shares do not carry an entitlement to vote at a general meeting.

15.4   FRS 4 – ACCOUNTING TREATMENT OF SHARES REDEEMABLE AT A PREMIUM

(a) Basic procedures

FRS 4 requires the shares to be treated as follows:

(1) The preference shares will usually be classed as non-equity. The amounts attributable following issue are the net proceeds (i e cash received less issue costs).
(2) The total finance cost over the period up to redemption is the difference between:

  (i)   proceeds on issue; and
  (ii) total payments to be made to the preference shareholders – either by way of dividends or payment on redemption.

(3) The finance cost should be allocated to each year's profit and loss account in a similar way to debt.

(4) Any difference between finance costs and dividends paid should be accounted for in the profit and loss account as an appropriation of profit.
(5) The balance sheet carrying amount should be increased by the finance cost for the period and reduced by payments.

Illustration 7

(1) Basic data

Company issued 100,000 £1 6% preference shares on 20 December 1993 at a premium of 5%. Issue costs were £3,000. The shares are redeemable on 31 December 2003 at a premium of 10%.

The total finance cost is:

	£
Net proceeds (105,000 – 3,000)	102,000
Redemption cost	110,000
Dividends (10 years × 6,000)	60,000
Total payments	170,000
Total finance costs	68,000

The total cost of £68,000 should be spread over the ten years so as to give a constant rate on the carrying amount. Strictly this should be done using the actuarial method, with a financial calculator or computer. For simplicity, however, assume a straight line method with an annual cost of £6,800 (£68,000 ÷ 10).

(2) The accounting entries are summarised below:

On issue of shares

	£	£
Dr cash	105,000	
Cr preference share capital		100,000
Cr share premium account		5,000
Dr share premium account	3,000	
Cr cash		3,000

Balance sheet extract 31 December 1993	
Non-equity shareholders funds	102,000

Notes

(i) It is not necessary to give an analysis of the individual components of shareholders funds between equity and non-equity interests.
(ii) FRS 3 requires the £102,000 to be shown in the movement of shareholders funds statements.

Entries in each subsequent year

	£	£
Dr profit and loss account (appropriation section)	6,800	
Cr redemption reserve (excess of premium on redemption over premium on issue)		
(10,000 – 5,000) ÷ 10		500
Cr cash (dividend paid)		6,000
Cr profit and loss reserve (issue costs £3,000 ÷ 10)		300

Notes

(i) The profit and loss account should distinguish between dividends on non-equity shares (£6,000) and other appropriations (£800).

(ii) The issue costs of £3,000 form part of the finance cost and so should be charged to profit and loss account over the life of the preference shares. However, as £3,000 has already been charged direct to reserve, reserves must be credited direct each year with a proportion of the £3,000.

(iii) At the end of 1994, the total of non-equity shareholders funds to be disclosed by way of note is calculated as:

	£
Carrying amount at 1.1.94	102,000
Finance cost	6,800
	108,800
less dividends paid	6,000
Carrying amount at 31.12.94	102,800

(iv) At the end of 2003, this will have increased by £800 per annum (total: $9 \times £800 = £7,200$) to £110,000 which is the amount payable on redemption.

15.5   PURCHASE AND REDEMPTION OF SHARES – CA 1985 RULES

(a) Redeemable shares

A company limited by shares or a company limited by guarantee and having a share capital may issue redeemable shares (ordinary or preference) provided it is authorised to do so by its articles.

The Companies Act 1985, ss 159–161 specify the following additional conditions:

(1) redeemable shares may not be issued unless at the time of issue there are issued shares of the company which are not redeemable;

(2) redeemable shares may not be redeemed unless they are fully paid;

(3) the terms of redemption must provide for payment on redemption.

(b) Financing the redemption

The method of redemption is restricted to the following three possibilities:

(1) by the proceeds of a new issue of shares of any class; or

(2) out of distributable profits; or

(3) by a combination of (1) and (2).

Where shares are redeemed wholly out of profits, an amount equivalent to the nominal value of shares redeemed is to be transferred from distributable profits to a capital redemption reserve.

Where shares are redeemed wholly or partly out of the proceeds of a fresh issue of shares, a transfer to capital redemption reserve is required to the extent that the proceeds of the issue fall short of the nominal value redeemed (Companies Act 1985, s 170).

> CRR transfer = nominal value redeemed − proceeds of new issue of shares

(c) Capital redemption reserve (CRR)

For the purposes of reduction of capital, the capital redemption reserve is treated as though it were paid-up share capital. However, the CRR may be applied in making a bonus issue of fully paid shares.

(d) Premium on redemption of redeemable shares

The basic rule is that any premium payable on redemption must be paid out of distributable profits of the company.

There is an exception to this rule, but it only applies if two conditions can both be satisfied:

(1) the shares to be redeemed were originally issued at a premium; and
(2) the redemption is to be financed by a fresh issue of shares.

In this situation, the premium or redemption may come out of share premium account (rather than distributable profits) but the amount of share premium account which may be used for this purpose is restricted to the lower of:

(i) the aggregate of premiums received on the original issue of the shares to be redeemed; and
(ii) the present balance on share premium account taking into account any premium relating to the fresh issue of shares.

(e) Cancellation of shares

Shares redeemed under the Companies Act 1985, ss 159–161 are to be treated as cancelled on redemption, and the company's issued share capital reduced accordingly.

However, the redemption of share capital is not to be taken as reducing the company's authorised share capital.

Illustration 8

	£
Sundry assets	840,000
Cash at bank	300,000
	1,140,000
Less liabilities	210,000
	930,000

	£
Authorised, called-up and fully paid capital	
200,000 £1 ordinary shares	200,000
400,000 £1 6% redeemable preference shares	400,000
	600,000
Profit and loss account	330,000
	930,000

By the terms of their issue the preference shares were redeemable at a premium of 5% on 1 January 19X5 and it was decided to arrange this as far as possible out of the company's resources subject to leaving a balance of £100,000 to the credit of the profit and loss account. It was also decided to raise the balance of money required by the issue of a sufficient number of ordinary shares at a premium of 25p per share.

Required: Journal entries and ledger account entries to reflect the above transactions, and a summarised balance sheet thereafter. Ignore taxation.

Workings

As redeemable shares were originally issued at par, the premium on redemption must come out of distributable profits. A further consideration is that the amount by which the nominal value redeemed exceeds the proceeds of the new issue should be transferred to capital redemption reserve.

	£
Existing balance on P/L	330,000
Required for premium on redemption	
5% × 400,000	20,000
	310,000
Final balance on P/L is required to be	100,000
∴ 'Available' for transfer to CRR	210,000

Proceeds of new issue

= nominal value redeemed − 210,000

= £400,000 − £210,000

= £190,000

So nominal value of shares to be issued at a premium of 25p per share

$$\frac{£190,000}{125p} = £152,000$$

Journal entries

	£	£
6% redeemable preference share capital	400,000	
Premium on redemption of preference shares	20,000	
Preference shares redemption account		420,000
Transferring 400,000 £1 redeemable preference shares redeemable at a premium of 5%		
Application and allotment (ordinary shares)	190,000	
Ordinary share capital		152,000
Share premium account		38,000
Issue of 152,000 ordinary shares at premium of 25p per share		
Cash	190,000	
Application and allotment (ordinary shares)		190,000
Cash received on issue of 152,000 ordinary shares		
Preference shares redemption account	420,000	
Cash		420,000
Redemption of 400,000 6% redeemable preference shares at a premium of 5%		
Profit and loss account	210,000	
Capital redemption reserve		210,000
Transfer out of profit of amount equal to nominal amount of shares redeemed otherwise than out of the proceeds of a new issue		
Share premium account	20,000	
Profit and loss account		20,000
Providing for premium on redemption out of share premium account		

Ledger accounts

6% REDEEMABLE PREFERENCE SHARE CAPITAL

		£			£
Jan 1	Preference shares redemption account	400,000	Jan 1	Balance b/f	400,000

PREMIUM ON REDEMPTION OF PREFERENCE SHARES

		£			£
Jan 1	Preference shares redemption account	20,000	Jan 1	Profit and loss account	20,000

PREFERENCE SHARES REDEMPTION ACCOUNT

		£			£
Jan 1	Cash	420,000	Jan 1	6% redeemable preference shares	400,000
				Premium on redemption	20,000

ORDINARY SHARE CAPITAL

		£			£
Jan 1	Balance c/f	352,000	Dec 31	Balance b/f	200,000
			Jan 1	Application and allotment	152,000
		352,000			352,000

SHARE PREMIUM ACCOUNT

		£			£
Jan 1	Balance c/f	38,000	Jan 1	Application and allotment	38,000

APPLICATION AND ALLOTMENT (ORDINARY SHARES)

		£			£
Jan 1	Share capital	152,000	Jan 1	Cash	190,000
	Share premium	38,000			
		190,000			190,000

PROFIT AND LOSS ACCOUNT

		£			£
Jan 1	Premium redemption of preference shares account	20,000	Dec 31	Balance b/f	330,000
	Capital redemption reserve	210,000			
	Balance c/f	100,000			
		330,000			330,000

CAPITAL REDEMPTION RESERVE

		£
Jan 1	Profit and loss account	210,000

CASH BOOK

		£			£
Dec 31	Balance b/f	300,000	Jan 1	Preference shares redemption account	420,000
	Application and allotment account (ordinary shares)	190,000		Balance c/f	70,000
		490,000			490,000

SUMMARISED BALANCE SHEET OF TRYM TRADERS PLC AFTER THE REDEMPTION OF PREFERENCE SHARES

	£
Sundry assets	840,000
Cash at bank	70,000
	910,000
Less liabilities	210,000
	700,000

		£
Authorised, called-up and fully paid capital:		
352,000 £1 ordinary shares		352,000
Capital redemption reserve		210,000
Share premium account		38,000
Profit and loss account		100,000
		700,000

Note: share capital and non-distributable reserves are maintained as a comparison of the position pre- and post-redemption shows:

	Pre-redemption £	Post-redemption £
Ordinary share capital	200,000	352,000
Preference share capital	400,000	–
Capital redemption reserve	–	210,000
Share premium	–	38,000
Total share capital and non-distributable reserves	600,000	600,000

(f) A problem area

The legislation may give rise to problems of interpretation in certain situations where the shares to be redeemed were themselves issued at a premium. It is possible that a literal interpretation of the legislation may result in a reduction in the total of share capital and non-distributable reserves.

Illustration 9

Several years ago, Redeemables plc issued 100,000 £1 redeemable preference shares at a premium of 8p per share. These shares are now due to be redeemed at a premium of 25p per share. The redemption is to be part-financed by a fresh issue of 80,000 £1 shares at a premium of 12.5p per share.

The balance on a share premium account prior to the fresh issue of shares was £12,000. Ignore other share capital of the company.

(1) Basic calculations

	£
(i) Transfer to CCR	
Nominal value of shares to be redeemed	100,000
Proceeds of new issue	90,000
Transfer to CRR	10,000

(ii) Premium on redemption of shares (£25,000)
Since shares to be redeemed were originally issued at a premium, share premium account may be used to the extent of lower of:

	£
(a) premium on original issue	8,000
(b) balance on share premium account (including premium on fresh issue of shares) = £12,000 + £10,000	22,000
ie lower amount is	8,000

(2) Journal entries

	£	£
Cash	90,000	
Share capital		80,000
Premium		10,000
Cash		125,000
Share capital	100,000	
Share premium	8,000	
Distributable profits	17,000	
Distributable profits	10,000	
Capital redemption reserve		10,000

(3) Comparisons of share capital and non-distributable reserves

	Pre-redemption £	Post-redemption £
Share capital	100,000	80,000
Share premium	12,000	14,000
Capital redemption reserve	–	10,000
Share capital and non-distributable reserves	112,000	104,000

There is some disagreement over the interpretation of the legislation. Some commentators have concluded that the legislation is deficient in that it may result in a reduction of capital and non-distributable reserves, as in the above example.

Others have commented that where part of the premium on redemption comes out of the proceeds of a fresh issue (ie £8,000 in the example above) it should reduce the aggregate proceeds available in determining the transfer to capital redemption reserve. Accordingly, a further £8,000 should be transferred out of distributable profit and into capital redemption reserve in order to maintain the total of share capital and non-distributable reserves.

This latter approach may be defended on prudence grounds even though the relevant sections of the Companies Act 1985 may be open to more than one interpretation.

(g) Purchase of own shares

A company limited by shares or a company limited by guarantee and having a share capital may purchase its own shares (including any redeemable shares) provided it is authorised to do so by its articles (Companies Act 1985, s 162).

However, a company may not purchase any of its shares if as a result of the share purchase there would be no member of the company holding shares other than redeemable shares.

There are three prescribed procedures for the purchase of shares by a company:

(1) off-market purchase;
(2) contingent purchase contracts;
(3) market purchase.

A detailed consideration of these, including necessary authorisations, is outside the scope of a financial accounting textbook.

All of the matters considered earlier relating to redeemable shares apply also to the purchase of own shares, except the terms and manner of purchase need not be determined by the articles.

(h) Purchase or redemption out of capital

(1) *Introduction*

This power is available to private companies only. Under no circumstances is it available to public limited companies.

The Companies Act 1985, ss 171–173 allow a private company limited by shares, or a private company limited by guarantee and having share capital, to make a payment out of capital provided it is permitted to do so by its articles.

The term 'payment out of capital' essentially means a redemption or purchase of shares other than out of the company's distributable profit, or out of the proceeds of a fresh issue of shares.

(2) *Conditions*

(i) The Act refers to the term *permissible capital payment* (PCP). This is the amount by which the purchase or redemption cost exceeds the total of available (ie distributable) profits, plus the proceeds of a fresh issue of shares made for the purpose of the redemption or purchase.

(ii) The difference between the PCP and the nominal value of shares redeemed or purchased is to be dealt with as follows:

  (a) If the total of PCP, plus the proceeds of a fresh issue of shares, is less than the nominal value of shares redeemed or purchased, the amount of the difference is to be transferred to capital redemption reserve.

  (b) If the total of PCP, plus the proceeds of a fresh issue of shares, is more than the nominal value, the excess may be used to reduce any of the following:

    (a) capital redemption reserve;
    (b) share premium account;
    (c) fully paid share capital;
    (d) revaluation reserve.

(iii) The Companies Act 1985 specifies stringent legal conditions in connection with purchase or redemption out of capital. While the Act attempts to offer private companies greater flexibility than public companies, it is particularly concerned with the protection of creditors.

  The legal conditions, a detailed consideration of which is outside the scope of this book, include:

  (a) the approval by the members of the company by means of a special resolution;

  (b) a statutory declaration of solvency by the directors with prescribed form and content and having annexed to it a special auditors' report;

  (c) publicity for proposed payment out of capital; and

  (d) rights of members or creditors to object.

Illustration 10

Private Ltd issued 1,000 £1 ordinary shares several years ago at par. Following the death of one of the major shareholders, the company now wishes to purchase 300 shares at a cost of £350. Distributable reserves amount to £270.

(1) Basic calculations

(i) Permissible capital payment (PCP)	£
Purchase cost	350
Distributable profits	270
PCP	80

(ii) CRR calculation	
Nominal value purchased	300
PCP	80
	220

(2) Journal entries

	£	£
Cash		350
Share capital	300	
Distributable profits	50	
Distributable profits	220	
CRR		220

Note: share capital and non-distributable reserves have been reduced by £80 ie the amount of the permissible share capital payment.

	Pre-purchase £	Post-purchase £
Share capital	1,000	700
CRR	–	220
Share capital and non-distributable reserves	1,000	920

15.6   THE DETERMINATION OF REALISED PROFITS

(a) Background

The term 'realised profits' was introduced into statute comparatively recently by the Companies Act 1985.

It is important in two separate contexts:

(1) Under the Companies Act 1985, in the determination of a company's distributable profits.
(2) Under the Companies Act 1985, in the context of the prudence concept ie deciding whether a particular profit is realised and may therefore be included in the profit and loss account.

(b) Definition of realised profits

The Companies Act 1985 refers to such profits as fall to be treated as realised profits in accordance with generally accepted accounting principles at the date the accounts are prepared.

The CCAB have indicated that SSAPs must be considered to be highly persuasive in determining principles generally accepted in determining realised profits.

(c) SSAP – disclosure of accounting policies

SSAP 2 states that revenues and profits are not anticipated but are recognised by inclusion in the profit and loss account only when realised in the form of cash or of other assets (such as debtors) whose cash realisation can be assessed with reasonable certainty.

(d) Post balance sheet events

The Companies Act 1985 requires all liabilities and losses which have arisen or are likely to arise in respect of the current financial year, or a previous year, to be taken into account. This should include those which have only become apparent between the balance sheet date and the date on which the financial statements are approved by the board of directors.

(e) Departures from the prudence concept

There may be special circumstances where a true and fair view could not be given without the inclusion of unrealised profits in the profit and loss account.

The Companies Act 1985 allows the directors to include unrealised profits where there are special reasons for doing so, in which case disclosure is required of the departure from the prudence concept, the reason for it and its effect.

Such situations are likely to be rare. A particular example is the treatment of translation differences on long-term foreign loans (see chapter 28).

(f) Long-term contracts

In its October 1982 technical release (The determination of realised profits and the disclosure of distributable profits in the context of the Companies Acts 1948 to 1981), the CCAB referred to the point that there was initially some confusion as to whether profits recognised in advance of completion of long-term contracts could be regarded as 'realised' in the context of the Companies Acts.

However, the CCAB concluded that since the profit recognition concepts of SSAP 2 were based on the concept of reasonable certainty as to eventual outcome, there was no conflict with the statutory accounting principles and the profits could be regarded as realised.

15.7 THE DETERMINATION OF DISTRIBUTABLE PROFITS

(a) Background

The Companies Act 1985 sets out conditions that must be satisfied before a company may make a distribution to its members. There are general rules which apply to all companies plus additional rules which apply only to public companies. Special rules apply to investment companies and insurance companies.

(b) Definition of distribution

A distribution is defined as any distribution in cash or otherwise except:

(1) An issue of fully or partly paid bonus shares.
(2) Redemption of preference shares out of the proceeds of a fresh issue of shares, plus payment of premium on redemption out of the share premium account.
(3) Reduction of share capital.
(4) Distribution of assets in a winding up.

(c) Restriction for all companies (plc and private)

(1) A distribution can only be made out of profits available for the purpose – namely, the aggregate of accumulated realised profits (not previously distributed or capitalised), less accumulated realised losses (so far as not previously written off by a reduction or reorganisation of capital).
(2) A profit is realised, provided it is treated as such under generally accepted accounting principles at the time when the accounts are prepared.

(d) Additional restriction for public companies

(1) A public company may not pay a dividend unless its net assets exceed its share capital plus undistributable reserves. The dividend must not reduce its net assets below this aggregate amount.
(2) Undistributable reserves are defined as:

(i)   share premium account;
(ii) capital redemption reserve;

(iii) the excess of accumulated unrealised profits over accumulated unrealised losses not previously written off by a reduction or reorganisation of capital;

(iv) any other reserve which the company is prevented from distributing, as a result of statute, or by its memorandum or articles of association.

(e) Illustration 11

Balance sheet prior to distribution

	£'000
Ordinary share capitaal	500
Share premium	250
Revaluation reserve	160
Retained profits	290
	1,200

Whether the company is public or private, its distributable reserves are restricted to £290,000.

(f) The treatment of provisions

(1) Any provision, other than one relating to a diminution in value of a fixed asset appearing on a revaluation of all the fixed assets, or of all the fixed assets other than goodwill, of a company, shall be treated as a realised loss.

(2) The 'revaluation of all the fixed assets . . .' referred to above need not necessarily be an actual valuation. As regards particular assets, a consideration of their value at a point in time will be regarded as a revaluation for these purposes. However, in this situation the exception will only apply if the directors are satisfied that the aggregate value of the particular assets is not less than the aggregate amounts at which they are stated in the accounts.

(3) Where valuations are 'considered' rather than actual, and this is important in considering the relevant accounts, a note to the accounts must state:

(i) that the directors have considered the value of certain fixed assets without actually revaluing them; and

(ii) that the directors are satisfied that the aggregate value of those assets is or was not less than the aggregate amount at which they are/were stated in the accounts.

Note: In view of the stringent conditions referred to above, it follows that a loss for diminution in value recognised in the profit and loss account will usually be regarded as a realised loss.

(g) Effect of the above rules

They may be summarised as follows:

Figure 1 – determination of whether a revaluation deficit is to be regarded as realised or unrealised

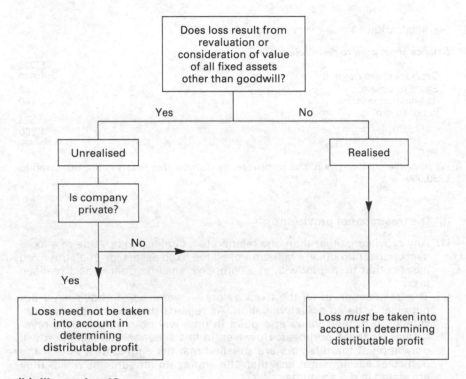

(h) Illustration 12

Balance sheet prior to distribution

	£'000
Ordinary share capital	500
Share premium	250
Revaluation deficits (net)	(120)
Retained profits	290
Net assets	920

Provided that the revaluation deficit results from the 'diminution in value of a fixed asset appearing on a revaluation of all the fixed assets . . ' a private company may distribute up to £290,000.

However, a public company's distributable profit is restricted to £170,000 (£290,000 less £120,000) since the dividend must not have the effect of reducing its net assets below its share capital plus undistributable reserves (i e a total of 500 + 250 = 750). The maximum reduction is thus (920 – 750) = £170,000.

(i) Specific points

(1) *Fixed asset revaluations incorporated into the balance sheet*

(i) When a fixed asset is revalued and the revaluation is incorporated in the accounts, SSAP 12 requires the depreciation charge to be based on the revalued amount.

(ii) The difference between the depreciation charge based on the revalued amount compared with that which would have applied had the asset not been revalued, may be regarded as a realised profit.

Illustration 13

The figure for an item of plant and machinery in a company's balance sheet was arrived at as follows:

	£
Historical cost	100,000
Accumulated depreciation (three years at 10%)	30,000
Net book value	70,000

The asset was revalued at £84,000 and the revaluation incorporated into the balance sheet. The surplus on revaluation of £14,000 was taken direct to revaluation reserve.

In subsequent years, the depreciation charge would be £12,000 (£84,000 divided by 7 years) as opposed to the previous £10,000 based on historical cost. For each subsequent year of the asset's remaining life, £2,000 of the revaluation reserve may be regarded as realised and hence distributable.

(2) *Development costs*

Development costs capitalised in accordance with SSAP 13 must in normal circumstances be regarded as a realised loss. The directors may in special circumstances depart from this principle; the special circumstances must be disclosed in the accounts.

It is generally assumed that the special circumstances are equivalent to the stringent conditions required to be satisfied by SSAP 13 in order to justify capitalisation of development costs.

(3) *Statutory current cost accounts*

The Companies Act 1985 permits a company, should it so choose, to adopt current cost accounting as its main accounting convention. This situation is likely to be extremely rare (see chapter 33).

Part of the current cost reserve will relate to realised items, such as depreciation adjustment, cost of sales adjustment, monetary working capital adjustment etc which were taken into account over a number of years in determining current cost profit.

The realised part of the current cost reserve is legally distributable under the Companies Act 1985 even though the effect of distributing this amount might be to impair the operating capability of the business.

(j) Investment companies

The Companies Act 1985 contains special rules regarding investment companies. These rules are detailed and complex and the notes below are intended to emphasise certain key points.

(1) *Definition*

An investment company is a public company which has given notice to the registrar of companies of its intention to carry on business as an investment company. An investment company must also comply with certain specific requirements including the prohibition by its memorandum or articles of the distribution of *capital* profits.

(2) *Distribution of profits*

Investment companies may base their distributions on two alternative sets of rules (i e choose whichever is more favourable in the circumstances) – either:

(i)   usual PLC rules (as above); or

(ii) a distribution out of accumulated realised revenue profits less *revenue* losses (realised or unrealised). This alternative is subject to the proviso that at the time of the distribution the amount of the company's assets is at least equal to one and a half times the aggregate of its liabilities (clearly no part of the distribution must take the assets below that figure).

(k) Other areas

The effect of elimination of purchased goodwill on the distributable profits of individual companies is dealt with in section 13.2(p). The treatment of dividends paid out of pre-combination profits is discussed in section 12.10.

16 ACCOUNTING FOR LIABILITIES AND PROVISIONS

Key Issues

* Creditors and loans
* FRS 4 – capital instruments
* Convertible loan stock
* Provisions

16.1 CREDITORS AND LOANS

(a) Companies Act 1985 requirements

The balance sheet formats and disclosure requirements were referred to in chapter 4 and may be summarised as follows:

(1) For each item shown under creditors, disclose:

   (i) aggregate amounts of debts repayable (other than by instalments) more than five years after B/S date;

   (ii) aggregate amount of debts repayable by instalments any of which fall due more than five years after the B/S date;

   (iii) for each item in (ii), the aggregate amount of instalments falling due after the five years.

(2) For each debt required to be disclosed within (1)(ii) above, disclose:

   (i) terms of payment or repayment and rate of interest payable; or

   (ii) if above statement would be of excessive length, a general indication of the terms of payment or repayment and rates of interest payable.

(3) For each item under creditors, supply:

   (i) aggregate amount of any debts in respect of which security has been given;

   (ii) indication of nature of securities given.

(4) Issues of debentures during the year – disclose:

   (i) reason for making issue;

   (ii) classes of debentures issued;

   (iii) for each class, amount issued and consideration received by company.

(5) Particulars of redeemed debentures which company has power to reissue.

(6) Where any of company's debentures are held by a nominee of or trustee for the company: state nominal amount of debentures and amount at which stated in the accounting records.

(7) Convertible debenture loans: amount of any convertible loans is required to be shown separately.

Illustration 1

Extend from annual report and accounts of Cowie Group plc for the year ended 31 December 1994.

17 Creditors

	The Group		The Company	
	1994	1993	**1994**	1993
	£000	£000	**£000**	£000
Amounts falling due within one year:				
Loan capital	**7**	27	**7**	7
Short term loans	**64,000**	32,000	**23,071**	32,000
Bank overdrafts	**3,187**	6,353	**–**	14,816
Syndicated and finance house loans (secured)	**270**	45,263	**194**	182
Obligations under finance leases	**733**	2,350	**1,442**	1,023
Payments received on account	**24,404**	13,965	**–**	345
Trade creditors	**30,633**	29,806	**899**	18,628
Creditors for taxation and social security	**19,981**	16,137	**6,078**	5,553
Other creditors	**9,155**	7,767	**1,635**	6,962
Accruals and deferred income	**23,003**	16,766	**2,626**	9,828
Proposed dividend	**10,304**	7,871	**10,304**	7,871
Amounts owing to Group undertakings	**–**	–	**12,840**	2,640
	185,677	178,305	**59,096**	99,855
Amounts falling due after more than one year:				
Syndicated and finance house loans (secured)	**270,309**	200,500	**309**	500
Loan capital	**11**	97	**11**	17
Payments received on account	**1,405**	1,584	**–**	–
Obligations under finance leases	**705**	1,364	**903**	1,994
Accruals and deferred income	**6,428**	3,912	**5,308**	3,853
	278,858	207,457	**6,531**	6,364
Loan capital and other borrowings repayment statement:				
Within 1 year or on demand	**68,197**	85,993	**24,714**	48,028
Between 1 and 2 years	**70,455**	100,705	**475**	845
Between 2 and 5 years	**200,570**	101,256	**748**	1,666
	339,222	287,954	**25,937**	50,539

Bank overdrafts and short term loans

Bank overdrafts and short term loans are secured by debentures giving fixed and floating charges over the assets of the Group or by guarantees given by Cowie Group plc.

Interest rate swaps and caps

The Group, at 31 December 1994, had entered into interest rate swap arrangements for periods of up to three years with various counterparties in respect of amounts totalling £220,000,000 (1993: £145,000,000). Under these arrangements the Group is required to pay interest on the above amounts at fixed rates and will receive interest on these amounts at rates linked to LIBOR. In addition, the Group had entered into interest rate cap arrangements in respect of amounts totalling £75,000,000 (1993: £145,000,000) where by the Group receives interest if the three months LIBOR rate rises above specified rates, of either 10.0% or 10.5%.

(b) Classification and analysis of liabilities – FRS 4, capital instruments

FRS 4 was referred to in chapter 15, section 15.3. FRS 4 requires that all capital instruments (except for shares) which contain an obligation to transfer economic benefits are classified as liabilities. The term 'obligation' also includes a contingent obligation.

In the case of convertible debt, FRS 4 specifically requires that conversion into shares should not be anticipated. Convertible debt must therefore be reported within liabilities, irrespective of the likelihood of conversion into shares (see section 16.3).

FRS 4 has extended the disclosure requirements for analysis of maturity of debt. The notes should include an analysis between amounts falling due:

(1) in one year or less or on demand;
(2) between one and two years;
(3) between two and five years; and
(4) in five years or more.

Note that debt maturity should be determined by reference to the earliest date on which the lender can require repayment.

16.2 ACCOUNTING TREATMENT OF DEBT REDEEMABLE AT A PREMIUM

FRS 4 sets out the following principles:

(1) Following the issue, debt should be stated at net proceeds (defined as fair value of consideration less issue costs).
(2) The total finance cost of the debt should be allocated over the period of the debt at a constant rate on the carrying amount. The finance cost is the difference between the proceeds on issue and the total payments to be made (either as annual interest charges or on redemption). The annual finance cost should be charged to profit and loss account.

    In principle the allocation of finance costs between different periods should be done using the actuarial method (as for finance leases under SSAP21).
(3) The balance sheet carrying amount each year will be calculated by adding the finance cost for the period to the opening balance and deducting the payments made for the period.

Illustration 2

A loan of £100,000 is taken out on 1 January 1994. Annual interest of £5,900 is payable at the end of each year. The loan is repayable on 31 December 1998 at a premium of £25,000. The effective periodic rate is approximately 10% per annum (determined by using a financial calculator or computer).

The relevant balance sheet and profit and loss account figures may be derived as follows:

Year ending 31 December	B/S liability at beginning of year £	P/L Finance cost (× 10%) £	Cash paid £	B/S liability at end of year £
1994	100,000	10,000	5,900	104,100
1995	104,100	10,410	5,900	108,610
1996	108,610	10,861	5,900	113,571
1997	113,571	11,357	5,900	119,028
1998	119,028	*11,872	5,900	125,000
		54,500	29,500	

Notes
(1) *£11,872 is a balancing figure as the rate was not precisely 10%.
(2) The total finance cost of £54,500 is made up of annual interest payments totalling £29,500 plus premium on redemption of £25,000.

In some cases, the straight line method of allocating finance charges may give an acceptable figure within the limits of materiality – in this case £54,500 ÷ 5 = £10,900 pa.

Note that this is a case where the sum of the digits method would **not** give acceptable figures.

16.3 CONVERTIBLE LOAN STOCK

Convertible loan stock should usually be separately disclosed on the face of the balance sheet under the overall heading of creditors.

Conversion of loan stock into shares should not be anticipated, however probable this is. Finance costs should be allocated over the loan period on the assumption that the stock will never be converted.

If, subsequently, part of the loan stock is converted into shares, the 'value' of the shares issued will be based on the carrying amount of the loan stock immediately prior to the conversion. Any excess of this amount over nominal value issued, will be credited to share premium account.

Note that the following disclosures are required:

(1) redemption dates;
(2) amount payable on redemption;
(3) number and class of shares into which the debt may be converted;
(4) dates or periods within which the conversion may take place;
(5) whether conversion is at the option of the issuer or at that of the holder.

16.4 PROVISIONS

(a) Definition

This term is defined by the Companies Act 1985 and includes:

(1) Provision for depreciation or diminution in value of assets – this includes provision for depreciation, stock and doubtful debts. Such provisions are deducted from the asset heading to which they relate.
(2) Provisions for liabilities or charges – amounts retained as reasonably necessary for the purpose of providing for any liability or loss which is either:

   (i) likely to be incurred; or
   (ii) certain to be incurred but uncertain as to amount or date on which it will arise.

This includes provisions for redundancy and reorganisation, repairs and maintenance, warranty expenditure and deferred taxation.

(b) Companies Act 1985 requirements

(1) Where amounts transferred to any provision for liabilities and charges, disclose:

   (i) amount of provision at beginning of year;
   (ii) amount transferred to the provision during the year;
   (iii) source and application of amounts so transferred;
   (iv) amount of provision at end of year.
(2) Where amounts are transferred from any provision for liabilities and charges except for the purpose for which provision was established, this should be disclosed as part of the movement on that provision.

(3) Other provisions (B/S item I3): where amount of a provision is material, give particulars of each provision included under this heading.

(4) Comparatives not required.

Illustration 3

Extract from annual report and accounts of Reckitt & Colman plc for the year ended 31 December 1994.

Note 18

18 Provisions for liabilities and charges

	Deferred tax (note 19) £m	Pensions £m	Post-retirement benefits other than pensions £m	Other provisions £m	Total £m
At beginning of year	20.64	16.39	57.81	39.78	134.62
Profit and loss account transfer:					
Operating items	15.21	4.22	5.02	138.64	163.09
Non-operating items	–	–	–	2.69	2.69
Provisions on acquisition	–	16.52	24.42	–	40.94
Utilised during the year	(16.74)	(2.09)	(5.35)	(29.99)	(54.17)
At 31 December 1994	19.11	35.04	81.90	151.12	287.17

Other provisions at 31 December 1994 consist primarily of amounts provided for reorganisation costs and for payments due to employees on termination of their services.

Illustration 4

Extract from annual report and accounts of Manganese Bronze Holdings plc for the year ended 31 July 1995.

20 Provisions for liabilities and charges

	Pension £000	Deferred taxation £000	Warranty £000	Total £000
Consolidated				
At 1 August 1994	708	–	1,112	1,820
Deferred tax asset at 1 August 1994	–	(369)	–	(369)
Transfer from profit and loss account	226	458	344	1,028
Offset against pension fund prepayment (see note)	(934)	–	–	(934)
At 31 July 1995	–	89	1,456	1,545
Company				
At 1 August 1994	708	–	–	708
Deferred tax asset at 1 August 1994	–	(234)	–	(234)
Transfer from profit and loss account	226	322	–	548
Offset against pension fund prepayment (see note)	(934)	–	–	(934)
At 31 July 1995	–	88	–	88

Note

During the year £1,200,000 was paid into the Pension Fund resulting in a net prepayment of £266,000 (see note 16).

17 CONTINGENCIES, COMMITMENTS, POST BALANCE SHEET EVENTS AND RELATED PARTY TRANSACTIONS

Key Issues

* Contingencies (SSAP 18, CA 1985)
* Commitments (CA 1985)
* Post balance sheet events (SSAP 17, CA 1985)
* Related party disclosures (FRS 8)
* 'Directors' interests in contracts (CA 1985)

17.1 CONTINGENCIES

(a) Terminology

A contingency is defined by SSAP 18 as a condition which exists at the balance sheet date where the outcome will be confirmed only on the occurrence or non-occurrence of one or more uncertain future events. A contingent gain or loss is a gain or loss dependent on a contingency.

(b) Contingent losses

Contingent losses may fall under SSAP 18 into any one of three categories, depending on the expected outcome:

(1) Those which will be accrued in financial statements. This will apply where it is 'probable that a future event will confirm a loss which can be estimated with reasonable accuracy at the date on which the financial statements are approved by the board of directors'.
(2) Those which are disclosed by way of memorandum note (this will include material contingent losses not falling within (1)).
(3) Those contingent losses where the possibility of the loss is remote, and where no disclosure is required.

(c) Post balance sheet information

Estimates of the outcome and financial effect of contingencies should take account of information available up to the date of approval of the financial statements. This may be particularly important, say, in the case of a substantial legal claim against the company.

(d) Contingent gains

Contingent gains should not be accrued. If material, such gains should be disclosed if it is probable that a gain will be realised.

(e) Disclosure in financial statements

Where disclosure is required, SSAP 18 requires that the following information be stated by way of note:

(1) the nature of the contingency;
(2) the uncertainties which are expected to affect the ultimate outcome;

(3) a prudent estimate of the financial effect, made at the date on which the financial statements are approved by the board of directors (or alternatively a statement that it is not practicable to make such an estimate);

(4) where appropriate, possible tax implications should be indicated.

Note: the amount disclosed, above, should be reduced by any amounts accrued and any components where the possibility of loss is remote.

(f) Companies Act 1985 disclosure requirements

The following should be disclosed regarding contingent liabilities:

(1) the amount or estimated amount of the contingent liability;

(2) its legal nature;

(3) whether any valuable security has been provided by the company in connection with that contingent liability and if so, what.

Disclosure is also required of:

(1) contracts for capital expenditure;

(2) pension commitments;

(3) any other commitments for which no provision is made in the accounts.

(g) Typical disclosure items

The most common contingencies, apart from those resulting from SSAP 15, relate to guarantees given by the parent company eg in relation to borrowings from subsidiaries, and associated companies and house purchase schemes.

Other examples include:

(1) discounted bills of exchange;

(2) partly paid investments in other companies;

(3) law suits or claims pending.

Illustration 1

Extract from annual report and accounts of Thorn EMI plc for the year ended 31 March 1995.

27 Contingent liabilities

(1) Litigation

Legal proceedings continue in the class action law suits referred to in the 1994 Annual Report and Accounts.

In addition, proceedings were commenced in respect of the following further class actions in the course of the year.

THORN Americas, Inc. and other members of the Group are defendants in a class action alleging, *inter alia*, that Rent-A-Center's Rental-Purchase Agreements are credit sales and do not comply with the requirements of New Jersey law. The amounts claimed in damages is unspecified.

THORN Americas, Inc. and other members of the Group are defendants in a class action alleging, *inter alia*, that Rent-A-Center's Rental-Purchase Agreements violate the Wisconsin Consumer Act and various federal laws. The amount claimed in damages is unspecified and the class action has not yet been certified by the court.

THORN Americas, Inc. is also defendant in a class action alleging, *inter alia*, that Rent-A-Center's Rental-Purchase Agreements violate the Pennsylvania Goods and Services Instalment Sales Act. The amount claimed in damages is unspecified and the class action has not yet been certified by the court.

These claims are being vigorously defended and their outcome is not expected to affect Rent-A-Center's business outside these states.

Save as disclosed, the Directors are not aware of any legal or arbitration proceedings pending or threatened against any member of the THORN EMI Group which may have any liability significantly in excess of provisions in the accounts.

(2) Guarantees, bills discounted and other contingent liabilities (excluding litigation referred to in (1) above) total £62.8m (1994: £79.9m) for the Group, of which £41.9m (1994: nil) relate to certain contracts entered into by former Group companies.
(3) Pursuant to the provisions of the Irish Companies (Amendment) Act 1986, the Company has guaranteed the liabilities of its Irish subsidiaries, thus exempting those companies from the requirement to file their annual accounts in Ireland.

Illustration 2

Extract from annual report and accounts of Rank Organisation plc for the year ended 1994.

31 Contingent liabilities

Group

	1994 £m	1993 £m
Guarantees by the Company and by subsidiary undertakings, bills discounted by Group companies and uncalled liability in respect of partly paid shares	58.9	63.4

A subsidiary undertaking is involved in class action suits in the USA. The actions are being vigorously contested.

Other subsidiary undertakings are defendants in separate litigation instituted in the USA in which some $250m in damages are claimed. This action is now in arbitration. The Directors of The Rank Organisation Plc, having been advised by their American lawyers, believe the case to be baseless.

Proceedings have been issued in the USA against the Group and other defendants in which the plaintiffs claim damages and the imposition of a constructive trust of at least $300m to satisfy the damages. The Directors, having been advised by their American lawyers, believe the claim to be baseless.

The Directors believe that none of these actions will result in a material adverse effect on the financial condition of the Group.

Company

	1994 £m	1993 £m
Guarantees of advances to subsidiary undertakings, bills discounted and uncalled liabilities in respect of partly paid shares:		
Provided as liabilities in the Group balance sheet	521.3	572.7
Others	17.5	17.5

No security has been given in respect of any contingent liability.

17.2 COMMITMENTS

The Companies Act 1985 requires disclosure as follows:

(1) Capital commitments:

    (i)   contracts for capital expenditure not provided for;
    (ii) capital expenditure authorised by directors but not yet contracted for.

(2) Pension commitment particulars:

    (i)   pension commitments included under any provision shown in the B/S;
    (ii) pension commitments for which no provision made;
    (iii) where applicable, separate particulars of pension commitments relating wholly or partly to pensions payable to past directors.

(See chapter 20.)

In addition SSAP 21 requires disclosure of leasing commitments (see chapter 18).

Illustration 3

Extract from annual report and accounts of Thorn EMI plc for the year ended 31 March 1995.

26 Financial commitments

	Group 1995 £m	1994 £m
Capital expenditure:		
Contracted	73.5	34.5
Authorised but not contracted	18.9	40.6
	92.4	75.1

The group has commitments, which are largely performance related, to pay advances to artists and repertoire owners amounting to approximately £351.8m at 31 March 1995 (1994: £335.9m). Annual commitments under operating leases at 31 March were as follows:

	Group 1995 £m	1994 £m
Land and buildings:		
Expiring in the first year	14.6	13.7
Expiring in the second to fifth years inclusive	60.1	45.3
Expiring after the fifth year	81.2	68.4
	155.9	127.4
Plant, equipment and vehicles:		
Expiring in the first year	7.6	22.3
Expiring in the second to fifth years inclusive	16.2	12.6
Expiring after the fifth year	1.0	–
	24.8	34.9

Commitments had not been entered into in respect of the Dillons stores at 31 March 1995 and consequently have not been included in the table above. Howevr, since the balance sheet date, contracts have been signed with an annual commitment of £9.1m for land and buildings (£1.2m expiring in the second to fifth years and £7.9m expiring after the fifth year).

Illustration 4

Extract from annual report and accounts of Albert Fisher Group plc for the year ended 31 August 1995.

22 Financial commitments

Deferred consideration
Under the agreements for the acquisition of certain subsidiary undertakings or the investment in certain associate undertakings, deferred consideration is payable based on the achievement of profits. The maximum deferred consideration outstanding in respect of periods ending on the dates detailed below is as follows

Payable in respect of periods ending on	Maximum deferred consideration £m
31 August 1995	1.3
31 August 1996	2.1
31 August 1997	1.5
31 August 1998	16.5

Deferred consideration where payable in local currencies has been expressed above using rates of exchange ruling on 31 August 1995.

Operating leases
Commitments of the group in respect of operating leases in the next 12 months are as follows

	Land and buildings £m	Other £m	Total 1995 £m	Total 1994 £m
Commitments expiring within twelve months	1.3	1.6	2.9	2.2
Commitments expiring within two to five years	2.7	5.4	8.1	7.2
Commitments extending over five years	2.3	0.7	3.0	2.8
	6.3	7.7	14.0	12.2

Future capital expenditure

	Group		Company	
	1995 £m	1994 £m	1995 £m	1994 £m
Contracted for but not provided	4.7	2.2	–	–
Authorised by the directors but not contracted for	8.9	6.3	0.1	0.1
	13.6	8.5	0.1	0.1

Pensions
The group has a number of pension schemes covering certain of its employees through-out the world. The principal schemes in the UK ae The Albert Fisher Group Pension Fund and the Hunter Saphir PLC Retirement & Death Benefit Scheme, both providing benefits for UK employees based on final pensionable pay. The assets of both these schemes are held separately to those of the group in trustee administered funds. The latest actuarial valuation of the main scheme, The Albert Fisher Group Pension Fund, was at 6 April 1995. The main actuarial assumptions used were those relating to the rate of return on investments (10% per annum), rates of increases in salaries including promotion (averaging 8% per annum) and the valuation of assets by valuing the discounted income, assuming a notional reinvestment in an equity index with dividend growth (5.5% per annum). Assets using this value were sufficient to cover 101% of the benefits accrued to members. At 6 April 1995, the market value of the assets was £14,284,000. Other schemes, apart from the Hunter Saphir PLC Retirement & Death Benefit Scheme, are principally of the defined contribution type and have assets held in separate trustee administered funds.

17.3   POST BALANCE SHEET EVENTS

(a) Introduction

SSAP 17 deals with post balance sheet events. The standard includes the following terms:

(1) Post balance sheet events are those events, both favourable and unfavourable, which occur between the balance sheet date and the date on which the financial statements are approved by the board of directors.

(2) Adjusting events are post balance sheet events which provide additional evidence of conditions existing at the balance sheet date. They include events which because of statutory or conventional requirements are reflected in financial statements.

(3) Non-adjusting events are post balance sheet events which concern conditions which did not exist at the balance sheet date.

(b) Adjusting events

These include two main categories:

(1) Events which provide additional evidence of conditions existing at the balance sheet date e g post balance sheet proceeds of sale of obsolete and slow-moving stocks would help substantiate year-end stock provisions.

(2) Events which because of statutory or conventional requirements are reflected in financial statements. An example is dividends receivable from associated companies.

The financial effects of adjusting events should be reflected in the financial statements for the year under review.

In addition to the above, SSAP 17 requires adjustment of year-end amounts where a post balance sheet event indicates that the application of the going concern concept is not appropriate.

(c) Non-adjusting events

The most common types of non-adjusting events are acquisitions or sales of subsidiaries, trading divisions or major investments. Shares issues made or announced after the year end are a further possibility.

SSAP 17 also requires disclosure of a material post balance sheet event where 'it is the reversal or maturity after the year end of a transaction entered into before the year end, the substance of which' was primarily to alter the appearance of the company's balance sheet' (ie 'window dressing' transactions).

(d) Further examples

The following extract is taken from the appendix to SSAP 17:

This appendix is for general guidance and does not form part of the statement of standard accounting practice. The examples are merely illustrative and the lists are not exhaustive.

The examples listed distinguish between those normally classified as adjusting events and as non-adjusting events. However, in exceptional circumstances, to accord with the prudence concept, an adverse event which would normally be classified as non-adjusting may need to be reclassified as adjusting. In such circumstances, full disclosure of the adjustment would be required.

Adjusting events

The following are examples of post balance sheet events which normally should be classified as adjusting events:

(1) FIXED ASSETS. The subsequent determination of the purchase price or of the proceeds of sale of assets purchased or sold before the year end.

(2) PROPERTY. A valuation which provides evidence of a permanent diminution in value.

(3) INVESTMENTS. The receipt of a copy of the financial statements or other information in respect of an unlisted company which provides evidence of a permanent diminution in the value of a long-term investment.

(4) STOCKS AND WORK-IN-PROGRESS

   (i)   The receipt of proceeds of sales after the balance sheet date or other evidence concerning the net realisable value of stocks.

   (ii) The receipt of evidence that the previous estimate of accrued profit on a long-term contract was materially inaccurate.

(5) DEBTORS. The renegotiation of amounts owing by debtors, or the insolvency of a debtor.

(6) DIVIDENDS RECEIVABLE. The declaration of dividends by subsidiaries and associated companies relating to periods prior to the balance sheet date of the holding company.

(7) TAXATION. The receipt of information regarding rates of taxation.

(8) CLAIMS. Amounts received or receivable in respect of insurance claims which were in the course of negotiation at the balance sheet date.

(9) DISCOVERIES. The discovery of errors or frauds which show that the financial statements were incorrect.

Non-adjusting events

The following are examples of post balance sheets events which normally should be classified as non-adjusting events:

(1) Mergers and acquisitions.
(2) Reconstructions and proposed reconstructions.
(3) Issues of shares and debentures.
(4) Purchases and sales of fixed assets and investments.
(5) Losses of fixed assets or stocks as a result of a catastrophe such as fire or flood.
(6) Opening new trading activities or extending existing trading activities.
(7) Closing a significant part of the trading activities if this was not anticipated at the year end.
(8) Decline in the value of property and investments held as fixed assets, if it can be demonstrated that the decline occurred after the year end.
(9) Changes in rates of foreign exchange.
(10) Government action, such as nationalisation.
(11) Strikes and other labour disputes.
(12) Augmentation of pension benefits.

(e) Disclosure in financial statements

As general rule, adjusting events will not normally require separate disclosure, unless they fall within the scope of SSAP 6 (for example, abnormal charges for bad debts and write-offs of stock and work-in-progress).

However, the appendix to SSAP 17 makes a reference to the prudence concept (see (d) above). A possible example, in the present economic climate, could be the closing of a significant part of the trading activities where a final decision was made after the year end but detailed reviews were still taking place up to the end of the year.

In deciding which non-adjusting events warrant disclosure, the guiding principle is to consider matters which are necessary to enable users of financial statements to assess the financial position.

Disclosure for non-adjusting events is required to be given in a note to the accounts (and therefore within the scope of the audit opinion) and includes:

(1) the nature of the event;
(2) an estimate of the financial effect, or a statement that is not practicable to make such an estimate;
(3) where necessary, an explanation of the taxation implications.

In addition, disclosure is required of the date on which the board of directors formally approve the financial statements.

Finally, the Companies Act 1985 requires particulars of any important post-balance sheet events to be disclosed in the directors' report.

Illustration 5

Extract from annual report and accounts of Granada Group plc for the year ended 30 September 1995.

29 Post balance sheet event

On 22 November 1995 Granada announced that it had made an offer to purchase the whole of the ordinary share capital of Forte Plc ('Forte') at 326.9p per share valuing Forte's issued share capital at approximately £3.3 billion. There is also a cash alternative of 321.67p per Forte Ordinary Share.

Illustration 6

Extract from annual report and accounts of Dalgety plc for the year ended 30 June 1995.

31 Post balance sheet events

(a) On 4 July 1995, the sale of the instant hot snacks business was completed for a consideration of £180m. The net assets of the business excluding goodwill were £11m.
(b) On 4 August 1995, the sale of the cooking sauce business was completed for a consideration of £58.6m. The net assets of the business excluding goodwill were £11m.
(c) Costs of these sales amounted to £1m and taxation on the sale is estimated to be £15m. This takes into account available capital losses and estimated roll-over capacity.
(d) The financial position of the Group following these sales is illustrated by the following abridged pro-forma balance sheet as at 30 June 1995.

	Summary of Group balance sheet as published £m	Pro-forma balance sheet after sales £m
Acquired brands	130	130
Tangible assets at cost	583	565
Investments	8	8
	721	703
Stocks	246	241
Debtors	450	446
Investments	2	2
Creditors	(554)	(549)
Net operating assets	865	843
Net borrowings	(451)	(213)
Net liabilities for dividends and tax	(87)	(102)
Provisions for liabilities and charges	(25)	(25)
Shareholders' funds	302	503

17.4 RELATED PARTY DISCLOSURES – FRS 8

(a) Introduction

FRS 8, Related party disclosures, was published on 26 October 1995. FRS 8 follows two earlier exposure drafts – the former ASC's ED 46, April 1989 and ASB's FRED 8, March 1994.

The stated objective of FRS 8 is to 'ensure that financial statements contain the disclosures necessary to draw attention to the possibility that the reported financial position and results may have been affected by the existence of related parties and by material transactions with them'.

FRS 8 aims to achieve this objective by requiring:

(1) specified disclosures of transactions and balances with related parties; and

(2) disclosure of control, i e the name of the party controlling the reporting entity and, if different, that of the ultimate controlling party. This disclosure of control is required whether or not any transactions between the reporting entity and the controlling parties have taken place.

(b) Scope

FRS 8 applies to all financial statements that are intended to give a true and fair view of a reporting entity's financial position and profit or loss for a period. Specific exemptions from disclosure are referred to below.

(c) Small companies

Shareholders' accounts of small companies, even those exempt from audit, are not exempt from FRS 8. This situation is unlikely to change as paragraphs 124 to 127 of the draft Financial Reporting Standard for Smaller Entities (FRSSE) contains disclosures identical to those in FRS 8.

Small company abbreviated accounts must include the relevant CA 1985 disclosures but need not include those of FRS 8. However, abbreviated accounts of medium-sized companies are required to show a true and fair view and must therefore include the necessary disclosures.

(d) Identifying related parties

The definition of related parties occupies two pages of the Standard and has two main strands:

(1) 'deemed' related parties, i e those that are regarded as related parties irrespective of circumstances;
(2) 'presumed' related parties, i e where it may be possible to present arguments which overturn the presumption.

(e) Deemed to be related parties

These are specified in para 2.5 of FRS 8 as follows:

Two or more parties are related when at any time during the financial period:

(1) one party has direct or indirect control of the other party; or
(2) the parties are subject to common control from the same source; or
(3) one party has influence over the financial and operating policies of the other party to an extent that that other party might be inhibited from pursuing at all times its own separate interests; or
(4) the parties, in entering a transaction, are subject to influence from the same source to such an extent that one of the parties to the transaction has subordinated its own separate interests.

Control is defined by FRS 8 as 'The ability to direct the financial and operating policies of an entity with a view to gaining economic benefits from its activities'.

(f) 'Deemed' related parties – further guidance

So that there is no doubt whatsoever, FRS 8 adds that the following are to be regarded as related parties of the reporting entity:

(1) its ultimate and intermediate parent undertakings, subsidiary undertakings, and fellow subsidiary undertakings;
(2) its associates and joint ventures;
(3) the investor or venturer in respect of which the reporting entity is an associate or a joint venture;

(4) directors of the reporting entity and the directors of its ultimate and immediate parent undertakings; and
(5) pension funds for the benefit of employees of the reporting entity or of any entity that is a related party of the reporting entity.

(g) Presumed to be related parties – Part 1

FRS 8 presumes the following to be related parties of the reporting entity unless 'it can be demonstrated that neither party has influenced the financial and operating policies of the other in such a way as to inhibit the pursuit of separate interests':

(1) the key management of the reporting entity and the key management of its parent undertaking or undertakings;
(2) a person owning or able to exercise control over 20 per cent or more of the voting rights of the reporting entity, whether directly or through nominees;
(3) each person acting in concert in such a way as to be able to exercise control or influence over the reporting entity; and
(4) an entity managing or managed by the reporting entity under a management contract.

FRS 8 defines the terms 'key management' and 'persons acting in concert' as follows:

Key management

Those persons in senior positions having authority or responsibility for directing or controlling the major activities and resources of the reporting entity.

Persons acting in concert

Persons who, pursuant to an agreement or understanding (whether formal or informal), actively co-operate, whether by the ownership by any of them of shares in an undertaking or otherwise, to exercise control or influence over that undertaking.

(h) Presumed to be related parties – part 2

The term related parties extends even further – it also catches certain individuals and entities who have a relationship with those 'deemed' or 'presumed' above.

FRS 8 presumes that the following are also related parties of the reporting entity:

members of the close family of any individual who falls under any of the categories in paras 16 to 18 above.

Definition of 'close family'

Close members of the family of an individual are those family members, or members of the same household, who may be expected to influence, or be influenced by, that person in their dealings with the reporting entity.

Illustration 7

Harold is a director of ABC Ltd and holds 35% of the shares in the company. Harold's brother George is a controlling partner in a business which manufactures building materials. The partnership usually sells between 25% and 35% of its annual sales to ABC Ltd.

As regards ABC Ltd, Harold is deemed to be a related party.

Additionally, since George is a member of the close family of Harold, both George and the partnership which George controls are presumed to be related parties of ABC Limited.

(i) Related party transactions – definitions and examples

Related party transactions

FRS 8 defines this as: 'the transfer of assets or liabilities or the performance of services by, to or for a related party irrespective of whether a price is charged.'

(j) Examples of related party transactions – FRS 8

FRS 8 provides the following examples of related party transactions that could, subject to materiality, require disclosure by a reporting entity in the period in which they occur:

(1) purchases or sales of goods (finished or unfinished);
(2) purchases or sales of property and other assets;
(3) rendering or receiving of services;
(4) agency arrangements;
(5) leasing arrangements;
(6) transfer of research and development;
(7) licence agreements;
(8) provision of finance (including loans and equity contributions in cash or in kind);
(9) guarantees and the provision of collateral security; and
(10) management contracts.

(k) Disclosure requirements

FRS 8's disclosure requirements fall into two main categories:

(1) disclosure of control;
(2) disclosure of transactions and balances.

(l) Disclosure of control

The disclosure requirement applies where the reporting entity is controlled by another party. The following should be disclosed:

(1) the related party relationship;
(2) the name of the controlling party;
(3) the name of the ultimate controlling party (if different from (2)).

This may result in the disclosure of controlling non-corporate persons, for example trusts, partnerships and individuals. In some cases, the name of the controlling party, or ultimate controlling party, may not be known. If this is so, that fact should be disclosed.

Note that the above disclosures are required even if no transactions have taken place between the controlling parties and the reporting entity.

(m) Disclosure of transactions and balances

FRS 8 requires financial statements to disclose material transactions undertaken by the reporting entity with a related party. Disclosure is required whether or not a price is charged.

The following should be disclosed:

(1) the names of the transacting related parties;
(2) a description of the relationship between the parties;
(3) a description of the transactions;
(4) the amounts involved;

(5) any other elements of the transactions necessary for an understanding of the financial statements;
(6) the amounts due to or from related parties at the balance sheet date and provisions for doubtful debts due from such parties at that date; and
(7) amounts written off in the period in respect of debts due to or from related parties.

As regards (5), the explanation section of FRS 8 cites as an example the need to give an indication that the transfer of a major asset had taken place at an amount materially different from that obtainable on normal commercial terms. Note that there is no requirement to determine a fair value for such transactions (FRS 8, appendix IV, para 20).

Illustration 8

John is a controling shareholder in XYZ Ltd. John's sister is a partner in a business which provides accountancy and consultancy services to XYZ Ltd.
John's adult son is a 60% shareholder in P Ltd which purchases a significant quantity of goods each year from XYZ Ltd.
Assuming the degree of influence normally expected from a close family relationship, the businesses run by the sister and son would be presumed related parties of XYZ Ltd.
As regards disclosures in XYZ Ltd., it will be necessary to disclose:

(1) the name of the controlling party, ie John;
(2) the names of the transacting related parties:

(i) John's sister's partnership;
(ii) John's son company;

(3) description of the family relationship;
(4) a description of the transactions:

(i) purchases of accountancy and consultancy services;
(ii) sale of goods;

(5) amounts involved;
(6) year-end balances:

(i) owing to the partnership;
(ii) owing from the company.

Illustration 9

For the whole year, the company was under the control of Mr Williams, a director, and members of his close family.
During the year, the company sold goods with a total value of £325,000 (1994 – £272,050) to a company controlled by Paul Williams, a son of the director. The transactions were in the ordinary course of business and at arm's length.
The balance owing to the company at the year-end was £36,500 (1995 – £21,700).

Illustration 10 (pre-FRS 8)

Extract from annual report and accounts of Fairway Group plc for the year ended 31 December 1994.

27. Transactions with related parties

During the year a subsidiary undertaking traded on an arm's length basis with Screen Marketing Services Limited ('Screen'), a company in which Mr M Brown was a shareholder. Mr Brown is the Managing Director of Spectrum Marketing Services Limited and a substantial shareholder in the Company. Details of the transactions are as follows:

Purchases from Screen	£415,565
Sales to Screen	£49,525
Rent charged to Screen	£91,645
Fixed assets sold to Screen	£69,585
Other expenses recharged to Screen	£9,156

Mr M Brown sold his shareholding in Screen on 28 November 1994.

(n) Companies Act 1985 – Directors' interests in contracts

Introduction

Directors have a general duty to disclose to the board of directors their interests in contracts. Once again, this aspect of the law is highly complex. Certain transactions caught within s 330 (loans etc to directors) may be unlawful, without more. Others, for example, substantial property transactions, may require the approval of the shareholders in general meeting.

This part of the notes is principally concerned with contracts for the provision of goods and services, including consultancy services, as well as contracts involving the transfer of property assets.

For private companies and unlisted plcs, the requirements to disclose are contained in Sch 6 of CA 1985.

Note also that references to directors are to include shadow directors.

Requirements to disclose

Part 2 of Sch 6 requires the accounts to give particulars of '. . . any other transaction or arrangement with the company in which a person who at any time during the financial year was a director of the company had, directly or indirectly, a material interest'.

Exemptions from disclosure

The following are exempt:

(1) transactions between different companies where the director's interest arises purely from being a director of those companies;
(2) a contract of service between the company and a director (CA 1985 requires the company to make copies of such contracts available for inspection by members of the company);
(3) transactions and arrangements which were not entered into during the financial year and which did not subsist at any time during the year;
(4) transactions in which the director's interest is not material (if a majority of the other directors decide in a formal meeting it is not material this should be minuted);
(5) transactions in which a director has a material interest provided either:

    (i) the aggregate value did not exeed £1,000; or
    (ii) if it did exceed £1,000, it did not exceed the lower of £5,000 or 1% of the value of the company's net assets at the end of the period.

Details to be disclosed

These include:

(1) the name of the director;
(2) the nature of the interest;
(3) the name of the person or company for whom the transaction or arrangement was made;
(4) the value of the transaction or arrangement.

These disclosures must also be included in abbreviated accounts filed with the Registrar.

D Profit and loss account considerations

18 HIRE PURCHASE AND LEASING

Key Issues

* Methods of financing asset purchases
* Hire purchase accounting
* Lessee accounting
  – background to SSAP 21
  – characteristics of finance leases
  – definitions and classification
  – methods of allocating finance charges
  – accounting entries
  – disclosures
* Interaction between SSAP 21 and FRS 5
* Lessor accounting
  – categories of lessors
  – operating leases
  – finance leases
  – methods of allocating earnings
  – accounting
  – disclosure
* Manufacturer/dealer lessor
* Sale and leaseback

18.1 INTRODUCTION – FINANCING OF FIXED ASSETS

A company may acquire the right to use a fixed asset over its useful life in one of a number of ways. These include:

(1) outright purchase for cash;
(2) outright purchase using the proceeds of a secured or unsecured loan;
(3) hire purchase (or lease purchase);
(4) finance leasing.

In the case of (1) and (2), legal title to the fixed asset is obtained at the date of purchase. In the case of (3), title is obtained when the final instalment has been paid and the option to purchase exercised. In the case of an agreement under a finance lease, as far as the United Kingdom is concerned legal title can never pass to the lessee.

18.2 HIRE PURCHASE – ACCOUNTING FOR THE HIRER

(a) Introduction

Under a hire purchase agreement the owner of goods leases them to a person called the hirer, on the terms that the hirer shall pay to the owner a number of instalments, until a price has been paid, when the ownership of the goods will either pass automatically to the hirer, or he may exercise an option to purchase them by the payment of a stated small sum. Thus the property in the goods does not pass to the hirer until he has paid the last instalment or exercised his option to purchase.

(b) Substance over form

Traditionally assets acquired under hire purchase agreements are brought into the balance sheet at cash price and depreciated over their useful economic life to the user. A corresponding obligation or liability is shown in the balance sheet. Payments to the hire vendor are allocated between capital and interest using some suitable basis. The capital part is used to reduce the balance sheet obligation, while the income part is debited to profit and loss account.

The justification for this treatment has been the substance over form argument: transactions and other events should be accounted for and presented in accordance with their substance and financial reality, and not merely with their legal form. Rights under hire-purchase agreements, prior to the obtaining of legal title, are for most practical purposes equivalent to those of immediate legal ownership.

FRS 5 requires an entity's financial statements to reflect the commercial substance of the transactions into which the entity has entered (see chapter 7, sections 7.1 and 7.2).

(c) Main accounting entries

These may be summarised as follows:

Debit	Credit	Notes
Asset account	Hire vendor	Cash purchase price (excluding interest)
Hire vendor	Cash	Deposit paid Instalments paid
Interest payable	Hire vendor	Hire purchase interest apportioned to the accounting period
Profit and loss	Interest payable	Balance on interest payable account

Notes:
(1) In the balance sheet, the fixed asset will appear at cash purchase price less any accumulated depreciation.
(2) The balance on the hire vendor's account will represent the instalments not yet paid less any interest apportioned to later accounting periods. For classification purposes, this balance must be analysed between amounts falling due within one year and those due after more than one year.
(3) Methods of apportioning interest between accounting periods are covered in detail in the section on lessee accounting (see section 18.5).

Illustration 1

Hawkins Ltd acquired a car on 1 January 19X3 under a two-year purchase agreement. This required an immediate deposit of £1,600 and four half-yearly instalments of £1,600 commencing on 1 July 19X3. The cash price was £7,544. The company's year end is 30 September.

Assume the finance charge of £456 (£8,000 – £7,544) is allocated as follows:

Year end:	£
30.9.X3	248
30.9.X4	184
30.9.X5	24
	456

Ignore depreciation on motor car.
The ledger accounts would appear as follows:

MOTOR CAR ACCOUNT

		£			£
1.1.X3	Hire vendor	7,544			

HIRE VENDOR ACCOUNT

		£			£
1.1.X3	Cash	1,600	1.1.X3	Motor car	7,544
1.7.X3	Cash	1,600	30.9.X3	Hire purchase interest	248
30.9.X3	Bal c/d	4,592			
		7,792			7,792
1.1.X4	Cash	1,600	1.10.X3	Bal b/d	4,592
1.7.X4	Cash	1,600	30.9.X4	Hire purchase interest	184
30.9.X4	Bal c/d	1,576			
		4,776			4,776
1.1.X5	Cash	1,600	1.10.X4	Bal b/d	1,576
			30.9.X5	Hire purchase interest	24
		1,600			1,600

INTEREST PAYABLE ACCOUNT

		£			£
30.9.X3	Hire purchase interest	248	30.9.X3	P/L	248
30.9.X4	Hire purchase interest	184	30.9.X4	P/L	184
30.9.X5	Hire purchase interest	24	30.9.X5	P/L	24

(d) Apportionment of hire purchase interest

The three main methods are:

(1) actuarial method;
(2) sum of the digits (rule of 78);
(3) straight-line method.

The basis of calculation and the respective merits of the various methods are dealt with in section 18.5.

(e) Hire purchase agreements terminated prematurely

Agreements may be terminated prematurely, when the hirer:

(1) With the consent of the hire-purchase vendor:

(i) wishes to complete the purchase; he pays the remainder of the cash purchase price, and so much of the finance charge still outstanding, as the vendor may require, as consideration for his consent and as compensation for his loss of future interest; or

(ii) sells or assigns the asset to a second hirer, who undertakes to pay the instalments as they fall due; or

(2) Fails to pay an instalment which falls due.

Dealing with each in turn:

(1) (i) completion of purchase – Hire vendor's account must be credited with the amount of the finance charge still required by the vendor, together with any administrative charge.

Illustration 2

Facts are as in illustration 1 but Hawkins Ltd wishes to complete the purchase on 2 October 19X3 and the hire vendor agrees to allow a rebate of 30% on the finance charge.

The final payment required to clear the transaction would be calculated as follows:

	£
Cash purchase price	7,544
Finance charge	456
Hire purchase price	8,000
30% rebate on £456	(137)
	7,863
Payments to date	(3,200)
Final payment	4,663

The hire vendor account would appear as follows:

		£			£
2.10.X3	Cash	4,663	1.10.X3	Bal b/d	4,592
				Hire purchase interest account (balancing figure)	71
		4,663			4,663

(1) (ii) sale or assignment of asset – The hire vendor's account is closed by a debit for the whole balance, asset disposal account being credited. Any consequent administration charge imposed by the hire vendor would be charged to profit and loss account.

(2) failure to pay instalments due – Where the agreement is terminated prematurely as a result of the failure to pay instalments and the owner repossesses the goods, the hirer is still liable for all unpaid instalments subject to any relief which may be available.

The accounting entries necessary are shown below in illustration 3.

Illustration 3

The facts are as in illustration 1 except that Hawkins Ltd is unable to pay the instalment of £1,600 due on 1 January 19X4. The hire vendor repossesses the car and the agreement is terminated by Hawkins Ltd paying £800 on 1 April 19X4. Hawkins Ltd had made a provision for depreciation of £2,400.

MOTOR CAR ACCOUNT

		£			£
1.1.X3	Hire vendor	7,544	1.4.X4	Disposals a/c	7,544

HIRE VENDOR ACCOUNT

		£			£
1.4.X4	Cash to terminate agreement	800	1.10.X3	Balance b/d	4,592
	Disposals (balancing figure)	3,792			
		4,592			4,592

MOTOR CAR ON HP – DISPOSAL ACCOUNT

		£			£
1.4.X4	Motor car a/c	7,544	1.4.X4	Provision for depreciation account	2,400
				Hire vendor	3,792
				P/L a/c – loss on disposal (balancing figure)	1,352
		7,544			7,544

18.3   LESSEE ACCOUNTING – BACKGROUND

(a) Introduction

A lease is a contract between a lessor and a lessee for the hire of a specific asset.

Traditional practice has been to charge lease payments to profit and loss accounts as incurred. While this treatment may be justified for operating leases, it is not appropriate for those types of leases referred to as finance leases.

Operating leases usually involve the lessee paying a rental for the hire of an asset for a period of time which is substantially less than the asset's useful economic life. With an operating lease, the lessor retains most of the risks and rewards of ownership.

By contrast, finance leases usually involve payments by the lessee to the lessor of the full cost of the asset together with a return on finance provided. Although the lessee never obtains legal title, the lessee has substantially all the risks and rewards which are usually associated with ownership.

(b) Typical characteristics of a finance lease

Characteristics will vary between different leases. The following characteristics are provided by way of illustration:

(1) Lessor retains title to asset. At the end of the lease, the asset is returned to the lessor *or* the asset is disposed of by the lessee as agent for the lessor. The lease may specify that the lessee obtains a substantial part (e g 95%) of the proceeds as a rebate of rentals.
(2) Payments to the lessor during the primary period are substantial and non-cancellable.
(3) Payments to the lessor during the secondary period are nominal in amount ('peppercorn rent'). The lessee may be given the option during the secondary period to renew on an annual basis.
(4) Lessee has uninterrupted use of the asset as long as leasing payments are made (rewards of ownership).
(5) Lessee is responsible for insurance and maintenance (risks of ownership).
(6) Lessee indemnifies lessor for claims.
(7) Lessee cannot dispose of asset.

(c) Arguments in favour of capitalisation of finance leases

SSAP 21 (Accounting for leases and hire-purchase contracts) accepts the traditional treatment of operating leases since it reflects both the economic substance and the legal form of the transaction.

However, both SSAP 21 and the exposure draft which preceded it (ED 29) have rejected the hitherto traditional treatment of finance leases and instead opted for capitalisation. The effect of capitalisation is to account for finance lease assets in a similar way to hire-purchase assets.

There are two main arguments in favour of capitalisation: substance over form, and the analysis of accounts argument.

(1) *Substance over form*

Substance over form recognises that a lessee's rights are for practical purposes little different from those of an outright purchaser. These rights represent an economic resource which is required in the business.

This argument is now expressed in terms of 'reporting substance' – see chapter 7 on FRS 5, Reporting the substance of transactions.

(2) *Analysis of accounts argument*

The traditional treatment of finance leases charges the lease payments to profit and loss account as such payments are made. The finance for such leasing arrangements is excluded from the balance sheet, a practice usually referred to as off-balance sheet finance. This practice may materially distort the view given by the following ratios:

(i)   Fixed assets as a proportion of total assets – since leased assets are excluded from the balance sheet.
(ii) Debt/equity (or gearing) – since potentially large liabilities are built up off balance sheet.
(iii) Return on capital employed (profit before interest and tax as a percentage of fixed assets plus net current assets).

SSAP 21 makes it clear that capitalisation of finance leases should assist both external and internal users. External users may be assisted in making investment or credit decisions. Internal users such as managers may be in a better position to appraise divisional performance.

(d) Arguments against capitalisation

The principal argument against is the rejection of the substance over form concept. It is argued that legal form should not be ignored. Proponents of this viewpoint maintain that leased assets and the corresponding obligations thereunder should not be reflected in the balance sheet. However, detailed memorandum information should be presented in the notes outside the double entry system. This argument has been rejected by both the ASB and the ASC for the reasons outlined in (c) above.

Other more minor arguments have been put up but have all been effectively rejected.

(e) Problems of capitalisation concept

Although the theoretical arguments have been forcibly advocated, certain problems remain. For example, the problem of distinguishing between finance leases and operating leases. Secondly, in some cases (such as where an asset could not be alternatively purchased for cash) it is not always clear how much should be capitalised at the outset of the lease.

(f) Companies Act implications

Two aspects should be considered:

(1) accounting treatment;
(2) disclosure requirements.

(1) *Accounting treatment*

The Companies Act 1985 does not define or distinguish between operating leases and finance leases. Thus, no accounting requirements are set out in the Companies Act.

(2) *Disclosure requirements*

Disclosure is required of:

(i) plant hire charges;
(ii) financial commitments which have not been provided for and which are relevant to assessing the company's state of affairs.
  Note that non-cancellable operating leases of land and buildings are included here. Also included are finance lease commitments in so far as not reflected in the balance sheet (eg in the periods before which capitalisation becomes mandatory under SSAP 21).

Finally, the overriding true and fair view requirements (see section 5.7) should always be borne in mind.

18.4   LESSEE ACCOUNTING – CLASSIFICATION

(a) Hire-purchase contracts

The accounting and disclosure requirements for finance leases generally apply equally to hire-purchase contracts. Special points which relate to hire-purchase contracts only will, however, be referred to separately.

(b) Finance leases

(1) *Definition*

A finance lease is a lease that transfers substantially all the risks and rewards of ownership of an asset to the lessee. This transfer is presumed to take place if, at the start of the lease, it can be shown that the present value of the minimum lease payments amounts to 90% or more of the fair value of the leased asset.

  These terms are explained immediately below. However, it should be appreciated that the majority of exam questions are unlikely to require elaborate calculations relating to this point.

(2) *Explanation of terms*

(i) PRESENT VALUE

This is obtained by discounting the minimum lease payments using the interest rate implicit in the lease as a discount factor.

(ii) MINIMUM LEASE PAYMENTS

(a) Minimum payments over the remaining part of the lease term. These will relate essentially to the non-cancellable payments during the primary period.

(b) If applicable, any residual amounts (at the end of the lease) which have been guaranteed by the lessee.

(iii) INTEREST RATE IMPLICIT IN THE LEASE

This is the discount rate, which when applied at the outset of the lease, equates the following:

(a) the present value of the amounts which the lessor expects to receive and retain. These amounts will include the minimum payments in (ii) above together with any unguaranteed residual value not accountable to the lessee;
(b) the fair value of the asset.

(iv) FAIR VALUE OF ASSET

This is the price for which an asset could be exchanged in an arm's length transaction. This amount should be reduced by the amount of capital-based grants that such an asset would normally be entitled to.

(3) *Illustration* 4

Langdale Ltd wishes to acquire the use of a new item of machinery. The company could purchase outright for cash of £16,200 or alternatively enter into a finance lease. The asset has an estimated useful life of ten years with a residual value of £800.
   The terms of the finance lease are as follows:

(i)   Primary period of five years – five rentals of £4,000 p a payable on first day of each year.
(ii) Secondary period – renewable on an annual basis for an indefinite period. Ignore secondary rentals.
(iii) Lessee responsible for insurance and maintenance.
(iv) At end of lease term, lessee entitled to 80% of proceeds of sale of asset as rebate of rentals.

Step 1

Calculate interest rate implicit in lease using a programmed calculator. To start with, identify the amounts which the lessor expects to receive and retain. These comprise:

(1) the lessee's minimum lease payments i e five lots of £4,000;
(2) unguaranteed residual value, less proportion accountable to the lessee i e 20% × £800 = £160.

It is then a question of determining what interest rate when applied to these amounts equates with a fair value of £16,200. This rate is determined as 12%.

	£
Check £4,000 × 1.0	4,000
£4,000 × 3.037 (annuity tables)	12,148
£160 × 0.322 (present value tables, year 10)	52
	16,200

Step 2

Calculate present value of minimum lease payments using a discount rate of 12%.

	£
£4,000 × 1.0 (payment now)	4,000
£4,000 × 3.037 (annuity four years)	12,148
	16,148

Step 3

Compare with 90% of fair value of leased asset, i e

90% × £16,200 = £14,580

Conclusion

There is a presumption that the lease is a finance lease. It is unlikely that this presumption could be rebutted since the lease does transfer substantially all the risks and rewards of ownership to the lessee.

(c) Operating leases

An operating lease is defined as a lease other than a finance lease.

(d) Unusual situations

In exceptional circumstances, the above presumptions may be rebutted. For example in very unusual circumstances, a lease that would otherwise be classified as finance may instead be classified as operating. This could be so if it could be shown that the lease did not transfer to the lessee substantially all the risks and rewards of ownership. The converse might in exceptional circumstances also be true.

18.5 LESSEE ACCOUNTING – FINANCE LEASES AND HIRE-PURCHASE CONTRACTS

(a) The concept of capitalisation

Although a lessee never obtains legal title, in the case of finance leases the lessee's rights and obligations are such that the risks and rewards from the use of the asset are substantially (not, of course, identically) similar to those of an outright purchaser.

SSAP 21 makes it quite clear that what is capitalised (and included in the balance sheet as an asset) is *not* the asset itself but the lessee's rights in the asset. Also capitalised is the corresponding obligation to pay rentals.

However, the standard points out that from a practical viewpoint, these rights are substantially similar to those of an outright purchaser. The outcome of this is that these rights are effectively classified as finance lease assets and are included together with owned assets under the general balance sheet heading of tangible fixed assets. However, the leased assets should be distinguished from owned assets and the amount disclosed (see under lessee accounting disclosures).

(b) Accounting treatment

(1) *Calculation of initial amount to be recorded as asset and obligation*

(i) THEORETICAL APPROACH

The amount to be capitalised should be the present value of the minimum lease rentals, discounted at the rate of interest implicit in the lease.

Illustration 5

Using the above example of Langdale Ltd, the amount to be capitalised would be £16,148.

(ii) PRACTICAL APPROXIMATION

In many cases, the fair value of the asset will provide a reasonable approximation to the above. Clearly, in the example of Langdale, it would be acceptable to capitalise £16,200.

In the subsequent illustrations, the amount to be capitalised will be taken as the fair value of the asset.

(2) *Depreciation of finance lease asset*

The asset should be depreciated over the shorter of:

(i) lease term – this includes:

  (a) the period for which the lessee has contracted to lease the asset (i e the non-cancellable primary period); plus
  (b) any further secondary periods under which the lessee has an option to continue leasing the asset (possibly renewing on an annual basis) and where it is reasonably certain at the start of the lease that the lessee will exercise the option; or

(ii) the asset's useful life.

The guidance notes point out that in most cases residual value will be small, and so for the purpose of depreciation calculations may be taken as nil. In the case of Langdale, the straight-line depreciation would be 10% (16,200 − 80% × 800) i e £1,556 taking account of residual value or £1,620 ignoring it. The difference of £64 is clearly not material.

(3) *Allocation of rentals*

Rentals paid to the lessor should be apportioned between financial charge and repayment of obligation. Possible approaches to allocation of finance charges are explained below.

(c) Allocation of finance charges

The key principle is that the total finance charge should be allocated to accounting periods during the lease terms so as to produce a constant periodic rate of charge on the remaining obligation outstanding.
  Possible approaches include:

(1) Actuarial method – this accords exactly with the above requirement.
(2) Sum of the digits (rule of 78) – this is an approximation to the actuarial method. The sum of the digits method is regarded as a reasonable approximation provided that the lease term is not very long (say, a primary period of less than seven years) and interest rates are not very high.
(3) Straight-line method – this does not produce a constant periodic rate of charge and is thus not normally regarded as acceptable. However, it may be used in practice in those situations where the total finance charges are not material.

Underlying calculations for each method are illustrated below.

(d) Illustration of calculations

(1) *Basic data*

An item of plant and machinery with a useful life of ten years may be purchased outright for cash for £21,400. Alternatively, use of the asset may be obtained by means of a finance lease. Under this arrangement, the lessee would be responsible for insurance and maintenance and would be required to make five annual payments of £5,800 all payable in advance. After the primary period of five years, the lessee would have the option to continue leasing the asset for an indefinite period for a nominal ('peppercorn') rental. The amount of the rental may be ignored.

It is assumed that the fair value of £21,400 provides an acceptable approximation to the present value of the minimum lease payments discounted at the rate of interest implicit in the lease.

(2) Depreciation calculation

If the straight-line method is used, and if residual value is ignored, the annual depreciation charge will be £2,140.

(3) Finance charge – actuarial method

Total finance charge to be allocated to periods = excess of rentals paid over amount capitalised (i e £29,000 − £21,400 = £7,600).
   The interest rate applicable is 18%. This may be calculated from annuity tables remembering that these tables assume the annuity is paid on the last day of each period.

Present value (£21,400 − £5,800) = £15,600
Annuity – four amounts of £5,800

$$\text{Annuity factor} = \frac{£15,600}{£5,800} = 2.69$$

From actuarial tables, interest rate is 18%.

The following table may then be constructed:

Year	B/F £	Rentals (in advance) £	Finance charge at 18% £	C/F £
1	21,400	(5,800)	2,808	18,408
2	18,408	(5,800)	2,269	14,877
3	14,877	(5,800)	1,634	10,711
4	10,711	(5,800)	889	5,800
5	5,800	(5,800)	–	–
		29,000	7,600	

The column headed finance charge gives the debit to profit and loss account for each period (e g 18% (£21,400 − £5,800) = £2,808).
   The carry forward column gives the balance sheet liability (obligation) at each year end.
   For example, at the end of year 1 the total obligation is £18,408 of which £14,877 is non-current and the balance of £3,531 is current.

(4) Finance charge – sum of the digits method

The sum of the digits may be calculated by the formula $\dfrac{N(N+1)}{2}$

where N is the number of periods over which the finance charge is to be allocated. For example, in the above illustration, the obligation is deemed to be reduced to nil by the first day of year 5. Consequently, the finance charge is to be allocated over four periods.
   The sum of the digits is (1 + 2 + 3 + 4) i e 10.

Alternatively, it may be calculated as $\dfrac{4(4+1)}{2} = 10$.

The finance charge allocation is as follows:

Year		£
1	$\frac{4}{10} \times £7,600$	3,040
2	$\frac{3}{10} \times £7,600$	2,280
3	$\frac{2}{10} \times £7,600$	1,520
4	$\frac{1}{10} \times £7,600$	760
Total		7,600

The obligation at each year end may be calculated by completing a table similar to that in (3) above.

(5) *Finance charge – straight-line method*

Annual finance charge $= \dfrac{£7,600}{4}$ ie £1,900.

18.6   LESSEE ACCOUNTING – OPERATING LEASES

Rentals under operating leases should be charged on a straight-line basis. This applies even if the payments are not made on this basis. No entry should be made in the balance sheet for either the right to use the asset or the obligation to pay rentals.

The standard requires the straight-line basis to be used unless 'another systematic and rational basis is more appropriate'. This could cover situations of rentals holidays where no payment is made during the first year in which the asset is in use. UITF 12, lessee accounting for reverse premiums and similar incentives, provides further guidance in this area (see section 9.6).

18.7   LESSEE ACCOUNTING DISCLOSURES – FINANCE LEASES

(a) Fixed assets

Two types of disclosure are possible:

(1) To disclose assets held under finance leases for each major class of asset, and to show:

   (i)   gross amounts of assets;
   (ii) accumulated depreciation;
   (iii) depreciation for the period.

(2) To integrate amounts for finance lease assets with those for owned assets. The only balance sheet information for leased assets would be the overall net book value.

Illustration of (2)
Using figures at the end of year 1 from the illustration above, the following note would appear at the foot of the fixed asset note:

   The net book value of fixed assets of £x includes an amount of £19,260 in respect of assets held under finance leases and hire-purchase contracts.

(b) Obligations under finance leases

(1) Amounts of obligations related to finance leases (net of finance charges allocated in future periods) should be disclosed separately from other obligations and liabilities.

(2) The above information may be shown either on the face of the balance sheet or in the notes to the accounts.

(3) Net obligations under finance leases should be analysed between:

    (i)   amounts payable in the next year;

    (ii) amounts payable in the second to fifth years inclusive from balance sheet date;

    (iii) the aggregate amounts payable thereafter.

(4) The analysis above may be presented, either:

    (i)   separately for obligations under finance leases.

  In this case, two alternatives are possible:

        (a) analysing the net obligations;

        (b) analysing the gross obligations and then deducting the future finance charges from the total;

or

    (ii) where the total of finance lease obligations is combined on the balance sheet with other obligations and liabilities, by giving the equivalent analysis of the total in which it is included.

Note that whichever alternative is adopted, the obligation must be split between current and non-current for balance sheet presentation purposes.

In the above illustration, using figures from the actuarial method at the end of year 1, the total obligation of £18,408 would be included as follows:

Creditors: amounts falling due within one year £3,531
Creditors: amounts falling due after more than one year £14,877.

(c) Profit and loss disclosures

The following amounts should be disclosed. For illustration purposes, figures have been taken from year 1 calculations from the earlier illustration of the actuarial method:

Profit is stated after charging:

	£
Depreciation of assets held under finance leases and hire-purchase contracts	2,140
Finance charges payable – finance leases and hire-purchase contracts	2,808

An additional note is required to comply with the Companies Act 1985:

Amounts charged to revenue in respect of finance leases and hire-purchase contracts are shown separately under the headings of depreciation (£2,140) and finance charges (£2,808) (total £4,948).

(d) Additional notes

(1) Disclosure is required for commitments existing at the balance sheet date for finance leases which have been entered into but whose inception occurs after the year end. (Inception of a lease is when the asset is brought into use or when the rentals first accrue, whichever is the earlier.)

(2) Accounting policies should also be disclosed. A suitable disclosure would be:

Fixed assets held under leases
Where assets are financed by leasing agreements that give rights approximating to ownership ('finance leases') the assets are treated as if they had

been purchased outright and the corresponding liability to the leasing company is included as an obligation under finance leases.

Depreciation on leased assets is charged to profit and loss account on the same basis as shown above.

Leasing payments are treated as consisting of capital and interest elements and the interest is charged to profit and loss account using the actuarial method.

All other leases are 'operating leases' and the relevant annual rentals are charged to profit and loss account on a straight-line basis over the lease term.

18.8   LESSEE ACCOUNTING DISCLOSURES – OPERATING LEASES

(a) The total of operating lease rentals charged as an expense in the profit and loss account should be disclosed and analysed between:

(1) amounts payable in respect of hire of plant and machinery; and
(2) other operating leases.
(b) The lessee should disclose operating lease payments which he is committed to make during the next year, analysed between those in which the commitment expires:

(1) within that year;
(2) in the second to fifth years, inclusive; or
(3) over five years from the balance sheet date.

Commitments in respect of leases of land and buildings should be shown separately from those for other operating leases.

Illustration 6

This is taken from the guidance notes to SSAP 21.

At 21 December 19X7 the company had annual commitments under non-cancellable operating leases as set out below.

	19X7 Land and other buildings £'000	£'000	19X6 Land and other buildings £'000	£'000
Operating leases which expire:				
Within one year	30	100	25	90
In the second to fifth years inclusive	80	50	75	40
Over five years	120	20	110	10
	230	170	210	140

The majority of leases of land and buildings are subject to rent reviews.

Illustration 7

Extract from annual report and accounts of Cadbury Schweppes plc for the year ended 31 December 1994.

Accounting policies (extract)

Fixed assets held under leases
Where assets are financed by leasing agreements that give rights approximating to ownership ('finance leases') the assets are treated as if they had been purchased outright and the corresponding liability to the leasing company is included as an obligation under finance leases. Depreciation on leased assets is charged to profit and loss account on the same basis as shown above. Leasing payments are treated as consisting of capital and interest elements and the interest is charged to profit and loss account.

All other leases are 'operating leases' and the relevant annual rentals are charged wholly to profit and loss account.

Note 10 (part of note)

The movements in tangible fixed assets were as follows:

	Group			Company		
	Land and buildings £m	Plant and equipment £m	Assets in course of construction £m	Land and buildings £m	Plant and equipment £m	Assets in course of construction £m
Cost or valuation						
At beginning of year	490.2	1,424.4	95.3	6.5	4.2	0.4
Exchange rate adjustments	(8.8)	(5.5)	(1.6)	–	–	–
Additions	12.0	55.9	171.2	0.6	2.0	0.4
Acquisitions of subsidiaries	4.2	7.2	–	–	–	–
Transfers on completion	14.4	134.8	(149.2)	–	0.8	(0.8)
Disposals	(5.9)	(61.0)	–	(0.2)	–	
At end of year	506.1	1,555.8	115.7	6.9	7.0	–
Depreciation						
At beginning of year	(36.7)	(685.0)	–	(0.3)	(1.8)	–
Exchange rate adjustments	1.8	(2.6)	–	–	–	–
Depreciation for year	(12.2)	(149.2)	–	(1.0)	(0.4)	–
Disposals	0.1	52.3	–	–	–	–
At end of year	(47.0)	(784.5)	–	(1.3)	(2.2)	–
Net book value at end of year	459.1	771.3	115.7	5.6	4.8	–

Additions to assets in course of construction include interest capitalised in the year of £1.5m (1993: £1.1m).

Cumulative interest capitalised on capital borrowed to fund construction is £2.6m (1993: £1.1m).

The value of land not depreciated is £141.5m (1993: £143.1m).

The net book value of plant and equipment held under finance leases was £120.3m (1993: £140.9m).

Plant and equipment also includes returnable containers of £53.1m (1993: £62.0m) whose value at most recent purchase price would be £73.7m (1993: £81.7m).

Leasing commitments

The future minimum lease payments to which the Group was committed as at 31 December 1994 under finance leases were as follows:

	1994 £m	1993 £m
Within one year	19.3	24.5
Between one and five years	47.9	56.5
After five years	26.2	31.1
	93.4	112.1
Less finance charges allocated to future periods	(29.3)	(33.2)
	64.1	78.9

The minimum annual lease payments in 1995, to which the Group was committed under non-cancellable operating leases as at 31 December 1994, were as follows:

	Property		Plant and Equipment	
	1994 £m	1993 £m	1994 £m	1993 £m
On leases expiring:				
Within one year	1.6	3.5	4.6	5.7
Between one and five years	7.1	7.8	12.9	12.4
After five years	9.9	8.3	–	–
	18.6	19.6	17.5	18.1

18.9   LEASE CLASSIFICATION AND FRS 5

FRS 5 does not change the accounting treatment of stand-alone operating leases and finance leases. However, para 45 of FRS 5 does state that '. . . the general principles of the FRS will also be relevant in ensuring that leases are classified as finance or operating leases in accordance with their substance. . .' (See also section 7.7(b).)

Illustration 8

Extract from annual report and accounts of First Choice Holidays plc, year ended 31 October 1994.

Financial Review (extract)

Accounting Adjustments
The adoption of FRS 5 has resulted in the Group reporting on its balance sheet two additional aircraft and one engine. These assets are held under leases with options to purchase at set dates and prices. As a prior year adjustment, these have added £55.2m to our fixed assets. These assets have been accounted for, in line with other 'on balance sheet' aircraft as sterling assets, to be revalued at each year end with their related financing also on balance sheet. One of the options is exercisable in the coming year and the financing for it is shown as a current liability.

Notes to the accounts – extract from note 1

Prior year adjustments
Two prior year adjustments have been made in preparing the 1994 Accounts. These have arisen as a result of the issue of Financial Reporting Standard No. 4 'Capital Instruments' (FRS 4) and Financial Reporting Standard No. 5 'Reporting the Substance of Transactions' (FRS 5). The effects of FRS 4 are disclosed in note 9.

Aircraft accounting (FRS 5)
Certain aircraft and engine contracts, previously treated as operating leases, have now been recognised in the balance sheet as a result of the issue of FRS 5. These contracts are now being accounted for as though they were finance leases save that the asset is being depreciated over a period to reflect the future ownership and the liability includes the amounts payable on exercise of the options in the contracts. The effect on the 1994 Accounts has been to increase profit after tax by £1.8 million. A summary of the prior year adjustment's effect on the 1993 Accounts is set out below. (Not reproduced.)

Illustration 9

Extract from annual report and accounts of BBA Group plc for the year ended 31 December 1994.

Accounting policies (extract)

Leases
Where assets are financed by leasing agreements (finance leases) that give rights similar to ownership, the assets are treated as if they had been purchased and the leasing commitments are shown as obligations to the lessor. The capitalised values of the assets are written off on a straight line basis over the shorter of the periods of the leases or the useful lives of the assets concerned. Lease payments are treated as consisting of capital and interest elements. Interest is allocated so as to produce a constant period rate of change to the profit and loss account.

   For all other leases (operating leases) the rental payments are charged to the profit and loss account on a straight line basis over the lives of the leases.

   Financial Reporting Standard No. 5 (FRS 5), which deals with accounting for the substance of transactions, became effective for accounting periods ending after 22 September 1994. Compliance with FRS 5 has led to the re-classification of certain leases, previously treated as operating leases, to those of finance leases. In order to present the prior year's results on a comparable basis, the Group profit and loss account, Group balance sheet and Group cash flow statement have been restated. The effect of this re-classification is to increase the profit/reduce the loss on ordinary activities before taxation by £0.6m in 1994 and £0.2m in 1993.

18.10 LESSOR ACCOUNTING – BACKGROUND

(a) Categories of lessors

Lessors may fall into any one of three categories:

(1) Companies such as finance houses which provide finance under lease contracts so as to enable a single customer to acquire the use of an asset for the greater part of its useful life. These leases will usually be finance leases.

(2) Companies which operate a business which involves the renting-out of assets for varying periods of time, usually to more than one customer (operating leases).

(3) Companies which are manufacturers or dealer lessors who use leasing to market their products. This could relate to either a finance lease or operating lease.

(b) Accounting approach

(1) In the case of an operating lease, the lessor retains both the legal title and the risks and rewards of ownership of the asset. The risks of ownership include the possibility of reduced demand for the lease of the asset as well as the risk of obsolescence. An operating lease asset should be capitalised and depreciated.

(2) In the case of a finance lease, the substance of the transaction is similar to that of a secured loan receivable. Consequently, the asset is treated as a finance lease receivable.

18.11 LESSOR ACCOUNTING – OPERATING LEASES

(a) Accounting treatment

(1) Assets held for use in operating leases should be classified as fixed assets, being depreciated over their useful lives.

(2) Rental income should be recognised on a straight-line basis over the period of the lease. This applies even if the payments are not made on a straight-line basis. However, the standard does permit another systematic and rational basis to be used if this is more representative of the time pattern in which the benefits are receivable.

Turnover should comprise the aggregate rentals receivable in respect of the accounting period.

(b) Lessor profit and loss account

Using format 2, the relevant profit and loss extract would appear as follows:

	£	£
Turnover		X
Staff costs	X	
Depreciation	X	
Other operating charges	X	
Interest payable	X	(X)
Profit on ordinary activities before tax		X

(c) Manufacturer/dealer lessor

Suppose a manufacturer/dealer enters into an operating lease. No sale has been made and so no immediate profit should be recognised.

If the asset has been manufactured, all reasonable manufacturing costs may be capitalised. If the asset has been acquired from a supplier, the purchased cost will be capitalised. The asset will be classified as a tangible fixed asset and depreciated over its useful life as far as the lessor is concerned.

Rental income will be credited to profit and loss account in the usual way.

18.12   LESSOR ACCOUNTING – FINANCE LEASES

(a) Introduction to accounting treatment

(1) *Profit and loss account*

The gross earnings from a finance lease comprise the excess of rentals received over the fair value of the asset. The way in which these earnings should be allocated over accounting periods is discussed below.

Illustration 10

The relevant extract from a profit and loss account prepared under format 2 would be:

	£	£
Gross earnings under finance leases		X
Staff costs	X	
Depreciation	X	
Other operating charges	X	
Interest payable	X	(X)
Profit on ordinary activities before tax		X

Note: The guidance notes to SSAP 21 suggest that the term 'turnover' should not be used in view of the special nature of the company's business. A term such as 'gross earnings under finance leases' may be appropriate.

However, it is considered that simply to disclose gross earnings would provide an incomplete measure of a lessor's activity. It is recommended that note disclosure should also be made of:

(i)   aggregate rentals receivable under finance leases;
(ii) cost of assets acquired for letting under finance leases.

(2) *Balance sheet*

The relevant asset should be described as finance lease receivables and included under the general heading of debtors. It will also be necessary to disclose by way of note the split of this total between amounts receivable within one year and those amounts receivable thereafter.

(b) Methods of allocating gross earnings: before-tax methods

(1) *Introduction*

The mechanism of each of the before-tax methods is described below.
The three methods are:

(i)   actuarial before-tax;
(ii) sum of the digits;
(iii) straight-line.

These methods are the mirror image of those previously considered for lessee accounting.

(2) *Actuarial before-tax*

Using the data in section 18.5(d):

Total gross earnings are £7,600
Allocation under actuarial method

Year	£
1	2,808
2	2,269
3	1,634
4	889

The lessor's profit and loss account extracts for the relevant years would appear:

	1	2	3	4
	£	£	£	£
Gross earnings under finance leases	2,808	2,269	1,634	889
Staff costs	(X)	(X)	(X)	(X)
Depreciation	(X)	(X)	(X)	(X)
Other operating charges	(X)	(X)	(X)	(X)
Profit on ordinary activities before/after tax	X	X	X	X
Dividends	(X)	(X)	(X)	(X)
Retained profit	X	X	X	X

Notes
(1) For each year in question, gross earnings under finance leases must be calculated for each individual lease (or group of similar leases) and the results then aggregated.
(2) All other items, such as staff costs and taxation, must be calculated directly for the company as a whole.

In the balance sheet, current assets/debtors would include the caption finance lease receivables. At the end of year 1, this would amount to £18,408. A note to the debtors figure should disclose the non-current amount of £14,877.

(3) *Sum of the digits method*

Gross earnings would be allocated as previously calculated:

Year	£
1	3,040
2	2,280
3	1,520
4	760
	7,600

The sum of the digits method is usually regarded as a reasonable approximation to the actuarial method.

(4) *Straight-line method*

Gross earnings would be allocated £1,900 per annum for four years.

(5) *Comment on the above approaches*

Both the actuarial before-tax, and the sum of the digits methods allocate gross earnings so as to give a constant periodic rate of return on the company's net investment in the lease.

Net investment is defined by SSAP 21 as:

(i)   gross investment in lease (minimum lease payments plus any unguaranteed residual value accruing to the lessor); *less*
(ii) gross earnings allocated to future periods.

However, the above approaches do not take account of the funds which the lessor has invested in the lease. For example, tax cash flows are ignored.

The net cash investment approaches (see below) take account of all relevant cash flows and thus are generally to be preferred.

(c) Methods of allocating gross earnings: after-tax methods

(1) *Introduction*

These methods base their approach on the funds invested in the lease by the lessor. The earnings allocation is related to the net cash investment (NCI).

NCI is defined as the net effect of the following:

(i)   cost of asset;
(ii)   government grants;
(iii)   rentals received;
(iv)   taxation payments and receipts (including the effect of capital allowances);
(v)   residual values at the end of the lease term;
(vi)   interest payments;
(vii)   interest received on cash surplus;
(viii) profit taken out of the lease.

The before-tax methods assume that the cash received by way of rentals is applied exclusively towards payment of notional interest on borrowings and repayment of capital.

The after-tax methods recognise that cash received has many 'calls' placed upon it. The following diagram illustrates some of the possibilities:

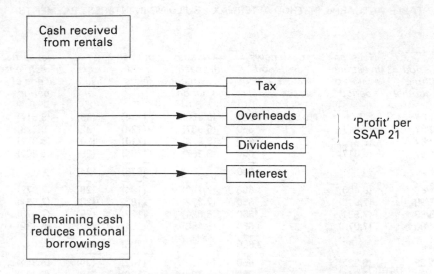

Cash is thus 'diverted' – for example, each lease must make some notional contribution towards payment of general overheads and dividends to shareholders.

(2) *Possible approaches*

There are two main approaches, each consisting of several variants:
(i)   actuarial method after tax;
(ii) investment period method (IPM).

(3) *Actuarial method after tax*

This method is illustrated by means of a detailed example taken from the guidance notes to SSAP 21.

(i) BASIC INFORMATION

A lessor leases out an asset on a non-cancellable lease contract with a primary term of five years from 1 January 1987. The rental is £650 per quarter payable in advance. The lessee has the right to continue to lease the asset after the end of the primary period for as long as he wishes at a peppercorn rent. In addition, the lessee is required to pay all maintenance and insurance costs as they arise. The leased asset could have been purchased for cash at the start of the lease for £10,000.

The lessor obtains writing-down allowances on the leased asset at the rate of 25%. The rate of corporation tax is 35%. The lessor's year end is 31 December and he pays or recovers tax nine months after the year end.

(ii) STAGE 1 – SET UP HYPOTHETICAL CASH FLOWS SHOWING NET CASH INVESTMENT (NCI) AT END OF EACH QUARTER

The table below appears in the guidance notes to SSAP 21. The comments following the table relate to certain of the figures and calculations.

TABLE ACTUARIAL METHOD AFTER TAX – BUILDING IN INTEREST PAYMENTS

Period (three months)	Net cash investment at start of period £	Cash flows in period (Notes a, b) £	Cash flows in period (Note c) £	Average net cash investment in period £	Interest paid (Note d) £	Profit taken out of lease (Note e) £	Net cash investment at end of period £
1/87		(10,000)	650	(9,350)	(234)	(33)	(9,617)
2/87	(9,617)		650	(8,967)	(224)	(32)	(9,223)
3/87	(9,223)		650	(8,573)	(214)	(30)	(8,817)
4/87	(8,817)		650	(8,167)	(204)	(29)	(8,400)
			2,600		(876)	(124)	
1/88	(8,400)		650	(7,750)	(194)	(28)	(7,972)
2/88	(7,972)		650	(7,322)	(183)	(26)	(7,531)
3/88	(7,531)		650	(6,881)	(172)	(25)	(7,078)
4/88	(7,078)	272	650	(6,156)	(154)	(22)	(6,332)
			2,600		(703)	(101)	
1/89	(6,332)		650	(5,682)	(142)	(20)	(5,844)
2/89	(5,844)		650	(5,194)	(130)	(18)	(5,342)
3/89	(5,342)		650	(4,692)	(117)	(17)	(4,826)
4/89	(4,826)	(8)	650	(4,184)	(105)	(15)	(4,304)
			2,600		(494)	(70)	
1/90	(4,304)		650	(3,654)	(91)	(13)	(3,758)
2/90	(3,758)		650	(3,108)	(78)	(11)	(3,197)
3/90	(3,197)		650	(2,547)	(64)	(9)	(2,620)
4/90	(2,620)	(245)	650	(2,215)	(55)	(8)	(2,278)
			2,600		(288)	(41)	
1/91	(2,278)		650	(1,628)	(41)	(6)	(1,675)
2/91	(1,675)		650	(1,025)	(26)	(4)	(1,055)
3/91	(1,055)		650	(405)	(10)	(1)	(416)
4/91	(416)	(440)	650	(206)	(5)	(1)	(212)
			2,600		(82)	(12)	
1/92	(212)			(212)	(5)	(1)	(218)
2/92	(218)			(218)	(5)	(1)	(224)
3/92	(224)			(224)	(6)	(1)	(231)
4/92	(231)	226		1	(1)	–	–
		6					
		(10,000)	13,000		(17)	(3)	
		(189)			(2,460)	(351)	

(a) The fair value of asset is £10,000 – at the outset, this is the NCI in the lease.

(b) Tax at the rate of 35% is payable at the beginning of period 4 in each year. It is calculated on rentals less interest paid and capital allowances, for example:

$$35\% \ (2,600 - 876 - 2,500) = £272$$
$$35\% \ (2,600 - 703 - 1,875) = £8$$
$$35\% \ (2,600 - 494 - 1,406) = £(245)$$

The figure at the bottom of the table of £(189) is the total of tax payments less recoveries.

(c) Rentals of £650 per quarter are payable in advance.

(d) Interest paid is calculated at 2.5% per quarter on the average net cash investment in each period.

(e) The profit taken out of the lease is determined on a trial and error basis. It is explained as follows:

> The profit taken out of the lease is calculated at 0.36% on the average net cash invested in each period until period 3/92, after which point the lessor no longer has funds invested in the lease. The calculations made to arrive at 0.36% will normally be carried out by financial institutions by computer program, but it can be attained by trial and error. The calculation is, initially, carried out ignoring the profit taken out of the lease and this will then leave a balance of surplus cash left over at the end which represents the approximate profit on the transaction.

> By dividing the total profit by the total average net cash investment in the period, an approximate percentage is obtained. As the profit taken out of the lease each quarter affects the average net cash investment in the following quarter, the net cash investment at the end of the whole transaction will not be zero until the percentage used is refined as in the above example to 0.36%. Note that NCI at end of 4/92 is nil.

> Finally, profit referred to above is not profit in the sense of net profit. It is effectively profit after charging notional interest and notional tax but before deducting overheads.

(f) Calculations for 1/87:

$$2.5\% \times 9350 = £234$$
$$0.36\% \times 9350 = £33$$

(iii) STAGE 2 – GROSS UP NOTIONAL PROFIT FIGURES TO DETERMINE ALLOCATION OF GROSS EARNINGS

	1987 £	1988 £	1989 £	1990 £	1991 £	1992 £	Total £
'Profit' (per table)	124	101	70	41	12	3	351
Gross up at 35% corporation tax	191	155	108	63	18	5	540
Interest (per table)	876	703	494	288	82	17	2,460
Gross earnings	1,067	858	602	351	100	22	3,000

Note: the *actual* gross earnings on the lease are £3,000 (rentals £13,000 less fair value of £10,000).

The *actual* allocation of gross earnings under this method is as follows:

	£
1987	1,067
1988	858
1989	602
1990	351
1991	100
1992	22
	3,000

To determine the company's gross earnings for a particular year, it is necessary to carry out the above calculations for each lease (or group of similar leases) and aggregate for the company as a whole.

(iv) PROFIT AND LOSS ACCOUNT FOR EACH YEAR

Once gross earnings have been determined, other items such as depreciation, staff costs, operating charges, interest payable, tax and dividends will be calculated on a global basis for the company as a whole.

(v) BALANCE SHEET ITEMS – DEBTORS: FINANCE LEASE RECEIVABLE

Once the gross earnings allocation has been completed, the balance sheet debtors may be calculated as follows:

Year	B/F	P/L	Cash	Bal C/f
	£	£	£	£
1987	10,000	1,067	(2,600)	8,467
1988	8,467	858	(2,600)	6,725
1989	6,725	602	(2,600)	4,727
1990	4,727	351	(2,600)	2,478
1991	2,478	100	(2,600)	(22)
1992	(22)	22	–	–

Notes

(1) The non-current part of the balance sheet debtor must be disclosed separately (eg £6,725 at the end of 1987).

(2) The NCI figures in the previous table are purely hypothetical figures. They do not appear as actual balances in the balance sheet. The notional NCI figures are used to calculate the gross earnings allocation.

(4) Investment period method (IPM)

The approach of this method is similar to that of the actuarial after-tax.

Under the IPM method, gross earnings of £3,000 are allocated between periods in proportion to the net cash investment for each period. The calculations are set out in the table below:

TABLE ALLOCATION OF GROSS EARNINGS UNDER IPM

Period	Net cash investment at end of period £	Gross earnings allocation £	Total gross earnings for year £
1/87	9,617	285	
2/87	9,223	274	1,070
3/87	8,817	262	
4/87	8,400	249	
1/88	7,972	236	
2/88	7,531	223	857
3/88	7,078	210	
4/88	6,332	188	
1/89	5,844	173	
2/89	5,342	158	602
3/89	4,826	143	
4/89	4,304	128	
1/90	3,758	111	
2/90	3,197	95	352
3/90	2,620	78	
4/90	2,278	68	
1/91	1,675	50	
2/91	1,055	31	99
3/91	416	12	
4/91	212	6	
1/92	218	6	
2/92	224	7	20
3/92	231	7	
4/92	–	–	
	£101,170	£3,000	£3,000

Note: The sum of the NCI 'weights' is £101,170. The NCI for quarter 1 of 1987 is £9,617. Thus the finance charge allocation is:

$$\frac{£9,617}{£101,170} \times £3,000 = £285$$

Once the finance charge allocations have been completed, the balance sheet debtors figures may be calculated.

(d) The acceptability of the various approaches

(1) *Hire-purchase transactions*

In principle, earnings allocations should be based on net cash investment (NCI). However, under a hire-purchase agreement, the capital allowances accrue to the user (unlike the position of a lease where the allowances accrue to the lessor). Consequently, it is perfectly possible that the finance company's NCI is not significantly different from its net investment.

So for hire-purchase transactions, either of the before-tax methods (actuarial before-tax, sum of the digits) will be acceptable. The straight-line method, however, would not be acceptable.

(2) *Finance leases*

Because of the significance of cash flows other than net investment, only one of the after-tax methods should be used.

18.13   MANUFACTURER/DEALER LESSOR

Selling profit may be taken in full to profit and loss account in the period in which the agreement is entered into.

However, profit taken is restricted to the excess of the fair value of the asset over the manufacturer's or dealer's costs less any grants receivable by the manufacturer or dealer.

Illustration 11

A manufacturer constructs a machine at a cost of £20,000. He normally sells the machine for £25,000, giving a profit on sale of £5,000.

The manufacturer also offers the machine on a five year finance lease with a rental of £5,800 per annum (the lessee accounting example). This is equivalent to a capital cost of £21,400.

Profit on sale should be restricted to £1,400 (i e £21,400 less £20,000). The remainder of the profit is gross earnings and will be allocated over the lease term.

18.14   LESSOR ACCOUNTING – DISCLOSURE REQUIREMENTS

(a) Introduction

Certain aspects of disclosure have already been referred to. For completeness, all the principal disclosure requirements of SSAP 21 are referred to below.

(b) Operating leases

Disclosure is required of:

(1) accounting policy for operating leases;
(2) aggregate rentals receivable in respect of an accounting period in relation to operating leases;
(3) gross amounts of assets held for use in operating leases and related accumulated depreciation charges.

(c) Finance leases and hire-purchase contracts

Disclosure is required of:

(1) net investment, at each balance sheet date, in:

   (i)   finance leases;
   (ii) hire-purchase contracts;

(2) accounting policy for finance leases;
(3) aggregate rentals receivable in respect of an accounting period in relation to finance leases;
(4) cost of assets acquired for the purpose of letting under finance leases.

Illustration 12

Extract from annual report and accounts of Cowie Group plc for the year ended 31 December 1994.

Accounting policies (extract)

(g) *Contract hire income*
Contract hire income is credited to the profit and loss account so that income and expenditure are matched over the duration of the related contracts.

(h) *Deferred revenue*
In respect of instalment credit agreements where the interest and charges are added to the amount financed at the commencement of the agreement, unearned interest and charges are calculated on the 'rule of 78' which attributes an appropriate part of the interest and charges to instalments receivable after the date of the balance sheet.

(i) *Maintenance of contract hire vehicles*
Income received in respect of maintenance is deferred and subsequently credited to profit and loss account so that it matches expenditure to be incurred over the duration of the related contracts.

(j) *Finance lease income and receivables*
Income from finance leasing contracts is credited to the profit and loss account in proportion to the funds invested. Finance lease receivables are stated in the balance sheet at the net investment in the leases after deduction of unearned charges.

(k) *Assets acquired under finance lease contracts*
Assets utilised by the Group which are acquired under finance lease contracts are recorded in the balance sheet as tangible fixed assets and the related obligations to pay future rentals (net of finance charges) are included in creditors.

Balance sheet (extract)

		The Group		The Company	
		1994	*1993*	*1994*	*1993*
	Notes	*£000*	*£000*	*£000*	*£000*
Fixed assets					
Goodwill	10	**8,214**	8,456	–	–
Tangible assets	11	**426,392**	366,180	**22,565**	69,207
Investments	12	**4,413**	4,313	**110,482**	46,749
		439,019	378,949	**133,047**	115,956
Current assets					
Stocks	13	**69,490**	67,001	**186**	51,639
Debtors	14	**57,203**	50,031	**11,759**	27,982
Instalment credit agreements	15	**36,446**	25,120	–	–
Finance lease receivables	16	**9,962**	5,843	–	–
Cash at bank and in hand		**424**	35	**24**	27
		173,525	148,030	**11,969**	79,648

Notes to the accounts

15 Instalment credit agreements

	The Group	
	1994	1993
	£000	£000
Amounts falling due within one year	**15,051**	11,215
Amounts falling due after more than one year	**21,395**	13,905
	36,446	25,120

16 Finance lease agreements

	The Group	
	1994	1993
	£000	£000
Amounts falling due within one year	**3,576**	2,723
Amounts falling due after more than one year	**6,386**	3,120
	9,962	5,843

The cost of assets acquired for the purpose of letting under finance leases in the year was £5,802,000.

Illustration 13

Extract from annual report and accounts of Courts plc for the year ended 31 March 1995.

Accounting policies (extract)

Profit recognition
The accounting policy in relation to deferred profit has been revised such that the unearned proportion of the service charge income as at the balance sheet date is deferred to future periods, and is deducted from the debtors shown on the balance sheet (see note 12).

As a result of the revision, turnover and operating profit include the service charge income earned during the period. The gross margin on sales made on extended credit terms is recognised at the time of sale. All expenditure to earn these sales is written off in the year in which it is incurred.

Directors' report (extract)

Accounting policy revisions
As stated in the Interim Report published in December 1994, following the introduction of FRS 5 (Reporting the Substance of Transactions) certain changes have been made whereby the property sale and leaseback transactions formerly reported as disposals are no longer recorded as such. The values of the properties, the associated indebtedness, the charges for both rentals and interest payable, the contingency property provision and the retained earnings have all been restated accordingly.

In addition, both in light of FRS 5 and following discussions with the Financial Reporting Review Panel as to the treatment of deferred profit and the applicability of SSAP 21 (Accounting for Leases and Hire Purchase Contracts), the accounting policy in respect of instalment and hire purchase transactions has been amended. Previously, in common with other companies in the retail sector providing extended credit, turnover was stated at the full invoiced amount of each transaction, including service charges billed on extended credit. However, no profit was recognised on instalment and hire purchase sales at the time of the sale and the gross margin and service charge income were transferred to a deferred profit reserve with only the proportion of the profit applicable to cash received during the year being included in pre tax profits for that year. The policy now is to include in turnover and operating profit only that portion of service charge income earned during the period under review. The gross margin on sales made on extended credit terms is now recognised at the time of sale. The unearned service charge is now deducted directly from debtors shown on the balance sheet. Consequently there is no longer any requirement for a deferred profit reserve.

Freehold buildings were formerly depreciated to the extent that their estimated future residual value was less than the value at which they were stated in the financial statements. The directors now consider it more appropriate, in the light of current best practice, to provide for depreciation of freehold buildings at a standard rate on a straight line basis.

The combined effect of these changes on the balance sheet as at 31st March 1995 has been to increase tangible fixed assets by £5.6m (1994 £13.2m), to decree investments in associates by £1.9m (1994 £2.0m), to decrease trade debtors by £32.8m (1994 £25.1m), to increase creditors due in less than 1 year by £7.0m (1994 £3.8m), to increase creditors falling due after 1 year by £Nil (1994 £7.0m), and to increase provisions for liabilities and charges by £9.5m (1994 £7.0m). There are no longer any amounts to be included in deferred profit reserve (formerly £49.3m), although an unearned service charge of £33.4m has been deducted from debtors (1994 £25.5m). Revaluation reserves have increased by £0.1m (1994 £Nil) and minority interests have increased by £3.8m (1994 £3.0m). Retained earnings have been restated, via a Prior Year Adjustment, increasing them by £13.7m.

The impact on the profit and loss account for the year ended 31st March 1995 has been to reduce reported turnover by the net movement in the unearned service charge of £8.6m (1994 £6.6m), to reduce operating profit before associated undertakings by £8.9m (1994 £6.4m), to reduce the share of profit from associates by £0.2m (1994 £0.4m) and to increase interest costs by £Nil (1994 £1.4m). There is no longer any requirement for a deferred profit transfer previously shown in the Profit and Loss Account below Operating Profit (formerly £11.8m), although a deferral of £8.6m (1994 £6.3m) has been deducted in arriving at turnover. The net effect on the pre-tax profit is thus an increase of £7.6m (1994 £3.5m). The tax charge has been increased by £2.0m (1994 £1.3m) and the minority interest by £0.7m (1994 £0.5m) resulting in an increase in both the profit available for distribution and in the retained profit for the year of £4.9m (1994 £1.7m).

Following the introduction of FRS 4 (Capital Instruments) shareholders' funds and minority interests have been analysed between equity and non-equity interests.

12 Debtors

	Parent		Group	
	1995	1994	1995	1995 Restated
	£'000	£'000	£'000	£'000
Amounts falling due within one year:				
Instalment and hire purchase debtors including unearned service charges	–	–	104,998	85,111
Less: Unearned service charges	–	–	(26,544)	(20,272)
	–	–	78,454	64,839
Other trade debtors	–	–	9,207	10,923
Amounts owed by subsidiary undertakings	45,175	45,391	–	–
Other debtors	785	442	6,004	5,109
Prepayments and accrued income	705	751	2,773	2,071
Taxation recoverable	298	–	472	186
	46,963	46,584	96,910	83,128
Amounts falling due after more than one year:				
Instalment and hire purchase debtors including unearned service charges	–	–	58,469	43,604
Less: Unearned service charges	–	–	(6,870)	(5,203)
	–	–	51,599	38,401
Other debtors	199	306	199	346
	199	306	51,798	38,747
Total debtors	47,162	46,890	148,708	121,875

The comparative figure for debtors has been restated by deduction of the unearned service charges at the period end as a result of the changes in accounting policies referred to in the Directors' Report [above].

18.15 SALE AND LEASEBACK

(a) Introduction

In commercial terms, sale and leaseback is one way in which a company may raise finance. A sale and leaseback transaction takes place when an owner sells an asset and immediately re-acquires the right to use the asset by entering into a lease with the purchaser.

For example, Northern Traders plc could sell its freehold head office building, on which there was no fixed charge, to Merchant Finance plc thus raising cash. Merchant Finance plc could then lease the property back to Northern Traders who would continue to use the building for its own purpose. It would be necessary to determine for accounting purposes whether the lease was an operating lease or a finance lease. The concept of accounting for substance (see chapter 7) is relevant here.

(b) The substance of the transaction

In the case of a sale and leaseback of an operating lease, the substance of the transaction is that the seller–lessee has disposed of substantially all the risks and rewards of ownership of the asset and has realised a profit or loss on disposal.

In the case of a sale and leaseback of a finance lease, the substance of the transaction is the raising of finance secured on an asset which is held by the enterprise and not disposed of. Paragraph 153 of the guidance notes to SSAP 21 states:

... If the leaseback is a finance lease, the seller-lessee is in effect re-acquiring substantially all the risks and rewards of ownership of the asset. In other words, he never disposes of his ownership interest in the asset, and so it would not be correct to recognise a profit or loss in relation to an asset which (in substance) never was disposed of.

(c) Accounting treatment – an introduction

Before looking at the detailed requirements of SSAP 21 consider a simple example. Northern Traders presently owns a property with a net book value of £200,000. The property is sold for cash to Merchant Finance. The price agreed of £250,000 is based on the fair value of the property at the date of sale.

The respective balance sheets of Northern Traders before and after the sale and leaseback are as follows:

	(a) before sale and leaseback £'000	after sale and leaseback	
		(b) operating L/B £'000	(c) finance L/B £'000
Property asset	200	–	200
Other net assets	650	900	900
Obligations under finance lease	–	–	(200)
	850	900	900
Ordinary share capital	100	100	100
P/L reserves	750	800	800
	850	900	900

Notes:

(1) The usual rules for distinguishing between operating and finance leases would apply in determining whether (b) or (c) was appropriate. A short lease with regular rent reviews would normally be classified as an operating lease whilst a long lease with a fixed rental may be classified as a finance lease.

(2) The profit on sale in situation (b) of £50,000 (£250,000 – £200,000) would be taken to profit and loss account (see (d) below, for sale at fair value and operating leaseback). Rentals paid subsequently by the lessee would then be charged to profit and loss account as incurred.

(3) In the case of a sale and leaseback of a finance lease, where proceeds exceed carrying amount, there are two possible treatments. The first, in para 46 of SSAP 21 is referred to below in (d) and (e).

The second and simpler alternative is that shown above. Note that carrying amount of the asset is left unchanged and the proceeds are effectively treated as a creditor. This is not referred to in SSAP 21 but is suggested as an alternative in para 155 of the guidance notes to SSAP 21. The justification of this treatment is that the substance of the transaction is the raising of finance and there is no reason why the asset value should be changed.

Subsequent payments under the terms of the finance lease should be split between capital and finance charge. The finance charge will be charged to P/L, the capital part will be deducted from the creditor figure.

(d) Accounting requirements of SSAP 21

The relevant paragraphs of SSAP 21 are reproduced below. These are also summarised in figures 1 and 2 on pages 331 and 332 below.

Para 46

Accounting by the seller-lessee
In a sale and leaseback transaction which results in a finance lease any apparent profit or loss (that is, the difference between the sale price and the previous carrying value) should be deferred and amortised in the financial statements of the seller/lessee over the shorter of the lease term and the useful life of the asset.

Para 47

If the leaseback is an operating lease:

(a) any profit or loss should be recognised immediately, provided it is clear that the transaction is established at fair value;

(b) if the sale price is below fair value, any profit or loss should be recognised immediately except that if the apparent loss is compensated by future rentals at below market price it should to that extent be deferred and amortised over the remainder of the lease term (or, if shorter, the period during which the reduced rentals are chargeable);

(c) if the sale price is above fair value, the excess over fair value should be deferred and amortised over the shorter of the remainder of the lease term and the period to the next rent review (if any).

Para 48

Accounting by the buyer/lessor
A buyer/lessor should account for a sale and leaseback in the same way as he accounts for other leases, that is, using the methods set out in paragraphs 38 to 45 of SSAP 21.

Three further paragraphs taken from the guidance notes to SSAP 21 are reproduced below. These do not appear in SSAP 21 but may be relevant in certain situations.

Figure 1

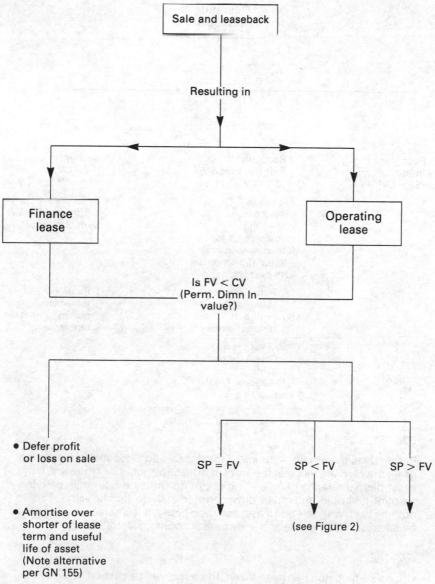

Figure 2

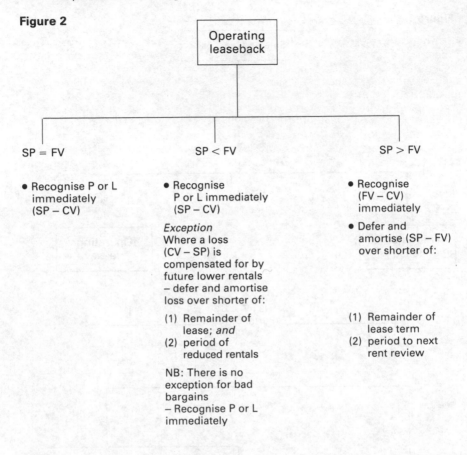

SP = FV	**SP < FV**	**SP > FV**
• Recognise P or L immediately (SP – CV)	• Recognise P or L immediately (SP – CV)	• Recognise (FV – CV) immediately
	Exception Where a loss (CV – SP) is compensated for by future lower rentals – defer and amortise loss over shorter of:	• Defer and amortise (SP – FV) over shorter of:
	(1) Remainder of lease; *and* (2) period of reduced rentals	(1) Remainder of lease term (2) period to next rent review
	NB: There is no exception for bad bargains – Recognise P or L immediately	

GN 151

Before dealing with the accounting for the sale and leaseback transaction itself, the carrying value of the asset in question should be reviewed. If the asset has suffered a permanent diminution in value below its carrying amount it should be written down immediately to its fair value. This is nothing to do with sale and leaseback specifically, but is a step which should be taken so that the sale and leaseback accounting is not distorted.

GN 152

Once that first step has been taken, the asset will be carried at fair value, or less. It is then necessary to determine whether the leaseback is an operating lease or a finance lease. This should be decided according to the criteria for all leases as set out in paragraphs 15 to 17 of the standard.

GN 155

As an alternative to calculating the apparent profit and deferring and amortising that amount, the same result can be achieved by leaving the previous carrying value unchanged, setting up the amount received on sale as a creditor, and treating the lease payments partly as principal and partly as a finance charge. This treatment will reflect the substance of the transaction, namely that it represents the raising of finance secured on an asset which is held and not disposed of.

(e) Finance leasebacks – applying the rules

The treatment referred to in GN 155 was illustrated in the example in (c) above.

Had para 46 of SSAP 21 (see (d) above) been applied the carrying amount of the asset in the balance sheet after the leaseback would have been under £250,000 and the balance sheet would have shown a balance of £50,000 under the caption 'deferred income'. This would be credited to profit and loss accounts of future years over a period equivalent to the shorter of the lease term and the asset's useful life.

The justification for this treatment is that in what is effectively a financing transaction, higher proceeds paid by the buyer/lessor will be compensated for by higher rentals paid by the seller/lessee. The credit to profit and loss account from deferred income will offset part of the effect of these higher rentals.

(f) Operating leasebacks – applying the rules

The following five situations will be used to illustrate the effect of the rules set out in (d) above. In the table below, SP refers to selling price, FV to fair value and CV to carrying value.

	Basic data for the five leaseback situations				
	SP = FV	SP < FV			SP > FV
	1	2	3	4	5
SP	100	80	60	60	110
FV	100	100	100	100	100
CV	70	70	70	70	70
Rentals					
Actual	4	3.5	1.5	4	5
Market	4	4	4	4	4
Years to next review	5	5	5	5	5

The effect on profit and loss account for each of the five situations is summarised in the table below. Reference should also be made to the notes below.

	Effect on profit and loss account				
			Lease		
	1	2	3	4	5
On leaseback					
– profit (loss)	30	10	Nil (but 10 is deferred & amortised)	(10)	30
Annual expense					
– actual rent	4	3.5	1.5	4	5
– amortisation	–	–	2.0	–	(2)
Total	4	3.5	3.5	4	3

NOTES

Lease (1) The transaction is established at fair value. The profit should be recognised immediately (SSAP 21, para 47(a)).

Lease (2) Although SP is below FV no actual loss arises. Profit of 10 (80 − 70) is calculated in the usual way.

Lease (3) The book loss of 10 (70 − 60) is compensated for by future rentals at a rate below market levels. The loss of 10 may be deferred and amortised (SSAP 21, para.47(b)). In this case 10 is charged over 5 years i e 2 per annum which is used to reduce the rental charge.

Lease (4) This is the situation of a bad bargain. Unlike lease (3), the low selling price is not compensated for at a below market rental. The loss cannot be deferred, it must be recognised in full in the current year.

Lease (5) This is the situation in SSAP 21, para 47(c). The profit recognised this year is restricted to FV − CV (i e, 100 − 70 = 30). SP − FV (110 − 100 = 10) must be deferred and recognised over a specified period. In this case, 10 is amortised over 5 years i e 2 p a which reduces the rental charge.

(g) Impact of FRS 5

FRS 5 refers to particular types of lease arrangements where FRS 5 contains provisions more specific than those in SSAP 21. An example given is a sale and leaseback arrangement with an option for the seller/lessee to repurchase the asset − application note B would be relevant.

Sale and repurchase agreements are referred to in section 7.13.

Illustration 14

Extract from annual report and accounts of Booker plc for year ended 31 December 1994.

Note 1 − changes in accounting policy and presentation (extract)

The financial reporting standard, FRS 5 − Reporting the substance of transactions, issued in 1994 by the Accounting Standards Board, requires that the assets and liabilities of an enterprise be recognised based on new definitions. Accordingly, a sale and leaseback arrangement entered into in 1992 by a US subsidiary is no longer recognised as a disposal. The effect of this change on the balance sheet at 31 December 1994 has been to increase tangible fixed assets by £16.3m (1993 £17.7m), to increase borrowings by £17.4m (1993 £18.8m), and to reduce profit and loss reserve by £11.7m (1993 £12.9m), substantially offset by a revaluation reserve of £10.6m (1993 £11.8m). The effect on profit tax for both years was immaterial. The comparative figures have been restated.

(Note 12, tangible fixed assets, states that '. . . a sale and leaseback transaction previously recorded as a disposal in 1992 has been reinstated, as a finance lease, under FRS 5. The reinstatement is at an open market existing use basis of valuation carried out at 31 August 1992. . .'

19 ACCOUNTING FOR TAXATION

Key Issues

* Tax under the imputation system
* SSAP 8 requirements
* Deferred taxation
  – timing and permanent differences
  – approaches to deferred taxation
  – the partial provision approach
* Presentation in accounts
* Value added tax
* Government grants

19.1 ACCOUNTING FOR TAX UNDER THE IMPUTATION SYSTEM

(a) Aim of this chapter

This chapter is concerned with the effect of tax transactions on ledger accounts and financial statements. It does not attempt to provide guidance on current tax legislation or deal with tax rate changes and transitional arrangements. For the purposes of the illustrations, assumed or hypothetical tax rates are used.

(b) Assumptions re tax rates

Unless otherwise indicated, the following tax rates are assumed to apply:

Corporation tax $\qquad\qquad$ 35%
Advance corporation tax $\qquad \frac{3}{7}$
Income tax $\qquad\qquad\qquad$ 30%

(c) The payment of corporation tax

Companies are assessed to corporation tax on their profits. Where no dividends are paid during the year, a single payment of corporation tax will be paid at some time after the year end (payment dates are referred to in (d) below).

In general terms, ignoring special situations, the payment of dividends will not affect the total amount of corporation tax paid over. However, the payment of dividends will affect the *timing* of the tax payments.

The payment of a dividend triggers off a payment of advance corporation tax (ACT). ACT is regarded as an on account payment of gross corporation tax. The residual balance owing is referred to as mainstream corporation tax (MCT).

(d) Tax payment dates

(1) *ACT*

ACT is paid on a quarterly basis by reference to the account period in which the dividend is paid. For example, if a dividend is paid in February, this falls in the quarter to 31 March and ACT is payable two weeks after the end of the quarter ie by 14 April.

(2) *MCT*

The payment date for MCT is nine months after the end of the year.

(e) Offset of ACT paid

ACT relating to dividends paid in a particular accounting year may be offset against the corporation tax on the profits of that period.

Illustration 1

A company paid a dividend of £14,700 on 3.8.X4. ACT of £6,300 (i e $\frac{3}{7}\times$£14,700) was paid over on 14.10.X4 (i e 14 days after quarter to 30.9.X4).

Corporation tax for the year ended 31 December 19X4 was estimated at £39,500. Show relevant extracts from financial statements.

Balance sheet

	£
Other creditors including tax and social security – corporation tax payable 1.10.X5 (39,500 – 6,300)	33,200

Profit and loss account

Tax on profit on ordinary activities	39,500
Dividends paid	14,700

(f) ACT on proposed dividends

Dividends proposed at the year end will not give rise to payment of ACT until the dividends are actually paid. However, since proposed dividends are accrued in the balance sheet, SSAP 8 requires ACT on proposed dividends to be included within creditors: amounts falling due within one year.

When ACT is paid, it will become available for offset against the corporation tax on the profits of the following year (i e the year in which the dividend payment is made).

Provided the ACT on proposed dividends is regarded as recoverable (i e against tax on the following year profits), the ACT debit should be deducted from deferred tax account. In the absence of a deferred tax account, the ACT should be regarded as a deferred asset.

Illustration 2

In the previous example, if the dividend of £14,700 was proposed at the year end what difference would this have made?

First of all, no ACT offset could be made against the corporation tax of £39,500. The reason is that the *dividend* is paid in the year following that to which the corporation tax relates. ACT paid may be offset against the corporation tax for 19X5.

Secondly, a creditor for ACT of £6,300 should be made. Also, in the absence of a deferred tax account, a deferred asset of £6,300 should be set up.

The relevant extracts are then:

(1) Balance sheet

Debtors			£
Deferred asset – ACT recoverable			6,300

Creditors – due within one year			
ACT	6,300	disclosed as	
MCT	39,500	single figure	45,800
Proposed dividends			14,700

(2) Profit and loss account

	£
Tax on profit on ordinary activities	39,500
Dividends proposed	14,700

(g) Dividends received

Where dividends are paid and received in a period, ACT will be paid on the net amount.

Illustration 3

A company paid a dividend of £8,400 on 5.6.X2 and received a dividend of £2,100 on 18.9.X2. Corporation tax on the profits for the year to 31.12.X2 was estimated at £54,100. Tax payments and receipts would be as follows:

	£
14.7.X2 ACT payment $\frac{3}{7} \times$ £8,400	3,600
18.9.X2 ACT reclaim $\frac{3}{7} \times$ £2,100	(900)
1.10.X3 MCT paid (54,100 – 2,700)	51,400
Total tax paid	54,100

For presentation purposes, SSAP 8 requires dividends received to be shown gross inclusive of tax credit. Thus, in the above illustration, dividends received would be included at £3,000. The tax credit of £900 should be shown as a separate part of the tax charge.

Note: that this grossing-up is purely for presentation purposes. It has no effect on ACT set-off.

Illustration 4

Profit and loss extracts for the above illustration:

		£
Dividends received		3,000
Tax on profit on ordinary activities		
Corporation tax	54,100	
Tax credits on dividends received	900	55,000
Dividends paid		8,400

(h) Income tax

Tax law requires companies to deduct income tax at the basic rate at source when paying loan interest, royalties etc.

A knowledge of the following terms is necessary to understand the treatment of income tax in accounts:

(1) Charges ie payments from which income tax must be deducted at source eg debenture interest, loan interest, mortgage interest, royalties.
(2) Unfranked investment income received ie income paid out of profits not subject to UK corporation tax eg loan interest received and income received from British government securities (from which income tax is deducted at source), local authority loans, and building society interest received.

The charge for royalties, debenture interest and annual charges in the profit and loss account is shown gross. Unfranked investment income is also shown gross. The double entry recording the payment of annual charges etc is: debit debenture interest etc, with the gross amount and credit cash with the cash paid to the debenture holder etc, and credit income tax account with the income tax deducted.

When unfranked investment income is received, debit cash with the cash received, debit income tax account with the income tax deducted by the payer at source, and credit unfranked investment income (UII) account with the gross amount.

In the balance sheet, an income tax account credit balance will be included in creditors. Accrued debenture and loan interest will be included in creditors, gross, and need not be disclosed separately on the balance sheet. Likewise, unfranked investment income receivable will be included in debtors at the gross amount.

Illustration 5

Company has year end of 31.12.X6. Debenture interest of £20,000 (gross) is paid net of tax on 23.6.X6. Debenture interest of £12,000 (gross) is received net of tax on 23.9.X6.

DEBENTURE INTEREST PAID

		£			£
23.6.X6	Cash	14,000	31.12.X6	P/L	20,000
23.6.X6	Income tax account (to gross up)	6,000			
		20,000			20,000

DEBENTURE INTEREST RECEIVED

		£			£
31.12.X6	P/L	12,000	23.9.X6	Cash	8,400
			23.9.X6	Income tax account (to gross up)	3,600
		12,000			12,000

INCOME TAX ACCOUNT

		£			£
14.7.X6	Cash (tax paid over)	6,000	23.6.X6	Debenture interest paid	6,000
23.9.X6	Debenture interest received	3,600	14.10.X6	Cash (tax reclaimed)	3,600
		9,600			9,600

Illustration 6

Company has year end of 31.12.X6. Debenture interest of £12,000 (gross) is paid net of tax on 23.6.X6. Debenture interest of £20,000 (gross) is received net of tax on 23.9.X6. The relevant ledger accounts are:

DEBENTURE INTEREST PAID

		£			£
23.6.X6	Cash	8,400	31.12.X6	P/L	12,000
23.6.X6	Income tax account (to gross up)	3,600			
		12,000			12,000

DEBENTURE INTEREST RECEIVED

		£			£
31.12.X6	P/L	20,000	23.9.X6	Cash	14,000
			23.9.X6	Income tax account	6,000
		20,000			20,000

INCOME TAX ACCOUNT

		£			£
14.7.X6	Cash (tax paid over)	3,600	23.6.X6	Debenture interest paid	3,000
23.9.X6	Debenture Interest received	6,000	14.10.X6	Cash (tax reclaimed)	3,600
			31.12.X6	Corporation tax account (6,000 – 3,600)	2,400
		9,600			9,600

Note: The unrecovered income tax of £2,400 is offset against corporation tax thus reducing the corporation tax payment.

(i) Requirements of SSAP 8

SSAP 8 (the treatment of taxation under the imputation system in the accounts of companies) requires the following:

(1) *Profit and loss account*

(i) TAX CHARGE
The tax charge in the profit and loss account should include the following items. Where items are material, they should be disclosed separately.

(a) The amount of UK corporation tax. The following elements should be specified:

   (1) corporation tax;
   (2) deferred tax;
   (3) tax attributable to franked investment income (i e tax credits on dividends received);
   (4) irrecoverable ACT;
   (5) relief for overseas taxation.

   (Points (4) and (5) are referred to later in this chapter.)
(b) Total overseas taxation, relieved and unrelieved. Disclosure is required of the amount of unrelieved overseas taxation which results from the payment or proposed payment of dividends.

(ii) CORPORATION TAX RATE
If the rate of corporation tax is not known for either the whole of the period or part of the period, the latest known rate of corporation tax should be used and disclosed. Prior to the Finance Act 1984, the corporation tax rate was specified in the budget on a retrospective basis. However, in the 1984 budget, corporation tax rates for future years were specified.

(iii) DIVIDENDS PAID AND PROPOSED
These should be included in the profit and loss account at the amount of cash payable to the shareholders, without the inclusion of ACT or tax credits.

(iv) DIVIDEND INCOME
Dividend income should be included at the amount of cash received or receivable plus tax credit. For example, suppose a company receives a dividend of £2,800 from a UK resident company. In theory, dividend income could be presented in two possible ways, only one of which is permitted by SSAP 8:

	Net approach £	Gross approach £
Investment income	2,800	4,000
Tax on profit on ordinary activities		
Tax credit on dividends received	–	(1,200)
Profit after tax	2,800	2,800

The difference between the two approaches is simply one of presentation. It can have no effect on tax payable or net profit. SSAP 8 requires the gross approach on the grounds of consistency i e all items which appear in the profit and loss account above the tax line should be included on a before-tax basis.

(2) *Balance sheet*

(i) DIVIDEND LIABILITY
Proposed dividends should be included in creditors (amounts payable within one year of the balance sheet date) without the addition of related ACT.

(ii) ACT ON PROPOSED DIVIDENDS
Whether or not this ACT is recoverable by offset against gross corporation tax, ACT payable should be included within creditors.

(iii) ACT RECOVERABLE ON PROPOSED DIVIDENDS
(a) ACT on proposed dividends is due for payment 14 days after the end of the quarter in which the payment is actually made.
(b) This ACT may be offset against the corporation tax on the profits of the accounting year in which the dividend is paid.

Illustration 7

Suppose a dividend is declared for the year ended 31 December 19X4. The dividend is paid on 15 April 19X5 so ACT is paid over 14 days after the quarter to 30 June 19X5 i e by 14 July 19X5.

ACT paid may be offset against the corporation tax on the profits for the year ending 31 December 19X5. The critical factor is the date when the dividend is paid. If the dividend payment falls in the year to 31 December 19X5, it may be offset against the corporation tax on the profits of that year. It may *not* be offset against the corporation tax on the profits for the year to 31 December 19X4.

The MCT for 19X5 will be due on 1 October 19X6. The ACT offset thus reduces a payment 21 months after the 31 December 19X4 balance sheet. The right of set-off is therefore in the nature of a deferred asset.

SSAP 8 requires the recoverable ACT either:

(1) to be deducted from the deferred tax balance if a deferred tax account exists; failing which
(2) to be treated as a deferred asset (under the heading of debtors).

Irrecoverable ACT is discussed below.

(iv) PREFERENCE SHARES
Where dividend rights on preference shares were established before 6 April 1973 at a particular gross rate, this was subsequently reduced to $\frac{7}{10}$ of its former rate.

Such preference shares would be described as, for example:

100,000 10% (now 7% + tax credit) preference shares of £1   £100,000

(j) Illustrations

In each of the illustrations below, corporation tax is to be taken at 35% and income tax at 30%. No deferred tax account is maintained. Ledger account entries are numbered for sequence of entries.

Illustration 8

Dividend paid on 8.9.X6 of £42,000. ACT paid on 14.10.X6 is £18,000 ($\frac{3}{7}$ × £42,000). Corporation tax for the year ended 31 December 19X6 is estimated at £203,000 and a dividend is proposed of £63,000.
Required: (a) ledger accounts;
              (b) extracts from financial statements.

ACT ACCOUNT

	£		£
14.10.X6		31.12.X6	
(1) Cash	18,000	(4) Corporation tax a/c	
		(ACT set-off)	18,000
31.12.X6			
Bal c/d	27,000	(5) ACT recoverable account	27,000
	45,000		45,000
		Bal b/d	27,000

MCT ACCOUNT

	£		£
31.12.X6		31.12.X6	
(3) ACT a/c	18,000	(2) P/L	203,000
MCT c/d	185,000		
	203,000		203,000

DEFERRED ASSET A/C – ACT RECOVERABLE

	£		£
(5) ACT a/c			
($\frac{3}{7} \times 63,000$)	27,000		

Profit and loss account (extracts)

		£
Tax on profit on ordinary activities		
Corporation tax at 35%		203,000
Dividends on ordinary shares		
Paid	42,000	
Proposed	63,000	105,000

Balance sheet extracts

	£
Debtors – Deferred asset:	
ACT recoverable	27,000
Creditors – Amounts falling	
due within one year	
Tax and social security	212,000
Proposed dividends	63,000

Working – tax and social security

	£
ACT payable	27,000
MCT payable	185,000
	212,000

Illustration 9

The following details relate to tax and dividends matters:

(1) Dividends relating to 19X8 were as follows:

Interim paid (2.10.X8)	14,000
Final proposed	21,000

(2) Dividends received on 3.8.X8 amounted to £7,700.
(3) Corporation tax on the profits for 19X8 has been estimated at £220,000.

(4) ACT payable at 31.12.X8 is £2,700 (ie $\frac{3}{7}$ (14,000 – 7,700))

Required:
(a) ledger accounts;
(b) extracts from financial statements.

ADVANCE CORPORATION TAX

	£		£
19X8		*19X8*	
31 Dec		31 Dec	
Bal c/d	11,700	(2) Corporation tax a/c (ACT set-off)	2,700
		(3) ACT recoverable account ($\frac{3}{7}$ × 21,000)	9,000
	11,700		11,700
		19X9	
		1 Jan	
		Bal b/d	11,700

MAINSTREAM CORPORATION TAX

	£		£
19X8		*19X8*	
31 Dec		31 Dec	
(2) ACT a/c	2,700	(1) P/L – tax charge	220,000
Bal c/d (MCT)	217,300		
	220,000		220,000
		19X9	
		1 Jan	
		Bal b/d	217,300

DEFERRED ASSET ACCOUNT – ACT RECOVERABLE

	£		£
19x8			
31 Dec			
(3) ACT a/c	9,000		

Comments on the above

(1) The receipt of dividend on 3.8.X8 has no immediate effect on ACT receipts or payments. No ACT can be claimed back as there were no ACT payments in previous accounting quarters.

(2) However, the above receipt does affect the ACT position as regards the dividend which is paid prior to the year end (ie the dividend of £14,000 paid on 2.10.X8).
ACT payable by reference to the dividend payment is $\frac{3}{7}$ (14,000 – 7,700), ie £2,700.
Thus, ACT is payable on 14.1.X9, and so is a creditor at the end of the year. Since the dividend to which the ACT relates was paid in 19X8, the £2,700 may be offset against the corporation tax on 19X8 profits of £220,000.

(3) ACT of £9,000 on the proposed dividend can only be offset against the corporation tax on 19X9 profits and so must be regarded as a deferred asset.

(4) The total ACT liability of £11,700 is payable as follows:

	£
14.1.X9	2,700
14.4.X9 (assuming dividend paid prior to 31.3.X9)	9,000
	11,700

Profit and loss extracts

		£
Income from investments		11,000

Tax on profit on ordinary activities:

Corporation tax at 35%		220,000
Tax credit on UK dividends received		3,300
		223,300

Dividends on ordinary shares:

Paid	14,000	
Proposed	21,000	35,000

Balance sheet extracts

Debtors – deferred asset: ACT recoverable		9,000
Creditors – amounts falling due within one year:		
Tax and social security		229,000
Proposed dividends		21,000

Workings

(1) *Tax and social security*

ACT payable	11,700
MCT payable	217,300
	229,000

(2) *Income from investments*

$$£7,700 \times \frac{100}{70} = £11,000$$

Note: It is recommended that the grossing up of dividend income is done on the face of the profit and loss account without any entry in the ledger accounts.

(k) Recoverability of ACT

It has been assumed that any ACT paid may be offset in full in arriving at MCT. This is so provided that the net ACT paid over does not exceed 30% (at basic rate income of tax at 30%) of the corporation tax income.

For tax purposes, any ACT not relieved in this way may be carried back for six years or carried forward indefinitely.

For accounting purposes, it is necessary to decide whether the recovery of the ACT is reasonably certain and foreseeable. If this is not so, ACT should be written off in the profit and loss account. The amount written off forms part of the tax charge, but has no effect on the possible future availability of loss relief for tax purposes.

ACT may be regarded as recoverable in the following circumstances:

(1) where current year or preceding year income is sufficient for set-off purposes;
(2) where a deferred tax account of sufficient size exists (ACT must not exceed 30% (at 30% IT rate) of the income timing differences on which deferred tax is calculated);
(3) where income of the next accounting period is expected to be sufficient for set-off purposes.

Illustration 10

The following details related to Wilson Ltd.
Assume corporation tax rate is 35% and ACT $\frac{3}{7}$.

	Chargeable income £	Dividend paid £	ACT paid £
19X6	600,000	235,000	100,714
19X7	150,000	165,000	70,714

19X6		£
Gross corporation tax is 35% × £600,000		210,000
Less ACT		100,714
So MCT =		109,286

(No restriction applies as ACT paid is below 30% of corporation tax income of £600,000. Unused set-off is £180,000 less £100,714 i e £79,286.)

19X7		
		£
Gross corporation tax is 35% × £150,000		52,500
Less ACT set-off: restricted to 30% × 150,000		45,000
So MCT =		7,500

Surplus ACT is £70,714 − £45,000 = £25,714. As this is below the unused set-off of £79,286, the £25,714 may be reclaimed from the Inland Revenue.

Illustration 11

Suppose the facts as in the previous illustration, but the dividend paid in 19X7 amounted to £320,000 (ACT $\frac{3}{7}$ × 320,000 = £137,143). MCT would be the same, but surplus ACT would amount to £137,143 − £45,000 = £92,143. The maximum repayment would be £79,286, so £12,857 would remain unrelieved. Unless evidence could be produced to demonstrate its recovery within the following year, £12,857 should be written off to profit and loss account and included as a separate part of the tax charge.

(l) Unrelieved overseas tax

There may be two possible causes of unrelieved overseas taxation:

(1) The rate of overseas tax on overseas profits exceeds the rate of UK corporation tax applied to those profits.

Illustration 12

	£	
UK profits	700,000	(35%)
Overseas profits	200,000	(60%)
Total	900,000	

Overseas tax is 60% × £200,000, i e £120,000.
Relief is restricted to 35% × £200,000 i e £70,000.

Profit and loss account (extract)

	£
UK corporation tax on profits at 35%	315,000
Less relief for overseas tax	70,000
	245,000
Overseas tax	120,000
	365,000

(2) Payment of a large UK dividend so as to restrict relief for overseas tax.

19.2 DEFERRED TAXATION

(a) Introduction

In the UK, corporation tax is assessed on a company's tax-adjusted profit. It is unlikely that this will be the same as its accounting or reported profit.

Illustration 13

The tax computation of Gardens plc is as follows:

	£'000	£'000
Accounting profit (= reported profit)		800
Add depreciation	260	
Interest payable	90	
Entertaining	40	390
		1,190
Less capital allowances	440	
Interest paid	70	510
Taxable profit		680

Assuming a corporation tax rate of 35%, corporation tax payable amounts to 35% of £680,000 ie £238,000.

(b) Timing differences and permanent differences

The difference between the two profit figures can be analysed between timing differences and permanent differences.

Timing differences reflect the fact that some items are recorded in different periods for tax as opposed to accounts purposes.

For example:

(1) Interest payable is treated for accounts purposes on an accruals basis. For tax purposes, interest payable is dealt with on a purely cash basis.
(2) Depreciation charges are allocated over accounting periods over the asset's useful life on an accruals basis. For tax purposes, the Inland Revenue allow capital allowances rather than depreciation. Again, the difference is one of timing.

Permanent differences are usually items which are reflected in the accounts but which are totally disregarded for tax purposes. For example, entertaining expenditure relating to UK customers is charged in the accounts but is never ever allowed for tax purposes.

Deferred tax is concerned with timing differences. Permanent differences are outside the scope of deferred tax.

Illustration 14

In the above illustration, accounting and taxable profit figures may be reconciled as follows:

	£'000	£'000
Accounting profit		800
Timing differences:		
Depreciation (440 – 260)	180	
Interest (90 – 70)	(20)	(160)
		640
Permanent differences:		
Entertaining		40
Taxable profit		680

(c) Examples of timing and permanent differences

(1) *Timing differences: short-term*

(i) Interest payable.
(ii) Interest receivable.
(iii) Royalties payable.

(iv) General bad debt provisions – not allowed for tax purposes until they become specific.
(v) Pension costs accrued.
(vi) Provisions for repairs and maintenance.

(2) *Timing differences: other*

(i)   Capital allowances/depreciation.
(ii) Revaluation surpluses reflected in the accounts but not taxable until the related fixed asset is disposed of.
(iii) Disposal of fixed assets where payment of tax is postponed as a result of roll-over relief.

(3) *Permanent differences*

(i)   Disallowable entertaining expenditure.
(ii) Depreciation on buildings which do not rank for tax allowances.
(iii) Disallowable fines.

(d) The full provision approach to deferred taxation

Under a previous standard (subsequently withdrawn), deferred tax had to be provided in full in company accounts irrespective of the circumstances of a company. Deferred tax was calculated by applying the corporation tax rate applicable to the company to the timing differences. The calculation is illustrated below, using for simplicity a company with a single fixed asset.

Illustration 15

A company acquired a fixed asset on 1.1.X1 at a cost of £80,000. The company's depreciation policy is to depreciate over ten years on a straight-line basis, ignoring residual value. The profit after depreciation is £100,000 in each of the years 19X1 to 19X5. Assume the corporation tax rate is 30% and 25% writing-down allowances are available for tax purposes. No first year allowances are available.
   Required: show the relevant extracts for both profit and loss account and balance sheet assuming deferred tax is provided in full on all timing differences.

(1) Calculations

(i) *Deferred tax*	*(1)* *Accounts NBV* £	*(2)* *Tax WDV* £	*Deferred tax account (1) – (2) times 30%* £
Cost of asset 19X1	80,000	80,000	0
Depreciation (Dep)/writing-down allowance (WDA) 19X1	8,000	20,000	3,600
A/cs NBV/tax WDV 31.12.X1	72,000	60,000	3,600
Dep/WDA 19X2	8,000	15,000	2,100
A/cs NBV/Tax WDV 31.12.X2	64,000	45,000	5,700
Dep/WDA 19X3	8,000	11,250	975
A/cs NBV/tax WDV 31.12.X3	56,000	33,750	6,675
Dep/WDA 19X4	8,000	8,437	131
A/cs NBV/tax WDV 31.12.X4	48,000	25,313	6,806
Dep/WDV 19X5	8,000	6,328	(502)
A/cs NBV/tax WDV 31.12.X5	40,000	18,985	6,304

(ii) Corporation tax

	19X1 £	19X2 £	19X3 £	19X4 £	19X5 £
Accounting profit	100,000	100,000	100,000	100,000	100,000
Add depreciation	8,000	8,000	8,000	8,000	8,000
Less capital allowances	(20,000)	(15,000)	(11,250)	(8,437)	(6,328)
Taxable profit	88,000	93,000	96,750	99,563	101,672
Corporation tax at 30%	26,400	27,900	29,025	29,869	30,502

(2) Extracts from financial statements

(i) Profit and loss account

	19X1 £	19X2 £	19X3 £	19X4 £	19X5 £
Profit on ordinary activities before tax	100,000	100,000	100,000	100,000	100,000
Taxation:					
Corporation tax	26,400	27,900	29,025	29,869	30,502
Deferred tax	3,600	2,100	975	131	(502)
	30,000	30,000	30,000	30,000	30,000
Total tax charge as percentage of accounting profit	30%	30%	30%	30%	30%

COMMENT

Assuming no permanent differences, if deferred tax is provided in full, irrespective of the circumstances of the company, then the tax charge bears a relationship to reported profit.

(ii) Balance sheet

	19X1 £	19X2 £	19X3 £	19X4 £
Creditors – amounts falling due within one year:				
Corporation tax	26,400	27,900	29,025	29,869
Provisions for liabilities and charges:				
Deferred tax	3,600	5,700	6,675	6,806

Illustration 16

A company's only short-term timing differences relate to interest receivable. Relevant details are as follows:

	19X2 £	19X3 £	19X4 £	19X5 £
Debtors – interest receivable at 31 December	10,000	12,000	8,000	8,000
Profit before interest	50,000	50,000	50,000	50,000
Investment income	10,000	30,000	40,000	42,000
Cash received	Nil	28,000	44,000	42,000
Corporation tax rate	30%	30%	30%	30%
Taxable income	50,000	78,000	94,000	92,000
Corporation tax	15,000	23,400	28,200	27,600

Required: relevant extracts from financial statements.

Calculation of deferred tax

	£ Timing differences	£ Deferred tax (= timing differences ×30%)
Interest debtor at 31.12.X1	Nil	Nil
19X2		
Excess of income in P/L over cash received	10,000	3,000
Interest debtor at 31.12.X2	10,000	3,000
19X3		
Excess of income over cash	2,000	600
Interest debtor at 31.12.X3	12,000	3,600
19X4		
Excess of cash over income	(4,000)	(1,200)
Interest debtor at 31.12.X4	8,000	2,400
19X5		
Excess of income over cash	–	–
Interest debtor at 31.12.X5	8,000	2,400

Extracts from financial statements

(i) Profit and loss account

	19X2 £	19X3 £	19X4 £	19X5 £
Operating profit	50,000	50,000	50,000	50,000
Investment income	10,000	30,000	40,000	42,000
Profit on ordinary activities before tax	60,000	80,000	90,000	92,000
Taxation:				
Corporation tax	15,000	23,400	28,200	27,600
Deferred tax	3,000	600	(1,200)	–
	18,000	24,000	27,000	27,600
Total tax charge as percentage of accounting profit	30%	30%	30%	30%

(e) The need for deferred tax

For many years, most accountants have recognised the need for deferred tax even if they have not agreed upon the basis on which it should be computed.

Two principal reasons have been given to underline the importance of deferred tax:

(1) The fact that profit after tax is regarded as an important indicator of performance. This figure enters into the earnings per share calculation for listed companies, from which is computed the price/earnings ratio.
(2) The importance from the balance sheet viewpoint of the relationship between shareholders' funds and other sources of funds.

The implications of these two points are considered below under discussion of the possible approaches to deferred tax.

(f) Criticisms of the full provision approach

The full provision approach is sometimes referred to as the full deferral approach or comprehensive tax allocation approach. This approach was at one time mandatory for all companies under the requirements of the subsequently withdrawn standard SSAP 11.

The full provision approach considers individual timing differences relating to individual fixed assets, specific loans receivable, and so on. For example, referring back to the two illustrations in section (d):

(1) As regards the fixed asset purchase in 19X1, an originating timing difference of £12,000 (ie £20,000 less £8,000) comes about in 19X1. A further originating timing difference of £7,000 (ie £15,000 less £8,000) occurs in 19X2. These timing differences will not reverse until those subsequent years such as 19X5 where depreciations exceed capital allowances.

   The reversal of these timing differences will result in a taxable income in excess of reported income, thus giving rise to larger than might be expected corporation tax liabilities in such years. The build-up of the deferred tax liability over the years 19X1 to 19X4 is then in anticipation of these liabilities.

(2) As regards loan interest receivable, the interest is recognised for accounts (reporting) purposes in the year of accrual, but not taxed until the subsequent year of receipt. The deferred tax liability is a provision for the tax that will eventually become assessable.

Why did the full deferral approach become subject to widespread criticism and eventually be replaced by an alternative approach? In order to appreciate the reasons, it is necessary to go back to years of 100% first year allowances and stock appreciation relief. Many companies investing in plant and machinery and stocks found that they were paying little or no corporation tax. This was not just a question of isolated years, but an annual occurrence. Effectively, any depreciation in the tax computation was more than out-weighed by capital allowances and stock relief.

In theory, if individual fixed assets were considered, then individual timing differences could be regarded as eventually reversing. In practice, if the company was looked at as a going concern, the directors of the company could often provide reasonable grounds to show that for the foreseeable future the aggregate of capital allowances each year would exceed the total depreciation charge for that year. In situations such as these, full deferral could be said to have two particular unfortunate consequences.

(i) As regards the tax charge in the profit and loss account, the effect of debiting deferred tax each year and adding this to corporation tax was to create an artificially high tax charge which had little meaning. This total charge was said to distort earnings per share, and possibly to counteract some of the fiscal aims of accelerated capital allowances.

(ii) As regards the deferred tax provision in the balance sheet, full deferral combined with a recurring annual situation of capital allowances in excess of depreciation resulted in an ever-increasing deferred tax balance. Such a liability was regarded by many accountants as fictitious and remote, possibly only ever becoming payable if the company went into liquidation. Users of financial statements might misunderstand the nature and effect of a deferred tax provision.

(g) Alternative approaches to deferred taxation

Two alternatives to full deferral have been advocated:

(1) Partial deferral – the approach in SSAP 15 and regarded as consistent with the Companies Act 1985. This approach is discussed in detail in section (h) below.

(2) Flow-through approach whereby the total tax charge in the profit and loss account is based on the estimated corporation tax assessment for the year in question. Deferred tax is effectively ignored. The main argument in favour of the flow-through approach is that it removes the need

for subjective judgement (which is an important aspect of partial deferral) and the possible calculation of unrealistic charges and provisions.

However, in some instances, the use of the flow-through approach could result in an imprudent approach to taxation. For example, a year in which substantial tax allowances were received might give an over-optimistic impression, only to be followed by a year of high tax charge. Such fluctuations would not assist users of accounts.

The flow-through approach was rejected by the Accounting Standards Committee and is incompatible with the requirements of the Companies Act 1985. The Companies Act 1985 requires provision to be made for amounts retained as reasonably necessary for the purpose of providing for any liability which is either likely to be incurred or certain to be incurred, but uncertain as to amount or date of payment.

(h) Partial deferral

Under the partial deferral approach, provision is made for the tax effects of all timing differences expected to arise within the foreseeable future. Under the partial deferral approach, timing differences are considered on an overall rather than individual basis.

Illustration 17

The following information relates to Redbank plc. The only timing differences relate to capital allowances/depreciation.

(1) Historical information

Year	Capital allowances £m	Depreciation £m	Excess of capital allowances over depreciation £m
19X0	40	30	10
19X1	48	41	7
19X2	52	43	9
19X3	57	45	12

(2) Projections at balance sheet date (31.12.X3)

19X4	56	46	10
19X5	55	48	7
19X6	59	50	9

Assume, that at 31.12.X3, the excess of accounts net book value of the fixed assets over the tax written down value amounted to £110 million and that the relevant corporation tax rate is 35%.

When timing differences are considered in aggregate, it appears that looking ahead three years (19X4, 19X5, 19X6) no reversal of timing differences is anticipated (since there is no expectation in any year that depreciation will exceed capital allowances).

Under the partial deferral approach, *no* deferred tax provision would be required. The total potential deferred tax of £38.5 million (i e 35% × 110) would be dealt with as follows:

	£m
(a) provided in the balance sheet	Nil
(b) unprovided (referred to in a memorandum note)	38.5
Total:	38.5

Illustration 18

Waterhead plc has always adopted the partial deferral approach to deferred taxation. However, in previous years, it has always been able to demonstrate that no provision is required for deferred tax.

The company is presently drafting its financial statements for the year ended 31 December 19X2. The projections for the next three years are as follows:

Year	Capital allowances £m	Depreciation £m	Capital allowances less depreciation £m
19X3	62	50	12
19X4	60	70	(10)
19X5	58	65	(7)

Should a deferred tax provision be set up in the balance sheet at 31 December 19X2? The main problem is that the company can foresee an overall reversal in timing differences in 19X4. In the 19X4 tax computation, it is predicted that taxable income will exceed accounting income by £10m thus giving rise to a correspondingly larger payment of corporation tax. The question is should the company pick up the liability in 19X4 (flow-through approach), or set up a provision as soon as the need is foreseen? Under the Companies Act 1985, a provision is required for a liability which is likely to be incurred.

In order to determine whether a provision should be set up at 31.12.X2 (as opposed to waiting until, say, 31.12.X3), it is recommended that the following table is set up. Corporation tax is taken as 35%.

Projections at 31.12.X2

Year	Capital allowances £m	Depreciation £m	Originating (reversing) timing differences £m	Cumulative originating (reversing) timing differences £m
19X3	62	50	12	12
19X4	60	70	(10)	2
19X5	58	65	(7)	(5) ←

The final column is the cumulative total of column 3. A maximum cumulative reversal of £5 million can be foreseen. A deferred tax provision should therefore be set up in the balance sheet. The amount required is 35% × £5m ie £1.75m. Since the provision at the beginning of the year is nil, a charge should be made to profit and loss account of £1.75m. At the subsequent balance sheet date, a similar exercise should be repeated. Assume this shows the following and that no revision is made for the 19X5 and 19X6 projections.

Projections at 31.12.X3

Year	Capital allowances £m	Depreciation £m	Originating (reversing) timing differences £m	Cumulative originating (reversing) timing differences £m
19X4	60	70	(10)	(10)
19X5	58	65	(7)	(17) ←
19X6	85	70	15	(2)

The maximum cumulative reversal which can be foreseen is £17m. A deferred tax provision at 31.12.X3 of 35% × £17m ie £5.95m is required.

A deferred tax charge of (5.95 less 1.75) ie 4.20 should be made in the profit and loss account.

Projections at 31.12.X4

Year	Capital allowances £m	Depreciation £m	Originating (reversing) timing differences £m	Cumulative originating (reversing) timing differences £m
19X5	58	65	(7)	(7) ←
19X6	85	70	15	8
19X7	82	73	9	17

Deferred tax provision required at 31.12.X4 is 35% × £7m i e £2.45m.
  Credit to profit and loss account in respect of deferred tax (5.95 less 2.45) i e £3.50m.

Projections at 31.12.X5

No reversals are foreseen, so no provision is required. The opening provision of £2.45m is no longer required and so may be credited to profit and loss account.

Summary of effect on financial statements

	19X1 £m	19X2 £m	19X3 £m	19X4 £m	19X5 £m
Balance sheet (31 Dec)					
Provision for deferred tax	Nil	1.75	5.95	2.45	Nil
Profit and loss account (tax charge)					
Corporation tax	X	X	X	X	X
Deferred tax	Nil	1.75	4.20	(3.5)	(2.45)
Total tax charge	X	X	X	X	X

At each balance sheet date a memorandum note would be required stating any unprovided deferred tax. This would be calculated as follows:

	£m
Total potential deferred tax	
35% (acs NBV − tax WDV)	X
less deferred tax provision (as calculated above)	X
∴ unprovided deferred tax (i e calculated as a balancing figure)	X

Comments
(1) The deferred tax balance is built up to £5.95m by 31.12.X3. In 19X4, the net add back in the tax computation is £10m i e a substantial corporation tax payment will become due nine months after the end of the year (30 September 19X5). The deferred tax provision is the amount retained to provide for the 19X4 and 19X5 liabilities.
(2) Had no deferred tax provision been established prior to 19X4, the tax charge for 19X4 would have been substantial. The effect of deferred tax is to achieve a total tax charge in 19X4 equivalent to approximately 35% of the reported accounting profit.

(i) The three approaches – an overview

The three approaches may be compared as follows:

	Full deferral approach	*Partial deferral approach*	*Flow-through approach*
ED/SSAP	ED 11/SSAP 11	ED 19/SSAP 15/ ED 33/SSAP 15 revised	N/A
Objective or subjective	Objective	Subjective	Objective
Acceptability (SSAPs, Companies Act 1985)	Unacceptable – unrealistic tax charge and liability	Acceptable – although dependent on subjective estimates, approach is generally regarded as realistic	Unacceptable – approach is imprudent and incompatible with Companies Act 1985

Note: all statements other than SSAP 15 revised have now been withdrawn. However, the Accounting Standards Board is presently reviewing the treatment of deferred tax.

(j) Principal requirements of SSAP 15 (Accounting for deferred taxation)

These requirements may be divided into two parts: accounting requirements and disclosure requirements.

(1) *Accounting requirements*

(i) *Approach*
SSAP 15 requires a partial deferred approach. Both full deferral and flow-through approaches are rejected. Deferred tax should be accounted for to the extent that it is probable that a liability or asset will crystallise. Undue prudence is discouraged in that SSAP 15 specifies that deferred tax should not be accounted for to the extent that it is probable that a liability or asset will not crystallise. The basis of calculation was covered in Illustration 18.

(ii) *Method*
Deferred tax should be computed under the liability method (see (k) below). The deferral method is thus unacceptable.

More detailed accounting requirements are referred under the relevant headings below.

(2) *Disclosure requirements*

(i) *Profit and loss account – disclosure:*

—deferred tax component of total tax charge on profit on ordinary activities;
—deferred tax relating to extraordinary items;
—unprovided deferred tax in a memorandum note analysing the amount into its major components;
—adjustments to deferred tax account. If they result from changes in tax rates they should form part of the total tax charge on profit on ordinary activities (separately disclosed if material). If the adjustments result from changes in the basis of tax or government fiscal policy they should be treated as extraordinary items.

(ii) *Balance sheet – disclosure:*
—deferred tax provided in B/S analysed into its major components;
—unprovided (ie memorandum only) deferred tax analysed into its major components;
—transfers to/from deferred tax account.

Illustration 19

Beckmire plc has summarised the following information relating to taxation matters:

(1) Deferred tax is provided for all timing differences on a partial deferral basis. At the present time, the only material timing differences relate to capital allowances and depreciation.
(2) The deferred tax balance at 1.1.X6 amounted to £875,200. During the year ended 31.12.X6, a transfer of £132,000 relating to the excess of capital allowances over depreciation is to be made to deferred tax account.
(3) At 31.12.X6, the excess of accounts net book value over tax written-down value amounts to £4,200,000. Corporation tax is 35%.
(4) Corporation tax on the profits for the year is estimated at £596,000.
(5) The total tax charge (corporation tax and deferred tax) has been reduced by £173,000 as a result of capital allowances.
(6) No dividends were paid during the year. A dividend amounting to £140,000 is proposed. ACT is to be taken as $\frac{3}{7}$.

Required: extracts from financial statements for the year ended 31 December 19X6.

Balance sheet extracts

Creditors: amounts falling due within one year

	£
Proposed dividends	140,000
Tax and social security	656,000

(Workings: £596,000 + $\frac{3}{7}$ × £140,000 = £656,000)

Provision for liabilities and charges

	£
Deferred taxation	947,200

(Workings: £875,200 + £132,000 − $\frac{3}{7}$ × £140,000 = £947,200)

Profit and loss account extracts

Tax on profit on ordinary activities:	£
Corporation tax	596,000
Deferred tax	132,000
	728,000

Note: the tax charge has been reduced by £173,000 as a result of capital allowances.

Notes to the accounts:
(1) *Accounting policy note*
   Provision is made for deferred taxation using the liability method on all timing differences except to the extent that these amounts are not regarded as likely to become payable in the foreseeable future.
(2) *Deferred tax*

	£
Balance at 1.1.19X6	875,200
Transfer during the year	132,000
	1,007,200
ACT on proposed dividends	60,000
	947,200

	Provided £	Unprovided £
Capital allowances	1,007,200	462,800
Other timing differences	X	X
	1,007,200	462,800
Advance corporation tax recoverable	60,000	
	947,200	

Working

Total potential deferred tax	
35% × £4,200,000	1,470,000
Provided in the accounts	1,007,200
∴ Unprovided	462,800

(k) Methods of computing deferred tax balances

In theory two methods of computing deferred tax balances are available. Where corporation tax rates fluctuate over a period of years, these two methods will give different results.

(i)   The liability method – whereby the deferred tax balance is revised to take account of changes in the rate of corporation tax. This is the method which is compatible with the overall requirements of the Companies Act 1985. The advantage of this approach is that deferred tax balances in the balance sheet represent the best estimates of amounts which would be payable or receivable if the particular timing differences reversed. Any adjustments to deferred tax as a result of tax rate changes should be treated as part of the tax charge or credit in the profit and loss account.

As stated above, this is the method required by SSAP 15.

(ii) The deferral method – whereby the tax effects of timing differences are calculated using tax rates applicable when the timing differences arise. No adjustment to deferred tax balance is made as a result of subsequent changes in the rate of corporation tax. This approach regards the deferred tax balance as a deferred charge or credit rather than an asset or liability. This appears to be inconsistent with the requirements of the Companies Act 1985 and is not accepted under SSAP 15.

Illustration 20

A company acquired an asset on 1 January 19X2 at a cost of £50,000. The company's depreciation policy is to depreciate on a straight-line basis over ten years. The asset ranks for a writing-down allowance (WDA) of 25% but no first year allowance. Assume that deferred tax is provided in full, and the corporation tax rate is 35% in 19X2, 33% in 19X3 and 34% in 19X4. Calculate the relevant amounts for the deferred tax under the two approaches for the years 19X2, 19X3 and 19X4.

Depreciation and WDA calculations

	Accounts NBV £	Tax WDV £
Cost of asset 19X2	50,000	50,000
Depreciation/WDA 19X2	5,000	12,500
NBV/WDV 31.12.X2	45,000	37,500
Depreciation/WDA 19X3	5,000	9,375
NBV/WDV 31.12.X3	40,000	28,125
Depreciation/WDV 19X4	5,000	7,031
NBV/WDV 31.12.X4	35,000	21,094

Deferred tax calculations

	Deferred tax account			
	Liability method		Deferral method	
	£	£	£	£
Balance 1.1.X2		0		0
P/L 19X2				
35% (12,500 – 5,000)		2,625		2,625
Balance 31.12.X2		2,625		2,625
P/L 19X3				
35% (9,375 – 5,000)	1,531		1,531	
Tax rate adjustment				
(21,875 – 10,000) × 2%	(237)		–	
		1,294		1,531
Balance 31.12.X3		3,919		4,156
P/L 19X4				
35% (7,031 – 5,000)	711		711	
Tax rate adjustment				
1% × 11,875 = 119				
1% × 2,031 = (20)	99			
		810		711
Balance 31.12.X4		4,729		4,867

Note: In any subsequent year where timing differences reversed, under the deferral method, deferred credits to profit and loss account would be evaluated at 35%.

(l) Assessing the amount to be provided

The assessment should be based on reasonable assumptions. These should take account of:

(1) post balance sheet events and management intentions;
(2) financial plans and projections – usually covering a three to five year period;
(3) prudence – a prudent view should be taken when financial plans or projections are susceptible to a high degree of uncertainty or are not fully developed for the appropriate period. (Note reference to prudence concept.)

(m) Separate consideration of deferred tax assets and deferred tax liabilities

The standard requires separate consideration of assets and liabilities. The procedures may be summarised as follows:

(1) Assess deferred tax liabilities. In determining the amount to be provided, short-term and other timing differences should be considered together.
(2) Consider each deferred tax asset category separately in order to determine whether an asset will crystallise. The standard is not specific on this matter but deferred tax assets could include the tax effects of losses, interest payable, provisions for repairs and maintenance etc. Such assets should only be regarded as crystallising if they are expected to be recoverable without replacement by equivalent debit balances.
(3) Those deferred tax liabilities required to be recognised in the accounts should be reduced by any deferred tax debit balances arising from any separate categories of timing differences and any advance corporation tax available for offset against those liabilities.

Illustration 21

Woodvale plc is preparing its accounts for the year ended 31 December 19X6. The following information is available regarding deferred tax.

(i)   *Capital allowances*
      At 31.12.X6 the accounts net book value of fixed assets exceeds the tax written down value by £170,000. Projections at 31.12.X6 show the following position:

	Capital allowances £'000	Depreciation £'000	Timing differences £'000
19X7	120	100	20
19X8	140	110	30
19X9	70	130	(60)
19X10	125	110	15

(ii) *Interest receivable*
      At 31.12.X6, the relevant total of interest receivable in the balance sheet is £80,000. The loan to which this relates falls due for repayment in 19X7. No further investment by Woodvale is anticipated.

(iii) *Interest payable*
      Woodvale took out a loan some years ago repayable in 19X35. The interest payable amounted at 31.12.X6 to £60,000. No further loans are foreseen within the next five to seven years.
(iv) The balance sheet at 31.12.X6 included a provision for repairs and maintenance amounting to £40,000. The expenditure is expected to be incurred during 19X7.

Required

The deferred tax to be provided at 31.12.X6 assuming the rate of corporation tax is 35%. The memorandum amount of unprovided deferred tax should also be shown.

Solution

(1) Deferred tax liabilities – taking all categories of timing differences together.

	Capital allowances £'000	Interest receivable £'000	Originating (reversing) £'000	Cumulative £'000
19X7	20	(80)	(60)	(60)
19X8	30	–	30	(30)
19X9	(60)	–	(60)	(90)
19X10	15	–	15	(75)

Maximum cumulative reversal foreseen is £90,000

∴ provision required is 35% × £90,000   –   £31,500

Capital allowances 35% × £10,000	=	3,500
Interest receivable 35% × £80,000	=	28,000
		31,500

Memo note – unprovided deferred tax
Capital allowances

Total potential 35% × 170,000	59,500
Provided (above)	3,500
Unprovided	56,000
Interest receivable unprovided	Nil

(2) Deferred tax assets:

£

  (i) *interest payable*
      –unprovided note
      35% × £60,000 =   21,000
  (ii) *provision for repairs*
      –provided 35% × £40,000 =   14,000
      –unprovided   Nil

Summary of disclosures – balance sheet

	Provided £'000	Unprovided £'000
Capital allowances	3,500	56,000
Short-term timing differences		
–liabilities	28,000	Nil
–assets	(14,000)	(21,000)
	17,500	35,000

(n) Deferred tax debit balances

(1) Deferred tax net debit balances – should not be carried forward as assets except to the extent that they are expected to be recoverable without replacement by equivalent debit balances.

(2) Deferred tax debit balances relating to advance corporation tax on dividends.

   (i) ACT on dividends payable or proposed – carry forward as assets provided that such ACT can be foreseen to be recoverable against tax on profits of the following year.

   (ii) ACT on dividends other than those payable or proposed at the year end – write off to P/L unless its recovery is assured beyond reasonable doubt.

(o) ASB's amendment to SSAP 15

The ASB's amendment to SSAP 15 allows deferred tax in respect of pensions and other post-retirement benefits to be considered separately from other timing differences.

Deferred tax in respect of post-retirement benefits may be dealt with either on:

(1) the full provision basis; or
(2) the partial provision basis.

19.3   PRESENTATION IN FINANCIAL STATEMENTS

(a) Introduction

Disclosure requirements for tax are set out in:

SSAP 8 (The treatment of taxation under the imputation system in the accounts of companies).
SSAP 15 (Accounting for deferred taxation).
Companies Act 1985 (Fourth Schedule).

The overall effect of these requirements is summarised below.

(b) Profit and loss account

P/L item	*Comments*
Income from fixed asset investments.	(1) Dividends to be included gross i e cash received plus tax credit.
	(2) Interest to be included gross of income tax.
Tax on profit on ordinary activities.	Disclose separately:

	(1) UK corporation tax:
	  (i) corporation tax;
	  (ii) deferred tax;
	  (iii) tax attributable to franked investment income (tax credits);
	  (iv) irrecoverable ACT;
	  (v) relief for overseas taxation.

	(2) Total overseas tax:
	  (i) relieved and unrelieved;
	  (ii) specify the part of unrelieved tax arising from payment of dividends.

	(3) Latest known rate of corporation tax.
Tax on extraordinary profit or loss.	
Dividends paid/proposed.	State at cash paid/payable to shareholders – do not include related ACT.

(c) Balance sheet

B/S item	Comments
Debtors ACT recoverable. Deferred tax.	} Indicate any part not recoverable within 12 months of balance sheet date.
Creditors: amounts falling due within one year	
Other creditors including tax and social security.	(1) Disclose tax and social security total separately. (2) This will include ACT, MCT, PAYE, NI, VAT.
Proposed dividends.	State cash paid/payable to shareholders – do not include related ACT.
Creditors: amounts falling due after more than one year	
Other creditors including tax and social security.	(1) Disclose tax and social security separately. (2) This will include MCT if payable in more than 12 months' time. (3) Disclose payment date.
Provisions for liabilities and charges Taxation, including deferred taxation.	Will usually relate to deferred tax only.
Capital and reserves Revaluation reserve.	Disclose deferred tax relating to movements on reserve.

(d) Other disclosure requirements

(1) Accounting policies statement.
(2) Particulars of special circumstances affecting the tax liability.
(3) Extent to which the tax charge for the period has been reduced by capital allowances and other timing differences.
(4) Where fixed asset valuation is disclosed by way of note, indicate tax implications if asset were to be realised at the balance sheet date at the valuation amount.

Illustration 22

Extract from annual report and accounts of Cowie Group plc for the year ended 31 December 1994.

Accounting policies (extract)

Deferred taxation
Provision is made on a liability basis for tax deferred by timing differences to the extent that there is reasonable probability that the tax deferral will crystallise in the foreseeable future.

5 Taxation

	1994 £000	1993 £000
Tax on profit on ordinary activities comprises the following:		
Corporation tax at 33%	**8,970**	7,583
Deferred taxation *note 19*	**1,594**	1,913
Tax on franked investment income	**51**	76
	10,615	9,572

Taxation on the exceptional items was £nil (1993: £nil) and was reduced to £nil by the utilisation of rollover relief.

19 Provisions for liabilities and charges

	The Group		The Company	
	1994 £000	1993 £000	1994 £000	1993 £000
Provisions for liabilities and charges, which represents deferred taxation only, is made up as follows:				
Provided in the accounts;				
Accelerated capital allowances	**5,551**	4,134	**–**	1,134
Short term timing differences	**1,664**	1,487	**1,468**	1,160
	7,215	5,621	**1,468**	2,294

The potential liability to deferred taxation not provided in the accounts, calculated at the rate of tax in force at the end of the year is as follows:

Accelerated capital allowances	**16,270**	11,658	**436**	2,826
Potential corporation tax in respect of revaluation surplus on properties and capital gains rolled over	**3,868**	3,498	**2,552**	2,418
	20,138	15,156	**2,988**	5,244

	The Group £000	The Company £000
The movement in deferred taxation is as follows:		
At 1 January 1994	5,621	2,294
Transfer from Profit and Loss Account	1,594	25
Transferred to Group undertaking	–	(851)
At 31 December 1994	7,215	1,468

19.4 ACCOUNTING FOR GOVERNMENT GRANTS

(a) Introduction

The original version of SSAP 4 was issued in April 1974. In July 1990, a revised version was issued in order to take account of Companies Act changes as well as changes in government assistance and grants.

(b) Scope

SSAP 4 covers all forms of government grants and assistance, including those from central government, local government and the European Community.

(c) Basic principles

Grants should be recognised in the profit and loss account so as to match them with the expenditure towards which they are intended to contribute.

Grants should not be brought into the accounts until conditions for receipt of the grants have been complied with and there is reasonable assurance that the grant will be received.

(d) Capital-based grants

Grants that are made as a contribution towards expenditure on fixed assets should be recognised over the expected useful lives of the related assets. Such grants should be accounted for by the deferred credit method and should not be netted off against the cost of the asset concerned (see section 9.5).

(e) Grants for achievement of non-financial objectives

An example would be a grant given on condition that jobs are created and maintained for a minimum period. Such a grant should be matched with the costs of providing jobs for that period.

(f) Liability to repay grants

Potential liabilities to repay grants in specified circumstances should only be provided for to the extent that repayment is probable.

(g) Disclosures

The following disclosures are required:

(1) the accounting policy adopted for government grants;
(2) the effects of government grants on the results for the period and/or the financial position of the enterprise;
(3) where the results of the period are affected materially by the receipt of forms of government assistance other than grants, the nature of that assistance and, to the extent that the effects on the financial statements can be measured, an estimate of those effects.

19.5   SSAP 5 (ACCOUNTING FOR VALUE ADDED TAX)

Value added tax (VAT) is a tax on the final consumer and, therefore, the trader is normally merely acting as a collector on behalf of the Inland Revenue. Amounts due to and from the Inland Revenue will be included in creditors and debtors, and need not be disclosed separately.

Turnover shown in the profit and loss account should exclude VAT.

Irrecoverable VAT attributable to fixed assets should be treated as part of their cost. Capital commitments should also include irrecoverable VAT.

Irrecoverable VAT should be included in costs eg where the trader suffers VAT on his inputs but is exempted, either in whole or in part, on his outputs.

20 ACCOUNTING FOR PENSION COSTS

Key Issues

* Companies Act 1985 disclosures
* Funding approaches
* Defined contribution and defined benefit schemes
* Scope of SSAP 24
* Actuarial methods and assumptions
* Accounting and funding
* Accounting objectives
* Variations from regular costs
* Special situations
* SSAP 24 disclosures

20.1 BACKGROUND

The subject of accounting for pension costs has been under consideration for many years. Various discussion papers have been issued. Two exposure drafts (ED 32 and ED 39) were issued prior to the publication in May 1988 of SSAP 24, Accounting for pension costs.

20.2 COMPANIES ACT 1985 IMPLICATIONS

Disclosure is required of:

(a) The amount of 'other pension costs so incurred' which forms part of the total of staff costs. Pension costs is defined as including:

  (1) contributions paid by the company to a pension fund or insurance company;
  (2) amounts set aside to a provision for employee benefits;
  (3) any amounts paid by the company in respect of pension payments without being set aside as under (2).

  Note that 'staff' includes directors provided that they are employed under contracts of employment.

(b) Pension commitments:

  (1) any pension commitments included under any provision shown in the company's balance sheet; and
  (2) any such commitment for which no provision has been made.

  Note that particulars are also required of commitments relating to pensions payable to past directors of the company.

20.3 FUNDING OF PENSION ARRANGEMENTS

Some of the main possibilities may be illustrated diagrammatically as follows:

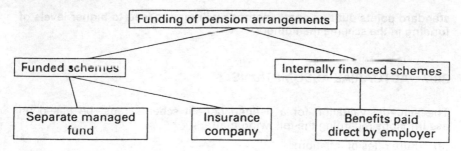

20.4 MAIN TYPES OF CONTRACTUAL SCHEMES

Two main groups of such schemes include defined contribution schemes and defined benefit schemes. Particular aspects of each may be contrasted as follows:

Aspect	Defined contribution schemes	Defined benefit schemes
(a) Benefit to employee?	Depends on funds available and performance of investments	May depend on employee's final pay prior to retirement
(b) Cost to employer?	Contributions payable in period (cost is easily measured)	Commitment is open-ended, final cost is often subject to considerable uncertainty
(c) Actuarial assumptions?	Not required	Crucial to calculation of pension costs in P/L ac
(d) Disclosures in annual accounts?	Relatively few	Extensive

20.5 SCOPE OF SSAP 24

SSAP 24 deals with accounting and disclosure of pension costs and commitments in the financial statements of enterprises that have pension arrangements for the provision of retirement benefits for their employees.

SSAP 24 applies where the employer has a legal or contractual commitment under a pension scheme or one implicit in the employer's actions, to provide or contribute to pensions for his employees.

SSAP 24 also deals with discretionary and ex gratia increases in pensions and ex gratia pensions.

The principles of SSAP 24 apply whether the scheme is funded or unfunded.

20.6 ACTUARIAL VALUATION METHODS

There are a number of actuarial methods available for determining the level of contributions needed to meet the liabilities of the pension scheme. The standard points out that some methods will tend to lead to higher levels of funding in the scheme than others.

20.7   ACTUARIAL ASSUMPTIONS

The actuarial valuation for a defined benefit scheme must be based on assumptions regarding the following matters:

(a) future rates of inflation;
(b) future pay increases;
(c) increases to pensions in payment;
(d) earnings on investments;
(e) numbers of employees joining the scheme;
(f) probability that employees will die or leave before they reach retiring age.

20.8   ACCOUNTING AND FUNDING CONTRASTED

Accounting is concerned with the allocation of the estimated total pension costs to the profit and loss accounts of particular periods. Funding is concerned with financial management and the availability of cash.

The funding amount may not always provide a satisfactory basis for determining the pension charge in the accounts. For example, three identical companies may have identical pension fund deficiencies following an actuarial valuation. Company A may increase the future outgoing contributions, company B may make a single lump sum payment while company C may spread the additional contribution over three years.

20.9   ACCOUNTING OBJECTIVES

(a) General objectives

To charge the cost of pensions against profits on a systematic basis over the service lives of employees in the scheme. This objective may be satisfied by different actuarial methods with different sets of assumptions.

(b) Specific objectives

(1) Defined contribution schemes – profit and loss account should be charged with contributions payable in respect of the period.
(2) Defined benefit schemes – the charge to the profit and loss account should consist of the following two elements:

  (i) regular cost (which provides a substantially level percentage of current and expected future pensionable payroll in the light of current actuarial assumptions);
  (ii) variations from regular costs to be charged over the expected average remaining service lives of employees.

(c) Balance sheet implications

Where the cumulative pensions cost charged to the profit and loss account differs from cumulative payments to date, the difference should be treated as a net pension liability or prepayment as appropriate.

20.10 VARIATIONS FROM REGULAR COSTS

These may arise in the following situations:

(a) experience surpluses or deficiencies;
(b) effects on actuarial value of accrued benefits of changes in assumptions or method;
(c) retroactive changes in benefits or conditions for membership;
(d) increases to pensions in payment or deferred pensions for which provision has not previously been made.

20.11 EXPERIENCE DEFICIENCY OR SURPLUS

(a) Definition

This is defined as the deficiency or surplus of the actuarial value of assets over the actuarial value of liabilities, on the basis of the valuation method used, which arises because events have not coincided with the actuarial assumptions made for the last valuation.

(b) Accounting

The surplus or deficiency should be spread over the expected average remaining service lives of employees (after allowing for future withdrawals). The standard allows a period representing the average remaining service lives to be used.

20.12 RETROACTIVE EFFECTS OF CHANGES IN ASSUMPTIONS OR METHOD

The effect of changes in assumptions should be accounted for in a similar way to an experience deficiency or surplus.

20.13 RETROACTIVE CHANGES IN BENEFITS OR CONDITIONS FOR MEMBERSHIP

Retroactive changes in benefits and membership are decided upon currently and it is not appropriate to charge any part of the costs arising from these decisions as a prior year adjustment. Past service costs should be written off over the average remaining service lives of employees.

20.14 INCREASES TO PENSIONS IN PAYMENT OR DEFERRED PENSIONS

Increases to pensions which are specified in the pension scheme rules or by law should be taken into account in the actuarial assumptions. The cost of such an increase should be charged over the remaining service lives of the employees.

20.15 SPREADING – METHOD AND PERIOD

SSAP 24 does not specify a particular method of spreading variations from regular costs. A straightforward approach is the straight-line method as illustrated in sections 20.20 and 20.21.

However, an alternative approach is suggested by SSAP 24 para 58, part 2 (definition of terms). This states:

... The average remaining service life is a weighted average of the expected future service of the current members of the scheme up to their normal retirement dates or expected dates of earlier withdrawal or death in service. The weighting can have regard to periods of service, salary levels of scheme members and future anticipated salary growth in a manner which the actuary considers appropriate having regard to the actuarial method and assumptions used.

Note that this offers but does not require an approach of a weighted rather than a simple average.

As regards period of spreading, this will be determined by the actuary. However, on the basis of evidence from published accounts, a period of between 10 and 15 years might be typical for many larger companies.

20.16 SPECIAL SITUATIONS

(a) Where a significant reduction in the number of employees covered by a pension scheme leads to a significant reduction in contributions in order to eliminate a surplus or deficiency:

    (1) if the reduction is part of a fundamental reorganisation, it should be treated as an exceptional item;

    (2) otherwise it should be accounted for as the variation in funding occurs.

(b) Prudence may require a material deficit to be recognised over a shorter period than the normal period. This should only apply where a major unanticipated event or transaction outside the normal scope of actuarial assumptions has occurred and it has necessitated significant additional contributions.

(c) Where the enterprise has taxed refunds from the scheme under the Finance Act 1986, there is a choice of accounting treatment between:

    (1) accounting for the refunds as they occur; or

    (2) spreading the refunds over the remaining service lives of members.

20.17 DISCLOSURE REQUIREMENTS – OVERRIDING PRINCIPLE

Sufficient information should be disclosed to give the user of the financial statements a broad understanding of the significance of the pension arrangements.

20.18 DISCLOSURES – DEFINED CONTRIBUTION SCHEMES

The following should be disclosed:

(a) nature of the scheme (ie defined contribution);
(b) accounting policy;
(c) pension cost charge for the period;
(d) any outstanding or prepaid contributions at the balance sheet date.

Illustration 1

The company operates a defined contribution pension scheme. The assets of the scheme are held separately from those of the company in an independently administered fund. The pension cost charge represents contributions payable by the company to the fund and amounted to £500,000 (19X4 £450,000). Contributions totalling £25,000 (19X4 £15,000) were payable to the fund at the year end and are included in creditors.

20.19 DISCLOSURES – DEFINED BENEFIT SCHEMES

The following should be disclosed:

(a) Nature of scheme (ie defined benefit).
(b) Whether scheme is funded or unfunded.
(c) Accounting policy (and if different, funding policy).
(d) Whether pension cost and liability (or asset) are assessed in accordance with advice of a professionally qualified actuary and if so disclose:

    (i) date of most recent formal actuarial valuation or later review used for this purpose;
    (ii) if the actuary is an employee or officer of the company or group – this fact should be disclosed.

(e) The pension cost charge for the period together with explanations of significant changes from the previous period.
(f) Provisions or prepayments (difference between costs recognised and funding amounts).
(g) Amount of deficiency on a current funding level basis. Indicate action, if any, being taken to deal with deficiency in the current and future financial statements.
(h) Outline of results of most recent formal actuarial valuation or later review of funding of scheme on an ongoing basis.

    Disclose:

    (i) actuarial method used and a brief description of the main actuarial assumptions;
    (ii) market value of scheme assets at the date of their valuation or review;
    (iii) level of funding expressed in percentage terms;
    (iv) comments on any material actuarial surplus or deficiency indicated by (iii) above.

(i) Expected effects on financial statements of commitments to make additional payments over a limited number of years.
(j) Accounting treatment of a refund (which is subject to deduction of tax) where a credit appears in the financial statements in relation to it.
(k) Details of expected effects on future costs of any material charges in the group's and/or company's arrangements.

Illustration 2 – small company

The company operates a pension scheme providing benefits based on final pensionable pay. The assets of the scheme are held separately from those of the company, being invested with insurance companies. Contributions to the scheme are charged to the profit and loss account so as to spread the cost of pensions over employees' working lives with the company. The contributions are determined by a qualified actuary on the basis of triennial valuations using the projected unit method. The most recent valuation was as at 31 December 19X4. The assumptions which have the most significant effect on the results of the valuation are those relating to the rate of return on investments and the rates of increase in salaries and pensions. It was assumed that the investment returns would be 9% per annum, that salary increases would average 7% per annum and that present and future pensions would increase at the rate of 4% per annum.

The pension charge for the period was £50,000 (19X4 £48,000). This included £5,200 (19X4 £5,000) in respect of the amortisation of experience surpluses that are being recognised over 10 years, the average remaining service lives of employees.

The most recent actuarial valuation showed that the market value of the scheme's assets was £1,200,000 and that the actuarial value of those assets represented 104% of the benefits that had accrued to members after allowing for expected future increases in earnings. The contributions of the company and the employees will remain at 11% and 5% of earnings respectively.

Illustration 3

Extract from annual report and accounts of Tesco plc for the year ended 25 February 1995.

Note 24 Pension commitments

The group operates a defined benefit pension scheme for full-time employees, the assets of which are held as a segregated fund, administered by trustees.

The pension cost relating to the scheme is assessed in accordance with the advice of an independent qualified actuary using the projected unit method. The latest actuarial assessment of this scheme was at 5 April 1993. The assumptions which have the most significant effects on the results of the valuation are those relating to the rate of return on investments and the rate of increase in salaries and pensions. It was assumed that the investment return would be 9% per annum with dividend growth of $4\frac{1}{2}$% per annum, that salary increases would average $6\frac{1}{2}$% per annum and that pensions would increase at the rate of 4% per annum.

At the date of the latest actuarial valuation, the market value of the scheme's assets was £480m and the actuarial value of these assets represented 111% of the benefits that had accrued to members, after allowing for expected future increases in earnings.

Benefit improvements to members have been agreed with the trustees which have resulted in an increased company cost. This increasing ongoing cost has been offset by the amortisation of the surplus as a level percentage of pay over nine years.

The pension cost of this scheme to the group was £29m (1994 – £28m).

The group also operates a defined contribution pension scheme for part-time employees which was introduced on 6 April 1988. The assets of the scheme are held separately from those of the group, being invested with an insurance company. The pension cost represents contributions payable by the group to the insurance company and amounted to £8m (1994 – £6m). There were no material amounts outstanding to the insurance company at the year end.

Following the European Court judgment in relation to part-time pension rights, the group is not expected to have any material liability in relation to part-time employees' pensions.

The group also operates defined contribution schemes in France. The contributions payable under these schemes of £1m (1994 – £1m) have been fully expensed against profits in the current year.

20.20 ACCOUNTING FOR PENSION SCHEME DEFICITS

(a) Means of dealing with an experience deficiency (see section 20.11) – this may be dealt with in a number of ways:

   (i) by an increase to the future ongoing contribution;
   (ii) by the payment of additional special contributions (single sum or spread over a relatively short period).

(b) Determining the pension charge in the profit and loss account – although (a)(ii) may be satisfactory for funding purposes, SSAP 24 does not regard such payments as providing a satisfactory basis for determining the pension charge in the profit and loss account.

Illustration 4

The actuarial valuation at 31.12.X4 of a pension scheme showed a deficiency of £90m. The actuary recommended that the company eliminate the deficiency by three lump sum payments of £30m in addition to the standard contributions of £10m per annum. The contributions would continue at £10m per annum thereafter.

The average remaining service life of employees in the scheme at 31.12.X4 was ten years. The charge in the profit and loss account for the years 19X5 to 19X14 will be:

	£m
Regular cost	10
Variation from regular cost $\dfrac{3 \times £30m}{10}$	9
Total charge	19

This ignores interest and assumes no changes in circumstances over the above period. In practice it is likely that valuations will occur at three year intervals. These valuations may reveal a deficiency or surplus which would then require an adjustment to the profit and loss account charge in subsequent periods.

The effect on the financial statements may be summarised as follows:

	Funding £m	P/L charge £m	B/S (prepayment) £m
19X5	10 + 30 = 40	19	21
19X6	10 + 30 = 40	19	42
19X7	10 + 30 = 40	19	63
19X8	10	19	54
19X9	10	19	45
19X10	10	19	36
19X11	10	19	27
19X12	10	19	18
19X13	10	19	9
19X14	10	19	–
Total over 10 years	190	190	

Comments

The estimate of average remaining service life of employees in the scheme is inevitably somewhat arbitrary and may not be applied consistently as between different companies.

20.21 ACCOUNTING FOR PENSION SCHEME SURPLUSES

(a) Means of dealing with an experience surplus – these include:

    (i)   by a reduction in the ongoing contribution rate;

    (ii) a contribution holiday (the employer ceases making contributions to the pension fund for a specified period, e g two years);

    (iii) withdrawing some of the surplus from the pension schemes (subject to agreement of trustees and Inland Revenue).

(b) Determining the pension charge in the profit and loss account – although (a)(ii) and (a)(iii) may be acceptable from a funding viewpoint, the payments concerned may not provide a satisfactory basis for determining the pension charge in the profit and loss account.

Illustration 5

The actuarial valuation at 31.12.X4 of a pension scheme showed a surplus of £260m. The actuary recommended that the company eliminate the surplus by taking a contribution holiday in 19X5 and 19X6 and then paying contributions of £30m per annum for 8 years. After 8 years, the standard contribution would be £50m per annum. The average remaining service life of employees in the scheme at 31.12.X4 was 10 years.

The annual charge in the profit and loss account for the years 19X5 to 19X14 will be:

	£m
Regular cost	50
Variation from regular cost	
$\dfrac{260m}{10}$	(26)
Total charge	24

Again, interest is ignored and it is assumed that there are no changes in circumstances over the above period. Triennial valuations may reveal a deficiency or surplus which would then require an adjustment to the profit and loss account charge in subsequent periods.

The effect on the financial statements may be summarised as follows:

	Funding £m	P/L charge £m	B/S (provision) £m
19X5	–	24	24
19X6	–	24	48
19X7	30	24	42
19X8	30	24	36
19X9	30	24	30
19X10	30	24	24
19X11	30	24	18
19X12	30	24	12
19X13	30	24	6
19X14	30	24	–
Total over 10 years	240	240	
19X15	50	50	–
19X16	50	50	–

20.22   UITF CONSENSUS 6

Consensus 6 deals with accounting for post-retirement benefits other than pensions. The aim of the Consensus is to give guidance on the accounting treatment and disclosure of post-retirement health care and other benefits.

Libilities should be set up using principles similar to those in SSAP 24.

Illustration 6

Extract from annual report and accounts of Tesco plc for the year ended 25 February 1995.

Accounting policies (extract)

Pensions
The expected cost of pensions in respect of the group's defined benefit pension scheme is charged to the profit and loss account over the working lifetimes of employees in the scheme. Actuarial surpluses and deficits are spread over the expected remaining working lifetimes of employees.

Post-retirement benefits other than pensions
The cost of providing other post-retirement benefits, which comprise private healthcare, is charged to the profit and loss account so as to spread the cost over the service lives of

relevant employees in accordance with the advice of qualified actuaries. Actuarial surpluses and deficits are spread over the expected remaining working lifetimes of relevant employees.

Note 25 Post-retirement benefits other than pensions

The company operates a scheme offering post-retirement healthcare benefits. The cost of providing for these benefits has been accounted for on a basis similar to that used for defined benefit pension schemes.

The liability as at 27 February 1993 of £8m, which was determined in accordance with the advice of qualified actuaries, is being spread forward over the service lives of relevant employees. A provision of £2m (1994 – £1m) is being carried in the balance sheet reflecting:

	1995 £m	1994 £m
At 26 February 1994	1	–
Charge to profit and loss account	1	1
Cash payments made	–	–
	2	1

It is expected that payments will be tax deductible, at the company's tax rate, when made.

Illustration 7

Extract from annual report and accounts of Reckitt and Colman plc for the year ended 31 December 1994.

Accounting policies (extract)

Pension commitments
The cost of providing pensions to employees who are members of a company pension scheme is spread over the expected service lives of the employees in the scheme. For defined contribution schemes the annual cost charged to the profit and loss account is the contributions made to the scheme. For defined benefit schemes the annual cost charged to the profit and loss account takes account of the contributions made to the scheme and any surpluses or deficits which are to be dealt with over the expected service lives of the employees. Provision is made for the estimated present value or ex-gratia pensions.

Post-retirement benefits other than pensions
The costs of providing post-retirement benefits are determined on an actuarial basis and are charged to the profit and loss account over the expected service lives of the relevant employees. To the extent that such costs do not equate to the cash contribution a provision or prepayment is included in the balance sheet.

26 Post-retirement benefits other than pensions

The group has implemented for the first time UITF 6 (Accounting for post-retirement benefits other than pensions) and has provided for the accumulated post-retirement benefit obligation determined on an actuarial basis. The balance sheet at 1 January 1994 had been restated to reflect the group's liability at that date.

Certain retired employees and dependents in the USA and the UK are eligible to receive medical and prescription benefits paid for by the group and provision for this is included in provisions for liabilities and charges.

In the USA salaried participants become eligible for retiree health-care benefits after they reach a combined age and years of service figure of seventy although the age and service must be a minimum of fifty and ten respectively. The number of current employees eligible to receive health-care benefits on retirement is 1,566. There are 1,624 retirees, inclusive of their dependants, presently eligible to receive these benefits.

The accumulated post-retirement benefit obligation in the USA, net of tax relief of £21.77m, was £34.05m at 1 January 1994 and has been taken to reserves in the 1994 accounts. The annual expense of providing for this cost on an actuarial basis has been estimated at £4.80m and this amount has been charged against profit. Tax relief will be available on these costs as payments are made. The main assumptions used in determining the required provision are a liability discount rate of 8.5% p a and medical cost inflation of 12% p a reducing progressively to 5% p a over the next five years.

In the UK the group pays the annual subscription to a private health plan for senior personnel and their dependants after retirement. Under this scheme the number of employees eligible to receive health-care benefits on retirement is 94. There are 173 retirees, inclusive of their dependants, presently eligible to receive these benefits.

The accumulated post-retirement benefit obligation in the UK, net of tax relief of £0.66m, was £1.33m at 1 January 1994 and has been taken to reserves in the 1994 accounts. The annual expense of providing for this cost on an actuarial basis is estimated at £0.22m and this amount has been charged against profit. Tax relief will be available on these costs as payments are made. The main assumptions used in determining the required provision are a liability discount rate of 9.5% p a and medical inflation of 12.5% p a for ten years and 7.5% p a thereafter.

Consequent to the acquisition of L&F Household, a provision of £24.42m has been made to recognise the existing post-retirement benefit obligation of its employees and retirees at 31 December 1994 and this is included in provisions for liabilities and charges. The provision has been calculated using the same assumptions as quoted for the USA above. The number of current employees eligible to receive health-care benefits on retirement is 1,788 and the number of eligible retirees is 532.

18 Provisions for liabilities and charges

	Deferred tax (Note 19)	Pensions	Post-retirement benefits other than pensions	Other provisions	Total
	£m	£m	£m	£m	£m
At beginning of year	20.64	16.39	57.81	39.78	134.62
Profit and loss account transfer:					
Operating items	15.21	4.22	5.02	138.64	163.09
Non-operating items	–	–	–	2.69	2.69
Provisions on acquisition	–	16.52	24.42	–	40.94
Utilised during the year	(16.74)	(2.09)	(5.35)	(29.99)	(54.17)
At 31 December 1994	19.11	35.04	81.90	151.12	287.17

Other provisions at 31 December 1994 consist primarily of amounts provided for reorganisation costs and for payments due to employees on termination of their services.

E   Group accounts

21 GROUP ACCOUNTS 1

Key Issues

* Why consolidated accounts are needed
* Terminology
  - group
  - parent
  - subsidiary
  - consolidated accounts
* Basic consolidation procedures
  - consolidated profit and loss account
  - consolidated balance sheet
  - treatment of goodwill on consolidation
* Inter-company dividends
* Minority interests

21.1 BACKGROUND

Most large organisations start in modest ways. A sole trader or partnership may decide to incorporate. The company which subsequently comes into being may initially expand through internal growth. At some stage, however, further expansion is often achieved by purchasing another business.

In some cases, such as the purchase of an unincorporated business, it is simply a question of introducing assets (including goodwill) into the company balance sheet. In other cases, the purchase involves the acquisition of a controlling shareholding in another company. Where one company owns a controlling interest in one or more other companies, a group comes into being.

21.2 THE NEED FOR GROUP ACCOUNTS

Suppose Elterwater Ltd has just paid £400 to acquire the entire shareholding (100 £1 shares) in Langdale Ltd.

Elterwater's summarised balance sheet immediately after the purchase is as follows:

	£	£
Fixed assets		
Tangible		890
Investments – shares in Langdale Ltd		400
Current assets		
Stocks	290	
Debtors	160	
Cash	30	
	480	

	£	£
Creditors payable within one year		
Trade creditors	215	
		265
		1,555
Called-up share capital		1,000
Profit and loss account		555
		1,555

The balance sheet of Elterwater, although accurate is hardly informative! While it reveals the cost of the investment in Langdale Ltd, it says nothing about the underlying assets of the economic entity, the group. The group consists of Elterwater (referred to as the parent company) and Langdale Ltd (referred to as a subsidiary of Elterwater).

Suppose the summarised balance sheet of Langdale immediately prior to acquisition by Elterwater was as follows:

	£	£
Tangible fixed assets		260
Stocks	70	
Debtors	125	
Cash	5	
	200	
Trade creditors	150	
		50
		310

	£
Called-up share capital	100
Profit and loss account	210
	310

In order to reveal the assets (less liabilities) under the control of the group, a consolidated balance sheet may be prepared.

In the consolidated balance sheet, items for tangible fixed assets, stock, debtors and creditors would consist of combined totals for the two companies.

The difference between the cost of the investment in Langdale (£400) and the net assets of Langdale (£310) is usually referred to as goodwill arising on consolidation and amounts to £90. In line with SSAP 22 (see chapter 13, section 13.2(h)), goodwill is usually eliminated against reserves, as soon as it arises.

Share capital and reserves of Elterwater as at the date of acquisition are eliminated on consolidation.

The consolidated balance sheet is as follows:

CONSOLIDATED BALANCE SHEET OF ELTERWATER LTD AND ITS SUBSIDIARY

Fixed assets	£	£
Tangible assets (890 + 260)		1,150

Current asssets		
Stocks (290 + 70)	360	
Debtors (160 + 125)	285	
Cash (30 + 5)	35	
	680	

	£	£
Less Creditors: amounts falling due within one year:		
Trade creditors (215 + 150)	365	
Net current assets		315
Total assets less current liabilities		1,465
Called-up share capital		1,000
Profit and loss account (555 – 90)		465
		1,465

Points to note

(a) An acceptable alternative treatment for goodwill on consolidation would be to treat it as an intangible fixed asset amortised over its economic useful life (see chapter 13).

(b) Share capital relates only to share capital of the parent company.

(c) Profit and loss account relates only to that of the parent company. Profits made by Langdale prior to acquisition by Elterwater are referred to as 'pre-acquisition' profits and from the company viewpoint are regarded as capital in nature. However, any profits which Langdale makes in the future (post-acquisition profits) would be regarded as revenue and included in the group profit and loss reserves in the consolidated balance sheet. This is discussed further below.

The usual form of group accounts is described in FRS 2 in the following terms:

> The objective of this FRS is to require parent undertakings to provide financial information about the economic activities of their groups by preparing consolidated financial statements. These statements are intended to present financial information about a parent undertaking and its subsidiary undertakings as a single economic entity to show the economic resources controlled by the group, the obligations of the group and the results the group achieves with its resources. (FRS 2, para 1)

The presentation of group accounts (consisting usually of a consolidated profit and loss account and a consolidated balance sheet) enables users of accounts to apply ratio analysis and other interpretative techniques to the results and financial position of the economic entity, the group.

21.3 LEGAL REQUIREMENTS

(a) Definitions

The Companies Act 1985, as amended by the Companies Act 1989, contains definitions relating to parent company and subsidiary. These definitions are dealt with in chapter 24. (See section 24.3.)

Chapters 21 and 22 will deal with the most usual situations giving rise to a parent company/subsidiary relationship. This is where company A (parent) holds a majority of the voting rights in B (subsidiary).

The term group refers to a parent company together with its subsidiary. (Note that the term holding company has been replaced by parent company.)

Further situations will be referred to in later chapters.

(b) Obligation to lay group accounts before the parent company

A company which, at the end of its financial year, has one or more subsidiary companies must present group accounts at the general meeting at which its (the parent company's) own accounts are presented.

(c) Form of group accounts

Special cases will be referred to in chapter 24 (see section 24.8).

Group accounts usually take the form of a single consolidated balance sheet and consolidated profit and loss account.

21.4   THE MECHANICS OF CONSOLIDATED ACCOUNTS

A company which has subsidiaries is required to present:

(a) Its own (ie parent company) accounts, comprising:

  (i)   parent company balance sheet; and
  (ii) parent company profit and loss account ((ii) is not required provided the consolidated profit and loss account is presented in a certain way and provides certain information). (See section 24.10.)

(b) Group accounts, usually comprising:

  (i)   consolidated balance sheet; and
  (ii) consolidated profit and loss account.

In this chapter, the preparation of both the consolidated profit and loss account, and the consolidated balance sheet will be considered together. Complications will be introduced gradually so that by the end of the chapter you should have a sound understanding of the mechanics of producing consolidated accounts.

For the purpose of illustration, format 1 of the Companies Act 1985 profit and loss account formats will be adopted.

21.5   A BASIC ILLUSTRATION

Illustration 1

H Ltd acquired the entire share capital of S Ltd several years ago. At the date of acquisition by H, the reserves of S Ltd amounted to £110. The final accounts for the current year to 31 December 19X2 are as follows:

PROFIT AND LOSS ACCOUNTS

year ended 31.12.X2

	H Ltd £	S Ltd £
Turnover	2,900	1,200
Cost of sales	1,800	880
Gross profit	1,100	320
Distribution costs	(200)	(90)
Administrative expenses	(300)	(80)
Profit on ordinary activities before tax	600	150
Corporation tax	300	75
Profit after tax	300	75
Balance brought forward	930	215
Balance carried forward	1,230	290

BALANCE SHEETS

at 31.12.X2

	H Ltd £	S Ltd £
Tangible fixed assets	3,030	865
Investment in S Ltd	700	–
Stocks	570	155
Debtors	330	120
Cash at bank	160	30
	4,790	1,170
Ordinary share capital	2,000	500
Profit and loss account	1,230	290
Loan stock	1,000	200
Current taxation	300	75
Creditors	260	105
	4,790	1,170

(a) Preparing the consolidated balance sheet

The method now used in this book is the analysis of equity method.

Share capital and reserves of the subsidiary and cost of investment in S are dealt with in the analysis of equity schedule and are eliminated on consolidation.

Before considering the approach in detail, it is worth noting three particular points:

(1) As S Ltd is a wholly owned subsidiary of H Ltd, the question of outside (or minority) interests does not arise.

(2) The parent company balance sheet includes an asset 'investment in S Ltd'. This does not appear in the consolidated balance sheet of the group – instead the individual assets and liabilities of S Ltd are included under their respective headings (stock, debtors etc).

However, as mentioned in section 21.2 above it is necessary also to take account of goodwill arising on consolidation. This is the amount by which cost of investment exceeds net assets of subsidiary as at date of acquisition. An acceptable treatment under SSAP 22 is to write off goodwill against reserves in the year in which the acquisition takes place.

Net assets at acquisition also equal shareholders' funds at acquisition, ie:

Assets – Liabilities = Net assets = Shareholders' funds = Share capital plus reserves.

So goodwill arising on consolidation is:

	£	£
Investment in S Ltd		700
Net assets of S Ltd at acquisition = OSC + reserves at acquisition (500 + 110)		610
Therefore, goodwill on consolidation written off against reserves		90

(3) The reserves of the parent company amount to £1,230.

However, group reserves in the consolidated balance sheet include:

	£	£
(i) the reserves of the parent company;		1,230
(ii) the post-acquisition reserves of the subsidiary (ie the amount by which the subsidiary's reserves have increased since the date of acquisition);		
Reserves at 31.12.X2	290	
Less reserves at acquisition	110	
So post-acquisition increase		180
Less goodwill written off		(90)
Reserves in consolidated balance sheet		1,320

Recommended approach

Prepare a schedule of analysis of equity as follows:

	Total £	Group share (100%) pre-acquisition £	Group share (100%) post-acquisition £
Ordinary share capital	500	500	–
P/L reserves at acquisition	110	110	–
P/L reserves since acquisition	180	–	180
	790	610	
Cost of investment		700	
Goodwill on consolidation (see below)		90	
Reserves of H			1,230
Goodwill w/o against reserves			(90)
Consolidated P/L reserves			1,320

Tutorial notes
(1) P/L reserves since acquisition amounting to £180 have been calculated as a balancing figure (290 – 110).
(2) It has been assumed that the group's policy for goodwill on consolidation is to write it off against reserves as soon as it arises (see chapter 13).

CONSOLIDATED BALANCE SHEET

at 31.12.X2

	£	£	£
Fixed assets			
Tangible assets (3,030 + 865)			3,895
Current assets			
Stock (570 + 155)		725	
Debtors (330 + 120)		450	
Cash at bank (160 + 30)		190	
		1,365	
Less creditors: amounts falling due within one year			
Creditors (260 + 105)	365		
Taxation (300 + 75)	375	740	
Net current assets			625
Total assets less current liabilities			4,520
Creditors: amounts falling due after more than one year – loan stock (1,000 + 200)			(1,200)
			3,320
Called-up share capital			2,000
Profit and loss account			1,320
			3,320

(b) Preparing the consolidated profit and loss account

Perhaps the most important point to remember is what we are aiming for – ie a completed profit and loss account. A good start is to draft a 'pro forma' with headings but leaving spaces for the numbers to be added later.

Using 'format 1', the headings are as follows:

CONSOLIDATED PROFIT AND LOSS ACCOUNT OF H LTD AND ITS SUBSIDIARIES
for the year ended 31 December 19X2

	£	£
Turnover		X
Cost of sales		X
Gross profit		X
Distribution costs	X	
Administrative expenses	X	
Profit on ordinary activities before tax		X
Taxation		X
Profit on ordinary activities after tax		X
Balance brought forward		X
Balance carried forward		X

Before filling in the figures, the following points should be borne in mind:

(1) The subsidiary is wholly owned. The complication of minority interests will be introduced later in the chapter.
(2) The subsidiary was owned throughout the year. Again, complications arising when a subsidiary is acquired during the current year will be dealt with later. (See chapter 22.)
(3) The consolidated profit and loss account does not deal with any profits of the subsidiary earned before acquisition by the parent company. Consequently the pre-acquisition reserves of S Ltd (£110) should *not* be included in either the brought forward or carried forward figures. This is most important!
(4) Finally, the balance carried forward should agree with the profit and loss account balances in the consolidated balance sheet!

In this simple example, the lines in the profit and loss account up to and including profit on ordinary activities after tax are arrived at by combining the respective amounts for H Ltd and S Ltd.

The balance brought forward is calculated as follows:

	£	£
H Ltd – full amount of b/f figure		930
S Ltd – post-acquisition part of b/f figure		
Reserves b/f	215	
Less reserves at acquisition (pre-acquisition)	110	
		105
		1,035
Less goodwill w/o in previous year (adjusted against opening reserves)		90
So figure for consolidated P/L is		945

The last line in the consolidated profit and loss account is arrived at simply by adding together the profit for the year and the brought forward figure.

Completing the consolidated profit and loss account:

CONSOLIDATED PROFIT AND LOSS ACCOUNT
for the year ended 31 December 19X2

	£	£
Turnover (2,900 + 1,200)		4,100
Cost of sales (1,800 + 880)		2,680
Gross profit		1,420
Distribution costs (200 + 90)	290	
Administrative expenses (300 + 80)	380	
		670
Profit on ordinary activities before tax		750
Taxation (300 + 75)		375
Profit on ordinary activities after tax		375
Balance brought forward (see above)		945
Balance carried forward		1,320

21.6   INTER-COMPANY DIVIDENDS

A subsidiary company is likely to make dividend payments to its shareholders. If the subsidiary is wholly owned, the full amount of the dividend will go to the parent company. As with any company, a subsidiary may pay its dividend in two parts – an interim and a final.

Illustration 2

Suppose H Ltd acquired the entire shareholding of S Ltd several years ago at a cost of £700 when the reserves of S Ltd amounted to £110.

The profit and loss accounts of the two companies for the year ended 31 December 19X2 are as follows:

	H Ltd £	S Ltd £
Turnover	2,900	1,200
Cost of sales	1,800	880
Gross profit	1,100	320
Distribution costs	(200)	(90)
Administrative expenses	(300)	(80)
Operating profit	600	150
Income from investments in group companies:		
Dividends received	10	–
Dividends receivable	20	–
Profit on ordinary activities before tax	630	150
Taxation	300	75
Profit on ordinary activities after tax	330	75
Dividends – paid	(70)	(10)
– proposed	(130)	(20)
Retained profit	130	45
Balance brought forward	930	215
Balance carried forward	1,060	260

Note carefully the relationship between:

(1) dividends paid and proposed by S Ltd; and
(2) dividends received (in cash) and receivable (in debtors) by H Ltd.

The balance sheets of the two companies are as follows:

	H Ltd £	S Ltd £
Tangible fixed assets	3,030	865
Investment in S Ltd	700	–
Stocks	570	155
Debtors	330	120
Dividends receivable	20	–
Cash at bank	100	20
	4,750	1,160
Ordinary share capital	2,000	500
Profit and loss account	1,060	260
Loan stock	1,000	200
Taxation	300	75
Creditors	260	105
Proposed dividends	130	20
	4,750	1,160

(a) Consolidated balance sheet workings

Note that dividends received and paid do not show up on the balance sheet – it is assumed that the respective companies' cash accounts have been adjusted.

The only additional complication is the dividend proposed and receivable amounting to £20. Their treatment in the analysis schedule is shown below:

ANALYSIS OF EQUITY OF S LTD

	Total £	Group share (100%) pre-acquisition £	Group share (100%) post-acquisition £
Ordinary share capital	500	500	–
P/L reserves at acquisition	110	110	–
P/L reserves since acquisition (260 – 110)	150	–	150
	760	610	
Cost of investment in S		700	
Goodwill on consolidation (see below)		90	
Reserves of H			1,060
Goodwill written off against reserves			(90)
Consolidated P/L reserves			1,120

Tutorial note
It is important to pay particular attention to the treatment of inter-company dividends. S has provided in its accounts for a proposed final dividend of £20. In the above example H has accrued its share of the dividend receivable – H's reserves of £1,060 clearly include the £20.

An alternative possibility could have been that H had not accrued for the dividend and so H's reserves would have appeared as £1,040. In this situation it would have been necessary to increase H's reserves by £20, thus giving an adjusted figure of £1,060. Consolidated reserves would still have amounted to £1,120.

CONSOLIDATED BALANCE SHEET
at 31.12.X2

	£	£	£
Fixed assets			
Tangible assets			3,895
Current assets			
Stock		725	
Debtors		450	
Cash at bank		120	
		1,295	
Less creditors: amounts falling due within one year			
Creditors	365		
Taxation	375		
Dividends	130		
Net current assets		870	425
Total assets less current liabilities			4,320

	£	£	£
Less creditors: amounts falling due after more than one year – loan stock			1,200
			3,120
Called-up share capital			2,000
Profit and loss account			1,120
			3,120

Tutorial note
The dividend proposed of £130 relates to the amount payable to the holding company shareholders.

(b) Consolidated profit and loss account workings

The only income from the subsidiary which is included in the parent company's profit and loss account is that relating to dividends received and receivable (i e £10 + £20 = £30).

While this reflects a fair situation for the holding company as a separate legal entity, it does not provide useful information for the group as a whole.

For the group accounts, it is far more useful to bring in the profit on ordinary activities after tax of £75, rather than simply include that part of the £75 which happens to be paid over (now or in the near future) as dividend (i e £30).

The essential point, therefore, is that the investment income of £30 is replaced by the various items which go to make up S's profit of £75.

This means that H's reserves in its own individual balance sheet will be smaller than the reserves in the consolidated balance sheet. The reason for this, of course, is that over a period of years, H's reserves include only dividends received from subsidiaries.

On the other hand, consolidated reserves include all attributable profits of subsidiaries irrespective of whether they are paid across as dividends (i e £30 in the above example) or ploughed back as retained profit (i e £45 above).

The consolidated profit and loss account should be tackled in the same way as before i e by drawing up a blank pro forma. Figures can then be slotted in as soon as they are calculated. This should save time and avoid unnecessary workings.

The completed consolidated profit and loss account is as follows:

	£	£
Turnover		4,100
Cost of sales		2,680
Gross profit		1,420
Distribution costs	290	
Administrative expenses	380	
		670
Profit on ordinary activities before tax		750
Taxation		375
Profit on ordinary activities after tax		375
Dividends – paid	70	
– proposed	130	200
Retained profit		175
Balance brought forward (W1)		945
Balance carried forward		1,120

W1	£	£
H Ltd – full amount		930
S Ltd – post-acquisition part		
at 31.12.X2	215	
at acquisition	110	
		105
		1,035
Less goodwill w/o		90
Group P/L balance b/f		945

21.7 MINORITY INTERESTS

(a) Background

Suppose H Ltd purchased only 80% of the shares in S Ltd; the remaining shares (20%) continuing to be held by outsiders.

$$\begin{array}{c} H \\ \uparrow \quad 80\% \\ S \end{array}$$

S Ltd is now a partly owned (as opposed to wholly owned) subsidiary with a minority interest of 20%. As S Ltd is a subsidiary, it must be reflected in the group's accounts.

In theory two possible approaches could be:

(1) to include 80% of the respective items (stocks, debtors, turnover, cost of sales etc) relating to S; or
(2) to include 100% of all such items but make a compensating adjustment to reflect 20% outside ownership.

The first approach has been used only on very rare occasions. Partly owned subsidiaries are normally consolidated using the second approach, in which items for minority interest appear in both the consolidated balance sheet and consolidated profit and loss account. Special situations are discussed later.

(b) Consolidated balance sheet procedures

The analysis schedule will now require an additional column for minority interest.

(c) Illustration 3

The basic data in section 21.5 will be used, the only difference being that £700 represents the cost of an 80% shareholding in S Ltd.

ANALYSIS OF EQUITY OF S LTD

	Total £	Group share pre-acquisition (80%) £	Group share post-acquisition (80%) £	MI (20%) £
Ordinary share capital	500	400	–	100
P/L reserves at acquisition	110	88	–	22
P/L reserves since acquisition (290 – 110)	180	–	144	36
	790	488		
Cost of investment in S		700		
Goodwill on consolidation		212		
Reserves of H			1,230	
Goodwill w/o against reserves			(212)	
Consolidated B/S totals			1,162	158

CONSOLIDATED BALANCE SHEET

at 31 December 19X2

	£	£	£
Fixed assets			
Tangible assets			3,895
Current assets			
Stock		725	
Debtors		450	
Cash		190	
		1,365	
Less creditors: amounts falling due within one year			
Creditors	365		
Taxation	375		
		740	
Net current assets			625
Total assets less current liabilities			4,520
Less creditors: amounts falling due after more than one year – loan stock			1,200
			3,320
Called-up share capital			2,000
Profit and loss account			1,162
			3,162
Minority interest			158
			3,320

Note: All of the assets of S Ltd have been consolidated, even though H's ownership is only 80%. This provides a more meaningful indication of assets employed within the group than would be the case if only 80% of the relevant amounts were included. The minority interest of £158 (equal to 20% of the net assets of S Ltd £790 – see balance sheet in section 21.5) indicates to holding company shareholders the extent of outside ownership.

(d) Consolidated profit and loss procedures

The basic approach is the same as that outlined earlier in the chapter. For all items up to and including profit on ordinary activities after taxation, the relevant consolidated profit and loss account line will include 100% of the respective item for S Ltd.

However, immediately after this line will appear a line for minority interest. This is calculated as 20% (in the above example) of the profit after tax of S Ltd ie 20% × £75 = £15.

Using the figures in section 21.5, the consolidated profit and loss account will appear as follows:

CONSOLIDATED PROFIT AND LOSS ACCOUNT

for the year ended 31 December 19X2

	£	£
Turnover		4,100
Cost of sales		2,680
Gross profit		1,420
Distribution costs	290	
Administrative expenses	380	
		670
Profit on ordinary activities before tax		750
Taxation		375
Profit on ordinary activities after tax		375
Minority interest		15
Profit attributable to members of H Ltd		360
Balance brought forward (W1)		802
Balance carried forward		1,162

W1	£	£
H Ltd – full amount		930
S Ltd – H's share of post-acquisition part		
– at 31.12.X2	215	
– at acquisition	110	
	105	
H's share 80% × £105		84
		1,014
Goodwill w/o		212
Group balance b/f		802

21.8 INTER-COMPANY DIVIDENDS AND PARTLY-OWNED SUBSIDIARIES

At this stage, it would be useful to consider the combined effects of the two previous sections. This will be developed by means of a further example using much of the data from the previous sections.

Illustration 4

H Ltd acquired 80% of the share capital of S Ltd at a cost of £700 when S's reserves amounted to £110. The draft final accounts of the year are as follows:

PROFIT AND LOSS ACCOUNTS

year ended 31 December 19X2

	H Ltd £	S Ltd £
Turnover	2,900	1,200
Cost of sales	1,800	880
Gross profit	1,100	320
Distribution costs	(200)	(90)
Administrative expenses	(300)	(80)
	600	150
Income from investments in group companies:		
Dividends received	8	–
Dividends receivable	16	–
Profit on ordinary activities before tax	624	150
Taxation	300	75
		× 80%
Profit on ordinary activities after tax	324	75
Dividends – paid	(70)	(10)
– proposed	(130)	(20)
Retained profit	124	45
Balance brought forward	930	215
Balance carried forward	1,054	260

(*Note:* relationship between dividends paid/proposed and dividends received/receivable.)

BALANCE SHEETS

at 31 December 19X2

	H Ltd £	S Ltd £
Tangible fixed assets	3,030	865
Investment in S Ltd	700	–
Stocks	570	155
Debtors	330	120
Dividends receivable	16	–
Cash at bank	98	20
	4,744	1,160
Ordinary share capital	2,000	500
Profit and loss account	1,054	260
Loan stock	1,000	200
Taxation	300	75
Creditors	260	105
Proposed dividends	130	20
	4,744	1,160

ANALYSIS OF EQUITY OF S LTD

	Total £	Group share (80%) pre-acquisition £	Group share (80%) post-acquisition £	MI (20%) £
Ordinary share capital	500	400		100
P/L reserves at acquisition	110	88		22
P/L reserves since acquisition	150		120	30
	760	488		
Cost of investment in S		700		
Goodwill on consolidation		212		
Reserves of H			1,054	
Goodwill w/o against reserves			(212)	
Consolidated B/S totals			962	152

Tutorial notes

(1) The reserves of H (£1,054) include H's share of dividend receivable from S (80% × £20 = £16).

(2) The proposed final dividend of S will be distributed as follows:

Payable to H   80% × 20 = 16
Payable to MI   20% × 20 = 4
                          ──
                          20

The inter-company dividend of £16 has already been taken into account. The dividend payable to MI of £4 will result in a payment outside the group and should be included as a separate item under creditors – amounts due within one year.

Consolidated balance sheet as at 31 December 19X2

	£	£	£
Fixed assets			
Tangible assets			3,895
Current assets			
Stock		725	
Debtors		450	
Cash		118	
		1,293	
Less creditors: amounts falling due within one year			
Creditors	365		
Taxation	375		
Proposed dividends			
Parent company	130		
Minority	4		
		874	
Net current assets			419
Total assets *less* current liabilities			4,314
Creditors: amounts falling due after more than one year – loan stock			1,200
			3,114
Capital and reserves			
Called-up share capital			2,000
Profit and loss account			962
			2,962
Minority interest			152
			3,114

Consolidated profit and loss account procedures

Once again, it is useful to start with a pro forma consolidated profit and loss account. This should contain a 'slot' for minority interest.

It is important (as always) to appreciate the difference between the parent company's own profit and loss, and the consolidated profit and loss account.

The parent company's profit and loss account should include dividends received or receivable from subsidiaries i e 80% × £30 = £24 in the above example.

However, simply to include dividends received does not give a meaningful view of group profitability. So in the consolidated profit and loss account, profits are substituted for dividends.

All lines down to and including profit on ordinary activities after tax include 100% of the respective items (sales, cost of sales etc) of S Ltd.

The consolidated profit and loss account may be completed:

CONSOLIDATED PROFIT AND LOSS ACCOUNT

for the year ended 31 December 19X2

	£	£
Turnover		4,100
Cost of sales		2,680
Gross profit		1,420
Distribution costs	290	
Administrative expenses	380	
		670
Profit on ordinary activities before tax		750
Taxation		375
Profit on ordinary activities after tax		375
Minority interest		15
Profit attributable to members of H Ltd		360
Dividends – paid	70	
– proposed	130	
		200
Retained profit		160
Balance brought forward		802
Balance carried forward		962

Note
(1) Minority interest is *always* calculated as the minority interest percentage of the subsidiary's profit after tax but before deducting dividends paid and proposed.
(2) The only dividends paid and proposed in the consolidated profit and loss account are those relating to the holding company.
(3) The balance brought forward is the same figure as calculated in the example in section 21.7.

21.9   MORE THAN ONE SUBSIDIARY

If the parent company has more than one subsidiary, it is useful to have a separate analysis of equity schedule for each subsidiary. However, for convenience, all minority items may be dealt with in a single account.

As regards presentation, only one item is shown for minority interest in the consolidated balance sheet and profit and loss account, even though the MI figures may relate to several groups of individuals owning shares in different companies.

21.10   GOODWILL ON CONSOLIDATION

The accounting treatment of goodwill on consolidation was discussed in detail in chapter 13.

For clarity, it is assumed for all group accounts illustrations, that the group policy is to eliminate goodwill on consolidation immediately on acquisition of a subsidiary, by means of a charge against reserves.

Under this policy, no entry is made in the profit and loss account. The amount written off will only be disclosed in the year of write-off. This approach is adopted by the majority of UK companies.

The amortisation alternative, although not illustrated here, would be acceptable provided it was consistent with the provisions of SSAP 22 (see section 13.2(j)).

22 GROUP ACCOUNTS 2

Key Issues

* Effects of subsidiaries acquired during the current year
* Preference shares in subsidiaries
* Debentures in subsidiaries
* Inter-company items
    – cash
    – loans
    – management charges
    – goods
    – fixed assets

22.1 SUBSIDIARIES ACQUIRED DURING THE CURRENT YEAR

(a) Introduction

First of all, what will be the effect of an acquisition during the year of a new subsidiary? The assets and liabilities of the new subsidiary should be included in the consolidated balance sheet as it is a member of the group at the year end.

As regards the consolidated profit and loss account, any profits earned by the subsidiary prior to acquisition should be excluded. The consolidated profit and loss account should include any post-acquisition profits.

(b) Possible approaches

Illustration 1

The profit and loss accounts of Fell Ltd and Tarn Ltd for the year ended 31 December 19X6 are as follows:

	Fell £	Tarn £
Turnover	900	600
Cost of sales	400	360
Gross profit	500	240
Distribution costs	(100)	(36)
Administrative expenses	(200)	(48)
Operating profit	200	156
Tax	90	72
Profit after tax	110	84

Fell acquired the entire share capital of Tarn on 30 September 19X6. How should the consolidated profit and loss account be presented?

The Companies Act 1985 (as amended by the Companies Act 1989) requires that only profit and turnover from the date of acquisition may be included.

This may be illustrated as follows:

CONSOLIDATED PROFIT AND LOSS ACCOUNT

for the year ended 31 December 19X6

	£
Turnover	1,050
Cost of sales	490
Gross profit	560
Distribution costs	(109)
Administrative expenses	(212)
Profit on ordinary activities before tax	239
Taxation	108
Profit on ordinary activities after tax/Profit attributable to the members of Fell Ltd	131

Tutorial note

All figures include three months for Tarn e g turnover is $(900 + \frac{3}{12} \times 600)$

(c) Pre-acquisition dividends received during the year

The parent company may well receive a dividend from a new subsidiary, shortly after its acquisition date. The problem is that this dividend may have been paid either wholly or partly out of pre-acquisition profits.

On receipt of the dividend, the parent company should normally apportion the dividend between:

(1) The pre-acquisition part – this should be credited to (i e effectively deducted from) cost of investment in subsidiary.
(2) The post-acquisition part – this should be credited to the parent company's profit and loss account.

The basis of apportionment is the date of acquisition in relation to the accounting year of the company paying the dividend.

Two short examples will be given: first, where only one dividend is paid for the year; secondly, where an interim and final dividend are paid. Note that recent developments in this area are discussed in chapter 25 (see section 25.10).

Illustration 2 – one dividend only

H Ltd acquired 100% of the share capital of S Ltd on 31.8.19X3. The year end of both companies is 31 December. In its accounts for the year ended 31 December 19X3, S Ltd proposes a dividend of £3,600. How should this be treated in the final accounts of H?

Diagrammatically

Pre-acquisition (8m)	Post acquisition (4m)
1.1.X3	31.8.X3	31.12.X3

The date of payment of the dividend (possibly in March or April of 19X4) is irrelevant. The only dates that matter are:

(1) the date of acquisition (31.8.X3);
(2) the year for which the dividend is declared (YE 31.12.X3).

So the post-acquisition part of the dividend is £1,200 ($\frac{4}{12} \times$ £3,600) and the pre-acquisition part £2,400 ($\frac{8}{12} \times$ £3,600).

The required journal entry in the books of H is:

	£		£
Debit dividend receivable (debtor)	3,600	*Credit* cost of investment in S	2,400
		Profit and loss account of H	1,200
	£3,600		£3,600

Illustration 3 – interim and final

H Ltd acquired 100% of the share capital of S Ltd on 31.8.19X3. The year end of both companies is 31 December. S paid an interim dividend of £1,000 on 7.7.19X3, and proposes a final dividend of £2,600. How should this be treated in the final accounts of H Ltd?

One approach considers that both elements of the dividend (totalling £3,600) relate to the year ended 31 December 19X3.

H does not receive £1,000 since it was paid to the previous shareholders of the company before H obtained control.

But H must set up a debtor for dividend receivable of £2,600. The maximum amount of this which may be regarded as post-acquisition is:

Four months' proportion of the total of the interim and the final dividend i e: $\frac{4}{12} \times$ (£1,000 + £2,600) = £1,200.

The balance of the final dividend (amounting to £2,600 − £1,200 = £1,400) must be regarded as capital.

The required journal entry is thus:

	£		£
debit dividend receivable	2,600	*Credit* cost of investment in S Ltd	1,400
		Profit and loss	
		account of H	1,200
	2,600		2,600

Illustration 4 – acquisition of a wholly owned subsidiary

Easedale acquired the entire share capital of Loughrigg on 30 September 19X3. The draft final accounts of the two companies are as follows:

PROFIT AND LOSS ACCOUNTS

for the year ended 31 December 19X3

	Easedale	Loughrigg
	£	£
Turnover	900	200
Cost of sales	500	112
Gross profit	400	88
Distribution costs	(90)	(16)
Administrative expenses	(150)	(32)
Operating profit	160	40
Dividends receivable (note 1)	2	–
	162	40
Taxation	80	20
Profit after tax	82	20
Proposed dividends	30	8
Retained profit	52	12
Balance b/f	120	40
Balance c/f	172	52

NOTE 1
Dividend receivable from Loughrigg is the post-acquisition part (ie $\frac{3}{12} \times$ £8 = £2. The balance of £6 has been deducted from the cost of investment of £175 (see balance sheet below).

BALANCE SHEETS
at 31 December 19X3

		Easedale £	Loughrigg £
Tangible fixed assets		200	90
Investment in S Ltd	175		
Less pre-acq div	6	169	–
Stocks		105	45
Cash		120	25
Dividends receivable		8	–
		602	160
Share capital		400	100
Profit and loss account		172	52
Proposed dividend		30	8
		602	160

ANALYSIS OF EQUITY OF LOUGHRIGG

	Total £	Group share pre-acquisition £	Group share post-acquisition £
Ordinary share capital	100	100	–
P/L reserves at acquisition	49	49	–
P/L reserves since acquisition	3	–	3
	152	149	3
Cost of investment in S		169	
Goodwill on consolidation		20	
Reserves of Easedale			172
Goodwill w/o against reserves			(20)
Consolidated P/L reserves			155

NOTE 2: CALCULATION OF PRE-ACQUISITION RESERVES

	£	£
Balance at 1.1.X3		40
Profit after tax for year	20	
Attributable to period 1.1.X3 to 30.9.X3		
$\frac{9}{12} \times 20$	15	
Less pre-acquisition part of final dividend	6	
		9
Therefore, pre-acquisition reserves		49

NOTE 3

Goodwill on consolidation is the amount by which the purchase consideration exceeds the net assets acquired. If a company pays a dividend before the date of sale, this affects the size of the bank balance, the purchase consideration and, of course, the goodwill.

However, a proposed dividend at the end of the year, paid to the new owner, has no effect on either assets taken over or purchase consideration. It cannot affect goodwill.

In the above example, had no dividend been proposed at the year end, the purchase consideration would still have amounted to £175 and the goodwill calculated at £20 as follows:

	£	
Cost of investment		175
Group share pre-acquisition		
OSC	100	
P/L (40 + 15)	55	155
		20

CONSOLIDATED BALANCE SHEET

at 31.12.X3

	£	£
Fixed assets		
Tangible assets		290
Current assets		
Stocks	150	
Cash	145	
	295	
Less creditors: amounts falling due within one year:		
Proposed dividend	30	
Net current assets		265
Total assets less current liabilities		555
Called-up share capital		400
Profit and loss account		155
		555

Consolidated profit and loss procedures

The key point to remember is that in method 2 we include a proportionate share ($\frac{3}{12}$) of the results of Loughrigg.

The consolidated profit and loss account will appear as follows:

CONSOLIDATED PROFIT AND LOSS ACCOUNT

for the year ended 31 December 19X3

	£	Workings
Turnover	950	$900 + \frac{3}{12} \times 200$
Cost of sales	528	$500 + \frac{3}{12} \times 112$
Gross profit	422	
Distribution costs	(94)	$90 + \frac{3}{12} \times 16$
Administrative expenses	(158)	$150 + \frac{3}{12} \times 32$
Profit on ordinary activities before tax	170	
Taxation	85	$80 + \frac{3}{12} \times 20$
Profit on ordinary activities after tax	85	
Proposed dividends	30	
Retained profit	55	

Statement of reserves	
Balance brought forward	120
Retained profit	55
Goodwill written off	(20)
Balance carried forward	155

NOTE 4
The balance brought forward relates to the parent company only. If a subsidiary is acquired during the current year, all of its reserves brought forward are pre-acquisition and have no effect on consolidated profit and loss reserves brought forward.

(d) Illustration 5 – acquisition of a partly owned subsidiary

This example introduces two further complications:

(1) the newly acquired subsidiary paid an interim dividend before the date of acquisition;
(2) the new subsidiary includes a minority interest.

The example is concerned solely with the profit and loss account.

(1) Basic information

The draft profit and loss accounts of Langdale Ltd and Elterwater Ltd were as follows:

	Langdale £	Elterwater £
Turnover	3,000	1,200
Selling and marketing expenses	(700)	(240)
Administrative expenses	(400)	(120)
Operating profit	1,900	840
Dividends receivable (note 2)	27	–
Profit before tax	1,927	840
Taxation	950	420
Profit after tax	977	420
Dividends – paid	(100)	(60)
– proposed	(300)	(120)
Retained profit	577	240
Balance b/fwd	1,000	700
Balance c/fwd	1,577	940

Notes

(1) The cost of investment was £1,850 and relates to a 90% shareholding acquired two months before the year end.

(2) The proposed dividend of £120 has been correctly treated in the accounts of the holding company:

Parent company share of final dividend = 90% × £120 = £108.

Maximum amount which may be treated as post-acquisition.

$$= 90\% \times \tfrac{2}{12} \times (£60 + £120)$$

$$= £27$$

(That is, pre-acquisition part of final dividend is £108 − £27 = £81 and has been deducted from cost of investment.)

(2) Procedures

(a) Consolidated profit and loss account should include $\frac{2}{12}$ of the following items:

Turnover	$\frac{2}{12} \times £1,200 = £200$
Selling expenses	$\frac{2}{12} \times £240 = £40$
Administrative expenses	$\frac{2}{12} \times £120 = £20$
Taxation	$\frac{2}{12} \times £420 = £70$

(b) Since the consolidated profit and loss account includes only two months' proportion of the respective revenue items, minority interest must be based on two months' profit after tax.

ie MI = 10% × $\frac{2}{12}$ × £420
= £7

CONSOLIDATED PROFIT AND LOSS ACCOUNT

for the year ended 31 December 19X3

	£
Turnover	3,200
Selling and marketing expenses	(740)
Administrative expenses	(420)
Profit on ordinary activities before tax	2,040
Taxation	1,020
Profit on ordinary activities after tax	1,020
Minority interest	7
Profit attributable to members of Langdale Ltd	1,013
Dividends – paid	(100)
– proposed	(300)
Retained profit (see note)	613

Note: It is good presentation (though not mandatory) to disclose the split of retained profit between:

	£
(a) profit retained by company, ie;	577
and	
(b) profit retained by subsidiary:	
$90\% \times \frac{2}{12} \times £240 =$	36
	613

22.2 PREFERENCE SHARES IN SUBSIDIARIES

(a) Introduction

Most types of preference shares entitle the holder to:

(1) dividend of fixed amounts, in priority to ordinary dividends;
(2) on liquidation, a return of capital of a fixed amount in priority to ordinary shareholders.

These preference shares have no effect whatsoever on the parent company/ subsidiary relationship as they are not voting shares.

(b) Approach to consolidation

(1) Consolidated balance sheet:

  (i) the difference between the cost of the investment in preference shares and the nominal value held should be adjusted through the goodwill calculation;
  (ii) the nominal value of preference shares held by outsiders should form part of minority interest (non-current part);
  (iii) preference dividends payable to outsiders are included as current items.

(2) Consolidated profit and loss account.
    The subsidiary should be consolidated in the usual way. However, the minority interest calculation requires particular care.

Illustration 6

H Ltd acquired the following shareholdings in S Ltd several years ago:

80% of the ordinary share capital.

10% of the preference share capital.

The draft profit and loss account of S Ltd for the current year is as follows:

		£
Turnover		7,000
Operating expenses		3,000
Profit on ordinary activities		4,000
Taxation		1,800
Profit after tax		2,200
Preference dividends	600	
Ordinary dividends	1,000	
		1,600
Retained profit		600
Balance brought forward		3,000
Balance carried forward		3,600

How should minority interest be determined for profit and loss account purposes?

(1) Minority interest

    Ordinary shares   20%
    Preference shares 90%

(2) The starting point is profit after tax (£2,200).

    (a) Minority interest in preference shares – fixed amount of 90% × £600 = £540.
    (b) Minority interest in ordinary shares – based on available profit
        (£2,200 − £600 = £1,600) ie 20% × £1,600 = £320.

    So total minority interest is £860.

(3) It is convenient to set the calculation out as follows:

	100% £	MI £
Profit after tax	2,200	
Preference dividends	600 × 90% =	540
Available for ordinary shareholders	1,600 × 20% =	320
MI in consolidated profit and loss account		860

Note: Had the ordinary and preference shares been acquired three months before the end of the year, only three months' results would be consolidated (as discussed in section 22.1) and the minority interest would also be based on three months. Minority interest would then amount to $\frac{3}{12}$ × £860 ie £215.

(c) A further illustration

It is useful to bring together the above points. For the sake of compactness, the accounting information has been summarised. More information would be required for Companies Act 1985 purposes.

    The draft profit and loss accounts of Hill Ltd and Side Ltd for the year ended 31 December 19X3 were as follows:

	Hill £	Side £
Turnover	11,000	5,000
Expenses	4,000	2,200
Operating profit	7,000	2,800
Taxation	3,500	1,400
Profit after tax	3,500	1,400

	Hill £	Side £
Proposed dividends		
Preference shares	–	(320)
Ordinary shares	(2,000)	(800)
	1,500	280
Balance brought forward	4,100	740
Balance carried forward	5,600	1,020

DRAFT BALANCE SHEETS

at 31 December 19X3

	Hill £	Side £
Fixed assets	21,660	13,590
Debtors	8,290	4,150
Cash	4,150	2,100
Creditors	(6,500)	(3,700)
Proposed dividends – ordinary	(2,000)	(800)
– preference	–	(320)
	25,600	15,020

	£	£
Ordinary share capital	20,000	10,000
Preference share capital (8% £1 shares)	–	4,000
Profit and loss account	5,600	1,020
	25,600	15,020

Additional information

(1) Fixed assets includes the cost of the following investments:

(i) 70% of the ordinary share capital of Side Ltd, acquired when its reserves amounted to £300 – cost of investment, £8,500.

(ii) 20% of the preference share capital of Side Ltd – cost of investment, £830.

(2) Hill Ltd has not yet made an entry in its books in respect of dividends receivable from Side Ltd. (Contrast this with the situation in previous examples.)

CONSOLIDATED BALANCE SHEET WORKINGS

			£
Dividends receivable by Hill			
Ordinary 70% × £800	=		560
Preference 20% × £320	=		64
Total			624

The reserves of Hill of £5,600 should thus be increased by £624 to £6,224.

ANALYSIS OF SHAREHOLDERS' EQUITY OF SIDE

	Total £	Group share (70%) pre-acquisition £	Group share (70%) post-acquisition £	MI (30%) £
Ordinary shares				
Ordinary share capital	10,000	7,000		3,000
P/L reserves at acquisition	300	210		90
P/L reserves since acquisition	720		504	216
	11,020	7,210		
Cost of investment		8,500		
Goodwill on consolidation		1,290		

		Group share (20%) £		MI (80%) £
Preference shares				
Preference share capital	4,000	800		3,200
Cost of investment		830		
Consolidation difference		30		

Hill Ltd reserves				
Per draft B/S	5,600			
Div. receivable	624		6,224	
Goodwill w/o against reserves	(1,290 + 30)		(1,320)	
Consolidated B/S totals			5,408	6,506

Tutorial notes
(1) Minority interest in proposed dividends is as follows:

		£
Ordinary dividend	30% × £800	240
Preference dividend	80% × £320	256
		496

This total should be included under creditors due within one year.
(2) It is usually acceptable to offset any difference on the purchase of preference shares (ie 830 − 800 = 30) against goodwill on consolidation relating to ordinary shares.

CONSOLIDATED BALANCE SHEET

at 31 December 19X3

	£	£	£
Fixed assets			
Tangible assets (W1)			25,920
Current assets			
Debtors		12,440	
Cash		6,250	
		18,690	

	£	£	£
Less creditors: amounts falling due within one year:			
Creditors	10,200		
Proposed dividends:			
Parent company	2,000		
minority	496		
		12,696	
Net current assets			5,994
Total assets less current liabilities			31,914
Called-up share capital			20,000
Profit and loss account			5,408
Minority interest			6,506
			31,914

W1

Fixed assets – per draft a/cs (21,660 + 13,590)	=	35,250
Less investments in subsidiary (8,500 + 830)	=	9,330
Tangible assets		25,920

CONSOLIDATED PROFIT AND LOSS ACCOUNT WORKINGS

(1) *Minority interest*

	100% £		MI £
Profit after tax	1,400		
Preference dividend	320	(80%)	256
Available for ordinary shareholders	1,080	(30%)	324
MI in consolidated profit and loss account			580

(2) *Retained profit allocation*

	£
Parent company	
Per draft accounts	1,500
Dividends to be accrued	624
	2,124
Subsidiary	
70% × £280	196
	2,320

(3) *Consolidated P/L reserves brought forward*

	£		£
Parent company			4,100
Subsidiary			
At 1.1.X3	740		
At acquisition	300		
Post-acquisition	440	× 70%	308
			4,408
Less goodwill w/o			1,320
			3,088

CONSOLIDATED PROFIT AND LOSS ACCOUNT

for the year ended 31 December 19X3

	£	£
Turnover		16,000
Operating expenses		6,200
Profit on ordinary activities before tax		9,800
Taxation		4,900
Profit on ordinary activities after tax		4,900
Minority interest		580
Profit attributable to parent company shareholders		4,320
Proposed dividends		2,000
Retained profit		2,320
Retained by parent company	2,124	
Retained by subsidiary	196	
	2,320	
Balance brought forward		3,088
Balance carried forward		5,408

In this case the MI is a mixture of MI in ordinary shares and MI in preference shares. Additional disclosures for both consolidated balance sheet and consolidated profit and loss account are required by FRS 4, showing the split of MI between equity and non-equity.

22.3 DEBENTURES IN SUBSIDIARIES

Mathematically, the approach is similar to that used for preference shares:

(1) Consolidated balance sheet:

    (1) The difference between the cost of the investment in debentures and the nominal value held should be adjusted through the goodwill calculation.

    (2) The nominal value of debentures held by outsiders should be presented as a non-current liability (ie under 'creditors amounts falling due after more than one year'). It should *not* be included under minority interest.

(b) Consolidated profit and loss account:

    Interest paid will include the outside share of debenture interest.

Illustration 7

A owns the entire share capital of B, but only owns 10% of the debenture stock. The abbreviated profit and loss accounts are as follows:

	A £	B £
Operating profit	200	200
Interest received	5	–
Interest paid	–	(50)
Retained profit	205	150

The inter-company interest amounting to £5 should be eliminated on consolidation. The effect of the above items on the consolidated profit and loss account would be:

		£
Operating profit		400
Interest paid (50 − 5)		45
Retained profit		355
Holding company	205	
Subsidiary	150	
	355	

22.4   INTER-COMPANY ITEMS

(a) Cash-in-transit

Cash-in-transit may be the cause of inter-company accounts failing to agree.

Illustration 8

At the year end, the current accounts in the books of H and S respectively show the following:

Books of H Ltd – account with S Ltd	£8,000
Books of S Ltd – account with H Ltd	£6,000

The difference is due to a cheque of £2,000 in transit.

   Procedure – amend books of H Ltd to £6,000 (so that inter-company balances may be offset) and remember to increase cash at bank by £2,000. A useful rule of thumb is:

(1) Items-in-transit between parent company and subsidiary – put 'journal' through parent company books.
(2) Items-in-transit between subsidiaries – amend books of recipient company.

(b) Loans

Assuming both sets of books are up-to-date, the inter-company balances should cancel each other out. Ensure that any loan interest charged has been correctly treated in both sets of books and that the charge is fair as regards the borrowing company (which may be a partly owned subsidiary).

(c) Management charges

Again, inter-company balances should cancel out. Management charges should be realistic. For example, if a parent company makes a management charge to a partly owned subsidiary, the charge will reduce the subsidiary's reserves and affect the rights of outside shareholders.

(d) Inter-company sales of goods

In a group of trading companies, it is not uncommon for companies to sell goods from one to another. If these goods are sold at a profit to the selling company, this raises the problem of unrealised inter-company profits.

Illustration 9

Eskdale owns 80% of the ordinary capital of Grange Ltd. During the current year, Grange sold to Eskdale goods costing £15,000 at a price which gives a profit of 25% on the selling price. By the year end, Eskdale had sold three-quarters of these goods to third parties.

(1) The draft accounts of the two companies showed the following:

	Eskdale £	Grange £
Turnover	200,000	85,000
Cost of sales	(130,000)	(60,000)
Other expenses	(25,000)	(9,000)
Profit on ordinary activities	45,000	16,000
Taxation	22,000	7,300
Profit after tax	23,000	8,700
Balance brought forward	50,000	20,000
Balance carried forward	73,000	28,700

(2) Stocks in the draft balance sheet amounted to:

	£
Eskdale	180,000
Grange	70,000

(3) Eskdale purchased its shares when the reserves of Grange amounted to £6,000.
(4) No goods were transferred between the two companies in previous years.

Points to consider
(1) Group turnover should include only sales to third parties. Inter-company turnover amounts to £20,000 ($\frac{100}{75} \times$ £15,000).
This must be taken into account in arriving at consolidated sales.
(2) The profit on the sale of the goods amounts to £5,000. Of this amount, 75% (ie £3,750) may be regarded as realised since this relates to the proportion of the goods which had been sold to third parties by the balance sheet date. Thus unrealised profits amount to £1,250. These should be eliminated before arriving at consolidated profit.
(3) How much of the £1,250 should be eliminated?
There are several viewpoints which can be put forward.

(i) Both reserves and stocks should be reduced by £1,250. This has the advantage that in the consolidated balance sheet, stock is stated at the lower of cost and net realisable value from the viewpoint of the group (as opposed to the viewpoint of individual companies!). This was widely followed in practice prior to the issue of the ASB's Interim Statement. Note that the amount of profit eliminated is the same whether the subsidiary is wholly owned or partly owned.

(ii) A second approach is to eliminate only that part of the profit relating to the group (ie 80% × £1,250 = £1,000) on the grounds that the profit attributable to outside shareholders is realised by sale outside that company. Under this approach, both consolidated reserves and consolidated stock are reduced by £1,000. A major disadvantage of this method is that it produces an unsatisfactory stock figure.

(iii) A third possibility is to reduce consolidated stock by £1,250 but to reduce group reserves by £1,000 and minority interest by £250. This reflects the parent company's ownership in the subsidiary. The method has merit, but would be difficult to operate for goods transferred within complex group structures. This is the approach now required by FRS 2.

ANALYSIS OF SHAREHOLDERS' EQUITY OF GRANGE

	Total £	Group share (80%) pre-acquisition £	Group share (80%) post-acquisition £	Minority interest (20%) £
Ordinary share capital	X	X		X
P/L reserves pre-acquisition	6,000	4,800		1,200
P/L reserves since acquisition	22,700	–	18,160	4,540
	XX	XX		
Cost of investement in Grange		X		
Goodwill on consolidation		XX		
Reserves of Eskdale			73,000	
Unrealised profit in stock			(1,000)	(250)
Goodwill w/o against reserves			(XX)	
Consolidated balance sheet totals			90,160	XXX

Stock in consolidated balance sheet	£
Eskdale	180,000
Grange	70,000
	250,000
Unrealised profit in stock	1,250
∴ Stock in consolidated B/S	248,750

CONSOLIDATED PROFIT AND LOSS ACCOUNT WORKINGS

		£
Turnover	200,000 + 85,000 − 20,000 =	265,000
Cost of sales	130,000 + 60,000 − 20,000 + 1,250 =	171,250
Profit on ordinary activities	45,000 + 16,000 − 1,250 =	59,750
Minority interest	20% × (£8,700 − 1,250) =	1,490
Reserves brought forward	50,000 + 80% (20,000 − 6,000) =	61,200

CONSOLIDATED PROFIT AND LOSS ACCOUNT FOR . . .

	£
Turnover	265,000
Cost of sales	(171,250)
Other expenses	(34,000)
Profit on ordinary activities before tax	59,750
Taxation	29,300
Profit on ordinary activities after tax	30,450
Minority interest	1,490
Profit attributable to members of parent company	28,960
Balance brought forward	61,200
Balance carried forward (ignoring goodwill w/o)	90,160

(e) Inter-company transfers of fixed assets

In a group which includes manufacturing companies, one company may manufacture and sell to another company assets which are retained by the transferee company as fixed assets.

From the group accounts viewpoint this poses two problems:

(1) The once and for all profit on the transfer of the asset;
(2) The effect each year on the depreciation charge.

The problem is solved by making consolidation adjustments in respect of unrealised profit.

Illustration 10

Oakfield Ltd and Woodlands Ltd are both partly owned subsidiaries of Cotham Ltd. Woodlands Ltd manufactures office furniture. During the year ended 30 September 19X2, furniture costing £2,000 to manufacture is transferred to Oakfield Ltd at a price of £2,400. The furniture is considered to have a useful life of ten years, with a nil residual value.

Contrasting the effect on the accounts of individual companies and those of the group:

(1) *Individual companies*
  (i) Woodlands Ltd – as a separate legal entity, the profit on sale to Oakfield is a realised profit.
  (ii) Oakfield Ltd – the annual depreciation charge of £240 is based on the cost to Oakfield as a separate legal entity.

(2) *Group accounts*
  (i) In 19X2, the transfer profit of £400 is unrealised. In the opposite direction, depreciation charge is £240 compared with £200 had the asset been transferred at cost. The net effect of these should be reflected as a consolidation adjustment.
  (ii) In 19X3 and subsequent years, if no consolidation adjustment were made, the depreciation charge each year would be overstated each year by £40.

The effect may be summarised as follows:

Year	Profit Overstated	Understated	Net
	£	£	£
19X2	400	40	360
19X3	–	40	(40)
19X4	–	40	(40)
19X5	–	40	(40)
19X6	–	40	(40)
19X7	–	40	(40)
19X8	–	40	(40)
19X9	–	40	(40)
19X10	–	40	(40)
19X11	–	40	(40)
Totals	400	400	–

The column entitled 'net' is the amount of the consolidation adjustment. For example, in 19X2 the net book value of the furniture in the books of Oakfield is £2,400 − £240 = £2,160. The consolidation adjustment is to reduce group profit and loss account by £360 and group fixed assets by £360. So in the group balance sheet, the furniture would be included at £2,160 − £360 = £1,800 (split cost £2,000 less depreciation £200) i e as if it had been transferred at cost.

Notes
(1) The adjustment (Dr £360 in 19X2 and credit £40 in 19X3) would appear in consolidated profit and loss reserves (as for stock in (d) above).

(2) The consolidation adjustments have no effect on the accounts of the individual companies – they are separate legal entities in their own right.
(3) As indicated for stock, the adjustment for unrealised profit could take account of minority interests. The approach adopted above, however, is recommended for exam purposes.

22.5   RESERVES OF SUBSIDIARIES

So far we have assumed that reserves of subsidiaries consist solely of accumulated profit and loss account balances. It is, of course, possible to have several categories of reserves including revaluation surplus (as a result of revaluing fixed assets) and share premium accounts.

The principles are still the same – each category of reserve must be split between pre-acquisition and post-acquisition.

Illustration 11

Henley Ltd acquired 60% of the ordinary share capital of Apsley Ltd several years ago when Apsley's reserves were as follows:

	£
Profit and loss account	12,000
Revaluation reserve	3,000
Share premium account	5,000

At the most recent balance sheet date, the reserves of the two companies were as follows:

	Henley £	Apsley £
Profit and loss account	102,000	19,000
Revaluation reserve	67,000	8,000
Share premium account	35,000	5,000

The effect on the consolidated balance sheet may be illustrated as follows.

ANALYSIS OF SHAREHOLDERS' EQUITY OF APSLEY LTD

	Total £	Group share (60%) of pre-acquisition reserves £	Group share of post-acquisition P/L £	Group share of post-acquisition revaluation reserve £	Group share of post-acquisition share premium £	MI (40%) £
Ordinary share capital	X	X				X
P/L reserves at acquisition	12,000	7,200				4,800
P/L reserves since acq.	7,000		4,200			2,800
Revaluation reserves at acquisition	3,000	1,800				1,200
Revaluation reserves since acquisition	5,000			3,000		2,000
Share premium at acquisition	5,000	3,000				2,000
	XX	XX				
Cost of investment		X				
Goodwill on consolidation		XX				
Reserves of Henley			102,000	67,000	35,000	
Goodwill w/o against reserves			(XX)			
Consolidated B/S totals			XX	70,000	35,000	XX

22.6 BONUS ISSUES

If a subsidiary company makes a bonus (or capitalisation) issue prior to acquisition, there are no problems since both share capital and reserves have been adjusted. If the bonus issue was shortly before the acquisition date but has not yet been reflected in the accounts, it is advisable to alter share capital and the relevant part of reserves, before proceeding with the consolidation adjustments.

However, bonus issues made after the acquisition date may present difficulties. The key point is to determine whether the bonus issue is made out of pre-acquisition reserves or post-acquisition reserves.

(a) Out of pre-acquisition reserves

If the bonus issue is made soon after acquisition, this must be the situation. The recommended procedure is to reduce subsidiary reserves and increase subsidiary share capital, then to proceed in the usual way.

(b) Out of post-acquisition reserves

It is important to determine whether the bonus issue is out of reserves of a capital nature (share premium account, capital redemption reserve etc) or out of profit and loss account.

In the former case, no adjustment is needed for group accounts purposes. In the latter case, group distributable reserves will be affected.

Illustration 12

The summarised balance sheets of H Ltd and S Ltd (a 90% owned subsidiary) are as follows:

	H Ltd £	S Ltd £
Net assets	84,000	42,000
Investment in S Ltd	16,000	–
	100,000	42,000
Share capital	30,000	10,000
Profit and loss account	70,000	32,000
	100,000	42,000

The investment in S Ltd was acquired when its reserves amounted to £2,000. S Ltd now proposes to make a 2 for 1 bonus issue out of post-acquisition reserves.

Considering the principal aspects of the consolidated balance sheet in turn:

(1) Consolidation goodwill is calculated as follows:

	£
Cost of investment	16,000
Group share of net assets (equal to share capital plus reserves) at acquisition 90% (10,000 + 2,000)	10,800
	5,200

A post-acquisition bonus issue cannot affect the goodwill figure.

(2) Minority interest is based on proportionate share of assets at balance sheet date i e 10% × £42,000 = £4,200.

(3) Consolidated profit and loss account reserve is calculated as follows:

H Ltd	70,000
S Ltd 90% (32,000 − 2,000)	27,000
	97,000
Less goodwill written off	5,200
	91,800

However, the fact that S Ltd is declaring a bonus issue out of post-acquisition profits is effectively saying that £20,000 (2 for 1 on share capital of £10,000) of profits which were previously distributable are now no longer regarded as distributable. The group proportion of this is £18,000. In order to present a true and fair view, this figure should be disclosed as a memorandum note in the group accounts.

(4) From the above it is clear that for exam purposes it is better not to adjust for the bonus issue, otherwise there is a danger that goodwill whether written off or capitalised, will be incorrect.

(5) The consolidated balance sheet (in summarised form) will appear as follows:

	£
Net assets	126,000
Goodwill on consolidation	–
	126,000
Share capital	30,000
Profit and loss account (see note)	91,800
Minority interest	4,200
	126,000

Note: Profit and loss account includes £18,000 not available for distribution.

23 VERTICAL AND MIXED GROUPS

Key Issues

* Vertical group
  – two methods of consolidating
* Mixed group

23.1 INTRODUCTION

This chapter is concerned with two special situations.

First of all the vertical group situation where company B is a subsidiary of company A, and company C is a subsidiary of company B.

Secondly, the mixed group situation where company A is a member of company B and has the right to appoint or remove directors holding a majority of voting rights at board meetings (see section 24.3(b)).

Each of these situations will be covered in turn and will be illustrated by examples.

23.2 VERTICAL GROUPS – A WORKED EXAMPLE

The summarised draft final accounts of Holbrook Ltd, Sevier Ltd and Tipton Ltd for the year ended 31 December 19X9 were as follows:

	Holbrook Ltd	Sevier Ltd	Tipton Ltd
Balance sheets	*£'000*	*£'000*	*£'000*
Tangible fixed assets	500	300	150
Net current assets	220	130	60
Investment in Sevier	410	–	–
Investment in Tipton		110	–
	1,130	540	210
Called-up share capital (£1 ordinary shares)	700	300	100
Profit and loss account	330	200	95
Proposed dividends	100	40	15
	1,130	540	210

	Holbrook Ltd	Sevier Ltd	Tipton Ltd
Profit and loss accounts	*£'000*	*£'000*	*£'000*
Turnover	800	180	80
Operating costs	480	70	44
Operating profit	320	110	36
Taxation	140	50	16
	180	60	20
Proposed dividends	100	40	15
Retained profit	80	20	5
Balance at 1.1.X9	250	180	90
Balance at 31.12.X9	330	200	95

The following information is also relevant:

(1) Sevier acquired 60% of the ordinary share capital of Tipton in 19X2 when the reserves of Sevier were £125,000 and those of Tipton, £60,000.
(2) Holbrook acquired 80% of the ordinary share capital of Sevier in 19X4 when the reserves of Sevier were £165,000 and those of Tipton, £85,000.
(3) Neither Holbrook nor Sevier has yet accrued their shares of dividends receivable.

Required: A consolidated profit and loss account and consolidated balance sheet for 19X9.

23.3 SUMMARY OF SHAREHOLDINGS

The position as regards reserves and shareholdings may be illustrated as follows:

(a) Reserves at dates of acquisition of share purchases

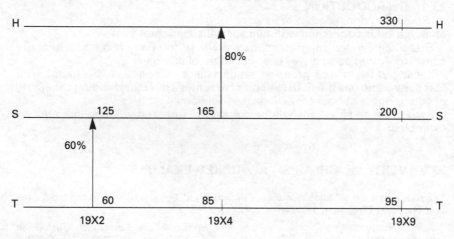

(b) Shareholdings

	Sevier	Tipton
Holbrook	80%	80% × 60% = 48% (I)
MI	20%	40% (D)
		20% × 60% = 52% (I)
	100%	100%

Notes
(1) T is a subsidiary of S. S is a subsidiary of H, therefore T is a subsidiary of H. This is so in spite of the fact that H's effective share of T is only 48% (80% × 60%).
(2) Group accounts are required dealing with H, S and T. 100% of the assets and liabilities of T should be consolidated. However, since H owns only 48% of T, minority interest should be based on 52%.
(3) In the shareholdings table, D refers to direct (i e a direct shareholding by H) while I refers to indirect (i e an indirect shareholding by H).

23.4 APPROACHES TO CONSOLIDATION

In principle, there are two possible methods:

(a) indirect (2-stage) consolidation;
(b) direct (1-stage) consolidation.

In practice, (a) is usually followed. For examinations, both methods should be known and will be illustrated below.

23.5   INDIRECT CONSOLIDATION

The group structure is:

H
↑ 80%
S
↑ 60%
T

Indirect consolidation involves two stages:

(a) Stage 1 – consolidation of Sevier group (i e Sevier and Tipton)
(b) Stage 2 – consolidation of Holbrook with the Sevier group.

23.6   STAGE 1 – CONSOLIDATION OF SEVIER GROUP

ANALYSIS OF EQUITY OF TIPTON

(Sevier share 60%, minority 40%)

	Total £	Group share pre-acquisition £	Group share post-acquisition £	Minority interest £
Ordinary share capital	100,000	60,000		40,000
Reserves at acquisition by Sevier	60,000	36,000		24,000
Reserves since acquisition	35,000		21,000	14,000
Total	195,000	96,000		
Cost of investment by Sevier		110,000		
Goodwill on consolidation written off against reserves		14,000	(14,000)	
Reserves of Sevier including dividends receivable from Tipton (200,000 + 60% × 15,000)			209,000	
Totals for Sevier group consolidated balance sheet			216,000	78,000

CONSOLIDATED BALANCE SHEET OF SEVIER GROUP AT 31 DECEMBER 19X9

	£	£	£
Fixed assets			
Tangible fixed assets			450,000
Net current assets		190,000	
Proposed dividends			
Parent company	40,000		
Minority (40% × 15,000)	6,000	46,000	
			144,000
Total assets less current liabilities			594,000

	£	£	£
Capital and reserves			
Called-up share capital			300,000
Profit and loss account			216,000
			516,000
Minority interest			78,000
			594,000

Tutorial note: the reserves of £216,000 are all post-acquisition as regards the Sevier group but include £15,000 (ie 60% × (85,000 − 60,000)) which are pre-acquisition as regards the Holbrook group.

23.7   STAGE 2 – CONSOLIDATION OF HOLBROOK AND SEVIER GROUP

ANALYSIS OF EQUITY OF SEVIER

(Holbrook share 80%, minority 20%)

	Total £	Group share pre-acquisition £	Group share post-acquisition £	Minority interest £
Ordinary share capital	300,000	240,000		60,000
Reserves at acquisition of Holbrook (see note below)	180,000	144,000		36,000
Reserves since acquisition per analysis of Tipton (216,000 − 180,000)	36,000		28,800	7,200
	516,000	384,000		
Cost of investment by Holbrook		410,000		
Goodwill on consolidation w/o against reserves		26,000	(26,000)	
Reserves of Holbrook including dividends receivable from Sevier (330,000 + 80% × 40,000)			362,000	
Consolidated balance sheet totals			364,800	103,200

Note
The consolidated P/L reserves of Sevier group at date of acquisition by Holbrook is calculated as follows:

	£
P/L reserves of Sevier	165,000
Sevier's share of post-acquisition reserves of Tipton 60% (85 − 60)	15,000
	180,000

Note this calculation very carefully: the increase in reserves from 60 to 85 is post-acquisition as regards the Sevier group but pre-acquisition as regards the Holbrook group.

Other workings

(1) Minority interest (non-current)

	£
Tipton	78,000
Sevier	103,200
	181,200

(2) Minority interest (current)

	£
Tipton 40% × £15,000	6,000
Sevier 20% × £40,000	8,000
	14,000

CONSOLIDATED BALANCE SHEET OF HOLBROOK GROUP
AT 31 DECEMBER 19X9

	£	£	£
Fixed assets			
Tangible assets			950,000
Net current assets		410,000	
Proposed dividends:			
Parent company	100,000		
Minority	14,000	114,000	296,000
Total assets less current liabilities			1,246,000
Capital and reserves			
Called-up share capital			700,000
Profit and loss account			364,800
			1,064,800
Minority interest			181,200
			1,246,000

23.8 CONSOLIDATED PROFIT AND LOSS ACCOUNT – INDIRECT METHOD

S GROUP

Stage 1

	£	£
Turnover		260,000
Operating costs		114,000
Operating profit		146,000
Taxation		66,000
Profit after tax		80,000
Minority interest (40% × 20,000)		8,000
		72,000
Proposed dividends		40,000
Retained profit		32,000
Balance b/f		
S	180,000	
T 60% (90,000 – 60,000)	18,000	
	198,000	
Less goodwill w/o	14,000	
		184,000
		216,000

Stage 2

	£	£
Turnover		1,060,000
Operating costs		594,000
Operating profit		466,000
Tax		206,000
Profit after tax		260,000
Minority interest		
Per S group P/L	8,000	
Tipton 12% × 20,000	2,400	
Sevier 20% × 60,000	12,000	
		22,400
		237,600
Proposed dividends		100,000
Retained profit		137,600
Balance b/f		
Holbrook		250,000
S group	184,000	
Pre-acq S	(165,000)	
Pre-acq T 60% × (85 – 60)	(15,000)	
	4,000	
H's share 80%		3,200
		253,200
Less goodwill w/o (Holbrook in Sevier)		(26,000)
		227,200
Balance c/f		364,800

23.9   DIRECT CONSOLIDATION

(a) This method omits the intermediate stage of the construction of the consolidated accounts of the Sevier sub-group (consisting of Sevier and its subsidiary, Tipton).

   The equity of each subsidiary (i e Sevier and Tipton) is analysed using the *effective* group percentages:

	Group	MI
Sevier	80%	20%
Tipton	80% × 60% = 48%	52%

(b)   ANALYSIS OF EQUITY OF SEVIER

(Group holding 80%, MI 20%)

		Total £	Group share pre-acquisition £	Group share post-acquisition £	Minority interest £
Ordinary share capital		300,000	240,000		60,000
Reserves at acquisition (19X4)		165,000	132,000		33,000
Reserves since acquisition					
Per acs	35,000				
Share of div. receivable 60% × 15,000	9,000				
		44,000		35,200	8,800
		509,000	372,000		
Cost of investment			410,000		
Goodwill w/o against reserves (see below)			38,000		
Carried forward to summary				35,200	101,800

(c)   ANALYSIS OF EQUITY OF TIPTON

(Effective group holding 48%, MI 52%)

	Total £	Group share pre-acquisition £	Group share post-acquisition £	Minority interest £
Ordinary share capital	100,000	48,000		52,000
Reserves at acquisition (NB: 19X4)	85,000	40,800		44,200
Reserves since acquisition	10,000		4,800	5,200
	195,000	88,800		
Cost of investment (allocated 80%:20%)		(88,000)		(22,000)
Group share w/o against group reserves		(800)		
Carried forward to summary			4,800	79,400

(d) **Summary**

	£	Group P/L reserves £	MI (non-current) £	MI (current) £
Holbrook				
Per acs	330,000			
Div receivable 80% × 40,000	32,000			
		362,000	–	–
Equity of S		35,200	101,800	
Proposed dividend S 20% × 40,000				8,000
Equity of T		4,800	79,400	
Proposed dividend T 40% × 15,000				6,000
Goodwill adjustments (38,000 − 800)		(37,200)		
Consolidated B/S totals		364,800	181,200	14,000

(e)   CONSOLIDATED BALANCE SHEET OF HOLBROOK GROUP
AT 31 DECEMBER 19X9

	£	£	£
Fixed assets			
Tangible assets			950,000
Net current assets		410,000	
Proposed dividends:			
Parent company	100,000		
Minority	14,000	114,000	296,000
Total assets less current liabilities			1,246,000
Capital and reserves			
Called-up share capital			700,000
Profit and loss account			364,800
			1,064,800
Minority interest			181,200
			1,246,000

(f)   CONSOLIDATED PROFIT AND LOSS ACCOUNT OF HOLBROOK GROUP
USING DIRECT CONSOLIDATION

	£	£
Turnover		1,060,000
Operating costs		594,000
Profit on ordinary activities before tax		466,000
Tax on profit on ordinary activities		206,000
Profit on ordinary activities after tax		260,000
Minority interest		22,400
Profit attributable to members of Holbrook		237,600
Proposed dividends		100,000
Retained profit		137,600
Parent company	112,000	
Subsidiaries	25,600	
	137,600	
Balance at 1.1.X9		227,200
Balance at 31.12.X9		364,800

(g) **Workings – consolidated profit and loss account**

(1) Minority interest

	£
Tipton 52% × £20,000	10,400
Sevier 20% × £60,000	12,000
	22,400

(2) Retained profit allocation

(a) Holbrook

	£
Per draft accounts	80,000
Dividend receivable from Sevier	
80% × £40,000	32,000
	112,000

(b) Subsidiaries

	£	£
Sevier		
Per draft accounts	20,000	
Dividend receivable Tipton		
60% × £15,000	9,000	
	29,000	
Group share 80% × £29,000		23,200
Tipton		
Group share 48% × £5,000		2,400
		25,600

(3) Balance at 1.1.X9

	£
Holbrook	250,000
Sevier 80% (180,000 – 165,000)	12,000
Tipton 48% (90,000 – 85,000)	2,400
	264,400
Less goodwill written off	37,200
	227,200

23.10 MIXED GROUPS – A WORKED EXAMPLE

The summarised draft balance sheets of Hiland Ltd, Fresno Ltd and Stockton Ltd at 31 December 19X9 were as follows:

	Hiland Ltd £'000	Fresno Ltd £'000	Stockton Ltd £'000
Tangible fixed assets	500	200	100
Net current assets	213	88	66
Investment in Stockton		42	
Investment in Fresno	255		
Investment in Stockton	57		
	1,025	330	166
Called-up share capital (£1 ordinary shares)	600	200	100
Profit and loss account	425	130	66
	1,025	330	166

The following information is also relevant:

(1) Fresno acquired 30% of the ordinary share capital of Stockton in 19X1 when the reserves of Fresno were £47,000 and those of Stockton were £24,000.
(2) Hiland acquired 90% of the ordinary share capital of Fresno in 19X3 when the reserves of Fresno were £60,000 and those of Stockton were £36,000.
(3) Hiland acquired 25% of the ordinary share capital of Stockton in 19X5 when the reserves of Fresno were £92,000 and those of Stockton were £44,000.

Required: A consolidated balance sheet at 31 December 19X9.

23.11   SUMMARY OF SHAREHOLDINGS

(a) Reserves at dates of acquisition of share purchases

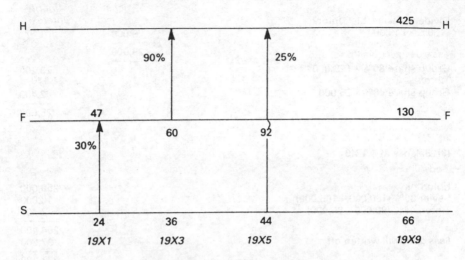

(b) Shareholdings

		Fresno	Stockton	
Hiland		90%	25% (D) 90% × 30% (I)	} 52%
MI		10%	45% (D) 10% × 30% (I)	} 48%
		100%		100%

23.12   APPROACH TO CONSOLIDATION

In this situation, the best approach is direct consolidation. The mechanics of this are similar to those for vertical groups.

ANALYSIS OF EQUITY OF FRESNO

(Group holding 90%, MI 10%)

	Total £	Group share pre-acquisition £	Group share post-acquisition £	Minority interest £
Ordinary share capital	200,000	180,000		20,000
Reserves at acquisition	60,000	54,000		6,000
Reserves since acquisition	70,000		63,000	7,000
	330,000	234,000		
Cost of investment		255,000		
Goodwill on consolidation		21,000		
Carried forward to summary			63,000	33,000

ANALYSIS OF EQUITY OF STOCKTON

(Group holding 52%, MI 48%)

	Total £	Group share pre-acquisition £	Group share post-acquisition £	Minority interest £
Ordinary share capital	100,000	52,000		48,000
Reserves at acquisition (19X5 when Stockton becomes part of Hiland Group)	44,000	22,880		21,120
Reserves since acquisition	22,000		11,440	10,560
	166,000	74,880		
Cost of investment				
direct		(57,000)		
indirect (allocated 90%:10%)		(37,800)		(4,200)
Goodwill		19,920		
Carried forward to summary			11,440	75,480

Summary

	Group P/L reserves £	MI £
Hiland	425,000	
Equity of Fresno	63,000	33,000
Equity of Stockton	11,440	75,480
Goodwill adjustments (21,000 + 19,920)	(40,920)	
Consolidated B/S totals	458,520	108,480

CONSOLIDATED BALANCE SHEET OF HILAND GROUP

as at 31 December 19X9

	£
Fixed assets	
Tangible assets	800,000
Net current assets	367,000
	1,167,000
Capital and reserves	
Called-up share capital	600,000
Profit and loss account	458,520
	1,058,520
Minority interest	108,480
	1,167,000

24 FRS 2 – ACCOUNTING FOR SUBSIDIARY UNDERTAKINGS

> **Key Issues**
> * Changeover to FRS 2
> * Requirement to prepare group accounts
> * What is a subsidiary undertaking?
> * Group accounting policies
> * Intra-group items
> * Accounting dates
> * Exclusion from consolidation
> * Minority interests
> * Exemptions from the preparation of group accounts
> * Significant restrictions on distributions

24.1 BACKGROUND

Prior to 1989, the main rules regulating the preparation of consolidated accounts were to be found in SSAP 14, Group accounts.

The subsequent enactment of the Companies Act 1989 (amending the Companies Act 1985) meant that SSAP 14 was in need of drastic revision. Pending the arrival of a new standard, the Accounting Standards Board (ASB) published an Interim Statement on consolidated accounts in December 1990.

FRS 2, Accounting for Subsidiary Undertakings, issued in July 1992, supersedes SSAP 14 and the relevant parts of the Interim Statement. It does not deal with accounting for associated undertakings and joint ventures (see chapter 27).

FRS 2 is linked closely to the Companies Act 1985 and should be referred to in conjunction with the Act. In some instances, FRS 2 summarises the Act; in others it provides further explanations of parts of the Act.

24.2 REQUIREMENT TO PREPARE CONSOLIDATED ACCOUNTS

FRS 2 requires a parent undertaking to prepare consolidated accounts unless it claims one of the three exemptions referred to below. The consolidated accounts should include all subsidiary undertakings, consolidated on a line-by-line basis

FRS 2 essentially adopts the definitions of parent undertaking and subsidiary undertaking introduced by the Companies Act 1989.

24.3 DEFINITIONS – PARENT UNDERTAKING AND SUBSIDIARY UNDERTAKING

In the explanation below, 'A' refers to the parent undertaking whilst 'B' refers to the subsidiary undertaking.

An undertaking (A) is deemed to be a parent undertaking of another undertaking (B) in any of the five following cases:

(a) A holds a majority of the voting rights in B;
(b) A is a member of B and has the right to appoint or remove directors holding a majority of the voting rights at board meetings;
(c) A has the right to exercise a dominant influence over B;
(d) A is a member of B and controls alone, following an agreement with other shareholders or members, a majority of voting rights in B;
(e) A has a participating interest in B and either actually exercises a dominant influence over B or, A and B are managed on a unified basis. Note that a participating interest is a shareholding of at least 20 per cent.

In practice most parent undertaking/subsidiary undertaking relationships are likely to fall within the first case i e whether or not A holds a majority of the voting rights in B. This case is also extended to sub-subsidiaries.

Situation (e) has also arisen in practice, but only in a small number of instances.

24.4 'DOMINANT INFLUENCE' AND 'MANAGED ON A UNIFIED BASIS'

FRS 2 includes the following definitions:

(a) Dominant influence

Influence that can be exercised to achieve the operating and financial policies desired by the holder of the influence, notwithstanding the rights or influence of any other party.

a In the context of paragraph 14(c) and section 258(2)(c) *the right to exercise a dominant influence* means that the holder has a right to give directions with respect to the operating and financial policies of another undertaking with which its directors are obliged to comply, whether or not they are for the benefit of that undertaking.

b *The actual exercise of dominant influence* is the exercise of an influence that achieves the result that the operating and financial policies of the undertaking influenced are set in accordance with the wishes of the holder of the influence and for the holder's benefit whether or not those wishes are explicit. The actual exercise of dominant influence is identified by its effect in practice rather than by the way in which it is exercised.

(b) Managed on a unified basis

Two or more undertakings are managed on a unified basis if the whole of the operations of the undertakings are integrated and they are managed as a single unit. Unified management does not arise solely because one undertaking manages another.

This definition does not include companies which are under common ownership only. There must be a connecting shareholding: one company must have a participating interest (i e a shareholding of at least 20%) in the other – see section 24.3(e) above.

24.5 ACCOUNTING POLICIES

The consolidated accounts should be prepared on the basis of consistent accounting policies. This consistency may be achieved by either:

(a) using identical policies for all companies in the group; or
(b) putting through adjustments at the consolidation stage to ensure that the consolidated accounts reflect uniform and consistent policies.

In exceptional cases, it may be impracticable to use consistent policies. The Companies Act 1985 then requires disclosure of:

(1) particulars of the departure (which should refer to the different accounting policies used);
(2) the reasons for the departure;
(3) the effect of the departure.

24.6   INTRA-GROUP ITEMS

(a) Balances, income and expenses

Inter-company balances and inter-company income or expense items should be elimated on consolidation.

(b) Unrealised profits

Profits or losses on inter-company transfers of assets should be eliminated in full to the extent that such assets are included in the consolidated balance sheet.

The amount of profit or loss eliminated should be allocated between group ownership and minority interest according to the ownership in the company which recorded the profit or loss.

The accounting treatment of inter-company items was dealt with in section 22.4.

24.7   ACCOUNTING DATES

(a) Preferred situation

Wherever practicable, all group companies should use the same accounting periods and year ends.

(b) Permitted alternatives

Where this is not possible, two alternative procedures may be applied:

(1) the option preferred by FRS 2 – the use of interim accounts prepared to the parent undertaking's accounting date;
(2) if (1) is not practicable – using the subsidiary undertaking's accounts made up to an earlier date, provided that is not more than three months earlier than the parent's balance sheet date.

(c) Interim accounts

Illustration 1

Group accounts are to be prepared covering the year to 31 December 19X4. A particular overseas subsidiary has a 30 September year end. The results of the subsidiary may be included as follows:

(1) nine months' proportion of the audited annual accounts to 30 September 19X4;
(2) three months' specially prepared accounts up to 31 December 19X4;
(3) it will also be necessary to prepare an interim balance sheet at 31 December 19X4, purely for consolidation purposes.

Illustration 2

Extract from accounting policies

Basis of consolidation
(i) The Group accounts consolidate those of the Company and its subsidiary undertakings for the period of 52 weeks (53 weeks when necessary) ending on the Sunday
nearest 30 April, except that the Directors do not consider it appropriate for legal and
fiscal reasons to change the accounting date of Frères Jacques SA from 31
December and so special financial statements have been prepared.

(d) Consolidation at different dates

Illustration 3

Suppose that the 30 September 19X4 accounts of a subsidiary are to be consolidated
with the accounts of the remainder of the group made up to 31 December 19X4.
Adjustments should be made for 'abnormal transactions' arising in the three months to
31 December 19X4.
  There are two categories of such transactions which may require adjustment:

(1) significant (but normal) transactions with other group companies, for example, in
the situation referred to earlier, a significant remittance of cash on 30 November
19X4 to the parent company;
(2) events such as major changes in exchange rates, major trade losses, and significant
fixed asset sales or discontinuance of business activities.

Note: ((b) above) the maximum gap permitted by the Companies Act 1985
between the parent's balance sheet date and the earlier date for the subsidiary
is three months.

Illustration 4

Extract from accounting policies.

Basis of consolidation

The Group accounts incorporate the accounts of West Cliff plc and its subsidiary
undertakings. The accounts have been prepared for the period ended 30 September
19X5 except that the accounts of the overseas rental companies have for administrative
reasons been prepared for the year ended 31 August 19X5; with account taken of any
significant transactions in the intervening period.

  FRS 2 and the Companies Act 1985 also specify additional disclosures for
option (b)(2) relating to the particular subsidiary undertakings concerned. For
each such subsidiary, the following should be disclosed:

(i)   its name;
(ii) its accounting date or period;
(iii) the reasons for using a different accounting date or period for it.

24.8   EXCLUSION FROM CONSOLIDATION

(a) Where exclusion of a subsidiary from consolidation is mandatory

FRS 2 requires a subsidiary to be excluded from consolidation where:

(1) severe long-term restrictions substantially hinder the exercise of the rights
of the parent undertaking over the assets or management of the subsidiary
undertaking;
(2) the interest in the subsidiary undertaking is held exclusively with a view to
resale and the subsidiary undertaking has not previously been consolidated;

(3) the subsidiary undertaking's activities are so different from those of other undertakings to be included in the consolidation that its inclusion would be incompatible with the obligation, to give a true and fair view.

The Standard makes it clear that exclusion on the grounds of different activities is likely to be rare. It takes the view that the usual approach will be for consolidation combined with segmental information possibly giving more information than that required by SSAP 25.

(b) Accounting and disclosure

The Standard includes detailed requirements for both accounting and disclosure – these are outside the scope of this text.

From a practical viewpoint, exclusion from consolidation will usually be relevant only for certain larger quoted companies.

Illustration 5 – held exclusively with a view to resale

Extract from annual report and accounts of De La Rue plc for the year ended 31 March 1995.

Accounting policies (extract)

Basis of consolidation
The consolidated accounts have been prepared under the historical cost convention as modified by the revaluation of certain fixed assets and in accordance with applicable UK accounting standards.

A number of subsidiaries acquired as part of the acquisition of Portals Group plc have been excluded from consolidation because they are held exclusively with a view to subsequent resale. These subsidiaries, listed on page 62, are recorded as assets held for disposal within current assets and are held at the Directors' valuation of anticipated net sale proceeds discounted to their present value at the balance sheet date. These subsidiaries have retained a year end of 31 December.

The results of all of the other subsidiaries of the Company have been consolidated. All of these subsidiaries and the associated companies prepare their annual financial statements to 31 March except for De La Rue Smurfit Limited which prepares its financial statements to 31 January and one associated company whose year end is 31 December.

Upon the acquisition of a business, fair values that reflect the conditions at the date of acquisition are attributed to the identifiable net assets acquired. Where the consideration paid for a business exceeds such net assets, the difference is treated as goodwill and is offset against reserves in the year of acquisition. The results of businesses acquired are included in the profit and loss account from the date of acquisition. On disposal of a business, the profit or loss on disposal is determined after including the attributable amount of purchased goodwill.

Part of balance sheet

		1995 Group £m	1994 Group £m	1995 Company £m	1994 Company £m
Notes					
	Fixed assets				
9	Tangible assets	**179.7**	116.0	**16.9**	17.3
10	Investments	**79.3**	53.2	**830.8**	381.4
		259.0	169.2	**847.7**	398.7
	Current assets				
11	Stocks	**87.4**	75.6	–	–
12	Debtors	**179.2**	117.9	**14.4**	29.1
13	Assets held for disposal	**160.0**	–	–	–
	Cash at bank and in hand	**106.4**	375.3	**13.3**	259.6
		533.0	568.8	**27.7**	288.7

	Current liabilities				
14	Creditors: amounts falling due within one year	**(493.2)**	(310.2)	**(277.7)**	(101.2)
	Net current assets	**39.8**	258.6	**(250.0)**	187.5
	Total assets less current liabilities	**298.8**	427.8	**597.7**	586.2
15	Creditors: amounts falling due after more than one year	**(52.1)**	(60.0)	**(272.2)**	(274.3)
16	Provisions for liabilities and charges	**(53.7)**	(41.2)	**(16.0)**	(9.1)
		193.0	326.6	**309.5**	302.8

Note 13

13 Assets held for disposal

Assets held for disposal represents the Group's investment in those companies listed as 'Businesses held for resale' on page 62. These companies, all of which were subsidiaries of Portals Group plc when the Group acquired Portals Group plc, are held exclusively with a view to resale. They are held at the Director's valuation of anticipated net sales proceeds discounted to their present value at 31 March 1995.

Included within other creditors is £3.3m owing to these businesses by the rest of the Group as at 31 March 1995, representing £2.6m of cash received and £0.7m of trading items. Apart from these transactions, during the period from acquisition to 31 March 1995 there were no material transactions between these businesses and the rest of the Group, and there were no dividends received or receivable from them.

(c) Disproportionate expense or delay

A final point is that the Companies Act 1985 (CA 1985) permits exclusion from consolidation where the information necessary for the preparation of group accounts cannot be obtained without disproportionate expense or delay.

It is important to note that FRS 2 does not permit this ground for exclusion for subsidiary undertakings that are individually or collectively material in the context of the group.

24.9 MINORITY INTERESTS

(a) General requirements

(1) The aggregate of the minority interest proportion of net assets or liabilities of subsidiary undertakings should be separately disclosed in the consolidated balance sheet.

(2) The consolidated profit and loss account should show separately:

   (i) the aggregate of the profit or loss on ordinary activities attributable to minority interests;

   (ii) the aggregate of any extraordinary profits or losses attributable to minority interests (this will usually be shown by way of note).

(b) Loss-making subsidiaries

In cases where the company is still in a satisfactory position, the effect on the minority interest is:

(1) In the consolidated profit and loss account, ignoring any other subsidiaries, the minority interest share of the loss will appear as a figure in brackets.

(2) In the consolidated balance sheet, the minority interest will be equivalent to a percentage of net assets of the subsidiary. However, if a company continues to lose money, the minority interest in successive consolidated balance sheets will become smaller and smaller!

(c) Subsidiaries with negative equity interest

(1) Leaving for a moment the question of minority interest, the first point is whether a subsidiary with a negative equity interest (debit balance on reserves in excess of share capital) should be consolidated?

   (i) If the going concern assumption can be justified, the subsidiary should be consolidated. To justify this, it will be necessary to demonstrate parent company guarantees, injections of fresh finance and so on.
   (ii) If the parent company intends to abandon the subsidiary and to allow it to go into liquidation, it would be misleading to consolidate. It would, of course, be important to ensure the parent company had made adequate provision for previous guarantees given in respect of the subsidiary.

(2) Suppose the going concern assumption is justified and the company is partly owned. How should minority interest be treated for consolidation purposes?

FRS 2 requires the group to make provision for 100% of the deficiency to the extent that it has any commercial or legal obligations to provide finance that may not be recoverable from the minority in respect of their share of the deficiency.

However, the explanation section to FRS 2 indicates that the normal route should be to recognise a debit balance for minority interest. The group should only provide for this debit balance in cases where it has a commercial or legal obligation as indicated above. Where the group has to provide, the debit balance should be set off initially against the minority interest in the balance sheet.

24.10   INDIVIDUAL PROFIT AND LOSS ACCOUNT OF PARENT COMPANY

A parent company which prepares group accounts need not publish its own profit and loss account provided the following conditions are satisfied:

(a) the individual profit and loss account must be approved by the board of directors;
(b) the group accounts must be prepared in accordance with the requirements of CA 1985 (as amended);
(c) the company's individual balance sheet must show by way of note the company's profit or loss for the financial year determined in accordance with CA 1985;
(d) the company's accounts must disclose the fact that the relevant exemption applies.

24.11   EXEMPTIONS FROM THE PREPARATION OF GROUP ACCOUNTS

(a) Grounds for exemption

Groups are exempt from preparing consolidated accounts in any of the following three cases:

(1) small and medium-sized groups (as defined by CA 1985).
(2) certain groups which are part of a larger group for which consolidated accounts are prepared (the EU parent exemption).

Both of the above exemptions are optional – full statutory consolidated accounts may be prepared if desired. Detailed conditions are set out in CA 1985.

(3) Groups which include only subsidiary undertakings falling into categories for which exclusion from consolidation is mandatory per FRS 2. These categories are: severe long-term restrictions and held exclusively with a view to subsequent resale.

Subsidiaries with different activities will usually be included in the consolidation.

(b) Exemptions for small and medium-sized groups

(1) *Definition of 'small' and 'medium-sized'*

A group is counted as 'small' if it satisfies two out of three of the following:

Turnover
– net   £2.8m
– gross   £3.36m

('Gross' means the aggregate of turnover figures for all group companies ignoring consolidation adjustments.)

Total assets
– net   £1.4m
– gross   £1.08m

(Again, 'gross' is before taking account of consolidation adjustments; total assets is fixed assets plus current assets, before deducting any liabilities.)

Aggregate number
of employees   50

For a medium-sized group, the respective figures are:

Turnover
– net   £11.2m
– gross   £13.44m

Total assets
– net   £5.6m
– gross   £6.72m

Employees   250

In addition, to qualify for exemption the group must not be ineligible. Irrespective of size, a group is regarded as ineligible if any of its members is:

(i)   a plc or a body corporate with the power to issue shares to the public;
(ii) a banking company;
(iii) an insurance company;
(iv) an authorised person under the Financial Services Act 1986 ie a Financial Services Company.

(2) *Audit requirement*

If the parent company's directors wish to take advantage of the above exemption, they must obtain a report from their auditors confirming the company's entitlement to exemption. The exemption does not apply unless the auditors state that the company is entitled to the exemption and the report is attached to the individual accounts of the parent company.

(3) Disclosure requirements

A parent company which claims exemption from the preparation of group accounts should give the following disclosures for each of its subsidiary undertakings:

(i)   name, country of incorporation/registration, nature of business;
(ii) classes of shares, proportion held;
(iii) capital and reserves at the year-end;
(iv) profit or loss for the year.

   A parent company is also required to disclose the aggregate amount of its total investment in the shares of subsidiary undertakings. This amount is determined according to the equity method of valuation. (See chapter 27.)

Illustration 6

XYZ Company Ltd
BALANCE SHEET (EXTRACT)

	19X8	19X7
	£	£
Investments (at cost)	322,000	XX

Notes to the accounts (extract)

(i) Accounting policies
Consolidation

1 The company has claimed exemption under Section 248 of the Companies Act 1985 from the preparation of group accounts on the grounds that the group is small/medium-sized.
2 The accounts present information about (parent) Ltd as an individual undertaking and not about its group.

(ii) Investments
Investments are stated at cost. The details of subsidiary undertakings are as follows:

Name	Country of incorporation or registration	Class of shares held	Proportion % held	Capital and reserves at 31.12.X3 £	Profit for year ended 31.12.X3 £	Valuation under the equity method £
A Ltd	England	Ordinary	100	250,000	35,000	250,000
B Ltd	England	Ordinary	80	90,000	14,000	72,000
						322,000

   The disclosure in note 2, under consolidation, is required by FRS 2 (see (d) below).
   In addition to the above, the profit and loss account and balance sheet formats set out in CA 1985, Sch 4 require separate disclosure of items such as:

(i)   Income from shares in (group undertakings);
(ii) Shares in (group undertakings);
(iii) Loans to (group undertakings);
(iv) Amounts owed by (group undertakings);
(v)   Amounts owed to (group undertakings).

   All of these items may be relegated to the notes to the accounts.

(4) *Filing requirements*

Where the above exemption applies, directors may be able to choose between:

(i) filing full group accounts; and
(ii) filing individual accounts for the parent company and subsidiaries. In the case of these individual accounts the minimum required to be filed will depend on whether the company concerned is small or medium-sized.

A subsidiary may file abbreviated accounts as a small company provided it is small in size and is not a member of an ineligible group.

A parent company may only file abbreviated accounts as a small company if the group which it heads up is small.

Illustration 7

A Ltd claims exemption from the preparation of group accounts on the grounds that the group is medium-sized.

The group structure and company size is as follows. For simplicity only turnover figures are given.

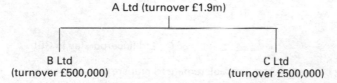

A Ltd (turnover £1.9m)

B Ltd
(turnover £500,000)

C Ltd
(turnover £500,000)

B Ltd and C Ltd may file abbreviated accounts as small companies.

Although A Ltd *appears* to be small, it is in fact classified by CA 1985 as medium-sized because the group it heads up has a turnover of £2.9m (ie 1.9 + 0.5 + 0.5) and thus exceeds the small company turnover of £2.8m (ignoring the asset and employee criteria).

Illustration 8

P Ltd claims exemption from the preparation of group accounts on the grounds that the group is medium-sized. The group structure and company size are as follows:

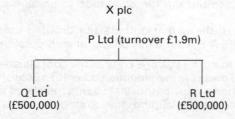

X plc

P Ltd (turnover £1.9m)

Q Ltd
(£500,000)

R Ltd
(£500,000)

P Ltd is entitled to the exemption as the combined size of P, Q and R is within the medium-sized threshold and the P group does not include any ineligible companies. However, none of P, Q and R can file abbreviated accounts as they are all members of an ineligible group (ie a group which includes a plc, X).

(c) EU parent (part of a larger group) exemption

(1) *Situations*

The EU parent situation relates to certain parent companies included in the accounts of a larger group. In particular situations, an intermediate parent company whose own immediate parent is established under the law of a member state of the EU may be exempt from the requirement to prepare group accounts.

The situations are:

(i) where the company is a wholly owned subsidiary of that EU parent undertaking;

(ii) where that EU parent undertaking holds more than 50% of the shares in the company and where shareholders holding either more than 50% of the remaining shares in the company or 5% of the total shares in the company have not served notice requiring the preparation of group accounts.

Illustration 9

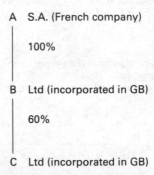

A   S.A. (French company)

100%

B   Ltd (incorporated in GB)

60%

C   Ltd (incorporated in GB)

B Ltd may be exempt from the requirement to prepare group accounts.

(2) *Conditions*

The exemption will only be given if detailed conditions are satisfied and additional disclosures given. In relation to the illustration above:

(i)   B Ltd must be part of a consolidation of a larger group whose immediate parent (A S.A.) is established under the law of a member state of the EU.

(ii) The accounts of the A group are drawn up and audited in accordance with the law of the relevant country (i e France in the above illustration).

(iii) B Ltd in its individual accounts states:

(1) that it is exempt from the obligation to prepare and deliver group accounts;

(2) the name of the parent undertaking drawing up the consolidated accounts (i e A S.A.) and its country of incorporation.

(iv) B Ltd delivers to the Registrar a copy of the consolidated accounts of the larger group. If these are in a language other than English it is necessary to attach in addition a copy of those accounts translated into English.

(v) the parent company claiming the exemption must be an unlisted company.

(3) *Disclosures*

The disclosure requirements are similar to those in (b)(3) above except that it is not necessary to disclose profit and loss for the financial year, and capital and reserves (3(iii) and 3(iv)).

In addition, it is not necessary to give the aggregate amount of investments under the equity method of valuation provided the directors state that in their opinion the aggregate amount of the parent company's investment in the subsidiaries concerned does not exceed the related underlying assets.

The exemption will only be given if detailed conditions are satisfied and additional disclosures given. In relation to the illustration above:

(i)   B Ltd must be part of a consolidation of a larger group whose immediate parent (A S.A.) is established under the law of a member state of the EU.
(ii) The accounts of the A group are drawn up and audited in accordance with the law of the relevant country (ie France in the above illustration).
(iii) B Ltd in its individual accounts states:

(1) that it is exempt from the obligation to prepare and deliver group accounts;
(2) the name of the parent undertaking drawing up the consolidated accounts (ie A S.A.) and its country of incorporation.

(iv) B Ltd delivers to the Registrar a copy of the consolidated accounts of the larger group. If these are in a language other than English, it is necessary to attach in addition a copy of those accounts translated into English.
(v)   the parent company claiming the exemption must be an unlisted company.

(d) Further disclosure requirements

Where a parent undertaking claims exemption from preparing group accounts for one of the three reasons referred to in (a) above, it must disclose by way of note:

(1) a statement that its accounts present information about it as an individual undertaking and not about its group; and
(2) a note of the grounds on which the parent undertaking is exempt from preparing consolidated accounts.

In addition, if the parent company claiming the exemption is itself part of a larger consolidation, it should disclose:

(1) the name of the parent undertaking of the largest group which includes P for which group accounts are prepared;
(2) the name of the parent undertaking of the smallest group which includes P and for which group accounts are prepared.

24.12   SIGNIFICANT RESTRICTIONS ON DISTRIBUTIONS

(a) FRS 2 requirements

FRS 2 deals with cases where the parent undertaking's access to distributable profits is materially limited by significant statutory, contractual or exchange control restrictions on a subsidiary's distributions. FRS 2 requires disclosure of the nature and extent of the restrictions.

(b) Situations

Most of the situations envisaged are likely to relate to overseas subsidiaries, although situations involving UK subsidiaries could include:

(1) profits capitalised by a subsidiary (for example, a bonus issue out of post-acquisition profits – see section 22.6);
(2) post-acquisition profits which have been applied by a subsidiary against its pre-acquisition losses (see below).

(c) Example

The balance sheets of H Ltd and its wholly owned subsidiary, S Ltd at 31.12.X2 are as follows:

	H Ltd £	S Ltd £
Investment in S Ltd	144	–
Net assets	1,156	340
	1,300	340
Called-up share capital	1,000	200
Profit and loss account	300	140
	1,300	340

At acquisition, the debit balance on S's reserves amounted to £32.

The usual consolidation procedures would calculate group revenue reserves as follows:

	£
Reserves of H	300
Post-acquisition reserves of S (32 + 140)	172
	472

However, it would be misleading to include this amount without an accompanying note stating that of this amount, £32 was not available for distribution. This makes sense since the maximum dividend which S could pay would be £140 and this would have the effect of increasing H's reserves to £440.

(d) Illustration 10

Note 33 – reserves (part of note)

The Group profit and loss account includes £367.5m (19X2 – £344.7m) in respect of subsidiaries and associated companies operating overseas which, if distributed as dividends, would involve liabilities to additional United Kingdom taxation as reduced by appropriate double taxation relief and, in certain territories, additional overseas taxation. The funds representing the reserves of subsidiaries operating overseas are in the main permanently employed in the business and are unlikely to be distributed as dividends. Remittances from certain territories in which subsidiaries and associated companies operate require the permission of the exchange control authorities in those territories.

25 ACQUISITION ACCOUNTING – FAIR VALUES, ACQUISITIONS, DISPOSALS AND FRS 3

Key Issues

* Consolidation methods
* Date control passes
* Features of acquisition accounting
* Fair values – measurement and disclosures
* Merger reserve – uses and limitations
* Changes in stake
* Share disposals
* Interaction with FRS 3

25.1 ACCOUNTING FOR BUSINESS COMBINATIONS

(a) Introduction

FRS 6, Acquisitions and mergers, sets out detailed criteria for determining the appropriate consolidation method for particular business combinations.

Those business combinations which satisfy the merger criteria must be accounted for using the merger accounting method of consolidation. FRS 6 anticipates that very few business combinations will satisfy the merger criteria. Merger accounting is dealt with in chapter 26. No further reference to it is made in this chapter.

FRS 6 states that: 'business combinations not accounted for by merger accounting should be accounted for by acquisition accounting . . .'

(b) Changes in the composition of a group

The phrase 'changes in the composition of a group' can refer to purchases or sales of shareholdings in subsidiary undertakings.

A key point is the date of change. An undertaking becomes a subsidiary undertaking on the date when control passes to its new parent. An undertaking ceases to be a subsidiary undertaking on the date on which its former parent undertaking relinquishes its control.

Control is the ability of an undertaking to direct the financial and operating policies of another undertaking with a view to gaining economic benefits from its activities.

Illustration 1

Extract from annual report and accounts of Grand Metropolitan plc for the year ended 30 September 1995.

Accounting policies (extract)

Basis of consolidation
The consolidated profit and loss account and balance sheet include the financial statements of the company and its subsidiary undertakings (subsidiaries) made up to 30 September. The results of subsidiaries sold or acquired are included in the profit and loss account up to, or from, the date control passes.

(c) Becoming a subsidiary undertaking

Where an undertaking becomes a subsidiary undertaking the appropriate date will be the date of acquisition or the date of merger in accordance with the Companies Act 1985. The accounting treatment and disclosure requirements FRS 6 and the Companies Act 1985 are dealt with in this chapter.

(d) Ceasing to be a subsidiary undertaking

Where an undertaking ceases to be a subsidiary undertaking, the consolidated profit and loss account should include:

(1) the results of the subsidiary undertaking up to the date that it ceases to be a subsidiary undertaking;
(2) any gain or loss arising on cessation (to the extent that these have not been already provided for in the consolidated accounts).

(See section 25.8 below.)

25.2 FEATURES OF ACQUISITION ACCOUNTING

FRS 6 includes the following key features of acquisition accounting:

(a) identifiable assets and liabilities of the companies acquired should be included in the acquirer's consolidated balance sheet at fair value at date of acquisition;
(b) results and cash flows should be brought in from the date of acquisition;
(c) previous year figures for the reporting entity should not be adjusted;
(d) the difference between:

  (i) the fair value of the net identifiable assets acquired; and
  (ii) the fair value of the purchase consideration;

is positive or negative goodwill.

Illustration 2

The draft balance sheet of S Ltd at acquisition appears as follows:

	£
Freehold property	150,000
Other assets	90,000
Liabilities	(60,000)
	180,000
Share capital	100,000
Profit and loss account	80,000
	180,000

H Ltd acquired the entire share capital. The purchase consideration was cash of £360,000. On the face of it, goodwill on consolidation is £180,000. But is this sensible? On closer inspection the freehold has an open market value of £250,000! Goodwill on consolidation is therefore to be calculated as £80,000.

In the consolidation working papers, it would be necessary to create a revaluation surplus account amounting to £100,000 (ie £250,000 less £150,000). All of this is pre-acquisition.

Analysis of equity would appear as follows:

ANALYSIS OF EQUITY

	Total £	Group share pre- acquisition £	Group share of post- acquisition P/L £	Group share of post- acquisition revaluation reserve £
Ordinary share capital	100,000	100,000		
P/L reserve at acquisition	80,000	80,000		
P/L reserve since acquisition	N/A		N/A	
Revaluation reserve (consolidation adjustment)	100,000	100,000		N/A
	280,000	280,000		
Cost of investment		360,000		
Goodwill on consolidation		80,000		
Reserves of holding company			X	X
Goodwill w/o against reserves			(80,000)	
Consolidated B/S totals			XX	XX

Disclosure implications are discussed in sections 25.3 and 25.6 below, which includes an illustration of a fair value table.

25.3 FAIR VALUES AND ACQUISITION ACCOUNTING

(a) Definition

Fair value is defined by FRS 7 as the amount at which an asset or liability could be exchanged in an arm's length transaction between informed and willing parties, other than in a forced or liquidation sale.

(b) Fair values and goodwill measurement

FRS 7 refers to positive or negative goodwill as the difference between:

(a) the cost of acquisition, and
(b) the fair value of the identifiable assets and liabilities acquired.

(c) Cost of acquisition

The cost of acquisition should consist of:

(a) amount of cash paid;
(b) the fair value of other purchase consideration;
(c) expenses of acquisition.

If the consideration includes an element which is contingent on one or more future events, such as profit performance, the cost of acquisition should include the fair value of amounts expected to be payable in the future. Cost of acquisition may therefore be subject to subsequent revision.

(d) Fair values of identifiable assets and liabilities acquired

FRS 7 specifies two general principles:

(a) the identifiable assets and liabilities should be those of the acquired entity that existed at the date of acquisition;

(b) the recognised assets and liabilities should be measured at fair values that reflect the conditions at the date of acquisition. Fair value is defined as the amount at which an asset or liability could be exchanged in an arm's length transaction between informed and willing parties, other than in a forced or liquidation sale.

The effect of the following should be excluded from the fair value calculation and treated as post-acquisition items:

(a) changes resulting from the acquirer's intentions or future actions;
(b) impairments or other changes, resulting from events subsequent to the acquisition;
(c) provisions or accruals for future operating losses or for reorganisations and integration costs expected to be incurred as a result of the acquisition. This exclusion applies irrespective of whether these relate to the acquired entity or to the acquirer. It is this aspect of FRS 7 which has been particularly contentious.

The standard gives guidance on the determination of fair values for the following specific categories:

(1) tangible fixed assets
(2) intangible fixed assets
(3) stocks and work in progress
(4) quoted investments
(5) monetary assets and liabilities
(6) contingencies
(7) business sold or held exclusively with a view to subsequent resale
(8) pensions and other post-retirement benefits
(9) deferred taxation.

Illustration 3 – extracts from FRS 7 (paragraph numbers refer to FRS 7)

Extracts, FRS 7, Statement of Standard Accounting Practice

Tangible fixed assets
9 The fair value of a tangible fixed asset should be based on:

(a) market value, if assets similar in type and condition are bought and sold on an open market; or
(b) depreciated replacement cost, reflecting the acquired business's normal buying process and the sources of supply and prices available to it.

The fair value should not exceed the recoverable amount of the asset.

Stocks and work-in-progress
11 Stocks, including commodity stocks, that the acquired entity trades on a market in which it participates as both a buyer and a seller should be valued at current market prices.
12 Other stocks, and work-in-progress, should be valued at the lower of replacement cost and net realisable value. Replacement cost is for this purpose the cost at which the stocks would have been replaced by the acquired entity, reflecting its normal buying process and the sources of supply and prices available to it – that is, the current cost of bringing the stocks to their present location and condition.

(e) The importance of fair value adjustments

Wherever possible, any adjustments to asset values should be put through the books of the acquired company. Failing this, consolidation adjustments should be put through the group accounts in order to ensure that goodwill on consolidation is a meaningful figure and does not partly reflect undervaluation of assets such as freehold property.

(f) Fair value disclosures

Detailed disclosures are set out in section 25.6 below. An important feature of these disclosures is the requirement by FRS 6 and CA 1985 for a fair value table.

In relation to a particular acquisition, FRS 6 requires the fair value table to show:

(1) the book values, as recorded in the acquired entity's books immediately before the acquisition and before any fair value adjustments;
(2) the fair value adjustments, analysed into:

    (i) revaluations;
    (ii) adjustments to achieve consistency of accounting policies; and
    (iii) any other significant adjustments, giving the reasons for the adjustments; and

(3) the fair values at the date of acquisition.

The table should disclose the amount of purchased goodwill or negative goodwill arising on the acquisition.

Illustration 4

28 Acquisition of Dartmouth Ltd

The effective date of acquisition of Dartmouth was 3 June 1994. The balance sheet at acquisition was as follows:

	Book value at acquisition £'000	Revaluation adjustments £'000	Accounting policy alignment £'000	Fair value to the Group £'000
Tangible assets	195	(55)	58	198
Investments	18	(9)	–	9
Goodwill	508	–	(508)	–
Current assets	330	–	–	330
Creditors and provisions	(910)	(1)	–	(911)
Net assets/(liabilities) at 3 June 1994	141	(65)	(450)	(374)
Share of net assets acquired				(367)
Goodwill written off to reserves				1006
Cost of acquisition				639
Satisfied by:				224
Cash				
Shares (525,000 ordinary shares of 25p each)				415
				639

Revaluation adjustments comprise a write-down of tangible assets following a revaluation of Dartmouth's properties (note 12) and a write-down in the carrying value of fixed asset investments.

The principal accounting policy changes which are required to bring Dartmouth's accounts into line with group policy are the reversal of depreciation on freehold and long leasehold buildings and the write off of goodwill.

Illustration 5

Extract from annual report and accounts of Cowie Group plc for the year ended 31 December 1994.

Note 24 (part of note)

24. Acquisitions

Leaside Bus Company Limited

	Acquired Book Value £000	Adjustment to Bus Accumlated Depreciation £000	Other Fair Value Adjustments £000	Net Cost £000	Contract Hire Business of Fleet Motor Management Cost £000	Other Cost £000
Net assets acquired:						
Tangible fixed assets	21,514	(3,812)	129	17,831	30,414	344
Stocks	336	–	–	336	–	–
Debtors	2,578	–	(121)	2,457	–	–
Investments	100	–	–	100	–	–
Creditors	(3,351)	–	(123)	(3,474)	(15,469)	–
Loans	(4,000)	–	–	(4,000)	–	–
	17,177	(3,812)	(115)	13,250	14,945	344
Goodwill				12,608	389	146
Satisfied by cash				25,858	15,334	490

	£000	£000	£000
Analysis of the net outflow of cash and cash equivalents in respect of the acquisitions:			
Loans acquired, settled at acquisition	4,000	–	–
Cash consideration	25,858	15,334	490
Net outflow of cash and cash equivalents in respect of the acquisitions	29,858	15,334	490

The adjustment to Bus Accumulated Depreciation in respect of Leaside Bus Company Limited represents the additional depreciation required to adjust the depreciation period of the related buses from 17 years to the Cowie Group practice of 14 years.

Other fair value adjustments represent adjustments to align acquired subsidiary accounting policies with those of the Group.

25.4 THE MERGER RESERVE (CA 1985, s 131)

(a) Section 131 and the merger reserve

FRS 6 does not deal directly with the accounting treatment of investments in the books of the parent company, although the matter is referred to in Appendix 1, FRS 6, note on legal requirements (see also section 25.10 below). However, the following provisions of the Companies Act 1985 are relevant:

(1) *Section 130*

If a company issues shares at a premium, whether for cash or otherwise, a sum equal to the aggregate amount or value of the premiums should be transferred to a share premium account.

(2) *Section 131*

This deals with the situation where the issuing company obtains at least 90% of the equity of another company. Section 130 does not apply to the premiums on any shares which are included in the consideration. Section 131 relief only applies to the issue of shares which take the holding to over 90%. SSAP 23 appendix refers to the term 'merger reserve'. This is the title widely referred to in practice, although it is not used by the Companies Act 1985.

Illustration 6

A already holds 15% of the share capital of company B. A issues 100,000 £1 ordinary shares (value £3) in order to obtain 80% of the share capital of B.

The journal entry in the books of company could be as follows:

Debit cost of investment in B	£300,000	*Credit* OSC	£100,000
		Merger reserve	£200,000

The possible uses of the merger reserve in the individual accounts of the parent company are referred to in section 25.10 below.

In the consolidated accounts, it is fairly common for consolidation goodwill to be written off against the merger reserve. This accounting treatment is illustrated in section 25.5 below.

25.5 ACQUISITION ACCOUNTING ILLUSTRATION

(a) Basic information

Panna Ltd and Rama Ltd decide to combine. Panna Ltd will issue 6,000 £1 shares in exchange for the entire share capital of Rama Ltd. The date of the combination is 30 September 19X3.

The draft financial statements of the two companies are as follows. No entries have yet been made in respect of the combination.

PROFIT AND LOSS ACCOUNT

for the year ended 31 December 19X3

	Panna £	Rama £
Turnover	22,000	20,000
Cost of sales	(8,000)	(6,000)
Distribution costs	(2,000)	(4,000)
Administrative expenses	(3,000)	(2,000)
Operating profit	9,000	8,000
Taxation	4,500	4,000
Profit after tax	4,500	4,000
Balance brought forward	8,000	5,500
Balance carried forward	12,500	9,500

Balance sheets at 31 December 19X3	Panna £	Rama £
Tangible fixed assets	16,000	11,000
Net current assets	13,500	9,500
	29,500	20,500
Called-up share capital (£1 shares)	8,000	8,500
Share premium	4,000	1,500
Revaluation reserve	5,000	1,000
Profit and loss account	12,500	9,500
	29,500	20,500

(b) Acquisition accounting procedures

Assume the combination is accounted for using acquisition accounting.

For this purpose assume that the following additional information is provided:

(i) The shares in Panna Ltd are issued at £5 per share.
(ii) At 30.9.X3, the fixed assets of Rama Ltd have a fair value of £15,000.
(iii) The balances on share premium account and revaluation reserve are pre-acquisition.
(iv) The balance on profit and loss account at 30.9.X3 was £8,500 (estimated by time apportionment).

(1) *Consolidated balance sheet procedures*

Before setting out the working papers, it is necessary to record the issue of 6,000 shares at an issue price of £30,000. The shares are issued at a premium of £24,000. The journal entry in the books of Panna Ltd is:

Debit cost of investment in		*Credit* ordinary share capital	6,000
Rama Ltd (6,000 × £5)	30,000	*Credit* merger reserve	24,000
		(see above)	

Remember also that the adjustment account must reflect the undervaluation of fixed assets of £4,000 (i e £15,000 − £11,000) – see analysis below.

Consolidated fixed assets are £16,000 + £15,000 i e £31,000.

Assume that goodwill arising on consolidation is written off against merger reserve (see section 25.4(a) above).

(2) *Analysis of equity*

	Total £	Pre-acquisition £	Post-acquisition P/L £	Post-acquisition share premium £	Post-acquisition revaluation reserve £
Share capital	8,500	8,500			
P/L at acq.	8,500	8,500			
since acq.	1,000		1,000		
Share premium	1,500	1,500		–	
Revaluation					
per acs	1,000	1,000			–
consol. adj.	4,000	4,000			–
	24,500	23,500			
Cost of investment		30,000			
Goodwill on consolidation written off against merger reserve of Panna		6,500			
Panna's reserves			12,500	4,000	5,000
Consolidated B/S totals			13,500	4,000	5,000

(3) *Consolidated balance sheet (acquisition accounting basis)*

	£
Tangible fixed assets	31,000
Net current assets	23,000
	54,000
Called up share capital	14,000
Share premium account	4,000
Merger reserve (24,000 − 6,500)	17,500
Revaluation reserve	5,000
Profit and loss account	13,500
	54,000

(4) *Consolidated profit and loss account procedures*

The key point to remember is that under acquisition, only three months' results of Rama Ltd would be included.

The consolidated profit and loss account is as follows.

CONSOLIDATED PROFIT AND LOSS ACCOUNT
(ACQUISITION ACCOUNTING BASIS)

for the year ended 31 December 19X3

	£
Turnover (22 + 5)	27,000
Cost of sales (8 + 1.5)	9,500
Gross profit	17,500
Distribution costs (2 + 1)	(3,000)
Administrative expenses (3 + 0.5)	(3,500)
Profit on ordinary activities before tax (9 + 2)	11,000
Taxation (4.5 + 1)	5,500
Profit on ordinary activities after tax	5,500
Balance brought forward	8,000
Balance carried forward	13,500

25.6 ACQUISITION ACCOUNTING DISCLOSURES

The disclosure requirements of FRS 6 are extremely detailed and run to almost eight pages – the note below aims to provide an overview.

(a) General disclosures

The consolidated accounts should disclose:

(1) the names of combining entities (other than parent);
(2) that the combination is accounted for using acquisition accounting;
(3) date of combination.

(b) Material acquisitions

Details of the following are required for *each* material acquisition:

(1) composition and fair value of consideration given;
(2) a fair value table (see (d) below);
(3) details of reorganisation and reconstruction provisions set up by the acquired entity in the twelve months prior to acquisition;
(4) details where fair values of assets and liabilities have been determined on a provisional basis;
(5) acquisition details required by FRS 3 (Reporting financial performance) and FRS 1 (Cash flow statements);
(6) details of certain costs incurred in reorganising, restructuring and integrating the acquisition;
(7) details of certain post-acquisition exceptional profits or losses which have been determined using fair values at acquisition, for example disposals of fixed assets which were part of the company acquired;
(8) details of movements on provisions for costs related to an acquisition;
(9) details of profits relating to the acquired entity for periods up to the date of acquisition;
    (i) current year up to date of acquisition;
    (ii) previous year.

(c) Minor acquisitions

The disclosure referred to in (b) (1) to (8) but not (9) should be given on an aggregate basis for non-material acquisitions.

(d) Fair value table

A fair value table should be provided for each material acquisition, and for non-material acquisitions in aggregate.

(e) Substantial acquisitions

Substantial acquisitions are defined as:

(1) for listed companies: class I or super class I transactions (see UITF 15 at (f) below);
(2) for other entities:

    (i) where the net assets or operating profits of the acquired entity exceed 15% of those of the acquiring entity; or
    (ii) where the fair value of the consideration given exceeds 15% of the net assets of the acquiring entity.

The disclosures below are required for all substantial acquisitions and also 'in other exceptional cases where an acquisition is of such significance that the disclosure is necessary in order to give a true and fair view':

(1) summarised profit and loss/gains and losses information for the acquired entity from the beginning of the year up to the date of acquisition;
(2) profit after tax and MI of the acquired entity for the previous year.

(f) UITF 15 – Disclosure of substantial acquisitions

FRS 6, Acquisitions and mergers, refers to specific disclosure requirements for 'substantial acquisitions' – the definition of which refers to 'class 1 or super class 1 transactions'.

Some time after the issue of FRS 6, the Stock Exchange abolished the category of 'class 1 transactions'.

UITF 15 requires the FRS 6 reference to class 1 transactions to be interpreted as meaning 'those transactions in which any of the ratios set out in the London Stock Exchange Listing Rules defining super class 1 transactions exceeds 15%'.

Illustration 7

Extract from annual report and accounts of Grand Metropolitan plc for the year ended 30 September 1995

Financial Review (extract)

Adoption of new accounting standards
In September 1994, the Accounting Standards Board issued FRS 6 – Acquisitions and Mergers and FRS 7 – Fair Values in Acquisition Accounting. In complying with these reporting standards, GrandMet has adopted their requirements in advance of their mandatory implementation date.

FRS 7 sets out new rules to be adopted when establishing the fair values of the assets and liabilities of an acquired entity. These rules require that the assets and liabilities be valued to reflect their condition at the date of acquisition and not reflect any intentions that the acquirer may have. As a result reorganisation and integration costs can no longer be provided for within the fair value balance sheet of an acquired entity. An exceptional charge to operating profit of £122 million was made in respect of the integration of the acquired Pet businesses into Pillsbury and European Foods.

The other main effect on GrandMet of complying with the new standards has been the increased level of disclosure concerning the group's acquisition of Pet. This is set out in the notes to the financial statements.

In compliance with these standards, comparative figures have not been restated.

Note 31 (extract)

31 Purchase of subsidiaries

(i) Pet Incorporated. The fair value balance sheet of Pet Incorporated prior to its acquisition on 9 February 1995, translated at the then exchange rate of £1 = $1.56, has been assessed as follows:

	Pet book values £m	Revaluati- on £m	Account- ing policy conformity £m	Busi- nesses held for sale £m	Fair value balance sheet £m
Goodwill	238	–	(238)	–	–
Brands	–	1,067	–	–	1,067
Tangible fixed assets	210	(37)	(2)	(22)	149
Businesses held for sale	–	–	–	161	161
Stocks	131	(3)	–	(22)	106
Debtors	128	(14)	–	(17)	97
Creditors and provisions	(175)	4	(8)	5	(174)
Net borrowings	(328)	6	–	–	(322)
Net assets	204	1,023	(248)	105	1,084
Goodwill					690
Purchase consideration (wholly cash)					1,774

The unaudited consolidated statements of income of Pet Incorporated for the period 1 July 1994 to 8 February 1995, translated at the average exchange rate for the period of £1 = $1.57, and the year ended 30 June 1994, translated at the average exchange rate for the year of £1 = $1.49, are set out below. This financial information has been prepared in accordance with US generally accepted accounting principles (US GAAP) and under Pet Incorporated's accounting policies prior to the acquisition.

	1 July 1994 to 8 February 1995 £m	Year ended 30 June 1994 £m
Net sales	613	1,062
Cost of goods sold	(320)	(506)
Gross profit	293	556
Selling, general and administrative expenses	(251)	(399)
Amortisation of goodwill	(5)	(8)
Operating income	37	149
Interest	(14)	(20)
Income from continuing operations before income taxes	23	129
Provision for income taxes	(17)	(50)
Income from continuing operations	6	79
Loss on disposal of discontinued operations, net of income taxes	–	(20)
Cumulative effect of accounting change, net of income taxes	–	(1)
Net income	6	58

US GAAP does not incorporate a statement of recognised gains and losses. However, such a statement would include the £6m net income shown above (with the effect of the accounting change separately disclosed) less dividends of £17m, and exchange adjustments of £nil (1994 – £58m, £21m and £7m respectively)

Illustration 8

Extract from annual report and accounts of Granada Group plc for the year ended 30 September 1995.

Note 24

	Book value £m	Fair value adjustment £m	Fair value to Group £m
24 Acquisition of business			
a Summary of the effect of the acquisition of Pavilion			
Tangible fixed assets	93.8	0.2	94.0
Stocks	3.2	–	3.2
Debtors	4.3	–	4.3
Creditors	(12.0)	(1.7)	(13.7)
Cash and cash equivalents	3.5	–	3.5
Corporation tax	(1.3)	0.5	(0.8)
Deferred taxation	(0.3)	–	(0.3)
Net assets acquired before borrowings	91.2	(1.0)	90.2
Cash paid			77.5
Borrowings acquired			49.0
Integration and acquisition provisions			9.4
Fair value of consideration			135.9
Goodwill			(45.7)
			90.2

Pavilion was acquired on 13 April 1995. The results for Pavilion for the period from 30 October 1994 to 13 April 1995 was a profit before tax of £2.3 million (1994 full year profit before tax: £4.9 million). Pavilion contributed £0.6 million to the cash flows of the Group and the profit and loss account of the Group included the following amounts related to Pavilion: depreciation £0.8 million; staff costs £4.7 million and other operating costs £46.9 million.

	1995 £m	1994 £m		**1995** £m	1994 £m
b Summary of the effect of the acquisition of other new businesses:					
Net assets acquired:			Discharged by:		
Fixed assets	24.3	6.9	Cash	**32.7**	11.3
Investments	–	(0.7)	Deferred consideration	**10.5**	–
Stocks	2.1	0.6			
Debtors	2.2	2.7			
Creditors	(13.1)	(16.1)			
Borrowings acquired	(21.8)	–			
Cash and cash equivalents	(2.2)	–			
Deferred taxation	3.7	–			
Goodwill on acquisitions	48.0	17.9			
	43.2	11.3		**43.2**	11.3

25.7 CHANGES IN STAKE

(a) Situations

FRS 2 deals with the specific cases of:

(1) acquiring a subsidiary undertaking in stages (step-by-step or piecemeal acquisition);
(2) increasing an interest held in a subsidiary undertaking;
(3) reducing an interest held in a subsidiary undertaking.

(b) Acquiring a subsidiary undertaking in stages

The Companies Act 1985, Sch 4A, para 9 requires that a subsidiary's assets and liabilities should be included in the consolidated accounts at fair value as at the date that it became a subsidiary undertaking. This statutory requirement also applies where the group's interest in the subsidiary undertaking is acquired In stages.

Illustration 9

H Ltd acquired a controlling interest in S Ltd in two stages, as follows:

(1) 30.6.19x2 20% holding at a cost of £33,000 when the fair value of the net assets amounted to £150,000.
(2) 31.3.19X3 40% holding at a cost of £92,000 when the fair value of the net assets amounted to £190,000.

The CA 1985 computation of goodwill arising on consolidation is:

	£
Cost of investment (33 + 92)	125,000
Group share of net assets at acquisition 60% × £190,000	114,000
∴ Goodwill on consolidation	11,000

FRS 2, para 89 refers to special cases, for example:

> . . . in special circumstances, however, not using fair values at the dates of earlier purchases, while using an acquisition cost part of which relates to earlier purchases, may result in accounting that is inconsistent with the way the investment has been treated previously, and for that reason, may fail to give a true and fair view. . .

One such case referred to by FRS 2 is where a group starts off with an interest which is treated as an associated undertaking. A further purchase of shares turns the undertaking into a subsidiary undertaking.

This is an example of a situation where the statutory calculation of goodwill would be misleading. FRS 2 therefore requires that goodwill should be calculated as the sum of goodwill arising from each purchase adjusted as necessary for any subsequent diminution in value.

Illustration 10

In the above illustration, assume that the 20% investment was treated as an associated undertaking (see chapter 27). At the date of purchase, the fair value of the company's net assets amounted to £150,000.

The FRS 2 calculation of goodwill is therefore:

	£
30.6.19X2 £33,000 − (20% × £150,000)	3,000
31.3.19X3 £92,000 − (40% × £190,000)	16,000
	19,000

The goodwill in the consolidated accounts would therefore be £19,000. However, the above is a departure from the statutory requirement in CA 1985, s 227(6) which requires particulars of the departure, the reasons for it and its effect, to be disclosed by way of note.

The difference between the two goodwill figures of £8,000 (£19,000 – £11,000) forms part of group reserves (relating to the associated undertaking) (ie 20% (190,000 – 150,000)).

(c) Increase in stake in undertaking that is already a subsidiary

Where a group increases its interest in an undertaking that is already a subsidiary, the subsidiary's assets and liabilities should be revalued to fair value. Goodwill arising on the increase in the interest in stake should be calculated by reference to those fair values.

Illustration 11

H Ltd acquires a 70% shareholding in S Ltd on 30.9.19X3 at a cost of £24,000 when the balance sheet of S Ltd was as follows. Assume that assets were already stated at fair value.

	£
Net assets	32,000
Ordinary share capital	10,000
P/L reserves	22,000
	32,000

The effect on the consolidated balance sheet, leaving in goodwill for purposes of explanation would be:

	£
Net assets	32,000
Goodwill £24,000 – 70% (£32,000)	1,600
	33,600
Minority interest 30% × £32,000	9,600
Cash paid	24,000
	33,600

On 30.11.19X5, H Ltd purchased a further 20% of the shares in S Ltd at a cost of £14,000. At that date, the balance sheet of S Ltd was:

	£
Net assets	42,000
Ordinary share capital	10,000
P/L reserves	32,000
	42,000

The fair value of the net assets was estimated at £50,000.

Following FRS 2, the effect on the consolidated balance sheet at 30.11.19X5 would be:

	£
Net assets	50,000
Goodwill (see below)	5,600
	55,600

Minority interest	
10% × £50,000	5,000
Group revaluation reserve	
70% (50,000 – 42,000)	5,600
Group P/L reserves	
70% (32,000 – 22,000)	7,000
Cash paid (24,000 + 14,000)	38,000
	55,600

Working – Goodwill calculation:

	£
30.9.19X3	1,600
30.11.19X5	
£14,000 − (20% × £50,000)	4,000
	5,600

In support of the above treatment, FRS 2, para 90 states:

> ... if the assets and liabilities were not revalued to fair values before calculating the goodwill arising on the change in stake, then the difference between the consideration paid and the relevant proportion of the carrying value of net assets acquired would be made up in part of goodwill and in part of changes in value ...

(d) Reducing an interest held in a subsidiary undertaking

Where a group reduces its interest in a subsidiary undertaking, it should calculate any profit or loss arising as follows:

	£	£
Proceeds of sale		X
The carrying amount of the net assets of that subsidiary undertaking attributable to the group's interest before the reduction	X	
Less the carrying amount attributable to the group's interest after the reduction	X	(X)
Less the appropriate proportion of goodwill not previously written off through P/L (per UITF 3)		(X)
Profit (loss) on disposal		X

25.8 ACCOUNTING FOR DISPOSALS OF SHARES IN SUBSIDIARY UNDERTAKINGS

(a) Date of change

Under FRS 2, the date for determining when a subsidiary ceases to be a subsidiary is when its former parent relinquishes control.

The explanation section of FRS 2 gives guidance on how to determine this date, as this is an area which can give rise to difficulties in practice.

In the more straightforward cases the date is determined as follows:

(1) control transferred by a public offer – the date the offer becomes unconditional (usually because a sufficient number of acceptances have been received);
(2) control transferred by a private transaction – the date an unconditional offer is accepted.

(b) Accounting implications

The consolidated profit and loss account should include:

(1) the results of the subsidiary up to the date that it ceases to be a subsidiary;
(2) any gain or loss arising on cessation (i e gain or loss on disposal of shares).

(c) Computation of gain or loss on disposal

The gain or loss is calculated as follows:

	£	£	£
Proceeds of sale			X
Carrying amount of net assets before cessation	(X)		
Less carrying amount of net assets after cessation	X	(X)	
Goodwill not written off through profit and loss account (see UITF 3 in section (e) below)		(X)	
Gain (or loss)			X

(d) Illustration 12 – Henry Group

Until fairly recently, Henry Ltd owned two wholly-owned subsidiaries – Percy Ltd and Thomas Ltd.

Both subsidiaries had been acquired several years ago when their reserves amounted to £25,000 and £4,000 respectively. Goodwill arising on consolidation had been written off immediately to profit and loss reserves.

Henry disposed of its entire shareholding in Thomas Ltd on 31 March 19X8 for cash proceeds of £92,000.

The draft accounts of the three companies for the year ended 31 December 19X8 were as follows:

DRAFT PROFIT AND LOSS ACCOUNTS

	Henry Ltd £	Percy Ltd £	Thomas Ltd £
Turnover	650,000	80,000	50,000
Operating expenses	(300,000)	(25,000)	(22,000)
Profit before tax	350,000	55,000	28,000
Dividend receivable	12,000	–	–
Taxation	(160,000)	(27,000)	(14,000)
Proposed dividends	(50,000)	(12,000)	(5,000)
Retained profit	152,000	16,000	9,000
Balance brought forward	430,000	40,000	12,400
Balance carried back	582,000	56,000	21,400

The draft profit and loss account of Henry Ltd does not reflect the gain or loss on the sale of shares in Thomas Ltd.

DRAFT BALANCE SHEETS

	Henry Ltd £	Percy Ltd £	Thomas Ltd £
Sundry net assets	956,000	168,000	76,400
Investment in Percy	172,000	–	–
Investment in Thomas	84,000	–	–
Dividends receivable	12,000	–	–
	1,224,000	168,000	76,400
Called up share capital	500,000	100,000	50,000
Profit and loss account	582,000	56,000	21,400
Proposed dividends	50,000	12,000	5,000
Sale of investment in Thomas	92,000	–	–
	1,224,000	168,000	76,400

The key workings are as follows:

(1) Goodwill on consolidation arising on the acquisition of Percy and Thomas

	Percy £	Thomas £
Cost of investment	172,000	84,000
Share capital	(100,000)	(50,000)
Pre-acquisition reserves	(25,000)	(4,000)
Goodwill arising	47,000	30,000

(2) Consolidated profit and loss reserves at 31 December 19X7

	£
Henry	430,000
Percy (40,000 − 25,000)	15,000
Thomas (12,400 − 4,000)	8,400
	453,400
Less goodwill written off direct to reserves (47,000 + 30,000)	77,000
Balance at 31 December 19X7	376,400

(3) Gain or loss on disposal of shares – group accounts

	£	£
Proceeds of sale		92,000
Net assets at date of sale = shareholders funds at 31 March 19X8		
OSC	50,000	
P/L b/f	12,400	
3 months profit after tax 3/12 × 14,000	3,500	
		65,900
		26,100
Less goodwill previously written off (see UITF 3, below)		30,000
		(3,900)

Notes:
(1) The loss of £3,900 recorded in the group accounts may be reconciled to the profit of £8,000 (92,000 − 84,000) recorded in the parent company's accounts as follows. The parent company profit and loss account records only dividends received whereas the group profit and loss account includes all attributable profits of subsidiaries whether paid out as dividends or retained:

	£
Profit in accounts of parent company		8,000
Post acquisition profits of Thomas included in group accounts		
Reserves at acquisition	4,000	
Reserves at disposal	15,900	
Increase		11,900
Loss in group accounts		(3,900)

(2) Tax on disposal of shares has been ignored.
    The group accounts may be completed as follows:

CONSOLIDATED PROFIT AND LOSS ACCOUNT

for the year ended 31 December 19X8

	£
Turnover (650 + 80 + 3/12 × 50)	742,500
Operating expenses (300 + 25 + 3/12 × 22)	330,500
Operating profit	412,000
Loss on sale of shares (exceptional item per FRS 3 – see section 25.9)	(3,900)
Profit before tax	408,100
Taxation (160 + 27 + 3/12 × 14)	190,500
Profit after tax	217,600
Proposed dividends	(50,000)
Retained profit	167,600

CONSOLIDATED BALANCE SHEET

at 31 December 19X8

	£
Sundry net assets (956 + 168)	1,124,000
Less proposed dividends	50,000
	1,074,000
Called-up share capital	500,000
Profit and loss account	574,000
	1,074,000

PROFIT AND LOSS RESERVES

	£
Balance at 1 January 19X8	376,400
Retained profit for the year	167,600
Goodwill written back to profit and loss account on disposal	30,000
Balance at 31 December 19X8	574,000

Notes:
(1) The goodwill write back is in accordance with UITF 3 (see below).
(2) The closing balance of £574,000 may be reconciled to the individual balances as follows:

	£
Henry's P/L (582 + 8)	590,000
Percy's post-acq. (56 – 25)	31,000
Goodwill w/o against reserves (Percy)	(47,000)
	574,000

(e) UITF Consensus 3 – goodwill on disposal of a business

(1) *Scope*

UITF 3 deals with the computation and disclosure of the profit or loss on the disposal of a previously acquired business, subsidiary or associate.

(2) *Computation*

The profit or loss on disposal should include the attributable amount of purchased goodwill where this has not previously been charged through the profit and loss account.

In the illustration in (d), the goodwill relating to the earlier acquisition of Thomas of £30,000 had been charged direct to reserves, without any charge through the profit and loss account. Without the goodwill adjustment, the consolidated profit and loss account would simply have picked up £26,100 (i e £92,000 − £65,900). The double entry to record the adjustment was debit P/L 30,000, credit P/L reserves (reserve movement) 30,000.

Suppose, as an alternative, Henry group goodwill policy was one of amortisation, with Thomas's goodwill written off over ten years. If the disposal was, say, four years after the acquisition the profit and loss accounts of the four years would each have been charged with £3,000 i e a total of £12,000. The required goodwill adjustment on disposal would then have been £18,000 (i e £30,000 total less £12,000 in respect of amounts amortised through P/L ac).

(3) *Disclosure*

The goodwill attributable to the business disposed of, and included in the P/L calculation should be disclosed on the face of the P/L or in a note.

Where it is impracticable to make a reasonable estimate of the purchased goodwill, the fact and the reasons should be disclosed.

(4) *Other possibilities*

The principles of UITF 3 are to apply to cases where negative goodwill arises and to business closures.

Illustration 13

Accounting policies (extract)

Goodwill
The net assets of businesses acquired are incorporated in the consolidated accounts at their fair value to the Group. The difference between the price paid for subsidiary undertakings and the fair value of net assets acquired is taken direct to reserves. At the time of any disposal of a business the goodwill which arose at the time of acquisition is written back from reserves to calculate the profit or loss on disposal.

(f) Part disposal, control retained

Suppose a parent sells a 25% shareholding in a previously wholly-owned subsidiary.

Ignoring tax, the group's gain or loss on disposal would be calculated as follows:

	£	£
Proceeds of sale of 25% holding		X
Carrying amount of net assets before disposal	X	
Less carrying amount × 75% of net assets after disposal	X	
	—	(X)
		X
Less 25% of any goodwill, to extent that it has not been written off through P/L		(X)
Gain (loss) on disposal		X

25.9 INTERACTION WITH FRS 3 – REPORTING FINANCIAL PERFORMANCE

(a) FRS 3 – a recap

The main elements of FRS 3 were referred to in chapter 8 and included:

(1) the treatment of exceptional items;
(2) the profit and loss account was to highlight the impact on results of new acquisitions and discontinued operations;

(3) the virtual abolition of extraordinary items;
(4) the new statements and notes:

   (i)   statement of total recognised gains and losses,
   (ii) note of historical cost profits and losses;
   (iii) movements in shareholders funds.

(5) the measurement of profit or loss on disposal of fixed assets which were included in the balance sheet on a revaluation basis;
(6) a revision in the definition of earnings per share.

The impact of FRS 3 on company disclosures is illustrated in section (e) below.

(b) Acquisitions and disposals of shares in subsidiaries

(1) *Acquisitions*

The aggregate results of acquisitions should be disclosed separately, down to operating profit level. For groups using the Companies Act 1985, format 1, this will require separate disclosure of turnover, cost of sales, distribution costs and administrative expenses.

This may be achieved by showing the impact on turnover and operating profit on the face of the consolidated profit and loss account, as indicated in the pro forma below. The required information for costs of sales, distribution costs and administrative expenses would be shown by way of note.

PRO FORMA CONSOLIDATED PROFIT AND LOSS ACCOUNT

for the year ended 31 December 19X8 (extract)

	£	£
Turnover		
Continuing operations		X
Acquisitions		X
		X
Cost of sales		(X)
Gross profit		X
Net operating expenses		(X)
Operating profit		
Continuing operations	X	
Acquisitions	X	
		X
Loss on sale of business		(X)
Profit on disposal of fixed assets		X
Profit on ordinary activities before interest		X
Interest payable		(X)
Profit on ordinary activities before taxation		X

Illustration 14

Referring back to section 25.5, FRS 3 would require items such as £5,000 turnover and £2,000 operating profit to be separately disclosed under the heading 'acquisitions'.

In the following year these items will be included in the comparative figures under 'continuing operations' and should not be separately disclosed.

FRS 3 requires comparatives to be restated on the basis of the status of an operation in the period being reported on. There will thus never be an item in comparative figures relating to acquisitions.

(2) *Disposals*

Profits or losses on the sale of an operation will be classed as exceptional items and are to be shown beneath the operating profit figure in the consolidated profit and loss account, as indicated in the pro forma above.

Illustration 15

Referring back to section 25.8, the loss on disposal of the shares in Thomas of £3,900 would appear under 'loss on sale of business' (or similar description), as shown in the pro forma.

The related turnover, expense and profit figures would only need to be separately disclosed under FRS 3 if the disposal was classified as a discontinued operation (see (c)).

(c) Deciding whether operations are continuing or discontinued

A company will have to satisfy several stringent conditions before it can classify particular operations as discontinued. If it cannot satisfy all of these conditions, the particular operations will automatically be regarded as continuing.

Discontinued operations are a company or group's operations that are sold or terminated and that satisfy all of the following conditions:

(1) *Timing*
The sale or termination must be completed either:

(i) in the current period, or
(ii) before the earlier of three months after the commencement of the subsequent period and the date on which the financial statements are approved.

(2) *For a termination*
The former activities have ceased permanently.

(3) *Extent of change*
The sale or termination must:

(i) have a material effect on the nature and focus of the reporting entity's operations (see extract below), and
(ii) represent a material reduction in its operating facilities resulting either from:

(a) its withdrawal from a particular market (whether class of business or geographical), or
(b) a material reduction in turnover in the reporting entity's continuing markets.

(4) *Separately identifiable*
The assets, liabilities, results of operations and activities must be clearly distinguishable physically, operationally and for financial reporting purposes.

The above aspects of FRS 3 are particularly complex and so the final paragraphs from the explanation section of FRS 3 are also included.

Extract FRS 3, paras 42–44

42 To be included in the category of discontinued operations, a sale or termination must have a material effect on the nature and focus of the reporting entity's operations and represent a material reduction in its operating facilities resulting either from its withdrawal from a particular market (whether class of business or geographical) or from a material reduction in turnover in its continuing markets. The nature and focus of a reporting entity's operations refers to the positioning of its products or services in their markets including the aspects of both quality and location. For example, if a hotel company which has traditionally served the lower end of the hotel market sold its existing

chain and bought luxury hotels then, while remaining in the business of managing hotels, the group would be changing the nature and focus of its operations. A similar situation would arise if the same company were to sell its hotels, in, say, the United States of America and buy hotels in Europe. The regular sales and replacements of material assets which are undertaken by a reporting entity as part of the routine maintenance of its portfolio of assets should not be classified as discontinuances and acquisitions. In the example, the sale of hotels and the purchase of others within the same market sector and similar locations would be treated as wholly within continuing operations.

43   To be classified as discontinued a sale or termination should have resulted from a strategic decision by the reporting entity either to withdraw from a particular market (whether class of business or geographical) or to curtail materially its presence in a continuing market (i e 'downsizing'). The sale or termination of a component of a reporting entity's operations which is undertaken primarily in order to achieve productivity improvements of other cost savings is a part of that entity's continuing operations and the effects of the sale or termination should be included under that heading.

44   To be classified as discontinued, the assets, liabilities, results of operations and activities of an operation must be clearly distinguishable, physically, operationally and for financial reporting purposes. If the financial results of a sold or terminated operation are not identifiable separately from the accounting records or to a material extent can only be derived through making allocations of income or expenses, then the operation cannot be classified as a discontinued operation. For example, a manufacturing facility that is closed down but which lacks an external market price for its output cannot be classified as a discontinued operation.

Illustration 16

A group has four main business activities – retail, leisure, personal care and footware. Balance sheet date is 4 June 1995. The retail business is disposed of on 31 March 1995, the leisure business on 25 July 1995. Under FRS 3 it is likely that the two disposals will count as discontinued operations in the 1995 accounts. If so, any turnover and profits in the year to 4 June 1995 relating to retail or leisure would be classed as discontinued. Comparative figures may need to be restated in accordance with paragraph 64 of FRS 3.

(d) Establishing a provision following a decision to sell or terminate an operation

Having decided to sell or terminate an operation, a company may wish to set up a provision to cover obligations incurred that will not be covered by future profits of that operation or by the disposal of the operation's assets.

   This raises three issues which are addressed by FRS 3:
(1) whether a decision to sell or terminate an operation has been made in the current period;
(2) the extent to which a provision may be set up to cover sale or termination expenses and operating losses up to the date of sale or termination;
(3) whether asset write-downs and any provisions set up should be classed under continuing operations or discontinued operations.

The evidence to support point (1) could be provided by a binding sale agreement or by a detailed formal plan for termination from which the company cannot realistically withdraw. Further considerations are discussed in the explanation section to FRS 3.

FRS 3 restricts the provision to:

(i) the direct costs of the sale or termination; and
(ii) any operating losses of the operation up to the date of sale or termination.

Both (i) and (ii) should take into account the aggregate of any profit which is likely to be recognised in the profit and loss account from the future profits of the operation or the disposal of its assets.

Any provisions set up and any write-downs of assets should appear under continuing operations unless the company can show that the operation qualifies for the period under review as a discontinued operation.

The illustrative examples in the appendix to FRS 3 (not reproduced in this text) give an example of possible disclosures.

(e) Illustration of disclosures under FRS 3

Illustration 17

Extract from annual report and accounts of Perry Group plc for the year ended 31 December 1994.

Consolidated profit and loss account

	Notes	1994 £'000	1993 £'000
Turnover			
Continuing operations		**353,263**	311,036
New operations		**9,581**	217
	1	**362,844**	311,253
Cost of sales		**340,645**	293,244
Gross profit		22,199	18,009
Administrative expenses		**15,409**	12,595
Operating profit			
Continuing operations		**6,272**	5,406
New operations		**518**	8
Operating profit	2	**6,790**	5,414
Continuing operations			
Profit on the sale of fixed assets		–	1,853
		6,790	7,267
Interest	3	**1,723**	2,112
Profit on ordinary activities before taxation	1	**5,067**	5,155
Taxation charge	6	**1,721**	1,350
Profit on ordinary activities after taxation		**3,346**	3,805
Dividends	7	**1,898**	1,588
Retained profit for the year		**1,448**	2,217
Earnings per ordinary share	8	**13.3p**	18.2p
Dividends per ordinary share	7	**7.5p**	7.0p

Movements of reserves are shown in notes 20 to 22.

Illustration 18

Extract from annual report and accounts of Cadbury Schweppes plc for the year ended 31 December 1994.

Group profit and loss account

Notes		Continuing operations £m	Acquisitions £m	*1994* **£m**	*1993* *£m*
2	**Turnover**	3,980.6	49.0	**4,029.6**	3,724.8
	Cost of sales	(2,095.6)	(33.2)	**(2,128.8)**	(1,974.4)
	Gross profit	1,885.0	15.8	**1,900.8**	1,750.4
	Distribution costs, including marketing	(1,011,4)	(7.1)	**(1,018.5)**	(964.9)
	Administration expenses	(354.5)	(3.9)	**(358.4)**	(331.3)
	Other operating income/ (charges)	(19.6)	0.1	**(19.5)**	(18.2)
	Trading profit	499.5	4.9	**504.4**	436.0
	Share of profits of associated undertakings	16.4	–	**16.4**	13.4
2	**Operating profit**	515.9	4.9	**520.8**	449.4
	Profit on sale of investment			–	11.9
2	Loss re properties			**(0.3)**	(1.5)
	Profit on ordinary activities before interest			**520.5**	459.8
5	Net interest			**(42.0)**	(43.5)
2	**Profit on ordinary activities before taxation**			**478.5**	416.3
6	Tax on profit on ordinary activities			**(155.2)**	(129.1)
	Profit on ordinary activities after taxation			**323.3**	287.2
	Equity minority interests			**(54.0)**	(44.2)
7	Preference dividends			**(7.4)**	(6.2)
	Profit for the financial year			**261.9**	236.8
7	Dividends to ordinary shareholders			**(130.5)**	(116.4)
	Profit retained for the financial year			**131.4**	120.4
8	**Earnings per ordinary share of 25p**			**31.46p**	30.59p

Illustration 19

Extract from annual report and accounts of Grand Metropolitan plc for the year ended 30 September 1995.

Consolidated profit and loss account

	Notes	1995 Before exceptional items £m	1995 Exceptional items (note 6) £m	1995 Total £m	1994 Before exceptional items £m	1994 Exceptional items (note 6) £m	1994 Total £m
Turnover							
Continuing operations		7,475		7,475	7,464		7,464
Acquisitions		490		490			
		7,965		7,965			
Discontinued operations		60		60	316		316
Total turnover	3	8,025		8,025	7,780		7,780
Operating costs	4	(6,993)	(122)	(7,115)	(6,757)	(272)	(7,029)
Operating profit							
Continuing operations		938	–	938	983	(272)	711
Acquisitions		81	(122)	(41)			
		1,019	(122)	897			
Discontinued operations		13	–	13	40	–	40
Total operating profit		1,032	(122)	910	1,023	(272)	751
Share of profits of associates	5	48	(15)	33	45	(8)	37
		1,080	(137)	943	1,068	(280)	788
Continuing operations							
Disposal of fixed assets			(9)	(9)		4	4
Sale of businesses	6		(44)	(44)		(38)	(38)
Discontinued operations							
Sale of businesses	6		198	198		18	18
Utilisation of prior year provisions			–	–		5	5
			145	145		(11)	(11)
Interest payable (net)	7	(168)	–	(168)	(123)	–	(123)
Profit on ordinary activities before taxation		912	8	920	945	(291)	654
Taxation on profit on ordinary activities	8	(255)	(29)	(284)	(269)	72	(197)
Profit on ordinary activities after taxation		657	(21)	636	676	(219)	457
Minority Interests							
Equity		(4)	–	(4)	(7)	–	(7)
Non-equity		(31)	–	(31)	–	–	–
Profit for the financial year		622	(21)	601	669	(219)	450
Ordinary dividends	9			(312)			(292)
Transferred to reserves				289			158
Earnings per share	10	29.8p	(1.0)p	28.8p	32.2p	(10.6)p	21.6p

4 *Operating costs*

	1995			1994		
	Continuing £m	Discontinued £m	Total £m	Continuing £m	Discontinued £m	Total £m
Raw materials and consumables	2,265	19	2,284	2,558	119	2,677
Other external charges	3,455	14	3,469	2,733	88	2,821
Staff costs (note 11)	1,027	12	1,039	1,102	53	1,155
Depreciation of tangible fixed assets	185	2	187	194	11	205
Decrease in stocks of finished goods and work in progress	98	–	98	79	1	80
Other operating income	(84)	–	(84)	(181)	–	(181)
Restructuring and integration costs (note 6)	122	–	122	272	–	272
	7,068	47	7,115	6,757	272	7,029

Total operating costs include: US excise duties of £310m (1994 – £345m); other excise duties of £532m (1994 – £423m); operating lease rentals for plant and machinery of £15m (1994 – £24m) and for other leases (mainly of properties) of £118m (1994 – £125m); and research and development expenditure of £43m (1994 – £43m). Other operating income includes profits arising from the franchising of outlets of £30m (1994 – £64m), income from listed investments of £10m (1994 – £7m) and income from operating leases of £19m (1994 – £18m).

Fees in respect of services provided by the auditors were: statutory audit of the group £4,381,000 (1994 – £3,998,000); other services to UK group companies £3,597,000 (1994 – £4,230,000); and other services to non-UK subsidiaries £1,988,000 (1994 – £1,401,000).

Operating costs for continuing operations in 1995 include advertising, marketing and promotion of £1,073m (1994 – £901m) and £531m relating to acquired businesses as follows: raw materials and consumables £147m; other external charges £191m; staff costs £60m; depreciation of tangible fixed assets £11m; and exceptional costs of £122m in respect of the integration of Pet Incorporated.

6 *Exceptional items*
(i) Operating costs. The £122m shown in the profit and loss account as exceptional operating costs comprises the cost of integration and reorganisation of Pet Incorporated. The major components of this charge are: costs to exit and move Pet's St Louis headquarters to Minneapolis, including severance of employees; manufacturing plant integration costs; management information systems integration costs; and packaging redesign costs.

Operating costs in 1994 included £272m of exceptional costs, comprising: restructuring costs of £143m in respect of Drinks; £55m in respect of the European operations of Food – Packaged; £31m in respect of Burger King to extend the re-engineering programme initiated during 1993; and £43m principally in respect of the write down of group properties and the consolidation and rationalisation of corporate support structures.

(ii) Sale of businesses. Losses on the sale of businesses treated as continuing operations include a loss of £42m relating to the disposal of Green Giant processing (1994 – includes a loss of £37m in respect of the US jug wine operations).

Profit on the sale of businesses treated as discontinued operations comprise £198m in respect of the disposal of Alpo Petfoods, which was sold in December 1994.

The net results on sale of businesses were after charging goodwill previously written off attributable to the businesses sold of £27m (1994 – £29m).

Discontinuing operations

A company may be in the process of selling or terminating a significant and distinct part of its business. If the sale or termination is not completed within three months of the year end, it will not count as discontinued.

Paragraphs 41 of FRS 3 states: '... In some cases it may be appropriate to disclose separately in a note to the profit and loss account the results of operations which although not discontinued are in the process of discontinuing, but they should not be classified as discontinued'.

Illustration 20

Extract from annual report and accounts of Galliford plc for the year ended 30 June 1994.

Financial Review (extract)

Profit and loss account
The consolidated profit and loss account shows not only the total loss for the year to 30 June 1994, but also a split between the operations to be discontinued and other continuing operations. The operations to be discontinued are those activities relating to our pipe-relining operation and the Chairman, in his statement, details the reasons behind the decision to withdraw from this business. The profit and loss account shows that, whilst the pipe-relining operation made a loss of £6 million after provisions, our other continuing operations made an operating profit of £116,000, an improvement of £632,000 compared with the previous year.

Consolidated profit and loss account

	Notes	1994 Continuing operations			1993 Restated (see notes 1 and 3)
		Operations to be discontinued £'000	Other continuing operations £'000	Total £'000	Total £'000
Turnover	2	10,824	208,935	219,759	215,730
Operating costs	4	13,743	208,775	222,518	215,476
Operating (loss)/profit		(2,919)	160	(2,759)	254
Provision for loss on operations to be discontinued	6	(3,081)	–	(3,081)	–
		(6,000)	160	(5,840)	254
Interest receivable			217	217	347
Amounts written off investments	13		(11)	(11)	(103)
Income from interests in associated undertakings			170	170	–
Income from other participating interests			–	–	57
Profit/(loss) before interest payable			536	(5,464)	555
Interest payable	7		420	420	143
Profit/(loss) on ordinary activities before taxation	2		116	(5,884)	412
Tax on (loss)/profit on ordinary activities	8			(1,411)	122
(Loss)/profit on ordinary activities after taxation attributable to members of Galliford plc	9			(4,473)	290
Dividends	10			888	888
Transferred from reserves	21			(5,361)	(598)
(Loss)/earnings per share	11			(5.04)p	0.33p

All operations are classified as continuing.
Additional disclosures have been given in respect of operations to be discontinued.

25.10   REALISATION OF THE MERGER RESERVE

(a) The problem of pre-combination dividends

Dividends paid out of pre-acquisition profits have in the past usually been treated as capital in the hands of the recipient company and not available for distribution to the recipient company's shareholders.

This view is still accepted where a subsidiary has been acquired other than by an issue of shares by the offeror. However, the view is now being challenged in the case of share-for-share issues. Consider the following illustration.

Illustration 21

A and B are two identical companies. Their respective balance sheets are set out below.

Suppose that A issues 300 shares (deemed to have a value of £5 each) in order to acquire the entire share capital of B.
  Two points may be made:

(1) The issue of shares falls within CA 1985, s 131 so if the investment is recorded at fair value of £1,500 (i e 300 shares issued valued at £5 each), the premium of £1,200 must be taken to a merger reserve and not to a share premium account.
(2) Under CA 1985, s 133, the investment in B may be recorded at nominal value issued i e at £300.

Balance sheets

	A (before)	B (before)	A (after –s 131)	A (after –s 133)
	£	£	£	£
Sundry assets	1,000	1,000	1,000	1,000
Investment in B	–	–	1,500	300
	1,000	1,000	2,500	1,300
OSC	300	300	600	600
P/L	700	700	700	700
Merger reserve	–	–	1,200	
	1,000	1,000	2,500	1,300

Now suppose B distributes its entire (and pre-acquisition) profit and loss account balance. How should this receipt be dealt with in the accounts of A?

(a) Where A's investment in B is recorded at £300 the former SSAP 23 appendix (accounts of the parent company) pointed out that '. . . where a dividend is paid to the acquiring or issuing company out of pre-combination profits, it would appear that it need not necessarily be applied as a reduction in the carrying value of the investment in the subsidiary'.
      Such a dividend received should be applied to reduce the carrying value of the investment to the extent that it is necessary to provide for a diminution in value of the investment in the subsidiary as stated in the accounts of the issuing company. To the extent that this is not necessary, it appears that the amount received will be a realised profit in the hands of the issuing company.
      If A credits the dividend to its P/L ac, investment in B will remain at £300. This will be matched by B's remaining asset of £300 after the dividend payments (i e 1,000 – £700 = £300).
      It is not necessary to provide for diminution in value.
(b) Where A's investment in B is recorded at £1,500 – the appendix to the former standard SSAP 23 referred to situations where the parent company records the investment at fair value and pointed out:

      it will in some cases . . . be necessary for the parent company to credit to the investment the dividend paid out of the subsidiary's pre-combination profits.

Thus the dividend received of £700 should be credited to cost of investment of £1,500 leaving an adjusted carrying amount of £800.

The £800 is represented by:

Tangible assets of B	300
Non-purchased goodwill	
(1,500 − 1,000)	500
	£800

The two balance sheets for company A may be compared as follows:

	Situation (a) £	Situation (b) £
Sundry assets	1,700	1,700
Investment in B	300	800
	2,000	2,500
OSC	600	600
P/L	1,400	700
Merger reserve	−	1,200
	2,000	2,500

Given that s 133 offers A a free choice of recording its investment in B at either £1,500 (fair value issued) or £300 (nominal value issued), it seems inconsistent that on the face of it A's distributable profit can be either £1,400 or £700.

With regard to (b), the appendix to the former standard SSAP 23 went on to say: In these circumstances, the question arises as to whether as a result of this treatment an equivalent amount of the merger reserve can legally be regarded as realised. No firm legal ruling on this is yet available.

Note the caution expressed; however FRS 6 returns to this aspect (see below).

These legal views appear to indicate that £700 of the merger reserve could be regarded as distributable, thus making total distributable reserves £1,400, i e the same as for situation (a).

(b) FRS 6, Appendix 1, legal requirements

Some guidance is provided by way of an appendix to FRS 6.

FRS 6, Appendix 1 – Note on legal requirements (extract)

Accounts of the parent company

15 The FRS deals only with the method of accounting to be used in group accounts; it does not deal with the form of accounting to be used in the acquiring or issuing company's own accounts and in particular does not restrict the reliefs available under sections 131–133 of the Companies Act.

16 Where a dividend is paid to the acquiring or issuing company out of pre-combination profits, it would appear that it need not necessarily be applied as a reduction in the carrying value of the investment in the subsidiary undertaking. Such a dividend received should be applied to reduce the carrying value of the investment to the extent necessary to provide for a diminution in value of the investment in the subsidiary undertaking as stated in the accounts of the parent company. To the extent that this is not necessary, it appears that the amount received will be a realised profit in the hands of the parent company.

Illustration 22

The Jack Simmons Group has recently disposed of a subsidiary. The subsidiary was originally acquired several years ago by means of a share-for-share exchange.

The shares originally issued as consideration were recorded at fair value, the premium of £250,000 being transferred to merger reserve. The consolidation followed acquisition accounting and goodwill of £60,000 was written off direct to merger reserve leaving a balance on merger reserve of £190,000.

The effect of the disposal on the reserves note for the company (following the legal advice in FRS 6 above) and the group (following UITF 3) would be as follows:

The group	*Merger reserve* £	*Profit and loss account* £
At 1.1.19X8	190,000	
Profit for the year		X
Goodwill written back to merger reserve on disposal	60,000	
Merger reserve realised on sale of subsidiary	(250,000)	250,000
At 31.12.19X8	–	X
The company		
At 1.1.19X8	250,000	X
Profit for the year		X
Merger reserve realised on sale of subsidiary	(250,000)	250,000
At 31.12.19X8	–	X

26 CONSOLIDATED ACCOUNTS – MERGER ACCOUNTING

Key Issues

* Rare use of merger accounting
* Key features
* Merger criteria
* Comparison with acquisition accounting
* Group reconstructions – a further application

26.1 BACKGROUND

Previous sections and chapters have considered acquisition accounting. This method of accounting has been used in the United Kingdom for the majority of business combinations. A particular feature of acquisition accounting is that turnover and results of new subsidiaries are only included in the consolidated profit and loss account as from the date of acquisition. Pre-acquisition profits of new subsidiaries are regarded as capital from the group viewpoint.

FRS 6 requires merger accounting to be used in only very restricted cases – the entries are referred to below.

In view of the limited uses of merger accounting this chapter deals with the subject in outline terms and does not attempt to cover all the detailed requirements of FRS 6.

26.2 KEY FEATURES

The key features of merger accounting are as follows:

(a) the financial statements of the combining companies are aggregated and presented as if the companies had been together since their respective incorporations;
(b) the full year's results of the combining companies must be included in the consolidated profit for the year even if the merger takes place during the year;
(c) comparative figures for both consolidated balance sheet and consolidated profit and loss account are restated as though the combining companies were together throughout the previous year.

26.3 ILLUSTRATION – ACQUISITION AND MERGER ACCOUNTING METHODS CONTRASTED

The circumstances of each business combination will determine the appropriate consolidation method – see section 26.4 below. However, for comparison purposes it is useful to compare the effect of the two methods using assumed figures.

Illustration 1

The balance sheets of A and B at 31.12.X6 are as follows:

	A £	B £
Net assets	500	500
Ordinary share capital (£1 shares)	200	200
P/L	300	300
	500	500

A and B are identical in all respects. A makes an offer on 31.12.X6 for the entire share capital of B. The offer takes the form of an exchange of shares – A issues 200 shares to the shareholders of company B. B then becomes a subsidiary of A. Assume that A's shares have a value of £4 per share.

(1) Acquisition accounting

A's acquisition of shares in B must now be reflected in A's balance sheet. The following journal entry will be needed:

	£
Dr investment in B	
(200 shares issued at a value of £4 each)	800
Cr ordinary share capital of A	
(nominal issued)	200
Cr merger reserve	
(premium on issue – see section 25.4(a) for explanation)	600
	800

The consolidated balance sheet of the A group will now appear as follows:

	£
Tangible net assets (500 + 500)	1,000
Goodwill on consolidation	300
	1,300

	£
Ordinary share capital	400
Merger reserve (non statutory share premium account)	600
Profit and loss account (note 2)	300
	1,300

Notes
(1) Consolidation goodwill of £300 will usually be written off against reserves. The merger reserve would be available for this purpose (see section 25.10).
(2) Under acquisition accounting, the pre-acquisition reserves of the acquired company are deemed to be capital. Group P/L reserves consist of:

	£
Parent company (A)	300
Post-acquisition reserves of subsidiary	Nil
	300

(2) Merger accounting

Under merger accounting, it will be usual for company A to record investment in company B at nominal value issued by A, ie journal entry would be:

	£
Dr investment in B	200
Cr share capital	200

The consolidated balance sheet of the A group on a merger accounting basis would then be:

	£
Tangible net assets	1,000
Ordinary share capital	400
Profit and loss account	600
	1,000

(3) *Comparison of the two approaches*

Note that merger accounting takes the view that nothing has really changed. Both former groups of shareholders still own the shares of the two group companies. As the combination is on the basis of a share-for-share exchange, no resources have left the group.

Merger accounts treat the merging companies as if they had been linked from the very beginning of their respective existences. Had they operated quite separately each company would possess distributable reserves of £300 ie a combined total of £600. As nothing has really changed, the merger accounting group balance sheet should reflect this reality.

It would not, of course, be possible to employ the above arguments had A acquired shares in B by the use of cash. In that case there would have been no continuing ownership by the former shareholders of B. Additionally, resources would have left the group.

26.4 MERGER ACCOUNTING CONDITIONS

(a) When merger accounting is mandatory

Business combinations meeting the stringent and detailed conditions set out in FRS 6, together with those in CA 1985, should be accounted for using merger accounting.

If these conditions are satisfied, merger accounting is mandatory. However, ASB anticipates that these conditions will be met on rare occasions only.

(b) FRS 6, Accounting for acquisitions and mergers

In outline the FRS 6 conditions are as follows:

A combination meets the definition of a merger only if it satisfies the five criteria set out in paragraphs 6–11 of the FRS. These criteria relate to:

(1) the way the roles of each party to the combination are portrayed;
(2) the involvement of each party to the combination in the selection of the management of the combined entity;
(3) the relative sizes of the parties to the combination;
(4) whether shareholders of the combining entities receive any consideration other than equity shares in the combined entity;
(5) whether shareholders of the combining entities retain an interest in the performance of only part of the combined entity.

(c) Companies Act 1989 requirements

The following additional requirements must be satisfied before merger accounting can be used:

(1) that at least 90% of the nominal value of the relevant shares in the undertaking acquired is held by or on behalf of the parent company and its subsidiary undertakings;

(2) that the proportion referred to in paragraph (1) was attained pursuant to the arrangement providing for the issue of equity shares by the parent company or one or more of its subsidiary undertakings;

(3) the fair value of any consideration other than the issue of equity shares given pursuant to the arrangement by the parent company and its subsidiary undertakings did not exceed 10% of the nominal value of the equity shares issued; and

(4) that adoption of the merger method of accounting accords with generally accepted accounting principles or practice.

26.5   MERGER ACCOUNTING – APPLYING THE RULES

Where the group can satisfy the conditions referred to above and chooses to prepare consolidated accounts on a merger basis, the following principles apply:

(1) Where the carrying value of investment in a subsidiary (usually equivalent to nominal value of shares issued) is less than the nominal value of the shares received from the offeree, the difference should be treated as a reserve arising on consolidation.

(2) Where the carrying value of investment in a subsidiary is greater than the nominal value of the shares received, the difference should be treated on consolidation as a reduction of reserves.

(3) In the consolidated profit and loss account, the full year's profits of the offeree should be included (note carefully).

(4) As regards comparative figures, these should be presented as if the companies had been combined throughout the previous period and at the previous balance sheet date (note very carefully).

The effect of these rules is shown in the illustration below.

(1) *The individual accounts of the parent company and section 133*

Illustration 2

Section 131 was referred to in section 25.4. Under s 131 the journal entry to record the parent's investment in the subsidiary would be:

Credit cost of investment in B	£300,000	Credit OSC Merger reserve	£100,000 £200,000

Section 133 refers to situations where the premium may be disregarded in determining the carrying amount.

In the above example, A could record its investment in B as follows:

Debit cost of investment	£100,000	Credit OSC	£100,000

Note two important points:
(1) the above statutory rules relate to the individual accounts of the parent company and not the consolidated accounts;

(2) in theory, company A may choose between recording the investment in B at
£300,000 or £100,000 irrespective of whether it intends to present consolidated
accounts on an acquisition basis or a merger basis.

In practice A would usually record the investment at £300,000 if it intended to
consolidate using acquisition accounting, and £100,000 if it intended to consolidate
using merger accounting.

(2) *Consolidation procedures – merger accounting*

Illustration 3 (see information in section 25.5)

(1) Carrying value in books of Panna Ltd of investment in Rama Ltd is £6,000 (i e nominal
value of shares issued in exchange). Share capital of Panna Ltd is now increased to
£14,000.

(2) Consolidated balance sheet workings:

		£
(i)	Carrying value of investment	6,000
	Nominal value received	8,500
	Reserve arising on consolidation	2,500

		P/L £	*Share premium* £	*Revaluation Reserve* £
(ii)	Reserve balances			
	Panna	12,500	4,000	5,000
	Rama	9,500	1,500	1,000
		22,000	5,500	6,000

Notes

(1) No distinction is made between pre-acquisition and post-acquisition reserves. The
combining companies are treated as though they had operated as a combined unit
since the date of incorporation.

(2) The fixed assets of the offeree company (Rama Ltd) are not revalued to determine
fair value. This is not so with acquisition accounting.

The consolidated balance sheet under merger accounting principles is as follows:

	£
Tangible fixed assets	27,000
Net current assets	23,000
	50,000
Called-up share capital	14,000
Share premium account	5,500
Revaluation reserve	6,000
Capital reserve on merger	2,500
Profit and loss account	22,000
	50,000

(3) In preparing the consolidated profit and loss account, remember to bring in a full
year's results for Rama Ltd even though the combination was on 30 September
19X3. Remember also that it is unnecessary (and inappropriate!) to adjust the
reserves of Rama Ltd between pre- and post-merger.

CONSOLIDATED PROFIT AND LOSS ACCOUNT
(ON A MERGER ACCOUNTING BASIS)
for the year ended 31 December 19X3

	£
Turnover	42,000
Cost of sales	14,000
Gross profit	28,000
Distribution costs	(6,000)
Administrative expenses	(5,000)
Profit on ordinary activities before tax	17,000
Taxation	8,500
Profit on ordinary activities after tax	8,500
Balance brought forward	13,500
Balance carried forward	22,000

26.6   GROUP RECONSTRUCTIONS

One area where merger accounting may be appropriate is that of group reconstructions.

FRS 6 defines the term 'group reconstructions' as including the following arrangements:

(a) the transfer of a shareholding in a subsidiary undertaking from one group company to another;
(b) the addition of a new parent company to a group;
(c) the transfer of shares in one or more subsidiary undertakings of a group to a new company that is not a group company but whose shareholders are the same as those of the group's parent;
(d) the combination into a group of two or more companies that before the combination had the same shareholders.

In the above cases FRS 6 permits the option of merger accounting but does not make it mandatory.

This is a complex area and is outside the scope of this book. Consequently no further reference is made in this chapter.

27 ACCOUNTING FOR FIXED ASSET INVESTMENTS INCLUDING ASSOCIATES

Key Issues

* Treatment of fixed asset investments
* Definition of associate
* Equity method of accounting
* Joint ventures and proportional consolidation
* Comparison of methods

27.1 INTRODUCTION – FIXED ASSET INVESTMENTS

The term fixed asset investments covers a broad spectrum including:

(a) investments in subsidiary companies;
(b) investments in associates;
(c) investments in joint ventures;
(d) other fixed asset investments (including trade investments).

Classification of investments is further referred to in section 27.8. The Companies Act 1985 permits an individual company to carry a fixed asset investment at either:

(1) historical cost (reduced by any provision for a permanent diminution in value); or
(2) current valuation.

In the profit and loss account dividends are usually included on a cash basis for (d) above. In the cases of (a), (b) and (c) it is usual to include also the share of any proposed dividends.

27.2 INVESTMENTS IN SUBSIDIARIES

(a) Individual accounts of the parent company

The accounting treatment was referred to in section 27.1 above.

(b) Accounts of the group

Subsidiaries are normally consolidated in the usual way unless:

(1) the parent company is exempt from the preparation of group accounts for one of the reasons discussed in section 24.11;
(2) the subsidiary is required to be excluded from consolidated accounts for one of the reasons discussed in section 24.8.

27.3 DEFINITION OF ASSOCIATED UNDERTAKING

(a) Background of SSAP 1

SSAP 1, Accounting for associated companies, was issued originally in January 1971 and revised in April 1982 following the enactment of the Companies Act 1981.

SSAP 1 has been further revised as a result of the ASB's Interim Statement on consolidated accounts. SSAP 1 is currently under review by the ASB.

(b) SSAP 1 definition

An associated company is a company not being a subsidiary of the investing group or company in which the interest of the investing group or company is for the long term and is substantial, and, having regard to the disposition of the other shareholdings, the investing group or company is in a position to exercise a significant influence over the company in which the investment is made.

Significant influence over a company essentially involves participation in the financial and operating policy decisions of that company (including dividend policy) but not necessarily control of those policies.

Representation on the board of directors is indicative of such participation, but will neither necessarily give conclusive evidence of it nor be the only method by which the investing company may participate in policy decisions.

The definition of associate now has two main elements:

(i) long-term holding;
(ii) investor in a position to exert significant influence. Note that significant influence means more than an entitlement simply to receive dividends but falls short of control.

(c) Companies Act 1989

An associated undertaking (or associate) means an undertaking in which an undertaking included in the consolidation has:

(1) a participating interest; and
(2) over whose operating and financial policies it exercises a significant influence. Joint ventures are dealt with separately. (See section 27.7.)

    (i) Participating interest is a complex term – it means an interest held by an undertaking in the shares of another undertaking which it holds on a long-term basis for the purpose of securing a contribution to its activities by the exercise of control or influence arising from or related to that interest.

        It is important to note that a 20% or more holding is presumed to be a participating interest unless the contrary can be shown.

    (ii) A holding of 20% or more of equity voting rights is presumed to exercise significant influence unless the contrary can be shown.

(d) Group and non-group situations

Holdings in associates are not restricted to group situations. The definition above envisages the two situations, illustrated below.

In the diagrams, H is the investing company, S is a subsidiary and A is an associated company.

Ⓐ
Investing
company
situation

H
|
A

Ⓑ
Investing
group
situation

H
|
S A

in Ⓑ, group accounts are prepared and the accounting problems revolve around how to incorporate the associate into the group accounts (ie consolidated balance sheet and consolidated profit and loss account).

Ⓐ is a comparatively uncommon situation – group accounts are not prepared. The accounting treatment differs as between the two situations (this is dealt with later).

The accounting treatment for A is illustrated in section 27.6.

The accounting treatment for B is illustrated in section 27.5.

27.4 ASSOCIATES – AN INTRODUCTION TO THE EQUITY METHOD OF ACCOUNTING

(a) Background to SSAP 1

Before 1970 a number of companies were conducting a substantial part of their business through other companies in which a substantial number of shares were held. As the proportion of shares held was 50% or less, such companies were not counted as subsidiaries. However, since the investing company was often in a position to exert significant influence over the activities of the investee company, it seemed sensible to distinguish them from trade investments in which a far smaller number of shares were held.

This distinction was followed by SSAP 1 (Accounting for associated companies) which introduced the concept of equity accounting for certain types of investments. Under the equity method, the *consolidated* profit and loss account of the investor includes a proportionate share of the profits of the investee rather than only dividend income.

Correspondingly, the reserves in the consolidated balance sheet include the group's share of post-acquisition retained profits of the investee.

The equity method is defined by FRS 2 as a method of accounting for an investment that brings into the consolidated profit and loss account the investor's share of the investment undertaking's results and that records the investment in the consolidated balance sheet at the investor's share of the investment undertaking's net assets including any goodwill arising to the extent that it has not previously been written off.

These points are illustrated below.

(b) Illustration 1

The H group holds 30% of the share capital of Associate Ltd. The profit and loss account of A Ltd showed the following position:

	£
Turnover	8,000
Operating expenses	3,500
Profit on ordinary activities before tax	4,500
Taxation	2,000
	2,500
Dividends proposed	1,000
Retained profit	1,500

The balance sheet of A Ltd was as follows:

	£
Fixed assets	6,500
Net current assets	500
	7,000
Ordinary share capital	2,000
Profit and loss account	5,000
	7,000

The shares were purchased several years ago at a cost of £1,100 when A's reserves amounted to £1,000.

(1) Consolidated profit and loss account

The consolidated profit and loss account is shown under the three following assumptions:

(a) H group has no investment in A Ltd;
(b) H group accounts for its investment in A Ltd using the cost method (the traditional method of accounting for fixed asset investments);
(c) H group accounts for its investment in A Ltd using the equity method.

For simplicity no information is given as regards subsidiary companies of company H. Assume, however, that H is required by law to prepare consolidated accounts.

	Consolidated profit and loss account		
	Situation (a)	Situation (b)	Situation (c)
Turnover	30,000	30,000	30,000
Operating expenses	(8,000)	(8,000)	(8,000)
Dividends receivable	–	300	–
Share of profit of investment	–	–	1,350
Profit on ordinary activities before tax	22,000	22,300	23,350
Tax			
Group	(11,000)	(11,000)	(11,000)
Share of investee's tax			(600)
Profit after tax	11,000	11,300	11,750
Dividends	5,000	5,000	5,000
Retained profit	6,000	6,300	6,750

Notes
(1) Under the cost method, only the share of dividend receivable (30% × £1,000 = £300) is included.
   Under the equity method, a proportionate share of profit before tax (30% × £4,500 = £1,350) and a proportionate share of tax (30% × £2,000 = £600) are included.
(2) The cost method does not include the group's proportion of the retained profits of the associate (30% × £1,500 = £450). This accounts for the difference between the two retained profit figures.
(3) The difference between the two approaches could have a significant effect on earnings per share (which is based on profit after tax).

(2) Consolidated balance sheet

(i) Reserves
The essential difference between the cost method and the equity method is that under the latter group reserves include a proportionate share of post-acquisition retained profits of A.

	£
Reserves of A	
At year end	5,000
At acquisition	1,000
	4,000
Proportionate share 30% × £4,000	£1,200

Group reserves would therefore include an additional amount of £1,200 attributable to the associate.

(ii) Fixed asset investment
Under the cost method, the investment would be included at £1,100.

Under the equity method, this would be increased by £1,200 (calculated above) to £2,300. However, there are two ways of presenting the balance sheet figure of £2,300.

PRESENTATION 1 (PURE EQUITY APPROACH)	£
Cost of investment	1,100
Post-acquisition reserves	1,200
	2,300

PRESENTATION 2 (UNDERLYING NET ASSETS APPROACH)	£
Net assets (30% × £7,000)	2,100
Premium on acquisition (see below)	200
	2,300

WORKINGS – CALCULATION OF PREMIUM	£
Cost of investment	1,100
Proportion of net assets at acquisition	
30% (2,000 + 1,000)	900
	200

Presentation 2 is the approach required by SSAP 1.

(c) Summary – comparison of accounting in the parent company and the consolidated accounts

	Parent company accounts	Group (consolidated) accounts
Balance sheet		
(i) *Fixed assets – shares in associates*	Usually at cost of investment less any amounts written off (in some cases shown at a valuation).	Total of: (i) group share of net assets (other than goodwill); (ii) group share of goodwill in associates' balance sheet; (iii) premium (discount) on acquisition of shares.
(ii) *Reserves* Profit and loss account	Dividends received and receivable by investing group.	Include also group share of retained post-acquisition profits.
Revaluation reserve	N/A	Include group share of post-acquisition revaluation reserve of associates.
Profit and loss account	Dividends received and receivable.	Group share of profits less losses of associates.

27.5 ACCOUNTING FOR ASSOCIATES IN GROUP ACCOUNTS: FURTHER CONSIDERATIONS

(a) Consolidated balance sheet in detail (CBS)

The consolidated balance sheet may include several items relating to associates:

Item in CBS	Comments
Fixed asset investments – shares in associates	Comprises: (i) group share of net assets (other than goodwill); (ii) group share of goodwill in associates' b/s; (iii) premium (discount) on acquisition of shares. (i) must be disclosed separately but (ii) and (iii) may be disclosed as a single figure.
Fixed asset investments – loans to associates	
Debtors – amounts owed by associates	Disclose separately. Do not net off against other items.

Creditors – amounts owed to associates:
    Due within one year
    Due after more than one year	

Reserves: Profit and loss account	Disclose group share of post-acquisition retained profits.
Revaluation reserve	Disclose group share of post-acquisition revaluation reserve.

The above information is sufficient for the majority of associates situations. However, if the associates' profits/assets/scale of operations are material in relation to the group, further disclosure may be required in the interest of a true and fair view. This might cover more detailed information concerning the tangible and intangible assets of the associate, as well as its liabilities.

(b) Consolidated profit and loss account in detail (CPL)

Item in CPL	Comments
Turnover	Investing group share of associates' turnover should *not* be disclosed (but separate disclosure may be required in certain situations – see below).
Cost of sales	
Distribution costs	Share relating to associates not included
Administrative expenses	
Other operating income	
Share of profits (less losses) of associates	Include (and disclose as a separate item) the investing group's share of associates' profit before interest and tax.
Interest receivable Interest payable	Include investing group's share of these items.
Taxation	Include (and disclose as separate item) the investing group's share of associates' tax on profit on ordinary activities.
Extraordinary items	Include (and, where material to group, disclose as a separate item) group share of extraordinary items.

SSAP 1 specifically states that the investing group should not include its share of associates' items such as turnover and depreciation in the aggregate amounts of these items disclosed in the consolidated financial statements.

However, SSAP 1 goes on to say that in some cases more detailed information would be required in the interest of a true and fair view. These cases are where the results of one or more associates are particularly significant in relation to the group, as regards profit and scale of operation. A separate note could then give more detailed profit and loss information, including turnover and other items.

(c) Examples of inclusion of associates in group accounts

The two examples below are intended to illustrate the principles and disclosures referred to above.

Illustration 2

Company	Cost of investment £	Percentage of ordinary shares held %	P/L reserves at date of acquisition (several years ago) £
S Ltd	7,000	80	3,000
A Ltd	550	30	400

The draft accounts for the year ended 31 December 19X4 are as follows:

Profit and loss account

	H Ltd £	S Ltd £	A Ltd £
Turnover	20,000	10,000	5,000
Cost of sales	5,000	3,000	2,000
Gross profit	15,000	7,000	3,000
Distribution costs	(2,000)	(500)	(600)
Administrative expenses	(1,000)	(600)	(700)
Operating profit	12,000	5,900	1,700
Dividends – S	800	–	–
– A	60	–	–
Profit on ordinary activities before tax	12,860	5,900	1,700
Taxation	5,000	2,200	800
Profit after tax	7,860	3,700	900
Dividends proposed	2,000	1,000	200
Retained profit	5,860	2,700	700
Balance at 1.1.X4	20,000	6,000	2,100
Balance at 31.12.X4	25,860	8,700	2,800

Balance sheets

	H Ltd £	S Ltd £	A Ltd £
Fixed assets			
Tangible	20,000	6,000	2,000
Investments – S	7,000	–	–
– A	550	–	–
Stock	7,000	8,100	800
Debtors	7,200	1,800	700
Dividends receivable	860	–	–
Cash at bank	1,750	800	1,050
Creditors (due within one year)	(6,500)	(3,000)	(550)
Proposed dividends	(2,000)	(1,000)	(200)
	35,860	12,700	3,800
Ordinary share capital	10,000	4,000	1,000
Profit and loss account	25,860	8,700	2,800
	35,860	12,700	3,800

Consolidated balance sheet

Key figures:

(1) *Goodwill on consolidation (re company S)*
7,000 – 80% (4,000 + 3,000) = £1,400

(2) *Minority interest*
(a) Non-current:
20% × £12,700   = £2,540
(b) Current:
20% × £1,000   = £200

(3) *Profit and loss account*

	£
H	25,860
S 80% (8,700 – 3,000)	4,560
A 30% (2,800 – 400)	720
	31,140

(4) *Associates*
(a) Investment

		£
Proportion of net assets 30% × £3,800		1,140
Premium £550 − 30% (1,000 + 400)		130
		1,270

(b) Dividend receivable
30% × £200 i e   £60

(5) *Assets and liabilities*
These are arrived at by combining respective items for H and S.
The consolidated balance sheet may now be completed:

	£	£	£
Fixed assets:			
Tangible assets			26,000
Investments – shares in associates			1,270
			27,270
Current assets:			
Stock		15,100	
Debtors		9,000	
Dividend receivable from associates		60	
Cash at bank		2,550	
		26,710	
Creditors – amounts falling due within one year:			
Creditors	9,500		
Dividends due to members of parent company	2,000		
Dividends due to minority shareholders	200	11,700	
Net current assets			15,010
Total assets less current liabilities			42,280
Capital and reserves			
Called-up share capital			10,000
Profit and loss account			29,740
			39,740
Minority investment			2,540
			42,280

Consolidated profit and loss account

Many items are arrived at by combining respective items for H and S. Items for which separate calculations are required include

		£
(1) Associated company		
Share of profit	30% × £1,700 =	510
Share of tax	30% × £800 =	240
(2) Minority interest	20% × £3,700 =	740
(3) Retained profit:		
Parent company		5,860
Subsidiary	80% × £2,700 =	2,160
Associates	30% × £700 =	210
		8,230
(4) Balance brought forward:		
Parent company		20,000
Subsidiary	80% (6,000 − 3,000) =	2,400
Associates	30% (2,100 − 400) =	510
		22,910
Less goodwill w/o		1,400
		21,510

The consolidated profit and loss account may now be completed:

	£	£
Turnover		30,000
Cost of sales		8,000
Gross profit		22,000
Distribution costs	2,500	
Administrative expenses	1,600	4,100
		17,900
Share of profits of associates		510
Profit on ordinary activities before tax		18,410
Tax on profit on ordinary activities:		
Investing group	7,200	
Associates	240	7,440
Profit on ordinary activities after tax		10,970
Minority interest		740
Profit attributable to shareholders of H		10,230
Dividends proposed		2,000
		8,230
Retained profit for year:		
Parent company	5,860	
Subsidiary	2,160	
Associates	210	
	8,230	
Balance at 1.1.X4		21,510
Balance at 31.12.X4		29,740

Illustration 3

Horton Ltd is the parent company of a small group of private companies. Some years ago, Horton Ltd purchased a 30% shareholding in Apsley Ltd at a cost of £160,000.

Charles, one of Horton's directors, was appointed to the board of directors of Apsley, and Apsley is regarded as an associate.

The balance sheets of the associate as at the date of purchase of the shares, and as at the consolidation date (31.12.X5) are shown below.

(1) Balance sheets	At date of purchase of shares £'000	At 31.12.X5 £'000
Ordinary shares	200	200
Profit and loss account	120	380
Revaluation reserve	75	125
Loans from companies in Horton Group	–	100
Current liabilities	60	105
Proposed dividends	–	50
	455	960
Fixed assets	290	560
Purchased goodwill	–	85
Current account with companies in Horton Group	–	90
Current assets	165	225
	455	960

(2) Profit and loss account for YE 31.12.X5

	£'000
Profit on ordinary activities	230
Tax	(110)
Proposed dividends	(50)
Retained profit	70
Balance sheet at 1.1.X5	310
Balance sheet at 31.12.X5	380

Required: The relevant extracts from the group financial statements for the year ended 31 December 19X5.

Consolidated balance sheet at 31.12.X5

Workings will be required for:

		£'000
(a)	Premium on acquisition:	
	Cost of investment	160.0
	Net assets at acquisition (fair value)	
	–group proportion 30% (455 – 60)	118.5
	Premium	41.5

(b) Proportion of net assets (other than goodwill) at 31.12.X5:
30% × (560 + 90 + 225 – 100 – 105 – 50)　　　186.0

(c) Proportion of goodwill:
30% × 85　　　25.5

(d) Attributable post-acquisition reserves at 31.12.X5:
Profit and loss account 30% × (380 – 120)　　　78.0
Revaluation reserve 30% (125 – 75)　　　15.0
　　　93.0

(e) Attributable post-acquisition reserves at 1.1.X5:
Profit and loss account 30% × (310 – 120)　　　57.0
Revaluation reserve (assume as for 31.12.X5)　　　15.0
　　　72.0

(f) Dividend receivable: 30% × 50　　　15.0

Relevant extracts are:

		£'000
(a)	Fixed assets – investments:	
	Shares in associates (note 1)	253.0
	Loans to associates	100.0

	£'000
NOTE 1	
Group's share of net assets other than goodwill	186.0
Goodwill	25.5
Premium on acquisition	41.5
	253.0

(b) Debtors – amounts owed by associates
(dividend receivable)　　　15.0

(c) Creditors – amounts owed to associates　　　90.0

(d) Revaluation reserve – total includes　　　15.0

(e) Profit and loss account – total includes　　　78.0

Additional disclosures:
Amounts in respect of associates relating to (d) and (e) should be separately disclosed.

Consolidated profit and loss account

Workings will be required for:

		£
Profit before tax	30% × 230	69.0
Tax	30% × 110	33.0
Retained by associates	30% × 70	21.0

Relevant extracts are:
(a) Share of profits of associates　　　69.0
(b) Tax on ordinary activities – associates　　　33.0
(c) Profit retained by associates　　　21.0

Statement of reserves

Amounts brought forward in respect of associates will include:

Revaluation reserve	15.0
Profit and loss account	57.0

Illustration 4

Extract from annual report and accounts of Cadbury Schweppes plc for the year ended 31 December 1994.

Accounting policies (extract)

(o) Associated undertakings
All companies where the Group has significant influence, normally both board representation and ownership of 20% of the voting rights on a long term basis, are treated as associated undertakings. The carrying value of associated undertakings reflects the Group share of the net assets of the companies concerned. The share of their profits is included in operating profit.

Illustration 5

Extract from annual report and accounts of Chrysalis Group plc for the year ended 31 August 1994.

Accounting policies (extract)

Associated undertakings
An associated undertaking is defined as an undertaking in which the Group has a participating interest and over whose operating and financial policy it exercises a significant influence.

A joint venture associated undertaking is defined as an undertaking operated on a joint venture basis and in which the Group has a 50 per cent interest in the ordinary share capital, or owns less than 50 per cent, but has in place arrangements that would enable the Group to increase its holding to 50 per cent of the ordinary share capital.

The Group's share of results in associated undertakings (including the Group's incorporated joint ventures) is included in the consolidated profit and loss account. Attributable post acquisition retained results of the associated undertakings are included in the consolidated reserves and in the book value of the Group's investments in those associated undertakings.

27.6 ACCOUNTING FOR ASSOCIATES: NON-GROUP SITUATIONS

(a) Introduction

This is the investing company situation which was illustrated in 27.3(d) as follows:

The problem is that the Companies Act 1985 permits the equity method to be used in consolidated accounts only. So, in the above example, H may include only dividend income from A in its profit and loss account. The investment in A should be included at cost.

However, SSAP 1 requires the equivalent information regarding the associate to be included in memorandum form. This will include balance sheet and profit and loss information.

(b) Balance sheet information

SSAP 1 requires that an investing company which does not prepare consolidated accounts (except for the wholly owned subsidiary situation) should
show the information referred to above either by.

(1) preparing a separate balance sheet; or
(2) adding the information in supplementary form to its own balance sheet.

(c) Profit and loss information

Similarly, such a company should either:

(1) prepare a separate profit and loss account; or
(2) add the information in supplementary form to its own profit and loss
    account. This should ensure that its share of associated company profits is
    not treated as realised for Companies Act purposes.

A statement accompanying SSAP 1 included the following illustration which
deals with option (2):

Illustration 6

Profit and loss account of investing company		£'000
Turnover		2,000
Cost of sales		1,400
Gross profit		600
Distribution cost	175	
Administrative expenses	125	300
Profit on ordinary activities before taxation		300
Tax on profit on ordinary activities		85
Profit on ordinary activities after taxation		215
Dividends – proposed		80
Amount set aside to reserves		135

Supplementary statement incorporating results of associated companies	£'000
Share of profits less losses of associated companies	50
Less tax	15
Share of profits after tax of associated companies	35
Profit on ordinary activities after taxation (as above)	215
Profit attributable to members of the investing company	250
Dividends – proposed	80
Net profit retained (£35,000 by associated companies)	170

Note: The earnings per share figure would be based on £250,000.

27.7 ACCOUNTING FOR JOINT VENTURES

(a) Definition

The joint venture situation referred to is where an undertaking included in the
consolidation manages another undertaking (the joint venture) jointly with
one or more undertakings which are not included in the consolidation.

(b) Accounting treatment – group accounts

Provided the joint venture is neither a body corporate nor a subsidiary, the
Companies Act 1989 permits it to be dealt with in the group accounts by the
method of proportional consolidation.

Proportional consolidation is a method of accounting where the investor's proportionate share of its assets and liabilities and revenues and expenses should be included with the equivalent items for the group on a line-by-line basis in the consolidated balance sheet, the profit and loss account and notes to the accounts (see section 27.9).

27.8 CLASSIFICATION OF FIXED ASSET INVESTMENTS

(a) Basic classification

Investments held by the parent company and subsidiary undertakings should distinguish between:

(1) subsidiary undertakings;
(2) participating interests which are treated for consolidation purposes as associated undertakings;
(3) other participating interests;
(4) other significant holdings (eg shareholdings of between 10% and 20% in equity shares).

(b) Participating interest

A participating interest is essentially a holding of 20% or more of the shares in a company (but not more than 50% of the voting shares).
  More formally, the Companies Act 1985 defines it as:

> ... an interest held by an undertaking in the shares of another undertaking which it holds on a long-term basis for the purpose of securing a contribution to its activities by the exercise of control or influence arising from or related to the interest.

A holding of 20% or more of the shares is presumed to be a participating interest unless the contrary is shown. Note that the interest is not restricted to a 20% holding of equity voting rights.
  Participating interests are likely to fall into two main categories:

(1) those where the investor is in a position to exert significant influence – these will then also fall under the heading of 'associated undertaking';
(2) those where the investor is not in a position to exert significant influence. This includes cases where another investor holds more than 50% of the voting shares. These are essentially 'trade investments'.

27.9 ACCOUNTING FOR INVESTMENTS IN GROUP ACCOUNTS – A SUMMARY

Having considered the situations in which various methods might be applied it would be useful to consider an example illustrating their basic operation.
  The methods which might be applicable in group accounts in different situations include:

(a) cost method;
(b) equity method;
(c) normal (conventional) consolidation;
(d) proportional (pro rata) consolidation.

Illustration 7

The H Group acquired 70% of the ordinary share capital of S Ltd several years ago when the reserves of S Ltd amounted to £30.

Summarised financial statements for 19X9 are set out below:

Balance sheets at 31.12.X9

	H Group £	S Ltd £
Fixed assets	1,105	600
Investment in S	350	–
Dividend receivable	35	–
Current assets	505	220
Current liabilities	(205)	(90)
Dividend payable	–	(50)
	1,790	680
Ordinary share capital	1,000	400
Profit and loss account	790	280
	1,790	680

Profit and loss accounts year ending 31.12.X9

	£	£
Operating profit	485	250
Dividends receivable	35	–
	520	250
Corporation tax	(230)	(110)
	290	140
Dividends paid	(100)	–
Dividends payable	–	(50)
Retained profit	190	90
P/L at 1.1.X9	600	190
P/L at 31.12.X9	790	280

The consolidated balance sheets under the various methods are set out as follows:

	Cost method £	Equity method £	Normal consolidation £	Proportional consolidation £
Goodwill	–	–	49	49
Tangible fixed assets	1,105	1,105	1,705	1,525
Investments	350	525	–	–
Current assets	505	505	725	659
Current liabilities	(205)	(205)	(295)	(268)
MI – dividend	–	–	(15)	–
– OSC and reserves	–	–	(204)	–
Dividend receivable	35	35	–	–
	1,790	1,965	1,965	1,965
Called-up share capital	1,000	1,000	1,000	1,000
Profit and loss account	790	965	965	965
	1,790	1,965	1,965	1,965

Balance sheet note – equity method

	£
Investments – pure approach	
Cost of investment	350
Reserves	175
	525
Investments – net assets/premium approach	
Net assets	476
Premium	49
	525

Workings – equity method

			£		£
(1)	Reserves	70% (280 – 30)		=	175
(2)	Net assets	70% × £680		=	476

(3) Premium

Cost of investment			350
OSC	400		
Reserves	30		
	430	× 70%	301
Premium			49

(4) Consolidated reserves

H group	790
S (as above)	175
	965

Workings – normal consolidation

(5) Goodwill – as (3) above   49

Note: for illustration purposes, goodwill is presented as an intangible fixed asset (for an acceptable treatment, see chapter 13).

(6) MI

		£
OSC and reserves	30% × £680	204
Dividend	30% × £50	15

Workings – proportional consolidation

(7) Fixed assets   1,105 + (70% × 600)   1,525

(8) Current assets   505 + (70% × 220)   659

The consolidated profit and loss accounts are:

	Cost method £	Equity method £	Normal consolidation £	Proportional consolidation £
Profit of group	485	485	735	660
Share of profit of S	–	175	–	–
Dividends receivable	35	–	–	–
	520	660	735	660
Corporation tax	230	307	340	307
Profit after tax	290	353	395	353
Minority interest	–	–	42	–
	290	353	353	353
Dividends paid	100	100	100	100
Retained profit	190	253	253	253
Balance b/f	600	712	712	712
Balance c/f	790	965	965	965

Workings – equity method

			£		£
(1)	Share of profit of	70% × £250		=	175

(2) Corporation tax

		£	£
H		230	
S	70% × £110	77	307

(3) Balance b/f

		£	£
H		600	
S	70% (190 – 30)	112	712

Workings – normal consolidation

(4) MI 30% × £140 = 42

Workings proportional consolidation

(5) Profit of group
H 485
S 70% × £250 175
─────
660
─────

Note on disclosure: In pro rata or partial consolidation, a possible variant would be to disclose separately the amounts in the consolidated balance sheet and profit and loss account relating to S. Such disclosure could either be on the face of the financial statements or in a separate note.

27.10 APPLICATIONS OF THE VARIOUS METHODS

Considering each method in turn, applications include:

(a) Cost method

(1) 'Trade' investments.
(2) Subsidiaries excluded from consolidation on the grounds that the investment is held exclusively with a view to resale.

(b) Equity method

(1) Associated companies.
(2) Subsidiaries excluded on the grounds of dissimilar activities. (Under FRS 2, this ground will be very rare.)

(c) Normal consolidation

All subsidiaries, except where FRS 2 or the Companies Act 1985 requires them to be excluded from consolidation.

(d) Proportional consolidation

Applications are rare but examples include non-corporate joint ventures (see section 27.7 above).

27.11 REVIEW OF SSAP 1

ASB is currently reviewing the treatment of associated companies and joint ventures, and has issued exposure draft FRED 11.

28 ACCOUNTING FOR OVERSEAS OPERATIONS

Key Issues

* Individual company transactions
* Treatment of long-term monetary items
* Choice of translation method
* Operation of closing rate/net investment method
* Operation of temporal method
* Equity investments financed by foreign borrowings
* Foreign branches

28.1 INTRODUCTION

Many UK companies at some stage become involved in transactions of an overseas nature. Involvement ranges from purchasing goods from an overseas supplier to conducting overseas operations through a subsidiary company or branch.

Clearly, the accounting problem is to find an acceptable approach to expressing the results of such operations in sterling so that they may be combined with those already expressed in sterling.

Put in these terms, the procedures seem routine and dull! Yet few topics, except for inflation accounting, have generated controversies to match those of foreign currency translation.

Previous attempts to produce an acceptable standard included ED 16 (1975), ED 21 (1977) and ED 27 (1981). It was only in 1983 that a definitive standard, SSAP 20 entitled 'Foreign currency translation', was finally issued.

28.2 APPROACH TO FOREIGN CURRENCY TRANSLATION

This chapter follows the approach of SSAP 20 in dealing separately with two aspects of the subject:

(a) Overseas business transactions entered into by individual companies. This includes overseas borrowings and purchases from overseas suppliers. This aspect is dealt with in section 28.3.
(b) The foreign operations of a UK company conducted through foreign enterprises, whether they be subsidiaries, associated companies or branches. This aspect is dealt with in the remaining parts of the chapter, and resolves around the preparation of consolidated financial statements.

28.3 ACCOUNTS OF INDIVIDUAL COMPANIES

(a) Objective

A company may enter into transactions which are denominated in a foreign currency. For example, a UK company may borrow $100,000 repayable in ten years' time. At each balance sheet date it will be necessary to express this in sterling for inclusion in the UK balance sheet expressed in sterling.

It is important to remember what we are trying to achieve. SSAP 20 states that 'the translation of foreign currency transactions ... should produce results which are generally compatible with the effects of rate changes on a company's cash flows and its equity and should ensure that the financial statements present a true and fair view of the results of management actions ...'.

(b) Basic rule

Assuming a UK company, the results of each transaction should normally be translated into £ sterling using the exchange rate in operation on the date on which the transaction occurred.

In certain circumstances, it may be acceptable to use an average rate for the period – this may be useful if there are a large number of transactions.

There are two important exceptions to this basic rule:

(1) where the transaction is to be settled at a contracted rate, the contracted rate should be used;
(2) where a trading transaction is covered by a related or matching forward contract, the rate of exchange specified in that contract may be used.

(c) Non-monetary assets

The term non-monetary assets includes plant and machinery, land and buildings, equity investments and stock.

As soon as non-monetary assets have been translated into sterling (normally using the rate at the transaction date per (b) above) and recorded in the books, they should not be retranslated at a later date.

Illustration 1

A UK company purchases plant and machinery for use in the United Kingdom from a Canadian company for $267,000. The exchange rate at the date of purchase was $1.8 = £1. So the company should record the fixed asset in its records at £148,333. The asset should not be translated again: subsequent changes in exchange rates will have no effect. The annual depreciation charge should be based on £148,333.

(d) Monetary assets and liabilities

The term includes debtors, cash, creditors and loans payable. Two possible situations may arise:

(1) the transaction has been settled by the balance sheet date, eg the amount owing to an overseas supplier has been paid in full;
(2) the transaction is still outstanding at the balance sheet date.

In each case, exchange differences will arise. These will normally be included as part of the profit on ordinary activities for the year. The two examples immediately below illustrate the above points.

Illustration 2

A UK company purchased goods from a French company in May 19X4 for Fr 10,500 when the exchange rate was Fr 11.6 = £1. The account was paid on 15 July 19X4 when the exchange rate was Fr 11.9 = £1.

The supplier's account in the records of the UK company would appear as follows:

A SUPPLIER

19X4	£	19X4	£
15 July Cash (10,500 ÷ 11.9)	882	May Purchases (10,500 ÷ 11.6)	905
31 Dec P/L a/c	23		
	905		905

Illustration 3

A UK company purchased goods from a German supplier in November 19X4 for DM 4,500 when the exchange rate was DM 3.9 = £1. The account has not been settled by 31 December 19X4, the company's year end. At that date the exchange rate was DM 3.8 = £1.

The supplier's account would appear as follows:

B SUPPLIER

19X4	£	19X4	£
31 December Balance c/d		November Purchases	
(4,500 ÷ 3.8)	1,184	(4,500 ÷ 3.9)	1,154
		31 December P/L	30
	1,184		1,184

Note
(1) In each case, the exchange gain or loss would form part of the profit (or loss) on ordinary activities before taxation. In the Companies Act 1985 formats they would normally be grouped within other operating income or expense, but there is no specific requirement to disclose separately.
(2) The exchange gain in A Supplier of £23 has already been reflected in cash flows (i e the amount paid was £882 as opposed to £905). The exchange loss in B Supplier is reasonably certain to be reflected in cash flows (it is only a matter of time before the bill is paid!).

(e) Long-term monetary items

Exchange gains on short-term monetary items (considered in (d) above) are fairly straightforward to deal with as they are already (or soon will be) reflected in cash flows.

With long-term monetary assets, for example a loan repayable in several years' time in a foreign currency, there are additional considerations. It will be difficult (if not impossible!) to predict the exchange rate when the loan comes up for repayment. The basic approach of SSAP 20 is:

(1) outstanding loans should be translated into sterling at each balance sheet date using the year end exchange rate;
(2) exchange differences arising between successive balance sheet dates should normally be reported as part of the profit or loss on ordinary activities.

Illustration 4

A UK company takes out a ten-year loan from an American bank in August 19X5 for US $800,000. The proceeds of the loan are converted to sterling and remitted to the UK when the exchange rate was 1.41 (so the proceeds amounted to £567,376).

At the company's year end at 31 December 19X5, the exchange rate was 1.42 and at 31 December 19X6 was 1.39.

The loan account in the books of the UK company would appear as follows:

US LOAN ACOUNT

19X5	£	19X5	£
31 December Balance c/d (800,000 ÷ 1.42)	563,380	August Cash	567,376
P/L a/c	3,996		
	567,376		567,376
19X6		19X6	
31 December Balance c/d (800,000 ÷ 1.39)	575,540	1 January Balance b/d	563,380
		P/L a/c	12,160
	575,540		575,540

The exchange gain in 19X5 of £3,996 would be included within other interest receivable and similar income, while the exchange loss of £12,160 would be included within other interest payable and similar charges.

In 19X5, the company's profit and loss account is credited with an unrealised gain of £3,996. This treatment is justified by SSAP 20, paras 10 and 11 as follows:

Paragraph 10

In order to give a true and fair view of results, exchange gains and losses on long-term monetary items should normally be reported as part of the profit or loss for the period in accordance with the accruals concept of accounting; treatment of these items on a simple cash movements basis would be inconsistent with that concept. Exchange gains on unsettled transactions can be determined at the balance sheet date no less objectively than exchange losses; deferring the gains whilst recognising the losses would not only be illogical by denying in effect that any favourable movement in exchange rates had occurred, but would also inhibit fair measurement of the performance of the enterprise in the year. In particular, this symmetry of treatment recognises that there will probably be some interaction between currency movements and interest rates and reflects more accurately in the profit and loss account the true results of currency involvement.

Paragraph 11

For the special reasons outlined above, both exchange gains and losses on long-term monetary items should be recognised in the profit and loss account. However, it is necessary to consider on the grounds of prudence whether the amount of the gain, or the amount by which exchange gains exceed past exchange losses on the same items, to be recognised in the profit and loss account, should be restricted in the exceptional cases where there are doubts as to the convertibility or marketability of the currency in question.

(f) Equity investments financed by foreign borrowings

This special situation is dealt with in section 28.7.

28.4 CONSOLIDATION OF FOREIGN SUBSIDIARIES – AN INTRODUCTION

(a) Objectives

The objectives are set out in SSAP 20:

(1) Results should be produced which are compatible with the effects of exchange rates on a company's cash flows.
(2) The consolidated accounts should reflect the results and relationships which existed in the foreign currency statments (eg the relationship between profits earned and assets employed).

(b) Method

There are two main methods available for translating the results of an over-seas operation into sterling – the closing rate method, and the temporal method. The two methods are not alternatives.

In any given situation, the method to be used will depend on the relationship between the parent company and the overseas entity (assumed, for the present, to be a subsidiary). This may be illustrated diagrammatically:

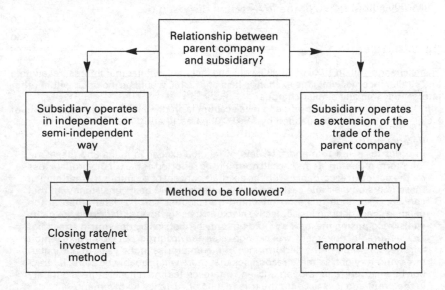

It is clear that SSAP 20 intends that the closing rate method will be appropriate in the vast majority of cases. This is confirmed by the English Institute's survey of published accounts of the leading UK companies.

(c) Foreign branches

Where a branch operates as a separate business with local finance, SSAP 20 states that the closing rate/net investment method should be used. If, how-ever, the branch operates as an extension of the company's trade and its cash flows have a direct impact on those of the company, SSAP 20 requires the temporal method to be used.

The examples below relate to foreign subsidiaries but clearly the same principles should be applied to foreign branches. Foreign branches are con-sidered further in section 28.8.

28.5   CLOSING RATE/NET INVESTMENT METHOD

(a) When appropriate

In broad terms, the method is appropriate whenever the subsidiary is indepen-dent or autonomous. Such situations may show the following characteristics.

(1) The parent company's investment is in the net worth of the foreign enterprise (as opposed to a direct investment in its assets and liabilities).
(2) The foreign enterprise will normally have both fixed assets and working capital, and these may be part-financed by local currency borrowings (as opposed to being entirely financed by the holding company).
(3) In its day-to-day operations, the foreign enterprise is not usually dependent on the reporting currency of the investing company (ie £ sterling).
(4) The parent company will expect dividends to be paid out of future profits, but its investment will remain until such future time as the foreign enterprise is liquidated, or the investment disposed of.

(b) Basic rules

Balance sheet	All assets and liabilities translated at closing rate of exchange.
Profit and loss account	Two options permitted under SSAP 20 – either: (1) all items at closing rate; or (2) all items at average rate.
Exchange differences	Two types of translation differences may arise: (1) exchange differences arising from the retranslation of the opening net investment at the closing rate; (2) differences between P/L at average rate and P/l at closing rate (only applicable if P/L option (2) is adopted). Both types of exchange differences should be recorded as reserve movements with no entry in the profit and loss account.

(c) Worked example

Many years ago, a UK company called Panther plc purchased a 70% holding of an overseas company called Clouseau SA. The investment cost £2,600 and at the date of acquisition, the reserves of Clouseau were Fr3,200.

The relevant exchange rates were as follows:

Date of acquisition	7.0 Fr to £1
31.12.X2	5.6 Fr to £1
Average for 19X3	5.1 Fr to £1
At payment of interim dividend	4.9 Fr to £1
31.12.X3	4.6 Fr to £1

The relevant final accounts are as follows:

Balance sheet at 31.12.X3

	Panther plc	Clouseau SA
	£	Fr
Tangible fixed assets – cost	92,000	56,000
– depreciation	(24,800)	(20,400)
Investment in Clouseau	2,600	–
Stock	19,600	14,120
Debtors	14,130	15,270
	103,530	64,990
Cash at bank	1,921	3,860
Dividends receivable	244	–
Loans	(10,000)	(6,000)
Creditors	(10,430)	(13,040)
Taxation	(10,400)	(6,880)
Proposed dividends	(7,000)	(1,600)
	67,865	41,330
Called-up share capital	30,000	15,000
Profit and loss account	37,865	26,330
	67,865	41,330

Profit and loss account for year end 31.12.X3

	£	Fr
Turnover	80,000	37,890
Cost of sales	(22,000)	(13,640)
Distribution costs	(16,500)	(2,090)
Administrative expenses	(14,600)	(7,200)
Dividends from Clouseau	415	–
Profit on ordinary activities before tax	27,315	14,960
Taxation	(10,400)	(6,880)
Profit on ordinary activities after tax	16,915	8,080
Exceptional items	9,300	–
	26,215	8,080
Dividends – interim (paid)	(5,000)	(1,200)
– final (proposed)	(7,000)	(1,600)
Retained profit	14,215	5,280
P/L balance at 1.1.X3	23,650	21,050
P/L balance at 31.12.X3	37,865	26,330

(d) Workings

The recommended approach is to tackle the workings in the following sequence:

(1) Translation of subsidiary's balance sheet.
(2) Consolidated balance sheet workings.
(3) Consolidated balance sheet.
(4) Translation of subsidiary's profit and loss account.
(5) Calculation of total exchange difference.
(6) Analysis of total exchange difference.
(7) Consolidated profit and loss account workings.
(8) Consolidated profit and loss account.
(9) Statement of reserves.

(e) Translation of balance sheet

	Fr	Rate	£'000
Fixed assets – cost	56,000		12,174
– depreciation	(20,400)		(4,434)
Stock	14,120		3,070
Debtors	15,270		3,319
Cash at bank	3,860	4.6	839
Loans	(6,000)		(1,304)
Creditors	(13,040)		(2,835)
Taxation	(6,880)		(1,495)
Proposed dividends	(1,600)		(348)
	41,330		8,986
Ordinary share capital	15,000		2,143
Pre-acquisition reserves	3,200	7	457
Post-acquisition reserves	23,130	Balancing figure	6,386
	41,330		8,986

Explanatory notes
(1) All assets and liabilities are translated into £ sterling using the closing rate of exchange of 4.6.
(2) Shareholders' funds of £8,986 do not appear in the consolidated balance sheet as such – they are subject to consolidation adjustments in order to arrive at goodwill on consolidation, minority interest and consolidated profit and loss reserves.

In order to make the subsequent calculations easier, it is convenient (although not absolutely necessary) to divide into the three parts shown above. Since reserves at acquisition are stated as Fr3,200, the post-acquisition reserves of Fr23,130 are the carry forward of Fr26,330 less Fr3,200. Share capital and pre-acquisition reserves are translated at 7 (these two figures are taken into account in calculating goodwill) and the figure of £6,386 is a balancing item. Remember that the workings are set out this way in order to ease the calculations! Other possible ways of setting out workings would have exactly the same effect on the consolidated balance sheet.

(f) Consolidated balance sheet workings

Analysis of equity

	Total £	Group share (70%) of pre-acquisition reserves £	Group share (70%) of post-acquisition reserves £	MI (30%) £
Ordinary share capital	2,143	1,500		643
P/L reserves at acquisition	457	320		137
P/L reserves since acquisition	6,386		4,470	1,916
	8,986	1,820		
Cost of investment		2,600		
Goodwill on consolidation w/o against reserves		780	(780)	
Reserves of Panther (including dividends received and receivable)			37,865	
Consolidated B/S totals			41,555	2,696
MI in proposed dividend (348 – 244)				104

CONSOLIDATED BALANCE SHEET

at 31 December 19X3

	£	£	£
Fixed assets			
Tangible assets			74,940
Current assets			
Stock		22,670	
Debtors		17,449	
Cash		2,760	
		42,879	
Less creditors: amounts falling due within one			
year			
Creditors	13,265		
Taxation	11,895		
Dividends payable:			
Parent company shareholders	7,000		
Minority shareholders	104		
		32,264	
Net current assets			10,615
Total assets less current liabilities			85,555
Creditors: amounts falling due after more than			
one year			(11,304)
			74,251
Called-up share capital			30,000
Profit and loss account			41,555
			71,555
Minority interest			2,696
			74,251

(g) Translation of subsidiary's profit and loss account

	Fr	Rate	£
Turnover	37,890		7,429
Costs of sales	(13,640)		(2,674)
Gross profit	24,250		4,755
Distribution costs	(2,090)	5.1	(410)
Administration expenses	(7,200)		(1,412)
Operating profit	14,960		2,933
Tax	6,880		1,349
	8,080		1,584
Dividends – paid	(1,200)	4.9	(245)
– proposed	(1,600)	4.6	(348)
Retained profit	5,280		991

Explanatory notes
(1) All profit and loss items have been translated at an average rate for the period. An acceptable alternative policy would have been to translate at closing rate.
(2) Dividends paid are translated at the rate of exchange at the date of payments, while dividends proposed are translated at the closing rate. This should correspond with the rates used by the parent company in its own separate accounts.

(h) Calculation of total exchange difference

So far we have:

(1) Split the closing reserves of the subsidiary between pre-acquisition and post-acquisition (see working (e)).
(2) Translated various profit and loss items (working (g)).

Before we can calculate the total exchange difference on translation for the year, we need to know the equivalent split of opening reserves between pre-acquisition and post-acquisition. In practice, this information would be available from the previous year working papers. As this information is not available, it is necessary to carry out a rather artificial exercise of reconstructing the previous year's closing balance sheet.

Net assets at 31 December 19X2 may be calculated as a global total by adding together share capital and reserves (Fr 15,000 + 21,050 = 36,050). Post-acquisition reserves (in francs) may again be calculated as a balancing figure.

	Fr	Rate	£
Sundry net assets	36,050	5.6	6,438
Ordinary share capital	15,000		2,143
Pre-acquisition reserves	3,200	7.0	457
Post-acquisition reserves	17,850	Balancing figure	3,838
	36,050		6,438

Explanatory notes
(1) First of all, the opening balance sheet in francs should be reconstructed. Although the breakdown of the net assets figure of Fr 36,050 is not known, this does not matter as all items included in this are translated at the same rate of exchange.
(2) The various items should be translated into £ sterling using the same procedures as in (e) above. The post-acquisition reserves of £3,838 are calculated as a balancing figure.

Calculation of total exchange difference

Post-acquisition reserves at 1.1.X3 (working (h))	3,838
Post-acquisition reserves at 31.12.X3 (working (e))	6,386
Increase	2,548
Retained profit (working (g))	991
Exchange difference (gain)	1,557

As the subsidiary is 70% owned, then 70% × £1,557, ie £1,089, will be shown as a movement on group reserves (with no entry in the consolidated profit and loss account for the year).

(i) Analysis of total exchange difference

Where the profit and loss account of the subsidiary is translated at the average rate of exchange, SSAP 20 distinguishes between two elements of the exchange difference:

(1) exchange differences arising from retranslation of the opening net investment at the closing rate; and
(2) the difference between the profit and loss account translated at an average rate and at the closing rate.

The total exchange difference of £1,557 above may be analysed as follows:

	Fr	Rate	£
Equity interest at 1.1.X3	36,050	5.6	6,438
Gain on retranslation at closing rate (bal figure)	–	–	1,399
Equity interest at 1.1.X3: Restated at closing exchange rate	36,050	4.6	7,837
Retained profit per p/l workings	5,280	–	991

Exchange difference – p/l at average rate
compared with closing rate

$$\frac{5,280}{4.6} - 991$$

	Fr	Rate	£
	–	–	158
Equity interest at 31.12.X3	41,330	4.6	8,986

Total exchange difference = (1,399 + 158) = £1,557
  Group share treated as movement on reserves during the year 70% × £1,557 = £1,089.

(j) Consolidated profit and loss account workings

For most items, it is simply a question of combining two sets of figures: those of the parent company, and the £ sterling figures for the subsidiary as calculated in (g) above.

The only other calculation required is that for minority interest. From working (g), MI is calculated as follows:

30% × £1,584 = £475

(k)   CONSOLIDATED PROFIT AND LOSS ACCOUNT
for the year ended 31 December 19X3

	£	£
Turnover		87,429
Cost of sales		24,674
Gross profit		62,755
Distribution costs	16,910	
Administration expenses	16,012	32,922
Profit on ordinary activities before tax		29,833
Tax		11,749
Profit on ordinary activities after tax		18,084
Minority interest		475
		17,609
Exceptional item		9,300
		26,909
Dividends – interim (paid)	5,000	
– final (proposed)	7,000	12,000
Retained profit		14,909
Retained by parent company		14,215
Retained by subsidiary		694
		14,909

Working: 70% × £991 (working (g)) = £694.

(l) Statement of reserves

This statement 'links in' the retained profit in the P/L and the group share of the exchange difference with the reserves in the consolidated balance sheet.

	£
So far we have calculated:	
(i) Retained profit (from consolidated P/L);	14,909
(ii) Group share of exchange difference (workings (h) and (i)).	1,089

We need to calculate the balance on consolidated P/L reserves at 1.1.X3 (this is the figure which appeared in last year's consolidated balance sheet).

	£
This is calculated as follows:	
Panther reserves at 1.1.X3	23,650
Panther's share of post-acquisition reserves at 1.1.X3 of Clouseau (working (h)):	
70% × £3,838	2,687
	26,337
Less goodwill w/o	780
	25,557

The statement of reserves which would be disclosed in the published accounts would be:

	£
Profit and loss account at 1.1.X3	25,557
Retained profit	14,909
Exchange differences	1,089
Profit and loss account at 31.12.X3	41,555

(Note that this last figure agrees with the consolidated balance sheet at 31 December 19X3.)

28.6 TEMPORAL METHOD

(a) When appropriate

The temporal method should be used in those relatively few cases where the foreign operations are carried out through foreign enterprises which operate as a direct extension of the trade of the investing company.

(b) Dominant currency

The temporal method should be used where it is considered overall that the currency of the investing company (ie parent company) is the dominant currency in the economic environment in which the subsidiary operates.

This assessment will require the following to be taken into account:

(1) the extent to which the subsidiary's cash flows have a direct impact on the cash flows of the investing company;
(2) the extent to which the functioning of the subsidiary depends directly on the holding company;
(3) the currency in which the majority of trading transactions are denominated;
(4) the major currency to which the operation is exposed in its financing structure.

(c) Possible situations

SSAP 20 gives the following as examples of situations where the temporal method may be appropriate:

(1) Where the foreign enterprise acts as a selling agency, receiving stocks of goods from the investing company and remitting the proceeds back to the company.
(2) Where the foreign enterprise produces a raw material or manufactures parts or sub-assemblies which are then shipped to the investing company for inclusion in its own product.
(3) Where the foreign enterprise is located overseas for tax, exchange control or similar reasons to act as a means of raising finance for other companies in the group.

(d) Basic rules

(1) *Balance sheet items*

Item	Examples	Exchange rate
Monetary assets and liabilities	Debtors Cash Creditors Loans	Closing rate
Non-monetary assets	Stock	Rate at date of acquisition of stock (but closing rate is usually acceptable)
	Fixed assets (cost less depreciation)	(1) Acquired before acquisition of subsidiary – rate at date of acquisition of subsidiary (2) Acquired after acquisition of subsidiary – rate at date of purchase of fixed assets

(2) *Profit and loss items*

Item	Exchange rate
Sales Expenses (excluding depreciation)	Average rate of exchange
Depreciation	Same rate as for fixed assets
Taxation	Closing rate (although some accountants consider that average rate should be used)
Dividends	Paid – rate at payment date Proposed – closing rate

(3) *Exchange differences*

These should be included in the profit and loss account and taken into account in arriving at profit on ordinary activities before taxation. They will normally be included under 'other operating income or expense'.

(e) Worked example

The previous example of Panther plc will be reworked using the temporal method. This is for purpose of illustration only, as the closing rate method would normally be appropriate for the circumstances of that company.

The 70% holding was acquired several years ago at a cost of £2,600 when the reserves of Clouseau amounted to Fr3,200.

The relevant exchange rates were:

Acquisition of subsidiary	7.0 Fr to £1
Acquisition of fixed assets	6.1 Fr to £1
31.12.X2	5.6 Fr to £1
Average for 19X3	5.1 Fr to £1
Payment of dividend	4.9 Fr to £1
31.12.X3	4.6 Fr to £1

The relevant final accounts are as follows:

Balance sheet at 31.12.X3

	Panther plc £	Clouseau SA Fr
Tangible fixed assets – cost	92,000	56,000
– depreciation	(24,800)	(20,400)
Investment in Clouseau	2,600	–
Stock	19,600	14,120
Debtors	14,130	15,270
Cash at bank	1,921	3,860
Dividends receivable	244	–
Loans	(10,000)	(6,000)
Creditors	(10,430)	(13,040)
Taxation	(10,400)	(6,880)
Proposed dividends	(7,000)	(1,600)
	67,865	41,330
Called-up share capital	30,000	15,000
Profit and loss account	37,865	26,330
	67,865	41,330

Profit and loss account for year end 31.12.X3

	Panther plc £	Clouseau SA Fr
Turnover	80,000	37,890
Cost of sales	(22,000)	(13,640)
Distribution costs	(16,500)	(2,090)
Administration expenses	(14,600)	(7,200)
Dividends from Clouseau	415	–
Profit on ordinary activities before tax	27,315	14,960
Taxation	(10,400)	(6,880)
Profit on ordinary activities after tax	16,915	8,080
Exceptional item	9,300	–
	26,215	8,080
Dividends – interim (paid)	(5,000)	(1,200)
– final (proposed)	(7,000)	(1,600)
Retained profit	14,215	5,280
P/L balance at 1.1.X3	23,650	21,050
P/L balance at 31.12.X3	37,865	26,330

Notes

(1) Loan interest has been ignored for this example.
(2) Cost of sales includes depreciation of 5,600 francs. There is no other depreciation.

(f) Workings

The recommended approach is to tackle the workings in the following sequence:

(1) Translation of subsidiary's balance sheet.
(2) Consolidated balance sheet workings.
(3) Consolidated balance sheet.
(4) Translation of subsidiary's profit and loss account.
(5) Calculation of total exchange difference.
(6) Consolidated profit and loss account workings.
(7) Consolidated profit and loss account.

(g) Translation of balance sheet

	Fr	Rate	£
Fixed assets – cost	56,000	6.1	9,180
– depreciation	(20,400)		(3,344)
Stock	14,120		3,070
Debtors	15,270		3,319
Cash at bank	3,860		839
Loans	(6,000)	4.6	(1,304)
Creditors	(13,040)		(2,835)
Taxation	(6,880)		(1,495)
Proposed dividends	(1,600)		(348)
	41,330		7,082
Ordinary share capital	15,000	7	2,143
Pre-acquisition reserves	3,200		457
Post-acquisition reserves	23,130	Balancing figure	4,482
	41,330		7,082

Explanatory note: As with the approach used for the closing rate method, the post-acquisition reserves of £4,482 is calculated as a balancing figure.

(h) Consolidated balance sheet workings

Analysis of equity

	Total £	Group share (70%) of pre-acquisition reserves £	Group share (70%) of post-acquisition reserves £	MI (30%) £
Ordinary share capital	2,143	1,500		643
P/L reserves at acquisition	457	320		137
P/L reserves since acquisition	4,482		3,137	1,345
	7,082	1,820		
Cost of investment		2,600		
Goodwill on consolidation w/o against reserves		780	(780)	
Reserves of Panther			37,865	
Consolidated B/S totals			40,222	2,125
MI in proposed dividend (348 – 244)				104

(i)   CONSOLIDATED BALANCE SHEET

at 31 December 19X3

	£	£	£
Fixed assets			
Tangible assets			73,036
Current assets			
Stock		22,670	
Debtors		17,449	
Cash		2,760	
		42,879	
Less creditors: amounts falling due within one year			
Creditors	13,265		
Taxation	11,895		
Dividends payable:			
Parent company shareholders	7,000		
Minority shareholders	104	32,264	
Net current assets			10,615
Total assets less current liabilities			83,651
Creditors: amounts falling due after more than one year			(11,304)
			72,347
Called-up share capital			30,000
Profit and loss account			40,222
			70,222
Minority interest			2,125
			72,347

(j) Translation of subsidiary's profit and loss account

	Fr	Rate	£
Turnover	37,890	5.1	7,429
Costs of sales (excluding depreciation)	(8,040)	5.1	(1,576)
Depreciation	(5,600)	6.1	(918)
Gross profit	24,250		4,935
Distribution costs	(2,090)	5.1	(410)
Administration expenses	(7,200)	5.1	(1,412)
Operating profit	14,960		3,113
Tax	(6,880)	4.6	(1,478)
	8,080		1,635
Dividends – paid	(1,200)	4.9	(245)
– proposed	(1,600)	4.6	(348)
Retained profit	5,280		1,042

(k) Calculation of total exchange differences

The approach adopted is similar to that for the closing rate method. Again, for reasons previously explained, it is necessary to reconstruct the opening balance sheet. The main point to note, however, is that opening net assets must be split between fixed assets and others, as different exchange rates are appropriate.

The calculations are set out below, followed by explanatory notes.

	Fr	Rate	£
Fixed assets			
(35,600 + 5,600)	41,200	6.1	6,754
Other assets less liabilities	(5,150)	5.6	(920)
	36,050		5,834
Ordinary share capital	15,000	7.0	2,143
Pre-acquisition reserves	3,200	7.0	457
Post-acquisition reserves	17,850	Balancing	3,234
	36,050	figure	5,834

Explanatory notes
(1) Assuming no acquisition or disposals of fixed assets during the year, it is possible to work back to the figure at the beginning of the year by adding back the depreciation charge.
(2) Post-acquisition reserves of Fr 17,850 are calculated as under the previous method (i e 21,050 – 3,200).
(3) Net liabilities of Fr 5,150 are calculated as a balancing figure.
(4) Amounts are translated into sterling using temporal principles.
(5) Post-acquisition reserves of £3,234 are calculated as a balancing figure.

Calculation of total exchange difference

	£
Post-acquisition reserves at 1.1.X3 (working (k))	3,234
Post-acquisition reserves at 31.12.X3 (working (g))	4,482
Increases	1,248
Retained profit (working (j))	1,042
Exchange difference (gain)	206

SSAP 20 does not attempt to analyse the component parts of the exchange gain – in fact such an analysis would have little meaning.

(I) Consolidated profit and loss account workings

Again for most items it is simply a question of combining two sets of figures.

(1) Minority interest

	£
Profit after tax (working (i))	1,635
Exchange gain taken to P/L	206
	1,841

MI: 30% × £1,841 = £552

(2) P/L balance as at 1.1.X3

	£
Panther reserves at 1.1.X3	23,650
Panther's share of post-acquisition reserves at 1.1.X3 of Clouseau (working (k)) 70% × £3,234	2,263
	25,913
Less goodwill w/o	780
	25,133

(m)   CONSOLIDATED PROFIT AND LOSS ACCOUNT

For the year ended 31 December 19X3

	£	£
Turnover		87,429
Cost of sales		24,494
Gross profit		62,935
Distribution costs	16,910	
Administration expenses	16,012	32,922
		30,013
Other operating income (exchange gain)		206
Profits on ordinary activities before tax		30,219
Tax		11,878
Profit on ordinary activities after tax		18,341
Minority interest		552
		17,789
Exceptional item		9,300
		27,089
Dividends – interim (paid)	5,000	
– final (proposed)	7,000	12,000
		15,089
Retained by parent company	14,215	
Retained by subsidiary (working)	874	
	15,089	
Profit and loss account balance at 1.1.X3		25,133
Profit and loss account balance at 31.12.X3		40,222

Working
70% (1,042 (j) + 206 (k))

28.7 EQUITY INVESTMENTS FINANCED BY FOREIGN BORROWINGS

(a) Background

Exchange gains or losses on foreign currency borrowings would normally be reported as part of the company's or group's profit on ordinary activities.

However, where the purpose of such borrowings is to provide a hedge against the risks associated with foreign equity investments, an alternative may be available.

SSAP 20 deals with this in two parts:

(1) in the accounts of the investing company;
(2) in the group accounts.

(b) Accounts of the investing company

(1) *Situation*

Where an individual company has used borrowings in currencies other than its own, either:

(i)   to finance foreign equity; or
(ii) where the purpose of such borrowings is to provide a hedge against the exchange risk associated with existing (ie previously acquired) equity investments;

then the company may be covered in economic terms against any movements in exchange rates.

(2) *Options*

Provided the company can satisfy the conditions set out below, the company *may* denominate its foreign equity investments in the relevant foreign currency and translate the carrying amount at each balance sheet date at the closing rate of exchange.

Any resulting exchange differences *should* be taken direct to reserves. Against these exchange differences *should* then be offset exchange gains or losses on related borrowings.

(3) *Conditions*

The three conditions to be satisfied are:

(i)   In any accounting period, exchange gains or losses arising on the borrowings may be offset only to the extent of exchange differences arising on the equity investments.

(ii) The foreign currency borrowings (whose exchange gains or losses are used in the offset process) should not exceed, in the aggregate, the total amount of cash that the investments are expected to be able to generate, whether from profits or otherwise.

(iii) The accounting treatment adopted should be applied consistently from period to period.

(4) *Illustration* 5

Suppose in the Panther example, the investment in Clouseau was part financed by a loan of 12,600 francs repayable in twenty years' time. Assume this loan is part of Panther's total borrowings.

(i) Ignoring SSAP 20 option

(a) The separate balance sheet of Panther will include:

Shares in group company		£2,600
Loan	$\left(\dfrac{\text{Fr}\,12,600}{4.6}\right)$	£2,739

(£2,739 is part of larger total of £10,000.)

(b) The loss on translation of the loan during the year is calculated as:

	£
$\text{Fr}\,\dfrac{12,600}{5.6}$	2,250
$\text{Fr}\,\dfrac{12,600}{4.6}$	2,739
Translation loss, charged to profit and loss account	489

(ii) SSAP 20 option

As an alternative, provided the above three conditions are satisfied, the company may take advantage of the option in SSAP 20 as follows:

(a) Shares in group company. Instead of showing this each year at an unchanged amount of £2,600, this equity investment may be denominated in francs, ie 18,200 francs (investment cost £2,600) when exchange rate was 7.0. This will then be retranslated each year at the closing rate of exchange:

Balance sheet 31.12.X2 $\dfrac{\text{Fr}\,18{,}200}{5.6}$ £3,250

Balance sheet 31.12.X3 $\dfrac{\text{Fr}\,18{,}200}{4.6}$ £3,957

(b) Loan in foreign currency borrowing:

Balance sheet 31.12.X2 $\dfrac{\text{Fr}\,12{,}600}{5.6}$ £2,250

Balance sheet 31.12.X3 $\dfrac{\text{Fr}\,12{,}600}{4.6}$ £2,739

(c) Exchange differences arising during the year:

	£
Exchange difference on investment (3,957 – 3,250)	707 Cr
Exchange difference on loan (2,739 – 2,250)	489 Dr
Net effect (credit)	218

If the company takes advantage of the option, £218 should be credited direct to reserves (with no entry in the profit and loss account).

(c) Group accounts

(1) *Situation*

Within a group, foreign borrowings may have been used to finance group investments in foreign enterprises (such as subsidiaries or associated companies) or to provide a hedge against the exchange risk associated with existing investments.

Any increase or decrease in the amount outstanding on the borrowings arising from exchange rate movements will probably be covered by corresponding changes in the carrying amount of the net assets underlying the net investments.

(2) *Option*

In the consolidated accounts, provided the conditions below are satisfied:

(i)   exchange gains or losses on such currency borrowings (which would otherwise be passed through the consolidated profit and loss account) *may* be offset as reserve movements against;
(ii) exchange differences on retranslation of the net investments.

(3) *Conditions*

The four conditions to be satisfied are:

(i)   the relationship between the investing company and the foreign enterprises concerned should be such as to justify the use of the closing rate method for consolidation purposes;
(ii) the other three conditions are those referred to on p. 506 except that 'net investments in foreign enterprises' applies instead of 'equity investments'.

(4) *Illustration* 6

Using the data from the Panther example:

(i) Ignoring SSAP 20 option

(a) Loss on translation of loan of £489 is debited to profit and loss account.
(b) Group share of exchange differences (70% × £1,557 = £1,089) to reserves.

(ii) SSAP 20 option

The difference on translation of the foreign currency borrowings may be offset against the difference on retranslation of the opening net investment:

	£
Gain on retranslation of opening net investment (see earlier workings) 70% × 1,399	979
Loss on translation of foreign currency borrowings	489
Exchange gain after offset	490
Group share of exchange difference on P/L translation: 70% × £158	110
So movement on reserves (credit) during the year is (490 + 110) i e	600

28.8 FOREIGN BRANCHES

(a) Translation method

The relationship between the branch and the head office will determine the translation method to be used. It is likely that most branches will conduct their business as an extension of the trade of the head office in which case the temporal method will be applicable.

This will not always be the case, however, and it is necessary to consider the definition of 'foreign branch' provided by SSAP 20.

(b) Definition

A foreign branch is either:

(1) a legally constituted enterprise located overseas, or
(2) a group of assets and liabilities which are accounted for in foreign currencies.

(c) Special situations

The extension of the definition ((b)(2), above), to a 'group of assets and liabilities' effectively means that certain branches (as defined) should be translated using the closing rate method.

The statement which accompanied the issue of SSAP 20 gave the following as examples of situations where a group of assets and liabilities should be accounted for using the closing rate/net investment method:

(i) a hotel in France financed by borrowings in French francs;
(ii) a ship or aircraft purchased in US dollars – with an associated loan in US dollars – which earns revenue and incurs expenses in US dollars;
(iii) a foreign currency insurance operation where the liabilities are substantially covered by the holding of foreign currency assets.

Both assets and liabilities will be translated at the exchange rate at the balance sheet date. Gains and losses on retranslation of opening 'equity' will be taken direct to reserves.

28.9   FOREIGN ASSOCIATED COMPANIES

By definition an associated company is not 'controlled' by the investor. Consequently, the closing rate/net investment method will usually be appropriate.

28.10   DISCLOSURE IN FINANCIAL STATEMENTS

(a) Accounting policies

The statement of accounting policies should disclose the translation method and the treatment of exchange differences.

(b) Disclosure of exchange gains

The net amount of exchange gains or losses on foreign currency borrowings less deposits should be disclosed, showing separately:

(1) the amount offset in reserves as under SSAP 20, paras 51, 57 and 58 (i e the options referred to above); and
(2) the net amount charged or credited to the profit and loss account.

This is not required for exempt companies as defined by SSAP 20.

(c) Movement on reserves

Net movement on reserves arising from exchange differences should be disclosed.

(d) Unrealised profits included in profit and loss account

If unrealised profits on long-term foreign loans are included in the profit and loss account, the Companies Act 1985 requires disclosure of:

(1) particulars of the departure (from the prudence concept);
(2) reasons for departure;
(3) effect of departure.

(You should refer back to section 28.3(e) above.)

Illustration 7

Extract from annual report and accounts of Reckitt and Colman plc for the year ended 31 December 1994.

Accounting policies (extract)

Foreign currency translation
Transactions denominated in foreign currencies are translated at the rate of exchange on the day the transaction occurs or at the contracted rate if the transaction is covered by a forward exchange contract.

   Assets and liabilities denominated in a foreign currency are translated at the exchange rate ruling on the balance sheet date or if appropriate at a forward contract rate. Exchange differences arising in the accounts of individual undertakings are included in the profit and loss account except that, where foreign currency borrowings have been used to finance equity investments in foreign currencies, exchange differences arising on the borrowings are dealt with through reserves to the extent that they are covered by exchange differences arising on the net assets represented by the equity investments.

   The accounts of overseas subsidiary and associated undertakings are translated into sterling on the following basis:

(1) Assets and liabilities at the rate of exchange ruling at the year-end date except for tangible fixed assets or undertakings operating in countries where hyper-inflation exists which are translated at historical rates of exchange.

(2) Profit and loss account items at the average rate of exchange for the financial year. An inflation adjustment is charged in arriving at local currency profits of undertakings operating in hyper-inflation countries before they are translated to reflect the impact of the hyper-inflation on the undertakings' working capital requirements.

Exchange differences arising on the translation of accounts into sterling are recorded as movements on reserves.

F Analysis of accounts

29 ANALYSIS OF ACCOUNTS – 1: INTERPRETATION OF ACCOUNTS

Key Issues

* Purpose of analysis
* Users and their needs
* Ratio analysis techniques
* Information available from published reports
* Limitations on usefulness of inter-company comparisons

29.1 INTRODUCTION

(a) Purpose of analysis

The process of interpreting accounts is essentially the art and science of translating figures in financial statements so as to reveal financial strengths and weaknesses. The analysis should hopefully help to identify the underlying causes which have contributed to these strengths and weaknesses.

Analysis is not necessarily restricted to historical cost based financial statements. It may also be applied to interim statements (see chapter 11) and forecast statements.

(b) Interested persons

The following users may have a particular interest in interpreting particular aspects of financial statements:

(1) the owners or, in the case of a limited company, the shareholders;
(2) debenture holders, or the holders of any other form of long-term loan capital;
(3) bank managers, financial institutions etc;
(4) investors and their professional advisers;
(5) financial journalists and commentators;
(6) creditors;
(7) HM Inspectors of Taxes.

(c) Areas of interest

These include:

(1) profitability trends, scope for improvement;
(2) solvency;
(3) ownership and control;
(4) financial strength;
(5) borrowing potential;
(6) gearing and interest cover;
(7) dividend cover.

(d) Profit and loss account

Analysts are likely to be concerned with:

(1) turnover:

  (i) variations in volume and price;
  (ii) sales mix changes (eg larger proportion of sales of higher-priced goods);

(2) gross profit ratios (gross profit as a percentage of sales);
(3) ratios of purchases and sales to creditors and debtors;
(4) ratios of stocks to cost of sales;
(5) fluctuations in expense elements (selling, distribution, administration, finance).

Comparisons may be made with figures of previous periods, with previously established budgets for the current period or with yardsticks for similar businesses.

(e) Balance sheet

(1) share capital including potential for future share issues;
(2) debentures – whether secured by fixed or floating charges;
(3) amount and adequacy of working capital;
(4) nature, purposes and limitations on use of reserves;
(5) valuations of property assets;
(6) goodwill – if it appears in a company balance sheet it is usually disregarded by analysts as the figure shown usually has little meaning.

29.2 RATIO ANALYSIS TECHNIQUES

(a) Introduction

Ratio analysis techniques help compare and interpret significant features in financial statements. Salient features may be brought into focus and areas requiring further investigation highlighted. Analysis helps to evaluate how we did last year, where we are now and possibly how we will fare in the future. Analysis may be concerned therefore with both control and prediction.

(b) Basis of comparison

Ratios calculated may be compared with:

(1) previous years (intra-firm comparisons);
(2) similar businesses (inter-firm comparisons).

Additionally ratios actually achieved for the current period may be compared with planned ratios established by management.

(c) Ratios in perspective

Ratio analysis should be regarded as an important part of an overall exercise involving interpretative techniques, including analysis of funds flow statements, scrutiny of accounting policies and so on. An analyst requires an overall picture of a business and should always avoid the danger of viewing ratios in isolation (refer also to section 29.4).

Auditors, for example, use ratio analysis techniques to provide corroborative evidence of the reasonableness of the view presented by the financial statements.

(d) Return on capital employed (ROCE)

Return on capital employed is often referred to as the primary ratio. The ratio comments on the efficiency of the management by contrasting the profit made by the business with the funds utilised to make that profit. It may be used to show the relative efficiency of the business as compared with the return on capital employed in other companies in the same industry, or in different industries, or in another country, or for the same concern in earlier years. The maintenance of the same ratio of profit to capital employed should be the lowest aim of every board of directors or proprietor: its improvement is probably a necessity in the face of mounting competition at home and abroad.

ROCE essentially expresses profit as a percentage return on net assets.

More specifically, profit is usually taken to refer to profit before deducting interest on long-term loans and tax. Net assets are fixed assets plus working capital (which is the same as shareholders' funds plus long-term liabilities).

There are several variants of ROCE, but the above is often regarded as the most useful and is the definition which will be adopted here.

(e) Secondary ratios

Closely allied to the primary ratio are (1) the profitability of sales disclosed by the ratio of percentage of net profit to sales, and (2) the intensity with which the capital is employed in the business as shown by the ratio of sales to capital employed. These ratios will support any conclusions drawn from the primary ratio and may indicate the reason for an unsatisfactory return on capital employed.

The relationship between the primary and secondary ratios may be illustrated as follows:

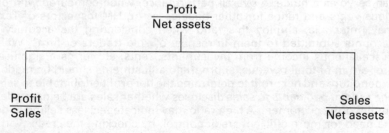

$$\frac{\text{Profit}}{\text{Sales}} \text{ is effectively a profit margin on sales.}$$

$$\frac{\text{Sales}}{\text{Net assets}} \text{ is sometimes referred to as asset turnover.}$$

(f) Pyramid of ratios

The above analysis can be taken further:

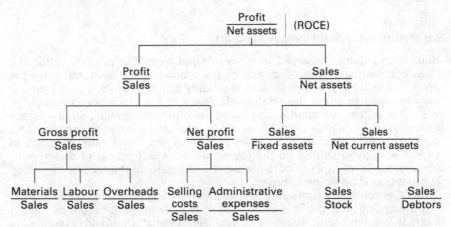

Certain of the above ratios are referred to in the following parts of the chapter.

(g) Ratio of profit to sales

(1) *The ratio of gross profit to sales* serves as an overall guide to the efficiency of production in a manufacturing business, while in non-manufacturing businesses it should correspond with the trade mark-up, which may be constant in respect of the whole of the sales, or variable in respect of known proportions of total turnover; in this type of business this ratio also serves as a valuable check upon the accuracy of the closing stock figure. Its limitations lie in the fact that as no account is taken of selling and distribution expenses it may be misleading; a product which is costly to produce, or purchase (in the case of a non-manufacturing concern), may incur very little in the way of selling and distribution expenses and vice versa.

(2) *The ratio of net profit to sales* discloses the ultimate proportion of sales and miscellaneous revenue accruing to the proprietors, or available for appropriation in the case of a limited company. Probably the most widely used ratio of all, this does not suffer from the disadvantages inherent in the ratio of gross profit to sales since it takes all expenditure into account and can serve as a guide to overall performance, when compared with previous years and ratios for other businesses eg HM Inspectors of Taxes may, inter alia, employ this ratio when considering the accuracy of accounts submitted to them in respect of sole traders or firms. Where miscellaneous income from investments, rents, etc forms a significant proportion of total revenue, appropriate adjustments should be made to expenditure and net profit to determine the net profit attributable to sales.

(3) *The ratio of bad debts to sales* discloses whether sales are being made to creditworthy customers. A high ratio may indicate reckless selling and/or the need for more efficient credit control, by checking the credit worthiness of new and existing customers and by the collection of outstanding debts before the affairs of customers get out of hand.

(4) *Production ratios*
These include:

   (i)   factory costs to sales;
   (ii) administration costs to sales;
   (iii) selling costs to sales;
   (iv) distribution costs to sales;
   (v)   research and development costs to sales.

Although the above could be expressed as ratios of total cost (being an equally important factor) it is considered that it is more advantageous to use sales since these ratios are probably best expressed as percentages, when the residual percentage will, after taking into account miscellaneous income, represent net profit; the relative effect upon net profits of trends or proposals will then be readily seen. To enhance their value, each of these would need to be broken down under the main items contained in each category e g it would be vital to analyse factory costs into materials, direct labour and factory overheads. Trends in the ratios over a number of years or periods would need to be studied, while the relative size of each heading and/or item should govern the extent of the investigations undertaken. It will be immediately apparent that if one item amounts to 1% of sales, while another accounts for 40%, greater potential savings are likely to result from a close scrutiny of the latter item. Some effort should be made by the analyst to distinguish between controllable costs and uncontrollable costs, which are due to external factors, such as a general increase in the price of certain raw materials, while it should be possible to correlate the behaviour of various costs, with a view to reducing total costs. This might apply where, for example, a reduction in direct labour has been achieved, or is proposed, by purchasing components and/or increasing the degree of mechanisation. The degree of correlation found from experience, or from one budget may provide a collateral check upon a number of flexible budgets.

The use of historical costs is implicit in the foregoing; however, trends based upon past performance are of limited value only in assessing efficiency due to the absence of an absolute or realistic yardstick. Comparison with carefully prepared budgeted or standard costs can, on the other hand, enhance the value of production and cost ratios immensely.

(h) Ratios of sales to net assets (capital employed)

The ratio of sales to capital employed discloses the 'rate of turnover' of the capital employed in the business. Unless overtrading is prevalent, a high ratio is a healthy sign, for the more times capital is turned over, the greater will be the opportunities for making profits. A low ratio, on the other hand, may be indicative of unused capacity, or undertrading, especially if this is accompanied by a high ratio of fixed factory overhead expenditure to sales. It may be advantageous to subdivide this ratio between fixed and working capital to discover whether fixed capital is overemployed, whilst the working capital ratio remains dormant, or vice versa: for this reason capital employed should, in this context, be taken to mean net assets. However, it will be necessary to study the behaviour of the constituent elements of working capital before reaching a decision, for a constant ratio may merely mask fluctuations of cash, stock, debtors and creditors. Attempts should be made to minimise the level of working capital by, for example, reducing the period of credit extended to debtors as sales increase.

Quoted investments should be excluded from working capital, since sales will not be directly influenced by these. Similarly, it may be advisable to exclude trade investments and shares in subsidiary companies from fixed capital, where the return on these is competitive, on the grounds that sales may have been unaffected by the employment of such funds. Much, however, will depend upon the circumstances in each case, which will need to be treated on its merits, for connections with associated and subsidiary companies will often provide outlets for additional sales. A more realistic picture may emerge by basing this ratio upon the average of fixed and working capital employed throughout the year, derived from interim accounts (if any) prepared at monthly or quarterly intervals.

(i) Stock ratios

These ratios indicate efficiency in the control of stocks of raw materials, work-in-progress and finished goods. Excessive stocks are to be avoided since, apart from incidental costs eg storage, insurance etc, working capital will be tied up which could perhaps be invested in securities or otherwise profitably employed. Where, moreover, superfluous stocks are in effect financed by an overdraft, the cost of such facilities is wasteful.

The ratios computed will be governed by the type of business; where, for instance, goods are produced for stock, there may be little or no work-in-progress, ratios being confined to raw materials and finished stock; where, however, the business is engaged upon job production, there should be no stocks of finished goods, but levels of raw material stocks and work-in-progress will need to be controlled.

It should be stressed that calculation of ratios is no substitute for efficient storekeeping, a perpetual inventory system and the objective calculation of minimum and maximum stocks for each item of raw materials and components.

(1) *Raw material stock to purchases* shows the rate of stock turnover. The ratio of closing stock to purchases indicates the number of days' (weeks' or months') purchases held in stock and can act as a guide to excessive stockholdings. A high ratio may signify the presence of obsolescent stocks, or inefficiency on the part of the buying department by purchasing too far in advance of requirements: if, however, such purchases were made at favourable prices prior to impending price increases, this may, on the contrary, denote efficiency on the part of the buyer. The ratio may be analysed between raw materials and components, and indeed different classes of raw materials, in order to pinpoint obsolescent items and forward purchases.

(2) *Work-in-progress to cost of production* indicates the length of the production cycle where a uniform product is manufactured. Comparison with earlier periods can provide a measure of efficiency or otherwise of the production department. In a medium-sized or large plant, figures would be available for each direct department, thus enabling the ratio for each department to be ascertained; bottlenecks indicated by these ratios can result in action being taken to expedite the production cycle in particular departments, resulting in a quicker overall production cycle, since this is clearly dependent upon the weakest link in the chain. Ratios based upon monthly figures may be even more enlightening since seasonal variations due, for example, to holidays and sickness, may come to light, both on a global and departmental basis, which, if capable of remedial action, may speed the production cycle still further. Where production is carried out in accordance with customers' specifications (ie job production) the production cycle will vary widely from one job to another, when the time taken to complete each job, and the level of work-in-progress, will need to be considered on its merits.

(3) *Finished stock to total turnover* shows how long finished goods are kept in store before being sold. Needless to say, stock should be held for as short a time as possible if profits are to be maximised. This ratio is best calculated by dividing annual turnover by the average of the stock figures at the close of each month, as ratios based upon opening or closing stock for the year, or the average of these, may be misleading, unless stocks are constant throughout the year. The question arises as to whether turnover and stock should be at selling price or cost price; however, provided both elements are either at cost or selling price, a realistic ratio should emerge. When the ratio increases, steps should be taken either to increase sales or to curtail output, if overproduction has occurred. In any event, sales and production

will need to be coordinated. Care should be taken to ensure that turnover of stock does not increase too much, signified by a very low ratio, otherwise it may prove difficult to meet customers' demands promptly. It should be noted that this ratio is sometimes expressed as a single figure, turnover being divided by stock.

(j) Ratio of credit sales to debtors

This shows the rate at which customers are paying for credit sales. This ratio should approximate to the credit terms allowed by the business and is, therefore, a comment on the efficiency of credit control. If three months' credit is extended to customers, then the normal ratio should be 4 to 1 (365 divided by 91). Thus, if annual turnover is £24,000, debtors should be approximately £6,000. This will, however, only apply if sales in terms of sterling are spread evenly over the year, since seasonal sales will give rise to variance; eg if the above turnover comprised sales of £5,000 for the first three quarters of the year and £9,000 for the last quarter, then debtors at the year end should be in the region of £9,000. The higher the ratio, the more favourable the effect upon working capital, because outsiders are being financed to a lesser extent while liquid resources will, other things being equal, increase.

(k) The solvency ratios

Although not referred to under the pyramid of ratios, these ratios are particularly important.

(1) The current (or working capital) ratio

This is determined by calculating the ratio of current assets to current liabilities. It shows whether there is an adequate amount of working capital to meet running expenses and service fixed assets. Movements will indicate how much of the concern's own resources are being utilised to finance current assets, as opposed to funds raised from current liabilities, eg an upward movement in stocks may be accompanied by a corresponding increase in creditors, rather than a decrease in cash. It should be remembered that the level of debtors and creditors represents the extent to which the business is financing, or is being financed by, respectively, outsiders. The extent of any unused overdraft facilities is important for, if the company has reached the limit of its short-term borrowing powers, difficulties will arise in times of emergency and expansion will be inhibited unless further long-term capital is raised.

Although it is desirable that current assets should exceed current liabilities, if only to provide ample coverage in the event of a liquidation, no two businesses are alike, and indeed it may be perfectly healthy for many businesses to work on a negative ratio. General criteria, such as the 'two to one' ratio should, therefore, be viewed with some scepticism. Again, due to seasonal idiosyncrasies the working capital position at the date of a balance sheet may represent maximum or minimum liquidity, not to mention 'window dressing', when an average over the year may provide a truer picture.

The principal factors which determine the optimum level of working capital may be summarised as follows:

(i)   The extent to which the business is subject to seasonal fluctuations and the vagaries of taste and fashion.
(ii) The amount of working capital required to finance any plans for expansion.
(iii) Terms of trade extended by suppliers and allowed to customers.
(iv) Bank overdraft facilities.

(v)   The length of the business cycle i e the finance tied up in production, or a specific order, from the time work commences until the receipt of cash. Much will obviously depend upon the nature of the product e g ocean-going liners or safety pins, while the level of work-in-progress will indicate the length of the cycle.

(vi)   The amount of working capital required to service fixed assets, which will be governed largely by the amount of capital sunk in these.

(vii)   The extent to which speculative activities are undertaken in the purchase of stock.

Attempts to expand turnover to a point when the working capital becomes inadequate to finance day-to-day operations produces a malady known as 'overtrading'. Symptoms of overtrading may take the following forms:

(i)   creditors will tend to increase in relation to debtors;
(ii)   a growth in the rate of long and/or short-term borrowing;
(iii)   minimal cash resources;
(iv)   an increase in stocks unaccompanied by an increase in turnover;
(v)   a diminution of gross and/or net profit;
(vi)   heavy expenditure on fixed assets.

A long production cycle will inevitably aggravate the shortage of liquid resources where this situation prevails.

An inadequate volume of business leads, on the other hand, to 'undertrading'. When trade diminishes beyond a certain point, a business will suffer the embarrassment of meeting its fixed and reduced variable costs from current assets which remain relatively static. The situation will be aggravated when the amount of fixed assets is large, since these will still have to be serviced, probably to a greater extent, due to underemployment.

(2) *Liquid (or quick) ratio*

The ratio, sometimes referred to as the acid test, is defined as:

$$\frac{\text{Current assets excluding stock}}{\text{Current liabilities}}$$

The ratio attempts to gauge the ability of a business to meet all its creditors from liquid resources, should they demand payment simultaneously. Although a useful guide to the solvency position of a business, it is somewhat unreal since many of the creditors are unlikely to demand payment at once. Quick assets comprise cash, quoted investments and bills receivable (as these may be discounted); in addition, an analysis of debtors may warrant the inclusion of some, considered to be readily realisable, but this is, however, a refinement. Businesses may be loath to realise investments where such action would result in a loss, while corporation tax payable on a chargeable gain may inhibit the realisation of investments where the reverse applies.

(I) The capital ratios

(1) *The capital gearing ratio* discloses the relationship between the ordinary share capital of a company and fixed interest capital, in the form of preference shares and debentures. A company with a preponderance of ordinary share (or equity) capital is said to be 'low-geared', while a company with a capital structure in which fixed interest capital is the higher, is said to be 'high-geared'. Gearing is neutral when ordinary and fixed interest capital are equal, resulting in a ratio of 1 to 1.

Reserves should be included as part of the equity of the company. Where a company's capital structure is low-geared, preference shareholders and debenture holders enjoy greater security, while the potential dividends payable to ordinary shareholders will not be subject to violent fluctuation with variations in profit. On the other hand, in a highly geared company variations in profit will tend to produce disproportionate changes in equity earnings, due to the burden of interest payable on fixed interest capital; in fact if profits fall too low, no dividend may be payable on the ordinary shares. Furthermore, where the structure is highly geared, a higher rate of interest would probably be offered to holders of prior charge capital to compensate for the greater risk attaching to their investment, both as regards security and income thereon.

(2) *The ratio of fixed assets to capital employed* reveals the disposition of funds between fixed and working capital: for the purposes of this ratio, fixed assets should be restricted to those of a tangible nature, while capital employed may be based on either gross or net assets, provided either basis is used consistently. Used in conjunction with the working capital ratio, this ratio may indicate the adequacy or otherwise of working capital to service fixed assets or an excess or deficiency of fixed assets, from which earnings can be generated. Comparison of the ratio for the current year with earlier years, against the background of the ratios of sales to working capital and sales to fixed capital, may indicate the optimum disposition of available funds. Comparison with ratios disclosed by the accounts of other businesses of a comparable type and scale may serve to support any conclusions drawn from study of internal ratios.

(m) The earnings or investment ratios

These relate to earnings on shares as opposed to earnings of the company itself and provide valuable information to actual or potential shareholders: they are also of great interest to higher management since a company depends upon its shareholders and would-be shareholders for its capital, and further funds for expansion. The following ratios are, therefore, closely associated with the capital ratios.

(1) *The ratio of net profit after corporation tax and preference dividend to equity capital* (ordinary shares plus reserves) shows the return on capital invested in the business by the ordinary shareholders regardless of the dividends paid or proposed on these shares. A more realistic and, invariably, conservative rate of earnings may be obtained by employing the real value of equity capital employed (ie the current value of the assets, less preference shares and liabilities) as the denominator. However, as mentioned earlier, assessment of the current value of the assets of a concern is no easy matter, and for this reason will not generally be available.

(2) *Earnings per share* (see chapter 30) has long been recognised as an important indicator of profitability.

(3) *The ratios of profit available for dividend to dividend paid,* or dividend cover, reveals the distribution and 'plough-back' policies of the directors. The ratio of retained earnings to net profit ie the complementary ratio, may also be computed to show the potential of an ordinary share for capital growth, while the margin of profit above that which is required to pay the expected dividend can be used to estimate the security of the share so far as dividend payments are concerned. Investors and would-be investors may use these ratios as criteria for decisions, so that they may have a direct effect on the demand for, and market price (in the case of a quoted company) of the shares.

The board of directors of a company should, therefore, always endeavour to maintain a careful balance between their dividend and 'plough-back' policies, for if dividends are too restricted, the market price of the shares may fall and a take-over bid ensue. On the other hand, distribution of dividends on too generous a scale may inhibit the ability of a company to expand without resort to fresh capital or loans, besides depleting its current liquid resources.

Care should be taken to deduct preference dividends from net profit when comparing the cover on ordinary shares.

(4) *The ratio of profit available for dividend to preference dividend* will reveal the number of times the preference divided is covered by earnings and thus indicate the preference shareholders' security, so far as income is concerned.

(5) *The dividend yield ratio* is the ratio of dividend received to the price paid for a share, or the current market price thereof. The yield acceptable to an investor will depend upon the risk attaching to the investment and the potential for capital growth; generally speaking, the greater the yield the greater the risk. Investors may be induced to accept a low yield where the market price of shares has fallen and the company is ripe for a take-over bid, or where the prospects are outstanding.

(6) *The price/earnings ratio* from an individual investor's viewpoint is ascertained by comparing the market price of an ordinary share with the earnings, or net profit per share, after deduction of corporation tax and preference dividends; this may be expressed as so many years' purchase of the profits: in other words, assuming stability of market price and ignoring the incidence of taxation of dividends, an investor's capital outlay will, at the present level of earnings, be recouped after so many years, either in the form of dividends received, or capital growth by virtue of retained profits. This ratio may provide a collateral check upon conclusions drawn from other earnings ratios, while calculations may be based upon forecast profits to provide a prospective price/earnings ratio.

This ratio may also be computed by comparing the Stock Exchange value of the ordinary shares of a company, ie price per ordinary share times the number of ordinary shares, with net profit after corporation tax and preference dividends, thus enabling the large investor and board of directors alike to compare the overall efficiency of a particular company with similar, or indeed, dissimilar companies (if the company in question is potentially adaptable): such comparisons will, however, only be valid if a reasonable degree of parity prevails between market prices, bearing in mind that these are subject to external influences eg government measures or the world economic climate, and/or domestic influences eg restrictive or overgenerous dividend policies.

29.3   RATIO ANALYSIS ILLUSTRATION

The figures below relate to the example of Veneering Manufacturers Ltd (see chapter 4).

The ratios are set out in the order in which they were discussed earlier in the chapter. Reference should be made to the comments made in respect of each ratio.

Return on capital employed

$$\frac{\text{(PBIT/FA + WC)}}{} \qquad \frac{133,600 + 6,000}{859,400} \times 100 \qquad 16.2$$

Gross profit

$$\frac{\text{Sales}}{} \qquad \frac{284,000}{791,000} \times 100 \qquad 35.9$$

PBIT

$$\frac{\text{Sales}}{} \qquad \frac{133,600 + 6,000}{791,000} \times 100 \qquad 17.6$$

Materials
$$\frac{\text{Sales}}{} \qquad \frac{352,400}{791,000} \quad \times\ 100 \qquad 44.5$$

Labour
$$\frac{\text{Sales}}{} \qquad \frac{137,900}{791,000} \quad \times\ 100 \qquad 17.4$$

Factory overheads
$$\frac{\text{Sales}}{} \qquad \frac{47,700}{791,000} \quad \times\ 100 \qquad 6.0$$

Administrative expenses
$$\frac{\text{Sales}}{} \qquad \frac{74,200}{791,000} \quad \times\ 100 \qquad 9.4$$

Selling and distribution expenses
$$\frac{\text{Sales}}{} \qquad \frac{107,300}{791,000} \quad \times\ 100 \qquad 13.6$$

Bad debts
$$\frac{\text{Sales}}{} \qquad \frac{2,500}{791,000} \quad \times\ 100 \qquad 0.3$$

$$\frac{\text{Sales}}{\text{Capital employed}} \qquad \frac{791,000}{924,300} \qquad \frac{0.8}{1}$$

Raw material stocks
$$\frac{\text{Purchases}}{} \qquad \frac{76,400}{319,000} \qquad \frac{0.24}{1}$$

Alternatively, raw material stocks could be described as 88 days' purchases (0.24 × 365).

Work-in-progress
$$\frac{\text{Cost of production}}{} \qquad \frac{12,800}{538,000} \qquad \frac{0.02}{1}$$

(That is, WIP is equivalent to eight days' production.)

Finished stock
$$\frac{\text{Turnover}}{} \qquad \frac{40,100}{791,000} \qquad \frac{0.05}{1}$$

(That is, finished stock is equivalent to 18 days' sales.)

Current sales
$$\frac{\text{Debtors}}{} \qquad \frac{791,000}{116,870} \qquad \frac{6.8}{1}$$

(That is, debtors are equivalent to 54 days' sales.)

Current assets
$$\frac{\text{Current liabilities}}{} \qquad \frac{460,450}{147,690} \qquad \frac{3.1}{1}$$

Liquid assets
$$\frac{\text{Current liabilities}}{} \qquad \frac{460,450 - 129,300}{147,690} \qquad \frac{2.2}{1}$$

Debt
$$\frac{\text{Equity}}{} \qquad \frac{150,000}{709,400} \qquad \frac{0.2}{1}$$

Fixed assets
$$\frac{\text{Capital employed}}{} \qquad \frac{582,700}{859,400} \qquad \frac{0.67}{1}$$

Net profit after tax and preference dividend
$$\frac{\text{Shareholders' equity}}{} \qquad \frac{67,700 - 5,600}{709,400} \ \times\ 100 \ = \qquad 8.7\%$$

Earnings per share $\dfrac{67,700 - 5,600}{400,000}$ = 15.5p per share

Dividend cover (ordinaries) $\dfrac{67,700 - 5,600}{20,000}$ = 3.1 times

Dividend cover (preference) $\dfrac{67,700}{5,600}$ = 12.1 times

Note: In the absence of a quoted share price, neither dividend yield nor earnings per share can be calculated.

29.4 INFORMATION AVAILABLE FROM PUBLISHED REPORTS

(a) Introduction

Some people appear to take the view that a company's position, performance and prospects can only be assessed by reference to information contained in the balance sheet, profit and loss account and related notes. This is often hardly the case! Useful information may be contained elsewhere in a company's annual report. Possible sources include:

(1) chairman's (or chief executive's) statement;
(2) divisional review;
(3) financial summaries and highlights;
(4) segmental analysis;
(5) cash flow statements;
(6) ratio analysis information including earnings per share;
(7) comparision of profits with those measured under United States generally accepted accounting principles (GAAPs).

(b) Chairman's statement

The statement of the chairman or chief executive often includes a concise review of the company's or group's progress. The statement may well give some indication of likely prospects for the forthcoming year. Such information, however, is not subject to minimum legal requirements regarding content nor is it technically within the scope of the auditors' report. Additionally the statement is likely to emphasise matters which the board wish to emphasise! Nevertheless to the average reader the statement is likely to be of significant interest.

(c) Divisional review

This may provide an informative perspective of business activities possibly with an indication of their relative importance in relation to sales and profits.

(d) Financial summaries and highlights

These are clearly aimed at the non-technical reader and aim to give a simple overview of financial highlights.

(e) Segmental analysis

Reporting requirements and the need for segmental analysis are referred to in chapter 32. As groups become larger and larger segmental analysis should take on an increasingly important role. Group accounts, after all, consolidate many different activities. Information about performance and contribution of segments becomes crucial in providing a counter-balance to the broadbrush approach of consolidation.

In practice, the amount and quality of segmental information vary from group to group. Some groups provide information over and above the mandatory minimum. Useful illustrations of segmental disclosures are given in chapter 32.

(f) Cash flow statements

Cash flow statements are dealt with in chapter 31.

(g) Ratio analysis information including earnings per share

All listed companies are required by SSAP 3 to present earnings per share information on the face of the profit and loss account (see chapter 30). It is evident that many financial analysts and commentators place great importance on this statistic notwithstanding some of the important limitations placed on its usefulness (see section 30.7).

Some companies present key ratios although such information is not mandatory. These ratios may be presented in the form of five-year (or even longer) summaries. A useful illustration, relating to the 1994 report of Cadbury Schweppes, is included below:

Illustration 1

Extract from financial review of Cadbury Schweppes plc for the year ended 31 December 1994.

Financial ratios

			1994	1993	1992	1991	1990
Trading margin	$\dfrac{\text{Trading profit}}{\text{Sales}}$	%	12.5	11.7	11.0	11.1	10.4
Return on assets	$\dfrac{\text{Trading profit}}{\text{Average operating assets}}$	%	35.7	31.8	29.3	31.7	31.1
Return on equity*	$\dfrac{\text{Earnings}}{\text{Average Ordinary Shareholders' funds}}$	%	21.0	22.9	24.2	28.9	28.7
Interest cover	$\dfrac{\text{Trading profit}}{\text{Net interest charge}}$	times	12.0	10.0	7.3	6.3	5.7
Fixed charge cover	See below	times	8.0	6.8	5.2	4.4	4.6
Dividend cover	$\dfrac{\text{Earnings per Ordinary Share}}{\text{Dividends per Ordinary Share}}$	times	2.0	2.1	2.0	2.2	2.2
Gearing Ratio*	$\dfrac{\text{Net borrowings}}{\text{Ordinary shareholders' funds} + \text{minority interests}}$	%	24.2	27.1	36.9	40.0	49.8
Operating asset turnover	$\dfrac{\text{Sales}}{\text{Average operating assets}}$	times	2.9	2.7	2.7	2.8	3.0
Earnings per Ordinary Share – published		p	31.46	30.59	26.41	27.10	24.51
IIMR		p	31.52	29.69	26.47	27.00	24.27
Dividends per Ordinary Share		p	15.60	14.40	13.00	12.31	11.33
Net assets per Ordinary Share*		p	158.16	141.30	118.83	100.89	86.73

*These ratios exclude preference shares at their redemption value (see Note 18).

Trading Profit = Operating Profit less the Group share of profits of associated undertakings.
Operating assets = Tangible fixed assets, stock, debtors and creditors after excluding post-acquisition restructuring provisions, borrowings, taxation, dividends and amounts payable to minorities and former minorities.

Fixed charge cover = $\dfrac{\text{Trading profit} + \text{Dividends from associates} + \frac{1}{3}\text{ operating lease rentals}}{\text{Net interest charge} + \text{preference dividends (gross)} + \frac{1}{3}\text{ operating lease rentals}}$

29.5   INTERPRETATION OF ACCOUNTS – POSSIBLE LIMITATIONS ON THE USEFULNESS OF INTER-COMPANY COMPARISONS

(a) Introduction

It may be difficult to make a valid comparison between two companies if they adopt significantly different policies regarding the treatment, for example, of leasing, goodwill, foreign currency translation and fixed asset revaluations. Some of the main areas of difficulty are referred to below. Further reference should be made to the relevant section covered earlier in the book.

(b) Historical cost accounts

Weaknesses and criticisms of accounts drawn up on a historical cost basis are referred to in chapter 33. These weaknesses clearly have implications for the validity of comparisons between companies.

(c) Goodwill

Companies may either eliminate goodwill against reserves as soon as it arises (without any effect on reported profit) or amortise over a number of years (thus reducing annual reported profit).

(d) Foreign currency translation

Groups which adopt a policy of translating financial statements of foreign subsidiaries using the closing rate/net investment method may translate the subsidiary's profit and loss account at either average for the year rates or year-end rates (see chapter 28).

(e) Implications of modified historical cost

Whether and to what extent a company adopts a modified historical cost can affect reported profits (the computations of depreciation charge and profit on sale of revalued assets were dealt with in chapter 12, section 12.7).

(f) Post balance sheet events

A post balance sheet event may be identified technically as being non-adjusting but a particular company may wish nevertheless to reflect it in current year accounts on prudence grounds. An example could relate to a closure decision taken shortly after the balance sheet date. Another company may reflect this transaction in the financial statements of the following year. Again this sometimes makes difficult valid inter-company comparisons.

(g) Off-balance sheet finance

This topic was referred to in chapter 7. One particular matter of concern was potential distortion of the debt/equity ratio. FRS 5 has improved the quality and usefulness of financial reporting in these areas.

(h) Business combinations satisfying the merger conditions of SSAP 23

In these circumstances group accounts may be prepared on either an acquisition basis or a merger basis. This again can cause problems when making inter-company comparisons. Earnings per share aspects of this are referred to in section 30.5(e).

(i) Impact of different policies

Reference should also be made to section 6.6.

30 ANALYSIS OF ACCOUNTS – 2: EARNINGS PER SHARE

Key Issues

* Usefulness of earnings per share information
* Calculation of EPS
  - basic EPS
  - impact of FRS 3
  - net and nil basis
  - changes in capital structure
  - fully diluted EPS
* Problems of comparability

30.1 BASIC CONSIDERATIONS

(a) Importance of earnings per share

From the viewpoint of a shareholder, earnings per share offers a basis of comparability of after-tax profits attributable to each share from one year to the next.

Investment analysts are also interested in earnings per share and use EPS to calculate the price/earnings ratio (PER). The price/earnings ratio (quoted price per share as a multiple of earnings per share) offers a useful basis for comparing companies within particular industrial and commercial sectors.

The additional information provided by FRS 3 (see chapter 8) has offered analysts alternative ways of measuring earnings per share (see 30.2).

(b) SSAP 3

SSAP 3 requires listed companies to publish earnings per share statistics on the face of the profit and loss account. The basis of calculation of EPS should be disclosed in a note to the accounts.

In certain circumstances, companies are required to display the fully diluted earnings per share in addition to the basic earnings per share. This is explained below.

(c) Definition

Prior to the issue of FRS 3, earnings per share was defined by SSAP 3 as the profit in pence attributable to each equity share based on the consolidated profit of the period after tax after deducting minority interests and preference dividends but before taking into account extraordinary items, divided by the number of equity shares in issue and ranking for dividend in respect of the period.

Illustration 1

The following extract is taken from the consolidated profit and loss account of CJ plc for the year ended 31 December 19X4. The company has 3m 25p ordinary shares in issue and which rank for dividend for the period:

	£
Profit on ordinary activities after tax	1,826,000
Minority interest	(70,000)
	1,756,000
Exceptional items	(200,000)
	1,556,000

Preference dividend	300,000	
Ordinary dividend	700,000	
		1,000,000
Retained profit		556,000

(1) Calculations

Earnings = £1,556,000 less £300,000
        = £1,256,000

$$\text{Earnings per share} = \frac{£1,256,000}{3 \text{ million}} \times 100 = 41.9\text{p}$$

(2) Disclosures

(i)   On face of consolidated profit and loss account.

	Year ended 31 December	
	19X4	*19X3*
Earnings per ordinary share of 25p	41.9p	X

(ii) Notes to the accounts.
The calculation of earnings per share is based on earnings of £1,256,000 (19X3 £-------) and 3m shares in issue throughout the two years to 31 December 19X4.

Illustration 2

CONSOLIDATED PROFIT AND LOSS ACCOUNT (EXTRACT)

	Note	*52 weeks to 31 July 19X2*	*Period to 2 August 19X1*
Earnings per ordinary share	10	15.2p	14.6p

Note 10: earnings per ordinary share

The calculation of earnings per ordinary share is based on profits after taxation or £14,911,000 (19X1 – £14,258,000) and on a weighted average of 98,328,004 (1991 – 97,795,812) ordinary shares in issue during the period. Fully diluted earnings per share are not materially different from the stated earnings per share.

(d) FRS 3

Under FRS 3, earnings are determined after taking extraordinary items into account. However, as indicated in chapter 8, extraordinary items are likely to be rare or non-existent.

30.2 THE IMPACT OF FRS 3 – REPORTING FINANCIAL PERFORMANCE

(a) Revised definition of EPS

FRS 3 amends the basic EPS definition. Earnings is now measured as profit after tax, minority interest, extraordinary items and preference dividend.

For large groups with diversified operations, EPS will reflect the effect of acquisitions, discontinued operations and a diverse range of exceptional items (see chapter 25).

(b) Publication of additional EPS information

FRS 3 also gives an opportunity to companies to present an additional earnings per share number, if they so choose. This may be calculated 'at any other level of profit'.

If a company wishes to follow this route, it should observe the following conditions and restrictions:

(1) the basic EPS required by FRS 3 should be at least as prominent as the additional EPS;
(2) there should be an explanation of the reason for calculating the additional EPS number;
(3) the additional EPS number should be presented on a consistent basis over time;
(4) the additional EPS should be reconciled to the basic EPS number based on the revised EPS definition referred to above.

The reconciliation should:

(i) list the items for which an adjustment is being made;
(ii) disclose the individual effect of each item on the calculation.

The explanation and the reconciliation should either:

(i) appear adjacent to the earnings per share disclosure; or
(ii) a cross-reference should be given as to where explanation and reconciliation can be found.

Illustration 3

Extract from annual report and accounts of De La Rue plc for the year ended 31 March 1995.

Group profit and loss account

Notes		1995 £m	1994 £m
	Turnover		
	Continuing operations	739.9	586.6
	Acquisitions	7.2	–
		747.1	586.6
	Discontinued operations	–	6.1
1		747.1	592.7
	Operating profit		
	Continuing operations: before acquisitions and reorganisation costs	107.3	96.1
	reorganisation costs	(4.9)	–
	acquisitions	1.1	–
		103.5	96.1
	Discontinued operations	–	0.2
1,2,3		103.5	96.3
4	Profit on the sale and termination of discontinued operations	–	14.1
4	Provision for losses on the disposal of properties in continuing operations	–	(8.0)
	Share of profits of associated companies	28.0	15.6
	Profit on ordinary activities before interest	131.5	118.0
5	Net interest receivable	15.1	11.8
	Profit on ordinary activities before taxation	146.6	129.8
6	Tax on profit on ordinary activities	(36.4)	(32.4)
	Profit on ordinary activities after taxation	110.2	97.4
	Equity minority interests	(1.4)	(1.5)
	Profit for the financial year	108.8	95.9
8	Dividends (including non-equity dividends)	(49.2)	(38.6)
19	**Transferred to reserves**	59.6	57.3
7	**Earnings per ordinary share**	55.1p	49.9p
7	**Headline earnings per ordinary share**	54.8p	47.5p
8	**Dividends per ordinary share**	23.00p	20.00p

There are no material differences between the results disclosed above and the results on an unmodified historical cost basis.

A reconciliation between earnings per share, as, calculated according to Financial Reporting Standard No. 3 'Reporting Financial Performance' (FRS 3) issued by the Accounting Standards Board, and headline earnings, as calculated according to the definition of headline earnings in Statement of Investment Practice No. 1 'The Definition of Headline Earnings' issued by the Institute of Investment Management and Research, is shown in note 7 of the Notes to the Group Profit and Loss Account.

Note 7

7 *Earnings per Share*	1995 55.1p	1994 49.9p

Earnings per share are based on the profit for the year attributable to ordinary shareholders of £108.8m (1994 £95.9m) as shown in the Group profit and loss account on page 38. The weighted average number of ordinary shares used in the calculations is 197,307,959 (1994: 192,020,693). The fully diluted earnings per share are not materially different from basic earnings per share in both 1994 and 1995.

Reconciliation of earnings per share	pence per share	pence per share
As calculated under FRS 3	55.1	49.9
Profit on the sale and termination of discounted operations	–	(6.4)
Provision for losses on the disposal of properties	–	4.0
Profit on the disposal of fixed assets	(0.3)	–
Headline earnings per ordinary share as defined by the IIMR	54.8	47.5

The Institute of Investment Management and Research (IIMR) has published Statement of Investment Practice No. 1 entitled 'The Definition of Headline Earnings'. The headline earnings per share shown above have been calculated according to the definition set out in the IIMR's statement. The reconciling items between earnings per share as calculated according to FRS 3 and as calculated according to the definition of the IIMR's headline earnings include the underlying tax effects.

The Directors are of the opinion that the publication of the IIMR's headline earnings figure is useful to readers of interim statements and annual accounts. Accordingly, it is their intention to continue to publish the IIMR's headline figure in future interim statements and annual accounts.

30.3   NET AND NIL BASIS

The tax charge of a company may contain some elements which are fixed (irrespective of the level of the dividends paid) and some which vary according to the level of dividend.

This gives rise to two possible measurements of EPS:

(1) The net basis, where the tax charge used to calculate the EPS includes irrecoverable ACT and any relieved overseas tax arising from the payment or proposed payment of dividends.
(2) The nil basis which excludes the above two items from the tax charge used as the basis of the EPS calculation.

SSAP 3 requires that earnings per share is determined on a net basis i e taking account of both fixed and variable elements of the tax charge.

However, where the nil basis calculation would differ significantly from the net basis, the nil basis should also be disclosed.

Illustration 4

Extract from the consolidated profit and loss account of Unrelieved plc for the year ended 31 December 19X6

The company had 2 million shares in issue throughout the year.

		£'000
Profit on ordinary activities before tax		1,200
Taxation		
Corporation tax	480	
Unrelieved advance corporation tax	115	595
Profit on ordinary activities after tax		605

Calculations

(1) Basic EPS net basis $\dfrac{1,200,000 - 595,000}{2,000,000} \times 100 = 30.2\text{p per share.}$

(2) Basic EPS nil basis $\dfrac{1,200,000 - 480,000}{2,000,000} \times 100 = 36\text{p per share.}$

As the nil basis differs significantly from the net basis, the nil basis should be disclosed in addition to the net basis.

30.4   LOSSES

Where a loss is incurred or where the amount earned for equity (ie after deducting preference dividends) is a negative figure, EPS should be calculated in the usual way and the result described as a loss per share.

30.5   BASIC EPS CHANGES IN THE CAPITAL STRUCTURE DURING THE YEAR

Possible situations include:

(a) bonus issue;
(b) issue for full consideration;
(c) rights issue.

(a) Bonus issue during the year

Where new equity shares have been issued by way of capitalisation of reserves during the financial year, the earnings per share should be based on the increased number of shares ranking for dividend after the capitalisation issue.

The corresponding earnings per share disclosed in respect of all earlier periods should be adjusted proportionately in respect of the capitalisation issue.

Illustration 5

In 19X4, the earnings of A plc amounted to £2,400,000 and the number of ordinary shares in issue and ranking for dividend amounted to 6m. EPS disclosed was therefore 40 pence per share.

Halfway through 19X5, the company made a bonus issue of 1 for 2. Earnings amounted to £2,700,000 and the number of shares, 9m.

In the accounts for 19X5, earnings per share would be disclosed as 30p per share. In order to achieve comparability with the previous year, the EPS of 19X4 should be restated to take account of the increased level of share capital.

That is, $\dfrac{£2,400,000}{9m} = 26.7\text{p}$

Figures disclosed in the 19X5 accounts would therefore be:

	19X5	19X4
Earnings per ordinary share of	30p	26.7p

Illustration 6

Extract from annual report and accounts of Haynes Publishing plc for the year ended 31 May 1994.

Note 11

11 *Earnings per share*
Earnings per share are calculated on the Group profit, after taxation, of £3,035,000 (1993: £2,692,000) and on the weighted average of 15,512,138 ordinary shares allotted. As a result of the 1 for 2 capitalisation issue on 25 November 1993 prior year earnings per share has been restated.

The fully diluted earnings per share has not been shown as it is not materially different.

(b) Issue of shares for full consideration

Where there has been an issue of shares for cash or other full consideration, ranking for dividend during the year, earnings per share on the weighted average share capital are shown.

Illustration 7

During the year ended 31 December 19X9, X plc earned £24,000. On 1 January 19X9, the ordinary share capital was 100,000 shares of 50p each. On 30 September 19X9, a further 200,000 ordinary shares of 50p each were issued.

$$\text{Earnings per share: } \frac{£24,000 \times 100}{150,000 \,(\text{i e } 100,000 + \frac{1}{4} \times 200,000)} = 16p$$

Note: The calculation of earnings per share is based on earnings of £24,000 and on the weighted average of 150,000 ordinary shares in issue during the year.

(c) Rights issue

An issue of shares to an existing shareholder at a price below the current market price is equivalent to an issue of shares at full market price plus a bonus issue. Previous years' earnings per share must be adjusted for the bonus element in the rights issue. Calculations should be based on the official middle price of the closing price on the last day of the quotation cum-rights. The calculation will be as follows:

$$\frac{\text{Earnings per share}}{\text{for previous years}} \times \frac{\text{Theoretical ex-rights price}}{\text{Actual cum-rights price}}$$

To avoid splitting the earnings during the current year between the periods before and after the rights issue, the share capital before the rights issue should be adjusted by the reciprocal of the factor used for calculating the previous years' earnings per share, viz:

$$\frac{\text{Actual cum-rights price}}{\text{Theoretical ex-rights price}}$$

Illustration 8

Y plc share capital of £2m all in ordinary shares of 25p each was increased on 1 July 19X9 to £3m by a rights issue of ordinary shares in the proportion of 1 for 4 at 50p per share = 2m shares for £1m. The middle market price of the ordinary shares on the last day of quotation cum-rights was 200p. Profits after tax were:

	£
Year ended 31 December 19X9	850,000
Year ended 31 December 19X8	800,000

Calculation of earnings per share
The holder of 100 ordinary shares would on taking up his entitlement subscribe for 25 new shares costing £12.50. His total holding of 125 shares would, assuming no other change in circumstances, be worth £212.50 or 170p per share.

The factor for adjusting past earnings per share is therefore:

$$\frac{\text{Ex-rights price}}{\text{Cum-rights price}} = \frac{£1.70}{£2.00} \text{ or } \frac{85}{100}$$

Previous year's earnings per share
As previously calculated:

$$\frac{£800,000}{8,000,000} \times 100 = 10p$$

Adjusted for bonus element in rights issue.

$$10 \text{ p} \times \frac{85}{100} = 8.5\text{p}$$

Earnings per share for current year (19X9)
Number of shares:

$$8 \text{ million} \times \frac{6}{12} \times \frac{\text{Cum-rights price}}{\text{Ex-rights price}}$$

(period)

$$8,000,000 \times \frac{6}{12} \times \frac{100}{85} = 4,705,880$$

Number of shares after rights issue

$$10,000,000 \times \frac{6}{12} = 5,000,000$$

(period)

Weighted average number of shares   9,705,880

Earnings per share:

$$\frac{\pounds 850,000}{9,705,880} \times 100 = 8.8\text{p}$$

Profit and loss account presentation

	Year ended 31 December 19X9	Year ended 31 December 19X8
Earnings per ordinary share of 25p	8.8p	8.5p

Note: The calculation of earnings per share is based on earnings of £850,000 (19X8 £800,000) and on the weighted average of 9,705,880 ordinary shares after adjustment of the number of shares in issue prior to the rights issue on 1 July 19X9 by the factor:

$$\frac{100\text{p}}{85} \quad \frac{\text{Cum-rights}}{\text{Ex-rights}}$$

The earnings per share for 19X8 have been adjusted accordingly.

(d) Acquisitions of subsidiaries for cash

The acquisition should be accounted for in the consolidated accounts on the basis of FRS 2 (Accounting for subsidiary undertakings). This will usually mean that profits are included from the date of control (see chapter 25). The earnings per share will be based on reported earnings and ordinary shares in issue throughout the year.

(e) Business combinations – share-for-share basis

The business combination should be accounted for on the basis of SSAP 23 (Accounting for acquisitions and mergers). This means that the consolidated accounts may be accounted for either on the basis of acquisition accounting or merger accounting (assuming the necessary conditions are satisfied).

In the case of a share-for-share exchange, the appendix to SSAP 3 states that for the purpose of calculating the earnings per share it should be assumed that the securities were issued on the first day of the period for which the profits of the new subsidiary are included in the earnings of the group.

FRS 2 and FRS 6 were issued some years after SSAP 3 and group accounts reporting practices have changed as a result. In addition the appendix to

SSAP 3 is not mandatory. The following alternative treatment is therefore suggested:

(1) Group accounts prepared on an acquisition basis:

    (i) Current year EPS should be calculated by dividing reported earnings by weighted number of equity shares in issue throughout the year. This ensures consistency between numerator and denominator, ie after the acquisition date group earnings reflect post-acquisition results of new subsidiary. This is matched in the denominator by a proportionate amount of increased shares as a result of the acquisition.

    (ii) Comparative EPS – no restatement is required.

(2) Group accounts prepared on a merger basis:

    (i) Current year EPS reflects a full year's earnings in respect of the new subsidiary. This should therefore be divided by the new number of shares (a weighted average would be inconsistent).

    (ii) Comparative EPS – this should be restated. Restated comparative earnings (inclusive of a full year's comparative earnings of the new subsidiary) should be divided by the new number of shares in issue as a result of the combination.

The method of group accounting will thus affect the EPS figure. The basis of calculation should thus be clearly stated.

30.6 FULLY DILUTED EARNINGS PER SHARE

(a) Possible situations

At the balance sheet date a company may have previously entered into commitments which could result in the issue at some future date of further ordinary shares.

Such an issue could adversely affect the interests of existing shareholders in terms of a reduction (or dilution) in earnings per share.

For this reason, SSAP 3 requires that in certain specified situations, a listed company should be required to publish its fully diluted earnings per share (based on certain hypothetical assumptions) in addition to its basic earnings per share (on the net basis as described above).

The situations where fully diluted earnings per share (FDEPS) are required to be shown are as follows:

(1) where the company has issued a separate class of equity shares which do not rank for any dividend in the period under review but which will do so in the future;

(2) where the company has issued debentures or loan stock (or preference shares) convertible into equity shares of the company;

(3) where the company has granted options or issued warrants to subscribe for equity shares of the company.

(b) FDEPS – additional considerations

(1) FDEPS need only be disclosed if the effect of the dilution is material (a reduction of more than 5% compared with basic EPS).

(2) Basis of calculation of FDEPS should be disclosed.

(3) FDEPS and basic EPS should be given equal prominence.

(4) FDEPS for the comparative period should not be given unless the assumptions on which the previous year's calculations were based still apply this year.

(c) FDEPS – calculations

(1) *Issue of shares ranking for dividend in a future period*

FDEPS is calculated by dividing actual earnings by the total equity shares in issue, whether or not they ranked for dividend this year.

(2) *Convertible stocks or shares*

FDEPS is calculated by adjusting:

(i) earnings for any savings of interest (net of corporation tax) or preference dividend as a result of conversion to ordinary shares;
(ii) maximum number of ordinary shares that could be in issue at a future date. (Clearly a hypothetical calculation, since present loan stock holders may or may not exercise their right to convert into ordinary shares.)

Illustration 9

Z plc share capital was £2m in ordinary shares of 25p each ie 8m shares. Some years previously the company had issued £2,500,000 8% convertible unsecured loan stock. Each £100 nominal of the stock will be convertible as follows:

On December 31 19X11 125 shares
                19X12 118 shares
                19X13 115 shares
                19X14 108 shares

Results

	Year ended 31 December 19X9	Year ended 31 December 19X8
	£	£
Profits before tax and interest	2,200,000	1,800,000
Interest on 8% convertible unsecured loan stock	200,000	200,000
Profits	2,000,000	1,600,000
Corporation tax, say	1,000,000	800,000
Profits after tax	1,000,000	800,000
Number of shares	8,000,000	8,000,000
Earnings per share	12.5p	10p

Fully diluted earnings per share

		£
Earnings as above		1,000,000
Add Loan interest	200,000	
Less Corporation tax, say	100,000	100,000
Adjusted earnings		1,100,000

Number of shares:

Up to 19X11, the maximum number of shares issuable after the end of the financial year will be at the rate of 125 shares per £100, viz: 3,125,000 shares, making a total of 11,125,000.

Fully diluted earnings per share 9.9p.

Profit and loss account presentation

	Year ended 31 December 19X9	Year ended 31 December 19X8
Basic earnings per ordinary share of 25p	12.5p	10p
Fully diluted earnings per ordinary share of 25p	9.9p	–

Note: The basic earnings per share is calculated on earnings of £1,000,000 (19X8 £800,000) and 8m ordinary shares in issue throughout the two years ended 31 December 19X9.

The fully diluted earnings per share is based on adjusted earnings of £1,100,000 after adding back interest net of corporation tax on the 8% convertible unsecured loan stock. The maximum number of shares into which this stock becomes convertible on 31 December 19X11 is 3,125,000, making a total of 11,125,000 shares issued and issuable.

Illustration 10

Extract from annual report and accounts of Granada Group plc for the year ended 30 September 1995.

Consolidated profit and loss account

	Note	£m	1995 £m	£m	1994 £m
Turnover:	1				
Continuing operations			2,314.1		2,097.7
Acquisitions – Pavilion and DVR			67.1		
			2,381.2		2,097.7
Depreciation on tangible assets:					
Rental assets		85.2		83.2	
Other assets		47.1		43.5	
		132.3		126.7	
Staff costs	2	528.4		482.9	
Net other operating costs	3	1,332.4		1,189.3	
			1,993.1		1,798.9
Continuing operations		378.2		298.8	
Acquisitions – Pavilion and DVR		9.9		–	
Operating profit	1		388.1		298.8
Net interest	7		36.8		33.4
Profit on ordinary activities before taxation			351.3		265.4
Tax on profit on ordinary activities	8		98.5		73.2
Profit on ordinary activities after taxation			252.8		192.2
Minority interests			0.2		0.2
Profit for the financial period			252.6		192.0
Dividends on equity and non-equity shares	9		80.7		70.1
Amount transferred to reserves	23		171.9		121.9
Earnings per share (basic)	10		41.3p		33.6p
Earnings per share (fully diluted)	10		39.1p		32.0p

Movements in reserves are set out in note 23

Note 10

10 *Earnings per share*
Basic earnings per share of 41.3p (1994: 33.6p) are based on earnings of £252.6 million (1994: £192.0 million) after adjusting to the preference dividend and the finance credit of non-equity shares and on 582.8 million ordinary shares, being the average number of shares in issue during the period (1994: 535.8 million).

Fully diluted earnings per share of 39.1p (1994: 32.0p) are based on earnings of £255.3 million (1994: £193.1 million) and on a weighted average of 653.3 million ordinary shares after allowing for full conversion of preference shares and the allotment of shares under option schemes (1994: 602.8 million).

(3) *Options and warrants*

In order to calculate FDEPS, SSAP 3 requires two sets of assumptions to be made:

(i)   That the maximum number of new ordinary shares had been issued under the terms of the options or warrants. It is also assumed that these are exercised on the first day of the period (or date of issue of options or warrants if this is later).

(ii) That the earnings are adjusted for notional interest on the cash proceeds which would be received by the company if the options or warrants were to be taken up. SSAP 3 requires the calculation to be based on the assumption that the proceeds of subscription had been invested in $2\frac{1}{2}\%$ consolidated stock on the first day of the period (using the quoted price of the previous day).

30.7   PROBLEMS OF COMPARABILITY

When comparing two companies, care should be taken to ensure that EPS has been calculated on a consistent basis as between the two companies.

The following are possible reasons why two identical companies might come up with different EPS figures:

(a) depreciation charges based on historical cost, valuation or some combination of the two (SSAP 12);
(b) goodwill amortised through profit and loss account over a number of years, or written off immediately against reserves (SSAP 22);
(c) profit and loss accounts of foreign subsidiaries translated at average or closing rate (SSAP 20);
(d) post-balance sheet events involving closure decisions taken after the balance sheet date where different interpretations may be placed on the prudence concept.

The above are simply intended as examples of situations which show how important it is to scrutinise accounting policies and notes to accounts before making a final comparison of two or more companies. FRS 3 has been particularly significant in terms of reference and usefulness of EPS information.

31 ANALYSIS OF ACCOUNTS – 3: CASH FLOW STATEMENTS

Key Issues

* Outline
* Exemptions
* Form and content – single companies
* The direct method and the indirect method
* Operating activities' cash flows
* Returns on investments and servicing of finance
* Taxation
ˣ Investing activities
* Financing
* Cash and cash equivalents
* Additional notes
* Problem areas
* Group cash flow statements
ˣ How cash flow statements are presented in practice
* Using cash flow statements

31.1 BACKGROUND AND SCOPE

(a) Introduction

FRS 1, Cash flow statements, was issued in September 1991.

A cash flow statement should include only inflows and outflows of cash and cash equivalents (see section 31.2 for definition).

A cash flow statement may also provide information additional to that which may be derived from the balance sheet, profit and loss account and notes. Examples are given in section 31.9 below.

(b) Exemptions from the preparation of cash flow statements

The standard is not mandatory for the following entities:

(i)   Small companies – ie companies which are eligible to file abbreviated accounts as small companies. Most small groups will, therefore, be entitled to exemption.
(ii) Certain wholly-owned subsidiary undertakings. These subsidiary undertakings are only exempt from publishing cash flow statements if the parent company is established under the law of an EU member state and publishes in English, consolidated financial statements which include a consolidated cash flow statement.
(iii) Building societies.
(iv) Mutual life assurance companies.

The following are not exempt from publishing cash flow statements (unless they fall within the wholly-owned exceptions in (ii) above).

(i)   PLCs – big and small.
(ii) Financial services companies (authorised persons under the Financial Services Act 1986).
(iii) Medium-sized companies.
(iv) Medium-sized groups:

> (1) if group accounts are prepared, the cash flow statement will relate to the group;
> (2) if the exemption from the preparation of group accounts is claimed, the cash flow statement will be that of the parent company. Note that unless individual subsidiary undertakings are classed as small, they will also have to produce cash flow statements.

31.2   FORMAT AND CONTENT – SINGLE COMPANIES

(a) Basic elements of the statement

Individual cash flows should be classified under certain standard headings according to the activities that gave rise to them.
   The standard headings required by FRS 1 are:

(i)   operating activities;
(ii) returns on investments and servicing of finance;
(iii) taxation;
(iv) investing activities;
(v)   financing.

The cash flow statement then concludes with changes in cash and cash equivalents.

(b) Operating activities – methods of computation

The net cash inflow from operating activities can be calculated and presented in two alternative ways – the direct method and the indirect method. Both methods are referred to in this chapter although in practice most companies use the indirect method.

(1) *Direct method*

The inflows and outflows relating to operating activities are derived directly from the company's records and summarised as follows:

	£
Cash received from customers	X
Cash payments to suppliers	(X)
Cash paid to and on behalf of employees	(X)
Other cash payments	(X)
Net cash inflow from operating activities	X

A worked example of the above computation is included in section 31.3 below.

Where the direct method is used, the above information should appear on the face of the cash flow statement. In practice, the use of this method is extremely rare.

(2) *Indirect method*

Under this method the net cash inflow (outflow) from operating activities is derived directly from operating profit. This approach is similar to that of SSAP 10.

Calculation of net cash inflow from operating activities:

	£
Operating profit	X
Depreciation charges	X
Increase in stocks	(X)
Increase in debtors	(X)
Increase in creditors	X
Net cash inflow from operating activities	X

Operating profit is determined on an accruals basis ie after adjusting for opening and closing stocks, debtors and creditors, and after charging depreciation. The above calculation thus converts accruals-based profit to net cash inflow.

Illustration 1

The balance sheets of Bamford Ltd at 31.12.X3 and 31.12.X2 were as follows:

	31.12.X3 £	31.12.X2 £
Tangible fixed assets – freehold property	301,000	391,000
Tangible fixed assets – plant and machinery	225,600	160,200
Stock	520,000	440,000
Debtors	83,100	53,100
Cash	70,300	1,700
Investment in Upton Ltd	200,000	–
	1,400,000	1,046,000

	31.12.X3 £	31.12.X2 £
Called-up share capital (£1 shares)	150,000	100,000
Profit and loss account	615,000	405,000
Share premium account	100,000	–
Long-term loans	–	170,000
Creditors	65,000	51,000
Corporation tax	350,000	230,000
Proposed dividends	120,000	90,000
	1,400,000	1,046,000

Additional information

(1) *Extracts from profit and loss account for year ended 31 December 19X3*

	£	£
Operating profit		760,000
Corporation tax		350,000
Profit on ordinary activities after tax		410,000
Dividends on ordinary shares		
Interim (paid)	80,000	
Final (proposed)	120,000	200,000
Retained profit		210,000
Balance at 1.1.X3		405,000
Balance at 31.12.X3		615,000

(2) During the year, depreciation charged on plant and machinery amounted to £16,400. There were no disposals of plant and machinery.
(3) Freehold property with a net book value at sale of £90,000 was sold for net book value.
(4) The investment in Upton Ltd is held as a fixed asset investment. No dividends were received during the year.
(5) A further 50,000 £1 shares were issued during the year for cash.

Net cash inflow is calculated as follows:

	£
Operating profit	760,000
Depreciation	16,400
Increase in stocks	(80,000)
Increase in debtors	(30,000)
Increase in creditors	14,000
Net cash inflow from operating activities	680,400

This reconciliation should not appear on the face of the cash flow statement but should be included by way of note.

The cash flow statement may be completed as follows:

	£	£
Net cash inflow from operating activities		680,400
Returns on investment and servicing of finance		
Dividends paid		(170,000)
Tax paid		(230,000)
Investing activities		
Payments to acquire fixed assets	(81,800)	
Sale of fixed assets	90,000	
Purchase of investments	(200,000)	
		(191,800)
Net cash inflow before financing		88,600
Financing		
Issue of shares	150,000	
Repayment of loans	(170,000)	
		(20,000)
Increase in cash		68,600

Workings:

(1) Purchase of plant

NBV b/f	160,200
Additions (balancing figure)	81,800
Depreciation	(16,400)
NBV c/f	225,600

(2) Dividends paid

Proposed 19X2	90,000
Interim 19X3	80,000
	170,000

The above presentation is of the reconciling type format – the cash flow changes are reconciled to changes in the cash balance.

An alternative format is also permitted by FRS 1. Using the above figures the statement would appear:

	£	£
Net cash inflow from operating activities		680,400
Returns on investment and servicing of finance		
Dividends paid		(170,000)
Tax paid		(230,000)
Investing activities		
Payments to acquire fixed assets	(81,800)	
Sale of fixed assets	90,000	
Purchase of investments	(200,000)	
		(191,800)
Net cash inflow before financing		88,600
Financing		
Issue of shares	(150,000)	
Repayment of loans	170,000	
		20,000
Increase in cash and cash equivalents		68,600
		88,600

Illustrations of the two approaches are included in section 31.8.

(c) Operating activities – further considerations

Cash flows from operating activities are essentially the cash effects of transactions and other events relating to operating or trading activities.

The reconciliation between operating profit and net cash flow from operating activities should be given as a note to the accounts.

The reconciliation should disclose separately:

(1) movements in stock, debtors and creditors;
(2) other differences between cash flows and profits.

(1) *Movements in debtors and creditors*

These two items are likely to include the following elements:

(i) trade debtors and trade creditors;
(ii) accruals and prepayments;
(iii) VAT debtors and creditors;
(iv) creditors and PAYE and NI.

The following should not be included:

(i)   other creditors – eg movement on creditors for fixed assets would be used to calculate the cash flow for fixed asset purchases disclosed under investing activities;

(ii) dividend creditors – dividends paid are disclosed under 'returns on investments and servicing of finance';

(iii) corporation tax debtors and creditors – these are used to calculate the taxation cash flows in the taxation section of the cash flow statement.

(2) *Other differences between cash flows and operating profits*

These will normally include:

(i)   depreciation on owned assets and on assets subject to finance leases;

(ii) provisions relating to 'operating profit items' – for example, provisions for:

   (1) warranty costs for goods sold,

   (2) repairs and renewals,

   (3) redundancy and reorganisation costs classified as exceptional items in the profit and loss account,

   (4) liabilities and charges;

(iii) profits and losses on sale of fixed assets.

(d) Returns on investments and servicing of finance

(1) *Cash inflows*

These include:

(i)   interest received (including any related tax recovered);

(ii) dividends received net of any tax credits.

(2) *Cash outflows*

These include:

(i)   interest paid including any tax deducted and paid over. This will include all interest paid irrespective of whether it is charged in the profit and loss account or capitalised in the balance sheet (eg under development properties);

(ii) dividends paid (excluding any ACT);

(iii) interest (or finance charge) element of finance lease rental payments. (See also section 31.5(a) below.)

(e) Taxation

In the majority of cases this part will simply include payments of corporation tax (including ACT). It will not include payments of PAYE and NI – these are part of the cash flows from operating activities.

VAT receipts and payments will usually be dealt with under operating activities cash flow. However, in cases where VAT is irrecoverable, the related tax should be dealt with under the appropriate heading in the cash flow statement.

(f) Investing activities

(1) *General considerations*

This part of the cash flow statement should include cash flows related to the acquisition or disposal of any asset held:

(i)   as a fixed asset;
(ii) as a current asset investment (but excluding assets held within cash equivalents (see section (h) below).

(2) *Cash inflows*

(i)   receipts from sales or disposals of fixed assets;
(ii) receipts from sales of investments in subsidiary undertakings (see section 31.6(d)).
(iii) receipts from sale of investments in other entities – proceeds of sale of investments in associated undertakings should be disclosed separately (see also section 31.6(c));
(iv) receipts from repayment of loans made to other entities by the reporting entity;

(3) *Cash outflows*

These include:

(i)   payments to acquire fixed assets;
(ii) payments to acquire investments in subsidiary undertakings (see section 31.6(d));
(iii) payments to acquire investments in other entities;
(iv) loans made by the reporting entity (other than cash equivalents).

(g) Financing

(1) *General considerations*

This part of the cash flow statement should include receipts from or repayments to external providers of finance of amounts relating to principal amounts of finance.

(2) *Cash inflows*

These include:

(i)   receipts from issuing shares or other equity instruments;
(ii) receipts from issuing:

    (1) debentures,
    (2) loans,
    (3) notes,
    (4) bonds,
    (5) other long and short-term borrowings (other than those included within cash equivalents).

(3) *Cash outflows*

These include:
(i)   repayments of amounts borrowed (other than those included within cash equivalents);
(ii) the capital element of finance lease rental payments;
(iii) payments to re-acquire or redeem the entity's shares;
(iv) expenses or commissions paid in relation to any issue of shares, debentures, loans, notes, bonds or other financing.

(h) Definitions of cash and cash equivalents

(1) *Cash*

Defined by FRS 1 as:

Cash in hand and deposits repayable on demand with any bank or other financial institution. Cash includes cash in hand and deposits denominated in foreign currencies.

(2) *Cash equivalents*

Defined by FRS 1 as:

Short-term, highly liquid investments which are readily convertible into known amounts of cash without notice and which were within three months of maturity when acquired; less advances from banks repayable within three months from the date of the advance. Cash equivalents include investments and advances denominated in foreign currencies provided that they fulfil the above criteria.

(Note reference in above to three months.)

(i) Additional notes

(1) Net cash flow from operating activities: the cash flow statement should include a reconciliation between operating profit and net cash flow from operating activities;
(2) balance sheet reconciliations:

   (i)   the movements in cash and cash equivalents should be reconciled to the related items in the opening and closing balance sheet for the period;
   (ii) a similar reconciliation should be provided for items within the financing section of the cash flow statement;
   (iii) both of the above reconciliations should disclose separately movements resulting from:

      (a) cash flows;
      (b) differences arising from changes in foreign currency exchange rates:

         – those relating to the retranslation of any opening balances of cash and cash equivalents and financing items, and
         – those resulting from the translation of cash flows of foreign entities at exchange rates other than the year-end exchange rate;

      (c) other investments.

(For illustrations of disclosures, please see sections 31.2(j) and 31.8 below.)

(j) Illustration of disclosures (Appendix to FRS 1)

Note: comparative figures are not included.

Illustration 2

XYZ LIMITED

Cash flow statement
for the year ended 31 March 19X2

	£'000	£'000
Net cash inflow from operating activities		6,889
Returns on investments and servicing of finance		
Interest received	3,011	
Interest paid	(12)	
Dividends paid	(2,417)	
Net cash inflow from returns on investments and servicing of finance		582
Taxation		
Corporation tax paid (including advance corporation tax)	(2,922)	
Tax paid		(2,922)
Investing activities		
Payments to acquire intangible fixed assets	(71)	
Payments to acquire tangible fixed assets	(1,496)	
Receipts from sales of tangible fixed assets	42	
Net cash outflow from investing activities		(1,525)
Net cash inflow before financing		3,024
Financing		
Issue of ordinary share capital	211	
Repurchase of debenture loan	(149)	
Expenses paid in connection with share issues	(5)	
Net cash inflow from financing		57
Increase in cash and cash equivalents		3,081

Notes to the cash flow statement

Note 1 – reconciliation of operating profit to net cash inflow from operating activities

	£'000
Operating profit	6,022
Depreciation charges	893
Loss on sale of tangible fixed assets	6
Increase in stocks	(194)
Increase in debtors	(72)
Increase in creditors	234
Net cash inflow from operating activities	6,889

Note 2 – analysis of changes in cash and cash equivalents during the year

	£'000
Balance at 1 April 19X1	21,373
Net cash inflow	3,081
Balance at 31 March 19X2	24,454

Note 3 – analysis of the balances of cash and cash equivalents as shown in the balance sheet

	19X2 £'000	19X1 £'000	Change in year £'000
Cash at bank and in hand	529	681	(152)
Short-term investments	23,936	20,700	3,236
Bank overdrafts	(11)	(8)	(3)
	24,454	21,373	3,081

Note 4 – analysis of changes in financing during the year

	Share capital £'000	Debenture loan £'000
Balance at 1 April 19X1	27,411	156
Cash inflow/(outflow) from financing	211	(149)
Profit on repurchase of debenture loan for less than its book value		(7)
Balance at 31 March 19X2	27,622	–

31.3   WORKED EXAMPLE – A SINGLE COMPANY USING THE DIRECT METHOD

(a) Basic approach

Under the direct method, individual components of operating activities cash flow (cash received from customers etc) are derived directly from the company's accounting systems.

(b) Illustration 3

The summarised balance sheets of Waddev plc are as follows:

	31.12.X8 £'000	31.12.X7 £'000
Capital employed:		
£1 ordinary shares	1,000	800
Revenue reserves	929	619
Share premium account	400	300
Bank loan	–	250
Trade creditors	184	158
Other creditors	–	50
Accrued expenses	35	25
Corporation tax	395	243
Proposed dividend	60	45
	3,003	2,490
Represented by:		
Freehold property	1,096	1,100
Plant and machinery (cost less aggregate depreciation)	726	732
Stock	537	365
Trade debtors	413	236
Prepayments	19	22
Cash at bank	212	35
	3,003	2,490

PROFIT AND LOSS ACCOUNT
for the year ended 31 December 19X8

	£'000	£'000
Turnover		2,960
Opening stock	365	
Purchases	2,073	
	2,438	
Less closing stock	537	
Cost of sales		1,901
Gross profit		1,059
Distribution costs and administrative expenses		197
Depreciation – buildings	4	
– plant	65	
– over provision on disposals of plant	(7)	62
Profit before tax		800
Corporation tax		395
Profit after tax		405
Dividends – paid	35	
– proposed	60	95
Retained profit added to reserves		310

The following information has been extracted from the company's accounting records:

(1) *Summary cash account*

	£'000	£'000
Balance at 1.1.X8		35
Receipts from customers		2,783
Issue of shares		300
Sale of fixed assets		128
		3,246
Payments to suppliers	2,047	
Payments for fixed assets	230	
Payments for overheads	115	
Wages and salaries	69	
Taxation	243	
Dividends	80	
Repayments of bank loan	250	3,034
Balance at 31.12.X8		212

(2) *Debtors control account*

	£'000
Debtors at 1.1.X8	236
Sales	2,960
Cash received	(2,783)
Debtors at 31.12.X8	413

(3) *Trade creditors control account*

Creditors at 1.1.X8	158
Purchases	2,073
Cash paid	(2,047)
Creditors at 31.12.X8	184

(4) *Other creditors (fixed assets)*

Creditors at 1.1.X8	50
Additions to fixed assets	180
Cash paid	(230)
Creditors at 31.12.X8	–

(5) *Distribution costs and administrative expenses control*

	£'000	£'000
Prepayments at 1.1.X8		(22)
Accruals at 1.1.X8		25
Sundry overheads		197
Cash paid		(184)
Prepayments at 31.2.X8	(19)	
Accruals at 31.12.X8	35	
Accruals less prepayments at 31.12.X3		16

Note: for the purposes of obtaining FRS 1 information for the direct method, the total payments of £184,000 have been analysed:

Employees	£69,000
Other	£115,000

(6) *Taxation account*

	£'000
Creditors at 1.1.19X8	243
P/L – tax charge	395
Cash paid	(243)
Creditors at 31.12.X8	395

(7) *Fixed assets – NBV summary*

	Property £'000	Plant £'000
NBV at 1.1.19X8	1,100	732
Additions	–	180
Depreciation charge	(4)	(65)
Disposals (NBV)	–	(121)
NBV at 31.12.X8	1,096	726

(8) *Fixed assets – disposal of plant*

	£'000
NBV of assets sold	121
Proceeds of sale	128
Depreciation over provided	(7)

Solution

WADDEV PLC – CASH FLOW STATEMENT

for the year ended 31 December 19X8
using the direct method

	£'000	£'000
Operating activities		
Cash received from customers		2,783
Cash payments to suppliers		(2,047)
Cash paid to and on behalf of employees		(69)
Other cash payments		(115)
Net cash inflow from operating activities		552
Returns on investments and servicing of finance – dividends paid		(80)
Taxation – corporation tax paid		(243)
Investing activities		
Purchase of tangible fixed assets	230	
Sale of tangible fixed assets	(128)	(102)
Net cash inflow before financing		127
Financing		
Issue of share capital	300	
Bank loan repaid	(250)	50
Increase in cash and cash equivalents		177

Note to the cash flow statement

Reconciliation of operating profit to net cash inflow from operating activities.

	£'000
Operating profit	800
Depreciation charges	62
Increase in stocks	(172)
Increase in debtors	(177)
Decrease in prepayments	3
Increase in trade creditors	26
Increase in accrued expenses	10
Net cash inflow from operating activities	552

(Other notes required by FRS 1 have not been reproduced. For guidance, please see section 31.2(i) and (j) above.)

31.4 WORKED EXAMPLE – A SINGLE COMPANY USING THE INDIRECT METHOD

(a) Basic approach

Under the indirect method, cash flow statement items are essentially derived from: a comparison of opening and closing balance sheets; a profit and loss account; additional information. The method illustrated below makes use of a simple work sheet which readily lends itself to a computer spreadsheet.

It is important to bear in mind that the effect of non-cash items is excluded from the cash flow statement. For example, suppose a company issues debenture stock as consideration for the acquisition of a property. Neither the increase in debentures nor the increase in the property will appear in the cash flow statement.

(b) How the work sheet should be completed

The key items in the cash flow statement may be derived by completing the following steps:

(1) Enter the closing and opening balance sheets in columns A and B respectively.

(2) Calculate the difference between each respective item in columns A and B. Enter the result in column C, taking care over brackets! Column C should total to zero.

(3) The retained profit of £310,000 in column C should be 'grossed up' for the effects of tax and dividends. This is achieved by entering operating profit of £800,000 in column D, the total dividend appropriation of £95,000 in column E, and the total tax charge in column F.

(4) The changes in the stock, debtors and creditors items affecting operating profit should be extended into column D. Other creditors relates to fixed assets and so the change (i e decrease) of £50,000 is extended into column G. The total depreciation charges of £4,000 for building and £58,000 for plant should also be entered in column D. The items in column D represent the components of the operating profit/cash inflow reconciliation. The total of column D, £552,000, represents the net cash inflow.

(5) The change in dividend creditors is extended into column E. The total of column E represents dividends paid.

(6) The change in tax creditors is extended into column F. The total of column F represents tax paid.

(7) For land and buildings/plant, the combined effect of columns C and D is extended into column G and analysed between acquisitions and disposals.

WORKSHEET – CASH FLOW STATEMENT OF WADDEV PLC
for the year ended 19X8 (£'000)

Item	Balance sheet 31.12.X8 B/S A	Balance sheet 31.12.X7 B/S B	Change C (A–B)	Cash flow statement headings Operating activities D	Returns E	Tax F	Investing activities G	Financing H	Cash and Cash Equivalent I
Land & buildings	1,096	1,100	(4)	(4)					
Plant & machinery	726	732	(6)	(58)			(128) / 180		
Stocks	537	365	172	172					
Debtors	413	236	177	177					
Prepayments	19	22	(3)	(3)					
Cash	212	35	177						177
	3,003	2,490							
Trade creditors	184	158	(26)	(26)					
Other creditors	–	50	50				50		
Accrued expenses	35	25	(10)	(10)					
Tax	395	243	(152)			(152)			
Dividends	60	45	(15)		(15)				
Loan	–	250	250					250	
OSC	1,000	800	(200)					(300)	
S. Prem	400	300	(100)					(300)	
P/L	929	619	(310)	(800)					
	3,003	2,490	0	(552)	95 / 80	395 / 243	(128) / 230	250 / (300)	177

When these are combined with the 'other creditors' change and totalled, the figures of £128,000 and £230,000 represent the receipts and payments in respect of fixed asset transactions.

(8) In this example columns H and I are straightforward

Solution

(c) Waddev plc – cash flow statement

For the year ended 31 December 19X8 using the indirect method.

	£'000	£'000
Net cash inflow from operating activities		552
Returns on investments and servicing of finance		
– dividends paid		(80)
Taxation – corporation tax paid		(243)
Investing activities		
Purchase of tangible fixed assets	230	
Sale of tangible fixed assets	(128)	
		(102)
Net cash inflow before financing		127
Financing		
Issue of share capital	300	
Bank loan repaid	(250)	
		50
Increase in cash and cash equivalents		177

The notes to the cash flow statement are the same as for the direct method (see section 31.3 above).

31.5 PROBLEM AREAS – SINGLE COMPANIES

(a) Finance leases

Finance lease payments are split between the finance charge element (returns on investments and servicing of finance) and the capital element (financing).

Where significant finance lease commitments have been entered into during the year, these may need to be reported by way of note to the accounts under the heading 'major non-cash transactions'.

(b) Non-cash transactions

The basic principle is that transactions which do not result in cash flows of the reporting entity should not be reported in the cash flow statement.

However, para 43 of FRS 1 states:

Material transactions not resulting in movements of cash or cash equivalents of the reporting entity should be disclosed in the notes to the cash flow statement if disclosure is necessary for an understanding of the underlying transactions.

Although FRS 1 refers to the notes to the cash flow statement, these may be integrated with other notes to the accounts.

Possible examples include:

(i) significant finance lease commitments entered into shortly before the end of the year;

(ii) convertible loan stock converted during the year into equity shares;

(iii) property assets exchanged for equity in another entity;

(iv) transactions with both cash and non-cash elements eg purchase of shares in a subsidiary undertaking by a combination of cash and shares consideration.

(c) Obtaining information for the direct method

The direct method may result in additional work. For example, FRS 1 requires that cash flows (eg cash received from customers, cash payments to suppliers) should be net of any attributable value added tax.

One company which used the direct method in its 1991 accounts made the following comment one year later in its 1992 accounts:

> The directors have decided to replace the 'direct' disclosure of operating cash flows used in the 1991 accounts with the 'indirect' method as the administrative costs outweigh the benefit of the addtional disclosure.

(d) Classification problems

(1) Current asset investments may either be classified under investing activities or changes in cash equivalents (see section 31.2).
(2) Short-term borrowings may fall under either financing or cash equivalents.
(3) Debtors and creditors will require particular care eg creditors in respect of the purchase of fixed assets (see section 31.2(c) above).

31.6   GROUP ACCOUNTS CONSIDERATIONS

(a) General approach

A group cash flow statement should deal only with flows of cash and cash equivalents external to the group.

In practice many subsidiary undertakings are likely to be wholly-owned and therefore exempt from preparing cash flow statements under the exemption referred to earlier. In addition, a large number of groups (if not the majority) are likely to opt for the indirect method.

Whenever possible therefore, the group cash flow statements will be derived directly from the consolidated accounts. This approach will be simpler as the effect of inter-company transactions will already have been eliminated on consolidation.

(b) Dividends paid to minority shareholders

These should be disclosed separately under the heading returns on investments and servicing of finance.

(c) Associated undertakings

Care should be taken over the cash flows of any entity such as an associated undertaking, which is equity-accounted in the consolidated accounts. The group cash flow statement should only include the entity's cash flows to the extent that they result in actual cash flows between the group and the entity concerned.

Examples of such cash flows could include:

(i)   dividends received (returns on investment and servicing of finance);
(ii)   shares in associated undertakings (investing);
(iii) loans from associated undertaking (financing).

(d) Acquisitions and disposals of subsidiary undertakings

Amounts of cash and cash equivalents paid or received in respect of acquisitions and disposals of subsidiary undertakings will be included under the 'investing' heading. FRS 1 effectively requires a one-line approach.

Note that the amounts should be net of any cash and cash equivalent balances transferred as part of the purchase or sale of the subsidiary undertaking.

The group cash flow statement should include a note giving a summary of the effects of acquisitions and disposals indicating:

(1) how much of the consideration comprised cash and cash equivalents; and
(2) the amounts of cash and cash equivalents transferred as a result of the acquisitions and disposals.

The group cash flow statement should include the cash flows of the subsidiary undertaking for the same period as that for which the subsidiary undertakings results are included in the profit and loss account.

Para 42 states:

> Material effects on amounts reported under each of the standard headings reflecting the cash flows of a subsidiary undertaking acquired or disposed of in the period should be disclosed, as far as practicable, as a note to the cash flow statement. This information need only be given in the financial statements for the period in which the acquisition or disposal occurs.

(e) Foreign subsidiaries

Cash flows of foreign subsidiaries should be included in the group cash flow statement on the same basis as that used for translating the results of the subsidiaries for consolidated profit and loss account purposes.

The effect of exchange rate changes should be dealt with in the balance sheet reconciliation note. This is dealt with in para 44 of FRS 1 and for some groups will be a particularly complex area. It is also a sensitive area in view of recent controversies surrounding SSAP 20!

(f) Non-cash transactions

An example relevant to groups is the acquisition of a subsidiary undertaking partly by the issue of shares, partly by the payment of cash (see section 31.7).

(Illustrations of presentations for groups are included in the appendix to FRS 1, illustrative example 2 (not reproduced), see sections 31.7 and 31.8.)

31.7 WORKED EXAMPLE – A GROUP

(a) Basic information

The consolidated balance sheets of Southdale plc at 31.12.X3 and 31.12.X2 were as follows:

	31.12.X3 £	31.12.X2 £
Tangible fixed assets	1,068,900	640,600
Goodwill on consolidation	320,000	250,000
Shares in associated undertakings	245,000	206,000
Stock	586,000	492,000
Debtors	307,000	164,000
Cash	71,100	32,100
	2,598,000	1,784,700

	31.12.X3 £	31.12.X2 £
Called-up share capital	210,000	50,000
Profit and loss account	701,000	580,000
Revaluation reserve	320,000	100,000
Share premium account	160,000	–
Minority interest:		
Ordinary share capital and reserves	325,000	295,000
Dividends payable	16,000	13,700
Corporation tax	380,000	360,000
Proposed dividends	190,000	165,000
Creditors	296,000	221,000
	2,598,000	1,784,700

Additional information

(1) Extracts from consolidated profit and loss account for year ended 31 December 19X3

	£	£
Operating profit		850,000
Profit of associated undertaking		120,000
Profit on ordinary activities before tax		970,000
Corporation tax		
Group	380,000	
Associated undertaking	50,000	430,000
Profit on ordinary activities after tax		540,000
Minority interest		69,000
		471,000
Dividends on ordinary shares		
Interim (paid)	160,000	
Final (proposed)	190,000	350,000
Retained profit		121,000
Balance at 1.1.X3		580,000
Balance at 31.12.X3		701,000

(2) During the year, the group acquired a wholly owned subsidiary, Dunster Ltd.
The details of the acquisition were:

	£
Purchase consideration:	
160,000 £1 ordinary shares issued at £2	320,000
Cash	20,000
	340,000
Tangible fixed assets	140,000
Goodwill on consolidation	70,000
Stock	70,000
Debtors	85,000
Cash	5,000
Creditors	(30,000)
	340,000

(3) Details of tangible fixed assets:

	Freehold property £	Machinery and vehicles £	Total £
NBV at 1.1.X3	410,000	230,600	640,600
Additions	55,000	195,000	250,000
Revaluation	220,000	–	220,000
Depreciation	(10,000)	(31,700)	(41,700)
	675,000	393,900	1,068,900

(Comparative figures are required in published accounts (see section 31.8) but are ignored in this example.)

(b) Workings

(1) *Associated undertaking*
The relevant information may be summarised as follows:

	£	£
Investment (shares)		
31.12.X3		245,000
31.12.X2		206,000
Increase (= retained profit)		39,000
Share of profits	120,000	
Share of tax	50,000	70,000
∴ Dividends received		31,000

(2) *Dividends paid to parent company shareholders*

	£
Last year proposed final	165,000
This year interim paid	160,000
	325,000

(3) *Minority interest*
To the extent that a partly owned subsidiary pays dividends to its minority shareholders, there is an outflow of cash from the group.

Dividends paid to minority shareholders may be calculated as a balancing item by reconstructing a minority interest account as follows:

MINORITY INTEREST ACCOUNT

	£		£
Cash paid (balancing figure)	36,700	Balances at 1.1.X3	
Balances at 31.12.X3		OSC + reserves	295,000
OSC + reserves	325,000	Dividends	13,700
Dividends	16,000	P/L	69,000
	377,700		377,700

(4) *Taxation paid (parent company and subsidiaries)*

	£
Last year tax liability	360,000

(c) Using a worksheet

The worksheet on pp 558–559 extends the approach developed in section 31.4 above. The following additional points are relevant:

(1) Acquisition details should be entered in column D so that purchase of a subsidiary may be calculated as a one-line item, net of cash balances transferred (i e £20,000 – £5,000 = £15,000).
(2) Dividends paid are dealt with in two columns:

    (i) column G–dividend paid to parent company shareholders (£325,000);
    (ii) minority shareholders (£36,700) – see also alternative 'T' account working above ((b)(3)) – column I.

(3) Dividends received from associated undertaking (£31,000) was explained above ((b(1)).
(4) In column K, the contra-adjustment of £220,000 is to eliminate the effect of the non-cash item (revaluation £220,000).
(5) The shares issued do not appear in the financing section (column L) as they were not issued for cash consideration. They are adjusted for in column D.

| | Consolidated balance sheets | | | Acqn details | |
Item £	B/S 31.12.X3 A	B/S 31.12.X2 B	Change C (A–B)	New Sub D	Change E (C–D)
Fixed assets	1,068,900	640,600	428,300	140,000	288,300
Goodwill	320,000	250,000	70,000	70,000	–
Assoc undertaking	245,000	206,000	39,000		39,000
Stocks	586,000	492,000	94,000	70,000	24,000
Debtors	307,000	164,000	143,000	85,000	58,000
Cash	71,100	32,100	39,000	5,000	34,000
Investing in subsidiary	–	–	–	(20,000)	20,000
	2,598,000	1,784,700			
OSC	210,000	50,000	(160,000)	(160,000)	–
P/L	701,000	580,000	(121,000)		(121,000)
Reval res	320,000	100,000	(220,000)		(220,000)
Share prem	160,000	–	(160,000)	(160,000)	–
MI: non-cash	325,000	295,000	(30,000)		(30,000)
MI: current	16,000	13,700	(2,300)		(2,300)
Tax	380,000	360,000	(20,000)		(20,000)
Dividends	190,000	165,000	(25,000)		(25,000)
Creditors	296,000	221,000	(75,000)	(30,000)	(45,000)
	2,598,000	1,784,700	0	0	0

SOUTHDALE PLC CASH FLOW STATEMENT

for the year ended 31.12.19X3

	£	£
Net cash inflow from operating activities		854,700
Returns on investments and servicing of finance		
Dividends received from associated undertaking	31,000	
Dividends paid		
Parent company	(325,000)	
Minority shareholders	(36,700)	
		(330,700)
Net cash outflow from returns on investments and servicing of finance		
Taxation		
UK corporation tax paid		(360,000)
Investing activities		
Purchase of tangible fixed assets	(110,000)	
Purchase of subsidiary undertakings (net of cash and cash equivalents acquired)	(15,000)	
Net cash outflow from investing activities		(125,000)
Net cash outflow before financing		39,000
Facing		
Issue of ordinary share capital		–
Net cash inflow from financing		–
Increase in cash and cash equivalents		39,000

Cash flow statement headings

Operating Activities F	Div paid G	Returns Assoc div H	MI div I	Tax J	Investing activities K	Financing L	Cash and cash equivalents M
(41,700)					110,000 220,000C		
		39,000					
24,000							
58,000							
					(5,000) 20,000		39,000
(850,000)	350,000	(120,000) 50,000	69,000	380,000			
					(220,000)C		
			(30,000) (2,300)				
				(20,000)			
	(25,000)						
(45,000)							
854,700	325,000	(31,000)	36,700	360,000	110,000(FA) 15,000(Sub)		39,000

Notes to the cash flow statement

(1) *Reconciliation of operating profit to net cash inflow from operating activities*

	£
Operating profit	850,000
Depreciation charges	41,700
Increase in stocks	(24,000)
Increase in debtors	(58,000)
Increase in creditors	45,000
Net cash inflow from operating activities	854,700

(2) *Analysis of changes in financing during the year*

	Share capital (including premium) £
Balance at 1 January 19X3	50,000
Shares issued for non-cash consideration	320,000
Balance at 31 December 19X3	370,000

(3) *Major non-cash transaction*
Part of the consideration for the purchase of a subsidiary undertaking comprised shares. Further details of the acquisitions are set out below:

PURCHASE OF SUBSIDIARY UNDERTAKING

	£
Net assets acquired	
Tangible fixed assets	140,000
Stocks	70,000
Debtors	85,000
Cash at bank and in hand	5,000
Creditors	(30,000)
Goodwill	70,000
	340,000
Satisfied by	
Shares allotted	320,000
Cash	20,000
	340,000

ANALYSIS OF THE NET OUTFLOW OF CASH AND CASH EQUIVALENTS IN RESPECT
OF THE PURCHASE OF SUBSIDIARY UNDERTAKINGS

	£
Cash consideration	20,000
Cash at bank and in hand acquired	(5,000)
Net outflow of cash and cash equivalents in respect of the purchase of subsidiary	15,000

31.8   ILLUSTRATIONS FROM PUBLISHED ACCOUNTS

Illustration 4

Extract from annual report and accounts of Peter Black Holdings plc for the year ended 3 June 1995.

Consolidated cash flow statement

Notes		1995 £'000	1994 £'000
18	**Net cash inflow from operating activities**	**11,446**	10,730
	Return on investments and servicing of finance		
	Interest received	**454**	128
	Interest paid	**(411)**	(402)
	Dividends paid	**(2,546)**	(2,135)
	Net cash outflow from return on investments and servicing of finance	**(2,503)**	(2,409)
	Taxation		
	Tax paid	**(3,000)**	(3,095)
	Investing activities		
	Purchase of tangible fixed assets	**(6,839)**	(6,341)
	Disposal of tangible fixed assets	**1,980**	730
19	Disposal of business	**4,653**	3,397
	Net cash outflow on investing activities	**(206)**	(2,214)
	Net cash inflow before financing	**5,737**	3,012
	Financing		
20	Increase of ordinary share capital including premium	**394**	775
21	**Increase in cash and cash equivalents**	**6,131**	3,787

Illustration 5

Extract from annual report and accounts of Cowie Group plc for the year ended 31 December 1994.

Group cash flow statement

	Notes	1994 £000	1994 £000	1993 £000	1993 £000
Net cash inflow from operating activities	22		**192,116**		166,213
Returns on investments and servicing of finance					
Interest and finance charges paid		**(23,487)**		(24,235)	
Dividends paid		**(11,775)**		(8,117)	
Dividends received	3(c)	**253**		338	
Net cash outflow from returns on investments and servicing of finance			**(35,009)**		(32,014)
Taxation					
Corporation and Advance Corporation Tax paid			**(6,239)**		(5,929)
Investing activities					
Acquisition of businesses	24	**(45,682)**		(38,846)	
Disposal of investments		–		7,833	
Purchase of contract hire vehicles		**(182,560)**		(153,330)	
Disposal of contract hire vehicles		**69,839**		83,933	
Inception of instalment credit and finance lease agreements		**(36,479)**		(23,528)	
Purchase of other fixed assets		**(20,811)**		(11,300)	
Disposal of other fixed assets		**13,936**		6,408	
Net cash outflow from investing activities			**(201,757)**		(128,830)
Net cash outflow before financing			**(50,889)**		(560)
Financing					
Issue of ordinary share capital		**(12)**		(30,700)	
Expenses paid in connection with shares issued		**2**		982	
Loan capital repaid	23	**106**		7	
(Inflow)/outflow from syndicated loans, net	23	**(25,000)**		30,000	
Finance lease obligations and finance house loans repaid, net	23	**2,460**		13,567	
Net cash (inflow)/outflow from financing			**(22,444)**		13,856
Decrease in cash and cash equivalents	25		**(28,445)**		(14,416)
			(50,889)		(560)

Notes to the accounts

22 *Reconciliation of operating profit to net cash inflow from operating activities*

	1994 £000	1993 £000
Profit before interest	65,995	62,616
Depreciation	108,527	99,109
Increase in stocks, excluding acquisitions	(2,153)	(3,306)
(Increase)/decrease in debtors, excluding acquisitions	(3,324)	11,870
Repayments of capital from instalment credit agreements and finance lease receivables	21,034	16,403
Increase/(decrease) in creditors, excluding acquisitions	2,602	(16,508)
Dividends received	(253)	(338)
Amortisation of goodwill	242	242
Profit on disposal of investments	–	(3,364)
Surplus on disposal of properties	(554)	–
Adjustment to carrying value of investment	–	(511)
	192,116	166,213

23 *Changes in financing during the year*

	Syndicated Loans		Loan Capital		Finance Lease Obligations and Finance House Loans	
	1994 £000	1993 £000	1994 £000	1993 £000	1994 £000	1993 £000
At 1 January	245,000	275,000	124	131	4,477	9,593
Repayments	–	(30,000)	(106)	(7)	(2,574)	(14,355)
Cash inflow from financing	25,000	–	–	–	114	788
Acquisitions	–	–	–	–	–	8,451
At 31 December	270,000	245,000	18	124	2,017	4,477

(Note 24 is reproduced in section 25.3).

25 *Analysis of the balances of and changes in cash and cash equivalents*

	At 31 December		Changes in Year	
	1994 £000	1993 £000	1994 £000	1993 £000
Cash at bank and in hand	(424)	(35)	(389)	(11)
Bank overdraft	3,187	6,353	(3,166)	2,427
Short term loan	64,000	32,000	32,000	12,000
	66,763	38,318	28,445	14,416

31.9 USING CASH FLOW STATEMENTS

(a) The usefulness of cash flow statements

Several parts of FRS 1 refer to the needs of users. The explanation section states that 'historical cash flow information may assist users of financial statements in making judgements on the amount, timing and degree of certainty of future cash flows . . .'. The section also states 'Accordingly, cash flow statements should normally be used in conjunction with profit and loss accounts and balance sheets when making an assessment of future cash flows'.

However, given the frequent volatility of cash flows between one year and another, a comparison of two years' figures is likely to be of only limited help. Cash flow statements may well be of greater assistance once several years' statements are available.

(b) Additional information provided by cash flow statements

Some of the disclosures required by FRS 1 will provide information beyond that available from the balance sheet, profit and loss account and notes. In addition, some companies produce information in excess of that required by FRS 1.

A cash flow statement is therefore more than merely a 'reclassification and summarisation of information . . .' (see section 31.1(a)). The following are examples of areas where additional information may be available:

(i)   for companies using the direct method, information relating to cash received from customers and cash paid to suppliers;

(ii)   memorandum information relating to non-cash transactions eg finance lease arrangements entered into during the year;

(iii) information regarding cash and cash equivalents, particularly where the three month part of the cash equivalent definition has significant impact on classification of assets and liabilities (see section 31.2(h) for definition);

(iv)   cash information eg cash payment for fixed assets, which might otherwise be difficult to calculate from accruals-based accounts;

(v)   for groups, cash flow information relating to acquisitions and disposals of subsidiaries;

(vi)   the impact of foreign exchange differences;

(vii) for some groups, additional information regarding investing activities.

31.10   REVIEW OF FRS 1

ASB is currently reviewing FRS 1. An exposure draft, FRED 10, has been issued.

32 ANALYSIS OF ACCOUNTS – 4: SEGMENTAL REPORTING

Key Issues

* Why segmental analysis is necessary
* Legal and Stock Exchange requirements
* SSAP 25 disclosures for larger companies
* Disclosures for smaller companies

32.1 THE NEED FOR SEGMENTAL ANALYSIS

In the words of International Accounting Standard 14 (Reporting financial information by segment):

> Rates of profitability, opportunities for growth, future prospects and risks to investments may vary greatly among industry and geographical segments. Thus, users of financial statements need segment information to assess the prospects and risks of a diversified enterprise which may not be determinable from the aggregated data. The objective of presenting information by segments is to provide users of financial statements with information on this relative size, profit contribution, and growth trend of the different industries and different geographical areas in which a diversified enterprise operates, to enable them to make more informed judgements about the enterprise as a whole. [IAS 14, para 5.]

32.2 COMPANIES ACT 1985 REQUIREMENTS

The Companies Act 1985 requires notes to accounts to give the following analyses:

(1) analysis of turnover between substantially different classes of business;
(2) analysis of profit or loss before tax between substantially different classes of business;
(3) analysis of turnover between substantially different geographical markets (determined by location of customers).

32.3 STOCK EXCHANGE REQUIREMENTS

The Stock Exchange requires annual accounts to provide a geographical analysis of turnover and of contribution to trading results of those trading operations carried on by the company (or group) outside the UK and Eire.

32.4 SSAP 25 – SEGMENTAL REPORTING

SSAP 25, issued in June 1990, requires disclosure of segmental information, both by class of business segment and by geographical segment.

The disclosures specified by SSAP 25 extend well beyond those required by either the Companies Act 1985 (for all companies) or by the Stock Exchange (for listed companies).

However, these additional disclosures are mandatory only for the following entities:

(a) a PLC;
(b) an entity which has a PLC as a subsidiary;
(c) a banking or insurance company or group;
(d) an entity which exceeds the criteria multiplied by 10 for defining a medium-sized company.

The full disclosures for the above entities are set out in section 32.6.

32.5 TERMINOLOGY

SSAP 25 provides the following definitions of terms:

(a) A class of business is a distinguishable component of an entity that provides a separate product or service or a separate group of related products or services.
(b) A geographical segment is a geographical area comprising an individual country or group or countries in which an entity operates, or to which it supplies products or services.
(c) Origin of turnover is the geographical segment from which products or services are supplied to a third party or to another segment.
(d) Destination of turnover is the geographical segment to which products or services are supplied.

32.6 DISCLOSURE REQUIREMENTS

Entities referred to in section 32.4 above must disclose the following information:

(a) For each class of business and geographical segment:
    (i) definition of class;
    (ii) turnover analysed between external customers and other segments;
    (iii) result before tax, minority interest and extraordinary items;
    (iv) net assets.
(b) Geographical segmentation of turnover by origin.
(c) Geographical segmentation of turnover to third parties by destination (or state, if appropriate, that this is not materially different from the figure in (b)).
(d) Where associates account for 20% or more of total results or net assets, segmental information regarding results and net assets of associates.
(e) Comparative figures (unless this is the first period for which segmental information has been provided).
(f) Where segment definitions or segment reporting policies have changed:
    (i) nature of the change;
    (ii) reason for the change;
    (iii) effect of the change.

Previous year's figures should be restated.

32.7 RELAXATIONS FOR SMALLER ENTITIES

Certain of the disclosures in section 32.6 above are not mandatory for smaller entities. These are:

(a) turnover derived from other segments;
(b) geographical segment analysis of results;
(c) analysis of net assets;

(d) geographical analysis of turnover by origin;
(e) associated company information.

The smaller entities which are exempt are entities that do not fall within any of the categories in section 32.4 above.

32.8   SUMMARY OF SSAP 25 REQUIREMENTS

(a) Disclosures by classes of business segments: overview

	'smaller' enterprises	*plc's etc & 'larger' enterprises*
Definition of classes of business	M	M
Turnover:		
total	O	M
inter-segment	O	M
external (3rd parties)	M	M
Results (before Int, Tax, MI, Extr)	M	M
Net assets (FA & WC)	O	M
Associated undertakings (if significant):		
segment results	O	M
net assets	O	M

Note:
O = optional   FA = fixed assets
M = mandatory   WC = working capital

(b) Disclosures by geographical segments (markets): overview

	'smaller' enterprises	*plc's etc & 'larger' enterprises*
Definition of geographical segments	M	M
Turnover:		
by destination external (3rd parties)	M	M
by origin total	O	M
inter-segment	O	M
external	O	M
Results (before Int, Tax, MI, Extr)	O	M
Net assets (FA & WC)	O	M
Associated undertakings (if significant):		
segment results	O	M
net assets	O	M

Note:
O = Optional   FA = Fixed assets
M = Mandatory   WC = Working capital

32.9 ILLUSTRATIONS FROM PUBLISHED ACCOUNTS

Illustration 1

Extract from annual report and accounts of Cadbury Schweppes plc for the year ended 31 December 1994.

Note 2 (part of note)

(a) Sales and Profit on Ordinary Activities Before Taxation
These were contributed as below:

	Sales		Profit	
	1994	*1993*	*1994*	*1993*
	£m	*£m*	*£m*	*£m*
Area of activity:				
Confectionary	**1,827.3**	1,660.1	**238.1**	211.3
Beverages	**2,202.3**	2,064.7	**282.7**	238.1
	4,029.6	3,724.8	**520.8**	449.4
Profit on sale of investment			–	11.9
Loss re properties			**(0.3)**	(1.5)
Net interest			**(42.0)**	(43.5)
Profit on Ordinary Activities Before Taxation			**478.5**	416.3

An analysis of sales by geographical destination is given below:

	1994	*1993*
	£m	*£m*
United Kingdom	**1,636.0**	1,556.6
Europe	**824.1**	762.2
Americas	**794.5**	664.8
Pacific Rim	**543.1**	513.0
Africa & Others	**231.9**	228.2
	4,029.6	3,724.8

Additional information (not part of statutory accounts covered by pages in audit report).

Sales, operating profit, operating assets and trading margin analysis

1994	Total *£m*	United Kingdom *£m*	Europe* *£m*	Americas *£m*	Pacific Rim *£m*	Africa & Others *£m*
Sales						
Confectionary	1,827.3	896.2	368.9	96.5	324.5	141.2
Beverages	2,202.3	833.1	406.2	670.5	214.5	78.0
	4,029.6	1,729.3	775.1	767.0	539.0	219.2
Operating Profit						
Confectionary	238.1	110.9	37.4	19.4	52.3	18.1
Beverages	282.7	120.0	14.7	113.0	14.6	20.4
	520.8	230.9	52.1	132.4	66.9	38.5
Operating Assets						
Confectionary	863.2	356.6	191.4	41.4	197.5	76.3
Beverages	591.1	219.0	155.4	107.7	93.6	15.4
	1,454.3	575.6	346.8	149.1	291.1	91.7
	%	%	%	%	%	%
Trading Margin						
Confectionary	12.8	12.4	10.1	20.1	16.1	10.5
Beverages	12.2	14.4	1.9	16.9	6.8	18.3
	12.5	13.4	5.8	17.3	12.4	13.3

*See Note 19 for the effect of acquisitions

1993 Sales	Total £m	United Kingdom £m	Europe £m	Americas £m	Pacific Rim £m	Africa & Others £m
Confectionary	1,660.1	826.9	312.3	53.0	311.5	156.4
Beverages	2,064.7	786.8	429.2	590.6	196.5	61.6
	3,724.8	1,613.7	741.5	643.6	508.0	218.0
Operating Profit						
Confectionary	211.3	94.2	33.3	12.3	53.9	17.6
Beverages	238.1	100.7	16.7	89.3	14.9	16.5
	449.4	194.9	50.0	101.6	68.8	34.1
Operating Assets						
Confectionary	743.2	332.0	129.3	30.8	174.6	76.5
Beverages	627.7	223.1	181.5	141.5	75.1	6.5
	1,370.9	555.1	310.8	172.3	249.7	83.0
	%	%	%	%	%	%
Trading Margin						
Confectionary	12.5	11.4	10.7	23.2	17.3	8.9
Beverages	11.1	12.8	2.7	15.1	7.6	19.5
	11.7	12.1	6.0	15.8	13.5	11.9

The analysis shown above is based on geographical origin.

Illustration 2

Extract from annual report and accounts of Cowie Group plc for the year ended 31 December 1994.

1 Turnover and profit and ordinary activities before taxation

	Turnover		Profit	
	1994 £000	1993 £000	1994 £000	1993 £000
By business:				
Finance	230,098	230,256	27,773	23,696
Motor	650,019	518,457	10,106	8,526
Bus and coach operations	27,045	14,438	3,364	1,604
Bus and coach distribution	20.375	16.134	2,883	2,262
Agricultural, industrial and horticultural	6,624	20,466	60	356
Head office and miscellaneous	–	–	(579)	1,566
	934,161	799,751	43,607	38,010

2 Segmental report

	Finance		Motor		Other		Group	
	1994 £000	1993 £000	1994 £000	1993 £000	1994 £000	1993 £000	1994 £000	1993 £000
Turnover:								
Total sales	243,914	245,534	782,322	619,059	54,196	51,087	1,080,432	915,680
Inter-segment sales	13,816	15,278	132,303	100,602	152	49	146,271	115,929
Sales to third parties	230,098	230,256	650,019	518,457	54,044	51,038	934,161	799,751
Profit before taxation	27,773	23,696	10,106	8,526	6,065	3,980	43,944	36,202
Head office and miscellaneous							(337)	1,808
Group profit before taxation							43,607	38,010

Net assets:								
Segment net assets	54,329	45,641	63,853	61,014	45,178	23,976	163,360	130,631
Unallocated net (liabilities)/assets							(22,566)	4,965
Group net assets							140,794	135,596

Segment net assets represent the net operating assets less net operating liabilities of the businesses within the segment, including interest bearing liabilities.

Profit before taxation from other operations is stated after deducting amortisation of goodwill amounting to £242,000 (1993: £242,000).

G Price change information

33 PRICE CHANGE ACCOUNTING

Key Issues

* Weaknesses of historical cost convention
* Approaches to price change accounting
* Current value systems
  - current replacement cost (entry values)
  - net realisable value (exit values)
  - economic value
  - mixed systems
* Accounting for the effect of changing prices handbook
* Operating capital maintenance concept
  - depreciation adjustment
  - cost of sales adjustment
  - monetary working capital adjustment
  - gearing adjustment
* Real terms version of CCA

33.1 BUSINESS PROFIT OR BUSINESS INCOME

An economist might refer to business profit or income as being the maximum a company could distribute during the year and still expect to be as well off at the end of the year as it was at the beginning of the year. Alternatively, this could be described in terms of the maximum which could be distributed and still keep the capital of the business intact.

Business capital may be measured in several ways, each of which can give rise to different profit figures, for example:

(a) money capital of shareholders' funds (historical cost accounting);
(b) purchasing power of the money capital of shareholders' funds (current purchasing power accounting);
(c) productive or operating capacity (current cost accounting).

The possible approaches are discussed later in this chapter.

33.2 THE ACCRUALS CONCEPT

The accounting approach revolves around the accruals concept (SSAP 2, Disclosure of accounting policies). Under the accruals concept, revenues and costs are accrued and matched with one another. For example, in a manufacturing company, pre-tax profit is determined by matching cost of sales against sales to arrive at gross profit, and then deducting operating expenses such as distribution costs and administrative expenses.

SSAP 2, para 14(b) states:

The accruals concept implies that the profit and loss account reflects changes in the amount of net assets that arise out of the transactions of the relevant period (other than distributions or subscriptions of capital and unrealised surpluses, arising on revaluation of fixed assets) . . . Under the accruals concept, the balance sheet reflects the effect of transactions still to be completed, for example, amounts to be paid or collected, stock to be sold, or fixed assets with a remaining number of years' service potential.

33.3   WEAKNESSES OF THE HISTORICAL COST CONVENTION

The main weaknesses may be considered under the following headings:

(a) Profit and loss account

Historical cost accounting (HCA) matches current revenues (expressed in up-to-date prices) with historical costs. In some cases these costs will relate to price levels of previous accounting periods (for example, depreciation of fixed assets).

When prices rise, the matching process may result in inflated profits being reported. Unless some part of the historical cost profit is retained within the business, business capital will not be maintained in real terms.

(b) Balance sheet

The historical cost of assets (depreciated where relevant) does not present a current measure (expressed in up-to-date prices) of resources employed in a business.

In the United Kingdom, some companies mitigate this weakness by incorporating revaluations of fixed assets (for example, freehold land and buildings) into the balance sheet. This practice is usually referred to as modified historical cost (MHC).

(c) Interpretation of accounts

Historical cost accounts can give misleading impressions of growth and profitability. This criticism is particularly apparent in the case of ten-year summaries included by listed companies in their annual reports. Statistics such as turnover, pre-tax profit, earnings per share and assets employed can give a distorted view of a company's performance and position. Clearly, much of this is due to the fact that money, the value of which changes over time, is an imperfect unit of measurement.

Following on from the above, the following specific comments can be made:

(1) Return on capital employed (ROCE) can be distorted as a result of profits being overstated in real terms and assets such as fixed assets being understated.
(2) Historical cost accounts may fail to show:

    (i)   whether a company is earning sufficient funds to enable it to maintain its capital in real terms;
    (ii) the extent to which funds can prudently be distributed in the form of dividends.

It should be noted that many accountants consider that the above weaknesses apply when inflation rates are running at relatively low figures, say 5% per annum.

33.4 APPROACHES TO ACCOUNTING FOR PRICE CHANGES

(a) Introduction

The aim of this chapter is to discuss some of the proposals put forward by the former Accounting Standards Committee over the past 20 or so years.

In the United Kingdom, the search continues to find an alternative to historical cost accounting which will attract the widespread support of accountants and various user groups.

(b) A summary of statements since 1973

Date	Reference and title of statement	Issued by
1973	ED 8 – Accounting for changes in the purchasing power of money	ASC
1974	SSAP 7 (provisional) – same title as ED 8	ASC
1975	Report of the Sandilands Committee	Government
1976	ED 18 – Current cost accounting	ASC
1977	Hyde guidelines on current cost accounting	ASC
1979	ED 24 – Current cost accounting	ASC
1980	SSAP 16 – Current cost accounting	ASC
1984	ED 35 – Accounting for the effects of changing prices	ASC
1986	Accounting for the effects of changing prices: a Handbook	ASC

All statements other than the 1986 handbook have been withdrawn.

The following section briefly discusses the current purchasing power approach set out in ED 8/SSAP 7.

33.5 CURRENT PURCHASING POWER (CCP) ACCOUNTING

(a) Background

In the United Kingdom, the first proposal for CPP accounting came in the form of ED 8 (Accounting for changes in the purchasing power of money). A provisional accounting standard, SSAP 7, with the same title, was issued in May 1974. However, CCP suffered a major blow in September 1975 as a result of the publication of the report of the Sandilands Committee which rejected CPP in favour of current cost accounting (CCA).

(b) Capital maintenance concept

CCP is concerned with maintaining the purchasing power (measured in terms of the retail price index) of the shareholders' equity. Under CPP, no profits result until the shareholders' equity at the beginning of the year has been maintained in purchasing power terms.

(c) Principal proposals of SSAP 7

Although SSAP 7 has been withdrawn, it is useful to consider briefly its main proposals:

(1) Annual accounts of listed companies were to be accompanied by a supplementary statement which showed in terms of pounds of purchasing power at the accounting year end:

   (i) the financial position at the year end; and
   (ii) the results for the year.

(2) The conversion of the basic accounts used to provide the information for the supplementary statement was by means of a general index of prices i e the retail price index (RPI).

33.6   CURRENT VALUE SYSTEMS

The weaknesses of historical cost accounting were considered in section 33.3. Over the years, accountants have come up with various proposals aimed at overcoming these drawbacks (see section 33.4). These proposals have fallen into two main groups:

(a) Current purchasing power accounting (ED 8, SSAP 7), considered in section 33.5.
(b) Current value systems (for example, current cost accounting as proposed by the Sandilands report: ED 18, Hyde Guidelines, ED 24, SSAP 16, ED 35).

Strictly speaking, the term 'current value systems' refers to a family of approaches which includes:

(1) current replacement cost (entry values);
(2) net realisable value (exit values);
(3) economic value;
(4) a mixed system which combines features of (1), (2) and (3).

Current cost accounting (CCA) is an example of a mixed system.

33.7   CURRENT REPLACEMENT COST (ENTRY VALUES)

(a) Main elements

The main elements of current replacement cost (CRC) are as follows:

(1) *Balance sheet*

(i)   Fixed assets – at net current replacement cost (NCRC).
(ii)   Stocks – at current replacement cost (CRC).
(iii) Other items – at historical cost.

(2) *Profit and loss account*

(i)   Depreciation charge – based on current replacement cost.
(ii)   Cost of sales – based on current replacement cost.
(iii) Other items – at historical cost.

Note: Mixed systems, such as CCA, cover aspects such as monetary working capital adjustment and gearing. These are dealt with later in the chapter, and are not further referred to here.

(b) Terminology

Current replacement cost of stock means the cost at which stock could have been replaced in the normal course of business at the balance sheet date or at the date of sale, whichever is relevant.

For fixed assets, net current replacement cost is calculated by determining gross replacement cost at the balance sheet date, less a proportionate deduction for accumulated depreciation.

(c) Illustration 1

Green Traders Ltd commenced business on 1.1.X2. On that date the company issued 1,000 shares of £1 each at par. The proceeds were applied as follows:

	£
Fixtures and equipment (estimated life, ten years)	600
Purchase of goods for resale 400 units at £1	400
	1,000

The goods were sold on 30.6.X2 for proceeds of £600. The goods were immediately replaced at a total cost of £480 (ie 400 units at £1.20). These goods were still in stock at the year end 31.12.X2 when their replacement cost was £1.30 per unit.

The gross replacement cost of equipment at the year end was £720. Equipment is depreciated on a straight-line basis assuming nil residual value.

Required: profit and loss account and balance sheets on a replacement cost (entry value) basis.

Calculations

(1) *Goods sold*

	£
(i) Under HCA, profit is (600 − 400), ie:	200

(ii) Under RCA, the total gain of 200 is analysed between operating profit and *realised* holding gains:

	£
Operating profit = sales − replacement cost of sales = £600 − (400 × £1.20)	120
Realised holding gain = replacement cost at date of sale − historical cost = £480 − £400	80
	200

(2) *Goods unsold*

(i) Under HCA, no account is taken of the increase in replacement cost between 30.6.X2 and 31.12.X2 as the gain is unrealised.

(ii) Under RCA, the increase in replacement cost (400 × £1.30 less 400 × £1.20) ie £40 is classified as an *unrealised* holding gain.

(3) *Fixtures and equipment*

(i) Under HCA, depreciation charge in the profit and loss account is £60. Accounts net book value in the balance sheet £540.

(ii) Under RCA, depreciation charged in the profit and loss account may be based on either average values or year-end values. The average approach is generally to be preferred as the equipment is consumed over a period of one year. RCA depreciation on an average basis is 10% ((600 + 720) ÷ 2) ie £66.

(iii) Under RCA, net current replacement cost at the balance sheet date is calculated as follows:

	£
CRC	720
Accumulated depreciation (one year) $\frac{1}{10} \times 720$	72
NCRC	648

(4) *Replacement reserve*

The replacement reserve will include realised and unrealised holding gains. The movement on the account may be summarised as follows:

	Total	Realised holding gains	Unrealised holding gains
	£	£	£
Goods:			
Sold	80	80	–
Unsold	40		40
Fixed assets:			
Depreciation	6		
(66 – 60)		6	
Net book value at year end	108		
(648 – 540)			108
Totals at 31.12.X2	234	86	148

Replacement cost accounts

(1) PROFIT AND LOSS ACCOUNT

for the year ended 31 December 19X2

	£
Sales	600
Replacement cost of sales	480
Gross profit	120
Depreciation	66
Operating profit	54

(2) BALANCE SHEET

as at 31 December 19X2

	£
Fixtures and equipment	648
Stock	520
Cash	120
	1,288
Ordinary share capital	1,000
Profit and loss account	54
Replacement reserve	234
	1,288

Note: The replacement reserve includes realised holding gains of £86 and unrealised holding gains of £148.

(d) Advantages and disadvantages of the replacement cost approach

(1) *Advantages of RCA*

RCA focuses attention on the effect of price changes on the non-monetary assets of the business.

In the balance sheet, stock is stated at its replacement cost at the balance sheet date. Fixed assets are stated at net current replacement cost. This is effectively the remaining number of years' service potential of the asset measured in terms of current replacement price. The replacement cost balance sheet thus offers an up-to-date measure of resources employed in the business.

Replacement cost profit is arrived at by matching current cost of sales and depreciation against sales. Replacement cost profit offers a far better guide than historical cost profit of the amount a business can distribute to shareholders without impairing its productive capacity or ability to produce goods and services in the future.

The analysis of gains between operating profit and holding gains provides useful information for those who wish to assess the two aspects of a company's performance.

(2) *Disadvantages of RCA*

(i) RCA does not take account of changes in the purchasing power of money. Unlike CPP, RCA is not a system of accounting for inflation.
(ii) Estimation of current replacement costs at particular dates can involve subjective judgements. It can be argued that this is a cost to be weighed against possible benefits deriving from more useful information than that contained in HCA.
(iii) By itself, RCA is not a comprehensive system of accounting for price changes. For example, it fails to take account of the effect of price changes on monetary items.

33.8 NET REALISABLE VALUE (EXIT VALUES)

(a) Basic approach

Under exit value accounting, balance sheet values are based on the prices which assets such as fixed assets and stocks could obtain if sold in an orderly manner at the balance sheet date. The illustration below sets out a simple approach to exit value accounting.

(b) Illustration 2

Suppose the following additional information relates to the accounts of Green Traders Ltd:
   Net realisable values of fixed assets and stocks at 31.12.X2 were £550 and £700 respectively.
   Summarised financial statements would appear as follows:

(1) Revenue statement

	£	£
Realised gross profit (per HCA) (600 – 400)		200
Less depreciation		
NRV at 31.12.X2	550	
Acquisition cost	600	(50)
Add unrealised gain on stock		
NRV at 31.12.X2	700	
HC	480	220
Increase in reserves		370

(2) Balance sheet

	£
Fixtures and equipment	550
Stock	700
Cash	120
	1,370
Ordinary share capital	1,000
Reserves	370
	1,370

(c) Advantages and disadvantages of exit value or net realisable value approach

(1) *Advantages of net realisable value (NRV)*

(i) Net realisable value is a concept which non-accountants find easy to understand.
(ii) If all businesses were to include assets in the balance sheet at net realisable value, accounts would become easier to compare.

(2) *Disadvantages of NRV*

(i)   NRV is inconsistent with the going concern concept. For a going concern business, NRV of fixed assets is of little relevance.
(ii) NRV focuses on total gains. It makes no attempt to segregate operating gains (unlike RCA).
(iii) NRV is hardly a practicable concept for the majority of non-monetary assets, as it will often be difficult to determine.

As with RCA, NRV is, by itself, unsatisfactory. However, NRV may provide a useful element of a mixed value system such as that set out in SSAP 16.

33.9   ECONOMIC VALUE METHOD (EV)

(a) General approach

Under the economic value approach, the current value of an individual asset is based on the present value of the future cash flows that are expected to result from ownership of the asset.

To calculate this present value, it is necessary to know the following:

(1) the cash amount of the future benefits;
(2) the timing of these benefits;
(3) an appropriate discount factor, for example, the cost of capital to the company.

(b) Illustration 3

A company owns a particular item of machinery. At 31.12.X3, the asset is expected to generate the following cash flows (measured in terms of excess of sales over operating costs)

	£
19X4	8,000
19X5	11,000
19X6	12,000

Assuming a cost of capital of 14%, the economic value may be calculated using present value tables:

	Net inflow £	Present value factor	NPV £
19X4	8,000	0.877	7,016
19X5	11,000	0.769	8,459
19X6	12,000	0.675	8,100
Total			23,575

The asset would be stated in the balance sheet at 31.12.X3 as £23,575.

(c) Problems with the EV approach

The EV approach suffers from several practical drawbacks including the following:

(1) The calculations of EV are dependent on the reliability of estimated future cash flows. Estimation of these amounts would give rise to many practical difficulties, and the resulting information would be subjective to an unacceptable extent.
(2) EV can only be applied to the business as a whole. It would be difficult to provide a detailed analysis of profit. Profit would be determined by comparing EVs at successive balance sheet dates and adjusting for capital introduced and dividends.

(d) Relevance of EV approach

As with RCA and NRV, economic value may provide a useful component of a mixed value system.

33.10 MIXED SYSTEMS

(a) The concept of deprival value

The Sandilands Committee Report (1975) recommended an approach to asset valuation based on the concept of value to the business.

Value to the business is effectively the same as deprival value, a term used in earlier accounting literature. The deprival value of an asset is the minimum compensation a business would require if deprived of the use of an asset.

(b) Determination of deprival value

This may be illustrated diagrammatically as follows:

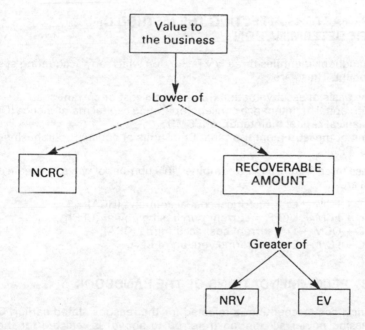

In the majority of cases, the future cash flows (EV) expected to be generated by a fixed asset will exceed its net current replacement cost. If deprived of the asset, the business would simply require sufficient compensation to replace with an equivalent asset (in terms of productive capacity, remaining years' service potential and so on). Value to the business would be NCRC.

However, in restricted cases the amount expected to be recoverable from an asset may be lower than its NCRC. In such a situation, the business would not wish to replace the asset. Minimum compensation required if deprived of the asset would be either expected sales proceeds (NRV) or cash flows that would otherwise have been earned (EV).

(c) Application to the UK

The deprival value concept is embodied in the 1986 Handbook, Accounting for the effects of changing prices, referred to below.

33.11   ACCOUNTING FOR THE EFFECTS OF CHANGING PRICES HANDBOOK

The term current cost accounting refers to a family of current value techniques which draw mainly upon replacement cost (or entry value) accounting techniques but also, to a lesser extent, net realisable values (exit values) and economic values.

The main pronouncements on CCA were listed in section 33.4. Clearly there are variations between each, but the purpose of the remainder of this chapter is to describe in broad terms the mechanics of CCA rather than to examine the various statements.

For this purpose, the discussion will centre around *Accounting for the effects of changing prices: a Handbook* (ASC, 1986) as this represents the latest state of play as regards thoughts on CCA.

Readers will be only too aware of the controversies surrounding the subject of accounting for price changes and the failure of the main accountancy bodies to find a solution acceptable to the majority of accountants and key user groups.

33.12   FACTORS AFFECTING THE METHOD OF PROFIT DETERMINATION

The handbook identifies three key factors on which any accounting system is dependent. These are:

(a) the basis of asset valuation (i e historical cost or current cost);
(b) the capital maintenance concept (operating capital maintenance (OCM) or financial capital maintenance (FCM));
(c) unit of measurement (nominal £s or units of constant purchasing power (UCPP)).

These three factors can be combined in a number of ways, the main ones of which are:

(1) HC + FCM + £s = historical cost accounting (HCA);
(2) HC + FCM + UCPP = current purchasing power (CPP);
(3) CC + OCM + £ = current cost accounting (CCA);
(4) CC + FCM + £ = real terms version of CCA.

33.13   RECOMMENDATIONS OF THE HANDBOOK

Historical cost accounting is rejected for the reasons stated earlier. Current purchasing power accounting (referred to above) is rejected for the main reason that since input prices specific to a particular company may fluctuate independently of general prices indices, CPP asset figures may bear no relationship to current values.

The two methods considered acceptable are:

(a) current cost accounting – operating capital maintenance version;
(b) current cost accounting – real terms version.

Each of these is considered in turn.

33.14   OPERATING CAPITAL MAINTENANCE CONCEPT OF CCA

(a) Operating capability

This concept is based on the entity's operating capability. Operating capability means the amount of goods and services which the business is able to supply in the period with its existing resources. In accounting terms, operating capability is represented by net operating assets of fixed assets and working capital. The term monetary working capital is defined below, but in broad terms it refers to debtors less creditors. For a trading company, this may be expressed as follows:

Operating capability	Financing
Fixed assets	Shareholders' funds
Working capital (a) stock (b) monetary working capital	Borrowings

In broad terms, monetary working capital refers to trade debtors less trade creditors. Some accountants, however, do not consider monetary working capital to be part of net operating assets (this is further referred to below in section 33.18(e).

(b) Effect of input price changes

A key concern in the OCM concept is the effect of input price changes (raw materials, wages, overheads, plant and machinery etc) on the funds required to maintain an entity's operating capability.

Input price increases do have funding implications. For example:

(1) A going-concern business will eventually have to replace its fixed assets, even if the form of the replacement assets bears little resemblance to the assets which are being replaced. Replacement costs will inevitably be much greater than historical costs. It is important that sufficient funds are retained within the business as opposed to being paid out as dividends. Historical cost profit is an unreliable measure of the entity's ability to pay out dividends.
(2) Stocks consumed or sold will eventually have to be replaced at prices considerably in excess of original cost.
(3) Entities in a net debtor position (debtors in excess of creditors) will find that an increasing amount of funds must be tied up in debtors simply to maintain in real terms the present level of business operations. Conversely, entities in a net creditor position (for example, supermarkets) may find that higher replacement costs of stock are financed by a semi-automatic increase in creditors.
(4) To the extent that part of the net operating assets is financed by shareholders, additional funds *will* be required. However, to the extent that lenders will fund part of the operating assets, additional replacement costs of fixed assets and stocks may be financed by additional borrowings.

The OCM version of CCA deals with each of the above points by means of a specific adjustment to historical cost profit:

(i)   depreciation adjustment (DA);
(ii) cost of sales adjustment (COSA);
(iii) monetary working capital adjustment (MWCA);
(iv) gearing adjustment (GA).

These adjustments are described later in the chapter. Again note that some accountants are opposed to the inclusion of MWCA and GA in a current cost accounting system.

(c) Current cost profit figures

Under some versions of OCM (such as that in SSAP 16), two separate current cost profit figures may be highlighted. The first profit figure considers the viewpoint of the entity, irrespective of how it is financed as between shareholders and lenders of funds. The second takes account of financing and considers the viewpoint of the shareholders.

(1) *Current cost operating profit*

This is the surplus arising from ordinary activities of the business after allowing for the impact of price changes on the funds needed to continue the business and maintain its operating capability. Note that this profit figure is determined before charging interest and tax and takes no account of the way in which operating capability is financed as between shareholders' funds and borrowings.

(2) *Current cost profit on ordinary activities before taxation*

This is the surplus arising after allowing for the impact of price changes on the funds needed to maintain the shareholders' proportion of operating capability. This profit figure is determined after interest and gearing adjustment.

This may be expressed diagrammatically as follows:

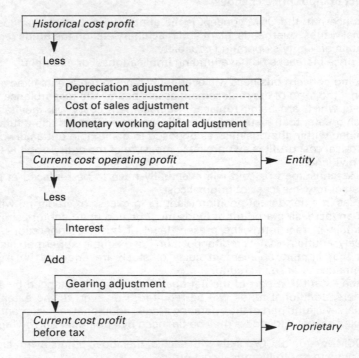

33.15   ILLUSTRATION – PREPARING CURRENT COST ACCOUNTS

The extracts below are taken from the historical cost financial statements of Lynton Traders plc. The current cost calculations will be set out in the following sections and the current cost financial statements summarised in section 33.20(a).

(a) Profit and loss account for the year ended 31 December 19X7

	£	£
Sales		16,500
Opening stock	2,200	
Purchases	12,100	
	14,300	
Closing stock	2,500	
Cost of sales		11,800
Gross profit		4,700
Depreciation		(340)
Operating expenses		(1,080)
Interest payable		(180)
Profit on ordinary activities		3,100
Tax		(1,200)
Profit after tax		1,900
Proposed dividends		(800)
Retained profit		1,100
Balance at 1.1.19X7		5,700
Balance at 31.12.19X7		6,800

(b) Balance sheet at 31 December 19X7

	31.12.X7 £	31.12.X6 £
Land and buildings – cost	7,000	7,000
– depreciation	(200)	(160)
Fixtures and equipment – cost	3,000	3,000
– depreciation	(1,050)	(750)
Stock	2,500	2,200
Debtors	2,900	2,700
Cash	1,700	160
Creditors	(2,050)	(1,800)
Taxation	(1,200)	(1,050)
Dividends	(800)	(600)
6% Loan Stock 19X24	(3,000)	(3,000)
	8,800	7,700
Ordinary share capital	2,000	2,000
Profit and loss account	6,800	5,700
	8,800	7,700

(c) Additional information

(1) Land and buildings were acquired on 1.1.19X3. The split of total cost is estimated as land, £5,000 and buildings, £2,000. Buildings are depreciated at 2% per annum on a straight-line basis.

Estimated open market values on existing use basis are as follows:

	31.12.X7 £	31.12.X6 £
Land	16,000	14,000
Buildings	6,300	6,000
Total	22,300	20,000

(2) Equipment was acquired on 30.6.19X4 and is depreciated at 10% per annum on a straight-line basis. Suitable government-produced indices for CCA purposes are as follows:

30.6.19X4	122
31.12.19X6	153
Average 19X7	163
31.12.19X7	173

(3) Stock, debtors and creditors at each balance sheet date are estimated to have an age of two months. Suitable indices are:

31.10.19X6	132
31.12.19X6	134
Average 19X7	140
31.10.19X7	144
31.12.19X7	146

(4) During 19X7, the retail price index showed the following:

31.12.19X6	124
Average 19X7	131
31.12.19X7	138

(5) The company has produced supplementary current cost accounts since 19X3.
At 31.12.19X6, the balance on current cost reserve was £14,684 (£920 realised, £13,764 unrealised).

(6) Deferred tax and ACT on proposed dividends have been ignored.

Note: All individual calculations will be made to the nearest £. In practice, of course, it is important to avoid the impression of spurious accuracy when much of CCA relies on subjective judgement.

33.16 FIXED ASSETS AND DEPRECIATION

(a) Basic aims

The profit and loss account is charged with a current rate for services provided (i e use of asset) during the period. The balance sheet shows the current cost of purchasing the asset's remaining service potential (i e remaining number of years of useful life).

(b) CCA balance sheet

Fixed assets should be stated at value to the business (i e the deprival value concept referred to in section 33.10).
Value to the business may usefully be described diagrammatically as follows:

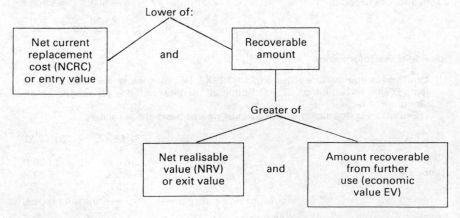

In most situations, value to the business will be represented by NCRC. Recoverable amount may be appropriate in restricted cases, e g:

(1) A group of assets is losing money ie operating costs exceed revenues. There is no prospect of improvement. The company's best option is to sell the assets as soon as possible. NRV is the appropriate basis.
(2) A group of assets is suffering from declining revenues. In two years' time, operating costs are expected to exceed operating revenues. The company has no intention of replacing the assets. However, at the present time, the company is better off continuing to use the assets (and earning cash flows ie economic value) rather than selling the assets immediately. Economic value is the appropriate basis.

(c) Calculating value to the business

Assume that net realisable value and economic value are not appropriate in any of the situations below.

(1) *Non-specialised land and buildings*

Value to the business can only be determined by specific valuation (ie open market value, existing use basis) as location is the main factor affecting valuation. Index numbers are inappropriate. Non-specialised land and buildings include shops, offices, showrooms and general purpose industrial units.

Illustration 4

The appropriate figures for Lynton at each year end would be as follows:

	£
31.12.X7	22,300
31.12.X6	20,000

(2) *Specialised land and buildings*

This would include specialised chemical factories, oil refineries, power stations and so on. Value to the business would be determined in two stages.

(i) Determine open market value of land using specific valuation techniques, and *add*:
(ii) depreciated replacement cost of buildings. The calculation is similar to that for plant and machinery (see below):

---

(1) First calculate GRC using construction index numbers:

$$HC \times \frac{\text{Index at B/S date}}{\text{Index at acquisition}} = GRC$$

(2) Then deduct proportionate accumulated depreciation.

---

(3) *Plant and machinery*

Ideally, NCRC should be calculated using direct valuation techniques (specific valuation, quotation, supplier's price list).

In practice, government-produced index numbers (eg PINCCA, Price Index Number for Current Cost Accounting) are used.

NCRC is calculated as follows:

(1) Calculate GRC	£
$\text{Historical cost} \times \dfrac{\text{index at B/S date}}{\text{index at acquisition}}$	A
(2) *Deduct accumulated depreciation*	$\underline{\underline{\begin{matrix} B \\ \overline{C} \end{matrix}}}$

Illustration 5

Using figures for Lynton, the respective CCA balance sheet figures would be calculated as follows:

	31.12.X7 £	31.12.X6 £
Gross replacement cost:		
$£3,000 \times \dfrac{153}{122}$		3,762
$£3,000 \times \dfrac{173}{122}$	4,254	
Accumulated depreciation:		
$£750 \times \dfrac{153}{122}$		941
$£1,050 \times \dfrac{173}{122}$	1,489	
	2,765	2,821

(d) Depreciation charge

The depreciation charge in the profit and loss account should be based on the value to the business of assets consumed during the year. This approach will be followed here. However, it should be noted that some accountants regard a depreciation charge based on year end GRC as a reasonable approximation.

The depreciation adjustment (sometimes referred to as additional depreciation) is the difference between the historical cost depreciation charge and the current cost depreciation charge.

The *amount* of the depreciation adjustment has no significance. For example, a company which adopts a modified historical cost convention may need only a relatively small depreciation adjustment. What *is* important is the size of the current cost operating profit after a full current cost depreciation charge has been allowed for.

Illustration 6

Using the information on Lynton, the calculation of the depreciation charge may be approached in two stages:

(1) Fixtures and equipment

The depreciation adjustment will be calculated using index numbers:

	£
Historical cost depreciation 10% × £3,000	300

Index number at acquisition 122
Averge index for 19X7 163
Current cost depreciation

	£
$£300 \times \dfrac{163}{122}$	401
So depreciation adjustment is	101

(2) Land and buildings

As the land and buildings are non-specialised index numbers are inappropriate. Also depreciation relates to the buildings element only.

	£
Historical depreciation	
2% × £2,000	40

Current cost depreciation based on 31.12.X6 values

OMV at 31.12.X6

Remaining years' life i e $\dfrac{£6,000}{46 \text{ years}}$ =	130

Current cost depreciation based on 31.12.X7 values

OMV at 31.12.X7

Remaining years' life i e $\dfrac{£6,300}{45 \text{ years}}$ =	140

Current cost depreciation based on average values	
½ (130 + 140) i e	135
HC depreciation	40
Depreciation adjustment	95

(3) Summary

Depreciation adjustment:	£
Fixtures and equipment	101
Land and buildings	95
Total	196

33.17 STOCKS AND THE COST OF SALES ADJUSTMENT

(a) Basic aims

The CCA profit should be determined by matching sales with cost of sales measured in current value terms and not historical cost terms. Stocks should usually be stated in the balance sheet at current replacement cost (entry values).

(b) CCA balance sheet

Stock should be stated at the lower of:

Current replacement cost (entry value);
and
Net realisable value (exit value).

The term current replacement cost means the cost at which the stock item could have been replaced (either by purchase or by manufacture) in the normal course of business at the valuation date. Valuation date may, of course, refer either to the date of sale or the balance sheet date.

(c) Determination of CRC

CRC may be calculated by any of a number of methods. The method chosen will depend on the nature and size of the business and its accounting systems.
Possible approaches include:

(1) supplier's price list or quotation;
(2) stock or costing records;
(3) index numbers:

   (i) produced in-house;
   (ii) published by the government statistical service.

Illustration 7

Assuming the index number approach is acceptable, CRC may be calculated as follows:

$$\text{CRC} = \text{HC} \times \frac{\text{index at valuation date}}{\text{index at acquisition}}$$

(d) CCA profit and loss account

A principal objective of CCA is to match sales revenue with the current (i e up-to-date) costs of earning that revenue.

Illustration 8

A wholesaler buys 100 Wods on 1 January 19X4 at a cost of 120p each. He sells the entire stock on 31 January for proceeds of 180p at which date the replacement cost of each Wod has risen to 135p.
Historical cost profit is £180 − £120 = £60.
Under CCA, this is analysed between:

		£
(1) Operating profit:		
Sales less current cost of sales		
ie (180 − 135)		45
(2) Holding gain (realised):		
Replacement cost at date		
of sale	135	
Historical cost	120	15
		60

In the terminology for SSAP 16, the realised holding gain of £15 is referred to as a cost of sales adjustment (COSA).
Supplementary CCA information could be presented as follows:

	£
Historical cost profit	60
Cost of sales adjustment	15
Current operating profit	45

The current cost operating profit offers a better guide to dividend policy than the equivalent historical cost profit. For example, if the business used £45 out of the proceeds of sale of £180, there would still be £135 left to finance replacement of 100 Wods at 135p. Capital (in terms of operating capability) would have been kept intact in real terms.

In principle, the cost of sales adjustment (COSA) should be calculated separately for each individual transaction and then aggregated to determine the COSA for the business as a whole. In practice, this approach is not necessarily feasible or necessary and a number of short-cut methods are available which offer reasonably acceptable approximations.

(e) Methods of calculating COSA

The following are examples of the main approaches:

(1) Determination of actual costs incurred at the valuation date (eg where a business possesses a computerised stock system).
(2) Suppliers' price lists – a time-consuming approach which might be practicable for high-value items.
(3) Indices applied to historical costs.
(4) Standard costs.
(5) Last-in-first-out – for the purposes of profit determination, LIFO may give a reasonable approximation to current costs. However, the LIFO balance sheet stock figure will need to be updated to current costs.
(6) Price indices used together with the averaging method (advocated by the Sandilands Committee Report).

(f) Averaging method

The averaging method assumes that purchases, sales and price increases occur evenly through the period. It is important that the price indices selected for this method reflect the purchasing experience of the company. The method also requires that historical cost stock figures are determined on a FIFO or average cost basis.

The calculations are illustrated using the figures from Lynton Traders. It is assumed that the above assumptions are valid for the whole year.

Illustration 9

The relevant part of the HCA profit and loss account of Lynton Traders is:

	£	£
Sales		16,500
Opening stock	2,200	
Purchases	12,100	
	14,300	
Closing stock	2,500	
Cost of sales		11,800
Gross profit		4,700

A problem with HCA is that cost of sales does not reflect price levels ruling at the date of sale.

Both sales and purchases are stated in prices which represent a spread throughout the year. However, both opening and closing stock are stated in terms of prices which obtained two months before each year end. If both opening and closing stocks are restated in terms of average prices for the year, an approximate figure of current cost of sales may be calculated.

	HCA £	Adjustment factor	Adjusted for CCA £
Sales	16,500	–	16,500
Opening stock	2,200	140	2,333
		132	
Purchases	12,100	–	12,100
	14,300		14,433
Closing stock	2,500	140	2,430
		144	
Cost of sales	11,800		12,003
Gross profit/operating profit	4,700		4,497

Cost of sales adjustment = current cost of sales less historical cost of sales
= £12,003 – £11,800
= £203

Since neither sales nor purchases affect the calculation of COSA, COSA may be determined in a more compact way:

	HCA £	Adjustment factor	Adjusted for CCA £
Opening stock	2,200	140	2,333
		132	
Closing stock	2,500	140	2,430
		144	
Increase (decrease) in stock	300		97

The amount by which closing stock exceeds opening stock (£300) could reflect either or both of two factors – different physical quantities or the fact that the cost per unit of closing stock is higher than the equivalent figure for opening stock.

However, the comparison of £2,333 and £2,430 is in terms of price levels at the same date (ie mid-year prices) and thus reflects different stock volumes in real terms.

COSA = total stock – volume stock = 300 – 97 = 203
(price effect)   change   change

Two additional points may be noted:

(1) Neither of the adjusted stock figures may be used for CCA balance sheet purposes since they do not represent current costs ruling at the balance sheet dates.
(2) If the assumptions referred to earlier are not valid for the year as a whole, it may be possible to show they are valid for shorter periods. For example, suppose a company can satisfy the conditions for three-month periods, it could calculate four separate quarterly COSA calculations and then aggregate them for the year as a whole.

(g) CCA balance sheet

As explained in section (c), if the index number approach is adopted, CRC at the year end may be calculated as follows:

$$CRC = HC \times \frac{\text{Index at year end}}{\text{Index at acquisition}}$$

Illustration 10

For Lynton Traders the calculations are as follows:

	31.12X7	31.12.X6
	£	£
HC	2,500	2,200
CRC		
£2,200 × 134/132		2,233
£2,500 × 146/144	2,535	

It is assumed that at both balance sheet dates, NRV is in excess of CRC.

33.18   MONETARY WORKING CAPITAL

(a) Basic aims

The term monetary working capital is defined in (b), below. In broad terms, monetary working capital (MWC) is the excess of trade debtors over trade creditors. Some businesses, for example supermarkets, have an excess of creditors over debtors. Monetary working capital may thus represent net assets or net liabilities.

For businesses which buy and sell on credit terms, MWC is an important part of their operating capability. For businesses in a net debtor position, a rise in the price of inputs (wages, materials etc) during the year will mean that additional funds must be tied up in MWC if the business is not to reduce in size.

This is not simply a problem for manufacturing and trading companies. A service company, for example an engineering consultancy firm, will have considerable funds tied up in debtors and unbilled work. If the payroll costs during the year increase by 10% and fees are accordingly increased, the level of year-end debtors will also need to be allowed to increase. The monetary increase in debtors does not represent an increase in real terms. However, the increase does place an imposition on funds which might otherwise have been used for an alternative purpose.

The monetary working capital adjustment (MWCA) represents the amount of additional (or reduced, in the case of a net creditor position) finance needed for monetary working capital as a result of changes in input prices of goods and services. It is important to appreciate that the MWCA is regarded as a funding adjustment.

(b) Definition of monetary working capital

Monetary working capital may be defined as the net aggregate of the following items:

(1) Trade debtors, prepayments and trade bills receivable.
(2) Certain special categories of stocks where a cost of sales adjustment is regarded as inappropriate.
(3) Trade creditors, accruals and trade bills payable.

Notes
(1) In most cases, cash and overdrafts are classified as borrowings and taken into account in arriving at the gearing adjustment
(2) Hire-purchase and leasing obligations, ACT, MCT and deferred tax are regarded as borrowings and not monetary working capital

(c) Current cost profit and loss account

The MWCA must be taken into account in arriving at current cost operating profit. Any method of calculating MWCA which achieves the objectives referred to in (a) above is acceptable.

However, in practice the averaging method is usually adopted. The calculations for the averaging method are similar to those for the cost of sales adjustment (COSA). The price indices used to calculate COSA are normally used also to determine MWCA.

Illustration 11

In the case of Lynton Traders, MWC at each balance sheet date is as follows:

	31.12.X7 £	31.12.X6 £
Debtors	2,900	2,700
Creditors	(2,050)	(1,800)
MWC	850	900

Since both debtors and creditors have an average age of two months, the calculations may be based on net MWC. Where ageings of debtors and creditors differ significantly, separate calculations should be carried out and the results combined.

Using the averaging method, MWCA may be determined as follows:

	HCA £	Adjustment factor	Adjusted for CCA £
Opening MWC	900	$\frac{140}{132}$	954
Closing MWC	850	$\frac{140}{144}$	826
Increase (decrease) in MWC	(50)		(128)

MWCA (price effect) = total MWC change − volume MWC change
$$= -50 - (-128)$$
$$= £78$$

Since the company is in a net debtor position, MWCA of £78 is a deduction in arriving at current cost operating profit.

For companies in a net creditor position, assuming prices are rising throughout the year, MWCA is added in arriving at current cost operating profit.

(d) Current cost balance sheet

All monetary items are stated in the CCA balance sheet at the same amounts as in the HCA balance sheet.

(e) Criticisms of the MWCA

Paragraph 3.11 of the Handbook states that '. . . the treatment of monetary working capital remains the subject of much debate. This is because some commentators do not view the allowance as being consistent with the operating capital maintenance concept. Some do not consider monetary working capital to be part of net operating assets.'

33.19   GEARING ADJUSTMENT

(a) Basic aims

Part of the operating capability of a business is financed by borrowings. The interest cost of these borrowings is charged to profit and loss account.

During a period of rising prices, the non-monetary assets (fixed assets, stocks) financed by these borrowings increase in monetary amount, while the amount of the loans remains unchanged. The HCA profit and loss account fails to reflect the gains even though interest is charged.

Some accountants consider that in an OCM system, a gearing adjustment is required. However, the Handbook refers to two types of gearing adjustments and each of these will be discussed below. Note that as under MWCA, some accountants are opposed to any concept of gearing adjustment (see below).

(b) Type 1 gearing adjustment

This version of the gearing adjustment indicates the benefit (assuming rising prices) to shareholders which is realised in the period measured by the extent to which a proportion of net operating assets is financed by borrowings.

The overall effect of depreciation adjustment, COSA and MWCA is to recognise the funding implications of increased replacement costs. However, these adjustments are concerned with the entity as a whole and take no account of the way in which the operating capability (or net operating assets) is financed as between shareholders and borrowings.

To the extent that part is financed by borrowings, parts of the above adjustments are not regarded as necessary in determining the position as regards the shareholders (the proprietary aspect).

(c) Type 2 gearing adjustment

This may be regarded as those parts of the total adjustments made to allow for the impact of price changes on the net operating assets, including the net surplus on the revaluations of assets arising during the period, that may be regarded as associated with items that are financed by borrowings.

(d) Definitions

For the purpose of measuring the two different gearing adjustments the definitions of borrowings and shareholders' funds are important.

These may be related to a current cost balance sheet as follows:

Operating capability	Financing
Fixed assets (Including trade investments, associated companies, intangibles)	Shareholders' funds • Ordinary share capital • Preference share capital • Reserves (adjusted to take account of restatement of fixed assets and stocks from HC to CC)
Working capital	• Proposed dividends • Minority interest
Stocks	Net borrowings • Loans and debentures • Overdraft (cash) (unless included within MWC)
Monetary working capital	• Tax liabilities, deferred tax • Hire-purchase and leasing obligations • (Marketable securities)

(e) Type 1 gearing adjustment calculation

There are three main stages to the calculation:

(1) Determine average gearing ratio:

> average net borrowings
> ―――
> average net borrowings + average shareholders' funds on CCA basis.

At this stage, a detailed analysis of shareholders' funds is not yet possible as the CCA profit and loss account has not been completed.

(2) Summarise current cost operating adjustments.

> COSA
> MWCA
> DA

(3) Apply average gearing ratio to current cost operating adjustments.

Illustration 12

Using information from Lynton Traders:

	19X7 £	19X6 £
Net borrowings		
Loan stock	3,000	3,000
Taxation	1,200	1,050
Cash	(1,700)	(160)
Totals	2,500	3,890
Shareholders' funds		
Per HCA B/S		
OSC	2,000	2,000
P/L	6,800	5,700
Restatement of non-monetary		
assets from HC to CC:		
Stock		
(2,535 – 2,500)	35	
(2,233 – 2,200)		33
Land and buildings		
(22,300 – 6,800)	15,500	
(20,000 – 6,840)		13,160
Fixtures and equipment		
(2,765 – 1,950)	815	
(2,821 – 2,250)		571
	25,150	21,464

Average net borrowings $= \frac{1}{2}(2,500 + 3,890)$
$= 3,195$

Average shareholders' funds $= \frac{1}{2}(25,150 + 21,464)$
$= £23,307$

Average gearing ratio $= \dfrac{3,195}{3,195 + 23,307} \times 100$

$\qquad\qquad\qquad\qquad\qquad\qquad\qquad\qquad$ 12.1%

Current cost operating adjustments

Depreciation adjustment	196
Cost of sales adjustment	203
Monetary working capital adjustment	78
	477

∴ Gearing adjustment
= 12.1% × £477 = £58

33.20 CURRENT COST FINANCIAL STATEMENTS

The information below is presented in summarised form. For the purposes of illustration a current cost balance sheet has been presented although this is not strictly necessary for presentation purposes.

(a) Current cost profit and loss account for the year ended 31 December 19X7

	£	£
Turnover		16,500
Profit before interest and taxation on the historical cost basis		3,280
Current cost operating adjustments		
Depreciation adjustment	196	
Cost of sales adjustment	203	
Monetary working capital adjustment	78	477
Current cost operating profit		2,803
Gearing adjustment	(58)	
Interest payable	180	122
Current cost profit before tax		2,681
Taxation		1,200
Current cost profit for the financial year		1,481
Dividends		800
Retained current cost profit of the year		681
Retained current cost profit B/F		4,780
Retained current cost profit C/F		5,461

(b) Current cost balance sheet at 31 December 19X7

	£	£
Fixed assets		
Land and buildings		22,300
Fixtures and equipment		2,765
		25,065
Current assets		
Stock	2,535	
Debtors	2,900	
Cash	1,700	
	7,135	
Current liabilities		
Creditors	2,050	
Taxation	1,200	
Dividends	800	
	4,050	
Net current assets		3,085
Total assets less current liabilities		28,150
Loan stock 19X24		(3,000)
		25,150
Ordinary share capital		2,000
Profit and loss account		5,461
Current cost reserve		17,689
		25,150

(c) Movement on current cost reserve

	Total £	Unrealised £	Realised £
Balance at 1.1.X7	14,684	13,764	920
Depreciation adjustment	–	(196)	196
Cost of sales adjustment	–	(203)	203
Monetary working capital adjustment	78		78
Gearing adjustment	(58)		(58)
Revaluation surpluses reflecting price changes:			
Fixed assets	2,780	2,780	–
Stock	205	205	
Balance at 31.12.X7	17,689	16,350	1,339

Workings

(1) *Retained current cost profit brought forward*

	£
Per historical cost accounts	5,700
Less current cost adjustments charged to CCA profit and loss a/cs of previous years (= realised element of opening balance on CCR)	920
	4,780

(2) *Reconciliation of unrealised element of opening balance on current cost reserve*

(i) Restatement of opening fixed assets from HC to CC:

	Fixtures and equipment £	Land and buildings £	Total £
HCA	2,250	6,840	9,090
CCA	2,821	20,000	22,821
Restatement	571	13,160	13,731

(ii) Restatement of opening stocks from HC to CC:

HCA	2,200
CCA	2,233
Restatement	33
Total	13,764

(3) *Reconciliation of unrealised element of closing balance on current cost reserve*

(i) Restatement of closing fixed assets from HC to CC:

	Fixtures and equipment £	Land and buildings £	Total £
HCA	1,950	6,800	8,750
CCA	2,765	22,300	25,065
Restatement	815	15,500	16,315

(ii) Restatement of closing stock from HC to CC:

HCA	2,500
CCA	2,535
Restatement	35
Total	16,350

(4) Revaluation surpluses reflecting price changes

	Fixed assets £	Stock £	Total £
Opening assets	13,731	33	13,704
Closing assets	16,315	35	16,350
Increase (decrease)	2,584	2	2,586
DA/COSA	196	203	399
Movement during year	2,780	205	2,985

(d) Type 2 gearing adjustment

Under this alternative, the gearing adjustment is defined as those parts of the total adjustments made to allow for the impact of price changes on the net operating assets, including the net surplus on the revaluation of assets arising during the period, that may be regarded as associated with items that are financed by net borrowings.

Illustration 13

Using the figures from Lynton Traders:
Gearing ratio: 12.1%

	£
Total adjustments:	
Net surplus on revaluation of:	
Fixed assets (see 33.20(c))	2,780
Stocks (see 33.20(c))	205
MWCA	78
	3,063

Gearing adjustment
= 12.1% × £3,063
= £370

Note: the difference between the two measurements of gearing adjustment is one of timing. The type 1 adjustment follows the prudence concept and only counts realised gains. By contrast, the type 2 adjustment applies the gearing adjustment to all gains arising during the period whether realised or unrealised.

Eventually all unrealised gains become realised as an asset is depreciated or sold.

33.21   THE REAL TERMS VERSION OF CCA

(a) Introduction

This version of CCA refers to a system of accounting for the effects of changing prices which measures whether a company's financial capital (shareholders' funds) is maintained in real terms. Assets are measured at current cost.

(b) Real terms profit

The measurement of real terms profit involves the following four stages:

(1) calculate shareholders' funds at the beginning of the period (based on current cost asset values);
(2) restate (1) in terms of £s of the reporting date (i e multiply by factor RPI at end of period divided by RPI at beginning);
(3) calculate shareholders' funds at the end of the period (again based on current cost asset values);

(4) compare (3) with (2) to determine whether a real terms profit has been made (allow for capital introduced, capital withdrawn and dividends).

(c) A simple layout

The calculation of total real gains is illustrated by reference to Lynton Traders (see section 33.15). Assume additionally that the increase in the Retail Price Index during the year amounted to 5%.

Unrealised holding gains during the year were calculated in section 33.20(c)(4) and amounted to:

	£
Stock	2
Fixed assets	2,584
	2,586

The inflation adjustment to shareholders' funds is 5% of £21,464 (see section 33.19(e)(3)) i e £1,073. Total real gains may be calculated as follows:

	£	£
Historical cost profit (before tax)		3,100
Add: unrealised holding gains during the year	2,586	
Less: inflation adjustment to shareholders' funds	1,073	
Real holding gains		1,513
Total real gains		4,613

(d) A more comprehensive layout

This layout has the advantage of presenting within the same statement both current cost operating profit (which is useful where the concept of operating capital maintenance *is* relevant to a particular company) and total real gains.

Using the data from Lynton Traders the comprehensive layout of real terms system profit and loss would be as follows:

	£	£
Sales		16,500
Less Cost of goods sold	11,800	
Cost of sales adjustment	203	
Depreciation	340	
Depreciation adjustment	196	
Other expenses	1,080	(13,619)
Current cost operating profit		2,881
Less Loan interest		(180)
Current cost profit		2,701
Add Realised holding gains		
Cost of sales adjustment	203	
Depreciation adjustment	196	
	399	
Unrealised holding gains	2,586	2,985
Total gains		5,686
Less inflation adjustment to		
shareholders' funds		1,073
Total real gains		4,613

Note: Unlike the OCM version of this example, no adjustments for MWCA and gearing adjustment have been made. The Handbook states that both these adjustments are inconsistent with the approach to monetary items implicit in the financial capital maintenance concept.

H Capital changes

34 CAPITAL REORGANISATIONS AND RECONSTRUCTIONS

> **Key Issues**
>
> * Reduction of capital
> * Amalgamations
> * Reconstructions

34.1 REDUCTION OF CAPITAL

(a) Introduction

The Companies Act 1985, ss 135–141 deals with reduction of capital. The term may apply to any of the following three situations, namely where a company wishes to:

(1) extinguish or reduce the liability in respect of share capital not fully paid up; or
(2) cancel any share capital which is lost or unrepresented by available assets; or
(3) pay off any paid-up share capital which is in excess of the company's requirements.

(b) Legal considerations

Section 135 sets out three conditions, all of which must be satisfied:

(1) The company must have the necessary authority under its articles.
(2) A special resolution for reducing share capital must be passed.
(3) The confirmation of the court must be obtained.

The following additional comments may be made:

(1) Where the proposed reduction involves either diminution of liability on unpaid share capital, or the payment to shareholders of any paid-up share capital, creditors are entitled to object and may require to be paid off or to have their liability secured.
(2) The court will take particular account of the rights of creditors and the equitable adjustment of any loss between the various classes of shareholders according to their capital and dividend rights.
(3) Once the company's special resolution has been confirmed by the court, it is binding on all members of the company. Members who did not vote in favour of the resolution cannot demand to be bought out. However, a company could not carry through a scheme which provided for the reduction of fully paid shares to partly paid shares and then for a further call to be made on shareholders unless the written consent of every member was obtained.
   It would be possible to effect such an arrangement under s 582 whereby the company could be wound up voluntarily and its business or property transferred to another company in exchange for partly paid shares therein. Under s 582, any member who did not vote in favour of the scheme could demand to be bought out.

(c) Writing off capital unrepresented by available assets

The procedures are as follows:

(1) Set up the fund for the capital reduction by debiting the various share capital accounts and crediting capital reduction account with the amounts by which the capital is to be reduced.
(2) Apply the fund in eliminating a debit balance on profit and loss account and in writing off or writing down assets.

Note: where drastic alterations in capital are involved, it is preferable to close the old capital accounts by:

(i)   crediting all the capital to the capital reduction account; and
(ii) debiting the capital reduction account and crediting the new share capital accounts with the new shares issued.

Illustration 1

The summarised balance sheet of Moorhead Ltd at 31 March 19X8 was as follows:

	£	£
Fixed assets		
Goodwill		25,000
Patents and trade marks		10,000
Deferred advertising expenditure		25,000
		60,000
Land and buildings	88,000	
Plant and machinery	86,000	174,000
Investments – shares in Saltash Ltd		30,000
		264,000
Current assets		
Stock	73,000	
Debtors	98,500	
	171,500	
Current liabilities		
Creditors	85,000	
Bank overdraft	60,000	
Debenture interest	2,500	
	147,500	
Net current assets		24,000
		288,000

	£	£
5% debenture stock (secured on land and buildings)		50,000
Directors' loans		23,000
Authorised, issued and called-up share capital:		
200,000 £1 ordinary shares	200,000	
100,000 £1 6% preference shares	100,000	
	300,000	
Profit and loss account	(85,000)	215,000
		288,000

Additional information

(1) Preference share dividends are three years in arrears.
(2) There is a contingent liability for damages amounting to £10,000.

(3) A capital reduction scheme, duly approved, settled the following terms:

    (i)   The preference shares to be reduced to 80p each and the ordinary shares to 25p each, and the resulting shares then to be converted into preference and ordinary stock respectively and consolidated into units of £1. The authorised capital to be restored to £100,000 6% cumulative preference stock and £200,000 ordinary stock. The preference shareholders waive two-thirds of the dividend arrears and receive ordinary stock for the balance.

    (ii) All tangible assets to be eliminated, and bad debts of £7,500 and obsolete stock of £10,000 to be written off.

    (iii) The shares in Saltash Ltd are sold for £60,000.

    (iv) The debenture holder agreed to take over one of the company's properties (book value £18,000) at a price of £25,000 in part satisfaction of the debenture and to provide further cash of £15,000 on a floating charge. The arrears of interest are paid.

    (v) The contingent liability materialised but the company recovered £5,000 of these damages in an action against one of its directors. This was debited to his loan account of £8,000, the balance of which was repaid in cash on his resignation.

    (vi) The remaining directors agreed to take ordinary stock in satisfaction of their loans.

Required:

(1) Journal entries to record the above, including the cash transactions;
(2) Capital reduction account;
(3) The revised balance sheet after giving effect to the entries in (1).

Ignore taxation.

Suggested solution

(1) *Journal entries*

	£	£
Preference share capital account	20,000	
Ordinary share capital account	150,000	
Capital reduction account		170,000

20p per share written off 100,000 6% cumulative preference
shares of £1 each and 75p per share written off 200,000 ordinary
shares of £1 each in accordance with capital reduction scheme.

	£	£
Preference share capital account	80,000	
Ordinary share capital account	50,000	
6% cumulative preference stock account		80,000
Ordinary stock account		50,000

Conversion of 100,000 preference shares of 80p each
and 200,000 ordinary shares of 25p each into stock and
consolidation into 80,000 £1 units of 6% cumulative preference
stock and £50,000 £1 units of ordinary stock respectively.

	£	£
Capital reduction account	6,000	
Ordinary stock account		6,000

Allotment of 6,000 £1 ordinary stock units in satisfaction of
one-third of the arrears of preference dividend, the other
two-thirds being waived.

	£	£
Capital reduction account	162,500	
Goodwill		25,000
Patents and trade marks		10,000
Deferred expenditure – advertising		25,000
Profit and loss account		85,000
Debtors		7,500
Stock		10,000

Writing off of intangible assets, bad debts and obsolete stock.

	£	£
Cash	60,000	
Shares in Saltash Ltd		30,000
Capital reduction account		30,000

Sales of shares in Saltash Ltd for £60,000 and transfer of profit (£30,000) to capital reduction account.

	£	£
5% debenture	25,000	
Land and buildings		18,000
Capital reduction account		7,000

Transfer to debenture holder at a valuation of £25,000 in part satisfaction of debenture for £50,000 of property of book value of £18,000 and transfer of profit to capital reduction account.

	£	£
Debenture interest	2,500	
Cash		2,500

Payment of accrued interest on £50,000 5% debenture.

	£	£
Cash	15,000	
Second debenture		15,000

Cash received for a new debenture carrying a floating charge over the assets of the company.

	£	£
Capital reduction account	5,000	
Directors' loan account	5,000	
Cash		10,000

Payment of £10,000 in settlement of contingent liability and recovery of £5,000 thereof by set-off against director's loan.

	£	£
Directors' loans	18,000	
Cash		3,000
Ordinary stock account		15,000

Repayment to former director of balance of loan and allotment of ordinary stock in satisfaction of other directors' loans.

	£	£
Capital reduction account	33,500	
Capital reserve account		33,500

Balance on capital reduction account transferred to capital reserve.

(2) *Capital reduction account*

	£		£
Ordinary stock account allotment of ordinary stock in satisfaction of arrears of preference dividend	6,000	Preference share capital – reduction of 20p per share on 100,000 shares	20,000
Cash – discharge of contingent liability	10,000	Ordinary share capital – reduction of 75p per share on 200,000 shares	150,000
Amounts written off:		Shares in subsidiary company:	
Goodwill	25,000	Profit on sale	30,000
Patents and trade marks	10,000	Property – profit on sale	7,000
Deferred expenditure	25,000	Cash – recovery of	
Profit and loss account	85,000	damages from director	5,000
Debtors	7,500		
Stock	10,000		
Capital reserve – balance transferred	33,500		
	212,000		212,000

(3) *Balance sheet – after reduction of capital*

	£	£
Tangible fixed assets:		
Land and buildings		70,000
Plant and machinery		86,000
		156,000
Current assets:		
Stocks	63,000	
Debtors	91,000	
	154,000	
Creditors – amounts falling due within one year:		
Bank overdraft	500	
Trade creditors	85,000	
	85,500	
Net current assets		68,500
Total assets less current liabilities		224,500
Creditors – amounts falling due after more than one year:		
5% debenture (secured)	25,000	
Second debenture (secured)	15,000	
		(40,000)
		184,500
Capital and reserves:		
Called-up share capital:		
71,000 £1 ordinary stock units		71,000
80,000 £1 6% cumulative preference stock		80,000
		151,000
Capital reserve		33,500
		184,500

Note: Authorised share capital consists of:	£
200,000 £1 ordinary stock units	200,000
100,000 £1 6% cumulative preference stock	100,000
	300,000

Illustration 2

Extract from annual report and accounts of GPG Ltd for the year ended 30 September 1991.

608   *Capital reorganisations and reconstructions*

26 Reserves

The movements on the reserves are:

	Capital reserve £000	Goodwill reserve £000 Note (a)	Other non-distributable reserves £000 Note (b)	Total other reserves £000	Profit and loss £000
Group					
At 1 October 1990	23	(7,917)	15,457	7,563	(45,432)
Capital reduction scheme					
Cancellation of share premium account					
(see note (c) below)	–	–	–	–	17,878
Reduction of 10 pence per ordinary share					
(see note (c) below)	–	–	–	–	32,363
Currency and other adjustments	–	–	–	–	52
Transfer to profit and loss account					
(see note (d) below)	–	7,917	–	7,917	(7,917)
Restatement Reserve transfer					
(see note (e) below)	–	–	(3,419)	(3,419)	3,419
Retained profit for the year	–	–	–	–	10,924
At 30 September 1991	23	–	12,038	12,061	11,287
Company					
At 1 October 1990	–	–	15,457	15.457	(51,731)
Capital reduction scheme					
Cancellation of share premium account					
(see note (c) below)	–	–	–	–	17,878
Reduction of 10 pence per ordinary share					
(see note (c) below)	–	–	–	–	32,363
Restatement Reserve transfer					
(see note (e) below)	–	–	(3,419)	(3,419)	3,419
Retained profit for the year	–	–	–	–	8,453
At 30 September 1991	–	–	12,038	12,038	10,382

(a) The goodwill reserve at 1 October 1990 represented the remaining goodwill that arose from the acquisition of MCG.

(b) The opening other non-distributable reserves include an amount of £11,838,000 which represents the balance remaining of the share premium account which was cancelled by the Court on 27 March 1987. Under the terms of the Court scheme amounts can be transferred from this non-distributable reserve to the profit and loss account in certain specified circumstances.

(c) Following approval of a scheme of capital reduction by shareholders on 19 April 1991, the High Court confirmed the cancellation of the share premium account and the reduction in share capital to eliminate the deficit on distributable reserves (see note 25).

(d) The transfer to the profit and loss account represents the transfer of the remaining goodwill in relation to MCG.

(e) The transfer to the profit and loss account from the restatement reserve represents the reduction in this exchange reserve following the disposal of MCG.

(f) The cumulative amount of goodwill resulting from acquisitions which has been written off, after deducting goodwill attributable to subsidiaries disposed of, is £10,307,000 (1990: £48,541,000).

(d) Repayment of share capital in excess of company's requirements

An illustration of this was the capital reconstruction of the General Electric Company Ltd in 1977.

The overall effect of the reconstruction was that £178.3m standing to the credit of share premium account and resulting from the earlier acquisitions of Associated Electrical Industries Ltd in 1967 and English Electric Company Ltd in 1968 was convortod to £178.3m of floating rate unsecured capital notes 1986. It was considered that the total of shareholders' funds was excessive in relation to the total capital of the company.

Part of the floating rate capital notes could be:

(1) redeemed by the company over the period 1979–1985;
(2) purchased by the company on the open market and handed over to trustees for cancellation;
(3) redeemed at the option of loan stockholders after 1982.

In any event, all the loan stock was to be redeemed by November 1986.

(e) Capital reductions involving compromises or arrangements with creditors

These should be carried out under the terms of ss 425–427 of the Companies Act 1985 (see section 34.3 below).

34.2 AMALGAMATIONS

(a) Introduction

The term 'amalgamation' is not defined in law, but is usually taken to refer to the merging of two or more companies. One possibility is that, for example, company A absorbs company B. An alternative would be for a new company, C, to be formed to absorb companies A and B.

The companies to be absorbed will go into voluntary liquidation and the purchasing company will usually take over the whole of the assets and assume the ordinary trade liabilities of the other(s), any debentures being either paid off in cash or exchanged for debentures or other interests in the purchasing company.

An amalgamation may be brought about under two possible schemes under the Companies Act 1985:

(1) s 582; or
(2) ss 425–427.

(b) Amalgamations under s 582

The essential feature of a s 582 amalgamation is that one company (the transferor company) is either in voluntary liquidation or is about to go into liquidation and transfers the whole or part of its undertaking to another company (the transferee company). The consideration for the transfer consists wholly or partly of shares in the transferee company which are to be distributed amongst members of the transferor company.

The scheme will usually require the passing of two special resolutions:

(1) approval of the scheme for the sale of the undertaking in exchange for shares in the transferee company;
(2) putting the company into members' voluntary liquidation.

The scheme must not involve a compromise or arrangement with creditors. Shareholders of the transferor company who did not vote in favour of the scheme may require the liquidator to purchase their interest for cash.

(c) Amalgamations under ss 425–427

This may be appropriate where it is thought necessary to alter the rights of the creditors or members. The scheme requires the sanction of the court, for example to:

(1) transfer to the transferee company the whole or part of the undertaking of the transferor company;
(2) allot shares or debentures to shareholders or debenture holders of the transferor company;
(3) dissolve the transferor company without winding it up.

(d) Accounting entries for closing the books of the transferor

The entries in the books will be similar to those required for the purpose of closing the books of a partnership on dissolution, ie:

Debit	Credit	With
Realisation account	Asset accounts	Book value of assets taken over by the purchasing company
Cash	Asset accounts	Proceeds of assets not taken over by purchasing company
Asset accounts	Realisation account *or*	Profit on disposal of assets *not* taken over by the purchasing company
Realisation account	Asset account	Loss on disposal of assets *not* taken over by the purchasing company
Share capital reserve account	Sundry members account	Balances attributable to sundry members
Sundry members account	Profit and loss account	Debit balances attributable to sundry members
Purchasing company	Realisation account	Total purchase consideration (including agreed amounts payable to creditors, debenture holders etc taken over)
Sundry members account Sundry debenture holders etc Cash Creditors	Purchasing company	Allocation of purchase consideration (eg shares, debentures, cash) Discharge of creditors etc taken over
Sundry debenture holders *or* Realisation account	Realisation account *or* Sundry debenture holders	Remaining credit balance Remaining debit balance
Realisation account	Cash	Realisation expenses
Realisation account Sundry members account Liability accounts	Sundry members account *or* Cash	Balance on realisation account Closure of cash book by payment to members of residual cash and/or settlement of liabilities deferred until receipt of cash from the purchasing company

Note: In some examples, liabilities taken over by the purchasing company are credited to the realisation account and the purchase consideration excludes the amounts the purchasing company has agreed to pay in settlement of the liabilities. It is, however, considered easier to adopt the above method because no difficulties will arise when the liabilities are not taken over at book values.

A provision for bad and doubtful debts must be dealt with on its merits. If the debts are taken over by the absorbing company at their book value, the provision for doubtful debts account should be transferred to the credit of realisation account; if the debts are taken over at their full value, the provision, since it is being ignored, must be transferred to the credit of sundry members account. If book debts are not taken over any bad debts incurred can be charged to the provision account, and the balance, if a debit, taken to realisation account, or if a credit, to sundry members account.

(e) Accounting entries for the books of the transferee company

Debit	Credit	Notes
(1) Asset accounts Goodwill	Liabilities Vendor account Capital reserve	Assets and liabilities at acquisition values; the vendor account is credited with the purchase consideration. Goodwill is debited with the excess of the purchase consideration over the net assets acquired; capital reserve is credited if the net assets acquired exceed the purchase consideration.
(2) Vendor account	Share capital Cash etc	Discharge of purchase consideration by issue of shares, paying cash etc

Note: goodwill should be accounted for in accordance with SSAP 22.

(f) Illustration 3

The Associated Engineering Co plc is absorbed by the United Engineering Co plc, the consideration being the assumption of the liabilities, the discharge of the debentures at a premium of 5%, by the issue of 5% debentures in the United Co, a payment in cash of £3 per share, and the exchange of three £1 shares in the United Co, at an agreed value of 150p per share, for every share in the Associated Co.

The summarised balance sheet of the Associated Co at the date of transfer was as follows:

	£	£
Fixed assets:		
Goodwill		25,000
Land and buildings		76,500
Plant and machinery		220,000
Patents		7,500
		329,000
Investments on compensation fund account		5,000

	£	£
Current assets:		
Stock	106,000	
Debtors	45,000	
Cash at bank and in hand	35,000	
	186,000	
Less creditors	30,000	
Net current assets		156,000
		490,000
5% debentures		(150,000)
		340,000
60,000 £5 ordinary shares		300,000
General reserve		32,000
Profit and loss account		3,000
		335,000
Accident insurance fund		5,000
		340,000

Required:
(1) Close off the books of the Associated Co giving journal entries.
(2) Show the opening journal entries in the books of the United Co.

Suggested solution

(1) *Journal of the Associated Co*

	£	£
Realisation account	520,000	
Sundry assets		520,000
Assets sold to the United Engineering Co as per balance sheet		
Creditors	30,000	
Realisation account		30,000
Liabilities taken over by the United Engineering Co		
Realisation account	7,500	
Debentures account		7,500
Premium of 5% now provided for		
United Engineering Co plc	607,500	
Realisation account		607,500
Purchase price as per agreement		
Cash	180,000	
Shares (United Engineering Co):		
180,000 shares of £1 each fully paid at £1.50 per share	270,000	
Debentures account – 5% debentures exchanged	157,500	
United Engineering Co plc		607,500
Discharge of purchase consideration		
Accident insurance fund	5,000	
General reserve account	32,000	
Profit and loss account	3,000	
Realisation account – profit on transfer	110,000	
Share capital account	300,000	
Sundry members account		450,000
Balances transferred		

	£	£
Sundry members account	450,000	
Cash		180,000
United Engineering Co shares account		270,000

3 shares of £1 each valued at £1.50 per share, and £3 per share
in cash for each of 60,000 shares distributed to shareholders.

---

(2) *Ledger accounts (for additional explanation only)*

REALISATION ACCOUNT

	£		£
Sundry assets	520,000	Creditors	30,000
Premium on debentures	7,500	United Engineering Co plc	
Sundry members account		– purchase consideration	607,500
profit on absorption	110,000		
	637,500		637,500

SUNDRY LIABILITIES

	£		£
Realisation account	30,000	Creditors	30,000
	30,000		30,000

DEBENTURES

	£		£
United Engineering Co plc	157,500	Balance b/f	150,000
		Realisation account – premium	7,500
	157,500		157,500

SUNDRY MEMBERS

	£		£
Cash	180,000	Share capital	300,000
Shares in United Engineering		Accident insurance fund	5,000
Co plc	270,000	General reserve	32,000
		Profit and loss account	3,000
		Realisation account – profit	110,000
	450,000		450,000

SHARES IN UNITED ENGINEERING CO PLC

	£		£
United Engineering Co plc	270,000	Sundry members account	270,000
	270,000		270,000

GENERAL RESERVE

	£		£
Sundry members	32,000	Balance b/f	32,000
	32,000		32,000

ACCIDENT INSURANCE FUND

	£		£
Sundry members	5,000	Balance b/f	5,000
	5,000		5,000

PROFIT AND LOSS ACCOUNT

	£		£
Sundry members	3,000	Balance b/f	3,000
	3,000		3,000

UNITED ENGINEERING CO PLC

	£		£
Realisation account –		Cash	180,000
purchase consideration	607,500	Shares	270,000
		Debentures	157,500
	607,500		607,500

(3) *Journal for opening entries in books of United Engineering Co plc*

UNITED ENGINEERING COMPANY'S JOURNAL

	£	£
Land and buildings	76,500	
Plant and machinery	220,000	
Patents	7,500	
Stocks	106,000	
Debtors	45,000	
Investments	5,000	
Cash at bank and in hand	35,000	
Goodwill	142,500	
Associated Engineering Company plc		607,500
Creditors		30,000
	637,500	637,500

Assets and liabilities taken over as per purchase agreement.

	£	£
Associated Engineering Company plc	607,500	
Cash		180,000
5% debentures account		157,500
Share capital account – 180,000 shares of £1 each		180,000
Share premium account		90,000
	607,500	607,500

Discharge of purchase consideration, the shares being taken
as issued at £1.50 per share.

Notes to illustration
(1) ACCIDENT INSURANCE FUND
The fund has been raised by the Associated Engineering Co out of profits and is
represented by specific investments. Since there remains a credit balance on the fund
account at the date of the sale of the undertaking, the Associated Co has made a profit of
£5,000 by undertaking its own risks, instead of insuring outside.

Therefore, although the United Engineering Co takes over the investments representing such insurance profit, it only buys them as investments, and should not bring
the fund account into its books. In the vendor company's books the balance of this fund
account will be transferred to the sundry members account in common with the other
accumulated profit balances.

(2) GOODWILL
The final figure of goodwill, £142,500, shown in the United Engineering Co's books is
arrived at by taking the difference between the valuation of the assets acquired and the
purchase consideration plus liabilities taken over.

	£
The amount can be proved as follows:	
Goodwill as per vendor company's books	25,000
Profit on absorption	110,000
Premium on debentures unrepresented by assets	7,500
	142,500

(3) PREMIUM ON SHARES
In the vendor company's books the premium forms part of the cost of the shares in the
purchasing company acquired; it forms part of the price received for goodwill, since it

increases the profit on realisation disclosed by the realisation account. In the purchasing company's books, the share premium increases the cost of goodwill; it must be credited to share premium account and can only be dealt with in accordance with the provisions of Companies Act 1985, s 130.

34.3 RECONSTRUCTIONS

(a) Possible situations

The term 'reconstruction' may refer to any of the following:

(1) the alteration of the capital structure of a single company, eg a company in severe financial difficulties which needs to reach a compromise with its creditors;
(2) a demerger, where the various activities of a single company are to be transferred to separate companies under separate management following liquidation of the first company;
(3) the transfer of the undertaking of one company to another company owned by substantially the same shareholders.

Reconstructions may be effected under either s 582 or ss 425–427 of the Companies Act 1985.

(b) Reconstructions under s 582

Section 582 was referred to in section 34.2(b) above. Under s 582 it is not possible to reach a compromise with creditors – that is possible only under s 425. Section 582 protects the rights of creditors and offers dissentient shareholders the right to demand to be bought out at a fair price.

Section 582 may be used to transfer the undertaking of one company to another company owned by substantially the same shareholders. The section may also be used for demerger situations.

(c) Reconstructions under ss 425–427

These sections may be required if on a reconstruction the company proposes a compromise or arrangement between itself and its creditors. Reconstructions under these sections require the sanction of the court.

Illustrations of situations affecting rights of creditors are given below.

(d) Compromise with creditors

When a company has sustained a considerable loss of capital and is unable to satisfy its creditors in full, the reconstruction scheme commonly provides for a reduction of the original capital, a compromise with the creditors either for cash or for the issue of fully paid shares or debentures and the provision of new working capital by the issue to the existing shareholders of partly paid up shares, in exchange for shares held in the old company.

Illustration 4

The final trial balance of the Patent Bottle Company plc was as follows:

	£	£
Share capital:		
50,000 shares of £1 each fully paid		50,000
Creditors		26,500
Patent rights	48,000	
Debtors	4,500	
Stock	10,000	
Profit and loss account	13,850	
Cash	150	
	76,500	76,500

Further information

Efforts to secure sufficient new capital to pay off the liabilities and place the concern on a sound basis having proved unsuccessful, it was decided to reconstruct, and the following scheme was submitted to, and approved by, the shareholders and creditors:

(1) The company to go into voluntary liquidation, and a new company having a nominal capital of £100,000 to be formed, called the New Patent Bottle Co plc, to take over the assets and liabilities of the old company.
(2) The assets to be taken over at book value, with the exception of the patent rights, which were to be subject to adjustment.
(3) The creditors to be discharged by the new company on the following basis:

	£
Preferential creditors to be paid in full	500
Unsecured creditors to be discharged by paid composition of 50p in the £	13,400
Unsecured creditors to be discharged by the issue of 6% debentures fully paid at a bonus of 10%	12,600
	26,500

(4) 50,000 shares of £1 each, 50p paid up, to be issued to the shareholders in the old company, payable 25p on application and 25p on allotment.
(5) The costs of liquidation amounting to £250 to be paid by the new company as part of the purchase consideration.

Required:
(1) Close off the books of Patent Bottle Co plc.
(2) Show opening entries in books of New Patent Bottle Co plc.
(3) Prepare a balance sheet of New Patent Bottle Co plc, assuming all the shares and debentures have been allotted, and all the cash for the shares has been received.

Suggested solution

(1) *Closing off books of old company*

	£	£
Realisation account	62,650	
Patent rights		48,000
Debtors		4,500
Stock		10,000
Cash		150
Sundry assets transferred		

	£	£
Realisation account	1,260	
Creditors		1,260
Bonus of 10% of £12,600 payable in 6% debentures fully paid as per agreement		

	£	£
Purchasing company	46,310	
Realisation account		46,310
Purchase consideration payable under scheme as follows:		
50,000 shares of £1 each, 50p paid up to be issued to shareholders	25,000	
£13,860 6% debentures fully paid to be issued to creditors in part payment	13,860	
Cash to creditors in part payment of unsecured creditors and in full discharge of preferential creditors	7,200	
Cash for liquidation expenses	250	
	46,310	

	£	£
Realisation account	250	
Cash		250
Payment of liquidation expenses		

	£	£
Shares account – 50,000 shares of £1 each, 50p paid up	25,000	
Debentures account – £13,860 6% debentures	13,860	
Cash	7,450	
Purchasing company		46,310
Assets handed over by New Co to liquidator in settlement of purchase consideration		

	£	£
Creditors	27,760	
Debentures		13,860
Cash		7,200
Realisation account		6,700
Discharge of amounts due to creditors as per agreement and		
Transfer of balance to realisation account		

	£	£
Sundry members	11,150	
Realisation account		11,150
Loss on realisation		

	£	£
Sundry members	13,850	
Profit and loss account		13,850
Balance transferred		

	£	£
Share capital	50,000	
Sundry members account		50,000
Share capital transferred		

	£	£
Sundry members	25,000	
Shares in New Co		25,000
Issue of 50,000 shares £1 each, 50p paid up in New Co in exchange for shares in old		

REALISATION ACCOUNT

	£		£
Patent rights	48,000	Purchasing company – purchase consideration	46,310
Debtors	4,500	Creditors, rebate allowed	6,700
Stock	10,000	Sundry members account, loss	11,150
Cash	150		
Creditors – 10% bonus	1,260		
Cash – expenses	250		
	64,160		64,160

PURCHASING COMPANY

	£		£
Realisation account – purchase consideration	46,310	Shares in purchasing company	25,000
		Debentures in purchasing company	13,860
		Cash	7,450
	46,310		46,310

SUNDRY CREDITORS

	£		£
Debentures in New Co	13,860	Balance b/f	26,500
Cash	7,200	Realisation account	1,260
Realisation account	6,700		
	27,760		27,760

SUNDRY MEMBERS

	£		£
Realisation account, loss	11,150	Share capital account	50,000
Profit and loss account	13,850		
Shares in New Co	25,000		
	50,000		50,000

CASH BOOK

	£		£
Purchasing company	7,450	Creditors	7,200
		Liquidation expenses	250
	7,450		7,450

(2) *Opening entries in the books of new company*

JOURNAL

	£	£
Patent rights	31,660	
Debtors	4,500	
Stock	10,000	
Cash	150	
Vendor		46,310
Asset taken over per scheme of reconstruction		
Vendor	46,310	
Share capital account – 50,000 shares of £1 each, 50p paid up		25,000
6% debentures		13,860
Cash		7,450
Shares and debentures issued and cash paid in settlement of purchase consideration		
Application and allotment account	25,000	
Share capital		25,000
25p per share payable on application and 25p on allotment of 50,000 shares issued		

CASH BOOK

	£		£
Vendor	150	Vendor	7,450
Application	12,500	Balance c/f	17,700
Allotment	12,500		
	25,150		25,150

(3) *Balance sheet of New Patent Bottle Co plc*

	£	£
Fixed assets:		
Patent rights at cost		31,660
Current assets:		
Stock	10,000	
Debtors	4,500	
Cash	17,700	
		32,200
		63,860
6% debenture stock		(13,860)
		50,000
Called-up share capital:		
50,000 £1 ordinary shares fully paid		50,000

Note to balance sheet – authorised share capital is 100,000 £1 shares.

Notes
(i) PAYMENT OF CREDITORS
As the liquidator is responsible to the creditors of the old company to see that the conditions of the scheme of reconstruction are carried out, the liabilities will be discharged through him, and the transactions will consequently be recorded in the books of the old company.
(ii) THE ADJUSTED VALUE OF THE PATENT RIGHTS
The value placed upon the patent rights is the difference between the purchase price payable to vendor and the assets taken over upon which an agreed value was placed.

(e) Capital reduction schemes involving compromise or arrangement with creditors

(1) *Introduction*

Section 135 of the Companies Act 1985 is only available for straightforward reductions which do not affect the rights of creditors. Reductions affecting rights of creditors should be carried out under the terms of the Companies Act 1985, s 425.

(2) *Basic approach*

Capital reduction schemes are only worth considering if the company has recovery prospects; the rights of the various classes of persons interested must be considered. The object of the scheme is the resumption of dividend payments.

The first step is to determine the amount required to eliminate any fictitious assets, and write down overvalued assets; overvaluation of assets may result in excessive charges to profit and loss account for depreciation, causing profits to be understated or losses overstated.

Debit balances on profit and loss account should be written off; goodwill, patents, trade marks, patterns etc should be written down to their book values.

(3) *Rights of creditors and shareholders*

Having determined the total amount to be written off, the rights of the debenture holders, creditors and various classes of shareholders must be considered. The following factors are relevant:

(i) DEBENTURE HOLDERS
They can sometimes be persuaded to make sacrifices to give the company a new lease of life.

If it can be proved that on a forced realisation of assets such as would ensue if the company were driven into liquidation, the assets, after providing for preferential creditors and the costs, would not realise sufficient to repay the debentures in full, but that there is every prospect of the security being enhanced in the future if the company is reorganised, then the debenture holders may consent to cooperate by sacrificing some of their capital.

Some recompense is usually required eg an increased rate of interest, and/or an interest in the equity by the issue to them of fully paid ordinary shares for a proportion of their capital contribution to the amount required for writing off assets.

(ii) OTHER CREDITORS
Creditors other than preferential creditors in a winding up, may agree to a share in a reduction, particularly if the debenture holders have agreed to a sacrifice, since in a liquidation they would obtain little or nothing. It must be proved to creditors that they will obtain more by accepting a reduction than by forcing the company into liquidation.

Usually, neither debenture holders nor creditors can be expected to share in the reduction, the amount required being provided by writing down share capital alone.

(iii) ORDINARY SHAREHOLDERS
The bulk of the loss, usually the whole of it, must fall upon the shareholders. If creditors are to come into the scheme, the shareholders must surrender something to them eg a share in the equity that will enable the creditors to reap some reward in future years for their immediate sacrifice.

As regards the position of the various classes of shareholders, where capital has been lost then the brunt of the loss must fall on the *ordinary* shareholders. However, if this meant the loss of their entire interest in the company, they would not agree to the scheme. The company may have retained in the past profits which could have been distributed as dividends in order to strengthen the company's finances. As the company fell on lean times, such reserves may have been drawn upon to pay preference dividends, with the result that the ordinary shareholders may have already made a sacrifice for the benefit of the preference shareholders.

(iv) EFFECTS OF WRITING DOWN CAPITAL
It is essential to appreciate the effect of writing down capital. For example, suppose the capital of a company is £100,000 divided into 60,000 6% preference shares of £1 each, and 40,000 £1 ordinary shares. Profits, after the preference dividend of £3,600 has been paid, are divisible among the ordinary shareholders. It does not matter to what nominal value the ordinary shares are written down; the amount of the dividend per share remains the same, and the market value of the shares will not be affected by the reduction in nominal value. Writing down ordinary shares therefore entails no real sacrifice so long as the shareholders' interest in the divisible profits is not reduced.

A reduction in the nominal value of the preference shares, however, or in their rate of dividend, will reduce the value of their shares.

Again, if the preference shareholders have the right to preferential repayment of capital, but are entitled to no right to share in a surplus on a winding up, the ordinary shareholders will receive all the assets remaining after repaying the preference capital, no matter what the nominal value of the ordinary shares may be. Writing down ordinary shares imposes only a nominal sacrifice upon the holders of such shares.

Where preference shareholders are entitled to share in a surplus, the writing down of the ordinary shares does involve a sacrifice of rights, since a bigger proportion of any surplus would then go to the preference shareholders. The ultimate winding up rights, however, are not so immediately important as the dividend, ie going concern rights, and therefore, where preference shareholders are called upon to share in a reduction of capital, it is only equitable that ordinary shareholders should surrender part of their rights to the preference shareholders.

(v) PREFERENCE SHAREHOLDERS

Preference shareholders should only be asked to share in a reduction if the amount to be written off exceeds the ordinary share capital. Either their capital and/or their rate of dividend may be reduced. They should be compensated by a share in the equity, so that they may recoup their losses should the company's fortunes improve.

Arrears of cumulative preference dividends must be dealt with on their merits. If they are cancelled, the preference shareholders should be compensated by the issue of shares or other consideration for the whole or part of the arrears, the cancellation of which will benefit the ordinary shareholders.

(vi) FAIRNESS OF THE SCHEME

The test of whether the scheme is reasonably equitable is to compute how the estimated future income will be divisible under the new share capital holdings compared with the old, bearing in mind that all classes of shares can anticipate immediate dividends instead of waiting until the debit balance on profit and loss account is eliminated by profits. The benefit of immediate dividends is greater, the lower the priority the class of shares has. Deferred shares, as a rule, will have to be cancelled, or given a very minute interest in the reorganised company. If, however, they hold valuable rights pari passu with the ordinary shares, they will have to rank equitably with the latter.

(4) *Illustration* 5

The following is the summarised balance sheet of Sea Mills plc as at 31 December 19X6:

	£	£
Fixed assets:		
Goodwill		100,000
Patents and trade marks		80,000
		180,000
Freehold land and buildings	135,000	
Plant and machinery	85,000	
		220,000
		400,000
Current assets:		
Stock	79,900	
Debtors	110,000	
Cash in hand	100	
	190,000	
Current liabilities:		
Creditors	64,000	
Bank overdraft	24,000	
Debenture interest	12,000	
	100,000	
Net current assets		90,000
		490,000

	£	£
6% debentures (secured by a floating charge)		100,000
Authorised, issued and called-up shared capital:		
250,000 £1 ordinary shares	250,000	
250,000 £1 6% cumulative preference shares	250,000	
	500,000	
Profit and loss account	(110,000)	390,000
		490,000

Additional information

(1) The dividends on the preference shares are five years in arrear.
(2) The directors state that the current trading results show a marked improvement, and that they anticipate a net profit of £20,000 per anum will be maintained in future years.
(3) The directors desire to resume the payment of dividends as soon as possible and are accordingly considering the reduction of the company's capital.
(4) The debenture holders, to assist in the revival of the company, have expressed their willingness to exchange their arrears of interest for an interest in the equity of the business of one-half of the nominal value of the arrears, and to provide £25,000 further cash (on a floating charge) to repay the bank overdraft and to provide working capital of £1,000.
(5) The preference shares are described by the articles as not preferential to capital, but any arrears of dividends are to form a first charge upon any surplus on winding up. The preference shareholders have expressed their willingness to a reduction in the rate of dividend to 5% and to forgo two-thirds of their arrears, provided that they receive an interest in the equity equal in nominal value to the remaining third.

Required:
(1) To draft a suggested scheme for the reduction of capital which should include the elimination of goodwill (acquired from James Mills on the formation of the company in exchange for 100,000 ordinary shares which he still holds) and the profit and loss account balance, the reduction of the value of patents and trade marks by £50,000, and the provision of a capital reserve through which any adjustments arising out of the capital rearrangements etc may be dealt with. After reduction, the ordinary shares are to be converted into 5p shares.
(2) To redraft the balance sheet, giving effect to the scheme you suggest.

Suggested solution

(1) *Suggested scheme*

(i) *Elimination of capital*

The capital must be reduced by £285,000, made up as follows:

	£
To eliminate goodwill	100,000
To eliminate profit and loss account balance	110,000
To write down patents and trade marks	50,000
To provide for one-third of arrears of preference dividend	25,000
	285,000

(ii) *Reorganisation of capital*
Since the preference shares are not entitled to a prior return of capital at first sight the loss of capital should be borne equally between the ordinary and preference shareholders. It makes no difference that the preference shareholders are to receive a share in the equity of £25,000 for the cancellation of £75,000 dividend arrears. But since the preference shareholders have consented to a reduction in their rate of cumulative dividend to 5%, which, of itself, will reduce the value of their shares, they should be required to suffer a correspondingly smaller reduction in their nominal capital.

The capital should be reorganised as follows:

(a) The 250,000 6% cumulative preference shares of £1 each to be reduced to shares of 67½p each and sub-divided into:

	£
250,000 5% cumulative preference shares of 50p each	125,000
875,000 ordinary shares of 5p each	43,750
	168,750

	£
This represents a reduction in capital of	81,250

In addition, the preference shareholders to receive 500,000 ordinary shares of 5p each = £25,000, in satisfaction of one-third of their arrears of dividend, the balance to be cancelled.

(b) The 250,000 ordinary shares of £1 each to be reduced to shares of 20p each and converted into 1,000,000 ordinary shares of 5p each.

This represents a reduction in capital of	200,000

(c) The debenture holders to be allotted 120,000 ordinary shares of 5p each in satisfaction of half their arrears of interest, the balance to be cancelled.

This represents a reduction of	6,000
Total reduction	287,250

Of this amount. £285,000 will be applied in writing down the assets and providing for the £25,000 arrears of preference dividend as shown above. The balance of £2,250 may be applied in meeting the costs of the reduction scheme and any adjustments arising out of it, and in reducing the book value of such other of the assets as may be determined by the directors.

The paid-up capital of the company will now consist of:

	£
250,000 5% cumulative preference shares of 50p each	125,000
2,495,000 ordinary shares of 5p each	124,750
	249,750

The resolution for reduction of capital should at the same time provide for the restoration of the authorised capital to £500,000, leaving £250,250 unissued capital, which would be available for issue at some future date, if required.

(iii) Effect on security holder's income

The effect of the above reorganisation of capital, assuming an annual profit of £20,000 to be maintained, will be to cause the profits to be divided between the existing preference and ordinary shareholders in approximately the following proportions. Although on a profit of £20,000, the preference shareholders will receive a little less than previously, their holding of ordinary shares will give them the control of the company, and they will take a major share in any increase in distributable profits over £20,000.

	£	£
Existing preference shareholders will receive:		
Dividend of 5% on £125,000 new preference shares	6,250	
Dividend of, say, 10% on £68,750 new ordinary shares	6,875	
		13,125
Existing ordinary shareholders will receive:		
Dividend of, say, 10% on £50,000 new ordinary shares		5,000

Debenture holders will receive:

Dividend, of say, 10% on £6,000 new ordinary shares		600
		18,725
Carry forward		1,275
		20,000

Note: It is assumed that the debenture interest would already have been provided for before arriving at the profit of £20,000.

(2) *Sea Mills plc – redrafted balance sheet at 31 December 19X6*

	£	£
Fixed assets:		
Intangible fixed assets:		
Patents and trade marks		30,000
Tangible fixed assets:		
Freehold land and buildings	135,000	
Plant and machinery	85,000	
		220,000
		250,000
Current assets:		
Stock	79,900	
Debtors	110,000	
Cash	1,100	
	191,000	
Creditors – amounts falling due within one year		
Creditors	64,000	
Net current assets		127,000
Total assets less current liabilities		377,000
Creditors – amounts falling due after more than one year:		
6% debentures (secured by floating charge)		(125,000)
		252,000
Capital and reserves:		
Called-up share capital:		
2,495,000 5p ordinary shares		124,750
250,000 50p 5% cumulative preference shares		125,000
		249,750
Capital reserve		2,250
		252,000

Note: Authorised share capital is £500,000.

INDEX

Abbreviated accounts
directors' statement, 183
filing concessions, 180
illustration of, 181–183
information required, 181
medium-sized companies, for, 183, 184
problem areas, 183
qualifying conditions, 180
smaller companies, for, 180–183
special auditor's report, 183

Accounting policy
changes in, accounting for, 170

Accounting practice
variations in, 116, 117

Accounting records
statutory requirements, 95, 96

Accounting reference dates
meaning, 95
notification, 95

Accounting reference periods
duration of, 95
meaning, 95

Accounting standards
Board. *See* ACCOUNTING STANDARDS BOARD
compliance with, 98
conceptual framework, 117–130
current, 99
Dearing Committee recommendations, 97
role of, 103
small company concessions, 184, 185
true and fair view, 102, 103

Accounting Standards Board
aims, statement of, 117
development of SORPs, policy on, 106, 107
establishment of, 97
Exposure Drafts, 100
off balance sheet finance, 131
other bodies, relationship with, 98
Statements of Principle, 98, 117

Accounting Standard Committee
off balance sheet finance, 131

Accounts
abbreviated. *See* ABBREVIATED ACCOUNTS
approval of, 94
audit, 94
basic data, 80–82
chairman's statement, 524
defective, revision of, 104
disclosure requirements, 69–79
divisional review, 524
earnings per share. *See* EARNINGS PER SHARE
extraordinary items, 157. *See also* SSAP 6
filing, 94
financial summaries and highlights, 524
form and content, 94
formats, 64–68
fund flow statements. *See* FUND STATEMENTS
illustration of, 80–93
information in, ratio analysis of, 524
interpretation of—
    areas of interest, 513
    inter-company comparisons, 526
    interested persons, 513
    published reports, information from, 524, 525
    purpose of, 513
non-statutory, 187, 188
partnership. *See* PARTNERSHIP
post-balance sheet events, accounting for, 290–293. *See also* SSAP 17
prior period adjustments, 160–162. *See also* FRS 3
ratio analysis techniques—
    capital ratios, 520, 521
    comparison, basis of, 514
    credit sales to debtors ratio, 519
    earnings ratios, 521, 522
    illustration of, 522–524
    investment ratios, 521, 522
    perspective, in, 514
    primary ratio, 515
    profit to sales ratios, 516, 517
    pyramid of ratios, 516
    return on capital employed, 515
    sales to net assets ratio, 517
    secondary ratios, 515
    solvency ratios, 519, 520
    stock ratios, 518
required information, 82
segmental analysis, 524, 564. *See also* SEGMENTAL ANALYSIS
signing, 94